Fireworks 3 Bible

Fireworks 3 Bible

Joseph W. Lowery
with Simon White

IDG Books Worldwide, Inc.
An International Data Group Company

Foster City, CA ✦ Chicago, IL ✦ Indianapolis, IN ✦ New York, NY

Fireworks 3 Bible

Published by
IDG Books Worldwide, Inc.
An International Data Group Company
919 E. Hillsdale Blvd., Suite 400
Foster City, CA 94404
www.idgbooks.com (IDG Books Worldwide Web site)

ISBN: 0-7645-3475-0

Printed in the United States of America

10 9 8 7 6 5 4 3

1B/TR/QV/QQ/FC

Distributed in the United States by IDG Books Worldwide, Inc.

Distributed by CDG Books Canada Inc. for Canada; by Transworld Publishers Limited in the United Kingdom; by IDG Norge Books for Norway; by IDG Sweden Books for Sweden; by IDG Books Australia Publishing Corporation Pty. Ltd. for Australia and New Zealand; by TransQuest Publishers Pte Ltd. for Singapore, Malaysia, Thailand, Indonesia, and Hong Kong; by Gotop Information Inc. for Taiwan; by ICG Muse, Inc. for Japan; by Intersoft for South Africa; by Eyrolles for France; by International Thomson Publishing for Germany, Austria and Switzerland; by Distribuidora Cuspide for Argentina; by LR International for Brazil; by Galileo Libros for Chile; by Ediciones ZETA S.C.R. Ltda. for Peru; by WS Computer Publishing Corporation, Inc., for the Philippines; by Contemporanea de Ediciones for Venezuela; by Express Computer Distributors for the Caribbean and West Indies; by Micronesia Media Distributor, Inc. for Micronesia; by Chips Computadoras S.A. de C.V. for Mexico; by Editorial Norma de Panama S.A. for Panama; by American Bookshops for Finland.

For general information on IDG Books Worldwide's books in the U.S., please call our Consumer Customer Service department at 800-762-2974. For reseller information, including discounts and premium sales, please call our Reseller Customer Service department at 800-434-3422.

For information on where to purchase IDG Books Worldwide's books outside the U.S., please contact our International Sales department at 317-596-5530 or fax 317-572-4002.

For consumer information on foreign language translations, please contact our Customer Service department at 1-800-434-3422, fax 317-572-4002, or e-mail rights@idgbooks.com.

For information on licensing foreign or domestic rights, please phone +1-650-653-7098.

For sales inquiries and special prices for bulk quantities, please contact our Order Services department at 800-434-3422 or write to the address above.

For information on using IDG Books Worldwide's books in the classroom or for ordering examination copies, please contact our Educational Sales department at 800-434-2086 or fax 317-572-4005.

For press review copies, author interviews, or other publicity information, please contact our Public Relations department at 650-653-7000 or fax 650-653-7500.

For authorization to photocopy items for corporate, personal, or educational use, please contact Copyright Clearance Center, 222 Rosewood Drive, Danvers, MA 01923, or fax 978-750-4470.

Library of Congress Cataloging-in-Publication Data
Lowery, Joseph (Joseph W.)
    Fireworks 3 Bible / Joseph W. Lowery with Simon White
        p. cm.
    ISBN 0-7645-3475-0 (alk.paper)
    1. Computer graphics. 2. Fireworks (Computer file)
I. Title: Fireworks three bible. II. White, Simon, 1969-
III.Title
T385 .L696   2000
006.6'869--dc21   00-027582

ABOUT IDG BOOKS WORLDWIDE

Welcome to the world of IDG Books Worldwide.

IDG Books Worldwide, Inc., is a subsidiary of International Data Group, the world's largest publisher of computer-related information and the leading global provider of information services on information technology. IDG was founded more than 30 years ago by Patrick J. McGovern and now employs more than 9,000 people worldwide. IDG publishes more than 290 computer publications in over 75 countries. More than 90 million people read one or more IDG publications each month.

Launched in 1990, IDG Books Worldwide is today the #1 publisher of best-selling computer books in the United States. We are proud to have received eight awards from the Computer Press Association in recognition of editorial excellence and three from Computer Currents' First Annual Readers' Choice Awards. Our best-selling *...For Dummies®* series has more than 50 million copies in print with translations in 31 languages. IDG Books Worldwide, through a joint venture with IDG's Hi-Tech Beijing, became the first U.S. publisher to publish a computer book in the People's Republic of China. In record time, IDG Books Worldwide has become the first choice for millions of readers around the world who want to learn how to better manage their businesses.

Our mission is simple: Every one of our books is designed to bring extra value and skill-building instructions to the reader. Our books are written by experts who understand and care about our readers. The knowledge base of our editorial staff comes from years of experience in publishing, education, and journalism — experience we use to produce books to carry us into the new millennium. In short, we care about books, so we attract the best people. We devote special attention to details such as audience, interior design, use of icons, and illustrations. And because we use an efficient process of authoring, editing, and desktop publishing our books electronically, we can spend more time ensuring superior content and less time on the technicalities of making books.

You can count on our commitment to deliver high-quality books at competitive prices on topics you want to read about. At IDG Books Worldwide, we continue in the IDG tradition of delivering quality for more than 30 years. You'll find no better book on a subject than one from IDG Books Worldwide.

John Kilcullen
Chairman and CEO
IDG Books Worldwide, Inc.

Eighth Annual Computer Press Awards ≫1992

Ninth Annual Computer Press Awards ≫1993

Tenth Annual Computer Press Awards ≫1994

Eleventh Annual Computer Press Awards ≫1995

IDG is the world's leading IT media, research and exposition company. Founded in 1964, IDG had 1997 revenues of $2.05 billion and has more than 9,000 employees worldwide. IDG offers the widest range of media options that reach IT buyers in 75 countries representing 95% of worldwide IT spending. IDG's diverse product and services portfolio spans six key areas including print publishing, online publishing, expositions and conferences, market research, education and training, and global marketing services. More than 90 million people read one or more of IDG's 290 magazines and newspapers, including IDG's leading global brands — Computerworld, PC World, Network World, Macworld and the Channel World family of publications. IDG Books Worldwide is one of the fastest-growing computer book publishers in the world, with more than 700 titles in 36 languages. The "...For Dummies®" series alone has more than 50 million copies in print. IDG offers online users the largest network of technology-specific Web sites around the world through IDG.net (http://www.idg.net), which comprises more than 225 targeted Web sites in 55 countries worldwide. International Data Corporation (IDC) is the world's largest provider of information technology data, analysis and consulting, with research centers in over 41 countries and more than 400 research analysts worldwide. IDG World Expo is a leading producer of more than 168 globally branded conferences and expositions in 35 countries including E3 (Electronic Entertainment Expo), Macworld Expo, ComNet, Windows World Expo, ICE (Internet Commerce Expo), Agenda, DEMO, and Spotlight. IDG's training subsidiary, ExecuTrain, is the world's largest computer training company, with more than 230 locations worldwide and 785 training courses. IDG Marketing Services helps industry-leading IT companies build international brand recognition by developing global integrated marketing programs via IDG's print, online and exposition products worldwide. Further information about the company can be found at www.idg.com. 1/26/00

Credits

Acquisitions Editor
Kathy Yankton

Project Editor
Laura E. Brown

Technical Editor
Derren Whiteman

Copy Editors
Lane Barnholtz
Laura Hester
Marti Paul

Media Development Specialist
Joe Kiempisty

Permissions Editor
Jessica Montgomery

Media Development Manager
Stephen Noetzel

Project Coordinators
Linda Marousek
Danette Nurse
Joe Shines

Graphics and Production Specialists
Robert Bihlmayer
Jude Levinson
Michael Lewis
Victor Pérez-Varela
Dina F Quan
Ramses Ramirez

Illustrator
Gabriele McCann

Indexing
York Production Services

Cover Illustrator
Murder By Design

About the Authors

Joseph W. Lowery has been writing about computers since 1981. Besides writing for such magazines as *Wired* and the *Seybold Report on Internet Publishing*, he has written several books, including *Fireworks 2 Bible*, *Buying Online for Dummies*, and the upcoming *Dreamweaver UltraDev Bible* and *Dreamweaver 3 Bible, Gold Edition* (IDG Books Worldwide). He has garnered the attention and respect of many at Macromedia, and he has been featured as a presenter at Macromedia User Conferences and as a speaker for Macromedia Web World. Joe also teaches at Seybold Conferences. His latest forum is teaching Dreamweaver courses at eHandsOn, an online training center offered by eHandsOn Corp. that teaches Web site design and production using Macromedia Dreamweaver and Fireworks. A professional Web developer, Joe lives in New York City with his wife, Debra Wanner, and his daughter, Margot.

Simon White is a writer, artist, and musician who serves as Creative Director for Mediafear, a full-service Web design shop specializing in multimedia-rich sites. He has contributed to a number of books focusing on Web design and graphics, and he is a Macromedia evangelist. Simon lives in San Francisco — near the beach — with his wife, Kelly, and a couple of Macs. He can be reached at simonwhite.com.

To all those who keep me

turning the pages:

James Ellroy, Elmore Leonard,

Jim Thompson, James W. Hall,

Martin Cruz Smith, Thomas Perry,

Mitchell Smith, William Gibson,

Thomas Harris, Michael Connelly and . . .

the list (thankfully) goes on and on.

JWL

For my mother, who has an artist's heart,

and my father, the über-geek.

SW

Preface

Remember that burst of pleasure when you first realized how exciting the Web could be? I'll let you in on a little secret: Macromedia Fireworks makes creating graphics for the Web fun again. Images produced with Fireworks are as sophisticated and rich as those created with any other combination of programs, plus they're Web-ready — as optimized as possible and bundled with HTML and JavaScript code for amazing interactive effects.

I'll be the first to admit my bias. I'm a Dreamweaver power user, and it seems only natural to combine Macromedia's exciting Web-graphics solution with their premier Web-authoring tool . . . in fact, Macromedia encourages you to do so with their Dreamweaver Fireworks Studio. But while I'm confessing, let me also note that I have no patience for tools that don't do the job. The wonderful revelation about Fireworks is that this program eliminates production bottlenecks I didn't even know existed — all while producing stunning imagery that stays editable through revision after easy revision.

When I set out to write this book, I decided to really push Fireworks. Rather than using it merely to optimize a series of images (which is does superbly) or to create a compact animation (which it also does superbly) from work created in other programs, I used Fireworks exclusively for all image manipulation and creation. Consequently, both my productivity and my creativity went through the roof. Fireworks 3 Bible was designed to give you all of the information and techniques you need to achieve the same results.

Who Should Read This Book?

The Web is, without a doubt, one of the key phenomena of our time, and it has attracted an enormous amount of talent, both artistic and technical. After all, how often does a new mass medium appear? The range of Web designers extends from first-generation artists drawn to the exciting Internet possibilities to print professionals who need to expand their creative horizons. *Fireworks 3 Bible* talks to all those groups, offering solutions to everyday graphics problems, as well as providing a complete reference for the program.

What Hardware and Software Do You Need?

Fireworks 3 Bible includes full coverage of Macromedia Fireworks 3. If you don't own a copy of the program, the CD-ROM that accompanies this book contains a fully functional, 30-day trial version. Written to be platform-independent, this book covers both Macintosh and Windows versions of Fireworks 3.

Fireworks for Windows requires a Pentium processor (Pentium II or higher recommended) and Windows 95 or Windows NT 4.0 Service Pack 3 or later version, which includes Windows 98 and Windows 2000.

Fireworks for Macintosh requires a PowerPC processor (G3 or higher recommended) and Mac OS 8.1 or later version.

On either platform, Fireworks also requires the following:

- ✦ 64MB of available RAM
- ✦ 100MB of available disk space
- ✦ 640-×-480-pixel, 256-color display (1,024 × 768 pixel or higher and millions of colors recommended)
- ✦ Adobe Type Manager 4 or later version, if you work with Type 1 (PostScript) fonts

Please note these are the minimum requirements. As with all graphics-based design tools, more capability is definitely better for using Fireworks, especially in terms of RAM and processor speed.

How This Book Is Organized

Fireworks 3 Bible can take you from raw beginner to full-fledged professional if read cover to cover. However, you're more likely to read each section as needed, taking the necessary information and coming back later. To facilitate this approach, *Fireworks 3 Bible* is divided into seven major, task-oriented parts. When you're familiar with Fireworks, feel free to skip around the book, using it as a reference guide as you build up your own knowledge base.

The early chapters present the basics, and all chapters contain clearly written steps for the tasks you need to perform. In later chapters, you'll encounter boxed sections labeled "Fireworks Techniques." Fireworks Techniques are step-by-step instructions for accomplishing specific Web design tasks, for example, using a mask to add an interesting border to an image. Naturally, you can also use Fireworks Techniques as stepping-stones for your own explorations into Web-page creation.

If you're running Fireworks while reading this book, don't forget to use the CD-ROM. An integral element of the book, the CD-ROM offers a number of additional Fireworks textures, gradients, and HTML templates, in addition to trial programs from major software vendors.

Part I: Come See the Fireworks

Part I begins with an overview of the Fireworks philosophy and design. To get the most out of the program, you need to understand the key advantages it offers and the deficiencies it addresses. Part I takes you all the way from setting up documents to getting the most out of Fireworks.

The opening chapters give you a full reference to the Fireworks interface and all of its customizable features. Chapter 1 will be of special interest to users of previous versions of Fireworks; it's a complete guide to all of the newly added features in Fireworks 3. Later chapters in Part I provide an overview of everything that Fire-works can do — this feature-rich program will often surprise you.

Part II: Mastering the Tools

The Fireworks approach to graphics is fundamentally different from any other tool on the market. Consequently, you'll need to travel the short learning curve before you can get the most out of Fireworks. The early chapters in Part II cover all the essentials, from basic object creation to full-blown photo manipulation.

Color is a key component of any graphic designer's tool kit, and color on the Web requires special attention, as you'll see in Chapter 7. The object-oriented nature of Fireworks is explored in chapters on creating simple strokes and combining paths in a variety of ways to help you make more sophisticated graphics. Fireworks excels at creating graphical text for the Web — you'll see how in Chapter 10.

Part III: Achieving Effects

Fireworks graphics really begin to gain depth in Part III. The variety of fills and textures available — as well as the ability to add your own — are critical for the wide range of image production for which a Web designer is responsible. Chapter 12 explores the exciting world of Fireworks Live Effects and Xtras (new in Fireworks 3), which are exciting not just because they're easy to use and they look great, but also because of the positive impact that their always-editable nature will have on your workflow.

Most of the time, a graphic will actually contain a number of images. Chapter 13 explains the Fireworks methods for arranging and compositing multiple objects in order to achieve stunning results. Fireworks' mask-group feature in particular is an especially creative and powerful tool that takes the hard work out of alpha channels. Although Fireworks is a great drawing tool, it's also adept at handling bitmap imagery.

Part IV: Coordinating Workflow

Web design is an ongoing process, not a single event. Part IV is dedicated to helping you streamline your workflow efficiently as you acquire images via scanning or importing, manipulate them in Fireworks, and then optimize them on export, either for the Web or for import into other creative tools, such as Macromedia Director or Flash.

While it's true that Web graphic design is an art form, it's also a business — and one element of that business is applying a consistent look and feel to each element of a particular Web site. Fireworks Styles enable you to save formatting instructions from one object and apply them to other objects again and again. The Library palette (new in Fireworks 3) is a place to store *Symbols*, objects you use again and again, such as logos and navigation buttons. Fireworks Symbols further minimize repetitive work by linking similar objects so that changes need only be made once. Chapter 18 describes how Fireworks 3 helps you update and maintain your graphics through the URL Panel and the surprising Find and Replace feature. The final chapter in Part IV covers the new Commands and History palettes, tools which automate your workflow by recording and scripting common tasks.

Part V: Entering the Web

Fireworks broke new ground as the first image editor to output HTML and JavaScript code. With its full-featured hotspots, image maps, and sliced images embedded in HTML tables, Fireworks is incredibly Web savvy. Part V explains the basics of Web interactivity for those designers unfamiliar with the territory and also offers specific step-by-step instructions for linking JavaScript behaviors to graphics.

If you work with Dreamweaver (or work with someone who does), you'll want to check out Chapter 22 in order to get the most out of the integration possibilities between Fireworks and Dreamweaver.

Part VI: Animation

Animations have become important to the Web. Not only do they offer an alternative to static displays, but GIF animations are used extensively in the creation of banner ads. Animation in Fireworks 3 is surprisingly full-featured and easy to use. We'll walk step-by-step through the creation of a banner ad and discover tweening, onion skinning, and other basic animation techniques.

Part VII: Programming With Fireworks

One of the most amazing things about Fireworks 3 is the way it can be controlled by scripts written in JavaScript, the most common scripting language for Web authoring. Fireworks offers many ways to customize the way you work with the program. We'll look at each of them and discover the extensive Fireworks JavaScript API (Application Programming Interface).

Appendixes

Appendix A is a Web Primer, a place to get a good grounding on the ways of the Web. Appendix B is a handy reference guide to productivity-boosting keyboard shortcuts on both Macintosh and Windows systems. The material on the accompanying CD-ROM is detailed in Appendix C.

Conventions Used in This Book

The following conventions are used throughout this book.

Windows and Macintosh conventions

Because *Fireworks 3 Bible* is a cross-platform book, it gives instructions for both Windows and Macintosh users when keystrokes for a particular task differ. Throughout this book, the Windows keystrokes are given first, and the Macintosh keystrokes are given second in parentheses, as in the following example:

To undo an action, press Ctrl+Z (Command+Z).

The first action instructs Windows users to simultaneously press Ctrl and Z, and the second action (in parentheses) instructs Macintosh users to press Command and Z together. In Fireworks for Windows, the key shortcuts are displayed in the menus in plain English. In Fireworks for Macintosh, as in other Macintosh programs, the key shortcuts are specified in the menus by using symbols that represent the modifier keys.

You'll notice that in most—but not all—key shortcuts, the Windows Ctrl key corresponds to the Macintosh Command key, and the Windows Alt key corresponds to the Macintosh Option key.

Screen captures in odd-numbered chapters are of Fireworks running on Windows 98; in even-numbered chapters, they're of Fireworks running on Mac OS 9. In the rare event that a particular feature or example is markedly different on each platform, both are shown.

For the purposes of this book, "Windows" refers to Windows 95, Windows 98, Windows NT 4.0 Service Pack 3, or Windows 2000. Similarly, "Macintosh" or "Mac OS" refers to Mac OS 8.1, 8.5, 8.6, or 9.0. If you are using a later version of Windows or Mac OS, you may find some differences in features external to Fireworks.

Key combinations

When you are instructed to press two or more keys simultaneously, each key in the combination is separated by a plus sign. For example:

Ctrl+Alt+T (Command+Option+T)

The preceding line tells you to press and hold down the two modifier keys (either Ctrl+Alt or Command+Option, depending upon your platform), and then press and release the final key, T.

Mouse instructions

When instructed to *click* an item, move the mouse pointer to the specified item and click the mouse button once. A *double-click* means clicking the mouse button twice in rapid succession.

A *right-click* means clicking the secondary mouse button once. Macintosh users who use a one-button mouse can substitute a *Control-click* for a right-click. To do so, press and hold down Control on your keyboard and click the mouse button once.

When instructed to select an item, you may click it once as previously described. If you are selecting text or multiple objects, you must click the mouse button once, hold it down, and then move the mouse to a new location. The item or items selected invert color. To clear the selection, click once anywhere in an empty part of the document background.

Menu commands

When instructed to select a command from a menu, you see the menu and the command separated by an arrow symbol. For example, when instructed to execute the Open command from the File menu, you see the notation File ⇨ Open. Some menus use submenus, in which case you see an arrow for each submenu, as in Modify ⇨ Transform ⇨ Free Transform.

Typographical conventions

Italic type is used for new terms and for emphasis. **Boldface** type is used for text that you need to type directly from the computer keyboard.

Code

A special typeface indicates HTML or other code, as demonstrated in the following example:

```
<html>
<head>
<title>Have a Nice Day!</title>
</head>
<body bgcolor="#FFFFFF">
</body>
</html>
```

This code font is also used within paragraphs to designate HTML tags, attributes, and values, such as <body>, bgcolor, and #FFFFFF.

The (¬) character at the end of a code line means that you should type the next line of code before pressing Enter (Return).

Navigating Through This Book

Various signposts and icons are located throughout Fireworks 3 Bible for your assistance. Each chapter begins with an overview of its information, and ends with a quick summary.

Icons are placed in the text to indicate important or especially helpful items. Here's a list of the icons and their functions:

Tips provide you with extra knowledge that separates the novice from the pro.

Notes provide additional or critical information, and technical data on the current topic.

Sections marked with a New Feature icon detail an innovation introduced in Fireworks 3.

Cross-Reference icons indicate places where you can find more information on a particular topic.

The Caution icon is your warning of a potential problem or pitfall.

The On the CD-ROM icon indicates the CD-ROM contains a related file.

Further Information

You can find more help for specific problems and questions by investigating several Web sites. Macromedia's own Fireworks Web site is the best place to start:

```
<http://www.macromedia.com/software/fireworks>
```

I heartily recommend that you visit and participate in the official Fireworks news-group:

```
<news://forums.macromedia.com/macromedia.fireworks>
```

You're also invited to visit my Web site for book updates and new developments:

```
<http://www.idest.com/fireworks>
```

You can also e-mail me:

```
<mailto:jlowery@idest.com>
```

I can't promise instantaneous turnaround, but I answer all my e-mail to the best of my ability.

Acknowledgments

It may be my name on the cover, but it wouldn't be there if it weren't for the help of an awful lot of generous people. First and foremost among these folks is Simon White. Simon White, and his company MediaFear, is known among the Fireworks and Dreamweaver newsgroup regulars as one of the most knowledgeable and generous experts around. I'd especially like to thank Simon for his major contributions to this book, not to mention his availability as a sounding board for some of my more off-the-wall concepts. It's always refreshing to find someone whose artistic vision is so well-formed and energized with whom I can laugh about the bizarre world that is book authoring. You'll find numerous examples of Simon's work throughout the book and especially in the color-plate section.

Fireworks is a massive program, and I have to thank Derren Whiteman, technical editor, for keeping all of our technical ducks in a row. On the editorial side of life, IDG stalwarts Kathy Yankton and Laura Brown kept me on track and — relatively — on schedule. Special thanks also to copy editors Lane Barnholtz, Laura Hester, and Marti Paul.

The Fireworks community has grown considerably over the past year and their generosity even more so. Special thanks to those designers who graciously allowed me to include their work on the CD-ROM: Kleanthis Economou, Massimo Foti, Linda Rathgeber, Eddie Traversa, and Simon White. Several other top designers contributed work to demonstrate the power of Fireworks, including Lisa Lopuck, Donna Casey, and Ruth Peyser — warm hugs and great thanks all 'round. I owe a debt of gratitude — and probably a drink or two — to another Fireworks community member, author Sandee Cohen. Sandee's work continues to inspire, and I wish her continued success.

Of course, I wouldn't be writing this book — and you certainly wouldn't be reading it — if it weren't for the fantastic vision of the Fireworks team. Fireworks is a marvelously complex program, and there is a true glory in bringing it to life. A hearty thank you and a round of applause to you all: Dennis Griffin, Doug Benson, David Morris, John Ahlquist, Jeff Ahlquist, Matt Bendicksen, Steven Johnson, Jeff Doar, and Eric Wolff. I'd also like to single out Mark Haynes for not only the specific questions he helped me with, but for all the users he's helped aboard the Fireworks team with his tireless answers in the newsgroup. Finally, let me offer a special thanks to Diana Smedley, Fireworks Product Manager, for her early support and encouragement, as well as the openness and access she granted me. — JWL

For many in the Macromedia user community, Joseph Lowery is the wise man sitting cross-legged at the top of the mountain. And quite deservedly so — a multitude of beginners and professionals alike have found Web design enlightenment in the pages of his books. I learned to use Dreamweaver with the first edition of Joe's *Dreamweaver Bible*, and then I had the good fortune to go on to learn quite a bit from him about writing, as well. His generous tutelage has been invaluable, and I thank him for it.

What would a book be without editors? I learned something from each and every one, and greatly appreciated the experience. Kathy Yankton launched the boat. Laura Brown steered it. Lane Barnholtz, Laura Hester, and Marti Paul made sure there were no leaks, and Derren Whiteman tuned the engine. I'm very grateful.

I'd also like to thank Derren for the extra help he provided along the way and for his seemingly unending supply of joie de vivre. His contributions to my efforts go beyond his official capacity as this book's technical editor.

And finally, thank you Kelly Konis White. — SW

Contents at a Glance

Preface. ix
Acknowledgments xvii

Part I: Come See the Fireworks. 1
Chapter 1: Welcome to Fireworks. 3
Chapter 2: Understanding the Interface 23
Chapter 3: Customizing Your Environment. 99
Chapter 4: Setting Up Documents 115

Part II: Mastering the Tools. 137
Chapter 5: Creating and Transforming Objects. 139
Chapter 6: Working with Images 165
Chapter 7: Managing Color 193
Chapter 8: Choosing Strokes 219
Chapter 9: Structuring Paths 255
Chapter 10: Composing with Text 285

Part III: Achieving Effects 313
Chapter 11: Fills and Textures 315
Chapter 12: Live Effects and Xtras 347
Chapter 13: Arranging and Compositing Objects 397

Part IV: Coordinating Workflow 435
Chapter 14: Capturing and Importing 437
Chapter 15: Exporting and Optimizing. 471
Chapter 16: Working with Fireworks Styles 519
Chapter 17: Using Symbols and Libraries 531
Chapter 18: Updating and Maintaining Web Graphics 553
Chapter 19: Automating Workflow with Commands and the History Panel. . . . 581

Part V: Entering the Web 603
Chapter 20: Mastering Image Maps and Slices 605
Chapter 21: Activating Fireworks with Behaviors 639
Chapter 22: Integration with Dreamweaver. 665

Part VI: Animation **687**

Chapter 23: Animation Techniques 689

Chapter 24: Animating Banner Ads 723

Part VII: Programming with Fireworks **737**

Chapter 25: Customizing Fireworks 739

Chapter 26: Fireworks API. 759

Appendix A: A Web Primer 809

Appendix B: Keyboard Shortcuts 831

Appendix C: What's on the CD-ROM 847

Index 853

End-User License Agreement 896

CD-ROM Installation Agreements. 901

Contents

Preface. ix

Acknowledgments xvii

Part I: Come See the Fireworks   1

Chapter 1: Welcome to Fireworks 3

Fireworks — the Next-Generation Graphics Package 4
    Combining the best features 4
    Enchanced vector-drawing program 5
    Screen oriented 5
    Internet based 5
Of Pixels and Paths: The Best of Both Worlds 6
    Vector tools with organic bitmaps. 7
    Bitmap compatibility 8
    Live effects 9
    Styles. 10
    Animation 11
Linking to the Web 12
    Hotspots and slices 12
    URL panel 13
    Images with Behaviors. 13
    Optimizing for the Web 14
    Dreamweaver integration 15
Production Tools 16
    Automation 16
    Batch processing. 17
What's New in Fireworks 3. 17
    User interface. 18
    Graphics creation 18
    Web connectivity. 19
    Image optimization. 19
    Workflow management 20

Chapter 2: Understanding the Interface 23

The Fireworks Environment 24
The Document Window 25

Document Controls 27
    Original/Preview tabs 29
    Magnification settings 30
    Display options 31
    Other controls 32
Opening the Toolbox 33
Accessing Toolbars (Windows Only) 37
    Main toolbar 37
    Modify toolbar 39
    Status bar 41
Managing the Floating Panels 41
    Grouping and moving panels 42
    Panel Layout Sets 43
    Hiding and revealing panels 44
    Windowshade 44
    Examining common features 44
    Optimize panel 46
    Object inspector 47
    Stroke panel 49
    Fill panel 51
    Effect panel 52
    Color Table panel 54
    Swatches panel 55
    Color Mixer panel 56
    Tool Options panel 57
    Layers panel 58
    Frames panel 59
    History panel 60
    Info panel 62
    Behaviors inspector 63
    URL panel 64
    Styles panel 65
    Library panel 66
    Find and Replace panel 68
    Project Log panel 69
Using the Menus 70
    File menu 70
    Edit menu 74
    View menu 77
    Insert menu 80
    Modify menu 81
    Text menu 87
    Commands menu 89
    Xtras 91
    Window menu 93
    Help menu 95

Chapter 3: Customizing Your Environment **99**

  Setting Preferences 99
    General preferences 100
    Editing preferences 102
    Folder preferences 105
    Import preferences 107
  Adjusting HTML Properties 108
    Slicing an image 108
    Using image map options 112
  Selecting Print Options 113

Chapter 4: Setting Up Documents **115**

  Creating New Documents 115
    Two approaches 115
    The canvas options 117
    Steps to create a new document 120
  Opening Existing Images 121
    File Formats 122
    Opening Multiple Images 125
  Storing Files 127
    Closing a file 128
    Reverting to a saved file 128
  Modifying Canvases 128
    Altering the canvas size 129
    Trimming the canvas 134
    Picking a new canvas color 135
    Rotating the canvas 135

Part II: Mastering the Tools   137

Chapter 5: Creating and Transforming Objects **139**

  Understanding Objects in Fireworks 139
  Examining Paths 140
    Applying a stroke 140
    Open and closed paths 142
    Center point 142
    Direction 143
  Starting from Shapes 143
    Rectangles and squares 144
    Ellipses and circles 147
    Polygons and stars 148
  Drawing Lines and Freeform Paths 152
    Straight lines 153
    Freeform Pencil and Brush 154

Constructing Bézier Curves 156
    Drawing lines with the Pen 157
    Creating smooth curves with the Pen 158
    Mixing lines and curves 159
    Adjusting curves 160
    Using the keyboard modifiers 162

Chapter 6: Working with Images 165

Understanding Bitmap Images in Fireworks 166
    Examining Image Edit mode 166
    Opening existing images 169
    Scaling images 170
    Inserting an image into a document 172
    Inserting an empty image 172
    Using Image-Edit-mode tools 173
Fireworks Technique: Limiting Your Drawing Area 185
Selecting Images 186
    Selecting all 186
    Selecting none 187
    Selecting inverse 187
    Feathering an existing selection 188
    Selecting similar 188
    Modify marquee 189
Applying Object Tools to Images 189
Converting an Object to an Image 190

Chapter 7: Managing Color 193

Working with Color on the Web 193
    Bit depth 194
    Hexadecimal colors 195
    Web-safe colors 196
    Platform differences 197
    Working with color management 199
Mixing Colors 199
    Using the Color Mixer 199
    Choosing a color 200
    Accessing the color models 201
Selecting Swatches of Color 205
    Choosing from the color wells 205
    Using the Eyedropper 206
    Accessing the system color picker(s) 206
    Opting for no color 208
    Using the Swatches panel 209
    Accessing the Color Table 212
Fireworks Technique: Converting Pantone Colors to Web-Safe Colors . . . 213

Chapter 8: Choosing Strokes 219

Using the Stroke Panel 219
    Stroke categories and types 221
    Stroke edge and size 222
    Stroke texture 222
Working with the Built-in Strokes 224
    Pencil 225
    Basic 226
    Air Brush 227
    Calligraphy 228
    Charcoal 228
    Crayon 229
    Felt Tip 230
    Oil 231
    Watercolor 232
    Random 233
    Unnatural 234
Creating New Strokes 235
    Managing your strokes 236
    Editing the stroke 238
Fireworks Technique: Making Dotted Lines 247
Orienting the Stroke 250

Chapter 9: Structuring Paths 255

Transforming Objects Visually 256
    Scaling 256
    Skewing 258
    Distorting 259
    Rotating 259
    Transforming Objects Numerically 261
Fireworks Technique: Creating Perspective 262
Managing Points and Paths 264
    Moving points with the Subselection tool 264
    Adding and removing points 265
    Closing an open path 267
    Working with multiple paths 268
Editing Paths 269
    Redrawing a path 269
    Freeform and Reshape Area 270
    Path Scrubber 275
    Path Operations 277

Chapter 10: Composing with Text 285

Using the Text Editor 285
    Previewing on the fly 287

Choosing basic font characteristics 288
Adjusting text spacing 290
Enabling Text Editor options 296
Re-Editing Text 297
Importing Text 297
Transforming Text 299
Adding strokes 299
Enhancing fills 301
Using the transform tools 301
Converting text to paths 303
Converting text to an image 303
Fireworks Technique: Cookie-Cutter Text 304
Fireworks Technique: A Font Safety Net 305
Text on a Path 306
Fireworks Technique: Masking Images with Text 310

Part III: Achieving Effects   313

Chapter 11: Fills and Textures 315

Using Built-in Fills 315
Turning off an object's fill 316
Solid 317
Web Dither 318
Managing Gradients 321
Applying a Gradient fill 321
Altering gradients 323
Using the Styles feature 327
Fireworks Technique: Making Transparent Gradients 328
Using Patterns 329
Adding new Patterns 330
Adding Patterns to a document 332
Altering Patterns 332
Fireworks Technique: Creating Seamless Patterns 334
Adding Texture to Your Fills 339
Adding new textures 341
Converting a color image to grayscale 341
Assigning an additional textures folder 341
Adding textures to a document 342
Filling with the Paint Bucket Tool 342

Chapter 12: Live Effects and Xtras. 347

Understanding Fireworks Effects 348
The Effect panel 348
Applying Live Effects 349
The Xtras menu 352

Working with Included Live Effects 353
    Adjusting color 355
    Adjusting tonal range. 355
    Three dimensions with Bevel and Emboss 361
    Adding depth with blurring 366
    Holdover effects. 367
    Shadow and Glow 367
    Sharpening to bring out detail. 371
Fireworks Technique: Making Perspective Shadows 372
Managing Live Effects 375
    Storing a customized effect 376
    Missing effects. 377
    Saving effects in Styles 377
Xtras, Read All About Them 378
    Path objects 379
    Image objects 379
    Pixel selections in an image object 379
    False pixel selections 380
    Multiple objects 381
Using Third-Party, Photoshop-Compatible Filters 382
    Installing third-party filter packages 382
    Using filters with multiple applications 383
    Using Shortcuts (Aliases) to plug-in folders 384
    Alien Skin Eye Candy 384
    Kai's Power Tools 5 390

Chapter 13: Arranging and Compositing Objects 397

Using Layers 397
    Working with layers. 398
    Hiding selected objects 402
Aligning and Distributing Objects 402
    Using a theoretical rectangle 402
    Aligning to the canvas 404
Layout Assistance 405
    Using rulers 405
    Working with guides 407
    The grid 410
Grouping Objects 411
    Subselecting and superselecting 413
    Mask groups 413
    Fireworks technique: quick photo edges 418
Opacity and Blending 420
    Controlling opacity 421
    Using blending modes 421
    Investigating the modes 423
    Fireworks technique: simulating a light source
        with blending modes 425

Fireworks Technique: Feathering Selections 427
Fireworks Technique: Applied Compositing 428

Part IV: Coordinating Workflow   435

Chapter 14: Capturing and Importing. 437

Image Capture Introductions. 437
    TWAIN-compliant devices 438
    Installing Photoshop Acquire Plug-ins (Macintosh only) 439
Page Scanning 440
The Scanning Process. 442
    Selecting a scan resolution 443
    Choosing a color depth 444
    Setting other options 445
    Scanning directly into Fireworks 446
Digital Cameras 447
    Capturing images directly in Fireworks 447
    Digital Camcorders 449
Inserting Objects from Other Applications. 450
    Copy and paste 450
    Drag and drop 451
Importing External Files 453
    Bitmap image files 453
    Vector art files. 458
    Text files 462
    Common problems 462
Screen Capture. 464
    Built-in screenshot tools 465
    Specialized applications 466
Opening Animations. 466
    Importing multiple files as a new animation. 467
    Importing Flash animations 468

Chapter 15: Exporting and Optimizing 471

Exploring Optimization Features 471
    Optimize panel 473
    Color Table panel 474
    Workspace preview 474
    Frame controls 481
Exporting Indexed Color 481
    Color palette. 483
    Number of colors 484
    Matte 487
    Lossy GIF compression. 487
    Dither. 489

Transparency 489
Remove unused colors. 493
Interlaced 493
Saved settings 494
Fireworks technique: creating GIF-friendly images 494
Exporting Photographic Images 497
JPEG 498
PNG 32 and 24 502
Other formats 503
Working in the Export Preview. 503
Cropping 504
Scaling exported images 506
Using the Export Wizards. 507
Additional Export Options 509
Exporting single slices 510
Exporting files. 511
Exporting as CSS layers 512
Exporting as Image Wells 514
Exporting vectors 515

Chapter 16: Working with Fireworks Styles 519

Understanding Styles 520
Applying Styles 521
Creating New Styles 522
Managing Styles 525
Fireworks Technique: Isolating Patterns and Textures from Styles 528

Chapter 17: Using Symbols and Libraries 531

Understanding Symbols and Instances 531
Introducing the Library Panel 534
Making and Modifying Symbols 536
Creating a Symbol. 536
Modifying Symbols 539
Creating Instances 541
Modifying Instances 542
Working with Buttons 543
Making and Modifying Button Symbols 543
Using Button Instances. 546
The Link Wizard. 547
Managing Libraries 548
Importing a Library. 548
Exporting and sharing Libraries 550

Chapter 18: Updating and Maintaining Web Graphics. 553

Preview in Browser 553

Managing Links with the URL Panel 556
    Accessing the URL History list 557
    Adding URLs to the URL Library 558
    Managing URL Libraries 560
Updating Graphics with Find and Replace 562
    Searching and replacing text 566
    Searching with Regular Expressions 566
    Altering font characteristics. 570
    Changing colors throughout a site 572
    Snapping colors to Websafe 573
    Updating URLs. 574
Working with the Project Log 575
Batch Processing Graphics Files. 577
    Basic procedure. 577
    Running Scriptlets 579

**Chapter 19: Automating Workflow with Commands and
the History Panel** **581**

Running Built-in Commands 582
    Animation 582
    Batch a Command 583
    Creative 584
    Document 586
    Panel Layout Sets 587
    Panel Layout. 589
    Web 589
Enhancing Productivity with the History Panel 591
    Super Undo and Redo 591
    Commands without coding 593
    Copying steps to the clipboard 596
Managing the Commands Menu 599
    Organizing installed Commands 599
    Adding more Commands. 601

Part V: Entering the Web   **603**

Chapter 20: Mastering Image Maps and Slices **605**

Understanding Image Maps and Hotspots 606
Using the Hotspot Tools 608
    Rectangular hotspot 608
    Circle hotspot 610
    Polygon hotspot. 611
    Assigning links to hotspots 611
    Converting an object to a hotspot 613

Exporting Image Map Code. 613
    Choosing an HTML style 614
    Inserting image map code in a Web page 616
Understanding Slices 622
Slicing Images in Fireworks. 623
    Rectangle slices 624
    Polygon slices 625
    Working with slice guides 626
    Copying an image to a slice 627
    Setting URLs in slices. 627
Exporting Slices 631
    Exporting slices as different image types 631
    Setting the Export options. 632
    Inserting slices in a Web page 633
Fireworks Technique: Animating a Slice 636

Chapter 21: Activating Fireworks with Behaviors **639**

Understanding Behaviors. 639
Using the Behaviors Panel 640
    Adding new Behaviors 641
    Modifying a Behavior. 642
    Deleting a Behavior 643
Creating Rollovers. 643
    How rollovers work. 643
    Rollover states 644
    Creating rollover images 645
    Applying the Simple Rollover Behavior 647
Exporting Rollovers for the Web. 648
    Exporting the code from Fireworks. 650
    Inserting rollover code in your Web page 652
Nav Bar Behavior 654
    Creating a Nav Bar 655
    Building buttons in the Button Editor 656
Advanced Rollover Techniques 659
    Making disjointed rollovers 659
    Creating external rollovers 660
    Working with hotspot rollovers. 661
    Displaying a status bar message 662

Chapter 22: Integration with Dreamweaver. **665**

Integration Overview 665
Optimizing Images with Fireworks 667
Editing Images with Fireworks 670
    Setting Fireworks as the graphic editor
        in Dreamweaver 670
    Recognizing Design Notes from Fireworks. 671

Exporting Dreamweaver Code 672
    Working with Dreamweaver Libraries 673
    Fireworks technique: adding CSS layers to Dreamweaver 676
Using Fireworks Behaviors in Dreamweaver 678
Fireworks Technique: Creating a Web Photo Album 681
Making Hybrid Commands 683

Part VI: Animation   687

Chapter 23: Animation Techniques 689

Understanding Web Animation 689
    Bandwidth, bandwidth, bandwidth. 690
    Making a statement 690
    Why animate a GIF? 691
The Fireworks Animation Toolkit 693
    Managing frames 693
    Animating objects. 698
    Using the VCR controls. 700
    Frame delay timing 701
    Using Onion Skinning. 702
    Export settings and options 704
Web Design with Animated GIF Images 709
    Animating background images 709
    Reusing animations. 709
    Scaling an animation 709
    Using the browser's background image 710
    Preloading an animation 710
    Animated rollovers 711
    Slice up animations 712
Tweening with Fireworks 712
    Fireworks technique: tweening Xtras. 715
    Fireworks technique: tweening depth 717
    Fireworks technique: fading in and out 719

Chapter 24: Animating Banner Ads 723

Banner Ad Basics 723
    Size — IAB/CASIE standards 723
    Weight 724
    Putting it in the page 725
    Advertise it 725
Fireworks Technique: Creating a Banner Ad 726
    Step one: Set the stage 726
    Step two: Write the script 726
    Step three: Create the cast of characters 727

Step four: Direct the action 729
Step five: Leave the excess on the cutting-room floor 732
Fireworks Technique: Using Blur to Save Frames 734

Part VII: Programming with Fireworks   737

Chapter 25: Customizing Fireworks 739

The HTML and JavaScript Engine 739
The Settings Folder 741
   Batch Code. 742
   Commands. 742
   Export Settings 743
   HTML Code 743
   JSExtensions. 744
   Libraries 744
   Patterns 745
   Styles 745
   Textures 745
   URL Libraries 746
   Xtras 746
The Fireworks 3 Preferences File 746

Chapter 26: Fireworks API 759

Nonstandard Data Types 760
   Colors 760
   File URLs 760
   Masks. 761
   Matrices 761
   Points. 762
   Rectangles 762
   Resolution 762
Global Methods 762
   alert(message) 762
   confirm(message). 763
   prompt(caption, text) 764
   WRITE_HTML(arg1[, arg2, ..., argN]) 764
   write(arg1[, arg2, ..., argN]) 765
Global Objects 765
   App 765
   Document 771
   Errors. 780
   Find 783
   Files 785
Hotspot Objects 789
   exportDoc 789

Image maps 791
Behaviors 793
Slice Objects 795
SliceInfo object 795
Slices object 797
Accessing the Fireworks API 799
Document functions 799
Fireworks functions. 800
History Panel functions 801
Building on the built-in Commands. 803

Apendix A: A Web Primer. 809

Appendix B: Keyboard Shortcuts 831

Appendix C: What's on the CD-ROM 847

Index 851

End-User License Agreement 896

CD-ROM Installation Agreements 901

Come See the Fireworks

P A R T

◆   ◆   ◆   ◆

In This Part

Chapter 1
Welcome to
Fireworks

Chapter 2
Understanding the
Interface

Chapter 3
Customizing Your
Environment

Chapter 4
Setting Up
Documents

◆   ◆   ◆   ◆

Welcome to Fireworks

✦   ✦   ✦   ✦

In This Chapter

The Fireworks
philosophy

Bringing vectors and
bitmaps together

Integrating with
existing images

Linking to the Web

Managing workflow

Enhancements in
Fireworks 3

✦   ✦   ✦   ✦

Every Fourth of July, I sit with my friends and family on a
neighbor's rooftop to watch the fireworks explode over
Manhattan. Almost every apartment building roof around us
holds a similar gathering. Everyone oohs and ahhs to their
own view of the spectacular light show, some of the patterns
and images familiar, while others have never been seen before.

The World Wide Web has become a global light show, running
around the clock. The graphics that fill Web pages explode
with brilliance, intensity, and meaning, and are viewed by
millions, each from their own perspective. The Web is a new
medium uniquely capable of both enlightening and entertain-
ing; it's also an extremely voracious medium, as thousands
upon thousands of new and updated Web sites emerge daily.
In addition to content, the Web needs graphics: all manner of
images, illustrations, logos, symbols, and icons. Some of the
imagery is static, others animated, and still others are interactive. Design has definitely encountered a whole new frontier.

To contribute the most to this new medium, new tools are
necessary. The Web is screen-, not print-based, and it has its
own set of rules and guidelines. Though some print-oriented
graphic tools have begun to extend themselves with the Internet in mind, a completely new tool was needed — a tool that
did everything Web designers needed and did it efficiently but
with flair. A tool capable of creating graphics light enough to
soar, yet powerful enough to brighten the night.

Enter Fireworks.

Fireworks—the Next-Generation Graphics Package

Fireworks is the premier Web graphics program from Macromedia. As a next-generation graphics package, Fireworks has definitely benefited from all of the great computer graphics programs that came before it. But whereas much of Fireworks functions in a manner similar to other graphics tools—which significantly shortens the learning curve—the program is purely focused on the Web and offers many innovative Web-only features.

Fireworks was built from the ground up with the Web in mind. Before creating Fireworks, Macromedia examined the way graphic designers were working and found that most designers used a wide variety of tools to achieve their goals. An initial design was usually laid out in a vector drawing program like FreeHand or Adobe Illustrator. But vectors aren't native to the Web, so the illustration was then ported to an image-editing program, such as Photoshop or Corel Photo-Paint. In these pixel-based programs, special effects, such as beveled edges, were laboriously added and text was merged with the bitmap before it was exported to an optimizing program. An optimizer, such as Debabelizer, was necessary to ensure that Web-safe colors were used and that the file size was the smallest possible for the bandwidth-limited Internet. Next came integration into the Web: linking URLs, image maps, rollovers, slices, and more. A slew of small specialty programs filled these needs. Moreover, many designers were forced to learn HTML and JavaScript; because no program did everything that was needed, many tasks had to be done manually. Adding to the intense difficulty of mastering all of the various programs was the problem of modifying an image. If a client wanted a change—and clients always want changes—the whole graphic had to be rebuilt from scratch.

Combining the best features

Fireworks offers a revolutionary new way to create Web graphics. It combines the best features of all the various programs:

✦ Vector drawing tools for easy layout

✦ Sophisticated, pixel-based image-editing tools for working with existing graphics and scanned images

✦ Live effects for straightforward but spectacular special effects

✦ An export engine for file optimization to Web standards, with onscreen comparison views so that a Web designer can select the best image at the smallest size

✦ HTML and JavaScript output tied to the graphics themselves

Best of all, virtually every single aspect of a Fireworks graphic can be altered at any stage. In other words, in Fireworks everything is editable, all the time. Not only is this a tremendous time-saver, but it's also a major production enhancement—and the Web requires an extraordinary amount of material and maintenance. Not only are new sites and Web pages constantly going online, but existing pages need continual updating. The underlying philosophy of Fireworks—everything editable, all the time—reflects a deep awareness of the Web designer's real world situation.

Enchanced vector-drawing program

If you're coming from a print background and you're used to working with tools like Photoshop, it's important to grasp certain Fireworks fundamentals. First, you should realize that Fireworks is not primarily an image-editing program, although it has excellent image-editing tools. Fireworks is basically a vector-drawing program that outputs natural-looking bitmap images. Once you get the hang of drawing with vectors—also known as paths and far more flexible than bitmaps—and applying bitmap strokes and fills, you'll never want to go back.

Screen oriented

Second, Fireworks, as a Web graphics engine, is screen—not print—oriented. The resolution of an image on a monitor is typically far lower than the resolution of the same image in print. Images are generally worked on and saved in their actual size; the technique of working with a larger image for fine detail and then reducing it to enhance the resolution won't work with Fireworks—in fact, it will backfire and you'll lose the very detail you were trying to instill. However, you can zoom in (up to 6,400 percent) for detailed correction. Just keep in mind that ultimately, all images are viewed at 100 percent in the browser.

Internet based

Which brings us to the final point for designers new to the Web: Fireworks is not just screen based, it's Internet based. Many Fireworks options are geared toward Web realities, such as the importance of a minimum file size, the limitations of Web-safe colors, and capabilities of the majority of browsers. Fireworks is extremely respectful of the Web environment and, when properly used, will help you conserve production, browser, and Internet resources.

 For a visual explanation of what Fireworks makes possible, turn to the color insert.

Of Pixels and Paths: The Best of Both Worlds

Although the Web is ultimately a pixel-based medium, paths — also called vectors — are much easier to control and edit. Fireworks bases most of its graphics creation power on paths, while offering a complete range of image-editing options. By switching effortlessly between paths and pixels, Fireworks smoothly integrates them both.

Fireworks treats separate graphic elements as independent objects that can be easily manipulated, arranged, and aligned. This object orientation is also extremely useful for production work. A single path object that defines the basic outline of a button, for example, can quickly be duplicated and positioned to build a navigation bar where each button is identical, except for the identifying text. For all the variety in Figure 1-1, only three separate path objects were drawn.

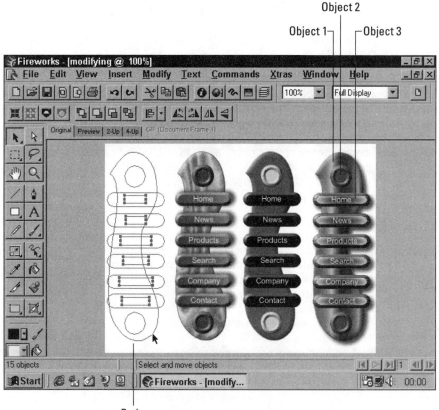

Figure 1-1: Reuse simple path shapes as you create and modify graphics in Fireworks.

Vector tools with organic bitmaps

For ultimate flexibility, Fireworks separates the stroke, fill, and effects of an object from the object itself. This enables the Web designer to create almost endless combinations for custom artwork while keeping each element individual and editable. If the client loves the orange glow around a button, but wants the text to be centered instead of flush right, it's no problem in Fireworks. Changing one aspect of a graphic — without having to rebuild the image from scratch — is one of Fireworks' key strengths.

While Fireworks depends on vector objects to create the underlying structure of its graphics, what goes on top of that structure (the stroke, fill, and effects) is displayed with pixels, as shown in Figure 1-2.

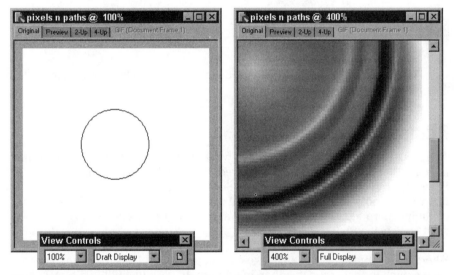

Figure 1-2: In Draft Display, an object's underlying path is clearly visible, but in Full Display mode — especially at a high magnification setting — you see that its visible elements are entirely pixel-based.

Bitmap components are calculated with numerous variables and as a result, give an organic feel to Fireworks objects. Bitmaps are recalculated and reapplied each time the path structure is changed, as shown in Figure 1-3. This procedure eliminates the distortion that occurs with other programs that just reshape the pixels. In a sense, when you alter a path in Fireworks, the program quickly redoes all of the work that you have done since you initially created the object.

Figure 1-3: Change the shape of a Fireworks object and the bitmap fill, stroke, and other properties are recalculated and reapplied.

To find out more about strokes, see Chapter 8. You can learn more about fills in Chapter 11.

Bitmap compatibility

As a next-generation graphics tool, Fireworks gracefully respects much of the imagery that has been previously created. With a full range of import filters, Fireworks can open and edit files from Photoshop, CorelDraw, FreeHand, and many more tools. Fireworks offers a full complement of bitmap selection tools, including Marquee, Lasso, and Magic Wand, as well as pixel-level drawing tools, such as Pencil and Eraser.

Filters are a large aspect of an image-editing program's featureset, and Fireworks is no slouch in that respect, either. In addition to various built-in filters, such as Gaussian Blur, Invert, and Sharpen, Fireworks is compatible with the Photoshop filter standard. Consequently, it works with any third-party plug-in that adheres to the standard, including Kai's Power Tools or Alien Skin's Eye Candy. In fact, two of the Eye Candy filters — Motion Trail, shown in Figure 1-4, and Cutout — are included with Fireworks 3 as Eye Candy LE (Limited Edition). What's more, you can easily include all of the third-party plug-ins that you use in Photoshop by just editing a single preference.

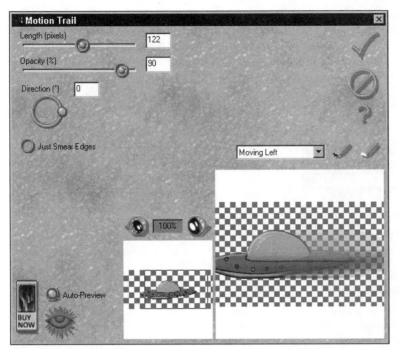

Figure 1-4: Alien Skin's Motion Trail filter is included with Fireworks as part of Eye Candy LE.

Want to know more about using third-party filters in Fireworks? Turn to Chapter 12.

Live Effects

One of the most challenging aspects of Web graphics used to be special effects, such as applying beveled edges and drop shadows. Fireworks takes all the complex, painstaking layer and mask manipulation these effects used to require and replaces it with Live Effects. Live Effects provide almost one-step ease with sophisticated variations for such effects as Inner Bevel, Outer Bevel, Drop Shadow, Glow, and Emboss.

Not only are these effects straightforward to create in Fireworks, but they adapt to any changes made to the object itself — hence, the name Live Effects. This feature is important for modifying graphics, and it speeds up production work tremendously. You can even batch process a group of files, reducing them in size, and the effects are scaled and reapplied automatically.

In addition to working with Fireworks' built-in Live Effects, Fireworks 3 will happily co-opt many Photoshop-compatible image filters that you may have installed as Xtras. These filters appear on the menu in the Effect panel, as shown in Figure 1-5, and are as "live" as any other Live Effect. In other words, you can apply Photoshop filters to path objects while they remain editable, and the effects themselves can be edited, removed or reordered at any time, too. What's more, effect combinations can be named and saved for later use.

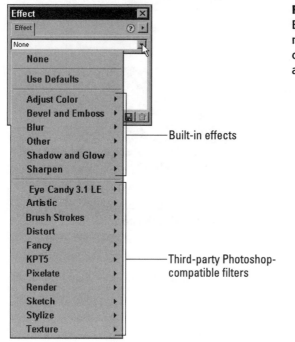

Figure 1-5: The redesigned Effect panel in Fireworks 3 now treats many Photoshop-compatible filters as always-editable Live Effects.

For detailed information on Live Effects, see Chapter 12.

Styles

Styles allow you to consistently apply the same look and feel to any number of objects. Fireworks Styles quickly replicate strokes, fills, effects, and even text settings. Web designers can use Styles to keep a client's Web site consistent looking across the board. Additionally, because Styles can be exported as files and shared, a lead designer can create a base Style for a Web graphic that can then be applied on a production basis to the rest of the site.

Styles also provide a way to audition different looks for a single object because you can quickly and easily apply complex groups of settings one after the other, as shown in Figure 1-6.

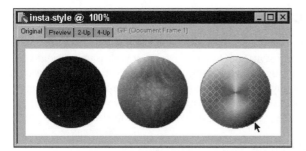

Figure 1-6: The same geometric shape, created in Fireworks, with and without Styles applied.

Macromedia offers a huge range of prebuilt Styles, in addition to the handful of Styles that are available in the Styles panel by default. Find them on the Fireworks CD-ROM or at `<http://www.macromedia.com/fireworks/download/styles>`.

Cross-Reference   Styles are a major time and work saver; to learn more about them, see Chapter 16.

Animation

Before Fireworks, one of the bevy of tools in a Web designer's arsenal was often a package to create animated GIFs (Graphics Interchange Format), often specifically for creating banner ads. This type of separate program is no longer necessary: Fireworks enables Web designers to build, preview, and export animated GIFs in any size or shape. Naturally, you can take advantage of all Fireworks path and bitmap tools to create and edit your animation.

Any Fireworks object can be turned into a Symbol and stored in the Library. Copies of Symbols are called Instances. Multiple Instances can be tweened — you make the beginning and end of an animation, and Fireworks extrapolates the middle for you — to create an animation in record time. Tweening can imply motion across the canvas or a change in an effect setting or other property. You could, for example, create an animated fade by tweening a fully opaque Instance with one that's fully transparent.

Cross-Reference Animation is a specialized but integral aspect of Web graphics. To find out more about it, turn to Part VI.

Linking to the Web

What do you call a graphics program that doesn't just output graphics? In the case of Fireworks, I call it a major innovation. On the surface, a Web page appears to be composed of images and text, but underneath it's all code. Fireworks bridges the gap between the images of a Web page and its HTML and JavaScript code to create image maps, slices, rollovers, and much more. Fireworks even gives you the option of choosing different styles of code, depending on which Web authoring tool you use.

Fireworks is fully integrated with the Web in mind. Every aspect of the program, from Web-safe color pickers to export optimization, keeps the Internet target clearly in focus. Even functions common to other programs have been given a special Web-oriented twist. For example, the capability to output a graphic to print is invaluable to Web designers as a way to present comps to clients; in Fireworks, you can print an image the way it will appear on the Web or at a higher print resolution — it's your choice.

Hotspots and slices

Hotspots and *slices* are frequently used elements in Web page design. Until Fireworks came along, however, designers had to create them using a program outside their usual graphics tools or tediously handcraft them individually. A hotspot is used as part of a Web page image map and is made of a series of x,y coordinates — elements definitely not in traditional visual artist vocabulary. Fireworks lets you draw out your hotspot, just as you would any other object, and handles all the math output for you.

Slice is a general term for the different parts of a larger image that has been carved into smaller pieces for faster loading or to incorporate a rollover. The separate parts of an image are then reassembled in an HTML table. If it sounds to you like an overwhelming amount of work, you're right — if you're not using Fireworks. Slicing an image is as simple as drawing slice objects, as shown in Figure 1-7, and choosing Export. Fireworks builds the HTML table for you. Additionally, Fireworks lets you optimize different slices, exporting one part as a JPEG (Joint Photographic Experts Group) and another as a GIF (or whatever combination gives you the highest quality at the lowest file size).

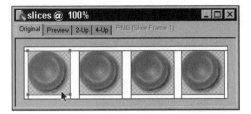

Figure 1-7: You draw the slice objects and Fireworks will do the cutting — and the HTML.

Explore more of what's possible with Fireworks hotspots and slices in Chapter 20.

URL panel

To take the fullest advantage of Fireworks HTML and JavaScript output, you need to attach hyperlinks or URLs to your images. You can import URLs from URL libraries, Bookmark files, or HTML pages through the URL panel. Not only does this sidestep the drudgery of manually entering Web links, it also eliminates any typing errors you might otherwise have made in the process. Once these URLs are in the URL panel, you can easily apply them to slices or to image map hotspots in order to Internet-enable navigation bar buttons.

Images with Behaviors

Static images are no longer enough on the Web; interactive images — images that react in some way when selected by the user — are a requirement for any state-of-the-art Web page. Fireworks handles this interactivity through a technique known as *Behaviors*. A Behavior is a combination of image and code: quite complex HTML and JavaScript code, to be exact. But when you apply a Behavior in Fireworks, all the code writing is handled for you.

Fireworks Behaviors can display a message when users pass their pointers over a particular image, or it can swap one image for another. Fireworks can even swap an image in one place if a graphic in another place is selected. Best of all, you can choose to output generic HTML code, or code that's optimized for your favorite Web authoring tool. Fireworks includes output templates for Macromedia Dreamweaver 3, Dreamweaver 3 Libraries, Dreamweaver 2, Adobe GoLive, and Microsoft FrontPage. If you've got the need and the savvy, you can also create custom templates.

New Feature

Fireworks also goes a step further in version 3 with the addition of the Button Editor, shown in Figure 1-8. The Button Editor makes it easy to create a self-contained, interactive button Symbol that can be previewed right in the document window.

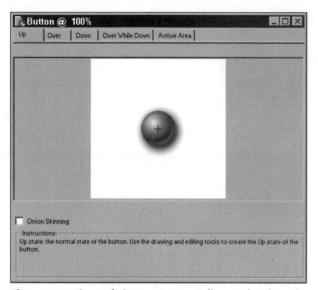

Figure 1-8: Fireworks's new Button Editor makes it easier than ever to make rollover buttons.

 Cross-Reference For more information about Behaviors, check out Chapter 21.

Optimizing for the Web

An overriding concern of many Web designers is file optimization: how do you get the best-looking image possible at the smallest size? Fireworks 3 allows you to compare the results of up to four different file compression views simultaneously, right in the document window. It's easy to monitor the way your work will look upon export; just click on one of the document window preview tabs, as shown in Figure 1-9.

In-place editing calls for some new controls within the Fireworks environment, and that means more panels. The Optimize panel contains the varied export options a Web artist requires, easily accessible at any time. And colors can be edited, locked, snapped to Web safe, or made transparent with a click of the mouse in the new Color Table panel. You'll also find the Frames panel has sprouted some animation timing controls.

What's more—and perhaps best of all—if you prefer the classic Fireworks 2 Export Preview dialog box and the Export to Size Wizard over in-place previews, you'll be happy to find that those features are still available.

 Cross-Reference To get the most out of exporting in Fireworks, check out Chapter 15.

Preview tabs

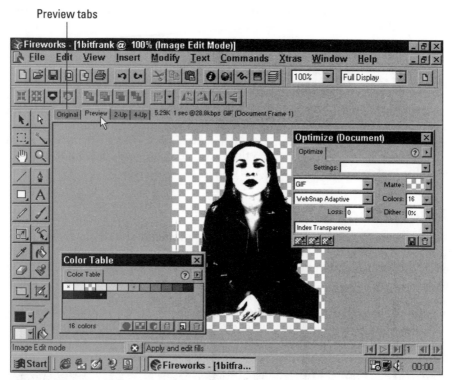

Figure 1-9: Quickly find the highest-quality image at the lowest possible size with Fireworks' Export Preview.

Dreamweaver integration

Dreamweaver 3 is a top-of-the-line Web authoring tool, now made even better through a tighter integration with Fireworks 3. Dreamweaver contains Commands that directly access Fireworks features or assist in importing Fireworks HTML code. In fact, the enhanced scriptability of Fireworks 3 allows Dreamweaver Commands to actually control Fireworks.

The integration is not just apparent from the Dreamweaver side, either. Fireworks outputs standard Dreamweaver code or Dreamweaver Library code with Fireworks Behaviors that are editable within Dreamweaver, as if they were applied in Dreamweaver itself. The two programs are also moving closer to each other from a usability viewpoint. For example, Fireworks now includes a Commands menu and History panel, just like Dreamweaver.

Cross-Reference For all of the details on maximizing the Fireworks 3-Dreamweaver 3 combination, see Chapter 22.

Production Tools

Though the Web offers plenty of room for creative expression, creating Web graphics is often—bottom-line—a business. To succeed at such a business you need a tool capable of high production output, and Fireworks 3 certainly fits the bill. You can insert whole pages of URLs at a time, rescale entire folders of images, or update all of the text embedded in a Web site's images.

Automation

Nothing eats up time and patience like having to do the same thing over, and over, and over again. Unfortunately, Web production features this kind of workflow all too often. The same steps are often required again and again. Chances are, if you have to do it more than once, you have to do it ten times.

In perhaps its simplest role, the new History panel (Figure 1-10) provides fine control over Undo steps, allowing you to reverse course at any time with pinpoint accuracy. Look a little deeper, though, and you'll notice that the History panel is also the heart of the enhanced automation setup of Fireworks 3.

Figure 1-10: Is the new History panel an enhanced Undo or a macro recorder? Both.

Select any step or group of steps in the History panel and you can instantly turn them into a Command that's automatically added to Fireworks' new Commands menu, shown in Figure 1-11. As useful as this is on its own, the History panel goes further still: each step is actually represented by JavaScript code, which can be copied to the clipboard and then pasted into a text editor for refinement.

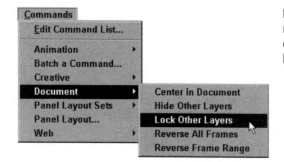

Figure 1-11: The Commands menu contains many useful options — but that's only the beginning.

Dive into Fireworks automation in Chapter 19.

Batch processing

The large number of images in a typical Web page has made batch processing a virtual necessity. It's not at all uncommon for a client to request that thumbnail images of an entire product line be created for an online catalog. With batch processing, just point to the folder of full-size images and tell Fireworks whether to scale them to a particular pixel size or to a particular percentage.

Another great timesaver is the Find and Replace panel. Find and Replace in a graphics program? What use could that possibly have? Very far-reaching uses, to be frank. Fireworks can search and replace text, fonts, colors, or URLs in any Fireworks file or a group of files. What's more, Fireworks 3 adds the capability to search for and snap non-Web-safe colors to their nearest Web-safe counterparts.

Chapter 18 has everything you need to know about batch processing in Fireworks.

What's New in Fireworks 3

Any way you look at it, the jump from the first version of Fireworks to Fireworks 2 was quite a leap; enhancing the drawing tools, refining the creative interface, and offering better integration of vector and bitmap editing. With Fireworks 3, the bar has been raised further, but this time the Fireworks engineering team focused less on Fireworks and more on you, the user. New features allow complete control of Undo steps, recording and automation of mundane tasks, fewer steps to get common tasks done, organization of Symbols in the Library, easier access to image optimization options, previews in the document window, Photoshop filters as Live Effects, import of Photoshop Layer Effects, and more. The list goes on and on, but the common theme is enhancing your efficiency, saving you time, and making Fireworks 3 a joy to use.

User interface

User interface enhancements may not qualify as a "feature" for some people, but they can have an incredible impact on your day-to-day work in an application, because changes are literally at your fingertips. Significant enhancements, such as those implemented in Fireworks 3, greatly increase productivity and workflow. One of the biggest improvements is a completely new way to preview your work: right in the document window, with export options set in floating panels.

User interface enhancements include:

✦ Preview directly in the document window

✦ Image optimization controls always available in the Optimize panel

✦ Animation timing now easily accessible in the Frames panel

✦ Improved floating-panel interfaces

Cross-Reference   For details on all the user interface changes, see the rest of the chapters in Part I.

Graphics creation

With each new release, Fireworks becomes a bigger and better drawing and bitmap-editing tool.

Graphics-creation enhancements include

✦ Adjust the contrast, brightness, hue and saturation of bitmaps with new Live Effects

✦ Correct the tonal range using Levels, Auto Levels, and Curves

✦ Instant access to textures and Patterns

✦ Save textures or Patterns with a document

✦ Choose from bicubic, bilinear, nearest neighbor, or soft interpolation scaling options within the Image Size dialog

✦ Rotate the canvas and all objects in one step

✦ Text blocks automatically resize vertically and horizontally as you enter text

✦ Font preview allows you to view a font before applying it

✦ Enhanced font substitution

Web connectivity

When Fireworks first appeared, its capability to output HTML code was like a rocket taking off. Now, other applications have followed suit, but Fireworks has continued to build on its excellent history, bringing the two worlds of Web designers — graphics and code — closer together.

Web connectivity enhancements include

✦ Enhanced Behaviors

✦ Button Symbols and Button editor

✦ Polygon Slices

✦ Copy to Clipboard code export

✦ Preview rollovers in the document window

✦ Update tables in Fireworks HTML

✦ Overlapping slices without HTML errors

Learn more about Web connectivity in Part V.

Image optimization

For many users, image optimization is at the heart of Fireworks. Getting the best possible image with the smallest possible file size is what it's all about. Fireworks 3 offers new methods for trimming file sizes and creating cross-platform graphics.

Image optimization enhancements include

✦ Snap to Web Color Find and Replace

✦ Lossy GIF optimization

✦ View Windows or Macintosh gamma

To learn more about Fireworks as an optimizing engine, see Chapter 15.

Workflow management

Workflow Management received special attention in Fireworks 3. In fact, it might be the overriding theme of Fireworks 3. Photoshop import has been greatly enhanced and Fireworks paths can now be exported for use in other vector drawing applications. Nearly complete automation allows for a small investment of time spent creating Commands – by recording your work in the History panel – to pay off big again and again as you reduce multiple mundane steps to a single menu item in the new Commands menu.

Workflow management enhancements include

✦ Improved Photoshop import

✦ Photoshop Layer Effects imported as Fireworks Live Effects

✦ Photoshop editable text remains editable

✦ Export paths as Flash SWF or Illustrator 7

✦ History panel allows complete Undo control

✦ Use Photoshop-compatible filters as always-editable Live Effects

✦ Commands menu

✦ Record Commands in the History panel

✦ JavaScript scriptability

✦ Greatly enhanced JavaScript API

✦ Symbol management with the Flash-style Library panel

✦ Tighter Dreamweaver integration

 Cross-Reference To get the most out of the new Fireworks workflow improvements, see Part IV.

Summary

"Pick the right tool for the job," the saying goes — and Fireworks 3 is definitely the right tool for the job of creating Web graphics. In many cases, it's the only tool you'll need to handle every aspect of this particular job: image creation, editing, optimization, and Web integration. It's no surprise that in the past, Web designers had to master many programs to even come close to what Fireworks 3 can accomplish. If you're looking at Fireworks 3 for the first time, keep these points in mind:

✦ Fireworks 3 replaces an entire bookshelf of programs that Web designers had previously adapted for their use. With only one program to master, designers can work more efficiently and creatively.

✦ Fireworks 3 is equally at home with vector-based objects and bitmap-based images. Moreover, it combines vector structures with bitmap surfaces in order to make editing easier and the results cleaner.

✦ Fireworks 3 works with Photoshop and many other existing file types — and can even use third-party Photoshop-compatible filters as Xtras or even as Live Effects.

✦ One of Fireworks 3's key capabilities is to connect you easily to the Web. To this end, Web-safe palettes are always available and HTML and JavaScript code — standard or custom — is just a click away.

✦ The more you work on the Web, the faster you realize just how much work there is to do. Fireworks 3 is a terrific production tool and makes updating graphics, via search and replace operations or batch processing, an automated process instead of a manual drudge.

✦ Fireworks 3 improved upon previous versions with a focus on the user; improving automation, lessening the steps involved in common tasks, providing easier access to previews, and offering new and enhanced floating panels.

In the next chapter, you'll take an extensive tour of Fireworks 3's user interface and all of its menu commands.

✦   ✦   ✦

Understanding the Interface

✦ ✦ ✦ ✦

In This Chapter

The Fireworks environment

Working in the document window

Familiarizing yourself with the Toolbox

Windows Toolbars

Optimizing the floating panels

Managing the menus

✦ ✦ ✦ ✦

Fireworks was designed to meet a need among Web graphics artists: to simplify the workflow. Before Fireworks, designers typically used different programs for object creation, rasterization, optimization, and HTML and JavaScript creation. Fire-works combines the best features of several key tools — while offering numerous innovative additions of its own — into a sophisticated interface that's easy to use and offers many surprising creative advantages. Once you've discovered the power of Fireworks, it's hard to design Web graphics any other way.

With Fireworks, the designer has tools for working with both vector-based objects and pixel-based images. You'll even find ways to combine the two different formats. When your document is ready to make the move to the Web, Fireworks acts as a bridge to the HTML environment by allowing you to create the necessary code in a point-and-click manner.

Fireworks 3 continues the trend toward an optimized workflow with several new features. First, you'll notice that you can now preview your work right in the document window and specify optimization through the new Optimize floating panel. The arrangement of the toolbox has changed slightly, and many menu items are more accessible or better organized.

As with any truly powerful computer graphics program, examining all the tools and options that Fireworks has to offer at one time can be overwhelming. However, that's not how most artists work. You may find it easier to familiarize yourself with a new tool by carrying out a specific task. It's fine to go all the way through this chapter — which covers every element of the Fireworks interface — but you'll probably get the most value from the chapter elements, especially the menu by menu description of commands at the end of the chapter, by using them as a reference guide.

The Fireworks Environment

Whether you start your graphics session by creating a new document or loading in an existing one, you'll find yourself working within a complete environment that includes standard menus, a toolbox, one or more document windows, and a selection of floating panels, as shown in Figure 2-1. Each document window contains a single Fireworks file; the menus, toolbox, and floating panels affect the file in the active document window.

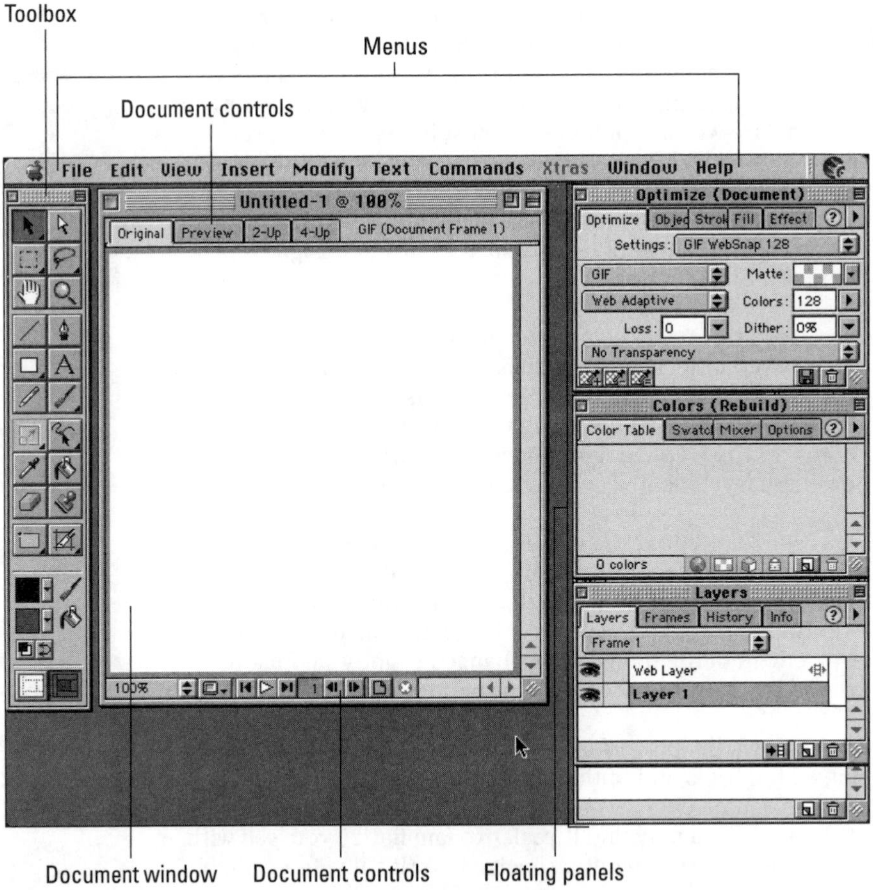

Figure 2-1: The Fireworks environment on both platforms includes menus, a toolbox, one or more document windows, and a complete set of floating panels.

Fireworks for Windows (Figure 2-2) features the same interface elements as its Macintosh cousin, but also adds three toolbars and a context-sensitive Status bar into the mix. Two of the toolbars mimic functions from the menus, such as opening a document or hiding a floating panel, while the third toolbar, View Controls, contains some of the document controls that are attached to each document window on the Mac (the rest are in the Status bar). The Windows version also uses a multiple document interface that contains all of the documents and interface elements within a parent Fireworks window that hides the desktop. Toolbars, and even the Toolbox, can be docked to the parent window or floated as required.

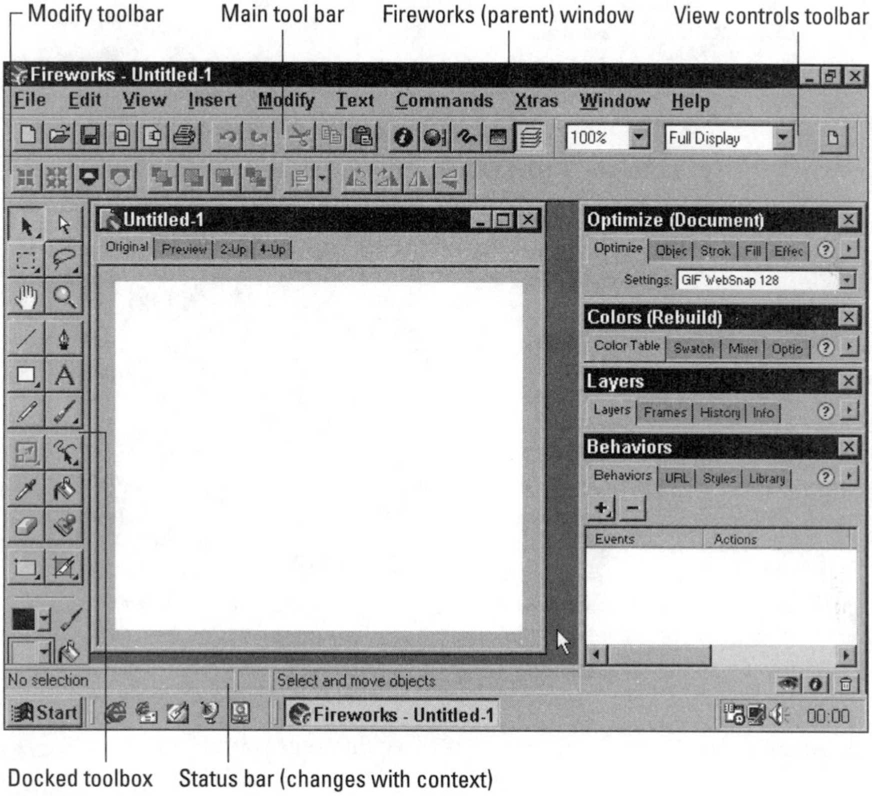

Modify toolbar   Main tool bar   Fireworks (parent) window   View controls toolbar

Docked toolbox   Status bar (changes with context)

Figure 2-2: The Windows version of Fireworks has additional toolbars and uses a multiple document interface.

We'll examine each element of the complete Fireworks environment throughout this chapter. Remember, you can refer back to Figures 2-1 or 2-2 at any time if you find yourself losing track of a particular item.

The Document Window

The document window is the central focus of your work in Fireworks. Each Fireworks document you open or create is contained within its own document window, and multiple documents can be opened and displayed simultaneously, as shown in Figure 2-3.

The menus, toolbox, and floating panels affect the file in the active document window. Objects are created and edited on the canvas within the document window.

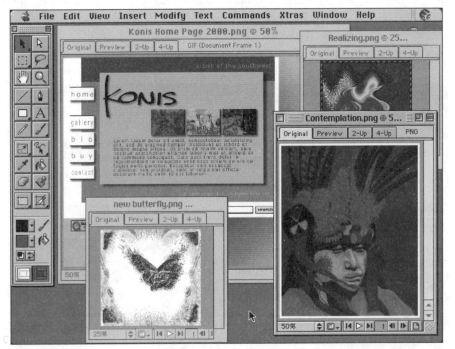

Figure 2-3: Each Fireworks file you open or create is contained within its own document window, and multiple documents can be opened simultaneously.

If you have multiple documents open and your workspace is getting cluttered, you can organize the document windows in three different ways:

✦ Choose Window ➪ Cascade to stack your open documents on top of each other in a diagonal, so that the title bar for each is visible.

✦ Select Window ➪ Tile Horizontal to see all open documents evenly distributed from top to bottom in the document window.

✦ Select Window ➪ Tile Vertical to view all open documents evenly distributed from left to right in the document window.

You can also hide document windows that you're not currently using. Macintosh users can click the Windowshade button on a document window to hide all but the title bar. Windows users can click the Minimize button on a document window to minimize its title bar to the bottom of the parent window. Windows users can also click Maximize to dock a document window to the parent window, hiding all other windows. Clicking the document window's Restore button undocks it.

In addition to multiple document windows for multiple documents, Fireworks can also display multiple document windows for the same document. To open a new view of a selected document, choose Window ➪ New Window or use the key shortcut Ctrl+Alt+N in Windows (Command+Option+N for Macintosh). The new view opens at the same magnification as the previous image, but, as Figure 2-4 shows, you can easily zoom in for detail work on one view while displaying the overall effect in another.

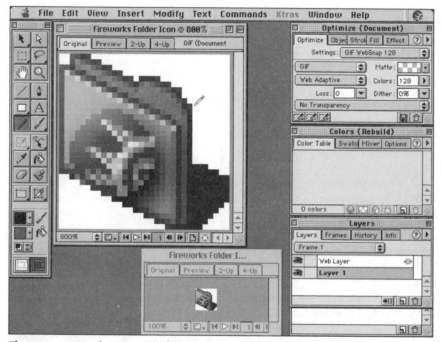

Figure 2-4: Use the New Window command to open a new view of the same image if both pixel-level modifications and the big picture are required.

On the CD-ROM You'll find the Mac OS 8/9 Fireworks folder icon pictured in Figure 2-3, as well as a Fireworks folder icon for Windows.

Document Controls

Fireworks enables you to control what you see in a document window in a number of ways. Tabs along the top of the document window enable you to preview your work in-place; you'll also find controls for magnification, display modes, animation, and more.

The document controls are all on the document window itself in Fireworks for Macintosh, as shown in Figure 2-5.

Original/Preview tabs

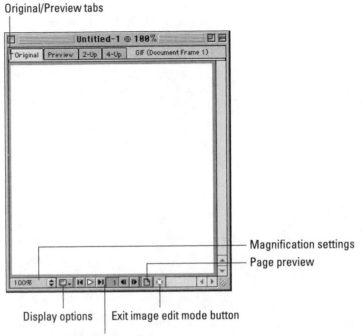

Magnification settings
Page preview

Display options   Exit image edit mode button

Animation controls

Figure 2-5: Fireworks document controls—located on the document window on the Macintosh—enable you to alter how your document is presented in the document window.

Fireworks for Windows spreads the document controls out a little bit, in keeping with the parent and child windows of its multiple document interface. Some are on the document window, some in the View Controls toolbar, and some in the Status bar, as shown in Figure 2-6. The controls always reflect and affect the settings of the currently active document window.

Tip   Windows users: although the View Controls toolbar is docked by default, you can float it by dragging it away from the parent window. To dock it again, drag it back or double-click its title bar.

Although the interfaces look slightly different on each platform, the functions of the various document controls are exactly the same. We'll look at each one, and what it does, in turn.

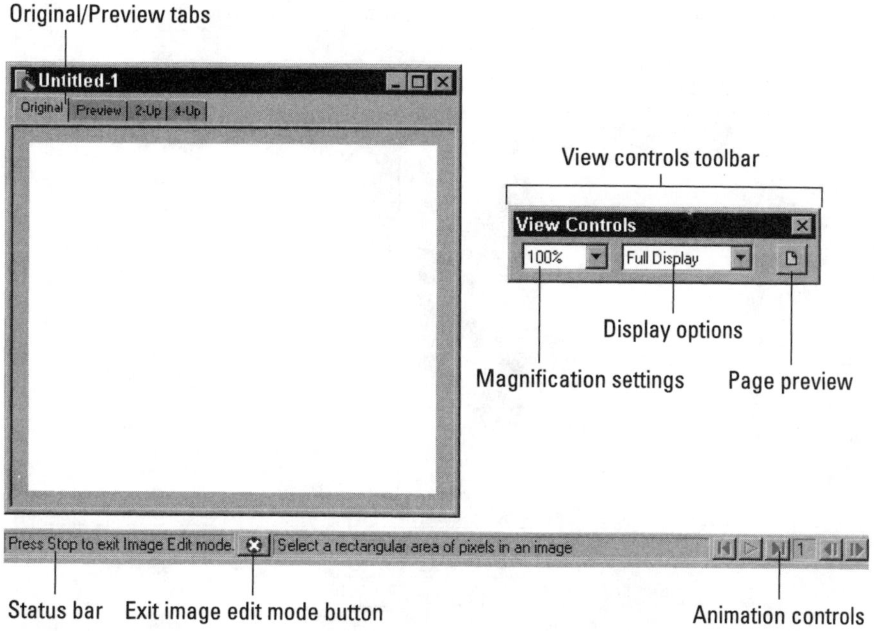

Original/Preview tabs

Figure 2-6: Fireworks for Windows' document controls are shared between the document window, the View Controls toolbar, and the Status bar.

Original/Preview tabs

When you open or create a document in Fireworks, the document window is set on the Original tab, so that you can interact with and edit the objects on the canvas. Choose one of the other tabs and Fireworks will create and display a preview of your work as it will appear in your exported final output.

New Feature

In Fireworks 3, previewing your work in place is now the default. Select the appropriate tab in the document window to switch from your Original, working view to a Preview, or a 2-up or 4-up preview. The Fireworks 2 style Export Preview dialog box is still available. Choose File ➪ Export Preview to display it.

You can switch from Original to one of the preview modes at any time. Fireworks generates a preview based on the settings you select in the Optimize panel, as shown in Figure 2-7. Control of the export palette is available in the Color Table panel.

Although the 2-Up preview gives you a side-by-side view of the Original and Preview views of a document, it only shows you half of each unless you manually expand your document window. If you have the screen real estate available, another way to get a side-by-side preview is to open a new document window for the same document (Window ➪ New Window, as described above) and set it to Preview.

Figure 2-7: A preview of your work is never more than a click away with Fireworks 3's in-place preview.

Cross-Reference   For more on previewing and exporting, see Chapter 15.

Magnification settings

Whether you're working with pixels or vectors, a polished, finished graphic often demands close-up, meticulous work. Likewise, the designer often needs to be able to step back from an image in order to compare two or more large images for overall compatibility or to cut and paste sections of a graphic. Fireworks offers a fast Magnification control with numerous keyboard shortcuts for rapid view changes.

Fireworks uses a series of zoom settings, from 6 percent to 6,400 percent, for its Magnification control. Because Fireworks always works with pixels (even when they're based on vectors), the magnification settings are predefined to offer the best image pixel to screen pixel ratio. When an image is viewed at 100 percent magnification, one screen pixel is used for each image pixel. Should you zoom in to 200 percent, two screen pixels are used for each image pixel. Zooming out reverses the procedure: at 50 percent, each screen pixel represents two image pixels. Fireworks' preset zoom method offers a full range of settings while maintaining an accurate view of your image.

Clicking the arrow button in the Magnification option list—on the document window on Macintosh and on the View Controls toolbar on Windows—displays the available settings. Highlight the desired zoom setting and release the mouse button in order to change magnifications. Fireworks also offers a variety of keyboard shortcuts to change the zoom setting, as detailed in Table 2-1. In addition to specifying a magnification setting, you can also have Fireworks fit the image in the current window. With this command, Fireworks zooms in or out to the maximum magnification setting possible—and still displays the entire image.

Table 2-1
Magnification Key Shortcuts

Magnification	Windows	Macintosh
100%	Ctrl+1	Command+1
50%	Ctrl+5	Command+5
200%	Ctrl+2	Command+2
400%	Ctrl+4	Command+4
800%	Ctrl+8	Command+8
3200%	Ctrl+3	Command+3
6400%	Ctrl+6	Command+6
Zoom In	Ctrl+Plus	Command+Plus
Zoom Out	Ctrl+Minus	Command+Minus
Fit Selection in	Ctrl+Zero	Command+Zero
Fit All in Window	Ctrl+Alt+Zero or double-click Hand tool	Command+Option+Zero or double-click Hand tool
Switch to Zoom tool temporarily	Hold down Ctrl+Spacebar	Hold down Command+Spacebar

Display options

Most of the time, Fireworks designers work in Full Display mode. In fact, this practice is so common that many designers don't realize that another mode is even available. The Display Mode option list offers two options: Full Display and Draft Display. Draft Display shows all vector-based objects with one-pixel-wide outlines and no fill; pixel-based images are shown as rectangles with an "X" in the middle.

What makes Draft Display so useful is that when a portion of a graphic is selected—either a pixel image or a vector object—that selection is rendered in Full Display mode while all the other parts of the picture are outlined, as shown in Figure 2-8. You can even select the entire image and then deselect sections, thus rendering them in Draft Display mode, so you can concentrate on particular areas of the image. The display mode can be toggled between Full and Draft Display with a keyboard shortcut, Ctrl+K (Command+K), or use the Display option list on the document window on Macintosh and on the View Controls toolbar on Windows.

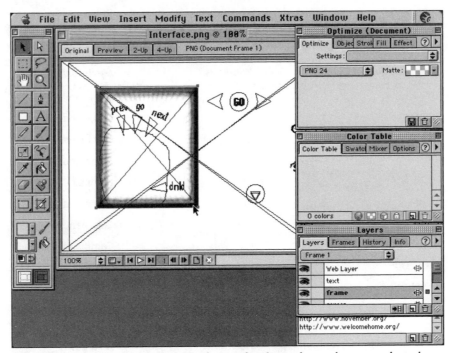

Figure 2-8: While you're in Draft Display mode, Fireworks renders any selected portion of your graphic in Full Display mode for editing.

Other controls

In addition to the controls we've already covered, Fireworks offers three more sets of document controls whose functions are fairly straightforward:

✦ **Page Preview:** Click the Page Preview button to see a quick dimensional overview of the current document. The width, height, and resolution are displayed in a small pop-up window. On Windows, click once to activate the control, and once again to deactivate it. On the Mac, click and hold to activate; release to deactivate.

✦ **Animation controls:** With these VCR-like buttons — on the document window in Macintosh and on the Status bar in Windows — you can play a frame-based animation straight through, using the timing established in the Frame panel. You'll also find buttons that enable you to move through the animation a frame at a time or to go to the first or last frame.

The Animation controls — and animation in general — are covered in Part VI.

✦ **Exit Image Edit Mode button:** Click the "stop" button on the bottom of the document window on Macintosh and on the Status bar on Windows to quickly exit Image Edit Mode and to enter Object Mode. When you're already in Image Edit Mode, the stop button is grayed out in Macintosh and invisible in Windows.

Opening the Toolbox

All Fireworks drawing and editing tools can be found in the Toolbox. Most tools work with both pixel-based images and path-based objects, although some change their behavior in order to do so. The eraser, for example, becomes a knife when you're working with paths.

Tools that are similar, such as the Lasso, Polygon Lasso, and Magic Wand, are grouped together into tool groups and accessed through a flyout. A tool group can be recognized by the small triangle in the lower-right corner of the button; clicking and holding the button causes the flyout to appear. Once the tool group is visible, you can select any of the tools in the group by moving the pointer over the tool and releasing the mouse. Figure 2-9 shows the toolbox with all of its flyouts *out*.

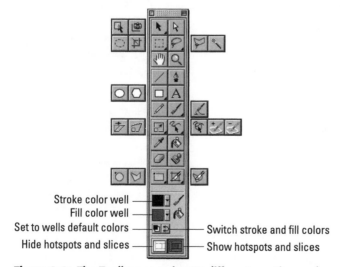

Figure 2-9: The Toolbox contains 37 different creation and editing tools for both graphics and Web objects.

Tip   Windows users have the option of floating the Toolbox or docking it to the Fireworks window. Double-clicking the title bar of the toolbox docks it to the parent window. Dragging it back out undocks it.

If you previously used Fireworks 2, you'll find the Toolbox largely unchanged. The crop tool has moved one floor down, from the Pointer flyout to the Marquee flyout—where Photoshop also keeps it—and the Slice tool has become a flyout that now contains the Slice tool and the Polygon Slice tool.

All of the tools have keyboard shortcuts. As befits a program that incorporates both pixel- and vector-editing tools, these single-key shortcuts parallel the shortcuts for some of the pixel-based tools in Photoshop, and vector-based ones in FreeHand. If two or more tools share a keyboard shortcut (as with M for Marquee and Ellipse Marquee), the key acts as a toggle between the tools; the letter R toggles through seven tools: the rectangle, the ellipse, and all of the Web tools. You Ωcan find the button for each tool, as well as its keyboard shortcut and a brief description the tool, in Table 2-2. More detailed information on each tool is presented throughout this book when the tool is used for various operations.

Note   Tools that are new or have moved in Fireworks 3 are displayed in bold text.

<table>
<tr><td colspan="4">Table 2-2
Fireworks Tools</td></tr>
<tr><td>*Button*</td><td>*Name*</td><td>*Shortcut*</td><td>*Description*</td></tr>
<tr><td></td><td>Pointer</td><td>V or Zero</td><td>Selects and moves objects</td></tr>
<tr><td></td><td>Select Behind</td><td>V or Zero</td><td>Selects and moves objects that are behind other objects</td></tr>
<tr><td></td><td>Export Area</td><td>J</td><td>Exports a selected portion of a document</td></tr>
<tr><td></td><td>Subselection</td><td>A</td><td>Selects an object within a group or points on a path</td></tr>
<tr><td></td><td>Marquee</td><td>M</td><td>Selects a rectangular portion of a pixel image</td></tr>
<tr><td></td><td>Ellipse Marquee</td><td>M</td><td>Selects an elliptical portion of a pixel image</td></tr>
<tr><td></td><td>Crop</td><td>C</td><td>Increases or decreases canvas size</td></tr>
</table>

Button	Name	Shortcut	Description
	Lasso	L	Selects a freely drawn area of a pixel image
	Polygon Lasso	L	Selects a polygon-shaped area of a pixel image
	Magic Wand	W	Selects similar color areas of a pixel image
	Hand	H or press and hold spacebar	Pans the view of a document
	Magnify	Z	Increases or decreases the magnification level of a document by one setting
	Line	N	Draws straight lines
	Pen	P	Adds points to paths
	Rectangle	R	Draws rectangles, rectangles with rounded corners, and squares
	Ellipse	R	Draws ellipses and circles
	Polygon	G	Draws polygons and stars
	Text	T	Inserts text objects
	Pencil	Y	Draws single-pixel freeform strokes
	Brush	B	Draws strokes using the Stroke panel settings
	Redraw Path	B	Redraws portions of a selected path
	Scale	Q	Resizes and rotates objects

Continued

Table 2-2 *(continued)*

Button	Name	Shortcut	Description
	Skew	Q	Slants, rotates, and modifies the perspective of objects
	Distort	Q	Reshapes and rotates objects
	Freeform	Period	Pulls or pushes a path with a variable-size cursor
	Reshape Area	Period	Reshapes an object's area with a variable-size cursor
	Path Scrubber (+)	U	Increases the stroke settings that are controlled by cursor speed or pen and tablet pressure
	Path Scrubber (-)	U	Decreases the stroke settings that are controlled by cursor speed or pen and tablet pressure
	Eyedropper	I	Picks up color from anywhere onscreen and applies it to the active color well
	Paint Bucket	K	Fills the selected area with color, gradients, patterns, or textures and enables fills to be adjusted
	Eraser / Knife	E	Deletes pixels from pixel-based images and cuts the paths of vector-based objects
	Rubber Stamp	K	Repeats portion of pixel images
	Hotspot	R	Draws an image-map hotspot area in a rectangular shape
	Ellipse Hotspot	R	Draws an image-map hotspot area in an elliptical shape
	Polygon Hotspot	R	Draws an image-map hotspot area in a polygonal shape
	Slice	R	Draws a slice object in a rectangular shape
	Polygon Slice	R	Draws a slice object in a polygonal shape

Tip

Certain tools have keyboard shortcuts that enable you to temporarily replace the active tool. Press and hold Ctrl (Command) in order to switch to the Pointer temporarily, and press and hold Alt (Option) in order to switch to the Eyedropper. You can also press and hold Ctrl+spacebar (Command+spacebar) in order to access the Zoom tool. Holding down the spacebar by itself temporarily retrieves the Hand tool.

Accessing Toolbars (Windows Only)

Some people hate toolbars, and some people love them. Either way, they're expected in Windows applications and are a welcome addition to Fireworks for Windows for many users.

There are three toolbars: Main, Modify, and View Controls. The Main toolbar contains common File and Edit menu functions and shows or hides commonly used floating panels. The Modify toolbar contains Modify menu functions, such as grouping, aligning or rotating objects. The View Controls toolbar contains document controls.

Note

The View Controls toolbar is covered earlier in this chapter in "The Document Window" section.

The toolbars are docked to the parent window by default, but you can position them anywhere within the Fireworks window by undocking them. To detach a docked toolbar, click and drag the toolbar. To dock a detached toolbar, drag the toolbar close to an edge of the Fireworks window until it snaps into position, or double-click its title bar.

Fireworks for Windows also has a context-sensitive Status bar that runs along the bottom of the Fireworks window. We'll look at that in this section, as well.

Main toolbar

The Main toolbar, shown in Figure 2-10, displays a row of buttons that access the most commonly used menu functions — 16 in all. The Main toolbar enables you to perform several key file operations, such as create a new document, open or save an existing document, and export or import an image, all with just one click. The most often-used editing features — Undo, Redo, Cut, Copy, and Paste — are also located on the Main toolbar. Finally, the Main toolbar brings five important floating panels into view or hides them. Table 2-3 describes each button in the Main toolbar.

Figure 2-10: The Main toolbar gives Window users one-click access to many commonly used commands.

Table 2-3
Main Toolbar

Button	Name	Description
	New	Creates a new document
	Open	Opens an existing document
	Save	Saves the current document
	Import	Imports a file into the current document
	Export	Exports the current document
	Print	Prints the current document
	Undo	Undoes the last action
	Redo	Redoes the last action that was undone
	Cut	Cuts the selected object to the clipboard
	Copy	Copies the selected object to the clipboard
	Paste	Pastes the clipboard into the current document
	Object	Displays/hides the Object panel
	Color Mixer	Displays/hides the Color Mixer panel
	Stroke	Displays/hides the Stroke panel
	Fill	Displays/hides the Fill panel
	Layers	Displays/hides the Layers panel

Modify toolbar

The Modify toolbar, shown in Figure 2-11, offers single-click access to four primary types of modifications:

✦ **Grouping:** Group or join two or more objects for easier manipulation. Buttons are also available for ungrouping and splitting combined objects.

✦ **Arranging:** Position objects in front of or behind other objects. Objects can also be moved on top of or underneath all other objects.

✦ **Aligning:** Align two or more objects in any of eight different ways, including centered vertically or horizontally.

✦ **Rotating:** Flip selected objects horizontally, vertically, or rotate them 90 degrees, either clockwise or counterclockwise.

Align pop-up

Figure 2-11: Group, arrange, align, or rotate selected objects with the Modify toolbar.

Instead of directly executing a command — like the other buttons on the Modify toolbar — the Align button opens a pop-up toolbar that contains a range of alignment buttons. In Fireworks, alignment commands — whether they're issued from this pop-up toolbar or from the Modify ➪ Align submenu — align objects to a theoretical rectangle around the selection, not to the canvas as you might expect. For example, if you select a circle on the left side of the canvas and a bitmap image on the right, clicking the Align Left button causes the bitmap image to align along the left edge of the circle, because it is the leftmost object in the selection. Table 2-4 details each button on the Modify toolbar.

 Read more about aligning objects in Fireworks in Chapter 13.

Table 2-4
Modify Toolbar

Button	Name	Description
	Group	Groups selected objects
	Ungroup	Ungroups previously grouped objects
	Join	Joins the paths of two path objects
	Split	Separates previously joined path objects
	Bring Front	Positions the selected object on top of all other objects
	Bring Forward	Moves the selected object one step closer to the top
	Send Backward	Moves the selected object one step closer to the bottom
	Send to Back	Positions the selected object underneath all other objects
	Align Left	Aligns the selected objects to the left edge of the selection
	Center Vertical Axis	Centers the selected objects on a vertical line
	Align Right	Aligns the selected objects to the right edge of the selection
	Align Top	Aligns the selected objects along the top edge of the selection
	Center Horizontal Axis	Centers the selected objects on a horizontal line
	Align Bottom	Aligns the selected objects along the bottom edge of the selection
	Distribute Widths	Evenly distributes the selected objects horizontally
	Distribute Heights	Evenly distributes the selected objects vertically
	Rotate 90° CCW	Rotates the selected object 90° counterclockwise

Button	Name	Description
	Rotate 90° CW	Rotates the selected object 90° clockwise
	Flip Horizontal	Flips the selected object horizontally
	Flip Vertical	Flips the selected object vertically

Status bar

The Status bar, shown in Figure 2-12, has four sections:

✦ **Selection indicator:** Displays the type of object or objects selected. If you're in Image Edit mode, the Status bar notifies you here.

✦ **Description:** Provides tooltips for each of the tools that are selected or moused over.

✦ **Exit Image Edit Mode button:** Appears only when you're in Image Edit Mode. Clicking it changes to Object Mode.

✦ **Animation controls:** Enable you to control frame-based animation in the document window.

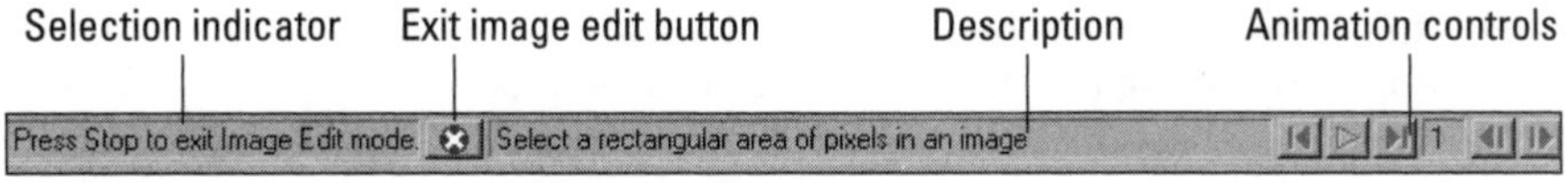

Selection indicator   Exit image edit button   Description   Animation controls

Press Stop to exit Image Edit mode. ⊗ Select a rectangular area of pixels in an image

Figure 2-12: The Status bar tells you what types of objects you have selected and offers context-sensitive tooltips.

Note   The Exit Image Edit Mode button and the Animation controls are also covered earlier in this chapter in "The Document Window" section.

Managing the Floating Panels

Fireworks maintains a great deal of functionality in its floating panels. In all, the program offers 19 different panels for modifying everything from the stroke color to a JavaScript behavior. Toggling whether a particular panel is shown or hidden is as simple as choosing its name from the Window menu or pressing its key shortcut.

Although there is an almost dazzling array of panels to choose from, the effect is not overwhelming because panels are docked together into groups. When a panel is docked behind another one, click its tab to bring it to the front.

By default, Fireworks combines the floating panels into four different groups, but you can customize the groupings to fit the way you work. If you're working with dual monitors, you might want to display every panel separately, so that all 19 are instantly available. On the other hand, you could conserve maximum screen real estate by grouping all the panels into one supergroup with tabs visible for each individual panel. The middle ground, though, is probably the best for most people: some docked, some not, and commonly used panels always visible.

The more you work in Fireworks, the sooner you'll arrive at a panel configuration that's best for you. I tend to group my floating panels on the right side of the screen and use the left area as my workspace. Once you come up with an arrangement you find useful, Fireworks 3 allows you to save that arrangement as a Panel Layout Set and recall it for later use.

Grouping and moving panels

Grouping and ungrouping floating panels is a straightforward process. To separate a floating panel from its current group, click the panel's tab and drag it away from the group. As you drag, you'll see an outline of the panel. Release the mouse button to place the panel onscreen.

Similarly, grouping one panel with another is also a drag-and-drop affair. Drag the panel's tab until the outline appears. When your pointer moves over a different panel, the outline snaps to the outline of the static panel. Release the mouse button and a tab, representing the panel being moved, is added to the right of the existing group.

In addition to the grouping feature, the floating panels also snap to the borders of the document window or another floating panel. This snapping feature enables the designer to move panels out of the way quickly and to align them in a visually pleasing manner. It may seem like a minor detail, but when panels are snapped to an edge, the workspace appears less cluttered and more useable.

The floating panels are easy to position around the screen. Just click on the panel's title bar and drag it to a new position. Likewise, you can easily resize and reshape any of the floating panels. In Windows, position your pointer over any border of the panel so that the cursor becomes a two-headed arrow and then drag the border to alter the size or shape of the panel. On the Mac, drag the resize widget on the lower right of the panel in order to alter the panel's size or shape. Each of the panels have a minimum size that you'll "bump" into if you try to make the panel too small.

Panel Layout Sets

Once you've discovered a particular arrangement of the floating panels that works for you, Fireworks 3 allows you to save that arrangement as a Panel Layout Set.

In Fireworks 3, the floating panels interface is even more usable because you can save Panel Layout Sets: the complete configuration and layout of all of the floating windows, saved for recall at a moment's notice.

To save a panel configuration as a Panel Layout Set, follow these steps:

1. Create an arrangement of floating panels that you'd like to save.

2. Choose Commands ⇨ Panel Layout. A JavaScript dialog box appears.

This is a JavaScript dialog box because all of the items under Fireworks' Commands menu are built with HTML and JavaScript. For more about Fireworks' new Command menu, see Chapter 19.

3. Enter a name for your new Panel Layout Set. Click OK when you're done.

The arrangement of your floating panels is saved as a new Panel Layout Set and is added to the Commands ⇨ Panel Layout Sets submenu.

To access a Panel Layout Set, choose Commands ⇨ Panel Layout Sets and then the name of the Panel Layout Set that you want to access.

Working with Dual Monitors

Fireworks works with dual monitors on Macintosh and on Windows systems that support the feature. You can set up this arrangement through the Monitors (or Monitors and Sound) Control Panel on Macintosh and through the Display Control Panel on Windows. Traditionally, the best strategy for using two monitors is to keep your documents on one monitor and your floating panels on the other. This works especially well if you have one large monitor and one small one, for documents and panels, respectively.

Another advantage of dual monitors is the capability to continuously preview your work at a different screen resolution or color depth than the one that you typically work at. Most designers and graphic artists work at a high resolution and color depth, such as 1600 × 1024 with 32-bit color, while most Web surfers are using 800 × 600, with varying color depths. Work on one monitor, and preview your work in a browser window simultaneously on the other. Adjust the settings of the preview monitor in order to view your work at a wide range of resolution and color depth combinations. Continuously previewing your work as it will ultimately be displayed helps to avoid surprises and the unnecessary revisions.

Caution   If you want to save your current panel layout, do so before accessing a Panel Layout Set. A restored Panel Layout Set supercedes the current layout.

Hiding and revealing panels

The floating panels are extremely helpful for making all manner of alterations to your documents, but they can also get in the way, visually, as well as physically. When working on a large image at 100 percent magnification, I often hide most of the panels, in order to better see and manipulate my image. Hiding — and revealing — all of the floating panels is a one-key operation. With just a press of the Tab key, the floating panels all disappear, or, if they are already hidden, reappear.

Although the Tab key is extremely convenient, you can choose a number of other methods to hide and reveal panels:

✦ Choose View ➪ Hide Panels to toggle the panels off and on.

✦ Use the other keyboard shortcut, Ctrl+Shift+H (Command+Shift+H).

✦ Windows users can select one of the panel buttons on the Main toolbar: Object, Color Mixer, Stroke, Fill, or Layers. If all of the chosen panels or all of the panels are hidden, selecting one of these buttons reveals them all again. If the panel is onscreen, but under another floating panel, selecting the panel's button once brings it to the front; selecting it again hides the panel.

Windowshade

Windowshading is an alternative to hiding the panels. It is a standard in Mac OS 8/9 but is found in the floating panels on both Macintosh and Windows versions of Fireworks. Double-clicking the title bar of a floating panel hides all but the title bar; double-clicking the title bar again reveals the whole panel. Mac users can also click the standard Windowshade button in a panel's title bar.

Examining common features

Although each floating panel does something different, they all share common interface elements. Many of the features, such as sliders and option lists, will be familiar to users of most any computer program. Some, such as color pickers, are more commonly found only in other graphics software. Figure 2-13 displays several different floating panels with different interface features highlighted.

Here's an overview of the most common Fireworks interface elements:

✦ **Tabs:** As mentioned previously, tabs appear when you dock a panel to one or more panels.

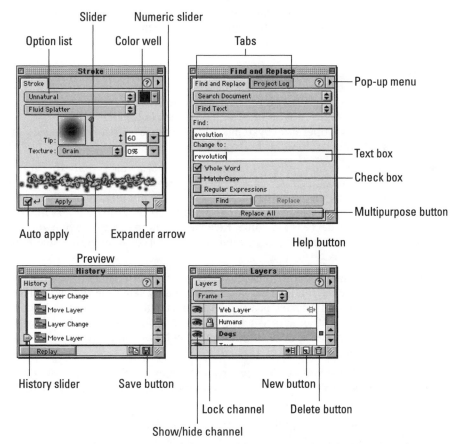

Figure 2-13: These floating panels exemplify many interface features found throughout Fireworks.

✦ **Pop-up menus:** All floating panels except for the Tool Options panel have a number of different options that you can access by selecting the pop-up menu button (a right-pointing arrow) in the upper right of the panel.

✦ **Help button:** All floating panels have a context-sensitive Help button that opens Using Fireworks at the appropriate page to help with the current operation.

✦ **Option lists:** For many selections, Fireworks uses option lists. Click the arrow button of an option list to see the available choices. In some circumstances, as with Patterns and textures, the option list displays a visual image, as well as a text listing of the options. This feature makes it easy in Fireworks to find what you're looking for.

Tip Windows users can type the first letter of an entry in an options list in order to jump to it. If multiple entries have the same first letter, pressing the letter again cycles through the entries.

✦ **Color wells:** Any color selection in Fireworks is handled through a color well that displays the current color for a certain aspect of the image. Click the color well to pop up the color picker with the active swatch. All color pickers have an Eyedropper tool for choosing onscreen colors and a Palette button for opening your operating system's color picker(s). Most Fireworks color pickers also have a No Color button for deselecting any color.

✦ **Numeric sliders:** Any entry that requires a numeric value — whether it is a percentage, a hexadecimal value, or just a plain number — uses pop-up sliders. Selecting the arrow button next to a variable number, such as a stroke's tip size, pops up a sliding control. Drag the slider and the numbers in the text box increase or decrease in value. Release the mouse button when you've reached the desired value. You can also directly type a numeric value in the adjacent text box.

✦ **Expander arrow:** Several floating panels — Stroke, Fill, and Effect — have an additional preview section that you can reveal by selecting the expander arrow. The expander arrow is a small white triangle in the lower-right corner of a floating panel that acts as a toggle. Select it once, and the floating panel expands to display the preview section; select it again, and the panel returns to its previous size.

✦ **Text boxes:** Enter values directly into text boxes. All Fireworks sliders have text boxes next to them so that you can quickly enter a number instead of using a mouse to move the slider.

✦ **Check boxes:** You can enable an option by clicking the associated check box or disable it by clicking it again in order to remove the check mark.

Optimize panel

The Optimize panel enables you to specify export settings for the current document. Choose a file type and file-type specific settings, such as Quality for JPEG images, and palette for GIFs. Depending on which file format you choose, the available options change accordingly.

New Feature Fireworks 3's new in-place preview would be nothing without the Optimize panel, where you set export options. In combination with the Color Table panel, the Optimize panel replicates the functions of the Export Preview dialog box — the only option for exporting in Fireworks 2 — right in the workspace itself.

Figure 2-14 shows the Optimize panel set to GIF WebSnap 128.

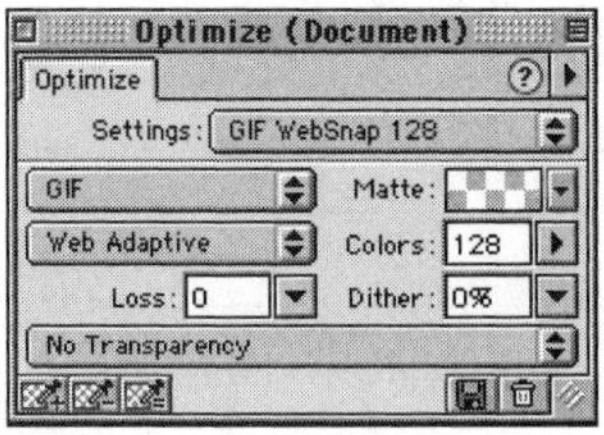

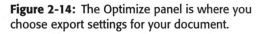

Figure 2-14: The Optimize panel is where you choose export settings for your document.

The Optimize panel's pop-up menu contains commands for fine-tuning your export settings. Table 2-5 details the commands.

Table 2-5	
Optimize Panel Pop-up Menu Commands	
Option	*Description*
Save Settings	Saves the current export settings
Delete Settings	Deletes the current saved export setting
Optimize to Size	Optimizes the current document to a particular export file size
Export Wizard	Starts the Export Wizard to assist in exporting a document
Remove Unused Colors	Toggles whether or not Fireworks removes unused colors from the export palette displayed in the Color Table panel
Interlaced	Toggles the interlaced option for formats that support it
Progressive JPEG	Toggles JPEG or Progressive JPEG
Sharpen JPEG Edges	Toggles sharpening of edges in exported JPEGs

Cross-Reference

Find more information about the Optimize panel in Chapter 15.

Object inspector

The Object inspector is primarily responsible for displaying and controlling how a selected object (or objects) interact with the canvas and other objects in your document. This floating panel displays one of nine different interfaces, depending upon what is selected. Figure 2-15 shows three examples of the Object inspector.

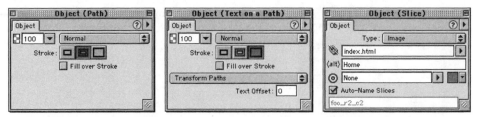

Figure 2-15: The Object inspector offers a variety of different options depending upon the type of object selected.

The type of object selected is identified at the top of the Object inspector. Following are the possible selections:

✦ **No Selection:** No image or object is selected. The Opacity and Blending Mode of the last selection are displayed.

✦ **Path:** When a vector-based object is selected, the term *Path* is displayed in the Object inspector along with Opacity and Blending Mode controls. Two additional stroke options are available. One is Stroke Placement, which determines whether the stroke is drawn outside, inside, or centered in the Path; the other is the aptly named Draw Fill Over Stroke option, which tells Fireworks to draw the fill on top of the stroke.

✦ **Image:** If a pixel-based image is selected, the Object inspector lets you alter the Opacity and Blending Modes, but only if you are not in Image Edit mode.

✦ **Text:** In addition to Opacity, Blending Modes, and Stroke options, the Object inspector for text enables you to change the Transformation method from Transform as Paths to Transform as Pixels. Text objects are explored in Chapter 10.

✦ **Text on a Path:** The Object inspector for Text on a Path is the same as that for Text with one addition: you can set the number of pixels by which the text is offset from the Path.

✦ **Mask Group:** A selected Mask Group's Object inspector can alter the Opacity, Blending Mode, type of group (regular or mask), and whether you mask to the image or path. You'll learn more about Groups and Mask Groups in Chapter 13.

✦ **Graphic or Button Symbol:** The Opacity and Blending Mode of a Symbol can be altered through the Object inspector, as well as whether it's pixels or paths are transformed when it's tweened. Button Symbols have further options, such as Button Text. Symbols are covered in Chapter 17.

✦ **Hotspot:** Much of the information necessary for a selected hotspot to function as a Web object is entered through the Object inspector: the URL, the <alt> tag, and the target. You can also set the color of the overlay and the hotspot's basic shape (Rectangle, Oval, or Polygon) here. Find out how to use hotspots in Chapter 20.

✦ **Slice:** In addition to the Web-specific information (URL, <alt> tag, and target), the selected Slice object can also choose export settings, the overlay color, and naming conventions. Turn to Chapter 19 to find out how to use this key Fireworks tool.

Most any selected object can be affected by the pop-up menu commands outlined in Table 2-6; you can even convert a Hotspot object to a Slice object and vice versa.

Table 2-6 Object Inspector Pop-up Menu Commands	
Option	**Description**
Make Hotspot	Converts the selected object into a hotspot
Make Slice	Makes a slice based on the selected object
Behaviors	Opens the Behavior inspector for the selected Hotspot or Slice object

Stroke panel

Any object created using one of the vector drawing tools — Pen, Brush, Rectangle, Ellipse, Line, or Text tool — is initially constructed with a path, the outline of the object. When a path is visible, it is said to be *stroked*. In Fireworks, strokes can be as basic as the one-pixel Pencil outline or as complex as the multicolored Confetti. The Stroke panel controls all the possible path settings and is a key tool in a graphic artist's palette.

Fireworks comes with a number of built-in stroke settings accessible through the Stroke panel, shown in Figure 2-16. You can also modify existing settings and save them as new strokes. Seven major options can affect the stroke:

Figure 2-16: The Stroke panel controls the appearance of an object's outline or path.

✦ **Stroke category:** Fireworks provides 11 stroke categories from which to choose: Pencil, Basic, Airbrush, Calligraphy, Charcoal, Crayon, Felt Tip, Oil, Watercolor, Random, and Unnatural. To hide the path entirely, choose None.

✦ **Specific stroke:** Once you've chosen a stroke category, a set of specific strokes, different for each category, is available. When you edit, rename, or save new strokes, the changes are reflected in the specific stroke option list.

✦ **Stroke color:** Selecting the arrow button next to the stroke color well displays the pop-up color picker from which you can select a color from one of the swatches, use the Eyedropper tool to select an onscreen color, or click the Palette button to open your operating system's color picker(s).

✦ **Stroke edge:** Use the stroke edge slider to soften or harden the stroke. The higher the slider, the softer the stroke; when the slider is all the way to the bottom, the stroke has no softness.

✦ **Stroke size:** The stroke size slider determines the stroke size in pixels. You can increase the size by moving the slider up; you can also enter the value (from 1 to 100) directly in the stroke size text box. The size of the brush is previewed dynamically in the Stroke panel.

✦ **Stroke texture:** In addition to color, size, and softness, you can also apply a texture to the stroke. Fireworks comes with 26 different textures, and you can also add your own.

✦ **Degree of stroke texture:** Once a texture has been selected, you must specify how intensely you want the texture applied by using the stroke texture slider or by entering a percentage value in the appropriate text box. The degree of stroke texture basically controls the opacity of the texture as it overlays the stroke.

If an object is selected while Auto-Apply is enabled, any changes made on the Stroke panel are automatically applied. Otherwise, you'll need to click the Apply button to see the effect of any new settings on your selected object.

You can manage current strokes and create new ones with the commands available in the Stroke panel pop-up menu, detailed in Table 2-7.

Table 2-7	
Stroke Panel Pop-up Menu Commands	
Option	**Description**
Save Stroke As	Saves the current stroke settings under a new name
Edit Stroke	Opens the Edit Stroke dialog box
Rename Stroke	Relabels the current stroke settings
Delete Stroke	Removes the current stroke from the menu

Cross-
Reference   Strokes are covered in detail in Chapter 8.

Fill panel

Just as the Stroke panel controls the outline of a drawn shape, the Fill panel controls the inside. Fills can be a solid color, a gradient, a pattern, or a Web dither. All fills can have textures applied with a sliding scale of intensity; moreover, textured fills can even appear transparent.

Once you've chosen the type of fill from the Fill panel, shown in Figure 2-17, you can go on to pick a specific color, pattern, edge, or texture. Following are the key options on the Fill panel:

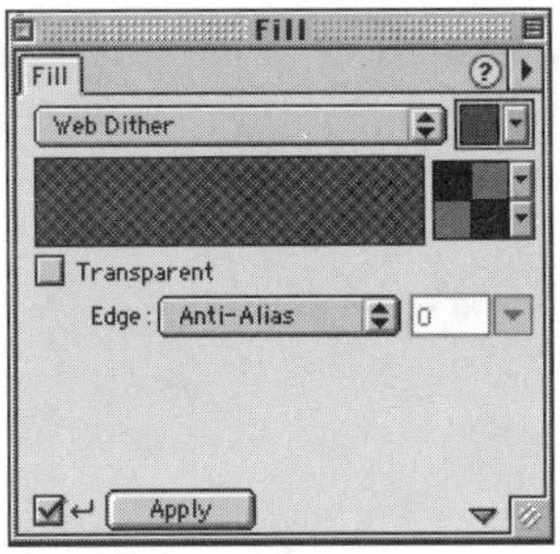

Figure 2-17: The Fill panel offers many options to modify the interior of a drawn shape.

✦ **Fill category**. Select a fill category from these options: Solid (single color fill), Web dither (two-color pattern), Pattern, or Gradient. The available standard gradients are Linear, Radial, Ellipse, Rectangle, Cone, Starburst, Bars, Ripples, Waves, Satin, and Folds.

✦ **Specific pattern or gradient color scheme:** If you choose Pattern or one of the gradient options, a second option list appears with choices for each type of fill.

✦ **Fill edge:** The fill itself can have a hard edge, an anti-aliased edge, or a feathered edge.

✦ **Degree of feathering:** If the fill is given a feathered edge, you can specify the degree of feathering (the number of pixels affected) with this slider control or by entering a value into the text box.

✦ **Fill texture:** The same textures available to the Stroke panel are available to a fill.

✦ **Degree of texture:** To make a texture visible, you must increase the degree of the texture's intensity by using the appropriate slider or text box. The higher the value, the more visible the texture.

✦ **Transparency of texture:** If the Transparency check box is selected, the lighter parts of the texture can be seen through.

The gradient fill type offers a number of options for creating and modifying your own gradient patterns. The commands are available from the Fill panel's pop-up menu and are detailed in Table 2-8.

Table 2-8	
Fill Panel Pop-up Menu Commands	
Option	*Description*
Save Gradient As	Saves the current gradient settings under a new name
Edit Gradient	Opens the Edit Gradient dialog box
Rename Gradient	Relabels the current gradient settings
Delete Gradient	Removes the current gradient from the menu

Cross-Reference   To delve deeper into fills, see Chapter 11.

Effect panel

In the early days of the Web, special graphics effects like drop shadows and beveled buttons required many tedious steps in programs, such as Photoshop. These days, Fireworks enables you to apply wondrous effects in a single step through the Effect panel. More importantly, like everything else in Fireworks, the effects are "live" and adapt to any change in the object. And you can easily alter them by adjusting values in the Effect panel.

The Effect panel options list contains the actual effects, split into two groups. The top group are Fireworks built-in effects. The bottom group are Photoshop-compatible image filters from your Fireworks Xtras folder and from another folder if you specified one in Fireworks Preferences.

New Feature   Fireworks 3 adds "live" Photoshop-compatible image filters to the Effect panel. Not all filters work with the Effect panel — however, they still appear in the Xtras menu — but a large number work, and the creative freedom that they provide is amazing. Add, remove, edit settings, or even change the order of effects, all while your objects remain editable.

Choosing an effect from the Effect panel option list applies it to the current selection and adds it to the active list in the Effect panel. Once an effect is in the active list, you can check or uncheck the box next to it in order to enable or disable it.

Selecting the *i* button next to an applied effect's name enables you to modify its settings. Photoshop-compatible filters each have their own unique dialog boxes. Many of Fireworks' built-in Live Effects open a small, pop-up edit window with their settings. Clicking anywhere outside the pop-up edit window dismisses it. Raised Emboss is an example of an effect with a pop-up edit window, shown in Figure 2-18.

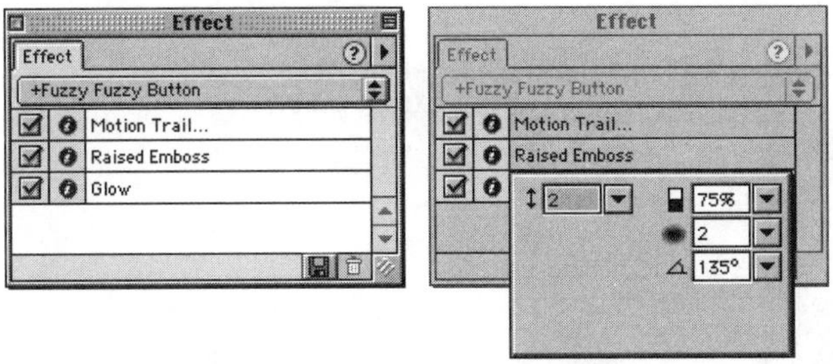

Figure 2-18: The settings for some Live Effects are displayed in an unusual pop-up edit window, such as this one for Raised Emboss.

As you develop specific effects, you can save them for later use with the pop-up menu commands listed in Table 2-9.

Table 2-9
Effect Panel Pop-up Menu Commands

Option	Description
Save defaults	Saves the current setup as the default for new effects
Save Effect As	Saves the current effect settings under a new name
Rename Effect	Relabels the current effect settings
Delete Effect	Removes the current effect from the menu
All on	Turns on all the effects currently active in the Effect panel
All off	Turns off all the effects currently active in the Effect panel
Locate Plug-ins	Shows a dialog box that allows you to select a folder of Photoshop plug-ins

Cross-Reference   Effects can add serious pizzazz to your graphics in a hurry. Find out more about them — with details on how to get the most from each Effects panel — in Chapter 12.

Color Table panel

The Color Table panel, shown in Figure 2-19, displays the current export palette when working with 8-bit images, such as GIFs. The Color Table panel provides feedback that allows you to minimize the file size of exported GIF images by reducing the number of colors in their palette.

Figure 2-19: The Color Table panel contains a document's current export palette.

The Color Table panel sports an extensive pop-up menu, detailed in Table 2-10:

Table 2-10	
Color Table Panel Pop-up Menu Commands	
Option	**Description**
Rebuild Color Table	Updates colors to reflect changes in the document
Add Color	Opens your operating system's color picker(s) so that you can manually add a color to the palette
Edit Color	Opens your operating system's color picker(s) so that you can change the selected color to a different color
Delete Color	Removes the selected color(s) from the palette
Replace Palette Entry	Opens your operating system's color picker(s) so that you can replace the selected palette entry with a different color
Snap to Web Safe	Snaps the selected color(s) to Web-safe
Transparent	Makes the selected color transparent
Lock Color	Locks the selected color so that it cannot be edited
Unlock All Colors	Unlocks all locked colors

Option	Description
Sort by Luminance	Selects sorting by luminance values
Sort by Popularity	Selects sorting by most-used color
Unsorted	Selects no sorting
Show Swatch Feedback	Toggles viewing icons that indicate a color is locked, transparent, or another attribute
Remove Edit	Restores selected color to what it was before editing
Remove All Edits	Restores all colors to what they were before editing
Load Palette	Loads a previously saved palette
Save Palette	Saves the current palette

Swatches panel

Whereas the Color Mixer defines the color universe, the Swatches panel identifies a more precise palette of colors. As the name implies, the Swatches panel contains a series of color samples, as you can see in Figure 2-20. You select a color by clicking on a swatch.

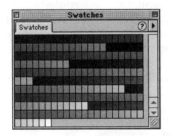

Figure 2-20: Palette management is coordinated through the Swatches panel.

Tip   To reset a swatch palette after you've modified it or sorted it by color, select the palette again from the Swatches panel's pop-up menu.

A major feature of the Swatches panel is tucked away in its pop-up menu: palette management. With the commands in the pop-up menu, you can switch to standard palettes (such as the Web 216, Windows, or Macintosh system palettes), save and recall custom palettes, or access the current export palette. The Add Swatches command is especially useful; it can load palettes previously stored in the Photoshop color table file format or pull the color information from a GIF file. Table 2-11 outlines all of the pop-up menu commands.

Table 2-11
Swatches Panel Pop-up Menu Commands

Option	Description
Add Swatches	Imports previously saved palettes from .aco or GIF files
Replace Swatches	Exchanges the current palette set for a previously saved one
Save Swatches	Stores the current palette set
Clear Swatches	Removes all palettes from the panel
Web 216 Palette	Switches to the Web 216 palette
Macintosh System	Switches to the Macintosh system palette
Windows System	Switches to the Windows system palette
Grayscale	Switches to a grayscale palette
Current Export Palette	Switches to the current export palette
Sort by Color	Sorts the swatches by color

Color Mixer panel

Web designers come from a variety of backgrounds: some are well-rooted in computer graphics, others are more familiar with print publishing, while an increasing number know only Web imagery. The Color Mixer lets you opt for the color model that you're most familiar with and that is best suited to your work.

The Color Mixer, shown in Figure 2-21, displays three different ways to choose colors:

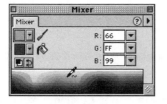

Figure 2-21: Select your stroke and fill colors from the color wells, the color ramp, or the color component sliders in the Color Mixer panel.

✦ **Stroke and Fill color wells:** Select a color well to open the pop-up color picker and gain access to the system color picker(s) through the Palette button.

✦ **Color ramp:** The full-spectrum preview of the chosen color model is known as the color ramp. You can select any color by clicking it.

✦ **Color component sliders:** Like the color ramp, the color component sliders change according to the chosen color model. Four of the five color models — RGB, Hexadecimal, CMY, and HSB — display three different sliders, whereas Grayscale shows only one, K (black).

Like the Toolbox, the Color Mixer also features a Default Colors button for restoring the preset stroke and fill colors, and a Swap button for reversing the colors. Choose a color model by selecting it from the pop-up menu, detailed in Table 2-12.

<table>
<tr><td colspan="2" align="center">Table 2-12
Color Mixer Panel Pop-up Menu Commands</td></tr>
<tr><td>*Option*</td><td>*Description*</td></tr>
<tr><td>RGB</td><td>Changes the color mixer display to Red, Green, and Blue</td></tr>
<tr><td>Hexadecimal</td><td>Changes the color mixer display to Hexadecimal Red, Green, and Blue, the standard way to specify colors in HTML</td></tr>
<tr><td>CMY</td><td>Changes the color mixer display to Cyan, Magenta, and Yellow</td></tr>
<tr><td>HSB</td><td>Changes the color mixer display to Hue, Saturation, and Balance</td></tr>
<tr><td>Grayscale</td><td>Changes the color mixer display to Grayscale, which is 256 shades of gray</td></tr>
</table>

Cross-Reference   A full understanding of the color possibilities and pitfalls is a must for any Web designer. Learn more about using the Color Mixer in Chapter 7.

Tool Options panel

Many tools from the Fireworks Toolbox have configurable settings accessible through the Tool Options panel. You have two basic ways to expose the Tool Options panel for a specific tool:

✦ Display the panel by choosing its tab or by choosing Window ➪ Tool Options, and then select the tool from the Toolbox.

✦ Double-click the tool in the Toolbox.

Like the Object panel, the Tool panel's options vary according to what is selected. Some tools, such as the Eraser shown in Figure 2-22, provide numerous choices. Several tools — including the Hand, Magnify, Line, Pen, Ellipse, Brush, and the Web tools — have no options. Each tool's options are covered in the section devoted to that tool.

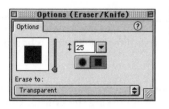

Figure 2-22: When the Eraser tool is double-clicked, several options become available through the Tool Options panel.

Note The Tool Options panel is the only panel that doesn't have a pop-up menu.

Layers panel

Layers in Fireworks enable the creation of extremely complicated graphics, as well as compatibility with files stored in Photoshop format. Fireworks layers permit multiple images and objects — each with their own stacking order — to be treated as a group and, in turn, placed on top of, or beneath, other layers. Moreover, each layer can be hidden from view for easier editing of complex images, and can be locked to prevent accidental editing. Layers can be shared across frames, allowing you to instantly add a static element to every frame of an animation.

All Web objects, such as slices and hotspots, are stored in the Web Layer, which can be hidden or locked, or have its stacking order changed, but cannot be deleted. The Web Layer is always shared across all frames.

The Layer panel, shown in Figure 2-23, is the central control center for layers. The layer list contains each layer's name, as well as Show/Hide and Lock/Unlock columns. Create or delete layers with the New Layer and Delete Layer buttons. The Distribute to Frames button places objects in the current layer on frames based on their stacking order, creating an instant animation.

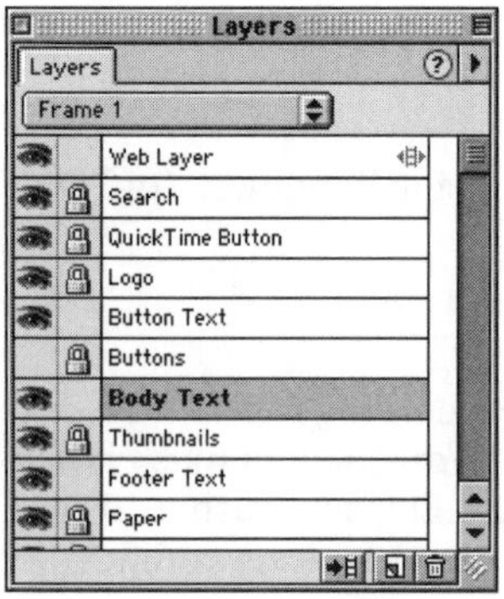

Figure 2-23: Objects on a layer can be hidden or locked with a single click on the Layers panel.

A good portion of Firework's layer management is coordinated through the Layers panel's pop-up menu commands, as described in Table 2-13.

Table 2-13	
Layers Panel Pop-up Menu Commands	
Option	**Description**
New Layer	Adds a new layer on top of all current image layers
Duplicate Layer	Clones the current layer
Layer Options	Opens the Layer Options dialog box in order to rename the layer and set the Share Across Frames option
Delete Layer	Removes the current layer
Hide All	Conceals all layers in the document
Show All	Reveals all layers in the document
Lock All	Prevents editing in the selected layer
Unlock All	Enables a locked layer to be edited
Share Layer	Enables all objects on the selected layer to be shared across all frames
Single Layer Editing	Restricts edits to the current layer

Frames panel

Frames have two primary uses in Fireworks: rollovers and animations. When used to create rollovers, each frame represents a different state of the user's mouse with up to four frames being used. To create an animated GIF, each frame in Fireworks corresponds to one frame of the animation. You can use as many frames for your animation as necessary (although file size often dictates that the fewest frames possible is best).

By default, frame timing is set to 20 milliseconds. Double-click the frame timing setting to edit it in the pop-up edit window, similar to the ones displayed by the Effect panel.

New Feature In keeping with Fireworks 3's new in-place document window previews, the Frames panel now allows you to specify animation timing, so you don't have to go into the Export Preview dialog box.

The Frames panel, shown in Figure 2-24, is laid out like the Layers panel, with a list of Frames featured prominently.

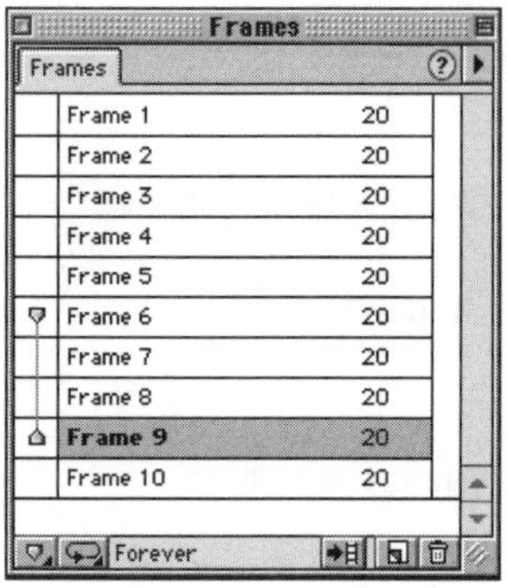

Figure 2-24: The Frames panel is Fireworks' center stage for creating rollovers and animated GIF images.

The Frames panel's pop-up menu, detailed in Table 2-14, enables you to further control your interaction with frames.

Table 2-14
Frames Panel Pop-up Menu Commands

Option	Description
Add Frames	Opens the Add Frames dialog box.
Duplicate Frame	Duplicates the current frame
Delete Frames	Deletes the current frame
Copy to Frames	Copies the selected object to a frame or a range of frames
Distribute to Frames	Distributes each selected object to a different frame as determined by the stacking order of the objects
Auto Crop	Sets the frame disposal method to Auto Crop
Auto Difference	Sets the frame disposal method to Auto Difference
Properties	Opens the pop-up edit window for the current frame

History panel

The History panel, shown in Figure 2-25, allows precise control over Fireworks' multiple level Undo command. The Undo Marker points to your preceding step. To roll back to even earlier steps, slide the Undo Marker up one or more notches. The number of steps the History panel keeps track of is the number of Undo steps you have specified in Fireworks preferences.

Caution The maximum number of Undo steps you can specify in Fireworks for Windows is 100. On the Mac, the number of Undo steps is limited only by the amount of RAM Fireworks has access to.

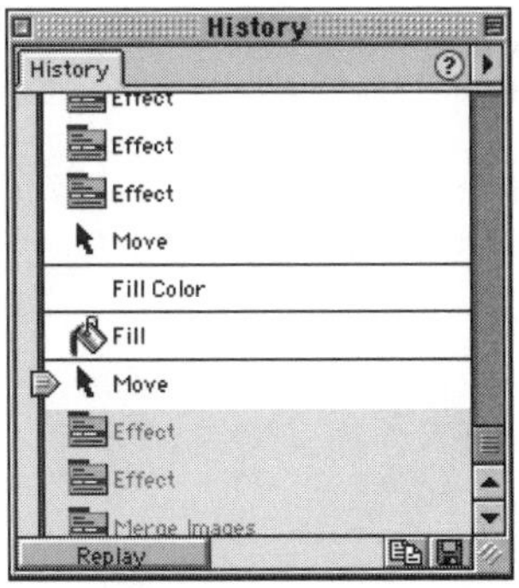

Figure 2-25: The History panel contains a record of your actions.

New Feature The History panel — new to Fireworks but familiar to Photoshop users — enables you to precisely control Fireworks' multiple-level Undo command, even to the point of saving your previous steps as a Command to use again and again.

The ability to save or replay your steps makes the History panel more than just an enhanced Undo. Saving your previous steps as a Command enables you to automate almost anything you do in Fireworks. If you have a project that requires you to tediously edit a number of images in the same way, do it once and save the steps as a Command that you can run on all of the other images.

The History panel's pop-up menu contains the commands detailed in Table 2-15.

<table>
<tr><td colspan="2" align="center">Table 2-15
History Panel Pop-up Menu Commands</td></tr>
<tr><td>*Option*</td><td>*Description*</td></tr>
<tr><td>Replay Selected Steps</td><td>Replays the selected steps</td></tr>
<tr><td>Copy Steps</td><td>Copies the selected steps to the clipboard</td></tr>
<tr><td>Save as Command</td><td>Saves the selected steps as a Command</td></tr>
<tr><td>Clear History</td><td>Deletes all steps</td></tr>
</table>

Find out more about the new History panel in Chapter 19.

Info panel

Often it's necessary to check an object's size or position when you're creating an overall graphic. The Info panel not only provides you with that feedback, but it also enables you to modify those values numerically for precise adjustments. In addition, the Info panel, shown in Figure 2-26, also lists the current pointer coordinates and the color values of the pixel found under the pointer, updated in real time.

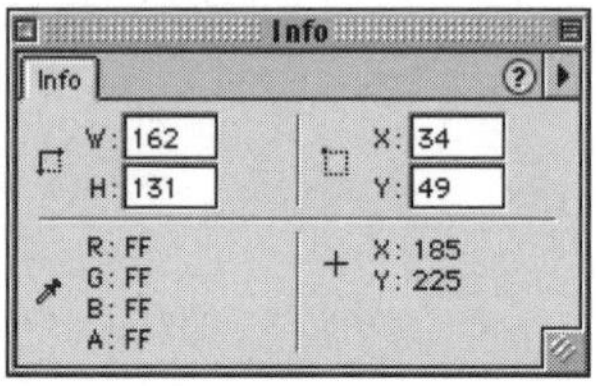

Figure 2-26: You can find any object's dimensions and position in the Info panel.

Usually with a series of text boxes, you can press the Tab key to simultaneously enter the input text and move to the next text box. However, with the Info panel, you must input your value and then press the Enter (Return) key to initiate any change.

The color model and measurement system shown in the Info panel can be altered by choosing another from the Info panel's pop-up menu, detailed in Table 2-16.

Table 2-16	
Info Panel Pop-up Menu Commands	
Option	**Description**
Hexadecimal	Changes the color settings display to Hexadecimal Red, Green, and Blue
RGB	Changes the color settings display to Red, Green, and Blue
CMY	Changes the color settings display to Cyan, Magenta, and Yellow
HSB	Changes the color settings display to Hue, Saturation, and Balance
Pixels	Changes the measurement display to pixels
Inches	Changes the measurement display to inches
Centimeters	Changes the measurement display to centimeters
Scale Attributes	Enables attributes to be scaled with the object

Behaviors inspector

One of the key features of Fireworks that separates it from other graphics programs is its capability to output HTML and JavaScript code along with images. The code activates an image and makes it capable of an action, such as changing color or shape when the user passes the mouse over it. The code is known in Fireworks as a *Behavior*. A Behavior is actually composed of two parts: an action that specifies what's to occur, and an event that triggers the action.

Behaviors require a Web object, such as a slice or a hotspot, to function. After you've selected the desired Web object, you assign a Behavior by choosing the Add Action button (the plus sign) from the Behavior inspector. Fireworks comes with four groups of Behaviors from which to choose: Simple Rollover, Swap Image, Set Nav Bar Image, and Set Text of Status Bar.

All assigned Behaviors for a given Web object are listed in the Behavior inspector, as shown in Figure 2-27. The events, such as OnMouseOver or OnClick, are listed in the first column and the actions in the second. The third column, Info, offers specifics that identify the Behavior. To remove a Behavior, select it and then choose the Remo-ve Action button (the minus sign). You can also delete a Behavior — or all of the Behaviors for a Web object — through the pop-up menu commands listed in Table 2-17.

Figure 2-27: Use the Behavior inspector to generate HTML and JavaScript code at the click of a mouse.

Table 2-17
Behaviors Panel Pop-up Menu Commands

Option	Description
Edit	Opens the dialog box for the selected Behavior
Delete	Removes the currently selected Behavior from its attached object
Delete All	Removes all Behaviors attached to the current object

Continued

	Table 2-17 *(continued)*
Option	**Description**
Show All	Shows all Behaviors in a group
Ungroup	Ungroups a group of Behaviors

Behaviors are a rich feature of Fireworks. To find out more about them, see Chapter 21.

URL panel

URLs are the life-blood of the Web. When a URL (Uniform Resource Locator, also known as a *link*) is attached to an image on a Web page, the user need only click once to jump to another section of the document, another page on the Web site, or another computer halfway around the world. For all their power, URLs can be difficult to manage; one typo in the often-complex string of letters and symbols can break a link.

The URL panel, shown in Figure 2-28, greatly eases the work required for managing URLs by listing all of the Internet addresses inserted in the current session or loaded from an external file. You can easily assign URLs with a click of a listed item; more importantly, you can maintain a list of links for a particular Web site so that you don't have to re-enter them each time. To add the current URL to the Library, select the Add button (the plus sign).

Figure 2-28: Adding links to your Web objects is easy with the URL panel.

You can access most of Fireworks' URL management utilities through the URL panel's pop-up menu, detailed in Table 2-18.

Table 2-18 URL Panel Pop-up Menu Commands	
Option	**Description**
Add Used URLs to Library	Adds the list of current URLs to the URL Library
Clear Unused URLs	Removes all URLs from the current listing
Add URL	Adds a new URL to the URL Library
Edit URL	Opens the Edit URL dialog box
Delete URL	Removes the selected URL from the URL Library
New URL Library	Creates a new URL Library
Import URLs	Loads a new set of URLs from a previously stored URL Library, a bookmark file, or an HTML page
Export URLs	Stores the current URL Library

Styles panel

If you've ever spent hours getting just the right combination of stroke, fill, and effects for an image — and then find you need to apply the same combination to all the navigation buttons throughout a Web site — you'll greatly appreciate the Fireworks Styles feature.

In Fireworks, a *Style* is a collection of attributes that can be applied to any object. The Styles panel is preset with a number of such designs, which appear as graphical buttons and text, with many more available on the Fireworks CD-ROM. To apply a Style, select the object and then select the Style; you can even select multiple objects (such as a row of navigation buttons) and apply the same Style to them all with one click. Styles are a terrific time-saver and a great way to maintain a consistent look and feel.

The Styles panel, shown in Figure 2-29, is composed of a series of icons, each representing a different Style. A Style can have the following attributes: fill type, fill color, stroke type, stroke color, effect, text font, text size, and text color. In addition to the preset Styles, you can also save your own combinations. Just highlight the object with the desired attributes and select the New Style button on the Styles panel. You can also accomplish this by choosing New Style from the pop-up menu. A full list of the Styles panel's pop-up menu commands appears in Table 2-19.

Figure 2-29: Automate applying a consistent look and feel to your objects by using the Styles panel.

Table 2-19
Styles Panel Pop-up Menu Commands

Option	Description
New Style	Creates a new Style based on the current object
Edit Style	Opens the Edit Style dialog box
Delete Styles	Removes a selected Style or Styles
Import Styles	Loads a new set of Styles after the currently selected Style
Export Styles	Stores the currently selected Style or Styles
Reset Styles	Reloads the default configuration of Styles
Large Icons	Displays the available Styles with icons twice as large as normal

Cross-Reference   Find out more about creating and applying Styles in Chapter 16.

Library panel

The Library panel contains Fireworks Libraries: collections of Symbols that can be saved and reopened as required. Symbols are edited right in the Library. Dragging a Symbol from the Library panel and dropping it into a document creates an Instance of that Symbol. Instances are copies of Symbols that remain linked to the Symbol and inherit changes to the Symbol. Instances are similar to a Windows file shortcut or Mac alias — right down to the arrow badge — and can be animated, tweened, and edited as a group. Symbols can be saved in Symbol Libraries and used again and again in multiple documents.

New Feature

Rather than mess with a confusing mix of Symbols and Instances in the document window, Fireworks 3 banishes Symbols to the Library panel and leaves Instances, the copies of Symbols, in the document window. Symbols can be saved in Libraries for later use.

The commands detailed in Table 2-20 are located in the Library panel's pop-up menu. Figure 2-30 shows the Library panel.

Figure 2-30: The Library panel enables you to store libraries of Symbols.

Table 2-20
Library Panel Pop-up Menu Commands

Option	Description
New Symbol	Creates a new Symbol
Duplicate	Duplicates the current Symbol
Delete	Removes the current Symbol from the Library
Edit Symbol	Opens the selected Symbol in its own window for editing
Properties	Displays the Symbol Properties dialog box for the current Symbol
Selected Unused Items	Selects unused Symbols in the Library
Update	Updates Symbols that were imported from other Libraries
Play	Consecutively displays all frames of a button
Import Symbols	Imports Symbols from a saved Library
Export Symbols	Exports Symbols to a saved Library

Find and Replace panel

Let's suppose you've just finished the graphics for a major Web site, chockfull with corporate logos, and you receive *the call*. You know, the one from the client who informs you that the company has just been acquired and instead of NewCo, Inc., it's now New2Co, Inc. Could you please redo all the graphics — by tomorrow?

Because Fireworks objects are always editable, the Find and Replace panel, shown in Figure 2-31, makes updating a series of Web graphics a snap. You can change all of the graphics in a selection, a file, a frame, or a series of files. Moreover, Find and Replace can handle more than just text; you can also alter fonts, colors, and URLs, or even snap all of the colors to their nearest Web-safe neighbor.

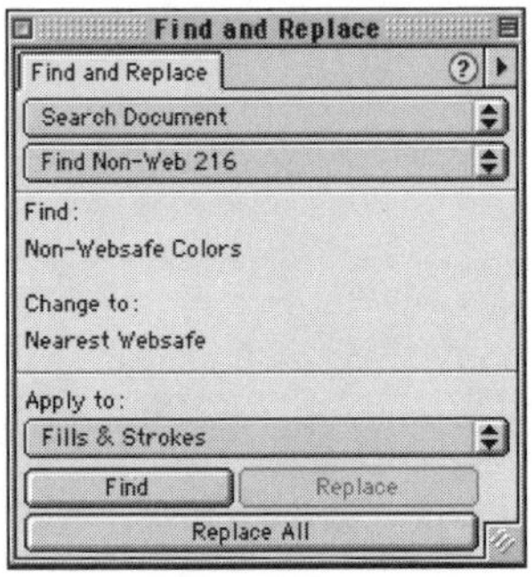

Figure 2-31: Need to make global changes in text, font, color, or URLs? Pull up the Find and Replace panel and get the job done fast.

The Find and Replace feature works with the Project Log panel, which tracks changes made to your documents. You can enable Project Log tracking through the pop-up menu commands listed in Table 2-21, as well as specify replacement options for multiple file operations.

<table>
<tr><td colspan="2">Table 2-21
Find and Replace Panel Pop-up Menu Commands</td></tr>
<tr><td>*Option*</td><td>*Description*</td></tr>
<tr><td>Add Files to Project Log</td><td>Tracks changes made in a Find and Replace operation in the Project Log</td></tr>
<tr><td>Replace Options</td><td>Displays options for multiple-file Find and Replace operations</td></tr>
</table>

Cross-Reference   You can really ramp up your production level of Web graphics if you master the Find and Replace feature. To learn more about it, see Chapter 18.

Project Log panel

With the power inherent in Fireworks automation tools, such as Find and Replace and Batch Processing, you need a way to keep track of the many changes that may have occurred. The Project Log panel, shown in Figure 2-32, details each change that has taken place and enables you to not only receive confirmation of the change, but also easily open any file that was affected.

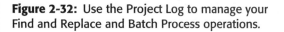

Figure 2-32: Use the Project Log to manage your Find and Replace and Batch Process operations.

In addition to listing images altered during an automated process, you can use the Project Log to keep a number of files close at hand, ready to be opened at will. Through the Add Files to Log command, in the pop-up menu detailed in Table 2-22, files can be made accessible, but not immediately opened. The pop-up menu also enables you to quickly make changes to files in the Project Log and to re-export them using their previous settings.

Table 2-22
Project Log Pop-up Menu Commands

Option	Description
Export Again	Exports selected files in the Project Log using their previous settings
Add Files to Log	Includes additional graphic files in the Project Log without initially opening them
Clear Selection	Removes the selected files from the Project Log
Clear All	Removes all files from the Project Log

To find out more about what's possible with the Project Log, turn to Chapter 18.

Using the Menus

Many of the commands and options available in the various Fireworks panels can also be found in the menus. You'll also find, however, many features that are unavailable anywhere else. This section provides a reference to every menu item in Fireworks, along with its corresponding keyboard shortcut, if available. Windows users won't see all of Fireworks' menus until a document—new or existing—is open.

Note   Commands in **bold** text are new or have changed menu locations in Fireworks 3.

File menu

It's standard practice to place basic computer operations—creating, saving, and printing files—in the File menu. Fireworks follows this practice and also includes commands for importing and exporting. All File menu commands are listed in Table 2-23.

<table>
<tr><th colspan="4">Table 2-23
File Menu Commands</th></tr>
<tr><th>Command</th><th>Description</th><th>Windows</th><th>Macintosh</th></tr>
<tr><td>New</td><td>Displays the New Document dialog box before creating a new document</td><td>Ctrl+N</td><td>Command+N</td></tr>
<tr><td>Open</td><td>Displays the Open dialog box before opening an existing document</td><td>Ctrl+O</td><td>Command+O</td></tr>
<tr><td>Open Multiple</td><td>Displays the Open Multiple dialog box before opening multiple documents</td><td>Ctrl+Shift+O</td><td>Command+Shift+O</td></tr>
<tr><td>Scan ⇨ Twain Acquire</td><td>Displays the interface dialog box for a Twain source, such as a scanner, if one is available and has been selected, before acquiring an image</td><td>n/a</td><td>n/a</td></tr>
<tr><td>Scan ⇨ Twain Source</td><td>Displays the Select Source dialog box before allowing you to select a Twain source to acquire an image from</td><td>n/a</td><td>n/a</td></tr>
</table>

Command	Description	Windows	Macintosh
Scan ⇨ Your Photoshop Acquire Plug-Ins (Macintosh only)	Lists currently installed Photoshop Acquire plug-ins. Typically, each plug-in enables you to acquire an image from a corresponding device.	n/a	n/a
Close	Closes the current document	Ctrl+F4	Command+W
Save	Saves a document, or displays the Save As dialog box for an unnamed document	Ctrl+S	Command+S
Save As	Displays the Save As dialog box before saving a document	Ctrl+Shift+S	Command+Shift+S
Save a Copy	Displays the Save Copy As dialog box before saving a copy of a document	n/a	n/a
Update HTML	Places or updates Fireworks HTML code in another HTML file on the same computer	n/a	n/a
Revert	Replaces the current document with the previously saved version of the same document	n/a	n/a
Import	Displays the Import dialog box before importing a file into any open document	Ctrl+R	Command+R
Export	Displays the Export dialog box before exporting a document in the format specified in the Optimize panel	Ctrl+Shift+R	Command+Shift+R

Continued

Table 2-23 *(continued)*

Command	Description	Windows	Macintosh
Export Special ⇨ Selected Slice	Displays the Export Preview dialog box before exporting just the selected slice as an image file	n/a	n/a
Export Special ⇨ Layers/Frames to Files	Displays the Export dialog box before exporting all Layers, Frames, or slices as separate image files	n/a	n/a
Export Special ⇨ CSS Layers	Displays the Export dialog box before exporting the document along with HTML formatted with CSS Layers	n/a	n/a
Export Special ⇨ Lotus Domino Image Well	Displays the Export **dialog box before** exporting the document as a Lotus Domino Image Well	n/a	n/a
Export Special ⇨ Flash SWF	Displays the Export Special dialog box before exporting in Flash SWF format for viewing with the Flash player, or import into Flash 3 or higher	n/a	n/a
Export Special ⇨ Illustrator 7	Displays the Export Specialdialog box before exporting in Adobe Illustrator 7 format for import into Illustrator or Macromedia FreeHand	n/a	n/a
Export Preview	Displays the Export Preview dialog box before exporting a document	Ctrl+Shift+X	Command+Shift+X

Command	Description	Windows	Macintosh
Export Wizard	Displays the Export Wizard before exporting a document	n/a	n/a
Batch Process	Displays the Batch Process dialog box before processing multiple image files	n/a	n/a
Run Script	Displays the Open dialog box before running a script	n/a	n/a
Preview in Browser ⇨ Preview in Primary Browser	Previews a document in your primary browser	F12	F12
Preview in Browser ⇨ Preview in Secondary Browser	Previews a document in your secondary browser	Shift+F12	Shift+F12
Preview in Browser ⇨ Set Primary Browser	Displays the Locate Browser dialog box before selecting a browser as your primary browser	n/a	n/a
Preview in Browser ⇨ Set Secondary Browser	Displays the Locate Browser dialog box before selecting a browser as your secondary browser	n/a	n/a
Page Setup	Displays the Page Setup dialog box (for printing)	n/a	n/a
Print	Displays the Print dialog box before printing a document	Ctrl+P	Command+P
HTML Properties	Displays the HTML Properties dialog box	n/a	n/a
Preferences	Displays the Preferences dialog box	n/a	n/a
Recent Files (Windows Only)	Displays the last four opened files; select any filename to reopen the file	n/a	n/a
Exit (Quit)	Quits Fireworks	Alt+F4	Command+Q

Edit menu

As evidenced by its name, the Edit menu holds the standard editing commands, such as Undo, Cut, Copy, and Paste, as well as numerous commands specific to Fireworks graphics, such as Paste Inside and Crop Selected Image. The Edit menu is detailed in Table 2-24.

	Table 2-24		
	Edit Menu Commands		
Command	**Description**	**Windows**	**Macintosh**
Undo	Reverses the last action. The number of Undo steps is set in Preferences.	Ctrl+Z	Command+Z
Redo	Redoes the last edit that was undone by Undo	Ctrl+Shift+Z	Command+Shift+Z
Cut	Moves the current selection to the system clipboard	Ctrl+X	Command+X
Copy	Copies the current selection to the system clipboard	Ctrl+C	Command+C
Copy as Paths	Copies a Fireworks path from the current selection to the system clipboard	n/a	n/a
Copy HTML Code	Displays the Copy HTML Code wizard that guides you through the process of exporting images and copying HTML code to the system clipboard for pasting into an HTML editor, such as Macromedia Dreamweaver	n/a	n/a
Paste	Copies the contents of the system clipboard to the current cursor position	Ctrl+V	Command+V

Command	Description	Windows	Macintosh
Clear	Removes the current selection from the document	Backspace (or Delete)	Delete
Paste Inside	Copies the contents of the system clipboard into a selected, closed path	Ctrl+Shift+V	Command+Shift+V
Paste Attributes	Copies the Fireworks-specific attributes of the contents of the system clipboard to a selected object	Ctrl+Alt+Shift+V	Command+Option+ Shift+V
Select All	Selects all objects in a document or all pixels in an image in Image Edit mode	Ctrl+A	Command+A
Deselect	Deselects all objects or pixels	Ctrl+D	Command+D
Superselect	Selects the entire group to which the current (sub)selection belongs	Ctrl+Up Arrow	Command+Up Arrow
Subselect	Selects an individual object within a group	Ctrl+Down Arrow	Command+ Down Arrow
Select Inverse	Selects all deselected pixels and deselects all selected pixels in Image Edit mode	Ctrl+Shift+I	Command+ Shift+I
Feather	Displays the Feather Selection dialog box before feathering the edges of a pixel selection in Image Edit mode	n/a	n/a

Continued

Table 2-24 *(continued)*

Command	Description	Windows	Macintosh
Select Similar	Selects pixels that are similarly colored to the selection while in Image Edit mode	n/a	n/a
Modify Marquee ⇨ **Expand**	Displays the Expand Selection dialog box before expanding the current selection in Image Edit mode	n/a	n/a
Modify Marquee ⇨ **Contract**	Displays the Contract Selection dialog box before contracting the current selection in Image Edit mode	n/a	n/a
Modify Marquee ⇨ **Border**	Displays the Select Border dialog box before selecting a border around the current selection in Image Edit mode	n/a	n/a
Modify Marquee ⇨ **Smooth**	Displays the Smooth Selection dialog box before smoothing the edges of the current in Image Edit mode	n/a	n/a
Duplicate	Creates a copy of the selected object, offset slightly from the original	Ctrl+Alt+D	Command+ Option+D
Clone	Creates a copy of the selected object, directly on top of the original	Ctrl+Shift+C Shift+C	Command+ Shift+C
Find and Replace	Displays the Find and Replace dialog box	n/a	n/a
Crop Selected Image	Displays crop handles around the selected image object	Ctrl+Alt+C	Command+ Option+C
Crop Document	Selects the crop tool	n/a	n/a

View menu

The View menu commands, listed in Table 2-25, control a Web artist's views during the creation phase. In addition to numerous magnification commands, the View menu also contains helpful layout aids, such as Rulers, Grids, and Guides. You'll also find several features to help you see just the graphic when you need to have a clear, uncluttered perspective.

Table 2-25
View Menu Commands

Command	Description	Windows	Macintosh
Zoom In	Increases the magnification level of a document by one setting	Ctrl+Plus	Command+Plus
Zoom Out	Decreases the magnification level of a document by one setting	Ctrl+Minus	Command+Minus
Magnification ⇨ 6%	Sets the magnification level of a document to 6%	n/a	n/a
Magnification ⇨ 12%	Sets the magnification level of a document to 12%	n/a	n/a
Magnification ⇨ 25%	Sets the magnification level of a document to 25%.	n/a	n/a
Magnification ⇨ 50%	Sets the magnification level of a document to 50%	Ctrl+5	Command+5
Magnification ⇨ 100%	Sets the magnification level of a document to 100%	Ctrl+1	Command+1
Magnification ⇨ 200%	Sets the magnification level of a document to 200%	Ctrl+2	Command+2
Magnification ⇨ 400%	Sets the magnification level of a document to 400%	Ctrl+4	Command+4

Continued

Table 2-25 *(continued)*

Command	Description	Windows	Macintosh
Magnification ➪ 800%	Sets the magnification level of a document to 800%	Ctrl+8	Command+8
Magnification ➪ 1600%	Sets the magnification level of a document to 1600%	n/a	n/a
Magnification ➪ 3200%	Sets the magnification level of a document to 3200%	Ctrl+3	Command+3
Magnification ➪ 6400%	Sets the magnification level of a document to 6400%	Ctrl+6	Command+6
Fit Selection	Sets the magnification level of a document so that all selected objects are visible	Ctrl+Zero	Command+Zero
Fit All	Sets the magnification level of a document so that all objects are visible	Ctrl+Alt+Zero	Command+Option+Zero
Full Display	Toggles Full Display	Ctrl+K	Command+K
Macintosh Gamma (Windows only)	Toggles the document display to simulate a typical Macintosh Gamma setting	n/a	n/a
Windows Gamma (Macintosh only)	Toggles the document display to simulate a typical Windows Gamma setting	n/a	n/a
Hide Selection	Hides selected objects	Ctrl+M	Command+M
Show All	Shows all hidden objects	Ctrl+Shift+M	Command+Shift+M

Command	Description	Windows	Macintosh
Hide Edges	Toggles display of selection borders	Ctrl+H	Command+H
Hide Panels	Toggles display of all open panels	Ctrl+Shift+H	Command+Shift+H
Rulers	Toggles display of rulers	Ctrl+Alt+R	Command+Option+R
Grid	Toggles display of the grid	Ctrl+ Apostrophe	Command+ Apostrophe
Grid Options ⇨ Snap To Grid	Toggles whether objects snap to the Grid or not	Ctrl+Shift+ Apostrophe	Command+Shift+ Apostrophe
Grid Options ⇨ Edit Grid	Displays the Edit Grid dialog box	Ctrl+Alt+G	Command+Option+G
Guides	Toggles display of Guides	Ctrl+ Semicolon	Command+ Semicolon
Slice Guides	Toggles display of Slice Guides	Ctrl+Alt+ Shift+ Semicolon	Command+Option+ Shift+Semicolon
Guide Options ⇨ Lock Guides	Toggles whether or not Guides can be edited and moved	Ctrl+Alt+ Semicolon	Command+ Option+Semicolon
Guide Options ⇨ Snap to Guides	Toggles whether objects snap to Guides or not	Ctrl+Shift+ Semicolon	Command+Shift+ Semicolon
Guide Options ⇨ Edit Guides	Displays the Edit Guides dialog box	Ctrl+Alt+ Shift+G	Command+ Option+Shift+G
Status Bar (Windows only)	Toggles display of the status bar	n/a	n/a

Insert menu

The Insert menu, detailed in Table 2-26, contains commands for inserting buttons, Symbols, Hotspots, Layers, Frames, and more.

<table>
<tr><th colspan="4">Table 2-26
Insert Menu Commands</th></tr>
<tr><th>*Command*</th><th>*Description*</th><th>*Windows*</th><th>*Macintosh*</th></tr>
<tr><td>**New Button**</td><td>Displays the Button Editor before creating a new button</td><td>n/a</td><td>n/a</td></tr>
<tr><td>**New Symbol**</td><td>Displays the Symbol Properties dialog box before creating a new symbol</td><td>Ctrl+F8</td><td>Command+F8</td></tr>
<tr><td>**Convert to Symbol**</td><td>Displays the Symbol Properties dialog box before converting an object to a symbol</td><td>F8</td><td>F8</td></tr>
<tr><td>**Libraries ⇨ Your Libraries**</td><td>Lists Libraries contained in the Libraries folder. Choose a Library to display the Import Symbols dialog box before importing a symbol from the Library.</td><td>n/a</td><td>n/a</td></tr>
<tr><td>**Libraries ⇨ Other**</td><td>Displays the Open dialog box before importing a Library</td><td>n/a</td><td>n/a</td></tr>
<tr><td>Hotspot</td><td>Inserts a hotspot object</td><td>Ctrl+Shift+U</td><td>Command+Shift+U</td></tr>
<tr><td>Slice</td><td>Inserts a slice object</td><td>n/a</td><td>n/a</td></tr>
</table>

Command	Description	Windows	Macintosh
Behaviors	Displays the Behaviors inspector, focused on the currently selected slice or hotspot	n/a	n/a
Image	Displays the Import dialog box before importing an image into the document	Ctrl+R	Command+R
Empty Image	Inserts an empty image object	Ctrl+Alt+Y	Command+Option+Y
Layer	Creates a new layer	n/a	n/a
Frame	Creates a new frame	n/a	n/a

Modify menu

Once you've created your basic objects, you'll undoubtedly spend as much, if not more time, tweaking and modifying them in order to get them just right. The Modify menu commands, detailed in Table 2-27, are quite numerous and specific.

Table 2-27 Modify Menu Commands			
Command	**Description**	**Windows**	**Macintosh**
Image Size	Displays the Image Size dialog box before changing the size of an image	n/a	n/a
Canvas Size	Displays the Change Canvas Size dialog box before changing the size of the canvas	n/a	n/a
Canvas Color	Displays the Canvas Color dialog box before changing the color of the canvas	n/a	n/a

Continued

Table 2-27 *(continued)*			
Command	*Description*	*Windows*	*Macintosh*
Trim Canvas	Shrinks the canvas to fit snugly around all objects	n/a	n/a
Rotate Canvas ⇨ Rotate 180°	Rotates the canvas 180°	n/a	n/a
Rotate Canvas ⇨ Rotate 90° CW	Rotates the canvas 90° clockwise	n/a	n/a
Rotate Canvas ⇨ Rotate 90° CCW	Rotates the canvas 90° counterclockwise	n/a	n/a
Symbol ⇨ Edit Symbol	Displays the selected symbol in its own canvas for editing	n/a	n/a
Symbol ⇨ Tween Instances	Displays the Tween Instances dialog box before creating intermediate steps between two selected symbol instances	Ctrl+Alt+ Shift+T	Command+Option+ Shift+T
Symbol ⇨ Break Link	Breaks the link between the selected symbol and its instances	n/a	n/a
Image Object	Switches to Image Edit mode	Ctrl+E	Command+E
Exit Image Edit	Exits Image Edit mode	Ctrl+Shift+D	Command+Shift+D
Path Edge ⇨ Hard	Removes anti-aliasing or feathering from the edges of a selection	n/a	n/a
Path Edge ⇨ Anti-Alias	Anti-Aliases the edges of a selection	n/a	n/a

Command	Description	Windows	Macintosh
Path Edge ⇨ Feather	Feathers the edges of a selection	n/a	n/a
Transform ⇨ Free Transform	Toggles the display of an object's transformation handles	Ctrl+T	Command+T
Transform ⇨ Scale	Sets transformation handles to resize and rotate objects	n/a	n/a
Transform ⇨ Skew	Sets transformation handles to slant, change perspective, and rotate objects	n/a	n/a
Transform ⇨ Distort	Sets transformation handles to distort and rotate objects	n/a	n/a
Transform ⇨ Numeric Transform	Displays the Numeric Transform dialog box	Ctrl+Shift+T	Command+Shift+T
Transform ⇨ Rotate 180°	Rotates an object 180 degrees	n/a	n/a
Transform ⇨ Rotate 90° CW	Rotates an object 90 degrees clockwise	Ctrl+9	Command+9
Transform ⇨ Rotate 90° CCW	Rotates an object 90 degrees counterclockwise	Ctrl+7	Command+7
Transform ⇨ Flip Horizontal	Flips an object horizontally	n/a	n/a
Transform ⇨ Flip Vertical	Flips an object vertically	n/a	n/a
Transform ⇨ Remove Transformations	Removes all transformations from an object		n/a n/a
Arrange ⇨ Bring to Front	Moves an object to the front of a layer	Ctrl+F	Command+F

Continued

Table 2-27 *(continued)*

Command	Description	Windows	Macintosh
Arrange ⇨ Bring Forward	Moves an object in front of the object just in front of it	Ctrl+Shift+F	Command+Shift+F
Arrange ⇨ Send Backward	Moves an object in back of the object just behind it	Ctrl+Shift+B	Command+Shift+B
Arrange ⇨ Send to Back	Moves an object to the back of a layer	Ctrl+B	Command+B
Align ⇨ Left	Aligns selected objects to the left edge of the selection	Ctrl+Alt+1	Command+Option+1
Align ⇨ Center Vertical	Aligns selected objects to the vertical center of the selection	Ctrl+Alt+2	Command+Option+2
Align ⇨ Right	Aligns selected objects to the right edge of the selection	Ctrl+Alt+3	Command+Option+3
Align ⇨ Top	Aligns selected objects to the top edge of the selection	Ctrl+Alt+4	Command+Option+4
Align ⇨ Center Horizontal	Aligns selected objects to the horizontal center of the selection	Ctrl+Alt+5	Command+Option+5
Align ⇨ Bottom	Aligns selected objects to the bottom of the selection	Ctrl+Alt+6	Command+Option+6

Command	Description	Windows	Macintosh
Align ⇨ Distribute Widths	Distribute selected objects horizontally throughout the selection	Ctrl+Alt+7	Command+Option+7
Align ⇨ Distribute Heights	Distribute selected objects vertically throughout the selection	Ctrl+Alt+9	Command+Option+9
Join	Joins two or more selected paths or endpoints	Ctrl+J	Command+J
Split	Splits an object into component paths	Ctrl+Shift+J	Command+Shift+J
Combine ⇨ Union	Combines two or more selected closed paths into a single object	n/a	n/a
Combine ⇨ Intersect	Combines overlapping parts of two or more selected closed paths	n/a	n/a
Combine ⇨ Punch	Combines two or more selected closed paths by punching holes in the back object with the front object(s)	n/a	n/a
Combine ⇨ Crop	Crops the back object of a selection with the front object of a selection of two or more closed paths.	n/a	n/a
Alter Path ⇨ Simplify	Displays the Simplify dialog box before removing points from a path while keeping its overall shape	n/a	n/a

Continued

Table 2-27 *(continued)*

Command	Description	Windows	Macintosh
Alter Path ⇨ Expand Stroke	Displays the Expand dialog box	n/a	n/a
Alter Path ⇨ Inset Path	Displays the Inset dialog box before expanding or contracting one or more closed paths	n/a	n/a
Merge Images	Merges one or more selected image objects into a single image object	Ctrl+Shift+ Alt+Z	Command+Shift+ Option+Z
Merge Layers	Flattens visible layers, discarding hidden layers	n/a	n/a
Group	Groups one or more selected objects	Ctrl+G	Command+G
Mask Group ⇨ Mask to Image	Groups one or more selected objects with the top image object used as an alpha mask	Ctrl+Shift+G	Command+Shift+G
Mask Group ⇨ Mask to Path	Groups one or more selected objects with the top path object used as an alpha mask	n/a	n/a
Ungroup	Ungroups a Group or Mask Group	Ctrl+U	Command+U

Text menu

Text in a traditional graphics program plays a relatively small, but key role. In a Web graphics program such as Fireworks, text becomes more important because graphics are the only way to incorporate heavily styled text into Web pages. The Text menu commands, described in Table 2-28, offer many shortcuts that enable you to manipulate text objects without opening the Text Editor.

Table 2-28 Text Menu Commands			
Command	*Description*	*Windows*	*Macintosh*
Font ➪ Your Font List	Changes the selected text object's typeface or the default typeface if no text object is selected	n/a	n/a
Size ➪ Other	Displays the Text Size dialog box	n/a	n/a
Size ➪ 8 to 120	Changes the selected text object's type size or the default type size if no text object is selected	n/a	n/a
Style ➪ Plain	Removes bold, italic, and underline formatting from the selected text	Ctrl+Alt+Shift+P	Command+Option+Shift+P
Style ➪ Bold	Makes the selected text bold	Ctrl+Alt+Shift+B	Command+Option+Shift+B
Style ➪ Italic	Italicizes the selected text	Ctrl+Alt+Shift+I	Command+Option+Shift+I
Style ➪ Underline	Underlines the selected text	Ctrl+Alt+Shift+U	Command+Option+Shift+U
Align ➪ Left	Left-aligns the selected text	Ctrl+Alt+Shift+L	Command+Option+Shift+L
Align ➪ Center	Centers the selected text	Ctrl+Alt+Shift+C	Command+Option+Shift+C

Continued

Table 2-28 *(continued)*

Command	Description	Windows	Macintosh
Align ⇨ Right	Right-aligns the selected text	Ctrl+Alt+Shift+R	Command+Option+ Shift+R
Align ⇨ Justified	Justifies the selected text	Ctrl+Alt+Shift+J	Command+Option+ Shift+J
Align ⇨ Stretched	Force-justifies the selected text	Ctrl+Alt+Shift+S	Command+Option+ Shift+S
Align ⇨ Top	Aligns vertically flowing text to the top of the text block	n/a	n/a
Align ⇨ Center	Aligns vertically flowing text to the vertical center of the text block	n/a	n/a
Align ⇨ Bottom	Aligns vertically flowing text to the bottom of the text block	n/a	n/a
Align ⇨ Justified	Justifies vertically flowing text to the top and bottom of the text block	n/a	n/a
Align ⇨ Stretched	Force-justifies vertically flowing text to the top and bottom of the text block	n/a	n/a
Editor	Displays the Text Editor dialog box	Ctrl+Shift+E	Command+ Shift+E
Attach to Path	Attaches the selected text block to a selected path	Ctrl+Shift+Y	Command+ Shift+Y
Detach from Path	Detaches the selected text block from a path if it's attached to one	n/a	n/a

Command	Description	Windows	Macintosh
Orientation ➪ Rotate Around Path	Orients attached text so that the bottom of each letter is closest to the path	n/a	n/a
Orientation ➪ Vertical	Orients attached text so that the side of each letter is closest to the path	n/a	n/a
Orientation ➪ Skew Vertical	Skews attached text vertically	n/a	n/a
Orientation ➪ Skew Horizontal	Skews attached text horizontally	n/a	n/a
Reverse Direction	Reverses the direction of text attached to a path	n/a	n/a
Convert to Paths	Converts text objects into vector objects	Ctrl+Shift+P	Command+Shift+P

Commands menu

The Commands menu is new in Fireworks 3. Commands are a way for the Fireworks user to extend the basic feature set and are relatively easy to create because they're written in JavaScript. Table 2-28 details the Commands that are included with Fireworks.

Table 2-28
Commands Menu Commands

Command	Description	Windows	Macintosh
Edit Command List	Displays the Edit Command List dialog box	n/a	n/a
Animation ➪ Rotate	Creates a multiframe animation by rotating the objects in a document	n/a	n/a
Animation ➪ Rotate and Scale	Creates a multiframe animation by rotating and scaling the objects in a document	n/a	n/a

Continued

Table 2-28 *(continued)*

Command	Description	Windows	Macintosh
Batch a Command	Displays the Open dialog box before running the selected Command on multiple documents	n/a	n/a
Creative ⇨ Convert to Grayscale	Converts the selection to grayscale	n/a	n/a
Creative ⇨ Convert to Sepia Tone	Converts the selection to a sepia tint	n/a	n/a
Creative ⇨ Create Picture Frame	Creates a faux-wood picture frame around the current document	n/a	n/a
Document ⇨ Center in Document	Centers the selection in the middle of the document	n/a	n/a
Document ⇨ Hide Other Layers	Hides all layers except the current layer	n/a	n/a
Document ⇨ Lock Other Layers	Locks all layers except the current layer	n/a	n/a
Document ⇨ Reverse All Frames	Reverses the order of the frames in a document	n/a	n/a
Document ⇨ Reverse Frame Range	Reverses the order of a range of frames in a document	n/a	n/a
Panel Layout Sets ⇨ Your Panel Layout Sets	Lists panel layout sets created with Commands ⇨ Panel Layout	n/a	n/a
Panel Layout Sets ⇨ 1024 x 768 / 800 x 600	Panel Layout Set examples that arrange the floating windows to the right of the screen, sized for optimal viewing at 1024×768 or 800×600, respectively	n/a	n/a

Command	Description	Windows	Macintosh
Panel Layout	Displays a dialog box where you can name the current panel layout and save it so that it appears under Commands ⇨ Panel Layout Sets	n/a	n/a
Web ⇨ Create Shared Palette	Creates a shared palette from multiple files	n/a	n/a
Web ⇨ Set Alt Tags	Displays a dialog box where you can specify alt text for a document's hotspots and slices	n/a	n/a

Xtras

In Macromedia parlance, an Xtra is a plug-in that extends the capabilities of a program. With Fireworks, Xtras are primarily image filters. As you can see in Table 2-29, Fireworks comes with four groups of filters, plus two Eye Candy filters, referred to as Eye Candy LE. Because Fireworks can read most Photoshop filters and plug-ins, you can greatly extend the available Xtras, either by including them in Fireworks' Settings/Plug-ins folder or by assigning the proper folder in Preferences.

Caution

Because all Fireworks Xtras are pixel-based image filters, any Xtra applied to a vector-based object first converts that object to an image. Many Xtras are also available in the Effect panel as Live Effects, which work on both pixel-based and path-based objects.

Table 2-29 Xtras Menu Commands			
Command	Description	Windows	Macintosh
Repeat Xtra	Repeats the most recently used Xtra	Ctrl+Alt+Shift+X	Command+ Option+Shift+X
Adjust Color ⇨ Auto Levels	Auto corrects the selection's levels	n/a	n/a
Adjust Color ⇨ Brightness/Contrast	Displays the Brightness/Contrast dialog box before adjusting the selection's brightness and/or contrast levels	n/a	n/a

Continued

Table 2-29 *(continued)*

Command	Description	Windows	Macintosh
Adjust Color ➪ Curves	Displays the Curves dialog box before adjusting the selection's color curves	n/a	n/a
Adjust Color ➪ Hue/Saturation	Displays the Hue/Saturation dialog box before adjusting the selection's hue and saturation levels	n/a	n/a
Adjust Color ➪ Invert	Changes each color in the selected image object(s) to its mathematical inverse	n/a	n/a
Adjust Color ➪ Levels	Displays the Levels dialog box before adjusting the selection's levels	n/a	n/a
Blur ➪ Blur	Blurs the selected image object(s)	n/a	n/a
Blur ➪ Blur More	Blurs the selected image object(s) across a larger radius than Blur	n/a	n/a
Blur ➪ Gaussian Blur	Displays the Gaussian Blur dialog box before blurring the selected image object(s)	n/a	n/a
Other ➪ Convert to Alpha	Converts the selected image object into an alpha mask	n/a	n/a
Other ➪ Find Edges	Identifies edges in the selected image object(s)	n/a	n/a

Command	Description	Windows	Macintosh
Sharpen ➪ Sharpen	Sharpens the selected image object(s)	n/a	n/a
Sharpen ➪ Sharpen More	Sharpens the selected image object(s) more than Sharpen	n/a	n/a
Sharpen ➪ Unsharp Mask	Displays the Unsharp Mask dialog box before sharpening the selected image object(s)	n/a	n/a
Eye Candy 3.1 LE ➪ **Cutout**	Displays the Eye Candy Cutout dialog box	n/a	n/a
Eye Candy 3.1 LE ➪ **Motion Trail dialog box**	Displays the Eye Candy Motion Trail	n/a	n/a

Window menu

The Window menu commands, listed in Table 2-30, give you access to all of Fireworks' floating panels and toolbars. In addition, several commands help you work with multiple images or multiple views of the same image.

Table 2-30 Window Menu Commands			
Command	Description	Windows	Macintosh
New Window	Creates a duplicate of the current document window	Ctrl+Alt+N	Command+Option+N
Toolbars ➪ Main (Windows only)	Toggles display of the Main toolbar	n/a	n/a
Toolbars ➪ Modify (Windows only)	Toggles display of the Modify toolbar	n/a	n/a

Continued

Table 2-30 *(continued)*

Command	Description	Windows	Macintosh
Toolbars ⇨ View Controls (Windows only)	Toggles display of the View Controls toolbar	n/a	n/a
Toolbox	Toggles display of the Toolbox	Ctrl+Alt+T	Command+Option+T
Optimize	Toggles display of the Optimize panel	n/a	n/a
Object	Toggles display of the Object inspector	Ctrl+I	Command+I
Stroke	Toggles display of the Stroke panel	Ctrl+Alt+B	Command+Option+B
Fill	Toggles display of the Fill panel	Ctrl+Alt+F	Command+Option+F
Effect	Toggles display of the Effect panel	Ctrl+Alt+E	Command+Option+E
Color Table	Toggles display of the Color Table panel	n/a	n/a
Swatches	Toggles display of the Swatches panel	Ctrl+Alt+S	Command+Option+S
Color Mixer	Toggles display of the Color Mixer	Ctrl+Alt+M	Command+Option+M
Tool Options	Toggles display of the Tool Options panel	Ctrl+Alt+O	Command+Option+O
Layers	Toggles display of the Layers panel	Ctrl+Alt+L	Command+Option+L
Frames	Toggles display of the Frames panel	Ctrl+Alt+K	Command+Option+K
History	Toggles display of the History panel	n/a	n/a
Info	Toggles display of the Info panel	Ctrl+Alt+I	Command+Option+I

Command	Description	Windows	Macintosh
Behaviors	Toggles display of the Behaviors inspector	Ctrl+Alt+H	Command+Option+H
URL	Toggles display of the URL panel	Ctrl+Alt+U	Command+Option+U
Styles	Toggles display of the Styles panel	Ctrl+Alt+J	Command+Option+J
Library	Toggles display of the Library panel	n/a	n/a
Find and Replace	Toggles display of the Find and Replace panel	n/a	n/a
Project Log	Toggles display of the Project Log panel	n/a	n/a
Cascade	Cascades the document windows	n/a	n/a
Tile Horizontal	Tiles the document windows horizontally	n/a	n/a
Tile Vertical	Tiles the document windows vertically	n/a	n/a
Your Open Documents List	Lists the currently open document windows	n/a	n/a

Help menu

Everyone needs help now and then, especially when working with a program as rich and deep as Fireworks. The Help menu provides quick access to Using Fireworks,various online resources, and a number of key tutorials that explain the basics of the program.

The Macromedia and Fireworks Web sites offer a tremendous range of support options. If you're troubleshooting a problem, you should start with the searchable TechNotes, which cover virtually every aspect of working with Fireworks. You'll also find links to useful tutorials, articles on Web graphics design, and interviews with industry leaders in Fireworks' main Support section.

One of the most important resources is the Fireworks newsgroup, hosted by Macromedia. This discussion group, located at <news://forums.macromedia.com/ macromedia.fireworks>, is an essential source for contacting other users of Fireworks. Fireworks support staff, as well as expert and novice users alike, frequent the newsgroup. Need a quick answer to a perplexing graphics problem? Can't figure out the final step in a procedure? Looking to have users with different systems and browsers check your site for compatibility? The Fireworks newsgroup can help in all of these areas and more.

The Help menu commands are detailed in Table 2-31.

Table 2-31
Help Menu Commands

Command	Description	Windows	Macintosh
About Balloon Help (Macintosh only)	Describes Balloon Help	n/a	n/a
Show Balloons (Macintosh only)	Toggles Balloon Help on or off	n/a	n/a
Using Fireworks	Opens the Fireworks online manual in your browser	F1	n/a
Index	Opens the Fireworks online manual in your Web browser with the index visible	n/a	n/a
Tutorial	Opens the tutorial in your primary browser	n/a	n/a
What's New in Version 3 (What's New)	Opens a list of what's new in Fireworks 3 in your browser	n/a	n/a
Fireworks Support Center	Connects to the Internet to view the Fireworks Support Center Web site	n/a	n/a

Command	Description	Windows	Macintosh
Fireworks Product Web Site	Connects to the Internet to view the Fireworks Product Web site	n/a	n/a
Register Fireworks	Connects to the Internet to register your copy of Fireworks with Macromedia	n/a	n/a
About Fireworks (Windows only)	Displays the About Fireworks dialog box	n/a	n/a

Tip   Mac OS 8/9 users can display the About Fireworks dialog box by choosing Apple Menu ⇨ About Fireworks.

Summary

With a program as feature-laden as Fireworks, it's helpful to have an overview of what's possible. The Fireworks user interface is very flexible and customizable. The more familiar you become with the layout of the program, the smoother your workflow will become. When you're looking at the Fireworks interface, keep these points in mind:

✦ In some ways, Fireworks combines tools from several different types of applications: a bitmap graphic program, a vector drawing program, an image optimizer, and an HTML editor.

✦ Export optimization settings and export previews are now done in-place in Fireworks 3, necessitating new panels, such as Optimize and Color Table, and modifications to previously existing panels, such as the Frames panel.

✦ All of the tools found in Fireworks' Toolbox have one-key shortcuts, such as V for the Select tool and Z for the Magnify tool.

✦ Customize your workspace in Fireworks 3 by grouping the floating panels however you'd like and then save that grouping as a Panel Layout Set.

✦ Many tools have special options you can access by double-clicking their Toolbox buttons, or by choosing the tool and then opening the Tool Options panel.

In the next chapter, you'll see how you can set up the Fireworks environment to suit your work style.

✦   ✦   ✦

Customizing Your Environment

✦   ✦   ✦   ✦

In This Chapter

Establishing
primary options

Linking to
external resources

Setting Photoshop
import preferences

Controlling
HTML output

Getting Fireworks
hard copy

✦   ✦   ✦   ✦

Y ou'll never find any two artists' studios that are exactly alike. And why should you? Creating—whether it's fine art, print images, or Web graphics—is a highly personal experience that requires the artist to be in comfortable, personalized surroundings. Fireworks 3 reflects this attitude by enabling you to personalize numerous preferences to facilitate your workflow, from importing existing images through graphic editing all the way to exporting your final product. This chapter describes options Fireworks offers to custom-fit the program to your personal style.

Setting Preferences

Most, but not all, of Fireworks' customization options are handily grouped in the Preferences dialog box. Though you can adjust these preferences at any time, they are generally used to fine-tune the program's overall functions between sessions. Consequently, changes to a number of the options do not take effect until you restart Fireworks.

To access these program-wide settings, choose File ⇨ Preferences. The Preferences dialog box opens with the first of its four panels displayed. The panels—detailed in the following sections—are labeled General, Editing, Folders, and Import. On Windows, move from panel to panel by selecting another tab. On the Mac, choose another option from the option list to move to another panel.

Cross-Reference Fireworks has an additional type of preference: the configuration and layout of the dockable floating windows. You can create your own combination of windows—Layers, Frames, Styles, Effects and so on—by dragging and dropping their tabs on one another. For details on this aspect of customizing your workspace, see Chapter 2.

General preferences

The General panel of the Preferences dialog box, shown in Figure 3-1, is divided into three sections: Undo Steps, Color Defaults, and Interpolation.

Tip   The screenshots of the Preferences dialog box in Figures 3-1, 3-2, 3-4, and 3-5 show the default, freshly-installed settings. If you're ever wondering what the default for a particular preference is, refer to these images.

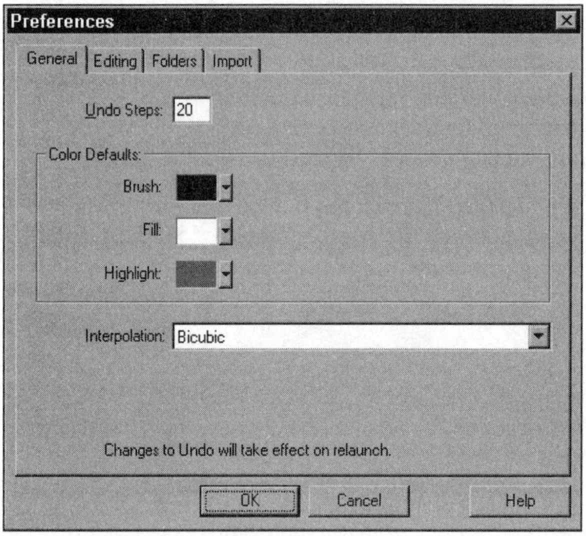

Figure 3-1: Set the number of Undo steps, change the color defaults, and specify the default interpolation method in the General panel of the Preferences dialog box.

Specifying undo levels

The capability to undo an action—whether it's a font color change, an image rotation, or an out-and-out deletion—is critical in computer graphics. Although some graphics programs only let you reverse or undo your last command, Fireworks not only gives you multiple undo levels, but the History panel provides a graphical way to interact with your previous steps. Of course, storing the changes that you make to a document in order to be able to undo that change requires a certain amount of memory. Rather than let an unlimited number of undo steps accumulate in the background until your computer starts to feel the strain, Fireworks lets you specify the number of undo levels that you think will strike the best balance between usability and utility.

Cross-Reference   For more about Fireworks 3's new History panel, see Chapter 19.

By default, Fireworks prepares itself to keep track of 20 undo levels. You can change this by altering the Undo Steps value. The amount of memory needed to undo an operation depends on the type of operation. For example, rotating a 500 × 600 pixel photograph requires far more memory than changing the color of a straight line.

Caution   Windows users can increase the number of Undo Steps up to a maximum of 100. Mac users can increase the number of Undo Steps further if Fireworks has access to enough RAM. See Macintosh Help (press the Help key or choose Help ⇨ Mac Help in the Finder) for information on how to give Fireworks access to more RAM.

If you alter the number of Undo Steps, the new setting takes effect for both the Edit ⇨ Undo menu command and the History panel after you restart Fireworks.

Color defaults

Although the Web designer has a full palette from which to choose, Fireworks starts with just three basic colors:

  ✦ **Brush:** The default Brush color is applied to any path that is drawn or stroked with any of the drawing tools, such as the Pencil, Pen, Brush, or Rectangle.

  ✦ **Fill:** The default Fill color is applied to any object when a Solid fill-type is selected in the Fill window.

  ✦ **Highlight:** To show a selected object, Fireworks temporarily changes the outline of the object to the Highlight color. When the object is deselected (or another object is selected), the Highlight color is removed.

You make all default color changes through the Color Defaults section of the General panel in the Preferences dialog box. To alter any of the Brush, Fill, or Highlight colors, select the arrow button next to their respective color wells. The Fireworks color picker is displayed. Choose any of the Web-safe color swatches shown or use the Eyedropper tool to select an onscreen color. For a wider selection of colors, select the Palette icon to display your operating system's color picker(s).

Tip   To turn off the automatic fill or stroke, select the No Color icon (the slash-in-circle symbol: ∅) from the pop-up color picker. Although a color is still displayed in the color well when No Color is selected, any objects created are drawn with Fill and/or Stroke option set to None.

You can alter both the Brush and Fill colors by choosing their respective color well on the Toolbox, the Color Mixer, or any number of other windows. The Highlight color can only be changed through Preferences. All color changes take place immediately after the Preferences dialog box closes.

Tip If you choose a gradient fill-type (such as Linear, Radial, or Cone) for an object, but no color combination, Fireworks uses the current Brush and Fill selections to create the gradient.

Interpolation defaults

When you resize an image, Fireworks analyzes the original, and based on that analysis creates a new image with either more or fewer pixels. This process is called interpolation. Fireworks offers four interpolation methods: bicubic, bilinear, soft, and nearest neighbor. When you resize an image, you can choose any of these four, but the interpolation preference you set here determines the default in the Image Size dialog box. Bicubic (the default) is the best general-purpose option. Unless you have a specific reason not to do so, I recommend leaving this preference at bicubic and modifying it as needed for special circumstances.

Cross-Reference For more about interpolation methods and resizing images, see Chapter 6.

Editing preferences

The Editing panel of Preferences, shown in Figure 3-2, offers some new options in Fireworks 3 to customize the workflow between Fireworks and an external HTML editor such as Macromedia Dreamweaver or Adobe GoLive. It also contains options for working with bitmap images.

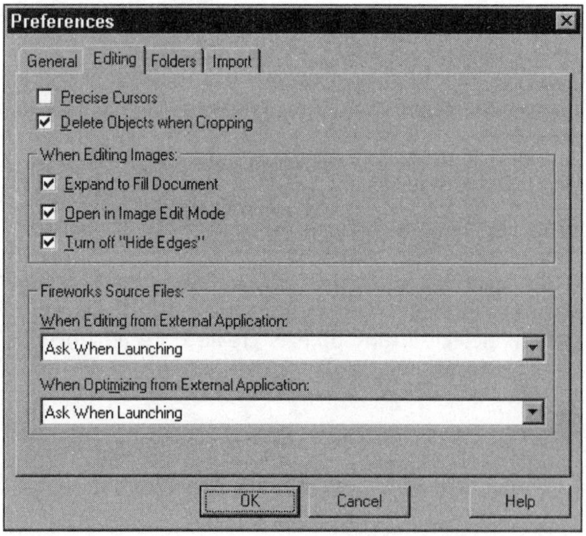

Figure 3-2: Customize your graphics creation style in the Editing panel of Fireworks Preferences.

Using precise cursors

By default, when a particular drawing or selection tool is selected, the cursor changes into a representative shape. For example, select the Pencil tool and the cursor changes to a pencil shape. The Precise Cursors option replaces all the affected individual cursor shapes with a crosshair cursor.

If the Precise Cursors option is selected, the following tools use the crosshair cursor:

✦ All selection tools including the rectangular and elliptical Marquee, and the Lasso, Polygon Lasso, and Magic Wand

✦ Drawing tools such as the Line, Pen, Rectangle, Ellipse, Polygon, Pencil, and Brush

✦ Modification tools such as Eraser and Paint Bucket

✦ All Web objects tools, including Hotspot Rectangles, Circle and Polygons, and the Slice tool

The Precise Cursor is very useful for detail work where the tool-specific cursor might block the designer's view, as illustrated in Figure 3-3.

Pencil tool cursor

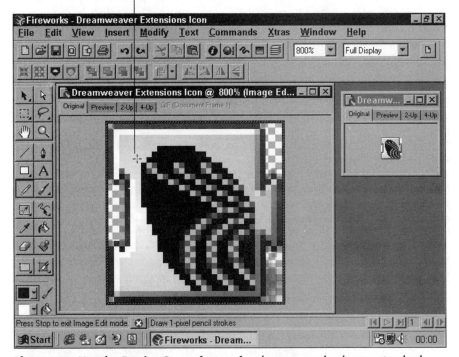

Figure 3-3: Use the Precise Cursor feature for close-up work where a standard cursor might hamper pixel-level accuracy.

Tip If you haven't enabled the Precise Cursors option in Preferences, the option can be toggled on or off with the Caps Lock key. Unless you find the standard cursors particularly distracting, I recommend keeping the Precise Cursors option disabled in Preferences and using the Caps Lock key whenever the crosshair cursor is needed.

Delete objects when cropping

New in Fireworks 3, the Delete Objects when Cropping preference specifies that path or image objects outside of a cropped area should be deleted. Fireworks 2 simply resized the canvas and left your objects alone. If you prefer that way of working, be sure to uncheck this preference setting.

Examining pixel-based image options

The When Editing Images options on the Editing panel affect only pixel-based images.

Because Fireworks creates and edits both pixel-based images and vector-based objects, a selected image is often just a portion of the overall document. When you choose the Expand to Fill Document option, anytime you enter Image Edit mode, the currently selected image object is expanded to the size of the entire document and surrounded by a "barber-pole" selection border. This allows you to make modifications to the image that extend beyond its original size. For example, if you have a 100×100 pixel image object in a 500×500 document, when you enter Image Edit mode, the image object is temporarily expanded to 500×500. You can make modifications to the image object freely, without worrying that you're " drawing outside the lines." If you paint a 10 pixel border around your 100×100 pixel graphic, when you exit Image Edit mode, the image object will collapse to 120×120 pixels.

When you open a document that contains a single bitmap image, Fireworks automatically enters Image Edit mode. If you'd prefer to have Fireworks stay in Object Edit mode no matter what, deselect the Open in Image Edit Mode preference.

Hide Edges, found under the View menu, normally makes all the selection outlines vanish. This includes the barber-poles around bitmap images in Image Edit mode, the "marching ants" around a pixel selection, and the hard blue lines around path objects. When the Turn Off "Hide Edges" option is enabled, the Hide Edges command is only temporary; making any selection causes the edges to reappear. In other words, the Hide Edges option means "hide edges until I make another selection." When Turn off "Hide Edges" is unchecked, the Hide Edges command hides edges until you choose it again and specifically ask to view selection borders. I've found that it's easy to lose track of selections if edges are hidden all the time, so I generally leave this option enabled.

Working with other applications

A common feature of the Web designer's workflow is to edit or optimize an image file that's already in an HTML page. A placed image may be too big in width or height, or even more commonly, too big in file size. Often, HTML editors such as Macromedia Dreamweaver or Adobe GoLive allow you to specify a default external image editor for image files. Of course, Fireworks is an excellent choice.

When you open an image for editing in Fireworks from an external application, Fireworks asks if you'd like to edit the actual GIF, JPEG or PNG file from the page, or whether you'd like to use a Fireworks PNG file as a source for editing. Using an original Fireworks PNG file (if one is available) is always preferable, because you'll maintain the highest quality possible, as well as retaining vector information and editable text.

Under the Fireworks Source Files section on the Editing panel of the Fireworks preferences, you can choose to always use a Fireworks PNG file, never use a Fireworks PNG file, or have Fireworks always ask. Additionally, you can specify a similar preference for optimizing an image in Fireworks, when you use the Dreamweaver command Optimize Image in Fireworks.

Folder preferences

One of the features of a truly great software program is the capability to extend its functionality. You can access additional resources in the Folders panel of the Preferences dialog box, as shown in Figure 3-4.

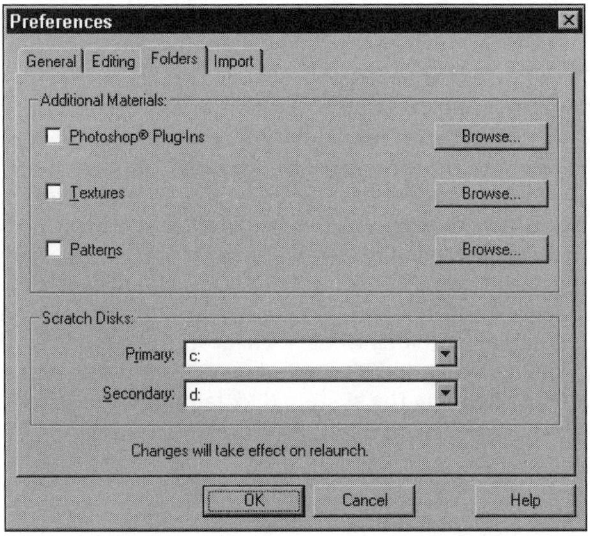

Figure 3-4: Access additional resources for Fireworks through the Folders panel of Preferences.

Additional materials

Three key areas for expansion are detailed in the Additional Materials section of the Folders panel.

✦ **Photoshop Plug-Ins:** Fireworks enables you to include additional image filters for applying effects to bitmap images. Fireworks works with Photoshop-compatible plug-ins — and compatibility with the myriad third-party filters that are available has been improved again in Fireworks 3.

✦ **A second Textures folder:** Textures are images that can be blended with other images to give the appearance of different surfaces.

✦ **A second Patterns folder:** Patterns are single images that repeat to fill a selected area.

Typically, designers use the Folder preferences to include resources that are currently available to another program, such as Photoshop. Fireworks has its own plug-ins (called Xtras), Textures, and Pattern folders from which it works, but is also willing to piggyback on another application to double the options that you have available when you're working in Fireworks.

Select the Browse button next to the Photoshop Plug-Ins, Textures, or Patterns checkboxes to navigate to a folder on your hard drive that contains the plug-ins, textures or Patterns that you want Fireworks to start using. Close the Preferences dialog box and restart Fireworks to complete the installation of these resources.

Cross-Reference   Patterns and textures add a great deal of richness to your graphics. For more details on how to apply them in Fireworks, see Chapter 11. For details on how to incorporate Photoshop plug-ins, turn to Chapter 12.

Scratch disks

The final option in the Folders preferences sets up an additional workspace for Fireworks called a *scratch disk*. Graphics manipulation requires a great deal of memory. When Fireworks needs to perform an operation that requires more memory than is currently available, a hard drive is used as a temporary workspace. By default, Fireworks uses the hard drive on which it is installed as the primary scratch disk. If another hard drive is available on a Windows machine (typically D:), Fireworks will choose it as the secondary scratch disk. On a Macintosh, the secondary scratch disk will be set to None until you choose another disk by name. If you have a choice, it's generally a good idea to have Fireworks use a drive other than the system disk as its primary scratch disk since your operating system and applications are probably already keeping the system disk fairly busy. A drive with lots of space on it is always preferable to one that's overflowing, though.

Tip

Defragmenting a hard drive unites file fragments and consolidates free space into contiguous chunks. This often leads to a general performance improvement in accessing the drive, and also makes big, empty spaces available for Fireworks so it can store its temporary data a little bit faster. Use a program such as Speed Disk, which is part of the Norton Utilities for Macintosh or Windows. Some versions of Windows include their own similar utility, Disk Defragmenter.

Import preferences

Photoshop is a well-established image-editing program that gains much of its power from its capability to layer one image on top of another with varying degrees of opaqueness and transparency. Fireworks handles Photoshop 3, 4, or 5 files quite elegantly, keeping the layers separate and the text editable. You can specify import options each time you import a Photoshop document, but setting the defaults that suit you best in the Import preferences will save you time and trouble later on, as shown in Figure 3-5.

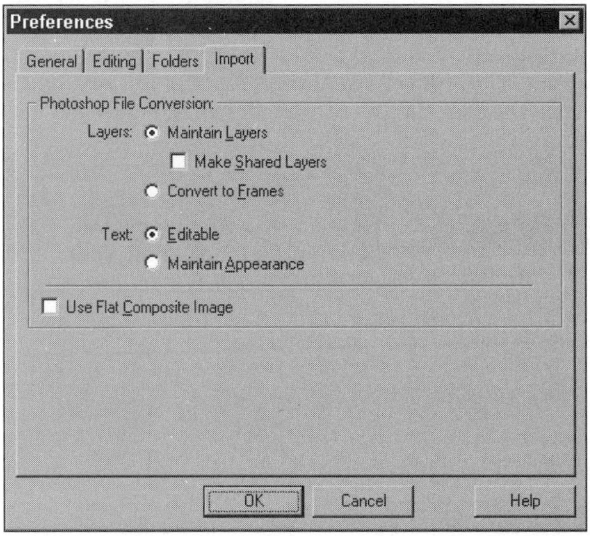

Figure 3-5: Specify the default options for importing Photoshop documents into Fireworks through the Import panel of the Preferences dialog box.

By default, the Maintain Layers option is selected and each layer of a Photoshop image is put in its own Fireworks layer. Check the Make Shared Layers option and Fireworks will share these layers across frames. Alternatively, you can choose to convert the Photoshop layers to Fireworks frames upon import by selecting Convert to Frames. To load a flat, single-layer version of the graphic, choose the Use Flat Composite Image option.

If you know that you'll never want to edit the text, or if you may not always have the matching fonts available, choose the Maintain Appearance option to "flatten" the text into images.

Adjusting HTML Properties

Fireworks files are similar to those from a page layout program in one important way: both are intended for publication. While the page layout program outputs files intended for a printer or service bureau, Fireworks generates files to be published on the Web. Because of the increased variations possible with its HTML output, Fireworks allows you to set a range of properties for each document.

Note   The HTML Properties command was previously called Document Properties in Fireworks 2.

The HTML Properties command enables you to set options for both slicing and image map operations. Briefly, slicing cuts an image into smaller sections, which are placed in an HTML table, whereas an image map is a graphic with one or more hotspots. The parameters chosen through the Document Properties command can be used for a single graphic or designated as the current default settings. Choose File ➪ HTML Properties to open the dialog box shown in Figure 3-6 and set these parameters.

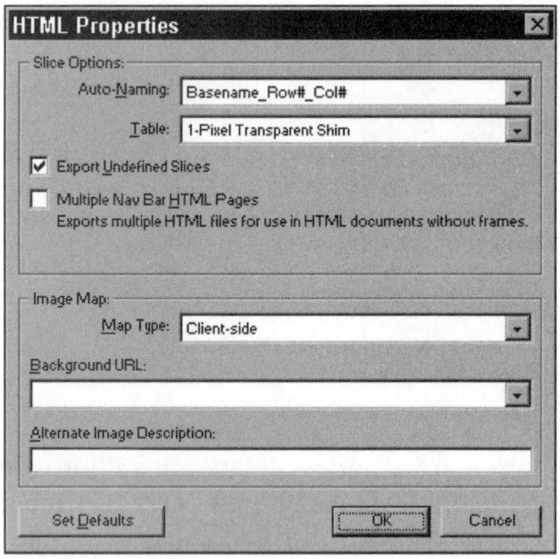

Figure 3-6: Control the HTML output of your document with the HTML Properties options.

Slicing an image

When Fireworks slices an image, each sliced section must be stored using a unique name. Rather than asking the designer to name each section on export, Fireworks automatically generates a filename. The naming convention combines a basename — the name entered in the Export process — before or after one of three different extensions, to make six different combinations. The following combinations are available from the Auto-Naming drop-down list on the Document Properties dialog box:

✦ **Basename_Row#_Col#:** Combines the basename with the number of the row and column of the HTML table used to display the slices; row numbers are prefaced with an "r" and columns with a "c". Examples: welcome_r1_c1; welcome_r1_c2; welcome_r1_c3; welcome_r2_c1.

✦ **Basename_Alphabetical:** Mixes the basename with an alphabetical suffix, in ascending order. For slices with many images, Fireworks uses a multiple letter combination, for example, AA, BB, CC, and so on, to name those images after the 26th one. Examples: welcome_A; welcome_B; welcome_C.

✦ **Basename_Numeric:** With this option, the unique name consists of the basename and an ascending number. Fireworks uses a smart-naming algorithm: if there are less than ten slices, the numbers 1 through 9 are used; however, if there are ten or more slices, a leading zero is used for the single digits. Examples: welcome_01; welcome_02; welcome_03.

✦ **Row#_Col#_Basename:** Uses the row and column numbers of the HTML table as described previously as a prefix to the basename. Examples: r1_c1_welcome; r1_c2_welcome; r2_c1_welcome.

✦ **Alphabetical_Basename:** Places the alphabetical reference before the basename. Examples: A_welcome; B_welcome; C_welcome.

✦ **Numeric_Basename:** Creates a unique name by combining the number of the slice with its basename. Examples: 01_welcome; 02_welcome; 03_welcome.

Both the numeric and alphabetical naming schemes follow the same pattern as they name objects in the HTML table. Objects are named row by row, left to right, as shown in Figure 3-7.

Slicing is one of Fireworks' richest features. For a complete discussion of slicing, see Chapter 20.

Shim options

An unfortunate fact-of-Web-life has made a device known as the table shim pretty much a necessity for many sliced images. When an image is sliced, each section is placed in a separate HTML table cell. Some browsers collapse the tables unless some content is included in each cell, rendering the image unattractive. Fireworks solves this problem by placing a 1-pixel shim in each outside column and row, as shown in Figure 3-8. The shims serve to keep the graphic looking as-designed, no matter what browser is used.

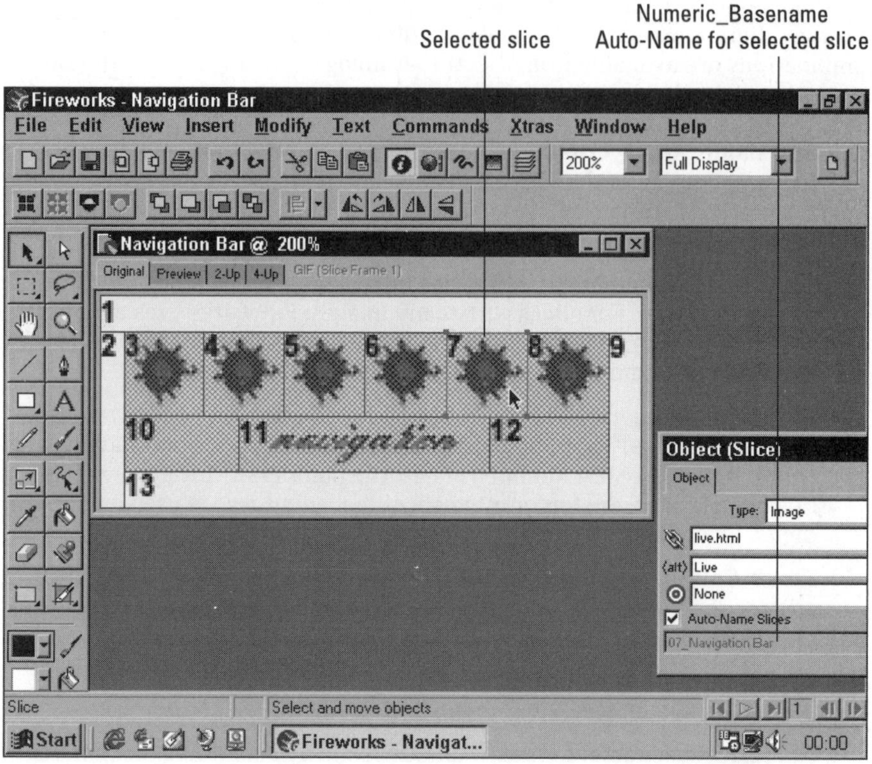

Figure 3-7: This figure depicts the slicing order as Fireworks moves top to bottom, left to right.

There are a range of possibilities for using shims. Select the Shims arrow button and select one of the options from the drop-down list:

✦ **Nested Tables — No Shims:** Fireworks attempts to maintain the proper look by nesting tables. If you use this option, be sure to test your final output in all required browsers to make sure shims aren't required.

✦ **Single Table — No Shims:** One table and no shims. As above, comprehensive testing is required to make sure your output is acceptable.

✦ **1-Pixel Transparent Shim:** This is the default method which places transparent shims around the outside of the image. Only one image file is added and used: a 1 × 1 pixel transparent GIF file called shim.gif with a tiny file size of 43 bytes. The shim.gif file is used repeatedly and resized in the browser, if necessary.

✦ **Shims from Image Slices:** The drawback to the transparent GIF shim is that separate sliced images could not butt up against each other — because of the 1-pixel barrier. You can opt to have the shim cut out of the image itself, thus avoiding use of the transparent shim.gif file. This solution works for many sliced images where graphics must be positioned side-by-side.

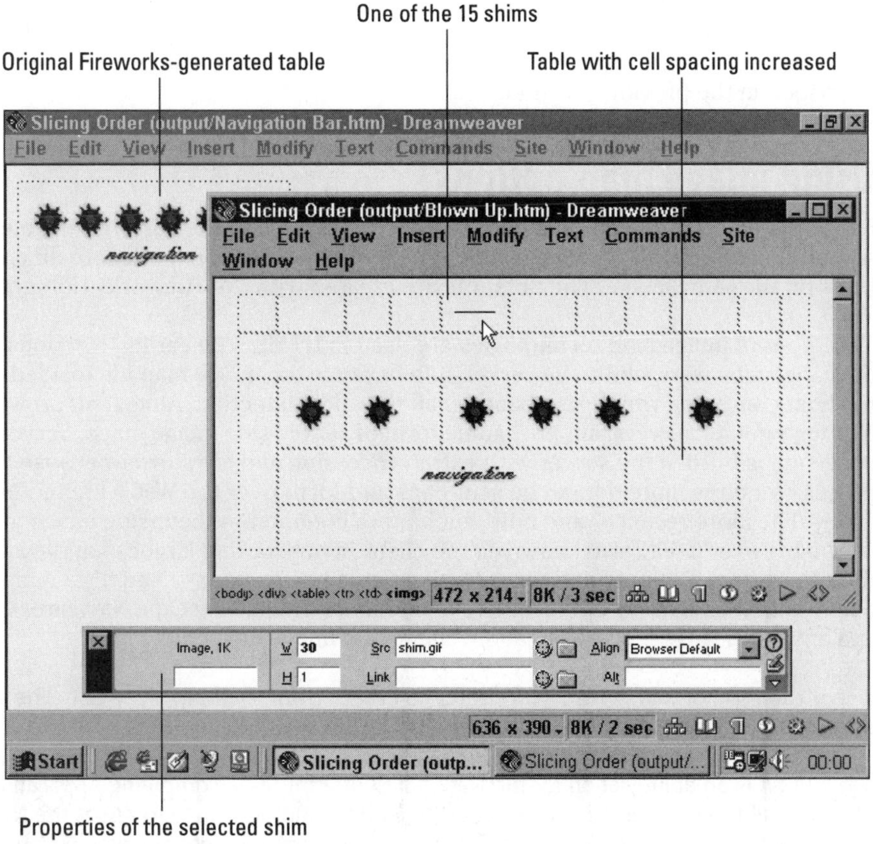

One of the 15 shims

Original Fireworks-generated table   Table with cell spacing increased

Properties of the selected shim

Figure 3-8: Opening this Fireworks-generated table in Dreamweaver and increasing the cell spacing allows us to see the extra cells—each containing a shim—across the top and down the right side. Note in the Property Inspector that the selected shim—which is really a 1 × 1 pixel GIF—is sized at 30 × 1.

> **Caution**
>
> Do not choose the Shims from Image option if your graphic has a rollover that extends to the edge. The shim cut from the image will not be affected by the rollover and will break the rollover button effect you're trying to achieve.

Exporting undefined slices

When you slice an image, you don't have to cover every portion of the canvas with a slice object. Although most of the time the entire graphic is translated into slices, you may prefer to store just the specifically sliced areas.

Let's look at an example. Say that a designer uses a single canvas to create multiple, similar graphic elements that will ultimately be used on separate pages. If the Export Undefined Slices option is left selected (it's the default), the entire graphic will be exported in a single table with the individual elements in the same relative position to each other — however, they could not be used on different Web pages. If, on the other hand, the Export Undefined Slices option is deselected, the sliced objects are exported as separate files, using the naming convention described in the previous section.

Using image map options

Fireworks offers three options for any image maps used in the current document. As noted earlier, an image map is a graphic that uses hotspots to denote different URLs on the same image. The hotspots are created with the Fireworks Hotspot tool.

Two types of image map technologies are used in HTML. The earliest versions of image maps were said to be server-side because the image map file resided on the host computer, which also handled all the click-detection. Almost all browsers, although not all servers, support some form of server-side image maps. Server-side image maps burden the server with extra processing and are slower because the process requires more data to be sent back and forth over the Web's limited bandwidth. The more recent — and now much more common — client-side image maps let the browser itself (also known as the client in networking jargon) handle all of the processing. The only drawback to client-side image maps — and it's a minor one — is that a few very old browsers can't handle them. Netscape Navigator 2+ and any other browser 3+ will handle client-side image maps just fine.

Select the type of image map you prefer to create from the Map Type list. The options are: Client-Side, Server-Side (NCSA), and Both.

Note

NCSA is an abbreviation for the National Center for Supercomputing Applications, one of the pioneers in early server-side Web technology. Fireworks uses the NCSA format for its server-side image map code. Several different server-side formats exist. Another common one is CERN. Make sure your servers support the NCSA format before making server-side image maps in Fireworks.

When a user clicks in a hotspot on an image map, the user's browser jumps to the associated Internet address or URL. Often, a designer wants to assign a general URL to the overall image, in case it is selected. This type of Internet address is known as the background URL, and you can enter either a relative or absolute URL in the Background URL text box on the Document Properties dialog box.

Similarly, when the user's pointer passes over a hotspot, some browsers will display a tooltip: short identifying text to give the user some more information about where the link leads. The information for the tooltip is set in the <alt> field of the Object window in Fireworks. For a tooltip to appear when the user's pointer is over the general image map, but not any specific hotspot, that information should be entered into the HTML Properties Alternate Image Description text box. This alternate text will also be all that a user sees if they have images turned off in their browser. You might like to identify your image as an image map here if you haven't provided additional text links on your pages for them to use.

Cross-Reference To understand the potential for image maps better, turn to Chapter 20.

Selecting Print Options

Although Fireworks is a tremendously Web-oriented program, occasionally a print-out of a graphic is useful. Quite often the designer is expected to present visual concepts to clients or other team members, occasionally in a printed format.

Fireworks' Print feature is very straightforward and uses standards set on both Macintosh and Windows operating systems. The File ➪ Page Setup command opens a standard dialog box, shown in Figure 3-9, which enables the user to determine the page size, paper source, orientation, and margins. Choosing the Printer button opens the standard dialog box with printer-specific options. When you're ready to print the selected image, just choose File ➪ Print and select the number of copies and other choices.

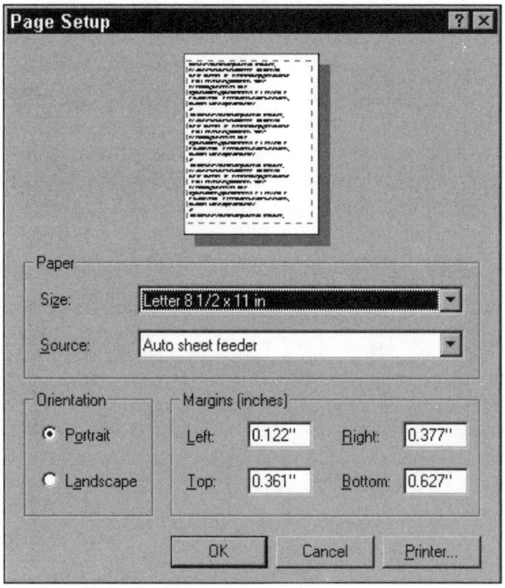

Figure 3-9: Use the Page Setup dialog box to establish your page size and orientation when printing from within Fireworks.

When Fireworks prints a selected image, the graphic is positioned in the center of the page at the preset resolution. You can change the resolution and the print size by selecting Modify ➪ Image Size and entering new values in the appropriate text boxes in the Image Size dialog box.

Tip If you often require printed proofs of Web designs, an excellent way to generate these is with Adobe Acrobat 4. Its Web Capture tool can grab a Web page or complete site from a local machine or the Web and turn it into a surprisingly good-looking PDF file, complete with navigable PDF bookmark links.

Summary

Setting your preferences not only lets you work more comfortably, but also more effectively. Fireworks 3 gives you control over many aspects of your graphics creation, output, and even printing. Here are a few key points to keep in mind about setting your Fireworks preferences:

✦ You can find most of the program's options by choosing File ➪ Preferences.

✦ Several preferences — such as including other Photoshop plug-ins, Patterns, and Textures folders — require you to restart Fireworks before they take effect.

✦ You can turn the crosshair cursor on and off by pressing the Caps Lock key, but only if you do not choose the Precise Cursors option in the Editing panel of Preferences.

✦ Each document opened or created can have its own set of special properties that affect the HTML output for slices and image maps.

In the next chapter, you'll learn how to create new canvases for your Web graphic creations as well as how to open existing works for modification.

✦　　✦　　✦

Setting Up Documents

In This Chapter

Prepping a
new canvas

Opening
existing images

Bringing in
multiple files

Saving your work

Adjusting canvas
size and color

O il painters have a fairly set ritual to complete before they can begin to paint. Although Web artists don't have to stretch or prime their canvases, choosing certain options prior to undertaking a new work can save time down the line. Of course, one of the major benefits of electronic illustration in general, and Fireworks in particular, is that you can modify virtually anything at any stage.

This chapter covers all you need to know about "prepping your canvas" in Fireworks. How big should it be and what kinds of things are you going to put on it? In addition you'll discover how to open, save and close Fireworks documents. We'll also look at how you can modify a canvas at any stage of the creative process.

Creating New Documents

Before you actually begin work, it's best to consider what you are aiming to create. The better you can visualize the final result, the fewer modifications you'll have to make along the way. This is not to say that trial and error is out of the question, but a little planning can save a lot of time and trouble later.

Two approaches

A fundamental question that you have to answer before you even choose File ⇨ New is what approach you're going to take in creating the multiple image files that typically make up Web pages. There are two basic approaches:

- ✦ Create multiple small images in multiple Fireworks documents and assemble them into a Web page later in another application, such as Macromedia Dreamweaver.

- ✦ Populate one Fireworks canvas with a complete Web page design, including all of the navigation elements, text, and images.

Before I started using Fireworks, I created Web page designs in Macromedia FreeHand and then copied individual elements into separate Adobe Photoshop documents for touching up and final rendering. Later, I found myself replicating this workflow, but substituting Fireworks for Photoshop. Each of the images for the Web site lived in their own Fireworks documents, as shown in Figure 4-1.

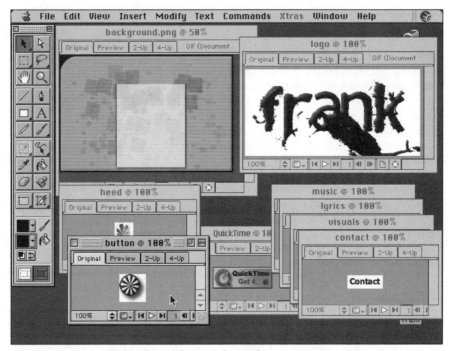

Figure 4-1: In a traditional workflow, each graphic is a separate document.

For many projects, though, your best option may be to create one large canvas, as shown in Figure 4-2, and populate it with your entire page design, either created from scratch or using a mix of from-scratch and imported elements. Fireworks is quite happy to allow you to draw, filter, effect, slice, specify hyperlinks, leave space for HTML text and finally, export the whole lot as HTML and JavaScript along with GIF and JPEG images. And if, at any time, you want to export a single layer or slice all on its own, Fireworks will let you do that, too.

Cross-Reference Turn to the color insert to see an example of a complete Web design in a single Fireworks document.

Whichever method you choose is a matter of your personal preference, of course. I'll go on record as recommending the one-canvas approach. Fireworks excels at one-stop Web graphics, and an integrated approach takes full advantage of the variety of tools Fireworks places at your disposal.

Figure 4-2: You can design and implement a complete Web page within one Fireworks document.

The canvas options

The "canvas" in Fireworks is a background for the visible area of a document. Fireworks gives you control over four basic elements of the canvas:

✦ **Width:** The horizontal dimension of a document, available in pixels, inches, or centimeters.

✦ **Height:** The vertical dimension of a document, also available in pixels, inches, or centimeters.

✦ **Resolution:** A print-style dots-per-inch (or centimeter) setting that Fireworks uses to translate inches or centimeters into pixels if you don't want to specify dimensions in pixels.

✦ **Canvas color:** The color of the underlying layer for your work. A transparent option is also considered a valid "color."

Width and height

Although it may appear otherwise sometimes, all Web graphic files are ultimately rectangular. A document's width and height determine not only a document's size, but also its shape. Whereas there are no theoretical limitations to the size of an image, the Web designer must always consider file size to be a vital factor and, everything else being equal, the larger the image, the bigger the file size. Typically, image dimensions are given in pixels, short for picture elements. Pixels are the red, green, and blue dots that make up a computer color monitor's screen. From time to time, it's helpful to switch to non-screen-based measurement systems, like inches or centimeters, and Fireworks gives you that option. But Web design is a pixel-oriented world and you'll find yourself primarily using them for measuring.

If you are building an entire page design in one Fireworks document, a typical size would be 600 pixels wide and 800 pixels tall for a page that is easily viewable at any display resolution and calls for an acceptable amount of scrolling at smaller resolutions (about two screen lengths). Another option is to make a page that's suitable for viewing on an 800 × 600 display with the browser filling the screen. If you start with a canvas that's 760 × 400 pixels (leaving space for browser toolbars), the user won't have to scroll at all once they size their browser window correctly.

Tip   Don't be afraid to make your canvas a little bigger than you actually require. I find that a little elbow room is nice while drawing, especially when using a pen and tablet ... you can experiment with strokes in the extra space before marking up your actual work. When you're done, delete the test strokes and choose Modify ⇨ Trim Canvas to quickly get rid of the extra space and get your document ready for export.

Resolution

Even if you sized your canvas in inches or centimeters, the canvas itself is an online (on-screen) item, made up of pixels, and it has to have a pixel measurement, too. The (print) Resolution setting allows you to specify how Fireworks should make the translation from dots to inches. If you sized your canvas to 8.5 by 11 inches in order to print a standard letter-sized page at 150 dots per inch (dpi), then put 150 in the Resolution box and you'll be able to print your document correctly when you're done.

If you're only using Fireworks to create online images — like most of us — the good news is that you can leave the Resolution setting at its default of 72 and continue to size your canvas and all of your objects in pixel measurements. As long as you leave it at 72 for all of the documents you make and work with, you can completely ignore it.

Why 72?

The screen image on the original Macintosh computer was 512 × 342 pixels and 7.1 × 4.5 inches. This works out to 72 dots per inch (dpi) for every Mac of that time period, because they all had the exact same display. If you wanted something to be exactly an inch wide on the screen (an inch on an on-screen ruler, for example) you would make it 72 pixels wide and it would work on all Macs. The number 72 is also convenient because there are 72 points (a standard typographical measure) in an inch, so one pixel could easily represent one point as well. These days, there is far too much variety in the display resolutions and dimensions of the computer displays we use for there to be an actual, real world common measurement, so 72 remains an arbitrary standard dpi setting. Although Windows and some Windows applications use 96, Fireworks on both platforms uses the standard 72.

Determining your display's actual dpi involves measuring its visible height and width and then dividing those measurements by your display resolution. A display with a visible area of 12 × 9 inches, running at 1024 × 768, has a resolution of 85 dpi. An 85 × 85 pixel object on that display would be one inch square.

Cross-
Reference
For more about online and print resolution settings, see Chapter 14.

Canvas color

Canvas color is very important, but also very flexible in Fireworks. When you're creating Web graphics, the canvas color often needs to match the background color of a Web page. You don't have to match the colors when creating your new page, but if you can, you should, and it will save you a step or two in the near future. You can modify the canvas color at any point in Fireworks by choosing Modify ➪ Canvas Color.

Initially, you have three basic choices for a canvas color: white, transparent, or custom. Although white is not the default color for all browsers, it's a common default background in Web authoring tools and a popular choice on the Web in general. Naturally, transparent is not really a color — it's the absence of color. However, as many Web pages use an image or pattern for a background, designers often choose the transparent option to enable part of the background to be visible through their graphics. This enables graphics — which are always saved in a rectangular format — to appear nonrectangular. Fireworks includes many techniques for outputting a graphic with a transparent background, but many artists like to work with a transparent canvas regardless.

The third choice, marked custom color, is really all the colors. Selecting the Custom Color radio button enables you to choose a color from the 216 Web-safe colors that display the same way in the major browsers on Macintosh and Windows computers running at 8-bit color. You can also choose a color from your operating system's color picker(s), or use the eyedropper to sample a color from anywhere on your display. The Custom Color option is great when you're trying to match a Web page background.

An understanding of color on the Internet is crucial for the Web graphics designer. See Chapter 7 for more information on using color in Fireworks.

Steps to create a new document

To create a new document, follow these steps:

1. Choose File ➪ New or use the key shortcut Ctrl+N (Command+N). Windows users can also click the New button on the Main toolbar. The New Document dialog box, shown in Figure 4-3, opens.

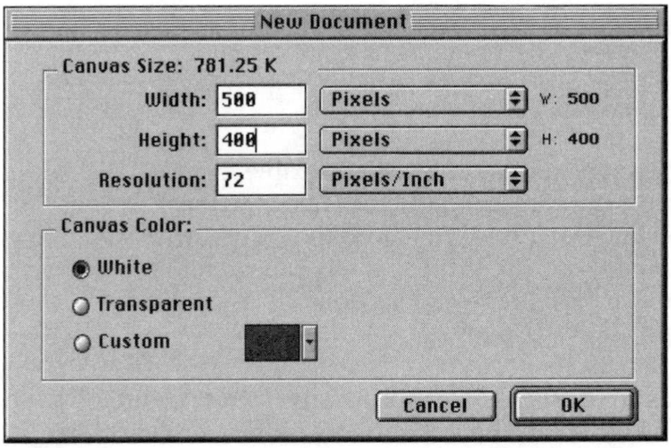

<table>
<tr><td colspan="2">New Document</td></tr>
<tr><td colspan="2">Canvas Size: 781.25 K</td></tr>
<tr><td>Width: 500</td><td>Pixels</td><td>W: 500</td></tr>
<tr><td>Height: 400</td><td>Pixels</td><td>H: 400</td></tr>
<tr><td>Resolution: 72</td><td>Pixels/Inch</td><td></td></tr>
<tr><td colspan="2">Canvas Color:</td></tr>
<tr><td>● White</td><td></td></tr>
<tr><td>○ Transparent</td><td></td></tr>
<tr><td>○ Custom</td><td></td></tr>
<tr><td colspan="2">Cancel   OK</td></tr>
</table>

Figure 4-3: Set your document's dimensions, print resolution and canvas color in the New Document dialog box.

2. To change the horizontal measurement of the canvas, enter a new value in the Width text box.

Press Tab when you're done to move on to the Height text box.

3. To change the vertical measurement of the canvas, enter a new value in the Height text box.

4. To enter a new resolution for the canvas, enter a value in the Resolution text box. The default resolution in Fireworks is 72 pixels per inch. Unless you have a specific reason to change it, leave it at 72.

5. To change the measurement systems used for Width, Height, or Resolution, select the arrow button next to the corresponding list box. You can choose Pixels, Inches, or Centimeters for both Width and Height; with Resolution, you can select either Pixels/Inch or Pixels/cm (centimeter).

Note

Whenever you switch Width or Height measurement systems, Fireworks automatically converts the existing values to the new scale. For example, if the new canvas was originally 144 pixels wide at 72 pixels per inch resolution, and the Width measurement system was changed to inches, Fireworks converts the 144 pixels to 2 inches. No matter which system you choose, Fireworks always displays the dimensions in pixels on the right side of the dialog box as W (width) and H (height).

6. Select a Canvas Color: White, Transparent, or Custom Color.

7. To choose a Custom Color, select the arrow button next to the color swatch and pick the desired color from the pop-up color palette.

8. For a more extensive color choice (beyond the 216 Web-safe colors in the pop-up display), either select the Palette button on the pop-up display or double-click the swatches to reveal the system color picker(s).

9. Click OK when you're done.

Tip

The New Document dialog box remembers your last settings the next time you create a new file, with one exception. If you've cut or copied a graphic to your system's clipboard and you select File ➪ New, the dialog box contains the dimensions of the image on the clipboard. This makes it easy to paste an existing image into a new file.

Opening Existing Images

Your Fireworks documents will fall into two distinct categories. Sometimes you'll start from scratch in Fireworks, and sometimes you'll import work from another application just to prepare it for the Web. Because Fireworks is terrific at optimizing images for the Web, you're just as likely to find yourself opening an existing file as creating a new one.

Tip

Use a lossless file format such as PNG or TIFF to move images between applications. The GIF and JPEG formats are unsuitable for use as master copies because information — and quality — is thrown away when you create them in order to achieve a smaller file size.

Opening a regular PNG file is just like opening a Fireworks document. Opening a file of another type creates a new Fireworks document that will need to be saved as a Fireworks PNG-format document under a new name. Export GIF, JPEG, or other files from your Fireworks document as required.

File Formats

As probably anyone who's ever touched a computer graphic is aware, different computer programs, as well as platforms, store files in their own file format. Fireworks opens a wide range of these formats. With formats from advanced graphic applications, such as Photoshop, Fireworks retains as much of the special components of the image — like layers and editable text — as possible. You can even open ASCII or RTF (Rich Text Format) files to import text into Fireworks.

Cross-Reference   Opening the native file formats of Macromedia FreeHand, Adobe Illustrator, or CorelDraw causes Fireworks to display a dialog box for setting special options. The Vector File Options dialog box is described in Chapter 14.

Table 4-1 details formats supported by Fireworks.

Table 4-1			
Supported File Formats			
Format	*Filename Extension*	*Macintosh Type Code*	*Notes*
Fireworks File Format	.png	PNGf	A PNG file with Fireworks-only information such as vectors added.
Fireworks 2.0	.png	PNGf	Converted to Fireworks 3 when opened, but can optionally be saved again as Fireworks 2 for later editing in Fireworks 2.
Fireworks 1.0	.png	PNGf	The Background is placed on its own layer.
Portable Network Graphic	.png	PNGf	Standard PNG documents that don't have extra Fireworks information.
Photoshop Document	.psd	8BPS	Version 3.0 or later only. Layers, editable text, and Layer Effects are preserved.
FreeHand Document	.fh7 or .fh8	AGD3	The vector-based format of FreeHand 7 or 8.
Illustrator 7 Document	.ai	uMsk	Adobe Illustrator 7's vector-based default format.

Format	Filename Extension	Macintosh Type Code	Notes
CorelDRAW 8 Document	.cdr	CDR8	CorelDRAW's vector-based format must have been saved without CorelDRAW's built-in bitmap or object compression to be openable in Fireworks.
GIF	.gif	GIFf	Graphics Interchange File Format. Static or animated. Each frame of an animated GIF is placed on its own frame in Fireworks.
JPEG	.jpg or .jpeg or .jpe	JPEG	Avoid importing JPEG images due to their lossy compression scheme and low quality.
xRes	.lrg	LRG	The default format of Macromedia's defunct xRes application.
Targa	.tga	TPIC	Common Unix image format.
TIFF	.tif or .tiff	TIFF	Tag Image File Format. High-quality lossless compression similar to PNG.
ASCII Text	.txt	TEXT	Plain text.
Rich Text Format	.rtf	RTF	Microsoft's styled text format, easily exported from Word.
Microsoft Bitmap (Windows only)	.bmp	BMP	Default image format for Windows 3+.
PICT (Macintosh only)	.pct or .pict or .p	PICT	Default image format for Mac OS 1-9. Combination vector/bitmap format. Fireworks renders any vectors as bitmaps.

To open an existing file in Fireworks, follow these steps:

1. Choose File ➪ Open or use the keyboard shortcut, Ctrl+O (Command+O). Windows users can also select the Open button from the Main toolbar. The Open dialog box appears, as shown in Figure 4-4.

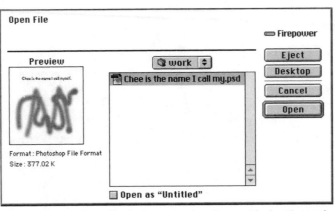

Figure 4-4: Preview files before opening them with the Fireworks Open dialog box.

2. Select the desired file in the Open dialog box. Fireworks identifies the file and displays a thumbnail of the image for certain file types in the Preview section of the dialog box.

Tip Windows users: to limit your view to a specific file format, click the arrow button next to the Files of Type drop-down list and select a format. To choose from every file type, select All Files (*.*) from the Files of Type drop-down list or type an asterisk in the File Name text field. To choose from Fireworks-compatible files, select All Readable Files from the Files of Type drop-down list.

3. To open a copy of the graphic, choose the Open as "Untitled" option.

4. Click OK when you're done. Fireworks opens the file, reducing the magnification, if necessary, so that the full image is displayed.

Tip You can also open files in Fireworks with the drag-and-drop method. In Windows, drop compatible image files on the Fireworks application icon, onto a shortcut to it, directly into the Fireworks window, or into an open document. On Mac OS 8/9, you can drop image files on the Fireworks application, onto an alias of it, or onto the Fireworks icon in the floating Application Switcher (drag the Application menu off the menubar to create the Application Switcher).

Opening Photoshop Files

Fireworks makes it relatively easy to open and work with Photoshop images. When you open or import a Photoshop file, Fireworks displays a dialog box to allow you to adjust how the file will be converted. By default, Fireworks maintains Photoshop's layers and editable text, but you can also choose to flatten the file if you don't need to edit it in Fireworks. Photoshop masks created from grouped layers are converted to Mask Groups and Photoshop's Layer Effects are converted to editable Fireworks Live Effects.

Fireworks 3 now retains Photoshop 5's Layer Effects and converts them to editable Live Effects, retaining a very similar look, and most importantly: editability.

Opening Multiple Images

It's the rare Web page that has but a single image on it. Most Web pages contain multiple graphics and, occasionally, a designer needs to work on several of them simultaneously. With the Open Multiple command, you can select as many files as you want to load into Fireworks, all at the same time. The files can come from the same folder or each from a different folder, if necessary. Select a range of files to open or double-click each file to add it to the List Window. You can easily remove files from the List Window, and when you're ready, Fireworks opens and displays all the files in a series of cascading windows.

Tip Macintosh users can also open multiple Fireworks documents by selecting a group of them in the Finder and double-clicking. Multiple image files that don't have a Fireworks Creator code can be selected as a group in the Finder and dropped on the Fireworks icon.

One significant advantage to the Open Multiple command: you can use it to create animated GIFs. In Fireworks, an animated GIF is a series of frames. When you choose the Open as Animation option in the Open Multiple dialog box, Fireworks inserts each chosen file in a single graphic, but on an individual frame. Then, preview the animation using Fireworks VCR controls or adjust the timing in the Export dialog box.

To open several files in one operation, follow these steps:

1. Choose File ⇨ Open Multiple or use the keyboard shortcut Ctrl+Shift+O (Command+Shift+O). The Open Multiple dialog box displays, as shown in Figure 4-5.

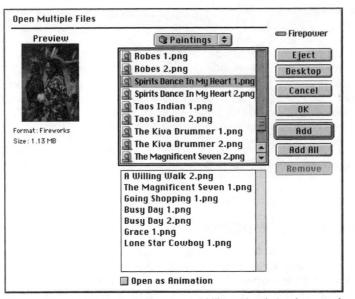

Figure 4-5: Select as many files as you'd like to load simultaneously with the Open Multiple command.

2. Navigate to the folder containing the images to open.

3. To add a single file to the list of files to be opened, double-click it. Windows machines display the full path of the image in the List Window.

4. To add a continuous range of files, select the first file, press and hold the Shift key, and then select the last file in the range. Select the Add button.

5. To select a number of files in the same folder that are not in a range, press and hold the Ctrl (Command) key. When you're ready, select the Add button.

6. To open an entire folder, select the Add All button.

Tip

You can also open an entire folder of images by dragging and dropping the folder on the Fireworks icon. Fireworks will open all images in the selected folder and any existing subfolders.

Caution

On the Macintosh, dropping a folder of files on the Fireworks icon opens them all in Fireworks as expected, but Fireworks will always finish the process with an error. Although the error seems to be harmless, a workaround is to open the folder, select all of the files with Command+A and drag the files themselves onto the Fireworks icon (or just double-click them if they have a Fireworks Creator code).

7. To place the selected images in a series of frames, choose the Open as Animation option. Each image is placed in a separate frame of a single graphic, in the order listed.

8. To delete a file from the list, select it and choose the Remove button.

9. When you're ready, select the Done button.

Storing Files

Every computer graphics professional has one — a nightmare story about the system crash that erased all the intense, meticulous, time-eating effort that went into an unsaved image. Saving your files is crucial in any graphics program, but it becomes even more important in Fireworks. To maintain the "everything's editable, all the time" capability, you must save your graphics in Fireworks' native format, PNG. Fireworks offers a very full-featured Export module to convert your graphics into whichever Web format you choose. However, a Fireworks file exported as a GIF or JPEG loses its all-encompassing editability — text can no longer be edited as text, vector-based objects are converted to bitmaps, effects are locked, and so on.

To keep the full range of Fireworks features active, it's essential that each file be saved as well as exported. Fireworks uses standard commands to save: File ➪ Save, the keyboard shortcut Ctrl+S (Command+S), and, for Windows users, a Save button on the Main toolbar. When you select any of these methods to store your file the first time, the Save dialog box (Figure 4-6) automatically opens. Choose between Fireworks or Fireworks 2.0 file formats in the option list at the bottom of the dialog box.

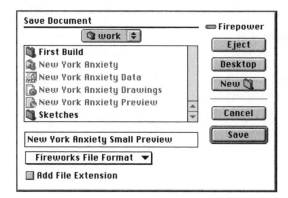

Figure 4-6: To maintain full editability, be sure to save every working graphic as a master Fireworks file in addition to exporting it as a GIF, JPEG, or other format.

 Cross-Reference To get all the details on exporting from Fireworks, see Chapter 15.

Saving a file after the initial save overwrites the existing file. If you would like to store multiple versions of the same file, Fireworks gives you two options: Save As and Save a Copy. Save As enables you to rename the file, and Save a Copy enables you to store a backup file in another folder (without saving the current document under its own name as well). Both are accessed in an identical manner. Choose File ➪ Save As or File ➪ Save a Copy to open the Save dialog box. Enter the new filename or navigate to a new folder in which to store the file (or both) and press the Save button.

Closing a file

When you're finished with a document, but want to continue working in Fireworks, you can close the file in one of several ways:

- ✦ Choose File ➪ Close.
- ✦ Use one of the keyboard shortcuts, Ctrl+W (Command+W) or Ctrl+F4 (Windows only).
- ✦ Click the document window's Close button.

If the document has not been saved since the last modification, Fireworks asks if you want to save the file before proceeding.

Reverting to a saved file

Part of the joy of computer graphics is the capability to try different approaches without fear of losing your earlier work. I'm a big fan of the Revert command, which enables you to completely alter a graphic and then restore it to its last-saved condition with one command. Between Revert, Undo, and Fireworks 3's new History feature, you have a lot of options for safe creative experimentation.

The Revert command is very straightforward to use. After you've made some changes to your graphic and want to return to the original, choose File ➪ Revert. Fireworks asks for confirmation to revert to the last saved version of the file, and, when confirmed, replaces the onscreen image with the stored version.

Modifying Canvases

What do you mean, you want to change the size of your canvas? And its color, too? Are you saying you're not perfect and didn't predict needing these alterations? Don't worry, you're certainly not alone. In fact, most of my images undergo some level of document surgery before they're done. It's the nature and the glory of computer graphics in general, and Fireworks in particular, to be very forgiving about changes.

In Fireworks, you can easily change the size of a complete image and its canvas, just the canvas dimensions, or the canvas color. It's very easy to expand the canvas in a particular direction, making it wider on the right, for example, either visually with the Crop tool, or numerically with the command Modify ➪ Canvas Size.

Altering the canvas size

Sometimes, the canvas is perfectly sized for all of the objects it contains, but you'll want to add another object, or apply a Glow or similar effect around an existing object, and there's no room. On the other hand, very often you'll start out with a canvas larger than necessary and you'll need to trim the canvas to fit the image. Whatever the situation, Fireworks has you covered.

Fireworks 3 offers three different methods for enlarging or reducing the canvas: numerically, using a menu command; visually, using the Crop tool; or according to the actual image, by trimming the canvas.

Specifying a new canvas size numerically

Quite often, I find myself needing to add a drop shadow and realize that I have to expand the canvas just a few pixels to the right and down for the effect to fit. With Fireworks, you can expand the canvas from the center out or in any of eight specific directions. Naturally, only the size of the canvas is modified; the objects it contains don't change at all, except for their placement on the canvas.

The key concept to understand when you're resizing the canvas numerically is the anchor. The placement of the anchor (handled through the Canvas Size dialog box) determines how the canvas changes to meet the newly input dimensions. By default, the anchor is placed in the center of the canvas. If, for example, the canvas dimensions were increased by 100 pixels horizontally and 100 pixels vertically with a center anchor, the canvas edge would increase by 50 on all four sides. However, if the upper-left anchor was chosen and the same increase in dimensions entered, the canvas would increase by 100 pixels on the right and bottom border; because the upper-left is the anchor, the canvas in that corner does not change. You can think of the anchor as specifying where on the new canvas the old canvas should be.

To resize the canvas numerically, follow these steps:

1. Choose Modify ➪ Canvas Size. The Canvas Size dialog box opens, as shown in Figure 4-7.

2. To alter the dimensions of the canvas horizontally, enter a new value in the width (the horizontal double-headed arrow) text box.

3. To alter the dimensions of the canvas vertically, enter a new value in the height (the vertical double-headed arrow) text box.

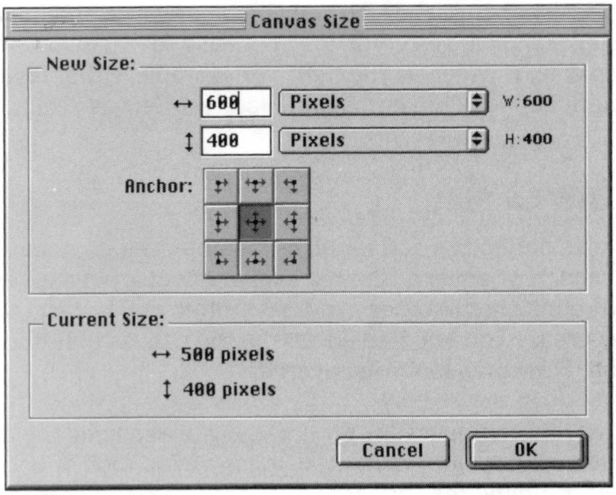

Figure 4-7: Enter new dimensions and select an anchor point in the Canvas Size dialog box to alter the canvas size.

Note

Fireworks always displays the original canvas size in pixels in the Current Size section of the dialog box.

4. To alter the canvas size by inches or centimeters rather than the default pixels, select the arrow button next to the width and height drop-down lists and choose the desired alternative. The dimensions in pixels appear to the right of the height and width text boxes.

5. Choose one of the buttons inside the Anchor grid to determine how the canvas will expand or contract.

Tip

When one of the elements in the Anchor grid is selected, by tabbing through the dialog box, you can use the arrow keys to select a different anchor.

6. Click OK when you're done.

Using the Crop tool

Resizing the canvas numerically is great when you have to match a specific width or height for your image. Unfortunately, it can also take a lot of trial and error to get the tightest fit for an effect like a glow or a drop shadow. The Crop tool provides a much faster method. Cropping is a familiar concept to anyone who has ever worked with photographs and needs to eliminate extraneous imagery. To *crop* means to cut off the excess. In addition to making the image smaller by cutting away the canvas, the Crop tool can expand the canvas as well.

The Crop tool works by enabling you to draw a rectangle with numerous sizing handles around an image. You then use these sizing handles to adjust the dimensions and shape of the cropped area. When the cropped region looks right, a double-click in the defined area completes the operation. The cropping border can stretch out past the edge of the canvas and, when double-clicked, the canvas is extended to the new cropped area.

To access the Crop tool, click and hold the Marquee tool in the Toolbox. Choose the Crop tool from the flyout menu. You can also use the keyboard shortcut by pressing C.

New Feature The Crop tool moved from the Pointer tool flyout in Fireworks 2 to the Marquee tool flyout in Fireworks 3 to make it more familiar to Photoshop users.

Using the Crop tool to extend the canvas, as shown in Figure 4-8, requires an additional step. When you first use the Crop tool and try to draw on the outside of the current canvas, you'll find that Fireworks snaps the cropping border to the edge of the canvas. As most designers are familiar with using the Crop tool to remove excess canvas, this is a convenient starting point for most operations. To extend the cropping border, you then need to drag any of the sizing handles to a new position outside the canvas.

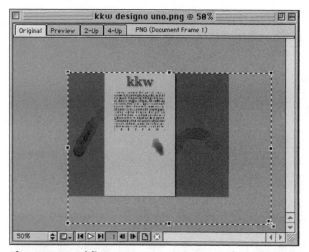

Figure 4-8: Adding some more canvas to the right and bottom of this Fireworks document is easy with the Crop tool.

Changing canvas size for a single image

If your document only contains a single bitmap image, many times you'll want to adjust the size of an entire completed image either up or down to make it fit properly in a Web page. Fireworks lets you make your adjustments either through specifying absolute pixel values or relative percentages with the Image Size command and automatically sizes the canvas appropriately, allowing you to work with single images like you would in Photoshop.

You can maintain the original proportions of your graphic or stretch it in one direction or another. The Image Size command enables you to resample your image as well as resize it. *Resampling* refers to the process of adding or subtracting pixels when the image is resized. Resizing always works better with object-oriented (or vector-based) graphics than with bitmap graphics, especially when you're scaling to a larger size. However, Fireworks offers you a choice of interpolation methods to help create a scaled image that looks great.

Fireworks lets you independently alter the onscreen pixel dimensions and the print size by changing the print resolution of the image. With this capability, you can print a higher or lower resolution of the image, at the original image size. It does, however, proportionately alter the pixel dimensions of the image for onscreen presentation. In Figure 4-9, for example, the original image on the top is 1440 × 657 pixels — although it's been zoomed to a 25% view in Fireworks — with a print size of roughly 20 × 9 inches at 72 pixels per inch. The image on the bottom has been resized by setting the resolution to one-quarter of the original pixel size by setting the resolution to 18 pixels per inch and is now only 360 × 164 pixels. The two images will print at the same size, though, with the resized one lacking one-quarter of the detail.

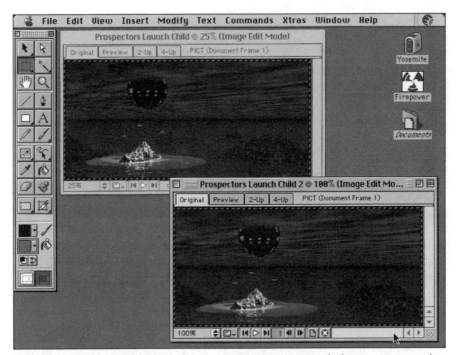

Figure 4-9: The bottom image, shown at 100%, was resampled at one-quarter the size of the original image, shown at 25%.

Note Once again, if you're using Fireworks exclusively to create online images — like most of us — stay entirely away from the Print Size settings and resize your images using the Pixel Dimensions settings in the Image Size dialog.

To alter the image size, follow these steps:

1. Choose Modify ➪ Image Size. The Image Size dialog box opens, as shown in Figure 4-10.

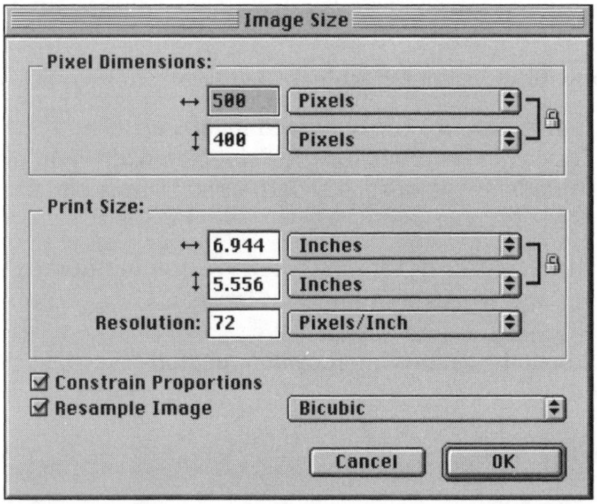

Figure 4-10: To proportionately enlarge or reduce your entire graphic, use the new Image Size command.

2. To alter the dimensions of the image proportionately, enter a new value in width (the horizontal double-headed arrow) or height (the vertical double-headed arrow) text boxes.

Tip If the default option, Constrain Proportions, is selected, changing one value causes the other to change as well.

Caution It's better to select the entire value in the text boxes first and then enter in your new number. If you try to backspace through each digit, you'll encounter an alert when you delete the final number. Fireworks warns you that you're entering an invalid number, as it interprets this as trying to reduce the dimensions below 1.

3. To alter the dimensions by percentage rather than by pixel measurement, select the arrow button next to the width or height drop-down lists and choose Percent.

4. To use the print size as a guide for adjusting the image size, enter a value in the Print Size width and height text boxes.

5. To alter the print size by percentage or centimeters rather than the default inches, select the arrow button next to the Print Size width and height drop-down lists and choose the desired alternative.

6. To change the number of pixels per inch, enter a new value in the Resolution text box.

7. To disable the proportional sizing, deselect the Constrain Proportions option.

8. To change the print size, but not the onscreen image, deselect the Resample Image option and choose new values for the Print Size width and height text boxes. When Resample Image is deselected, the Pixel Dimensions section becomes unavailable.

9. Choose an interpolation method from the interpolation method option list. Bicubic is the default and works well for most images.

A complete description of the various interpolation methods Fireworks offers is available in Chapter 6.

10. Click OK when you're done.

Trimming the canvas

What's the fastest, most accurate way to reduce the canvas to just the essential objects? Trim it, of course. If you've ever trimmed a real canvas with a razor-sharp matte knife, you know it's a very dramatic, fast operation. However, the Trim Canvas command is even faster — it handles four edges at once and there's no need to keep a supply of bandages at the ready.

The beauty of the Trim Canvas command is that it's all automatic — you don't even have to select any objects for Fireworks to trim to. Moreover, this feature even takes into account soft edges like glows or drop shadows, so you can't accidentally truncate your effect. In fact, it's a great command to use in combination with other canvas expanders, like the Crop tool or Canvas Size. Just open up the canvas more than you think necessary, make the alterations, and then choose Modify ➪ Trim Canvas. Presto! All the canvas edges are hugging the graphics as tightly as possible.

As the name indicates, Trim Canvas can only make your overall document size smaller; it can't expand it even if part of the image is moved off the canvas.

Picking a new canvas color

Although you set the canvas color when you create the document, you're by no means stuck with it. You can adjust the color at any point by choosing Modify ⇨ Canvas Color. Invoking this command opens the Canvas Color dialog box (Figure 4-11), which replicates the Canvas Color section of the New Document dialog box. Again, you have three choices: White, Transparent, and Custom Color. Of course, selecting the arrow button next to Custom Color opens the pop-up color picker with the palette of 216 Web-safe choices. For a wider color selection, click the Palette button on the pop-up color picker to display your operating system's color picker(s).

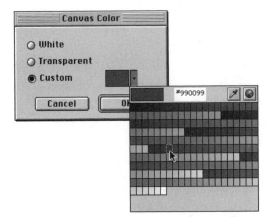

Figure 4-11: The pop-up color picker is useful for quickly picking a Web-safe color for the canvas.

Tip If you open a Photoshop or Fireworks 1.0 document, you may find that a solid-color Background layer is created. Hide this layer by clicking the Show/Hide Layer icon next to it in the Layers panel in order to see your document's actual canvas color.

Rotating the canvas

Although you can rotate objects with the Transform tools, the canvas itself always stays in the same place. If your canvas is not square, rotating a group of objects 90 degrees will often leave them hanging off the canvas. Instead of rotating objects, rotate the entire canvas. Choose Modify ⇨ Rotate Canvas and then one of the options: Rotate 180 degrees, Rotate 90 degrees CW (clockwise) or Rotate 90 degrees CCW (counter-clockwise).

New Feature Fireworks 3 now includes a brand-new command that allows you to rotate the canvas.

Summary

Setting up your document is the basis for all of the work you do in Fireworks. Whether you're starting with the fresh slate of a new document or opening an existing file, Fireworks gives you all the tools you need to build a solid foundation and modify it when necessary. When working with your objects from an overall document perspective, keep these points in mind:

✦ The more you can visualize your graphics and thus design the canvas, the less time you'll spend making modifications.

✦ When you're creating a new document, Fireworks enables you to set the height, width, print resolution, and color of the canvas.

✦ Fireworks can open more than a dozen different file formats, including common ones such as TIFF, FreeHand, and Photoshop.

✦ You can open a group of files simultaneously with the Open Multiple command.

✦ To get the most out of Fireworks, always save at least one version of your graphic in the native PNG format.

✦ You can alter the canvas size using any of three different methods: Canvas Size, the Crop tool, or Trim Canvas.

✦ You can modify the canvas color or rotate the canvas at any time.

In the next chapter, you begin exploring the heart of Fireworks graphics: objects.

✦   ✦   ✦

Mastering the Tools

PART

II

◆ ◆ ◆ ◆

In This Part

Chapter 5
Creating and
Transforming Objects

Chapter 6
Working with Images

Chapter 7
Managing Color

Chapter 8
Choosing Strokes

Chapter 9
Structuring Paths

Chapter 10
Composing with Text

◆ ◆ ◆ ◆

Creating and Transforming Objects

✦   ✦   ✦   ✦

In This Chapter

Mastering basic
object concepts

Forming geometric
shapes

Drawing freely with
the Pencil and Brush

Shaping Bézier
curves

✦   ✦   ✦   ✦

Objects are the foundation of Fireworks. Don't get me
wrong: all the other elements — images, effects, Web
objects — are vital, but objects are what give Fireworks its
flexibility, precise control, and editability. They're what
separate Fireworks from its contemporaries such as Adobe
Photoshop or ImageReady.

As you might suspect, a great number of Fireworks tools and
features focus on path objects. This chapter covers the basic
object operations — creation of the simple, geometric shapes
and freeform lines and drawings — that draw special attention
to one of the most difficult to master, but most rewarding concepts: Bézier curves.

Understanding Objects in Fireworks

An object, in Fireworks lingo, is a path or vector-based
graphic. Unlike bitmap graphics that use pixels to make
mosaic-like images, objects use lines, or more accurately, the
description of a line. Instead of plotting a series of pixels on
the screen, a vector-based graphic basically says, "start a line
at position X, Y and draw it to position A, B." Or, "draw a circle
with a midpoint at C, D and make it 1.5 inches in diameter." Of
course, you don't see all these instructions on the screen — it's
all under the hood of the graphics engine — but it's what
enables drawing programs, such as FreeHand and Adobe
Illustrator, to maintain a smooth line regardless of how the
image is scaled.

Whereas Fireworks objects maintain the underlying path structure, their surfaces are composed of pixels. Although this may seem to be a contradiction, it's really at the heart of Fireworks' brilliance as a graphics tool. Whenever you modify an object — slanting a rectangle, for example — Fireworks first applies the modification to the path structure and then reapplies the pixel surface. It is as if an image of a ballerina in a magazine suddenly became alive, leaped across the stage, and then became an image again.

Examining Paths

Objects begin as *paths*. Paths are lines with at least two points. Whether you draw a squiggly line with the Pencil tool or a multi-point star with the Polygon tool, the outline of your drawing is what is referred to as the path. By themselves, paths are invisible. Don't believe me? Try this:

1. Start up Fireworks and open a new document by choosing File ➪ New.

2. Select the Rectangle tool from the Toolbox.

3. Draw out a shape by clicking on the canvas and dragging the mouse out to form a rectangle.

4. Release the mouse when you have a visible shape. You'll see the path in the default highlight color, as shown in Figure 5-1.

5. Choose the Pointer tool from the Toolbox and click anywhere on the document, outside of the just-drawn rectangle. The highlight — and the rectangle's path — disappears.

6. If you pass your pointer over the existing rectangle, it will highlight temporarily so that you can select it again.

Applying a stroke

To make a path visible, you have to apply a *stroke* to see the outline. You can quickly apply a stroke to a selected object by choosing a color from the Stroke color well, located on the Toolbox or on the Color Mixer. This action applies a Pencil-type stroke five pixels wide with a soft or *anti-aliased* edge. Strokes can vary in color, width, softness, texture, and type of brush to name a few characteristics; several examples of different strokes are shown in Figure 5-2. You'll notice in the figure how, regardless of their different attributes, strokes always follow the path of an object.

Cross-Reference   Part of Fireworks' power is derived from the wide range of strokes possible. To learn more about strokes, see Chapter 8.

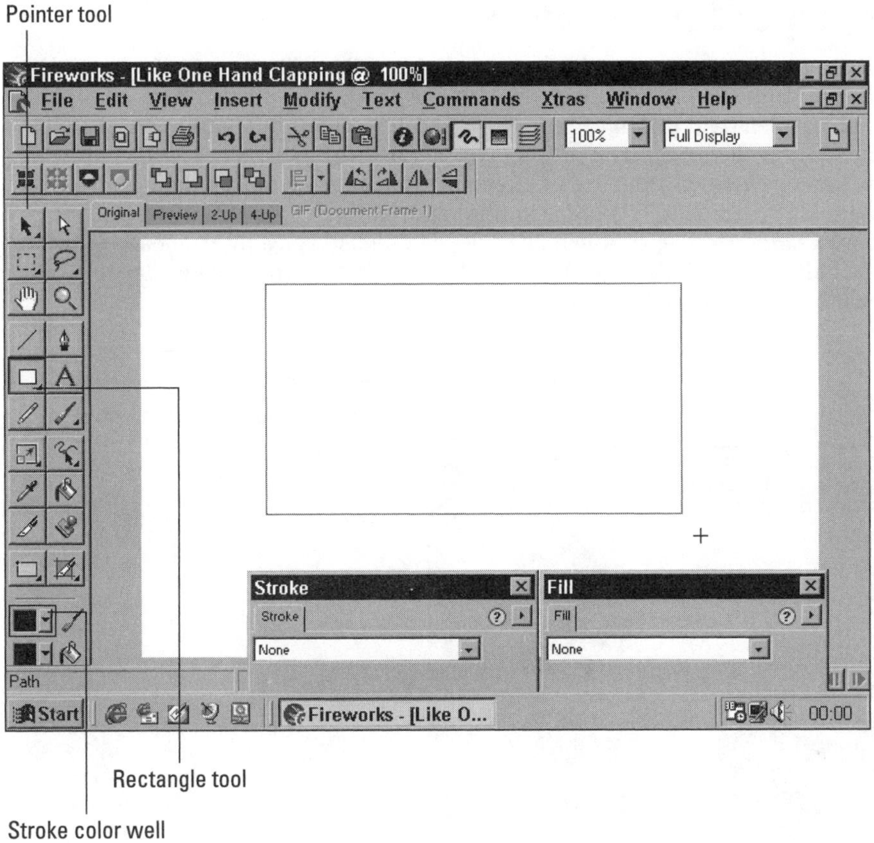

Pointer tool

Rectangle tool

Stroke color well

Figure 5-1: Drawing out a rectangle — with no stroke or fill selected — leaves you with just the path.

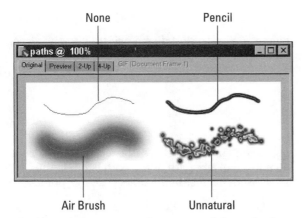

None   Pencil

Air Brush   Unnatural

Figure 5-2: You can see the same path in each of these different strokes.

Open and closed paths

There are two types of paths: *open* and *closed*. The difference between the two is simple: a closed path connects its two endpoints (the start and finish of the line), and an open path doesn't. Closed paths define different shapes, whether standard, such as an ellipse, square, or polygon; or custom, such as a freeform drawing. Just as a stroke gives the outline of a path substance, a *fill* makes the interior of a path visible. Like strokes, fills come in different categories, colors, and textures. In addition, a *pattern,* created from a PNG file, can be used as a fill. You can even change the softness of a fill's edge. As Figure 5-3 shows, regardless of what the interior fill is, it always follows the established path.

Selected with no fill   Solid fill

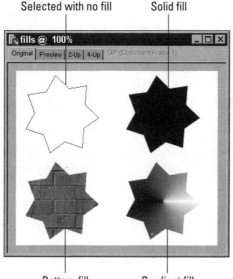

Pattern fill   Gradient fill

Figure 5-3: An object can be filled with a solid color, a gradient, or a Pattern.

Tip   Even though fills are most often applied to closed path objects, it's perfectly legal to apply a fill to an open path object—although the results are not as predictable. But then, that's one of the beauties of computer graphics—try it and if you don't like it, undo it.

Center point

One common feature that all objects in Fireworks share is a *center point*. A center point is an invisible point in the middle of any path; if the path is open, the center point is on the line. If the path is closed, it's inside the object. Center points are useful when you need to rotate an object. You can also adjust the center point of an object when its transform handles are visible in order to rotate it around a different axis, or control how its center aligns to other objects.

Cross-Reference You'll see how to work with rotation in Chapter 9.

Direction

The final point to keep in mind about objects is that their paths all have *direction*. Though it's more obvious with an object like a line that you start drawing at one point and finish at another, it's true even with rectangles and ellipses. Generally, Fireworks draws objects in a clockwise direction, starting at the upper left corner of rectangles or squares and the left center of an ellipse or circle, as shown in Figure 5-4. Path direction becomes important when you begin attaching text to a path — wrapping a slogan around a circle, for example. Fireworks includes several tools for adjusting the path's direction.

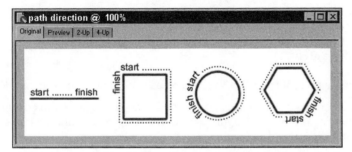

Figure 5-4: A path's direction determines how text is attached.

Starting from Shapes

Most Fireworks documents are amalgams of many, many objects of different types, sizes, colors, and attributes. Drawing shapes sounds easy, but you must master the capabilities of each basic object to get the greatest effect in the shortest amount of time.

Fireworks provides tools for creating a series of basic geometric shapes — rectangles, ellipses, and polygons — as well as those for drawing structured and freeform lines. All of these tools will be familiar to anyone who has worked with a vector drawing program in the last few years. In fact, most of the key shortcuts are industry-standard. This chapter, though, is written from a complete novice's point of view. Even if you've never used a computer to draw before, you'll have a full understanding of the basic tools in Fireworks after working your way through this chapter.

> **Tip**
>
> If you have access to a graphics tablet, don't be afraid to use it here. Drawing is always easier with a pen and tablet than with a mouse.

The quickest way to create a Web page design, particularly the often-required navigational buttons, is to use one of Fireworks' shape-building tools. Although at first glance there only seems to be three such tools — the Rectangle, Ellipse, and Polygon — these tools each have options that allow them to produce a wide range of objects.

Rectangles and squares

My dictionary defines a rectangle as "any four-sided figure with four right angles." A Web designer generally sees a rectangle as a basic building block for designs that are, after all, going to be viewed within the rectangular confines of a browser window. The Rectangle tool from the Toolbox is very straightforward to use and offers a number of very useful options.

Creating rectangles

Like almost every other computer drawing tool on the planet, Fireworks creates rectangles using the familiar click-and-drag method. To draw a rectangle in Fireworks, follow these steps:

1. Select the Rectangle tool from the Toolbox or use the keyboard shortcut, R.

2. Click once to select your originating corner and drag to the opposite corner to form the rectangle, as shown in Figure 5-5. As you drag your pointer, Fireworks draws a preview outline of the form.

Starting point

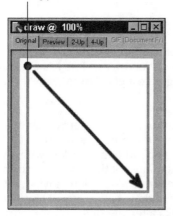

Figure 5-5: Once you've selected your originating corner with the Rectangle tool, you can drag out a box shape in any direction, as indicated by the arrow.

3. Release the mouse button when the rectangle is the desired size and shape. If any stroke or fill has been previously set, these attributes are drawn when you release the mouse button.

Using keyboard modifiers

You can use two keyboard modifiers with the Rectangle tool, Shift and Alt (Option), in order to apply two very commonly-required behaviors.

✦ **To create a square:** You can easily make your rectangle into a square by pressing Shift while you drag out your shape. Unlike some other graphics programs, you don't have to press Shift before you begin drawing; pressing Shift at any time while you're drawing causes Fireworks to increase the shorter sides to match the longer sides of the rectangle to form a square.

✦ **To draw from the center:** To draw your rectangle from the center instead of from the corner, press Alt (Option) when dragging out the shape. While Alt (Option) is held down, Fireworks uses the distance from your originating point to the current pointer position as the radius rather than the diameter of the shape. As with Shift, you can press Alt (Option) at any time when drawing to change to a center origin, as shown in Figure 5-6.

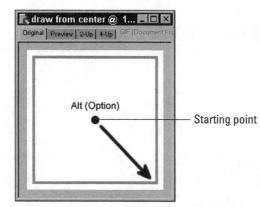

Figure 5-6: Holding down Alt (Option) while drawing a shape centers the shape around your starting point.

Tip Of course, you can use Shift and Alt (Option) together to draw a square from the center.

You can use the Info panel to check the pixel placement of your rectangle as you are drawing. One section displays the Width and Height (marked with a W and H) dynamically, while another displays the upper-left point of the rectangle, even if it is being drawn from the center.

Creating rounded corners

The standard rectangle and square, by definition, are composed of four right angles. However, Fireworks can create rectangles with rounded corners — and you can even set the degree of "roundness." The corner setting is visible on the Tool Options panel when the Rectangle tool is selected. The quickest way to access the Rectangle Tool options is to double-click the Rectangle tool; the Tool Options panel will automatically open. You can also display the Tool Options panel by choosing Window ➪ Tool Options or using the keyboard shortcut, Ctrl+Alt+O (Command+Option+O).

Once the Tool Options panel is available, choose how rounded you want the corners of your rectangle to appear by entering a value in the Corner text box or by using the Corner slider. The Corner scale is percentage-based: 0 represents a standard rectangle and 100 creates a fully rounded rectangle — also known as a circle. As Figure 5-7 shows, the higher the Corner value, the more rounded the rectangle's corners become.

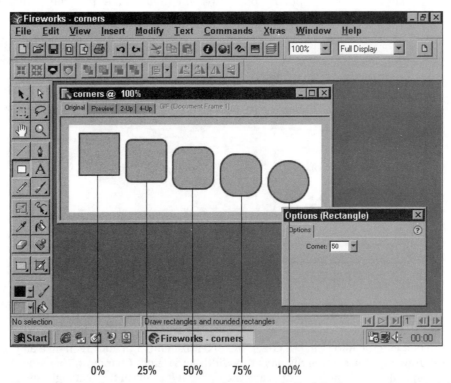

Figure 5-7: Use the Corner setting from the Rectangle Tool Options panel to determine the degree of roundness for your rectangle or square's corners before you draw them.

Exactly how Fireworks applies the corner percentage is most easily explained with an example. Let's say you draw a rectangle 100 pixels wide by 50 pixels tall and choose a Corner value of 50 percent. As shown in Figure 5-8, Fireworks plots the points of the corner 50 pixels along the top edge (50% of 100 pixels = 50 pixels) and 25 pixels along the side edge (50% of 50 pixels = 25 pixels). The resulting arc makes the corner. If you created an ellipse with a horizontal diameter of 50 pixels and a vertical one of 25, it would fit right into the newly rounded corner.

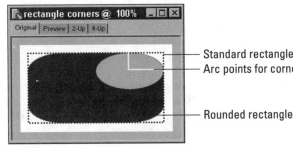

Standard rectangle
Arc points for corner

Rounded rectangle

Figure 5-8: Fireworks draws the rounded corner of a rectangle according to a percentage formula.

> **Tip**   Be sure to set the desired corner percentage on the Tool Options panel before you draw your rectangle. You can't convert a right-angle rectangle to a rounded-corner rectangle (or vice-versa) after it's been created.

Ellipses and circles

In Fireworks, ellipses and circles are created in exactly the same manner as rectangles and squares. Clicking the mouse once sets the origin point, and then the shape is drawn out as you drag the pointer. Even the Shift and Alt (Option) keyboard modifiers function in the same way as they do with rectangles. In fact, only two differences exist between the Rectangle and the Ellipse tool. First, it's pretty obvious that there's no need for an ellipse function equivalent to the Round Corners option for rectangles; ellipses are already rounded. Second — less apparent, but notable nonetheless — is the fact that the origin point of an ellipse or a circle never appears on its path. This is particularly important for novice designers who are trying to place an ellipse correctly.

Using an imaginary bounding box

When Fireworks draws an ellipse, an imaginary bounding box is used, as shown in Figure 5-9. The origin point of the bounding box acts as one corner, while the end point becomes the opposite corner. As with rectangles, if Alt (Option) is pressed, the center point is used as the origin. In either case, neither the origin nor the end point are located on the path of the ellipse. It's as though you're drawing a rectangle and Fireworks fits an ellipse inside it when you're done.

Starting point   Ellipse

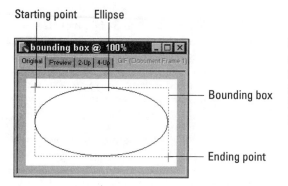

Bounding box

Ending point

Figure 5-9: When you drag out a circle or oval using the Ellipse tool, Fireworks draws the shape using an imaginary bounding box, indicated by the dashed rectangle.

Tip   It's particularly helpful to keep the concept of the imaginary bounding box in mind when you are trying to align ellipses of different sizes. The Align commands and snapping to the grid work using an ellipse's bounding box rather than the drawn path of the shape.

Drawing an ellipse or circle

To draw an ellipse or a circle, follow these steps:

1. Select the Ellipse tool from the Toolbox. If the Ellipse tool is not visible, click and hold the Rectangle tool until the flyout appears and then choose the Ellipse tool.

Tip   You can also press R until the Ellipse tool is selected. The R key shortcut cycles through the shape, hotspot, and slice drawing tools.

2. Click once to select the origin point and drag to the opposite corner to create the ellipse. As you drag your pointer, Fireworks draws a preview outline of the form.

3. Release the mouse button when the ellipse is the desired size and shape. If any stroke or fill has been set, these attributes are drawn when you release the mouse button.

4. To draw a circle, press the Shift key while you are drawing the ellipse.

5. To draw an ellipse or circle that uses the center point of the shape as the origin, press the Alt (Option) key while you are drawing.

Polygons and stars

In Fireworks, the Polygon tool creates many-sided objects where all the sides — and all the angles connecting the sides — are the same. The technical term for this type of geometric shape is an *equilateral polygon*. Fireworks permits the graphic designer to specify the number of sides, from 3 to 25. You can also use the Polygon tool to create a special type of polygon, a star. Star shapes can be drawn with anywhere from 3 to 25 points (and thus, 6 to 50 sides). Moreover, Fireworks gives you the option of either specifying the angles for the star points or having the program assign them automatically.

A drag-and-draw affair

As with rectangles and ellipses, making polygons is a drag-and-draw affair. Click once to set the origin point and then drag out the shape. However, that's where the similarities end. With polygons, there's only one possible origin point: the center; there is no keyboard modifier to switch to an outside edge. You'll also immediately notice as you draw your first polygon that you can quickly set both the size and the rotation. Dragging the pointer straight out from the origin increases the dimensions of the polygon; moving the pointer side to side rotates it around its midpoint.

Drawing a polygon

To draw a polygon, follow these steps:

1. Select the Polygon tool from the Toolbox by clicking and holding the Rectangle tool until the flyout appears and then choosing the Polygon button. Alternatively, press the keyboard shortcut, G.

2. To set the number of sides for a polygon:

   • First, choose Window ⇨ Tool Options or double-click the Polygon tool to open the Tool Options panel shown in Figure 5-10.

   • In the Tool Options panel, make sure the shape type is set to Polygon (instead of Star).

   • Next, enter a value in the Sides text box or use the Sides slider.

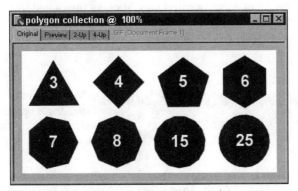

Figure 5-10: Polygons in Fireworks can have up to 25 sides — although anything above 15 tends to start looking like a circle.

3. Click and hold down the mouse button where you want the center of the poly-gon to appear and drag out the polygon shape. Fireworks displays a preview of the polygon as you draw.

4. Rotate the polygon to the desired position by moving your pointer from side to side.

5. Release the mouse button when you're done. Fireworks draws the polygon with the current stroke and fill settings.

Fireworks interprets the distance from the origin point to the release point as the radius to each of the points on the polygon. As you can see in Figure 5-10, just changing the number of sides results in a wide range of basic shapes.

Pressing the Shift key while drawing a polygon constrains a side's angle to a multiple of 45 degrees. Because, however, each shape as it is initially drawn is equilateral — with identical sides and angles — you'll only notice a couple of variations for each type of polygon. When drawing a hexagon and constraining the angle with the Shift key, you'll only notice three differently angled shapes, although you can actually draw eight (there are eight increments of 45 degrees in a full 360-degree circle).

Tip   For most polygons, you can draw it so that the bottom of the shape is parallel to the bottom of your canvas by either dragging straight up or straight to one side while holding down the Shift key.

Automatic angles

Although you can specify up to 25 sides for a polygon, polygons with more than 10 or 15 sides look very much like a circle. Not so with Fireworks stars, which, with the proper angle setting, can create very distinctive graphics with any number of sides. Fireworks offers both automatic and customizable angle options. When Automatic Angles is selected (the default), Fireworks draws stars so that the opposite arms are automatically aligned. With a five-pointed star, such as the one shown in Figure 5-11, the tops of the left and right arms are aligned.

Five-pointed star

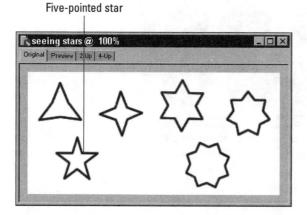

Figure 5-11: With the Automatic Angle option enabled, a star's opposing arms are aligned.

As is readily apparent in Figure 5-11, the automatic angles on stars with higher number of sides tend to flatten out the sharpness of the points. These types of angles are known as *obtuse* angles. An obtuse angle is one over 90 degrees. The opposite of an obtuse angle is an *acute* angle. Acute angles create much sharper points on stars, as shown in Figure 5-12. To create an acute star in Fireworks, you need to enter a custom value in the Angle text box.

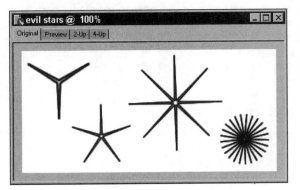

Figure 5-12: Create acute stars by lowering the Angle value in the Tool Options panel and drawing with Star selected for the Polygon tool type.

Creating a star

To create a star in Fireworks, follow these steps:

1. As with drawing a regular polygon, select the Polygon tool from the Toolbox by clicking and holding the Rectangle tool until the flyout appears and then choosing the Polygon button. Alternatively, press the keyboard shortcut, G.

2. Choose Window ➪ Tool Options or double-click the Polygon tool to open the Tool Options panel.

3. In the Tool Options panel, change the shape type by selecting the option arrow and choosing Star.

4. To change the number of points, enter a value in the Sides text box or use the Sides slider.

5. To change the angle of the star arms, enter a value in the Angle text box or use the Angle slider.

Tip   Use lower numbers for sharper points and higher numbers for blunter ones.

6. If you want to use the Fireworks predetermined angle for your star, choose the Automatic check box.

7. Click on the canvas to set the origin point for the center of the star and drag out to the desired size and rotation.

8. Release the mouse when you're done. As with any other shape, Fireworks applies the current stroke, fill, or effect setting, if any.

Precisely Adjusting a Shape's Dimensions and Position

Like any graphic design, Web graphics are a blend of visual flair and precise placement. To many artists, an image isn't right until it's aligned just so. Whereas much of Fireworks' interface enables very intuitive drawing with a mouse or graphics pad, you can also position and size objects numerically through the Info panel.

Typically, I use the Info panel to get a general sense of the dimensions of an object or its X, Y coordinates. However, I occasionally need to render an exact rectangle, one that's exactly 205 pixels wide by 166 high, say, and starts at 20 pixels in from the left and 35 pixels down. With Fireworks, you can rough out your shape and placement and then numerically resize and reposition the object. Values can be entered into each of the four text boxes on the Info panel representing the dimensions and the position of the bounding box surrounding the object. If the object is a circle or a triangle, for example, the height and width displayed would be that of the invisible rectangle encompassing them.

To specify a new dimension or placement of an object, follow these steps:

1. Select the object you wish to alter.

2. Double-click the value in the Info panel that you want to change. The four possibilities are

   • W (width)

   • H (height)

   • X (horizontal origin)

   • Y (vertical origin)

r (Return) — not Tab. Fireworks changes the

s 2–4.

of alignment and transformation tools as
o panel.

form Paths

ry according to how structured they are.
ol, which only draws single straight lines;
Brush tools, both of which are completely
ard the Line tool) is the Pen tool, which

Like a geometric shape, a path is invisible unless a particular stroke is applied to it. All paths accept strokes, but only closed paths also accept fills. If the two endpoints that define a line are joined, the path is said to be closed. When you're drawing paths, Fireworks displays a special cursor when two endpoints are about to be joined. If the two endpoints of a line are not joined, the path is said to be open. Unlike most vector drawing tools, Fireworks allows you to apply fills to open paths, as well as closed.

Straight lines

The Line tool is perhaps the simplest command in the entire Fireworks Toolbox. Click once to set the beginning of the line, drag in any direction, and release to set the end of the line. Two endpoints and a straight line in between; that's it and there's not a whole lot more to the tool. Straight lines are by definition open paths and thus can only display the stroke and not the fill settings. Effects and Styles can be applied to Line-created paths, as shown in Figure 5-13.

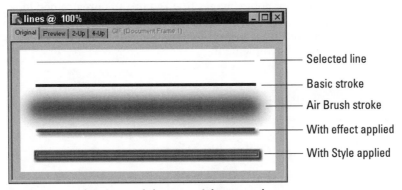

Figure 5-13: The Line tool draws straight-as-a-ruler lines that can take on a stroke setting and even an effect.

To use the Line tool, follow these steps:

1. Select the Line tool from the Toolbox or use the keyboard shortcut, N.

2. Position the pointer where you'd like the line to begin and click and hold the mouse button. Optionally, you can draw straight lines at a 45-degree angle if you press the Shift key while drawing the line.

3. When the line is at the desired size and angle, release the mouse button.

Freeform Pencil and Brush

The Pencil and Brush are also drag-and-draw tools, but without any of the restraints imposed on all the other tools. Anything you can draw with a mouse or graphics tablet, you can draw with the Pencil or Brush. As you move your pointer on the screen, Fireworks tracks the movements and plots points to replicate your drawing. Remember, these are vector-based objects, not pixel, and if you draw a perfectly straight line, Fireworks only needs two points to depict the line. All of the points that make up the line can be edited — moved, deleted, or increased — and the line changes accordingly.

Cross-Reference

Fireworks not only tracks your pointer's movement across the screen, it also follows the speed with which you draw your lines. With certain strokes, such as Watercolor and Charcoal, the velocity is translated visually when the stroke is rendered. For more details on varying your strokes, see Chapter 8.

Freehand drawing with the mouse is particularly difficult and many artists avoid it whenever possible. I prefer a graphics tablet and highly recommend them to others whenever I get the chance. For some images that require an unrestrained look — like the fellow in Figure 5-14 — the Brush is ideal. Choosing one of the Fireworks strokes that are pressure sensitive allows you to emulate the look of a Calligraphy pen, a pencil or other drawing implement.

With calligraphy stroke applied   Paths

Figure 5-14: Freehand drawing is best done with a graphics tablet using the Brush tool set to a pressure-sensitive stroke.

Applying strokes automatically

The major difference between these two tools and all the other geometric shape tools (including Line) is that both Pencil and Brush automatically apply a particular stroke, even if none is selected. This feature enables you to see all paths completed with these tools instantly — instead of having to wait until a stroke is selected and applied.

The stroke setting also holds the sole difference between the Pencil and the Brush. Any path drawn with the Pencil tool is rendered with a Pencil-category, single-pixel-width stroke with a hard edge, as seen in the Stroke panel shown in Figure 5-15 — even if a different stroke has been predetermined.

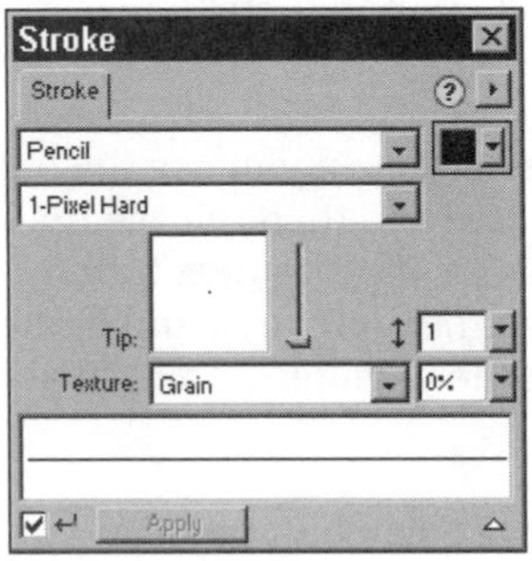

Figure 5-15: The Pencil enables you to draw freeform shapes that always use the same Pencil stroke that's shown here in the Stroke panel.

Note The only exception to the Pencil's adherence to these basic parameters is color. If you alter the stroke color, the Pencil tool draws with the new color.

The Brush tool also uses the same single-pixel Pencil type stroke, but only as a default, when no other stroke has been established. Once you select a different setting from the Stroke panel, the Brush tool uses that setting until it is changed.

As noted previously, both the Pencil and the Brush are capable of creating either open or closed paths. Remember, a closed path is one in which the beginning and final endpoints meet. With many graphic tools, this simple procedure becomes quite difficult, because it's often hard to position one pixel directly on top of another. Fireworks makes closing a path very straightforward. When you draw a path over the initial endpoint, a small black square appears on the lower right of the Pencil cursor. Releasing the mouse button when this cursor is displayed forces Fireworks to close the path.

Using the Pencil or Brush

To use the Pencil or Brush, follow these steps:

1. To draw with the Pencil, select the Pencil tool from the Toolbox or press the keyboard shortcut, Y.

2. To draw with the Brush, select the Brush tool from the Toolbox or press the keyboard shortcut, B.

3. Click and drag the pointer on the canvas. Fireworks renders the drawn path for a Pencil with a one-pixel width stroke, and the Brush with the current settings of the Stroke panel.

4. To draw a perpendicular line, press the Shift key while you're dragging the pointer. If your movement is primarily left to right, a horizontal line is drawn; if it is up and down, a vertical line is drawn.

Here's a rather peculiar feature of the Brush and Pencil tools: if you use the Shift key to constrain your Brush path to a perpendicular line and then release the mouse button—but not the Shift key—a small plus sign appears next to the Brush cursor. Draw another Brush stroke (still holding down the Shift key), and Fireworks connects the final point of your previous stroke with the beginning point of your new stroke.

Cross-Reference

The Pencil tool has one other use. If you are in Image Edit mode, modifying a pixel-based graphic, the Pencil changes any pixels it touches to the current Stroke color. You can find out more about editing pixel-based images in Chapter 6.

Constructing Bézier Curves

Remember those plastic stencils you used in school to trace different-size circles, stars, and other shapes? One of those "other shapes" was probably an asymmetrical, smoothly curving line that was referred to as a French curve. The Frenchman who invented this type of curve was a mathematician named Pierre Bézier. His theoretical work, collectively known as *Bézier curves,* forms the foundation for much of vector computer graphics, both in print through PostScript and on the screen through programs such as FreeHand, Illustrator, and, of course, Fireworks. The learning curve—pun definitely intended—for Bézier curves is a steep one, but it's one that every graphic designer using vectors must master. Bézier curves are amazingly flexible, often graceful to behold, and worth every bit of effort it takes to understand them fully. So let's get started.

Pierre Bézier's breakthrough was the realization that every line—whether it was straight or curved—could be mathematically described in the same way. Imagine a rainbow. The shape appears to start in one place, arch to the sky, and then land some distance away. The beginning and ending points of the rainbow are easily described; if we were plotting them on a piece of graph paper, we could set down their location as X and Y coordinates. But what about the arc itself? Consider an imaginary element in the sky that attracts the rainbow, almost magnetically, which causes the center of the rainbow to arch up, anchored by the beginning and ending points. Bézier postulated that every anchor point on a curve had two such magnetic elements, called *control points* — one that affects the curve going into the anchor point and one that affects it coming out of the anchor point, as shown in Figure 5-16. In the Bézier vernacular, an anchor point with curves on either side is called, naturally enough, a *curve point*. An anchor point with a curve on just one side is known as a *corner point*.

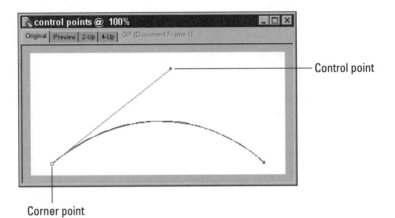

Figure 5-16: Bézier curves use control points to alter the shape of a curve.

Drawing lines with the Pen

Fireworks' primary tool for creating Bézier curves is the Pen, although all objects use Bézier curves. But how could a Bézier curve describe a straight line? When the control points are in the same location as the corner or curve points, the line is not pulled one way or the other; it remains straight. In fact, the Pen is terrific for creating connected straight lines. Unlike the Line tool, which draws a single straight line by clicking and dragging, the Pen draws a series of straight lines by plotting each point and letting Fireworks draw the connecting lines.

To draw a straight line with the Pen, follow these steps:

1. Select the Pen on the Toolbox or use its keyboard shortcut, P. The cursor changes to a cross with a small open box on the lower-right side.

2. Click once where you want the line to start.

3. Move your pointer to where you want the line to end. Fireworks draws a path from your starting point to the current cursor position, as shown in Figure 5-17.

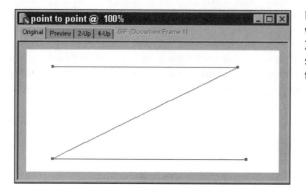

Figure 5-17: Create a Z with the Pen tool much like Zorro carves one with his sword, moving from point to point.

4. Click once to set the next point. Fireworks draws a straight line path from the first point to the second and renders the stroke settings, if any.

5. Repeat Steps 3 and 4 to continue adding straight lines.

6. Double-click to end the series of straight lines.

As with the Brush and Pencil tools, you can close an open path created by the Pen by moving the pointer over the beginning point. The cursor adds a solid black square on the lower right to indicate a possible closed path. Click once when you see the black square to complete the shape.

Creating smooth curves with the Pen

Laying out a series of straight lines is a fine feature, but the Pen tool really shines when it comes to drawing curves. The key difference between Pen-drawn lines and curves is that, with curves, you drag the pointer after you've set the anchor's position to drag out the control handles and start a curve, whereas with lines, there is no dragging whatsoever, you are just plotting corner points.

Follow these steps for creating a smooth curve, as illustrated in Figure 5-18.

1. With the Pen tool, click and hold where you want your curve to start. This creates an anchor point.

2. Drag the control handles out from your anchor point and adjust them to set the angle of your curve. Let go of the mouse button when you're done.

3. Without holding a mouse button down, draw the length of your curve from the anchor point to the next point.

4. Click to set a curve point and repeat steps 2-4 to continue adding curves, or double-click to finish.

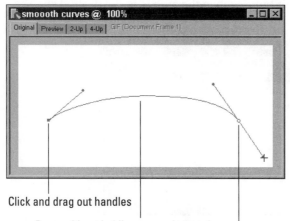

Click and drag out handles

Draw without holding mouse button down

Click to set curve point or double-click to finish

Figure 5-18: When you drag out one Bézier curve, you begin to create this curve.

Mixing lines and curves

You can, of course, combine the straight and curved line techniques with the Pen by alternating just clicking with both clicking and dragging. However, because dragging a control point affects curves on either side of the curve point, it is often difficult to place a straight line directly next to a curve. Fireworks uses the Alt (Option) key to constrain the control point that affects the previous curve, while permitting you to manipulate the current curve. As an example of this option, follow these steps to create a shape like the one shown in Figure 5-19.

1. Use the straight-line capability of the Pen to draw the outer edge of the arch by clicking once for each of the outside points, starting at the inside left corner and moving in a clockwise direction. After you've drawn all the straight lines, you'll have the outer shell of the arch, minus the inner arc, completed.

2. Move your pointer back over the beginning point. The closed path cursor is displayed.

3. Click and hold the mouse button as if you are going to drag it. Press the Alt (Option) key while continuing to hold down the mouse button.

4. Drag the control point in the direction of the arch. If Alt (Option) was not pressed, the connecting line (on the left side of the arch) would be affected by the control-point drag.

5. Release the mouse button when the arch is in the desired shape.

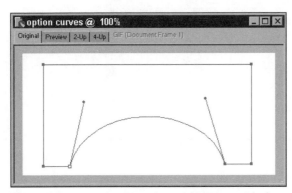

Figure 5-19: Use the Pen — in combination with the constraining Alt (Option) key — to draw straight and curved lines.

You can also use this constraining property to draw uneven curves, where you drag a little bit before pressing Alt (Option) and effectively lock the previous curve.

Caution Be sure the mouse button is down before you press Alt (Option) to constrain the control points. Pressing Alt (Option) by itself temporarily activates the Eyedropper tool for sampling color. Should you accidentally sample a color, choose Edit ➪ Undo or use the keyboard shortcut Ctrl+Z (Command+Z) and then proceed as intended.

Adjusting curves

The alternative name for the two control points in Bézier curves is *control handles*. As the name implies, control handles can be grabbed and manipulated. By changing the position of the control handle, you can adjust the shape of the curve. Here are a few guidelines for moving control handles:

✦ The closer the control handle is to its associated curve point, the flatter the curve.

✦ Alternatively, the further away the control handle is from its curve point, the steeper the curve.

✦ If a control handle overlaps its curve point, the curve becomes a straight line and the curve point becomes a corner point.

✦ You can convert straight lines into curves by pulling the control handle away from the corner point.

✦ After you've drawn a curve point, you can retract one of the control handles so that the next segment can be either a curve or a straight line.

All of the manipulations involving control handles can be accomplished after the fact using the Subselection tool; you'll find a discussion of how to use this point adjustment device in Chapter 9. However, you can perform a few of these operations while drawing with the Pen. The two key operations involve adding and removing a control handle.

Adding a control handle to a corner point

To add a control handle to a corner point, follow these steps:

1. Use the Pen to draw a path with a curve point. Two control handles are visible.

2. Move the pointer over the last curve point set. A small arrow appears on the Pen cursor, as shown in Figure 5-20.

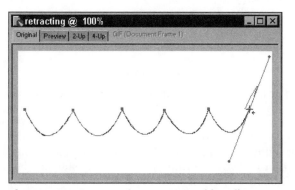

Figure 5-20: By retracting one control handle, you can continue the curve in the same direction.

3. Click once. The control handle that affects the curve to be drawn is retracted into the curve point.

4. To draw a straight line from the curve point, move your pointer away and click once.

5. To draw a curve, move your pointer away and click and drag out the control handles.

This technique is very handy for drawing a series of scallop or wave shapes where the curves all go in the same direction.

Extending a control handle from a corner point

The opposite of retracting a control handle is extending one. To extend a control handle from a corner point, you need to enlist the aid of a couple of keyboard modifiers: Ctrl+Alt (Command+Option) to be specific. When you extend a control handle while drawing, you are, in effect, changing your mind. Instead of proceeding with the straight line that you first indicated you want with the corner point, you can now draw a curve.

To extend a control handle from a corner point while drawing, follow these steps:

1. Draw a straight line segment with the Pen.

2. Move the pointer over the last point set. A small arrow appears on the Pen cursor.

3. Press Ctrl+Alt (Command+Option) and then click and drag a control handle out from the point. When you press the keyboard modifiers, the pointer changes to a white arrowhead.

4. Release the mouse button when you've positioned the control handle where desired.

5. Move the pointer to the position for the curve to end.

6. Continue drawing or double-click the final point to complete the shape.

In this technique, it's important that you press the keyboard modifiers before you drag the control handle. If you begin dragging before pressing the special keys, you'll move the anchor point instead of extending a control handle. This is actually a feature and enables you to move a previously set point by starting the drag and then pressing the Ctrl (Command) key; the Alt (Option) key has no effect on this sequence.

Using the keyboard modifiers

Bézier curves in Fireworks use a fair number of keyboard modifiers to achieve various effects. While I've explained the use of these special keys throughout this section in context, I thought it would be useful to put them all in one place (Table 5-1) for easy reference.

Cross-Reference

There's a lot more to manipulating Bézier curves and other Fireworks objects, as you'll find in Chapter 9.

Table 5-1
Bézier Curves Keyboard Modifiers

Windows Keys	Macintosh Keys	Description
Shift	Shift	Constrains the straight line or control handle to a 45-degree angle
Ctrl	Command	Moves a set curve or corner point or a control handle to a new position
Ctrl and double-click	Command and double-click	Completes an open path without adding another point
Ctrl+Alt	Command+Option	Extends a control handle from a corner point

Summary

I once had to indoctrinate a corporate design team into "The Fireworks Way" in a two-day training session. When it came to objects, I described them as being the "skeleton" of Fireworks graphics. After the graphic is completed — and the body of fills and clothing of strokes have been applied — you won't be able to see the underlying structure of the path object, but it is the basis of the image. As you begin to build your graphics with objects, keep these points in mind:

✦ Paths are the most basic element of Fireworks' vector-based objects. A path must be stroked and/or filled before it can be seen.

✦ The three basic geometric shape tools — Rectangle, Ellipse, and Polygon — can also create squares, rounded rectangles, circles, and stars.

✦ The Line tool creates one straight line at a time.

✦ Two freeform tools, Pencil and Brush, enable you to draw on the Fireworks canvas without restriction. The Pencil tool always defaults to a 1-pixel-wide stroke.

✦ The Pen draws Bézier curves, which use a series of corner and curve points in conjunction with control handles to make smooth curves and connected straight lines.

In the next chapter, you'll begin to learn about the other side of Fireworks graphics: bitmap images.

✦   ✦   ✦

Working with Images

In This Chapter

An image overview

Examining Image
Edit mode

Opening images
in Fireworks

Resizing images

Selecting image
elements

Defining a
drawing area

Working with
image tools

Path-based objects are the backbone of Fireworks, and are perfectly suited for the bulk of the work a Web artist does: building navigation bars, drawing shapes and lines and inserting editable text. These design elements benefit from the precision that vector drawing provides, and are the kinds of things you're likely to draw right from scratch in Fireworks.

Some kinds of images couldn't possibly benefit from a path-based substructure, though. Photographic images that started out life in a digital camera or scanner are pure bitmap, through and through. Think of product photographs for an online store, or digitized paintings for an online art gallery; incorporating them into a Web page won't involve drawing. Instead you'll cut and paste pixel selections and manipulate alpha masks and blending modes.

Almost all work with images takes place in Fireworks' Image Edit mode. Fireworks enters Image Edit mode whenever you use a bitmap tool such as the Magic Wand. It will seem like a subtle transition, but it's an important one. You're telling Fireworks to stop moving groups of pixels around in convenient vector containers; to shift gears and focus instead on the pure pixels themselves.

This chapter begins with a discussion of how Fireworks generally handles images. We'll delve into an exploration of the various tools available for bitmap editing: those dedicated to Image Edit mode, as well as the object tools that function slightly differently when applied to raster graphics. Finally, we'll cover how to change an object into an image and the benefits you might realize by doing so.

Understanding Bitmap Images in Fireworks

Here's a quick refresher course on bitmap images — just in case you're coming from the world of vector graphics and can't tell a pixel from a pig in a poke. The word *pixel* is derived from the term *picture element* (PIX for picture and EL for element). A pixel is the smallest component part of a bitmap image. In the early days of computer graphics, the color of each pixel was stored in 1 bit of memory; which was either on for black or off for white. Map these bits along an x and y axis and you can create an image out of them. Editing a bitmap basically involves adding or removing pixels, or changing their colors. Even when you erase part of an image, you're just setting the color of those excess pixels to whatever your background color is so that they appear to have been erased.

The best way I can think to describe the difference between a bitmap image (also called a *raster graphic*) and a path-based object is to ask you to think of a line, 100 pixels long and 1 pixel wide. With vector graphics, all you need to make this line visible is two points and a stroke in between. With a bitmap, you need exactly 100 pixels. To move one end of the object version of this line up a notch, you just need to move one of the endpoints. With pixel-based images, however, you have to erase all of the pixels in the line and redraw them in another location.

Examining Image Edit mode

As you can see, manipulating path-based objects and pixel-based images are two completely different operations. For that reason, Fireworks has two different modes: an Object Edit mode for vector objects (discussed in Chapter 5) and an Image Edit mode for bitmap images. Some tools work in one mode but not the other, whereas some tools seem to work the same, but actually return different results. It's not that one mode is better than the other; they are just used for different purposes.

You can ask Fireworks to change over to Image Edit mode, but you don't have to. Mode changes are tool-driven: start to use an image-editing tool and you automatically enter Image Edit mode. Pick an object-editing tool, start to work, and you're back in Object Edit mode. Sometimes the transition is accompanied by a helpful message from Fireworks explaining that the change is necessary. For example, if you try to use the Reshape Path tool in Image Edit mode, Fireworks warns you that it's only good for paths.

Tip   The mode-shifting warnings all include a "don't show again" checkbox, so you can switch them off when you feel comfortable enough to do so.

All of the objects you work on in Fireworks start out in one camp or the other — either they're all pixels or all paths. However, eventually the lines begin to blur (pun intended, maybe) and you find yourself moving back and forth between the two modes effortlessly and with no real conscious thought.

Starting Image Edit mode

In addition to automatically invoking Image Edit mode by choosing a particular tool, you can also enter it explicitly in several ways:

✦ Double-click an image object with the Pointer or Subselection tool. This is probably my most commonly used technique for accessing Image Edit mode.

✦ Choose Modify ➪ Image Object, or use the keyboard shortcut, Ctrl+E (Command+E).

✦ Choose Insert ➪ Empty Image, or use the key shortcut Ctrl+Alt+Y (Command+ Option+Y). This creates a new image object, which you can paint with pixel-based tools.

It's easy to tell when you're in Image Edit mode; in fact, Fireworks offers multiple different visual cues, as shown in Figure 6-1. First, a striped border surrounds the canvas, unless you uncheck the "Expand to Fill Document" preference, in which case the striped border only surrounds the image object itself. Second, you'll notice the phrase "(Image Edit Mode)" in the title bar of the graphic you're working on, and also in the title bar of the Object panel. Finally, the status-bar Stop button (a white X in a red circle) is active instead of grayed-out.

Tip

Windows users will also see the helpful hint "Press Stop to exit Image Edit mode" right next to the stop button itself.

Leaving Image Edit mode

When you leave Image Edit mode, any bitmap image, if selected normally, has a bounding box around it. In Fireworks, images can also be manipulated — moved, resized, aligned, distorted — as image objects. In Object Edit mode, image objects act like rectangular path objects filled with a bitmap image. You can even apply an effect, such as a drop shadow, to a selected image object.

The most obvious way to leave Image Edit mode and go to Object Edit mode is to select the Stop button. However, the Fireworks team created a number of other exits, as well. Here's a list of all the methods for leaving Image Edit mode:

✦ Choose Modify ➪ Exit Image Edit or use the key shortcut, Ctrl+Shift+D (Command+Shift+D).

✦ Press the Stop button on the status bar.

✦ If the Image Edit border surrounds just the image object and not the canvas, then the cursor changes into a Stop button when it's not over the object itself. Click once when you see the Stop button cursor.

✦ If the Image Edit border surrounds the entire document, choose a selection tool (Marquee, Ellipse Marquee, Lasso, Polygon Lasso, or Magic Wand) and double-click any open area.

Document title bar message   Striped border

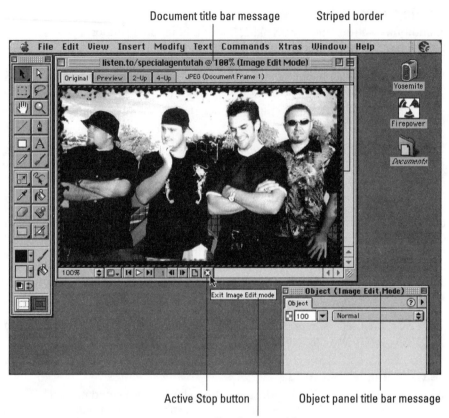

Active Stop button   Object panel title bar message

Stop button tooltip

Figure 6-1: Fireworks tells you that you're in Image Edit mode in a number of ways. Note the tooltip describing the function of the stop button.

To specify whether the image border surrounds just the image object or the whole canvas:

1. Choose File ⇨ Preferences.

2. Select the Editing tab in the Preferences dialog box.

3. Uncheck Expand to Fill Document under When Editing Images.

4. Choose OK.

The change takes place immediately.

Why would you want to have the Image Edit border surround more than just the image? Quite often, you need to expand the area of an image while you're editing — to blur the edges or make the shape nonrectangular, for example. If the Image Edit border tightly hugs the bitmap graphic, there's no room for expansion. By enabling the Expand to Fill Document option, you have plenty of canvas in which to maneuver. You're still just editing the one image object

Examining other Image mode functions

The other two options under the Editing tab in Preferences — Open in Image Edit Mode and Turn Off "Hide Edges" — can also prove useful. The Open in Image Edit Mode option (checked by default) tells Fireworks to automatically go into Image Edit mode when you open a document that doesn't contain any path objects — in other words, a single image. If you prefer, you can uncheck this option and always start out in Object Edit mode. You have to quit and restart Fireworks to enable this preference.

As helpful as the striped or barber-pole border is in identifying Image Edit mode, it can be a bit of a visual nuisance. To view your image temporarily without the striped border, choose View ➪ Hide Edges or the key shortcut Ctrl+H (Command+H). When you change modes, the Hide Edges command is automatically unchecked. If you'd prefer the edges stay hidden, uncheck Turn off "Hide Edges" (it's checked by default). This option takes effect immediately.

Opening existing images

I'm sure you've heard the expression, "Success is 1 percent inspiration and 99 percent perspiration." In the Internet graphics field, the formula is a bit different: "Web design is 20 percent creation and 80 percent modification." Of course, this is just my rough estimate — but it definitely feels like I spend most of my day revising an image already created by myself or someone else.

Fireworks offers multiple ways to open existing images — and it supports a wide range of image formats as well. Increasingly, more of your work will be stored in Fireworks' PNG-based format, which enables both object and image editing. However, many times you'll find yourself forced to work with a bitmap file created in another application such as Photoshop.

As with many computer programs, Fireworks loads images and other files through the File ➪ Open command. This displays the Open dialog box, which can preview various file types: PNG, TIFF, Photoshop, FreeHand, GIF, JPEG, and others. The Open Multiple command allows you to open several files at the same time. With the Open Multiple dialog box, as shown in Figure 6-2, you can select entire folders or gradually build a shopping list of files from one or more folders. It also has a very useful option, Open as Animation, that creates an animation from separate files by distributing them across frames.

Cross-Reference   For detailed information on how to use the Open and Open Multiple commands to load any type of file, see Chapter 14.

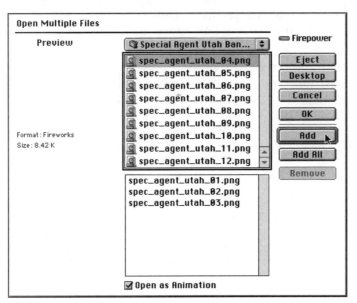

Figure 6-2: Opening an image sequence as an animation using Fireworks Open Multiple command.

Scaling images

Changing the size of a pixel-based image is something we probably take for granted, but it's actually a pretty complex task, requiring Fireworks to literally create a new image—with the newly specified dimensions—by analyzing the old image. Fireworks looks at groups of pixels and basically makes a best guess about how to represent them with either more or fewer pixels. Coming up with intermediate values based on analysis of known values is called interpolation.

New Feature   Fireworks image scaling interpolation methods are much more accessible in Fireworks 3. Previously, you had to run a Scriptlet to change interpolation methods. Now, the choices are available in the Image Size dialog box. You can also set your preferred default method in Fireworks Preferences.

Fireworks offers you four interpolation methods (Figure 6-3):

✦ **Bicubic:** With bicubic interpolation, Fireworks averages every pixel with all eight pixels surrounding it — above, below, left, right, and all four corners. This scaling option gives the sharpest results under the most conditions and is recommended for most graphics.

✦ **Bilinear:** Bilinear interpolation is similar to bicubic, but only uses four neighboring pixels (above, below, left, and right), instead of eight.

✦ **Nearest Neighbor:** The Nearest Neighbor algorithm causes Fireworks to copy neighboring pixels whenever a new pixel must be interpolated. Consequently, the Nearest Neighbor scaling option creates very pixelated, stairstep-like images.

✦ **Soft:** Soft interpolation was the original scaling option used in Fireworks 1 and it offers a smoothing blur to the scaled-down images. The Soft Interpolation scaling option is a good choice if your images are producing unwanted artifacts using the other scaling images.

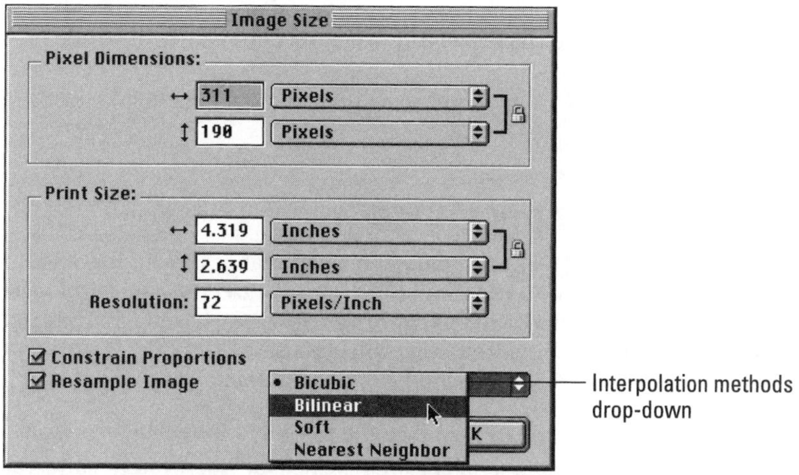

Figure 6-3: Fireworks offers four scaling options, which are now more accessible in Fireworks 3.

I've found that although I tend to use Bicubic Interpolation most of the time, I do turn to Bilinear and Soft Interpolation in some cases, usually when small text is involved. I haven't found much use for the blockiness produced by the Nearest Neighbor scaling option. Experimenting with the different interpolation methods is the best way to become familiar with their results.

Inserting an image into a document

Collage — the mixing of various images and other graphics — is a very important design tool on or off the Web. Whether you're overlapping images or just laying them side-by-side, Fireworks' Insert Image command enables you to include an existing graphic wherever necessary in an open document.

To include an image in a document, follow these steps:

1. Choose Insert ⇨ Image or use the keyboard shortcut, Ctrl+R (Command+R). Fireworks displays the Import dialog box.

2. Select your image and choose Open when you're done. The cursor changes to the Insert Image cursor: a corner bracket.

3. Position the Insert Image cursor wherever you'd like the upper-left corner of the image to be initially located and click once. The chosen image is inserted into the document as a new image object and selected.

If you need to adjust the position of the newly inserted image object, select the Pointer tool and click and drag it to a new place. For more precise placement, use the cursor keys to move the selected image object any direction, one pixel at a time.

Tip   When pressing Shift, the arrow keys move the selected image object in 10-pixel increments.

Inserting an empty image

So far we've seen how Fireworks can open a wide range of file formats for bitmap editing. But what if you want to create a bitmap image directly from within Fireworks? Whereas path-based objects are far more editable than bitmap images, occasionally only a bitmap will do. For those times, you can use a Fireworks feature that creates an editable bitmap area by choosing Insert ⇨ Empty Image or by pressing Ctrl+Alt+Y (Command+Option+Y).

Tip   The Empty Image command is extremely helpful when you need to paint a fairly large background with a brush such as the Airbrush, and don't want to use the Fill tool. You can then modify the Airbrushed background with any of the pixel-based tools, such as the Eraser.

When you insert an empty image, Fireworks immediately goes into Image Edit mode and selects the Marquee tool. If you want to limit your drawing area, use the Marquee tool to draw out a rectangle. Any drawing will now be clipped to the selected region. Otherwise, use any of the available tools to draw straight to the bitmap. When you leave Image Edit mode, the image object just created is sized to be only as large as necessary to encompass all the applied pixels. This automatically trimmed image object can naturally be repositioned or manipulated like any other image object.

Using Image-Edit-mode tools

The scoreboard shows a fairly equal number of Fireworks tools dedicated to working with images (five) as opposed to those that work only with objects (six). The vast majority of tools work in both modes, some in a different manner and others exactly the same. Naturally, the better you understand what a tool is intended for and how it is best used, the more fluid your workflow becomes. This section discusses tools that are intended for use in the Image Edit mode only.

The Image-Edit-mode-specific tools are primarily concerned with *selection,* and there's a very good reason for this emphasis. It's much harder to select pixels than it is to select paths. The most complicated path possible can be selected with just one click. Pixels are chosen either by their position with a tool such as the Marquee, or by their color with the Magic Wand. Quite often you need to use a combination of tools and methods to get the desired results.

Luckily, Fireworks offers a full range of selection tools: Pointer, Marquee, Elliptical Marquee, Lasso, Polygon Lasso, and Magic Wand. Each has its own way of working as well as a variety of user-definable options.

Pointer

Though technically the Pointer should be listed as one of the tools capable of being used in both modes, I included it here for a simple reason. Double-clicking the pointer on an image is one of the fastest and most intuitive methods of entering Image Edit mode. You can also use the Pointer to reposition the image once you're in Image Edit mode by clicking and dragging anywhere within the image object, as shown in Figure 6-4.

Tip

It's not obvious, but you can also use the Pointer to resize an image object, whether you're in Image Edit or Object Edit mode. You can drag the border surrounding the image to a new position, resizing the graphic much like the Distortion tool. You can even obtain proportional resizing by pressing Shift while dragging a corner Image Edit or image object border. The image object, however, is a tad easier to use because the sizing handles are apparent.

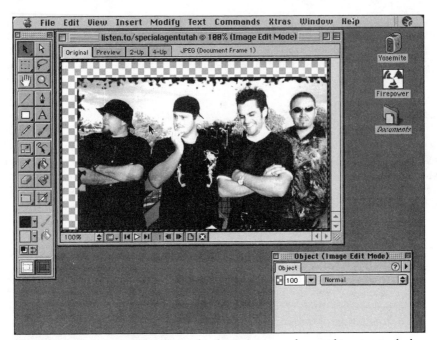

Figure 6-4: Even in Image Edit mode, the Pointer can be used to move whole image objects around the canvas.

Marquee

The Marquee tool is one of the most frequently used selection tools and not only because it's the default tool after entering Image Edit mode. The Marquee selection tool is quite similar to the Rectangle drawing tool. Both are generally used by selecting a point for one corner of the rectangular shape and dragging diagonally to the opposite corner. However, the Marquee tool doesn't draw a shape on the image; it temporarily surrounds and selects an area of pixels for another operation to take place, such as a copy or a fill.

Rectangular and Ellipse

There are actually two different Marquee tools. The first is the default rectangular Marquee, which is selected through its button on the toolbar or by pressing the keyboard shortcut, M. The second parallels the Ellipse drawing tool: the Ellipse Marquee selects an oval or circular area.

Caution   You might expect that holding down Shift while using the Marquee and Ellipse Marquee tools would constrain the shapes you draw to perfect squares and circles, as it would when using the Rectangle or Circle drawing tools, but this is not the case. To draw perfect squares and circles, double-click the Marquee or Ellipse Marquee tool to open its Options panel and choose Fixed Ratio from the Style box. Set the ratio at 1 to 1 and you'll be drawing perfect square and circle selections instead of rectangles and ovals.

To use the Marquee or Ellipse Marquee, follow these steps:

1. To select a rectangular or square region, select the Marquee tool from the Toolbox or through its keyboard shortcut, M.

2. To select an elliptical or circular region, select the Ellipse Marquee tool from the Toolbox by clicking and holding the Marquee tool and choosing the button from the flyout menu. Alternatively, you can press the keyboard shortcut, M, twice.

3. Click where you want one corner of your selection to begin and drag to the opposite corner. Fireworks displays a moving dashed line, called a marquee or, more familiarly, "marching ants" (Figure 6-5).

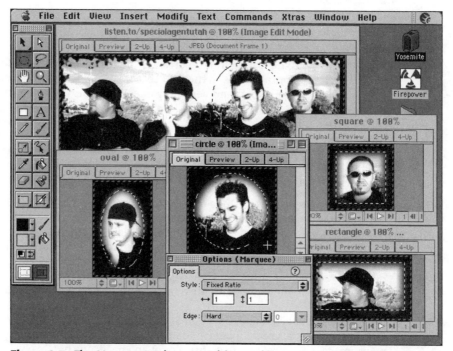

Figure 6-5: The Marquee tools are used for marking rectangular, square, oval, or circular areas for selection.

Tool Options panel

The two Marquee tools also share a set of options available from the Tool Options panel. You can display the Tool Options panel, as shown in Figure 6-6, by double-clicking either the Marquee or Ellipse Marquee tool, or by choosing one of the tools and then selecting Window ⇨ Tool Options. The Marquee Tool Options affect two separate areas: Style and Edge.

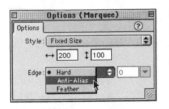

Figure 6-6: Use the Tool Options panel to set the Marquee to a predetermined size or ratio; you can also choose a type of edge for the selection: Hard, Anti-Alias, or Feather.

Style portion

Normally, the Marquee tools are unrestrained, meaning the selection can be any size or shape drawn out. However, sometimes it's helpful to be able to specify the needed selection dimensions. The Style portion of the Marquee Tool Options panel has three possibilities:

✦ **Normal:** This default state enables you to drag out your rectangular or elliptical selections freely.

✦ **Fixed Ratio:** Sets the horizontal-to-vertical ratio for the Marquee selection tools. Enter horizontal values in the first text box (marked with the side-to-side double-headed arrow) and vertical values in the second (marked with the up-and-down double-headed arrow). This option is useful when you know that the selection must be a particular proportion. If, for example, you knew that the selection should be twice as wide as high, you would enter a 2 in the horizontal text box and a 1 in the vertical text box. To get a perfect square selection, specify 1 to 1. When you use either Marquee tool with a Set Ratio option enabled, the selection size varies, but not the proportion.

✦ **Fixed Size:** Sets the dimensions to a particular pixel width and height. Enter the desired pixel values in the horizontal and vertical text boxes. When either Marquee tool is selected with this option enabled, a selection outlining the specified dimensions is attached to the pointer and can be easily repositioned on the screen. After you've located the area to be selected, clicking once drops the selection outline on the image. The Fixed Size option works especially well when you need to create a number of same-sized selections.

Tip If you enter a value in one of the Fixed Size text boxes, but leave the other blank, Fireworks creates a selection outline the width or height specified that spans the entire image. It's a great way to grab a slice of an image, one or two pixels wide or tall, and ensures that you get the full image without having to draw it. For this technique, it's best to use the Marquee tool rather than the Ellipse Marquee.

Types of edges

The Tool Options panel also controls the type of edge that the selection uses. The default edge-type is a hard-edged line — what you select is what you get. The other two types, Anti-Alias and Feather, act to soften the selection. Anti-Alias is the more subtle of the two options. When you choose the Anti-Alias option for your selection, any jagged edges caused by an elliptical or circular selection are blended into the background, much like bitmap type is anti-aliased to make it appear less jagged.

> **Tip**
>
> You can get a very smooth bitmap crescent by making a circular selection using the Ellipse Marquee tool on a solid color. Set the Edge type on the Marquee Tool Options panel to Anti-Alias and make your selection. Then, use the arrow keys to move the selection one or two pixels vertically and the same distance horizontally. You'll be left with a crescent shape that blends smoothly into its points.

Feathering a selection is much more noticeable. Basically, think of feathering as blending. After selecting the Feather option, the value box becomes active with a default of 10 pixels. Any feathered selection blends equally on either side of the selection outline. If, for example, you choose a small Feather value of 2 pixels for a rectangular selection, four rows of pixels will be altered—two inside the selection and two outside. If you delete a feathered selection, you'll be left with a hole in the image, blending smoothly into the canvas, because both the selection and the surrounding image are feathered. If you move a feather selection, the selection will have a faded edge, as shown in Figure 6-7.

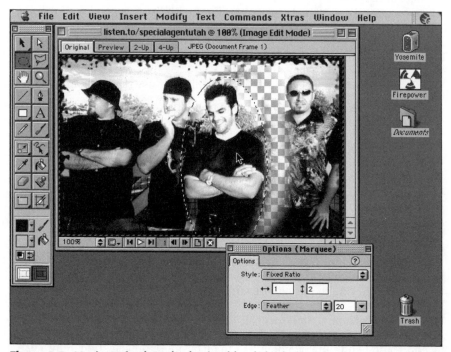

Figure 6-7: Moving a feathered selection blends both the selection and the remaining image to create a gentle transition.

Lasso and Polygon Lasso

Not all regions to be selected are rectangular or elliptical. The Lasso tools select irregularly shaped areas of an image. As the name implies, the Lasso tools surround or lasso the desired pixels to select them. The standard Lasso tool is a click-and-drag type instrument that enables freeform selection, much like the Pencil or Brush is used for freeform drawing. The Polygon tool, on the other hand, is more like the Pen in its straight-line mode, and makes selections through a series of connected straight lines.

All Lasso selections are by their very nature closed paths. As with the drawing tools, when you drag the pointer near the beginning of a Lasso selection, Fireworks displays a closed-path cursor with a black square in the lower-right corner, as shown in Figure 6-8. You can also close a Lasso tool selection by releasing the mouse button; Fireworks draws a line from the beginning point to the ending point, closing the shape. With the Polygon Lasso, double-click the last point to close the shape automatically in the same manner.

If you're selecting an area that has more curves than straight lines, use the Lasso. If your selection has some long straight lines, you may find the Polygon Lasso is more suitable, even if you also have some curves to deal with, because the straight lines will be quick and accurate. Lots of short lines with the Polygon Lasso will allow you to draw around curves.

To make a freeform selection, follow these steps:

1. To use the Lasso, select it from the Toolbox or use the keyboard shortcut, L.

2. With the Lasso, click at the starting point for your selection and drag the mouse around the desired area, releasing the mouse when you're done.

3. To use the Polygon Lasso, select and hold the Lasso tool until the flyout appears and then choose the Polygon Lasso or press the keyboard shortcut, L, twice.

4. With the Polygon Lasso, click at the starting point for your selection and then move the mouse to the next point on the outline surrounding the desired area and click again. Fireworks connects each point that you set down with a straight line.

5. Repeat Step 4 until you've outlined the entire area and then close the selection by moving your pointer over the starting point and clicking once or double-clicking to permit Fireworks to connect the first and final points.

As a matter of personal preference, I get a lot more use out of the Polygon Lasso than I do the regular drawing Lasso. Selecting an area of pixels is often a painstaking chore and I find the Polygon Lasso to be far more precise. Generally, I use the Lasso to outline some stray pixels for deletion only when there's little chance that I'll select part of the main image.

Closed path Polygon Lasso cursor

Figure 6-8: Drawing with the Polygon Lasso. One more click will close the path and create the selection.

You can determine the type of edge the Lasso tools use through the Tool Options panel. As with the Marquee tools, the three options are Hard Edge, Anti-Alias, and Feather, and they work in exactly the same manner as described in the previous Marquee section.

Magic Wand

The Magic Wand is a completely different type of selection tool from those already discussed. Instead of encompassing an area of pixels, the Magic Wand selects adjacent pixels of similar color. This type of tool enables you to select single-color backgrounds or other regions quickly.

Using the Magic Wand is very straightforward. Choose the Magic Wand tool from the flyout that appears by clicking and holding the Lasso tool, or use the keyboard shortcut, W. Now select any pixel in the image — it, and all pixels of a similar color next to it, are selected.

Tip   With both the Magic Wand and the Lasso, I find that the representational pointers sometimes get in the way. It's hard to see exactly which pixel you're pinpointing if there is a sparkly wand cursor obscuring the area. You can toggle Precise Cursors — a crosshair pointer — whenever you like by pressing the Caps Lock key.

The key phrase in the description of the Magic Wand is "pixels of a similar color." Many bitmap images, especially photographic JPEG's, tend to use a range of colors even when depicting a seemingly monochromatic area. You control what Fireworks defines as a "similar color" through the Tolerance setting on the Tool Options panel. The Tolerance scale goes from 0 to 255; lower tolerance values select fewer colors and higher values select more.

Here's how the Magic Wand and the Tolerance work. By default, the initial Tolerance is set to 32. The Tolerance value is applied to the RGB values of the selected pixel — the exact one selected by the Magic Wand. If the Tolerance value is 50 and the selected pixel's RGB values are 200, 200, and 200, Fireworks judges any adjacent pixel with an RGB from 150, 150, 150 to 250, 250, 250 as being similar enough to select. Pixels within that color range but not in some way touching the originally selected pixel will not be chosen.

In addition to varying the Tolerance, you can also determine the type of edge for a Magic Wand selection. Edge options, like those for Marquee and Lasso tools, are Hard Edge, Anti-Alias (the default), or Feather. For a detailed explanation of how these tools work, see the "Marquee" section earlier in this chapter.

Increasing or Reducing the Selection Area

Fireworks' selection tools are very full-featured, but, for complex selections, you need more flexibility. Adding several selections together, or using one selection tool to eliminate part of an existing selection, opens up a whole range of possibilities.

The key to adding or removing pixels is to use the keyboard modifiers as you draw your selections: Press Shift to add selections and Alt (Option) to remove them. You'll notice that the pointer indicates the operation; a plus sign appears when Shift is pressed and a minus sign appears when Alt (Option) is pressed.

For example, I often use Shift in combination with the Magic Wand to select additional areas of an image, rather than alter the Tolerance. Your first Magic Wand selection may have a couple of small gaps that need filling. Holding down Shift and clicking in those gaps is usually the quickest way to fill out the selection, as shown in the accompanying figure.

Just as you can add onto selections, you can take away from them, too. Use the Alt (Option) key when applying any of the selection tools to reduce an existing selection. The basic technique is to "carve out" the undesired selection; in the following figure, the donut shape was created by first drawing a circular selection and then pressing Alt (Option) while drawing a smaller circular selection inside. The soft edge was achieved through use of the Feather option, and then an Xtra was applied to the donut to create a frame around the subject's face. Obviously, the selection reduction feature enables you to create some very unusual shapes.

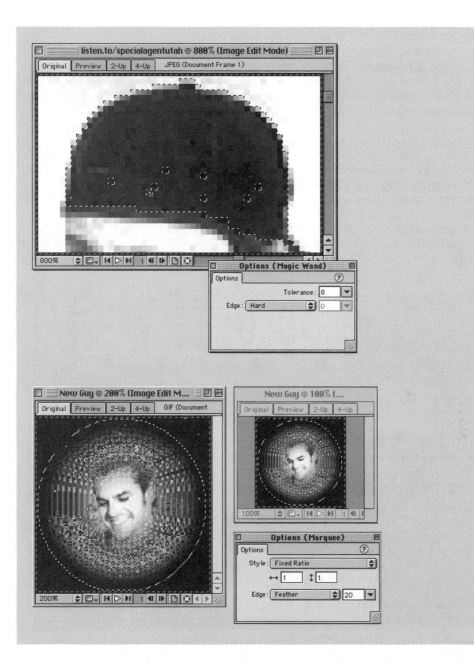

Rubber Stamp

If you're looking for a unique tool, look no further than the Rubber Stamp. One of the few pixel-based drawing tools, Rubber Stamp acts like a real rubber stamp: picking up a section of your document and stamping it out somewhere else. The Rubber Stamp tool makes it easy to pick up portions of an image and blend them into other areas of the graphic.

The Rubber Stamp is a two-part tool with both source and destination pointers. The source, or origin, pointer is initially placed on the area of the document that you want to duplicate. The destination pointer draws the duplicated section in a different location on the image. While you are drawing, the two pointers maintain the same relationship to each other; if you move the destination pointer to the left, the source pointer moves to the left as well. Because the "ink" that the Rubber Stamp tool uses is always changing while you move it (because the source pointer is also moving), you can achieve a smooth blend, as in Figure 6-9. It's a little tricky to get a handle on this tool, but well worth the time you spend mastering it.

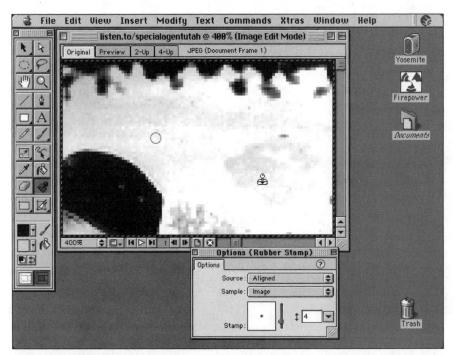

Figure 6-9: Using the Rubber Stamp tool to darken the sky in this image by drawing a section of the darker portion in the source circle onto the lighter portion underneath the tool.

To use the Rubber Stamp tool, follow these steps:

1. Select the Rubber Stamp tool from the Toolbox or use the keyboard shortcut, S.

2. Set the source pointer by clicking once on the image. If you attempt to set the source pointer on a path object, Fireworks tells you that the Rubber Stamp tool can only be used on floating image objects.

3. Move the destination pointer to where you want the copied image to appear and draw by clicking and dragging. As the source pointer moves over the image, following the movement of the mouse, the image is copied under the destination pointer.

Aligned Source and Fixed Source modes

You can use the Rubber Stamp in two basic modes, selectable from the Source options list found on the Rubber Stamp Tool Options panel. First, with the Aligned Source mode (default), you can always keep the relationship between the source and destination pointers constant, not just when you're drawing. This is useful if you want to copy different portions of the image to a remote area, but keep them proportionally spaced. For example, if I wanted to position two eyes as if they were floating in space above my model's head, I would copy one eye using the Rubber Stamp tool, release the mouse button, and position the source pointer over the second eye and then begin dragging and drawing again until the second eye was completed.

The other Rubber Stamp mode is Fixed Source. In Fixed Source mode, whenever the mouse button is released, the source pointer snaps back to its original starting place. This mode enables you to copy the same image in several locations. If, for example, I wanted to place a series of floating eyes around my model's head, I would use Fixed Source mode.

Tip   Press Alt (Option) to reset the origin for the Rubber Stamp.

Other options

Though the Rubber Stamp only draws pixels, you can use it to copy any part of your document, whether image or object. In the Sample option list, choose Image to copy only from the image and Document to copy from anywhere in the document. There is one small trick to using the Sample Document option, however. Because the Rubber Stamp tool is intended as a pixel-based tool, you can't start by clicking outside of the image; Fireworks won't permit it. You can, however, click once on the image to set the source pointer and then immediately move it by pressing Alt (Option) and resetting it on an area outside of the image. Then you can set the destination pointer normally and begin copying the image.

Two other controls are available on the Rubber Stamp Tool Options panel. The Edge Softness slider affects the hardness of the duplicated image's edge; the higher the slider, the softer the edge. To blend a copied image more, use a softer edge. You can also change the size of the source and destination pointers with the Stamp Size slider. The range of the Stamp Size slider is from 0 to 72 and the default is 16 pixels. The selected Stamp Size includes any feathering that may be required by the Edge Softness setting.

Eraser

As you might suspect, the Eraser removes pixels from an image, just like the trusty gum-based version erases pencil drawings. What you might not guess, however, is that the Eraser tool has numerous options and can achieve a variety of effects. The Eraser, which works only on pixel-based images, shares a Toolbox spot with its path-oriented counterpart, the Knife. To see the Eraser button appear on the Toolbox, select a bitmap image to enter Image Edit mode.

To use the Eraser, follow these steps:

1. Select the Eraser (or the Knife) from the Toolbox; alternatively, you can use the keyboard shortcut, E.

2. If necessary, select the image you want to work on.

3. Click and drag over the pixels you wish to remove. Fireworks deletes the pixels according to the preferences selected in the Tool Options panel, as shown in Figure 6-10.

In addition to being able to set the Edge Softness and Size of the Eraser on the Tool Options panel, as you can with the Rubber Stamp tool, you can also select its basic shape. By default, the Eraser is circular, but you can change it to a square by choosing the Square Eraser button.

The final set of choices on the Tool Options panel gives the Eraser a fair degree of power. With some graphics programs, you're always erasing to whatever the current background is or, in Fireworks jargon, the canvas color. In Fireworks, you can select what will replace the area erased from four different choices:

✦ Transparent

✦ Fill color

✦ Stroke color

✦ Canvas color

Note   If the image is floating over the canvas and you choose the Erase To Transparent option, it will look like you're erasing to the canvas color. However, if you move the image over another object, you'll see that the area erased is indeed transparent.

Figure 6-10: The Eraser tool removes pixels from your image according to the settings established on the Tool Options panel.

Fireworks Technique: Limiting Your Drawing Area

Not only can the selection tools modify your images after they're created, but they can also help to structure them while they're being made. When you place a selection on an image canvas — whether it's an existing image or an inserted Empty Image — any subsequent drawing is limited to that selected area. The selected area can be any shape possible with any or all of the selection tools: Marquee, Ellipse Marquee, Lasso, Polygon Lasso, and Magic Wand. In Figure 6-11, a feathered selection around the subjects' faces was inverted so that everything in the document except the faces was selected. The entire document was then painted over with the Paintbrush tool. Note that the Paintbrush could only paint in the selected area.

Tip

If you have a pixel selection in your document, an Xtra will only apply to the selected area as well. A Film Look Xtra was also applied to Figure 6-11 after painting, to dirty the background a little and cause the faces to stand out even more.

Deselected area   Selected area

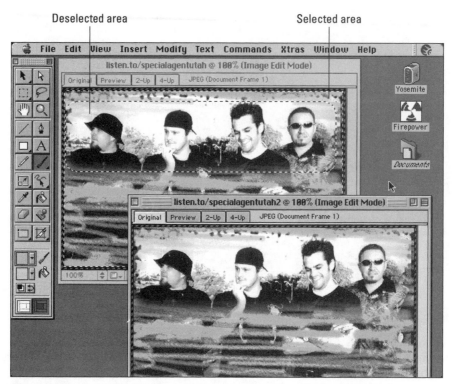

Figure 6-11: The subjects' faces aren't selected, so they don't get painted.

The only prerequisite for using this technique is to make sure that the selection is active before you begin drawing. The marquee or "marching ants" border designates an active selected area.

Selecting Images

The selection tools found in the Toolbox are handy, but they aren't the only selection options in Fireworks. The Edit menu contains several commands pertinent to selecting objects.

Selecting all

When you need to select all the objects — both images and paths — in the current document, choose Edit ⇨ Select All. I often find myself using the keyboard shortcut for this command, Ctrl+A (Command+A), in combination with the Delete key when I want to erase all the work in a document and start over. Of course, any operation that needs to be applied universally to every portion of a document benefits from the Select All command.

If you are in Image Edit mode and issue the Select All command, just the image is selected. If, on the other hand, you're in Object Edit mode, all the path-based objects and the pixel-based images are selected. Keep in mind, though, that the image is selected as an image object and image tools such as the Rubber Stamp that work only in Image Edit mode will not function.

Both Superselect and Subselect are concerned with groups and are therefore covered in Chapter 13.

Selecting none

The opposite of Select All is Deselect. I use this command so frequently, it goes on my Top 10 Keyboard Shortcuts to Memorize list: Ctrl+D (Command+D). It's a very straightforward and extremely useful command. Choose Edit ⇨ Deselect to remove all selections in the current document for any image, object, or text.

Selecting inverse

Sometimes I think I select inverse more than I select the pixels I want directly. Often, the background in an image contains fewer or flatter colors than the fore-ground, making it easier to select with the Magic Wand tool. Once the background is selected, use the Select Inverse command to invert the selection and select the foreground elements. On the other hand, if you want to select a background full of irregular colors and shapes, it may be easier to select the foreground elements and then invert the selection to select the background. This command can be a time-saver over and over again.

1. First, select your foreground object through whatever tool or combination of tools is required.

2. Choose Edit ⇨ Select Inverse or use the keyboard shortcut, Ctrl+Shift+I (Command+Shift+I). Fireworks inverts the selection so that the background is now selected (see Figure 6-12).

Figure 6-12: Selecting the foreground element and inverting the selection quickly isolated this complex, blended background.

Feathering an existing selection

You've seen the Feather option for all the Toolbox selection tools. However, you may have noticed that in each case, feathering has to be established prior to the selection being made, whether through the Marquee or the Magic Wand. But what do you do when you want to feather an existing selection? Make your selection and choose Edit ⇨ Feather to open the Feather Selection dialog box, as shown in Figure 6-13. Whatever value is entered into the Radius text box is then applied to the current selection.

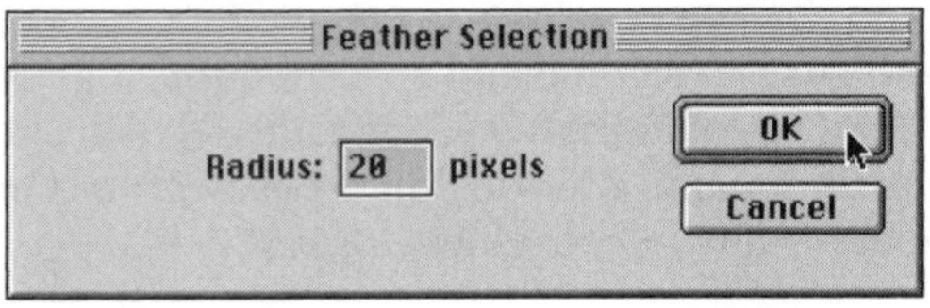

Feather Selection

Radius: 20   pixels

OK

Cancel

Figure 6-13: The Feather Selection dialog box permits you to feather the edges of the current selection.

Remember that the Feather command does not blur the selection's edges, but rather alters the selection's alpha channel, which controls transparency. To see the effect of a feathered selection, it's often necessary to move or cut and paste the selection. As with all the other feathering options, both the selection and the area adjacent to the selection are affected.

Cross-Reference

If you do just want to blur all or part an image, you'll want to use one of the Blur commands found under the Xtras menu. Find out more about these commands in Chapter 12.

Selecting similar

The Select Similar command is an extension of the Magic Wand selection tool. Whereas the Magic Wand selects pixels within a particular color range adjacent to the one initially chosen, Select Similar selects *all* the pixels in a document within that color range, whether they are adjacent to the original pixel or not. To use this command, choose Edit ⇨ Select Similar after setting the Tolerance level on the Magic Wand Tool Options panel.

Caution

This is a very powerful command and one that should be used with care. It's often extremely difficult to predict all the areas of an image that will be affected. You may find yourself using this command in concert with the new History panel.

Modify marquee

The Modify Marquee submenu contains four commands for adjusting marquee selections you've already created.

New
Feature

In Fireworks 3, getting just the right pixel selection is made easier by the four commands under Edit ➪ Modify Marquee. Expand or Contract a current selection, turn a selection into a border, or smooth its edges.

Expanding or contracting

Sometimes a hand-drawn marquee selection is just a few pixels too large or small. Make a selection and then choose Edit ➪ Modify Marquee ➪ Expand to open the Expand Selection dialog box and specify the number of pixels by which you want to expand the selection. Conversely, if you want to contract the selection, choose Edit ➪ Modify Marquee ➪ Contract and enter the number of pixels to contract the selection in the Contract Selection dialog box. Click OK when you're done in either case.

Border

To create an additional marquee around a current marquee, choose Edit ➪ Modify Marquee ➪ Border, enter the width of the border you want to create in the Select Border dialog box and click OK when you're done. Instead of your previous selection, what is now selected is a border around the previous selection.

Smooth

The Smooth command smooths the outline of a selection to turn a jagged, complicated marquee into a simpler one. This is especially useful for the jagged marquees that are easily created with the Magic Wand tool. Create a selection and then choose Edit ➪ Modify Marquee ➪ Smooth. Enter a sample radius in the Smooth Selection dialog box; a higher number means a greater smoothing effect. Click OK when you're done.

Applying Object Tools to Images

Whether you're creating a bitmap image from scratch or touching up an existing graphic, you'll need additional tools. In Fireworks, all of the geometric shapes — Rectangle, Ellipse, and Polygon — and most of the drawing tools — such as the Pencil and Brush — are applied in exactly the same way in Image Edit mode as in Object Edit mode. The primary difference is that what's drawn is easily editable when it's an object and not when it's an image. Sometimes, however, you don't have a choice and you have to work in Image Edit mode because that's the way your image started out. Table 6-1 explains how the object tools are used in Image Edit mode.

Table 6-1
Tools in Image Edit Mode

Tool	Effect
Rectangle and Square	Works the same way in Image Edit mode as with objects and uses the current Stroke and Fill settings.
Ellipse and Circle	Works the same way in Image Edit mode as with objects and uses the current Stroke and Fill settings.
Polygon and Star	Works the same way in Image Edit mode as with objects and uses the current Stroke and Fill settings.
Line	Works the same way in Image Edit mode as with objects and uses the current Stroke settings.
Pencil	Works the same way in Image Edit mode as with objects and uses the basic one-pixel stroke setting.
Brush	Works the same way in Image Edit mode as with objects and uses the current Stroke settings.
Pen	Ends Image Edit mode; tool must be selected again to use in Object Edit mode.
Text	Ends Image Edit mode and opens Text Editor.
Transform, Skew, and Distort	No effect in Image Edit mode. You can, however, use these tools to modify a selected image object.
Freeform, Reshape Area, and Path Scrubber	No effect in Image Edit mode; Fireworks will warn that these tools can be used only with paths.

Converting an Object to an Image

It's best to keep parts of your document in path form for easy modification, but occasionally you may want to convert a path-based object to a bitmap image. To accomplish this, select the object and then choose Modify ➪ Merge Images or use the key shortcut Ctrl+Shift+Alt+Z (Command+Shift+Option+Z). Fireworks converts the path outline to a rectangular bounding box surrounding all the pixels from the object's fill, stroke, and effect settings.

If you have selected multiple objects, you can convert them all at one time with this command. However, you lose the capability to reposition them individually as they all become part of one image; as the command's name implies, you are merging the images.

Caution Once you've converted an object to an image, you can't go back without using the Undo command or the History panel to actually reverse your work. Converted objects that have been saved and reloaded cannot return to their object state under any circumstances. Fireworks throws away the vector information when you convert a path object to an image object.

Summary

Bitmap images are used throughout the Web and Fireworks offers a robust set of tools for creating and manipulating them. Whereas images don't have the flexibility of path objects, editing them is an important part of the Web designer's job. When it comes time to begin modifying an existing image in Fireworks, keep these points in mind:

✦ Images are composed of pixels and each pixel is assigned a particular color. At the most basic level, editing images involves changing the colors of pixels.

✦ In Fireworks, images are modified primarily in Image Edit mode, which you can enter by double-clicking an image with the Pointer or working with any image-based tool such as the Marquee.

✦ All of the image selection tools in Fireworks — Marquee, Ellipse Marquee, Lasso, Polygon Lasso, and Magic Wand — have numerous options available through the Tool Options panel.

✦ By selecting an area of the image prior to drawing, you can limit your drawing area.

✦ One of the best techniques for separating a figure from the background is to select the simpler of the two and invert the selection with Edit ➪ Select Inverse.

✦ Most of the primary object drawing tools, such as the Rectangle, Pen, and Brush, work in Image Edit mode as well, with some restrictions.

In the next chapter, you'll see how to handle color in Fireworks.

✦   ✦   ✦

Managing Color

For any graphic designer, the importance of color is a given. Not only can color attract the eye and convey emotions, but it's also an important commercial consideration. On the Web, as with any mass medium, color also becomes a key factor in branding. After all, if you're working on a logo for the Coca-Cola Web site, you'd better make sure you're using genuine Coca-Cola red.

Fireworks outputs graphics for a screen-based medium. You won't find complex color separation, halftone, or calibration tools in Fireworks; those are instruments for the world of print. Moreover, Fireworks is not just screen-based, it's Internet-based — a distinction that signifies an important balance of freedoms and restrictions.

New Feature Fireworks 3 includes a comprehensive set of Xtras for making color adjustments to photographic images. Find them under the Xtras ⇨ Adjust Color submenu, and detailed descriptions of them in Chapter 12.

This chapter covers color on the Web — both its basic theory with the various standards, and its actual practice with Fireworks. If you're familiar with how computers handle color in general, feel free to skip the initial part of the chapter and dive right into the more hands-on Fireworks sections. If, on the other hand, you think RGB is a one-hit wonder band from the '80s and hexadecimal is a library catalog system, the first section should be pixel-perfect for you.

Working with Color on the Web

Color in the natural world comes at us full force, without any impediments. Color on the Web, however, passes through many filters. At the most basic level, the computer dictates how color is generated. Rather than using a system of blending inks as with print, the computer blends light — red, green, and blue light, to be precise. Next, the color settings and

In This Chapter

Web color fundamentals

Blending new colors

Picking palettes

Fireworks technique: converting print colors

capability of a viewer's specific system determine the range of colors to be used. The final filter for Web-based color is the browser, in all of its varied configurations and versions.

To get the most out of your Web graphics, you'll need a basic understanding of how computers create color. The smallest component of a computer screen that you can see is the pixel, which, you'll remember, is short for *picture element*. Pixels are displayed by showing three colors in combination: red, green, and blue, often referred to by their initials, RGB. The blend of red, green, and blue at full intensity creates white.

> **Tip**
>
> If you're coming from a print background, you'll probably be more familiar with the CMYK (cyan, magenta, yellow, and black) color model than the RGB model. It's generally not too difficult to make the transition; Fireworks offers ways to convert a color in one system to its equivalent in the other, as you'll see in the section, "Using the Color Mixer," later in this chapter.

If RGB blended at full intensity creates white, and if a pixel that's turned off displays black, how are other colors created? The intensity of each of the key colors in a pixel — red, green, and blue — and their combinations can be varied. For example, if you have red set all the way up and both blue and green off, you'll get pure red; if you add a full dose of blue to the red, you'll create a deep purple. However, having only the capability to turn a color on or off greatly limits the number of color combinations possible. What's needed is an increase in the number of steps or levels between on and off.

Bit depth

The number of accessible RGB levels is called the *bit depth*. A bit is the smallest element of computer memory, and each bit is basically an on-off switch. A computer display with a bit depth of 1 is capable of showing two colors — one color in the on position and another in the off position. Now, if the bit depth is doubled, twice as many colors can be defined.

Each time you increase the bit depth, the number of colors increases exponentially. Table 7-1 takes a look at how bit depth affects color range.

Table 7-1 Bit Depth and Color Range		
Bit Depth	**Number of Colors**	**Description**
1	2	Black and white, corresponding to the "on" or "off" possible with 1 bit
2	4	Typically, computers with 2-bit color depth (usually handhelds or portables) display 4 shades of gray.

Bit Depth	Number of Colors	Description
4	16	The minimum color depth of VGA (Video Graphics Adapter) displays, the most common computer display technology.
8	256	Most computers manufactured after 1995 can display 8-bit color or better.
16	65 536	Often called "Thousands of Colors" or "HiColor"
24	16 777 216	Referred to as "Millions of Colors" or "True Color"
32	16 777 216	True Color with an additional 8-bit alpha mask

In Table 7-1, I skipped some bit depths because they're not commonly used on computer displays. Note that 32-bit color has the same number of colors as 24-bit. Although with 32-bits you could potentially describe more than 4 billion colors, the human eye can't differentiate that many. Thirty-two-bit color is therefore a combination of 24-bit color, with its 16.7 million colors, and an 8-bit grayscale overlay (known as a *mask*) that primarily specifies transparency and how graphics should be composited. For example, a mask can be used to make a graphic appear round or have holes in it by showing parts of the graphic beneath it. This grayscale mask is known as an alpha mask, or the *alpha channel*.

Because bit depth is directly related to computer memory (remember that a bit is a chunk of memory), the higher the color range, the more memory required. And not just any memory, but video memory. Until recently, video memory was fairly limited, and most computer systems were shipped displaying only 256 colors (8-bit). Therefore, when designing for the Web, artists have been forced to work with the lowest common denominator and created work in 256 colors.

Note
Increasingly, computers surfing the Web have an increased bit depth and can display more colors. A recent poll showed that out of 7 million Web visitors, less than 15 percent were using 256 color systems. However, this doesn't mean that all graphics can now be in millions of colors. The more colors used in a GIF image, the larger the file size, and download speed over the Internet is a major consideration in Web design.

Cross-Reference
Examples of various bit depths can be found in the color insert.

Hexadecimal colors

In HTML, the language of the Web, RGB color values are given in *hexadecimal*. Hexadecimal (or *hex*, as it is more commonly called), is a base-16 number system, which means that instead of the numbers running from 0 to 9 and then repeating, there is an initial series of 16 number values:

```
0, 1, 2, 3, 4, 5, 6, 7, 8, 9, A, B, C, D, E, F
```

The single letters represent values that would normally take two digits in the decimal system: A equals 10, B equals 11, C equals 12, and so on. When you want to count beyond single hex digits — in other words, go higher than F — you place a one in front of the numbers and continue, just like you do in decimal when you want to go beyond single digits. Although this looks strange to our decimal-trained eyes, continuing the above hex series looks like this (keep in mind that "10" is actually 16):

```
10, 11, 12, 13, 14, 15, 16, 17, 18, 19, 1A, 1B, 1C, 1D, 1E, 1F, 20
```

In the decimal number system, two digits can be used to express any number up to 99; but in the hexadecimal number system, the highest two-digit number is FF. Although they're both two-digit numbers, in hex, you have to count 255 things to fill up two digits.

> **Tip**
>
> Don't cheat and convert FF to 1515 and think of it as one thousand, five hundred and fifteen. When you look at the decimal number 99, you assume that the first 9 is really 90, or 9 multiplied by (base) 10. When you look at the hexadecimal number FF, remember that the first F is really 15 multiplied by (base) 16, which is equal to 240 in decimal. Add the other F, and you can see how FF is equal to 255.

RGB values are expressed in hex with a set of three two-digit numbers, with each of the three values corresponding to 256 levels of red, green, and blue, respectively. For example, white in RGB values would be represented as 255, 255, 255 — each color being its most intense. The equivalent in hex is FF, FF, FF, which in HTML is written all together, like this: FFFFFF. Black is 0, 0, 0 in RGB and 000000 in hex, whereas a pure red would be 255, 0, 0 in RGB, and FF0000 in hex.

Though it may seem completely foreign to you initially, hexadecimal colors quickly become recognizable. You'll even start to notice patterns; for instance, any color where the hex triplets are all the same represents a shade of gray — 111111 is the darkest gray, and EEEEEE is the lightest.

Web-safe colors

As noted previously, the generally accepted lowest-common denominator in monitor displays is 8-bit, or 256 colors. Unfortunately, there's yet one more restriction on Web colors: the browser. Each of the major browsers from Microsoft and Netscape uses a fixed palette of 256 colors to render 8-bit images on both Windows and Macintosh operating systems. Once the 40 unique colors used for system displays in both Macintosh and Windows platforms are subtracted — because you generally would like your Web graphics to look the same on both Windows and Macintosh platforms — a common palette of 216 colors remains. Because any of these colors can safely be used by any system without dithering — faking the color with a combination of two others — they are collectively referred to as the *browser-safe* or *Web-safe* palette.

Tip   Interestingly enough—and thankfully—Web-safe colors are easy to spot when given in hexadecimal. Any hex color that contains some combination of 00, 33, 66, 99, CC, or FF—such as 0000FF, 336699, or FFCC00—is Web safe.

It's important to realize that the Web-safe palette is for use with flat-color images, such as illustrations, logos, and headline text—the kinds of images that are drawn or created right on a computer and exported in the GIF format. Using Web-safe colors in these images keeps flat areas of color flat. Photographic images are still exported with a 24-bit palette—usually in the JPEG format—and dithered by the browser if necessary.

Because of its importance in Web design, Fireworks makes extensive use of the Web-safe palette, and includes a number of features for efficiently working with it:

✦ By default, the pop-up color picker that is accessible from every color well in the program is set to the Web-safe palette.

✦ Holding down the Shift key when you use the Eyedropper tool causes the tool to convert any color that it samples to Web-safe.

✦ The Find and Replace panel can search for colors that fall outside the Web-safe palette and snap them to their nearest neighbor, in one document or a range of documents, all in one step.

Cross-Reference   For more about using the Find and Replace panel, see Chapter 18.

✦ The Fill panel has a Web Dither category that can convert any color into a pattern of Web-safe colors that closely approximates the color.

As you continue to work with Fireworks and in Web design in general, you'll become more and more familiar with the Web-safe palette.

Platform differences

Not only does the Web designer have to contend with a limited palette and a host of issues with the wide variety of browsers in the market, but many differences worth noting exist between the Windows and Macintosh platforms. Chief among these is the *gamma* setting.

The gamma setting, or more properly, the *gamma correction* setting, is designed to avoid having midtones onscreen appear too dark. The problem is that there are different gamma settings for different systems. The Macintosh typically defaults to a setting of 1.8; while Windows uses 2.2, which is also the standard for Television. The lower gamma setting on the Mac works well to emulate print output, but the display seems brighter when compared to Windows. Consequently, the same graphic appears darker on a Windows machine than on a Macintosh.

Tip

Mac users who want to set their system to 2.2 for Web or television work can do so if they have ColorSync enabled. Open the Monitors or Monitors and Sound Control Panel, click the Color button, and then follow the instructions to calibrate your display. Choose 2.2 as a gamma setting.

It's also worth noting that Windows machines are typically paired with much more diverse varieties of display hardware, while most Macs typically use a matching or even built-in display. Actual testing might lead us to find to find that typical Windows gamma varies more than typical Mac gamma; after all, we're talking about many different manufacturers instead of one Aiming squarely at 2.2 in your work won't necessarily guarantee that your work is viewed properly by all Windows users.

One solution to this problem—still, unfortunately, at the "coming soon" stage—can be found in Fireworks' native format, PNG. Images saved in a PNG format have built-in gamma correction so that they will be displayed correctly, regardless of the user's system. Although displaying a PNG image in a browser is old hat these days, support for the gamma correction elements of the format is still unavailable anywhere except in Internet Explorer for Windows.

In the future, the influence of Television on the Internet and the Internet on computing may result in a 2.2 gamma correction setting becoming standard on the Macintosh (I already run my Mac at this setting). For now, the best solution is to view your work under both settings and compromise a little when necessary in order to achieve acceptable results on both platforms. To aid in this, Fireworks provides a shortcut for viewing the "other" gamma setting: the Macintosh Gamma and Windows Gamma commands.

New Feature

Fireworks allows you to quickly and easily see how your work looks on the "other" common gamma correction setting. Fireworks for Windows can emulate the common Macintosh gamma setting of 1.8; while Fireworks for Macintosh can emulate the common Windows gamma of 2.2.

Choose View ➪ Macintosh Gamma in Fireworks for Windows in order to see a representation of what your work will look like on most Macs. Similarly, choose View ➪ Windows Gamma in Fireworks for Macintosh in order to view the way your work will look on most Windows machines.

Tip

Mac users: if you're using a gamma setting of 1.8 while preparing an image for Television, remember that Windows gamma is also TV gamma, so the Windows Gamma command doubles as a TV gamma preview.

Cross-Reference See the effects of Fireworks' new cross-platform gamma view in the color insert.

Working with color management

ColorSync (Macintosh only) and Kodak color management systems work with Photoshop and certain other applications to achieve accurate color representations across monitors, scanners, and printers. If you import an image from one of these applications into Fireworks, you may find that the color values are shifted slightly because Fireworks does not work with color management systems.

The easiest way to prevent this color shifting is to disable color management in the source application before exporting or saving an image. Alternatively, you can import the image into Fireworks and use the Hue slider on the Hue/Saturation Xtra to adjust all of the colors slightly, moving them all back to Web-safe values, for example.

Mixing Colors

The general color mechanism in Fireworks is the Color Mixer. With the Color Mixer, you can select your Fill and Stroke colors from the entire spectrum available to you in any of five different color models. You can also directly determine a color by entering the appropriate values through the sliders or text boxes.

Using the Color Mixer

To open the Color Mixer, choose Window ➪ Color Mixer or, in Windows, select the Color Mixer button from the Main toolbar. The Color Mixer, shown in Figure 7-1, is divided into three main areas:

✦ **Color wells:** The Stroke and Fill color wells display the active color for the selected object stroke and fill, respectively. The color defaults can also be applied and swapped through buttons in this section.

✦ **Color sliders:** Use the color sliders to choose a color by altering its components.

✦ **Color ramp:** The color ramp displays all colors of a particular color model and enables you to select them with an Eyedropper tool.

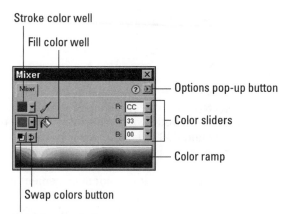

Stroke color well

Fill color well

Options pop-up button

Color sliders

Color ramp

Swap colors button

Default colors button

Figure 7-1: Open the Color Mixer to select your Stroke and Fill colors from the color ramp or set them with the color sliders.

Choosing a color

The Web artist alternates between creating new graphics fresh from the mind's eye and matching or adapting existing imagery. Both methods are valid ways of working, and Fireworks enables you to select the colors you need accordingly. Should you want to create visually, selecting your colors direct from the palette, you can sample colors either from a full-spectrum color ramp, the more limited showing of the active swatches, or directly off the screen from another image. If you'd prefer to work more formulaically, the color sliders enable you to enter a precise value in five different color models.

Using the color ramp

To select a color from the color ramp, follow these steps:

1. Open the Color Mixer by choosing Window ⇨ Color Mixer. Windows users can also select the Color Mixer button in the Main toolbar.

2. Select either the Stroke or Fill color well. The selected color well is highlighted with a border around it.

3. Move your pointer over the color ramp. The pointer changes into one of two Eyedropper tools. The Eyedropper tool with a wavy line indicates that a Stroke color is to be selected, whereas the Eyedropper tool with the solid block indicates that you're choosing a Fill color.

Tip

Initially, the color ramp display matches the chosen color model, such as RGB, Hexadecimal, or Grayscale. You can change the color ramp, however, by Shift+clicking it. With each Shift+click, the color ramp cycles through one of three displays: the Web-safe, full-color, and grayscale spectrums.

4. Choose any desired color in the color ramp by clicking it once.

Tip

If you click and drag your pointer across the color ramp, the wells and the slider settings update dynamically. This gives you a better idea of the actual color you're selecting — the swatch in the color well is large and the color values are easy to follow. If the color chosen is unsatisfactory, select Edit ➪ Undo in order to return to your previous setting.

5. After you've selected the color by releasing the mouse button, both the color well and sliders display the new color. If an object was selected when the new color was chosen, its Fill or Stroke color changes to match the new one.

Using Color Mixer sliders

Another method of selecting a color uses the Color Mixer sliders. As with other Fireworks sliders, you can enter the values either directly in the text boxes or by dragging the slider handle up or down. Which sliders are available depends upon the color model chosen. Sliders for RGB, CMY, and HSB all match their respective initials. Choosing the Hexadecimal model displays the R, G, and B color sliders. Selecting Grayscale shows just one slider, K, which represents the percentage of black.

If you're not trying to match a specific RGB or other value, you can visually — as opposed to numerically — mix your colors by moving the slider and watching the selected color well. If you have an object selected, its stroke or fill settings will update when you release the mouse button.

Accessing the color models

Aside from the previously described RGB and Hexadecimal, Fireworks offers three other possible color models. The capability to switch between different color models is important in Web design. Quite often the Web artist is asked to convert graphics from another medium, be it another computer-based medium or print. You can also switch from one system to another in order to take advantage of its special features. For example, switching the HSB enables you to select a tint of a particular color by reducing the saturation.

All color models are chosen by selecting the pop-up menu button in the upper-right corner of the Color Mixer. Choose a color model from the list that appears, as shown in Figure 7-2.

Figure 7-2: Choose from five different color models in the Color Mixer's pop-up menu.

RGB

Choosing the RGB color model enables you to select any one of 16.7 million colors that are available in the 24-bit color spectrum. Whereas not all of the colors are represented on the RGB color ramp (at a resolution of 72 pixels per inch, displaying all pixels would require over 19,000 square feet — that's a mighty big monitor), you can enter any required value in the color sliders shown in Figure 7-3. The color sliders use values from 0 to 255.

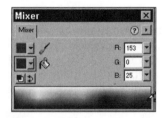

Figure 7-3: Work with the RGB color model to specify any one of 16.7 million colors.

Caution

If your computer display is not capable of showing as many colors as are viewable in the color model — for example, if your system is set on 256 colors and you choose RGB — you'll see some dithering in the color ramp. *Dithering* is the combination of two or more colors to simulate another color, and it appears as noticeable dots. However, although the display may dither, the colors that the Eyedropper tool chooses are accurate RGB values.

Hexadecimal

When you select the Hexadecimal color model, two things happen. The Color Mixer sliders translate their displayed values to hexadecimal values and the color ramp depicts a Web-safe spectrum, as shown in Figure 7-4. With a Web-safe color ramp (which is the default when Fireworks first starts up after installation), you'll notice what's referred to as *banding*. Banding occurs when the range of colors is not large enough to make a smooth gradation.

Caution

All values entered manually in the slider text boxes must be in the proper hexadecimal pair format. If you try to enter a numeric value outside of hexadecimal range, such as 225, Fireworks just drops the first number without properly converting the value.

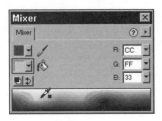

Figure 7-4: Although you can enter any valid hexadecimal RGB value in the color sliders with the Hexadecimal color model, only Web-safe colors are selectable in the default color ramp.

CMY

As mentioned previously, most designers coming from a print background are used to expressing color as a mixture of cyan, magenta, yellow, and black: CMYK, also known as the four-color process. In theory, the color range should be representable with just the first three colors, but in printing practice, the fourth color, black, is necessary to produce the darker colors.

Fireworks presents CMY colors as a range of numbers from 0 to 255. In some ways, CMY can be considered the opposite of RGB. RGB is referred to as an *additive* process because you add the colors together to reach white. CMY is a *subtractive* process because you take colors away to make white. When you choose CMY from the pop-up menu, the Color Mixer panel displays a slider for C (Cyan), one for M (Magenta), and one for Y (Yellow), as shown in Figure 7-5.

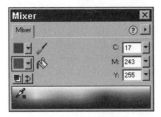

Figure 7-5: Print designers new to the Web will find the CMY color model familiar.

Fireworks isn't concerned with output to a print medium, so it can express the color spectrum with just cyan, magenta, and yellow, without resorting to the addition of black. This, however, does make it difficult to translate a CMYK color to a CMY color. The best workaround I've found is to use a common third model, such as RGB or a specific Pantone color.

HSB

HSB is short for Hue, Saturation, and Brightness. It is a color model available on numerous graphics programs, including Photoshop. Hue represents the color family, as seen on a color wheel. Because of the circular model, Hue values are presented in degrees from 0 to 360. Saturation determines the purity of the color, in terms of a percentage. A 100 percent saturation is equal to the purest version of any hue. The Brightness value, also expressed as a percentage, is the amount of light or dark in a color — 0 percent is black and 100 percent is the brightest that a color can appear. If the brightness is reduced to zero, the Hue and Saturation values are automatically reduced to zero, as well. After choosing HSB from the pop-up menu on the Color Mixer panel, the three sliders change to H, S, and B (Figure 7-6).

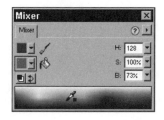

Figure 7-6: Use the HSB color model to easily lighten or darken a particular hue.

Don't attempt to directly translate HSB values from the similarly named HLS color model. HLS (Hue, Luminosity, and Saturation), a color model used in FreeHand and other drawing programs, also available in the Mac OS color picker, uses Luminosity rather than Brightness as its "light" component. The key difference between Luminosity and Brightness lies in how a color is affected at the higher end of the scale. In HSB, when full Brightness is combined with full Saturation, colors are at their most vivid. In HLS, full Luminosity, regardless of Saturation level, makes colors white.

Grayscale

Despite the richness of the realm of color — or maybe because of it — grayscale images have an undeniable power. Whether you're constructing graphics as a homage to black-and-white movies or blending black-and-white photographs in a full-color site, access to a grayscale palette is essential. Fireworks' grayscale palette is a full range of 256 tones, ranging from absolute white to absolute black.

When Grayscale is selected from the Color Mixer's pop-up menu, the three sliders of the other palette are reduced to one slider and marked K, for black. As shown in Figure 7-7, the black value is expressed as a percentage where 100 percent is black and 0 percent is white.

Figure 7-7: To access any one of 256 shades of gray, select the Grayscale color model.

Selecting Swatches of Color

Quite often the graphics for a Web site are designed with a particular palette in mind. The most common palette contains the 216 Web-safe colors, which is used to keep images from shifting colors on different platforms. Palettes are also devised to match a particular color scheme—either for an entire Web site or for one particular area. Each palette can be saved as a separate swatch file.

Fireworks provides very full palette support through its Swatches panel. Swatches can be modified, stored, loaded, or completely scrapped to start fresh. You can even grab the palette from a sample image.

Choosing from the color wells

The standard Fireworks pop-up color picker contains several tools. First, the Eyedropper tool enables you to select a color from any onscreen image—whether it's in Fireworks or part of another program. Next, the Palette button gives you instant access to your operating system's color picker(s). Finally, the No Color button can quickly set a stroke or fill to None, without your having to open their respective panels.

To access the colors in the current swatch set, select the arrow button next to any color well. When the pop-up color picker appears, as shown in Figure 7-8, move your pointer over any of the color swatches. As you move your pointer, you'll notice that the color chip in the upper-right corner dynamically updates to show the color underneath the pointer; the color name in hexadecimal is also displayed. Click once to choose a color.

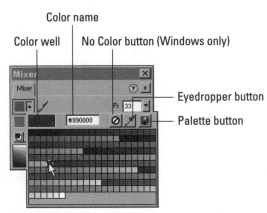

Figure 7-8: You can open the pop-up color picker from any color well in Fireworks.

Tip

If you've selected a color for a stroke or fill where previously there was none, Fireworks automatically enables the setting, turning the Stroke type to Pencil and the Fill type to Solid for the selected color.

Using the Eyedropper

The Eyedropper is a great tool for ensuring color fidelity across images. Need to match a particular shade of purple in the background graphic for the outline of the navigation bar you're building? Click once with the Eyedropper to grab that color; the selected color well is now filled with the chosen color.

The Eyedropper tool is straightforward to use. Once you've displayed the pop-up color picker, click once on the Eyedropper button; the pointer changes to its namesake shape. Now you can easily select a color from anywhere within Fireworks.

Moreover, the Eyedropper tool is not limited to sampling colors from Fireworks. You can pick up a color from any application or graphic displayed on your computer. There is, however, a slight difference in the way this feature works on each computing platform:

✦ With Macintosh systems, the Eyedropper works the same way outside of Fireworks as it does within Fireworks.

✦ With Windows systems, click and drag the Eyedropper tool from the pop-up color picker. Keep the mouse button held down as you move the mouse cursor outside of the Fireworks window. Release the mouse button when the cursor is over the color you want to sample.

Tip

It's possible — even likely — that the color you sample with the Eyedropper won't be Web-safe. To snap the sampled color to the closest Web-safe value, press Shift when you select your color.

Accessing the system color picker(s)

If you work with a number of graphics applications, you may find it more convenient to work with your operating system's color picker(s) than with those in Fireworks. To open the system color picker(s), click the Palette button on the Fireworks color picker. Closing the system color picker(s) automatically assigns the last selected color to the Fireworks color well.

The Macintosh system color picker dialog box has several color pickers from which to choose. These different schemes are detailed in Table 7-2.

Table 7-2
Color Models in the Macintosh Color Picker Dialog Box

Color Model	Description
CMYK	Standard model for color printing
Crayon	A box of crayons with names like Banana and Cool Marble. Click a crayon to select that color
HLS	Hue, Luminosity, and Saturation
HSV	Hue, Saturation, and Value model with a color wheel
HTML	RGB expressed in hexadecimal numbers, with an optional Web-safe snap
RGB	Standard model for computer displays, with an optional Web-safe snap

Choose a color model from the left part of the color picker dialog box, as shown in Figure 7-9, and specify settings on the right. The color that the Fireworks color picker is set to is shown in the upper right of the window as the "original" color, for comparison with the color you're currently choosing.

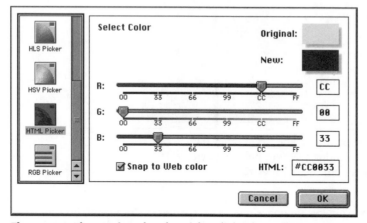

Figure 7-9: The Macintosh color picker dialog box offers numerous color models from which to choose.

Tip

If you hold down Option while you're in the Macintosh color picker dialog box, the cursor will change into an Eyedropper tool (just like in Fireworks). Use it to sample colors from anywhere on the screen.

In addition to these seven default color pickers, the Macintosh color picker system is extensible, so you may have other color pickers depending on the hardware and software you have installed. Color pickers are installed by Apple Display Software, for example, or you may have installed a third-party color picker yourself. My favorite—no pun intended—is FVPicker, available from <http://www.at-soft. net>, which enables you to store your favorite colors for easy recall.

The Windows system color picker is split into two parts, as shown in Figure 7-10. On the left, you'll find 48 color chips from the Windows system palette. Located on the right is a full-color spectrum with a value bar, for mixing colors. Both RGB and Hue, Saturation, and Luminance text boxes are available below the spectrum. To choose a color beyond the basic 48, you must create it by choosing a color from both the main spectrum and the value bar on the right and then add it to one of the 16 the custom color wells on the left.

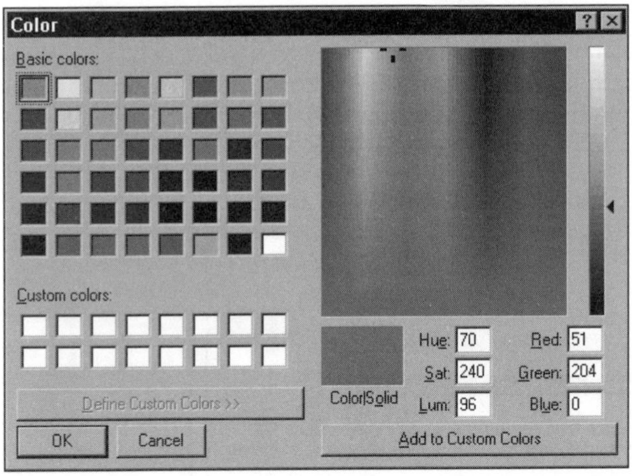

Figure 7-10: The Windows color picker offers easy access to colors from the Windows system palette, or create 16 of your own colors from the full spectrum.

Tip

In order to avoid overwriting a previously created custom color, be sure to select an empty custom color well in the Windows color picker before creating a new custom color.

Opting for no color

When it comes to stroke and fill colors, it's important to remember that "no color" is as valid an option as any color. To disable a fill or a stroke, just choose the No Color button from the Fireworks color picker. When you select the No Color button, the color chip displays the checkerboard pattern used to depict transparency in Fireworks.

Note The No Color button is available in the pop-up color pickers that are called from the Stroke and Fill color wells found in the Toolbox, but not on the other pop-up color pickers. On Windows, the No Color button can also be found in the color picker in the Color Mixer panel.

Using the Swatches panel

The Swatches panel is deceptively simple in appearance. Consisting of just colors (with the exception of the pop-up menu button), the Swatches panel enables you to choose a stroke, fill, or effect color from the active palette. Like all other Fireworks floating panels, the Swatches panel can be moved and resized — the latter feature is especially important if you want to show a larger palette.

Caution It's important to remember that the Swatches panel displays the current Fireworks palette, not the palette of the current document.

The most basic use of the Swatches panel is similar to that of the Color Mixer and the pop-up color picker. Select the color well you want to alter and then choose a color by clicking any of the color chips in the Swatches panel, as shown in Figure 7-11. There's no real feedback in the Swatches panel to identify the color other than visually; you'd need to have the Info panel visible to see the RGB or other components.

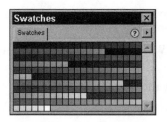

Figure 7-11: Pick a color, any color, from the Swatches panel.

As you'll see in the next section, you can choose from a number of preset color palettes. However, you can also add any custom mixed color — or color selected with the Eyedropper — to a swatch. The custom color then becomes available from anywhere in the program where you can click a color well or access the Swatch panel. New colors can be added, extending an existing palette or replacing a color on the palette. You can also delete standard or custom colors from a palette.

To add, replace, or remove a color in the Swatches panel, follow these steps:

1. Mix or sample the color you want to add so that it appears in the active color well.

2. Display the Swatches panel by choosing Window ⇨ Swatches or by clicking the Swatches tab if the panel is behind other panels in a group.

3. To add a new color to the current palette, position your pointer over an open area in the Swatches panel and click once. When over an open area, the Eyedropper pointer becomes a paint bucket.

4. To replace an existing color in the current palette, press Shift while you position your pointer over the color to be replaced and click once. If you press Shift when the pointer is positioned over an existing color, the pointer becomes a paint bucket.

5. To remove a color from the current palette, hold down Ctrl (Command), position the pointer over the color to be deleted, and click once. When you press Ctrl (Command), the pointer becomes a pair of scissors. For best results, position the scissors so that the crossing of the blades — the middle of the X — is placed directly over the color you want to delete.

To reset any standard palette that has been modified, select that palette from the pop-up menu.

Picking preset swatches

Fireworks has four standard palettes that you can select at any time:

✦ **Web 216 Palette:** Colors common between both major browsers, Netscape Navigator and Internet Explorer, on Macintosh and Windows

✦ **Windows System:** The color palette used by Windows to display its system elements

✦ **Macintosh System:** The color palette used by the Macintosh operating system

✦ **Grayscale:** A monochrome palette ranging from white to black

All palettes with the exception of Web 216 are composed of 256 colors

To switch palettes, select a different one from the Swatches panel's pop-up menu, as shown in Figure 7-12.

One additional palette is available from the pop-up menu: the Current Export palette. Choosing this option loads the current document's export palette from the Color Table panel — detailed later in this chapter — into the Swatches panel.

Figure 7-12: The Swatches panel's pop-up menu enables you to select different standard palettes or to load your own.

Managing swatches

The real power of Fireworks swatches is in the capability to load and store custom palettes. The remaining five commands on the pop-up menu are dedicated to managing swatches. Fireworks can load and save palettes in a format known as Active Color Table (ACT). Adobe Photoshop can also read and write ACT files, so it's easy to load Photoshop palettes in Fireworks.

However, you don't have to save your palettes as ACT files in order to work with them in the Swatch panel. Fireworks can also glean the palette from any GIF or other 8-bit indexed color file. Moreover, you have two different ways to access a previously stored palette. You can either append the saved palette to the current swatch, or you can use just the saved palette.

To load palettes into the Swatches panel, follow these steps:

1. In the Swatches panel, click the pop-up menu button.

2. If you want to extend the existing palette with a new palette, choose Add Swatches.

3. If you want to use the just saved palette, choose Replace Swatches.

   In either case, the Open dialog box appears for you to select a palette.

4. Choose the type of palette you wish to load:

   • Color table (filename typically ends in .act)

   Note On the Mac, a color table file may not have (and doesn't require) the .act filename extension. Color table files have a File Type code of 8BCT. Although Fireworks doesn't provide an icon for its color table files, color table files saved by Photoshop have an icon with color wells and the description CLUT on them.

   • GIF files (filename ends in .gif)

5. Locate the file and click Open when you're ready.

If you chose Add Swatches, the new palette is appended to the end of the existing Swatch. If Replace Swatches is used, the existing swatch is removed and the new palette is displayed in its place.

Tip   Although the feature is a bit hidden, you can also load Adobe Swatches in addition to Adobe Color Tables. Adobe Swatches have a file extension of .aco, rather than the Color Tables extension of .act. Fireworks for Windows only offers the ACT file type in its Open dialog boxes; enter ***.aco** in the File Name text box and press Return in order to force the dialog box to list files with the filename extension .aco.

In Fireworks, all palettes are saved in Active Color Table format. To save a current swatch, simply choose Save Swatches from the pop-up menu and name the file in the standard Save As dialog box.

You can erase the entire palette from the Swatches panel by choosing Clear Swatches from the pop-up menu. This removes any palette displayed in the Swatches panel, but it doesn't affect the default palettes at all. If you do issue the Clear Swatches command, the color wells revert to using the default Web-safe palette in the pop-up color pickers.

The final pop-up menu command in the Swatches panel is Sort by Color. As the name implies, Sort by Color displays the active palette by color value rather than by the default mathematical order. If new colors have been added — or a completely new palette loaded — those colors are sorted, as well. Please note that there is no way to undo a Sort by Color command; to restore a standard palette to its previous configuration, choose the particular palette from the pop-up menu.

Accessing the Color Table

If you've specified a reduced export palette in the Optimize panel — generally by specifying to export as a GIF — then the current document's export palette will be reduced accordingly and won't match any standard palette. The Color Table panel offers easy access to the export palette.

New Feature   In keeping with the new preview-in-place paradigm of Fireworks 3, the export palette of the current image is available right in the workspace, located in the Color Table panel.

To display the Color Table panel, shown in Figure 7-13, choose Window ➪ Color Table or click the Color Table tab if the Color Table panel is docked behind another panel.

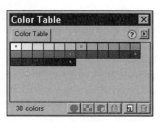

Figure 7-13: The Color Table panel enables you to access the current document's export palette.

If you've carefully reduced the export palette for your document to 16 or 32 colors, you probably don't need or want access to colors outside that range while you're still working with the document. Accidentally adding a new color at this point may simply undo optimization work you've already done. In the later stages of working with a GIF image, I'll often use the Swatches panel to load the export palette and then choose my colors there.

If the Color Table displays the message "(Rebuild)" in its title bar, the colors it's displaying are "out of date" because you've made some modification to the export palette in the Optimize panel. Choose Rebuild Color Table from the pop-up menu. Menu items on the pop-up menu — as well as the buttons along the bottom of the Color Table panel — enable you to add, remove, edit and lock colors as required.

For more about working with the Color Table panel, see Chapter 15.

Fireworks Technique: Converting Pantone Colors to Web-Safe Colors

Many Web designers have clients with specific concerns regarding the use of their logos, trademarks, and other brand identifiers. Many larger companies have spent large amounts of money to develop a distinct look in their print, television, and other-media advertising and marketing — and they want to ensure that their look continues over the Internet. Most designers work with a set series of colors — Pantone colors are among the most popular — that can be specified for print work. It should come as no surprise to discover that many of these colors fall outside of the Web-safe palette of 216 colors.

There is a way, however, to bring the two seemingly divergent worlds together. In fact, there are several ways. Pantone makes a product called ColorWeb Pro that converts their colors so they are usable in computer graphics. ColorWeb Pro is a small utility that enables you to look up a Pantone color by number and then displays a color chip with the equivalent RGB and/or HTML color values.

ColorWeb Pro runs in two modes: the Pantone Matching System, which allows you to choose from all 1,012 Pantone colors; and the Pantone Internet Color System, which converts your choice to a Web-safe color before sending it to Fireworks. If you're satisfied with a simple conversion from Pantone to Web-safe, use the Internet Color System to choose a Pantone color and convert it to Web-safe.

To get a more accurate representation of a Pantone color, you can combine the Pantone Matching System with Fireworks' Web Dither fill, sampling a Pantone color and allowing Fireworks to create a Web Dither equivalent. This opens many of the Pantone colors for use on the Internet where it counts the most — in the fill areas. Though this system is not perfect — I occasionally find Pantone colors that do not have a good duplicate in the Web Dither mode — it's quite close.

In Windows, ColorWeb Pro runs as an application that is basically a floating color chip. Double-clicking this chip opens the Pantone color pickers. Right-clicking the chip displays a context menu that enables you to specify options.

On the Mac, ColorWeb Pro simply installs its color pickers into the Mac's extensible color picker dialog box. Access these new color pickers as you would access any other system-level color picker: choose the Palette button from the Fireworks color picker or choose Add Color from the Color Table panel.

Caution Mac users may find that they already have Pantone color pickers because they were installed by ColorSync or Apple Display Software. In this case, installing the ColorWeb Pro demo overwrites your Pantone color pickers, necessitating a reinstall of ColorSync or Apple Display Software if you don't purchase ColorWeb Pro after the demo times out.

Using ColorWeb Pro for Windows

To convert a Pantone color to a Web Dither color in Fireworks for Windows, follow these steps:

1. Start ColorWeb Pro.

2. If the Pantone color chip doesn't stay on top of Fireworks, right-click (Control-click) the color chip and enable Stay on Top from the shortcut menu. Because you'll be working with both Fireworks and ColorWeb Pro, you need to see both programs simultaneously.

3. Double-click the Pantone color chip in order to display the Pantone Color Picker, as shown in Figure 7-14.

4. Locate the desired color either by entering its number in the Find Color text box or by selecting it. Click OK when you're done in order to return to the color chip.

5. Select the object you want to fill with a Pantone color.

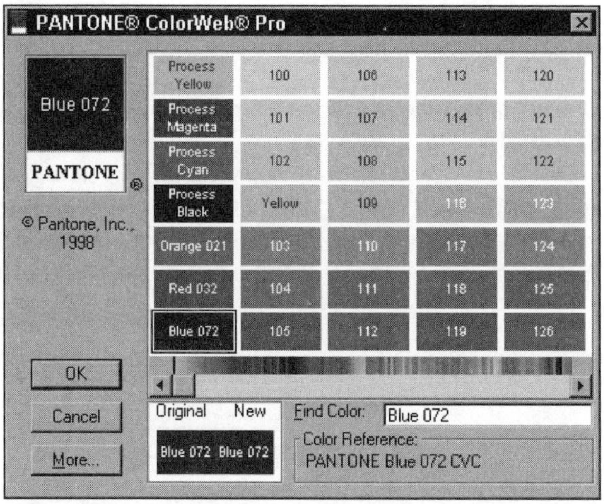

Figure 7-14: ColorWeb Pro offers you an extensive palette of Pantone colors.

6. Display the Fill panel by choosing Window ➪ Fill or use the key shortcut Ctrl+Alt+F.

7. Select the Fill color well arrow in order to open the pop-up color picker and choose the Eyedropper tool.

Caution Be sure to pick the main color well (the top one) and not either of the two dither color wells.

8. Use the Eyedropper to sample the Pantone color chip. Windows users must click the Eyedropper while it's over Fireworks, drag it to the Pantone color chip and then release to sample the color.

Fireworks calculates the closest match using the Web Dither technique. If the Pantone color is Web safe, both dither color wells hold the same color.

Using ColorWeb Pro for Macintosh

To convert a Pantone color to a Web Dither color in Fireworks for Macintosh, follow these steps:

1. Select the object you want to fill with a Pantone color.

2. Display the Fill panel by choosing Window ➪ Fill or use the key shortcut Command+Option+F.

3. Choose the Web Dither category from the Fill panel.

4. Open the Fill panel color picker and choose the Palette button in order to display the Macintosh color picker dialog box.

Caution   Make sure to choose the Fill panel color picker from the upper color well, not the lower Web dither color wells.

5. Select the Pantone DC (Pantone Digital Color) color picker from the left part of the Macintosh color picker dialog box, as shown in Figure 7-15. Choose the desired color on the right by entering its number in the text box or by selecting it. Click Done.

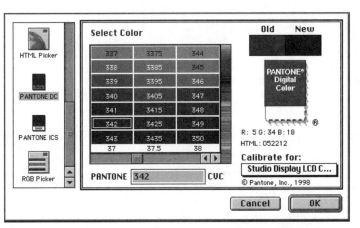

Figure 7-15: ColorWeb Pro offers you an extensive palette of Pantone colors within the Macintosh color picker dialog box.

Fireworks calculates the closest match using the Web Dither technique. If the Pantone color is Web safe, both dither color wells hold the same color.

Summary

Fireworks offers brisk color control, enabling the designer to select from the overall color model and specific palette that best serves. In Fireworks 3, color manipulation has been greatly simplified with the introduction of the pop-up color picker, available from any color well. As you begin to delve deeper into color with your Fireworks graphics, considers these points:

✦ RGB is the language of color for the screen. Pixels depend on a mixture of red, green, and blue in order to achieve their color variations. HTML uses hexadecimal notation to designate RGB colors.

✦ Fireworks enables you to switch between several color models, such as Hexadecimal, RGB, CMY, and grayscale.

✦ To ensure that your colors appear the same regardless of which browser you use to view them, work with Web-safe colors. Fireworks allows you to choose a Web-safe palette to pick colors from, and it enables you to snap selected colors to their nearest Web-safe equivalent.

✦ Fireworks uses three floating panels for color control: the Color Mixer, the Swatches panel, and the Color Table panel. The Color Mixer enables the designer to specify a new custom color or to modify an existing one. The Swatches panel displays a series of color chips that can come from a standard palette, such as Web 216, or from a custom palette. The Color Table panel displays the current document's export palette.

✦ The Eyedropper tool in the pop-up color picker can sample colors from any onscreen image, whether the image is in Fireworks or another application.

In the next chapter, you'll explore working with the fine lines of Fireworks graphics — strokes.

✦   ✦   ✦

Choosing Strokes

✦   ✦   ✦   ✦

In This Chapter

Applying strokes

Mastering the Stroke panel

Working with graphics tablets

Investigating with the standard strokes

Creating custom strokes

Fireworks technique: building a dotted stroke

Stroke orientation

✦   ✦   ✦   ✦

Strokes are one of the three key features of a Fireworks document. Along with fills and effects, strokes can give each element its own unique character. The stroke is what makes a path visible. It's far more than just "visibility," however — you can vary a stroke's width, color, softness, and shape, as well as control how it reacts to the speed, pressure, and direction of your drawing. Moreover, you can modify strokes already applied to any selected path and instantly see the results.

In addition to 48 built-in, standard strokes in Fireworks, you can customize your strokes with an almost infinite set of variations. Numerous options, such as color, stroke width, and edge softness, exist right on the Strokes panel for easy experimentation. Additionally, Fireworks enables you to custom build your own stroke from the ground up. You'll find explanations for all of the controls in this chapter, as well as step-by-step instructions for developing special strokes, such as dotted lines.

Using the Stroke Panel

The Stroke panel is your control center for all stroke settings. Though you can set the stroke color in two other places, the Toolbox and the Color Mixer, the Stroke panel is the only place to select all of the options.

Here's the typical process for setting up or modifying an existing stroke that uses all of the options available on the Stroke panel:

1. Choose Window ⇨ Stroke to open the Stroke panel (Figure 8-1). Alternatively, you can use the keyboard shortcut, Ctrl+Alt+B (Command+Option+B) or choose the Stroke tab, if it's onscreen.

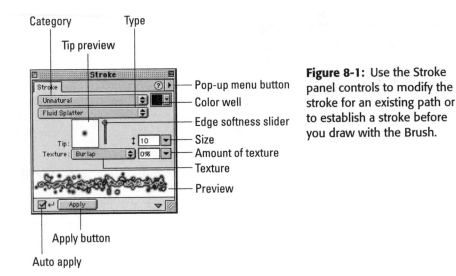

Category   Type

Tip preview

Pop-up menu button
Color well
Edge softness slider
Size
Amount of texture
Texture
Preview

Apply button

Auto apply

Figure 8-1: Use the Stroke panel controls to modify the stroke for an existing path or to establish a stroke before you draw with the Brush.

2. Select one of the 11 categories from the Category option list. To turn off the stroke, select None from the Category option list.

3. Choose any of the available types listed for each category from the Type option list. When you choose a type, the default settings for that type's size, edge softness, and texture are also selected.

4. If desired, select a new color from the stroke color well.

5. To change how the stroke blends, use the Edge Softness slider.

6. Alter the size of the stroke by using the Size slider or by entering a value directly in the Size text box. As you move the Edge Softness or Size slider, Fireworks previews the stroke. If the Apply check box is selected, changes are instantly reflected on a selected path.

7. Add a texture by choosing one from the Texture option list and setting its opacity through the Amount of texture slider.

As noted previously, you can either modify the stroke for an existing, selected path, or you can set up the stroke before you draw. To select a path, with or without a stroke already applied, first move the Pointer tool over the desired path and then click the highlighted path once. The path displays a red highlight if it is capable of being selected and, by default, a light-blue highlight after it has been selected.

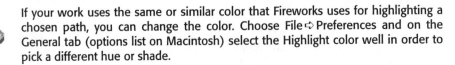

Tip   If your work uses the same or similar color that Fireworks uses for highlighting a chosen path, you can change the color. Choose File ➪ Preferences and on the General tab (options list on Macintosh) select the Highlight color well in order to pick a different hue or shade.

Sometimes it's easier to select the path for stroke modification by using the marquee feature of the Pointer tool. If you click and drag the Pointer, a temporary rectangle is drawn out. Any paths touched by this rectangle are selected. The Pointer marquee is a great way to select multiple paths if you want to simultaneously change the stroke settings for several paths. Alternatively, pressing Shift enables you to select multiple paths, one at a time, with the Pointer tool.

Tip You can quickly switch to the Pointer tool from any other tool by pressing and holding Ctrl (Command). When you release the key, the previously selected tool returns.

When you're setting up your next stroke, be sure that no path or object is selected — otherwise, that selected object will be modified if Auto Apply is enabled. Use the Pointer to click an empty canvas area or choose Edit ➭ Deselect — or its keyboard equivalent, Ctrl+D (Command+D) — to clear any previous selections.

Stroke categories and types

With the None option, Fireworks offers a dozen stroke categories. From the simplest, Pencil and Basic; to the most outrageous, Random and Unnatural, the stroke categories run the gamut, as evident in Figure 8-2. When you select a category, that category's types become available, with the first one in an alphabetical list chosen.

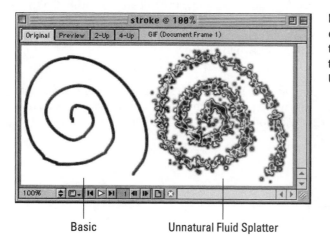

Basic   Unnatural Fluid Splatter

Figure 8-2: Choose any of the preset stroke types — from the Basic to the farthest out Unnatural Fluid Splatter.

The standard strokes are covered in detail later in this chapter, but two primary factors apply to all of the basic strokes. First, when a particular stroke category and type are selected, the default settings for that stroke are selected — even if you just modified it seconds ago and are returning from trying out another stroke. Second, every facet of all of the standard strokes can be modified, altered, and adjusted.

Cross-
Reference

Later in this chapter, in the section "Creating New Strokes," you'll see how to store and reuse a modified stroke.

Stroke edge and size

If you're reading this book in sequence, you've already discovered the concept of feathering as it relates to bitmap images in Chapter 6. As you'll remember, a feathered edge is one that blends into the background. Strokes can be "feathered" through the Edge Softness slider found in the Stroke panel. Moving the slider all the way to the bottom creates the hardest edge, with no blending, whereas sliding it to the top creates the softest edge, with maximum blending for the current stroke size.

As in feathering, edge softness is actually an application of the alpha channel, which controls transparency. There are 256 degrees of transparency in the alpha channel and only 100 degrees of edge softness, but the overall control is similar. Although you can select any degree of softness from the full range for any stroke, you won't see much of a difference if the stroke is thin. The thicker the stroke, the more softness variations are apparent. At the softest setting, Fireworks maintains roughly two-thirds of the stroke size. The object's opacity and the other one-third is blended into transparency equally on either side of the stroke.

You can change the thickness of a stroke either by entering a value in the Size box or by using the Size slider to select from the range of possible values: 1 to 72 pixels wide. The Tip preview is not big enough to show the full stroke width. On the Mac, the Tip preview stops being useful at about 50 pixels and just goes black; on Windows you'll notice "2x" or "4x" appears after about 50 pixels to indicate the actual width of large strokes, as shown in Figure 8-3.

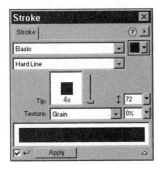

Figure 8-3: When you select a stroke size larger than the Tip preview can display, the Windows version of Fireworks compensates numerically.

Stroke texture

Applying texture to a stroke can give a line true character and depth. Fireworks comes with 26 standard textures built-in and a library of 21 more on the CD-ROM. Each of these textures can be applied to any stroke with a variable degree of intensity. Some of the preset strokes, such as the Textured Air Brush or the Basic Crayon, use a texture to create their distinctive look.

To apply a texture to a stroke, follow these steps:

1. On the Stroke panel, select the category and type of stroke to which you want to apply the texture.

2. If necessary, set the size, color, and edge softness for the stroke. Note: Many textures will not be apparent if the stroke width is too small.

3. Choose a texture from the Texture option list.

4. Set a degree of intensity for the Texture from the Amount of texture slider. You can also enter a percentage value (with or without the percent sign) into the Amount of texture text box.

 Note   You must enter a percentage value greater than 0 percent or no texture will be visible.

Textures, in effect, are image patterns that are overlaid on top of the stroke. The Amount of texture slider controls how transparent or opaque those textures become. At 0 percent, the texture is transparent and, for all intents and purposes, nonexistent. At 100 percent, the texture is as visible as possible. Figure 8-4 displays the same stroke with several variations of a single texture. As a general rule, textures containing highly contrasting elements show up better, whereas those with less contrast are more subtle and probably only useful on extremely thick strokes.

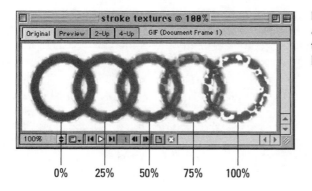

Figure 8-4: The higher the amount of the texture value, the more visible the texture becomes.

 On the CD-ROM   Can't get enough of those fabulous textures? You'll find another 50, courtesy of Massimo Foti and the Fantastic Corporation, in the Textures folder of the CD-ROM.

Using a Graphics Tablet

Using a mouse to create objects is often derided as being like "drawing with a bar of soap," and for good reason. In the past, graphics tablets — flat panels that you draw on with a pen-like stylus — were often expensive, insensitive, and unwieldy. But, like most technologies, graphics tablets have steadily become cheaper and better. These days, there are a range of sizes and specifications available for any Macintosh or Windows computer. For beginners or casual use, Wacom's Graphire is a 4 × 5-inch tablet that hardly costs more than a mouse. Wacom's professional range of Intuos tablets extends from 4 × 5 inches to 12 × 18 inches with features and options to satisfy any artist. However, a 4 × 5-inch tablet can be quite acceptable for the typically small canvases used for Web graphics.

There's really almost no learning curve to using a graphics tablet with Fireworks. Everything works as with the mouse, except that you have far more control. The first advantage is the accuracy provided by the tablet's one-to-one relationship with areas on the screen. The classic test is a signature — try signing your name with a mouse and then with a pen and tablet — there's a world of difference because similar horizontal and vertical movements of the mouse don't correspond to similar movements of the mouse pointer.

The more obvious advantage is that you're drawing with a pen, and the pressure that you apply directly affects the appearance of the strokes that you create. Press down harder and you'll get a heavier line, or use a lighter touch for a softer line. This often leads to a slightly more imperfect, or "human" look to the graphics that you create, and the imperfect appearance can be quite pleasing. Many standard Fireworks strokes are sensitive to pressure, including all of the Air Brush, Calligraphy, Charcoal, Oil, and Watercolor presets. How strokes respond to pressure is also adjustable, as you'll see later in this chapter when you look at how to create strokes.

Even if you're not much of an artist, I find that selecting tools, and drawing rectangles and ovals is easier with a graphics tablet. After a short while, you'll find yourself "reaching" for objects on your canvas without having to look at them or track them down with a mouse because they're always in the same place on your tablet. It's an intuitive and creative way to assemble computer graphics.

If you don't have a tablet, you can simulate increased or decreased pressure with your keyboard. Press 1 to decrease the pressure and 2 to increase it. Be aware, however, that unlike a graphics tablet, the pressure doesn't even out when you stop drawing. If you press 1 three times to decrease the pressure, the pressure will continue to be light until you press 2 three times to restore it to its default state or until you relaunch Fireworks.

Working with the Built-in Strokes

One of the key advantages of Fireworks' preset strokes is speed — just pick one and go. The other main advantage is consistency. You can use the Textured Air Brush time and again, and you'll always get the same effect. Even if you prefer to work only with custom strokes, you generally begin the creation process with one of the standard ones.

This section explores each of the stroke categories and the different presets each one offers. Fireworks starts the stroke categories with two of the simplest, Pencil and Basic. After these, the list proceeds alphabetically from Air Brush to Unnatural. The overall impression, however, is that the more often-used standard strokes are found at the top of the list, and the more elaborate decorative strokes at the end.

Pencil

When you start to draw with the Pencil tool, the path is rendered in the Pencil 1-Pixel Hard stroke, regardless of any previous stroke settings for other tools. If you use the Brush and no stroke settings have been established, you get the same Pencil 1-Pixel Hard stroke. You might say that the Pencil is one of the real workhorses of the preset strokes.

The Pencil is a fairly generic stroke, intended to give a simple representation to any path without any embellishments. You can see the differences between its four presets, listed in Table 8-1, and depicted in Figure 8-5. The 1-Pixel Soft Pencil stroke anti-aliases the path to avoid the jaggies that may be apparent with the 1-Pixel Hard setting. The Colored Pencil, at four pixels, is slightly wider and is designed to be affected by pressure and speed in the same way that a real colored pencil would be affected. The final preset, Graphite, is also affected by the pressure and speed at which the paths are drawn; in addition, a high degree of texture is added to further break up the stroke.

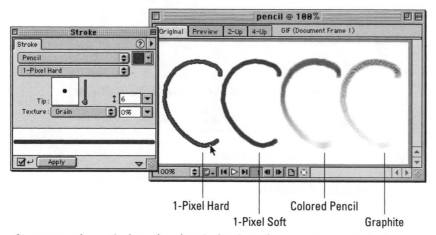

Figure 8-5: The 1-Pixel Hard and 1-Pixel Soft strokes remain constant when drawn, but the Colored Pencil and Graphite strokes are affected by pressure and speed.

Table 8-1
Pencil Type Attributes

Name	Size	Edge Softness	Texture	Amount of Texture
1-Pixel Hard	1	0 percent	None	n/a
1-Pixel Soft	1	0 percent	None	n/a
Colored Pencil	4	0 percent	None	n/a
Graphite	4	0 percent	Grain	80 percent

Basic

Another, slightly heavier variation of the simple path is the appropriately named Basic stroke. All of the Basic presets, detailed in Table 8-2, are 4 pixels wide and vary only with the basic shape of the line (square or round) and its anti-alias setting. Hard Line and Hard Line Rounded are not anti-aliased, whereas both Soft Line and Soft Line Rounded are. The variations, shown in Figure 8-6, are subtle, but can make quite a difference on some objects.

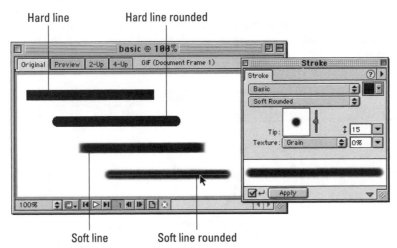

Figure 8-6: You can see the differences between the four Basic stroke types when you look closely at them.

Table 8-2
Basic Type Attributes

Name	Size	Edge Softness	Texture	Amount of Texture
Hard Line	4	0 percent	None	n/a
Hard Line Rounded	4	0 percent	None	n/a
Soft Line	4	0 percent	None	n/a
Soft Line Rounded	4	0 percent	None	n/a

Air Brush

I'll fess up—I'm an airbrush addict. I can't get enough of the variations that the Fireworks Air Brush stroke offers. Both presets (Table 8-3) are very sensitive to changes in speed and pressure, plus—like a real airbrush—the ink builds up if you stay in one spot, as seen in Figure 8-7. The Textured Air Brush is significantly different from the Basic Air Brush and offers a good example of what's possible when applying a texture to a stroke.

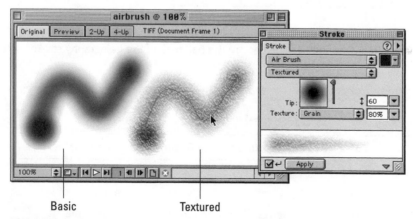

Basic   Textured

Figure 8-7: The difference between the two Air Brush presets is quite noticeable, as is the build-up on each at the end of the two strokes.

Table 8-3
Air Brush Type Attributes

Name	Size	Edge Softness	Texture	Amount of Texture
Basic	60	100 percent	None	n/a
Textured	50	100 percent	Grain	80 percent

Calligraphy

Calligraphy is an elegant handwriting art in which the thickness of a stroke varies as a line curves. The Calligraphy stroke in Fireworks offers five variations on this theme, as detailed in Table 8-4 and shown in Figure 8-8. Only the Bamboo preset does not create distinct thick-and-thin curved lines — that's because all the others use a slanted brush, whereas Bamboo's brush is circular, like a bamboo stalk. The Quill preset is pressure- and speed-sensitive and, along with the Ribbon and Wet presets, builds up ink as it rounds a curve, emphasizing the angles.

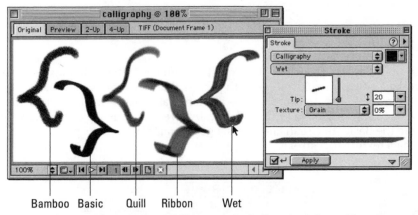

Bamboo Basic   Quill   Ribbon   Wet

Figure 8-8: Great lettering possibilities are the hallmark of the Calligraphy stroke.

Table 8-4
Calligraphy Type Attributes

Name	Size	Edge Softness	Texture	Amount of Texture
Bamboo	20	0 percent	Grain	50 percent
Basic	14	0 percent	None	n/a
Quill	20	20 percent	Grain	25 percent
Ribbon	25	0 percent	None	n/a
Wet	20	0 percent	None	n/a

Charcoal

The Charcoal strokes are notable for their textures, both within the strokes themselves and on their edges. As you can see in Table 8-5, each preset uses some degree of Grain texture. The Creamy and Pastel presets vary according to a stroke's pressure and speed — Creamy more so than Pastel. The key difference between the

Soft preset and the other preset strokes is that with the Soft preset the size of the brush changes randomly as you draw—the width fluctuates from a maximum of 20 pixels to a minimum of 5 pixels. Figure 8-9 shows a side-by-side comparison of the Charcoal presets.

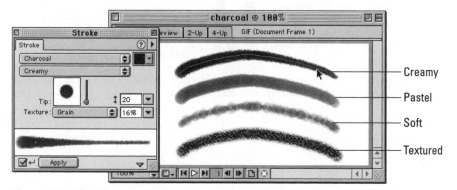

Figure 8-9: The Charcoal strokes offer a range of rough textures.

Table 8-5 Charcoal Type Attributes				
Name	*Size*	*Edge Softness*	*Texture*	*Amount of Texture*
Creamy	20	0 percent	Grain	16 percent
Pastel	20	0 percent	Grain	24 percent
Soft	20	20 percent	Grain	30 percent
Textured	20	60 percent	Grain	85 percent

Crayon

Kids can never understand why their parents like to draw with crayons as much as they do. The Crayon stroke in Fireworks captures that broken edge that gives real-world crayons character. The three Crayon presets are interesting to compare; if you look at the samples in Figure 8-10 and their details in Table 8-6, you'll see an obvious anomaly. The Rake preset has the smallest stroke size, but actually appears slightly thicker than both the Basic and Thick preset. This difference is because the Rake preset uses four tip; it's as if you were simultaneously drawing with four crayons. Because there are four tips, the lines overlap, and one tip can extend farther than the other three.

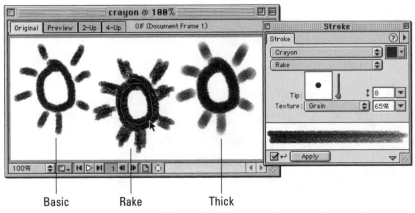

Basic   Rake   Thick

Figure 8-10: Return to your childhood — this time with scientific precision — through the Crayon strokes.

Table 8-6
Crayon Type Attributes

Name	Size	Edge Softness	Texture	Amount of Texture
Basic	12	0 percent	Grain	65 percent
Rake	8	0 percent	Grain	65 percent
Thick	20	0 percent	Grain	20 percent

Felt Tip

The four presets for the Felt Tip stroke, shown in Figure 8-11, offer different degrees of transparency that mimic the real-world drawing implements they're named after. The Highlighter and the Light Marker presets are largely transparent, in fact. The Light Marker also uses a slightly softer edge than the other presets, as noted in Table 8-7.

Table 8-7
Felt Tip Type Attributes

Name	Size	Edge Softness	Texture	Amount of Texture
Dark Marker	8	0 percent	None	n/a
Highlighter	16	0 percent	None	n/a
Light Marker	12	5 percent	None	n/a
Thin	4	0 percent	None	n/a

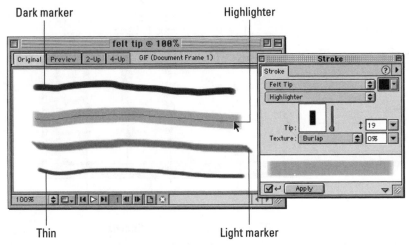

Figure 8-11: The various Felt Tip strokes achieve transparent and opaque effects when used over graphics or images.

Oil

When you look at the five Oil stroke presets in Figure 8-12, it's hard to believe that the second stroke from the left, Broad Splatter, is a single stroke. Although the size for Broad Splatter is only ten pixels — the same as for the Bristle and Splatter presets, all shown in Table 8-8 — the larger width is because it uses two tips instead of one, and they're spaced 500 percent apart. In other words, the Broad Splatter preset can be five times the width of its pixel size. All but the Splatter preset use multiple tips, as well, but because they're set to be less than 100 percent apart, the strokes appear as single lines.

Table 8-8
Oil Type Attributes

Name	Size	Edge Softness	Texture	Amount of Texture
Bristle	10	0 percent	Grain	20 percent
Broad Splatter	10	0 percent	Grain	30 percent
Splatter	10	0 percent	Grain	30 percent
Strands	8	43 percent	None	n/a
Textured Bristles	7	0 percent	Grain	50 percent

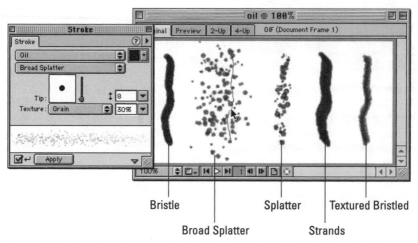

Figure 8-12: Looking for a stroke that doesn't look like a line? Try the Oil Splatter and Oil Broad Splatter presets.

Watercolor

Like any of the pressure and speed sensitive strokes, you can't get a true Watercolor feel if you draw using one of the geometric shapes; you have to use a freeform tool such as the Brush to achieve the more realistic look apparent in Figure 8-13. The Thin preset especially appears to run out of ink when completing a stroke. Both the Heavy and Thick presets are quite transparent and blend well when applied over an image because of their relatively soft edges (Table 8-9).

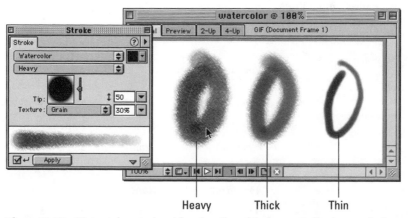

Figure 8-13: Watercolor strokes blend well and fade naturally due to their pressure and speed sensitivity.

		Table 8-9 **Watercolor Type Attributes**		
Name	**Size**	**Edge Softness**	**Texture**	**Amount of Texture**
Heavy	50	50 percent	Grain	30 percent
Thick	40	70 percent	Grain	5 percent
Thin	15	25 percent	None	n/a

Random

So much for natural media—it's time to create strokes that only a computer can create. In addition to the varying sizes, edge softness, and textures shown in Table 8-10, Random strokes also change the shape and color of the resulting stroke. The basic brush shape is evident both by the Random preset names—Dots, Fur, Squares, and Yarn—and in the sample strokes shown in Figure 8-14, but you'll have to turn to the color insert to really see the color variations. The Confetti preset is the most colorful and Dots the least colorful, but all the Random strokes exhibit some changing hues.

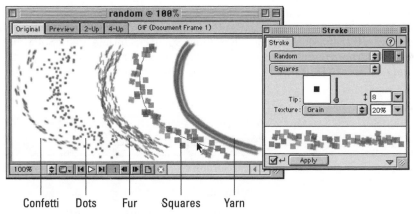

Confetti Dots Fur Squares Yarn

Figure 8-14: The Random strokes provide five fanciful alternatives to natural media strokes.

	Table 8-10 Random Type Attributes			
Name	**Size**	**Edge Softness**	**Texture**	**Amount of Texture**
Confetti	6	25 percent	None	n/a
Dots	3	20 percent	None	n/a
Fur	10	0 percent	None	n/a
Squares	5	0 percent	Grain	20 percent
Yarn	8	0 percent	None	n/a

Unnatural

I think it's a pretty safe bet that the Unnatural strokes were developed in a, shall we say, party-like atmosphere. How else do you explain the messiness of Fluid Splatter or the glow-in-the-dark feel of Toxic Waste—not to mention the otherworldliness of Viscous Alien Paint? No matter how they were developed, I find myself returning to them time and again when I need a unique and distinctive look for my graphics. Experiment by applying them to almost any object when you're up against a creative wall; the results are often surprising and useful. As you can see in Table 8-11, all the presets are roughly the same size with the exception of Chameleon. Several of the strokes have a transparent area: 3D Glow, Fluid Splatter, Outline, Paint Splatter, and Toxic Waste. Although you can get a sense of the preset variations from Figure 8-15, you'll have to turn to the color insert to see the Unnatural strokes in all their glory.

	Table 8-11 Unnatural Type Attributes			
Name	**Size**	**Edge Softness**	**Texture**	**Amount of Texture**
3D	20	12 percent	None	n/a
3D Glow	19	100 percent	None	n/a
Chameleon	6	0 percent	Grain	31 percent
Fluid Splatter	12	100 percent	None	n/a
Outline	19	100 percent	None	n/a
Paint Splatter	12	100 percent	None	n/a
Toothpaste	18	50 percent	None	n/a
Toxic Waste	18	100 percent	None	n/a
Viscous Alien Paint	12	30 percent	None	n/a

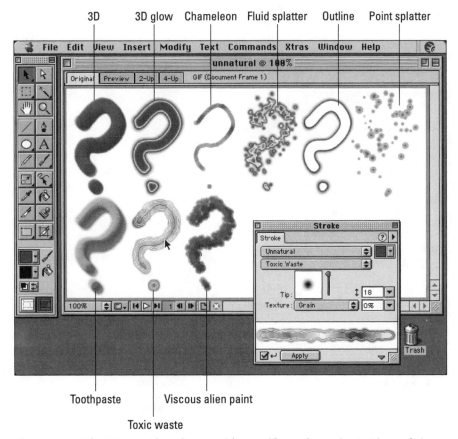

Figure 8-15: The Unnatural strokes provide an offbeat alternative to Fireworks' natural media strokes.

Creating New Strokes

What, the standard 48 strokes aren't enough? You need a slightly smaller Air Brush or a Calligraphy stroke with more texture? What about a dashed or dotted line instead of a solid one? Fear not; in Fireworks, custom strokes are just a click or two away. Not only can you store your minor adjustments as new strokes, but you can completely alter existing strokes and save them, either within the document or as a Fireworks Style that you can use in any document or export and share with a colleague or workgroup.

This section is divided into two parts. The first section explains how to manage your strokes so that the ones you need are always available. The second part delves into the somewhat complex—but altogether addictive—option of editing your strokes.

Managing your strokes

Stroke management is handled through the Stroke panel pop-up menu, which is shown in Figure 8-16.

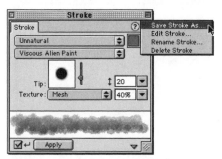

Figure 8-16: Manage your strokes through the Strokes panel pop-up menu.

The pop-up menu contains four menu commands:

✦ **Save Stroke As:** Stores the current stroke under a new name within the active document

✦ **Edit Stroke:** Displays the Edit Stroke dialog box, covered in detail later in this chapter

✦ **Delete Stroke:** Removes the current stroke, custom or standard, from the Stroke panel

Caution   Use the Delete Stroke command carefully — although Fireworks asks for confirmation, you can't undo removing a stroke.

✦ **Rename Stroke:** Relabels the current stroke

To store a modified stroke, follow these steps:

1. Modify any existing stroke by changing the Edge Softness, Size, Texture, and/or Amount of texture. The stroke color is not stored as part of the stroke.

2. Choose Save Stroke As from the pop-up menu. The Save Brush As dialog box appears. Fireworks 1 users will remember that strokes were previously known as brushes.

3. Enter a unique name for the stroke. If you choose a name already in use, Fireworks asks if you want to replace the existing brush.

4. After entering a new name, choose Save. The new stroke name is displayed alphabetically in the Type list options of the active Stroke category.

It's important to understand that any new or modified strokes are stored within the document in which they're used. The newly defined stroke will always be available for use in the document in which it was stored, even if no paths currently employ it. To use the stroke in another document, follow these steps:

1. Open the document containing the stroke you want to use.

2. Select a path using the new stroke. If no path currently uses the stroke, draw a temporary one and select it.

3. Open the new document in which you want to use the new stroke.

4. Copy the selected path to the new document either by using the Edit ➪ Copy and Edit ➪ Paste or by dragging and dropping the path from one document to the other. The new stroke setting is added to the Stroke panel when the path containing the stroke is pasted into the document.

5. If desired, delete the copied path from the new document; the stroke will still be available for later use in the document.

You can achieve the same effect of transferring strokes from one document to another in several other ways:

✦ Import a document containing one or more custom strokes. After you've clicked once to place the document, choose Undo. The graphics will vanish, but all custom strokes will be incorporated into the Strokes panel. With this technique, only custom strokes actually applied to paths in the source document are transferred.

✦ Copy the path with the custom stroke in one document and just paste the attributes to a path in the new document by selecting that path and choosing Edit ➪ Paste Attributes.

Perhaps the best way to always be sure your custom strokes are available is to use the Styles feature. To create a new Style using a custom stroke, follow these steps:

1. Select a path that uses the custom stroke.

2. If necessary, choose Window ➪ Styles, use the keyboard shortcut Ctrl+Alt+J (Command+Option+J), or click the Style tab, if visible, to display the Styles panel.

3. On the Styles panel, select the New Style button. The New Style dialog box displays, as shown in Figure 8-17.

4. In the Edit Style dialog box, enter a descriptive name for your stroke in the Name text box and deselect all checkboxes except Stroke Type.

5. Click OK when you're done. A new Style is entered in the Styles panel.

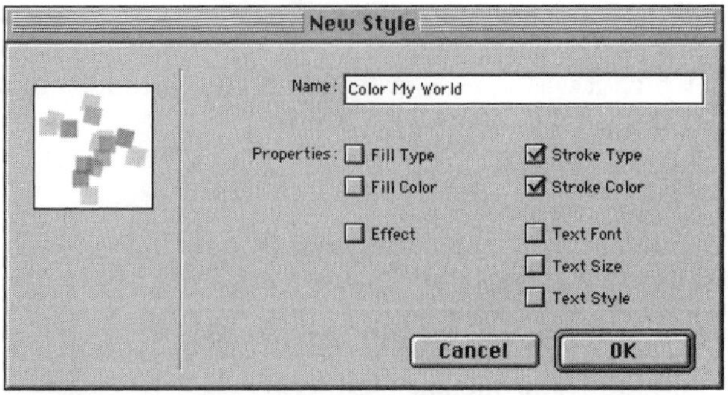

Figure 8-17: Declaring a stroke through the New Style dialog box stores the stroke definition for easy access from all Fireworks documents.

Any Style added in the fashion just described is always available for any Fireworks document. To apply the stroke, just highlight any Fireworks path object and select the new Style. Your custom stroke is then added to the Stroke panel.

Cross-Reference   To find out more about the powerful Styles feature, see Chapter 16.

Editing the stroke

Whereas you can make certain modifications through the Strokes panel, if you really want to customize your strokes, you have to use the Edit Stroke dialog box. Although the array of choices the dialog box offers can be a bit overwhelming, once you understand how to achieve certain effects, creating new strokes becomes easy, fun, and compelling.

You can access the Edit Stroke dialog box in one of two ways:

✦ Choose Edit Stroke from the Strokes panel pop-up menu.

✦ Double-click the Strokes panel Tip preview where the stroke shape is displayed.

The Edit Stroke dialog box is divided into three tabs: Options, Shape, and Sensitivity. Each of the tabs contains a preview panel that updates after every change is made. If you have selected a stroke prior to opening the Edit Stroke dialog box, you can also see the effect by using the Apply button.

Caution   In my explorations of the Edit Stroke dialog box, I uncovered one technique that worked differently than I expected. First, if you make a change to a stroke without selecting a path, the change does not register. Always select a path, even a temporary one, before you create a custom stroke.

The Options tab

The Options tab hosts a number of general, but important, attributes. In addition to providing controls for familiar parameters, such as a stroke's degree of texture and opacity, the Options tab, as shown in Figure 8-18, also holds the key to affecting the tightness of the stroke, how it reacts over time, and what, if any, edge effect is employed.

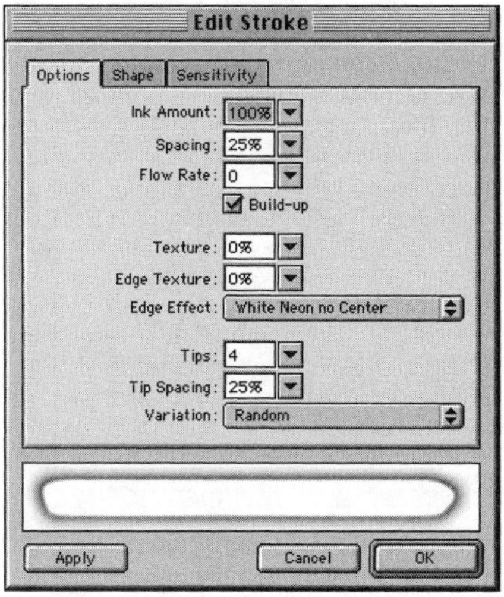

Figure 8-18: The Options tab of the Edit Stroke dialog box contains many key controls.

Ink Amount

The first stroke attribute on the Option tab is Ink Amount. Generally, this parameter is set at 100 percent, but lowering it is a possibility for any stroke. The Ink Amount value is responsible for a stroke's opacity: 100 percent is completely opaque, and 0 percent is completely transparent. The bottom of the two "CLICK" buttons in Figure 8-19 shows how a stroke is affected when the Ink Amount is reduced to 60 percent.

You can also alter an object's overall opacity through the Object panel, but changing just the Ink Amount value alters just the stroke. Combine the two and the effect is additive; if, for example, you see a stroke's Ink Amount at 50 percent and you reduce the opacity of the path object to 50 percent, the stroke would appear to be 25 percent opaque (because half of 50 percent is 25 percent). The Felt Tip Highlighter preset is a good example of a stroke that uses a reduced Ink Amount in order to obtain transparency.

Spacing

Technically, each stroke consists of a long series of stroke *stamps*. A stamp is the smallest unit of a stroke; you can see it by selecting a stroke and the Brush tool, and then clicking the mouse once, without moving. As you draw with the Brush or another tool, one stamp after another is laid down. How close those stamps are to each other is determined by the Spacing attribute. As detailed later in this chapter, you can create dotted lines by changing the Spacing value.

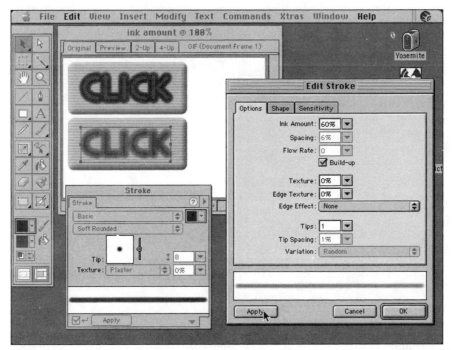

Figure 8-19: Reducing the Ink Amount of a stroke reduces its opacity.

Note

If you try to modify the Pencil 1-Pixel strokes or any of the Basic strokes, you'll find that no matter what you do, you won't be able to enable the Spacing or Flow Rate options. These strokes actually use a different rendering engine than all the other strokes, which sacrifices spacing and flow control to gain pinpoint pixel accuracy. To see the effects of changing either the Spacing or Flow Rate options, edit any other stroke.

The Spacing value ranges from 0 percent to 1,000 percent. If the Spacing attribute is set at 100 percent, stroke stamps in a straight line are positioned directly next to each other. If the Spacing is less than 100 percent, the stamps are overlaid on top of one another. If the Spacing is greater than 100 percent, the stamps are separated from one another. Strokes with a soft edge, such as the Air Brush, appear to be separated even when the Spacing is set to less than 100 percent, but this is only because the soft edge is incorporated into the stroke stamp. The effect in Figure 8-20 is achieved by increasing the spacing of a Felt Tip stroke to more than 200 percent.

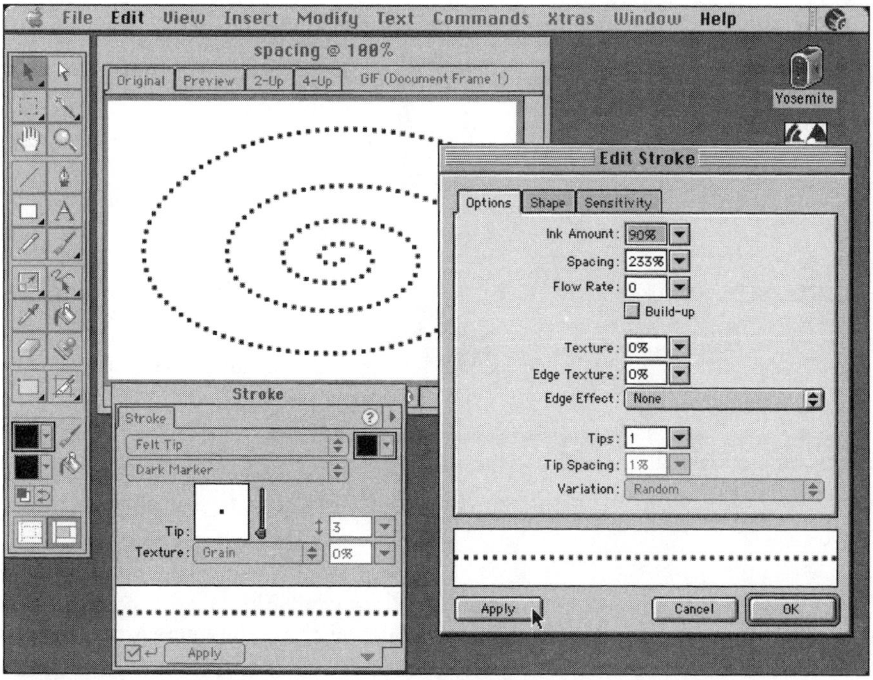

Figure 8-20: Create dotted line patterns by increasing the Spacing value.

Flow Rate and Build-up

Most stroke settings alter how a stroke changes as it's drawn across a screen. However, the Flow Rate percentage value represents how fast ink flows; the higher the number, the faster it flows. The Air Brush category is the best example of the use of Flow Rate. Both preset Air Brushes, Basic and Textured, use a fairly high value of 80 percent.

The Build-up option is another way of affecting a stroke's opacity. If Build-up is enabled, for example, as with the Air Brush preset, and the stroke crosses itself as in Figure 8-21, you'll notice a darker area at the overlap of the stroke. If you disable the Build-up option, the stroke has a much flatter, monochrome appearance.

Texture, Edge Texture, and Edge Effect

The Texture setting in the Edit Stroke dialog box is reflected on the Stroke panel as the Amount of Texture value. Increase the Texture value to make the chosen texture more visible on the opaque portion of the stroke; a value of 0 percent effectively turns off the texture.

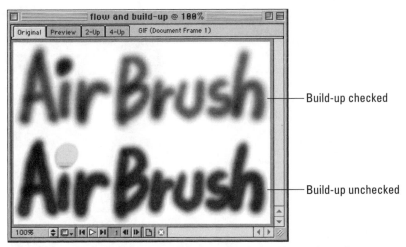

Build-up checked

Build-up unchecked

Figure 8-21: With the Build-up option enabled, the Air Brush stroke acts like a real airbrush, building up where it crosses itself.

Caution   The type of texture cannot be specified from within the Edit Stroke dialog box; it must be set through the Stroke panel. Whereas the texture type is saved with the stroke when the Save Stroke As command is selected, if another texture type is chosen temporarily, the original texture does not reappear when the custom stroke is reselected. Reload the document with the saved stroke in order to again establish the custom texture settings.

Just as the Texture value causes the chosen texture to appear over the opaque portion of the stroke, the Edge Texture setting causes the texture to appear over the transparent portion. Remember that in Fireworks, edge softness is created by affecting the stroke's alpha channels or transparency. By increasing the Edge Texture and lowering the Texture value, the soft edge of the stroke is textured more noticeably than the center.

Note   Edge Texture values, no matter how high, will in effect be invisible if the Edge Softness is at 0 percent.

In addition to altering an edge's texture, you can also create an Edge Effect. Technically speaking, the five Edge Effects are created by applying an algorithm affecting the alpha channel for both the stroke and its edge. In this case, descriptions are a poor second to a visual representation of the intriguingly named Edge Effects, shown in Figure 8-22. Because Edge Effects rely on the transparency of the stroke's edge, you can't apply an Edge Effect to a stroke with a 0 percent Edge Softness value.

White neon   Smooth neon   Harsh wet

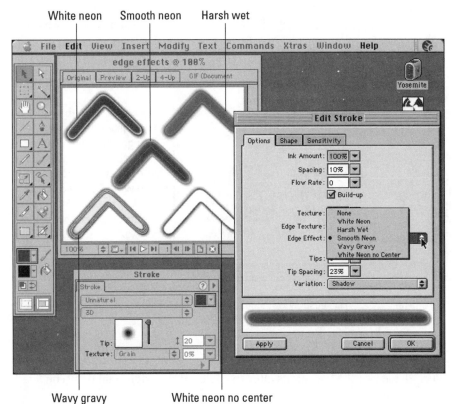

Wavy gravy   White neon no center

Figure 8-22: The five preset Edge Effects combine both stroke and edge transparency.

Tips, Tip Spacing, and Variations

Have you ever drawn with a fistful of colored pencils or noticed, too late, that your paint brush has dried with the bristles separated? In each case, the result is a series of separate strokes that curve and move together. In Fireworks jargon, each pencil or separate bristle is referred to as a *tip* and is determined by the Tips attribute. Every stroke must have at least one and can have as many as ten tips.

> **Note** For either the Tip Spacing or Variations attributes to become active, you must have more than one Tip.

Whether the number of tips is apparent or not is determined primarily by the Tip Spacing attribute. Similar to the Spacing parameter, Tip Spacing is set in a range from 0 percent (where each tip is drawn on top of one another) to 1000 percent (where each tip is as far apart as possible). You can see the results of an extreme experiment in Figure 8-23, where the Unnatural 3D stroke is set to use one, five, and ten Tips with a Tip Spacing of 1,000 percent. A single star was drawn for each graphic.

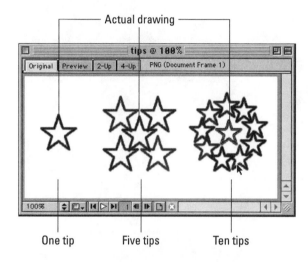

Actual drawing

One tip   Five tips   Ten tips

Figure 8-23: Although it looks like the stars in the two groups were cloned, only a single star was drawn in each group; multiple tips and wide Tip Spacing are the key to drawing many identical images with one stroke.

Variations are the final elements on the Options tab. When multiple tips are used, how the different tips are depicted is determined by which of the Variations are selected. Each of the Variations alter the color of the additional tips. The five Variations are

✦ **Random:** A new color is selected at random for each tip with each new stroke.

✦ **Uniform:** All tips use the base color selected in the Stroke color well.

✦ **Complimentary:** If the stroke uses two tips, one tip is displayed in the complimentary color (on the opposite side of an HLS (Hue, Lightness, Saturation) color wheel) of the base color. If more than two tips are specified, the additional tips are selected from evenly spaced hues that are located between the initial complimentary colors.

✦ **Hue:** Multiple tips are presented in hues similar (plus or minus 5 percent on an HLS color wheel) to the stroke color.

✦ **Shadow:** Additional tips are shown in alternating lighter and darker shades of the stroke color (the Lightness).

The Shape tab

Compared to the Object tab, the Shape tab of the Edit Stroke dialog box (Figure 8-24) is almost self-explanatory. Like the Strokes panel, it has two preview panes; the upper pane shows the stroke stamp, and the lower pane shows a representation of the stroke over distance.

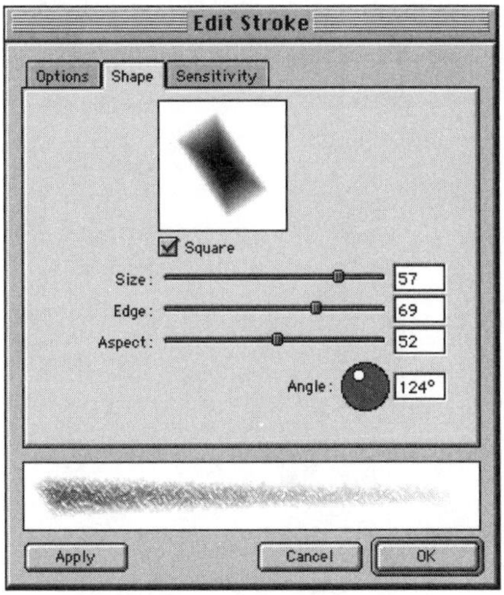

Figure 8-24: The look of the stroke stamp, and ultimately the stroke itself, is influenced by the attributes of the Shape tab.

The Shape tab offers the following five parameters:

✦ **Square:** When enabled, the Square option makes the stroke stamp square or rectangular according to the Aspect setting. If Square is disabled, the stroke stamp is circular or elliptical.

✦ **Size:** Sets the initial stroke width, in pixels, from 1 to 100. The value is displayed in Stroke panel.

✦ **Edge:** Determines the softness of the stroke's edge. This value is also reflected in the Stroke panel.

✦ **Aspect:** Sets the height to width aspect ratio. Values 0 and 100 make circles or squares — any other value creates rectangles or ellipses.

✦ **Angle:** Determines the angle of the stroke stamp. Values can be entered directly or by dragging the dial in a circle.

You can achieve a wide range of different shapes by combining different parameters from the Shape tab. I've found the Aspect and Angle controls to be especially useful. For example, I used them to create a diamond dotted stroke, as detailed later in this chapter.

The Sensitivity tab

The Sensitivity tab of the Edit Stroke dialog box, shown in Figure 8-25, permits you to establish somewhat interactive controls for custom strokes. By altering your drawing pressure, speed, or direction, your strokes can assume different sizes, angles, opacities, or colors. You can even set up the stroke to alter any of its properties randomly.

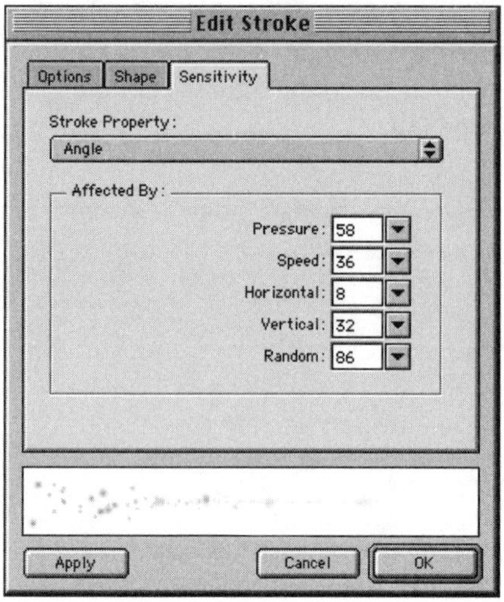

Figure 8-25: Create interactive strokes through the Sensitivity tab of the Edit Stroke dialog box.

The basic procedure for working in the Sensitivity tab is to select one of the stroke attributes from the Brush Properties option list and then set the desired control found in the Affected By area. For example, if you wanted your stroke to shift colors when it is drawn across the document but not down it, you would choose Hue from the Brush Properties option list and set the Affected By Horizontal value to a high percentage value. The higher the value, the more impact the condition (Pressure, Speed, and so on) will have.

The seven stroke attributes are

✦ **Size:** When the Size property is affected, the stroke always gets smaller than the initial width, never larger. If the setting is at 50 percent, the stroke loses, at most, one-half of its size.

✦ **Angle:** The angle of the stroke stamp can be affected by as much as 90 degrees if Angle property is selected and an Affected By value is set to its maximum, 100 percent.

✦ **Ink Amount:** As on the Options tab, Ink Amount refers to opacity. At the highest setting, the affecting condition can make the stroke transparent.

✦ **Scatter:** The amount of variance with which stroke stamps are drawn away from the path. Scatter is really only effective with the Random condition.

✦ **Hue:** The color of the stroke. Multicolored strokes, such as those in the Random category, make great use of this property.

✦ **Lightness:** The amount of white in a color. To make a stroke fade more as you draw faster, choose the Lightness property and increase the Speed condition.

✦ **Saturation:** The intensity of the color. The higher the value set in the condition, the more the Saturation lessens. A stroke with a high Speed setting for Saturation becomes grayer as the path is drawn faster.

The conditions that affect these properties each have a separate slider and text box for entering values directly:

✦ **Pressure:** The degree of pressure applied by a stylus used with a pressure-sensitive graphics tablet.

✦ **Speed:** The amount of speed used when a path is drawn either with a graphics tablet or a mouse.

✦ **Horizontal:** Drawing paths from left to right or vice versa.

✦ **Vertical:** Drawing paths from top to bottom or vice versa.

✦ **Random:** The selected property is affected without any additional input from the user.

The Affected By conditions can be used together. For example, setting Angle to be equally affected by both the Horizontal and Vertical conditions causes a stroke, such as Random Fur, to change direction as the path is drawn.

Generally, the Sensitivity tab settings tend to react more predictably with hand-drawn paths, such as those created with the Brush tool, than paths constructed with one of the geometric shapes, such as the Rectangle or Ellipse. However, experimentation is the key to uncovering unique effects with almost all of the Edit Stroke parameters, and you have nothing to lose by trying a particular setting.

Fireworks Technique: Making Dotted Lines

All the strokes in Fireworks' standard arsenal are more or less solid lines with nothing that can be used as a dotted line. Although there are a few exceptions, such as most of the Random presets, these tend to be too unconventional to use for a basic dotted line. As you've seen in the previous section, however, Fireworks offers you a tremendous degree of control in customizing your own strokes. The procedure for creating a dotted line is fairly straightforward and a good introduction to the world of custom stroke creation.

The key to creating a dotted line is in the Spacing control found on the Options tab of the Edit Stroke dialog box. When the Spacing value is 100 percent, each stroke stamp (the smallest component of a stroke) is right next to the one following it. If the value is less than 100 percent, the stroke stamps overlap and — here's the heart of the dotted line — when the value is greater than 100 percent, the stroke stamps are separated.

When creating any custom stroke, you want to start with the built-in stroke that's closest to your goal. Although either of the Basic or Pencil 1-Pixel strokes would be ideal, the key attribute for creating a dotted line, Spacing, is not available for these strokes. As explained earlier in this chapter, these strokes are rendered with an eye toward pixel precision that is incompatible with the Spacing and Flow attributes. However, one of the other Pencil presets, Colored Pencil, works quite well as a stroke on which to build a custom dotted line, with a minimum of adjustments required.

To create a simple dotted line, follow these steps:

1. Display the Stroke panel by choosing Window ⇨ Stroke or selecting its tab, if it is visible.

2. Choose Pencil from the Category option list.

3. Choose Colored Pencil from the Type option list.

4. Open the Edit Stroke dialog box by choosing Edit Stroke from the Strokes panel pop-up menu or by double-clicking the Tip preview pane.

5. On the Options tab of the Edit Stroke dialog box, change the Spacing value from 15 percent to 200 percent.

   You'll notice in the preview pane that you now have a dotted line, as shown in Figure 8-26.

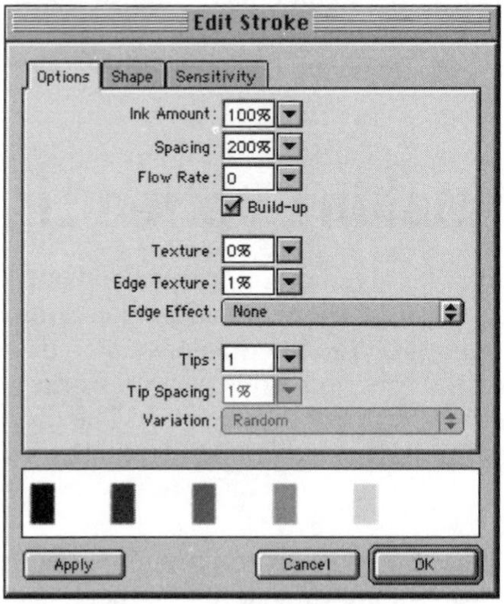

Figure 8-26: You can easily create a dotted line by modifying the Edit Stroke Settings.

6. Click OK when you're done.

7. From the pop-up menu, choose Save Stroke As.

8. In the Save Stroke As dialog box, enter a unique name for the custom stroke.

Test out your new dotted line by using almost any of the path drawing tools:—the Rectangle, Ellipse, Polygon, Brush, or Pen.

Now that you've seen how easy it is to customize a brush stroke, try a few variations, such as the ones in Figure 8-27. Each set of instructions assumes that you're working in the Edit Stroke dialog box.

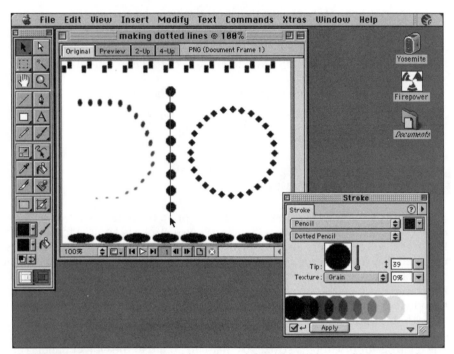

Figure 8-27: You can create a wide variety of dotted lines by modifying the Edit Stroke Settings.

To give the dotted line a harder, more consistent edge, make these changes:

✦ Change the Edge Texture value on the Options tab to 0 percent.

✦ On the Shape tab, change the Edge value to 0 percent.

✦ On the Sensitivity tab, change the Size Speed setting to 0, the Ink Amount Pressure and Speed settings to 0, and the Lightness Pressure and Speed settings to 0.

Make these changes in order to create a dotted line with circles instead of squares:

✦ On the Shape tab, deselect the Square option.

✦ Also on the Shape tab, change the Aspect value to 100.

To create a horizontal line with dashes, change these values:

✦ From the Shape tab, change the Aspect value to 50.

✦ Also on the Shape tab, change the Angle to 0.

To create a vertical line with dashes, change these values:

✦ From the Shape tab, change the Aspect value to 50.

✦ Also on the Shape tab, change the Angle to 270.

Change the following values in order to create a dotted line with diamonds:

✦ From the Shape tab, make sure the Square option is selected.

✦ Also on the Shape tab, change the Aspect value to 100.

✦ Change the Angle to 45.

Orienting the Stroke

Strokes are useful, whether they are intended for an open path, such as a line, or a closed path, such as a circle or rectangle. When a stroke is applied to a closed path, however, Fireworks offers an additional set of options. By default, when strokes are rendered they are centered on a path. Select any closed path object and you'll see the stroke rendered on either side of the actual path. The orientation of a stroke to a path can be changed: the stroke can also be drawn completely inside the path or outside the path. As you can see from Figure 8-28, wildly different effects are possible with this option.

The controls for orienting a stroke to a path are found in the Object panel. The three buttons, respectively from left to right, place the stroke inside the path, centered on the path, or outside the path. A fourth option, Draw Fill over Stroke, is located below the stroke orientation controls. By default, the stroke always appears on top of the fill color, Pattern, or gradient. However, by enabling the Draw Fill over Stroke option, you can reverse this preference.

Tip By combining the Draw Fill over Stroke option with a stroke rendered on the center of the path and a fill with a feathered edge, the stroke appears to blend into the fill while retaining a hard outer edge.

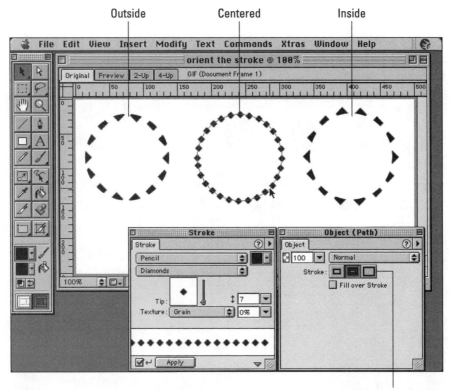

Figure 8-28: The same stroke is rendered outside the path, centered on the path, and inside the path.

One of my favorite applications of the stroke orientation controls is to use inside strokes as a sort of auxiliary fill, creating the effect of a more complex fill, as shown in Figure 8-29. Hard to believe Fireworks allows you to do this kind of thing completely with paths!

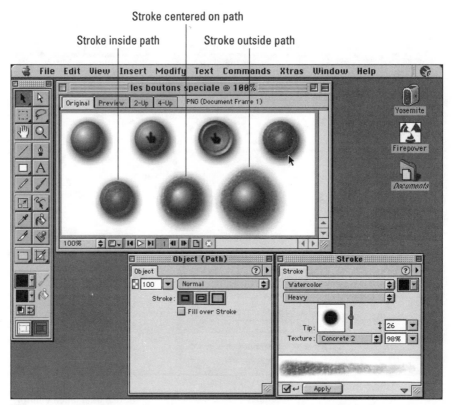

Figure 8-29: Inside strokes figure prominently in this set of buttons. The bottom row is the selected button shown again, this time after each of the three stroke orientation options has been applied.

Summary

In many ways, the stroke is the defining surface of a graphic. Fireworks offers a superb catalog of standard strokes and even more flexibility to create your own. As you begin to work with strokes, use these guidelines:

✦ Strokes make paths visible. An unstroked line cannot be seen unless the path is closed and a fill added.

✦ The Stroke panel offers immediate control over a stroke's color, size, edge, and texture. Two previews show the tip of the stroke, as well as how the stroke will look when it is applied to a path.

✦ Fireworks includes 48 different preset strokes spread over 11 categories. Many of the stroke presets are interactive and vary according to the speed and pressure with which you draw.

✦ Fireworks strokes can be customized with a great number of variations through the Edit Stroke dialog box.

✦ After you've customized your stroke, you can save it with the document by using the Stroke panel pop-up menu commands. You can also store your custom strokes within a Fireworks Style.

✦ Although Fireworks doesn't come with a preset dotted-line pattern, it's easy to create one.

✦ Fireworks works well with graphics tablets and takes great advantage of their pressure sensitivity.

In the next chapter, you'll see how you can employ advanced path techniques in Fireworks.

Structuring Paths

Even with the coolest stroke, the snazziest fill, and the wildest effect, you rarely get exactly the graphic you need the first time you draw an object. Maybe it needs to be a little bigger, smaller, taller, or wider, or maybe it's perfect — but it's facing the wrong way and it's upside down. Whatever the problem, Fireworks has the tools to fix it and, because Fireworks blends pixel surfaces with vector skeletons, you'll get amazingly sharp results.

Fireworks has the kinds of tools you'd normally expect to find in a full-fledged vector drawing application. You can combine several paths in any number of ways with evocatively named tools such as Union, Intersect, Punch, and Crop. Naturally, what you have joined together can be split apart and regrouped as needed. Paths can be simplified, expanded, or inset with Fireworks commands.

This chapter covers all the tools and techniques you'll find in Fireworks for transforming and combining objects. You'll also find a section that describes how you can use Fireworks to create perspectives in your imagery.

You really begin to appreciate the power of Fireworks' vector/ bitmap combination when you start transforming your objects. In a pure bitmap graphics application, if you increase the size of an image, you have to add pixels, whereas shrinking an image causes the program to throw away pixels — you rarely achieve ideal results in either situation. However, in Fireworks, when you rescale a path object, the path is altered (a snap for vector graphics) and the pixels are reapplied to the new path, just as if you had drawn it that way to begin with.

◆ ◆ ◆ ◆

In This Chapter

Transforming paths

Fireworks technique: creating perspective

Working at the point level on a path

Editing existing paths

Using path power tools

◆ ◆ ◆ ◆

Transforming Objects Visually

Fireworks includes methods for transforming objects both visually and numerically. The visual method relies on three key tools found in the Toolbox: Scale, Skew, and Distort.

Note   Although I primarily use path objects as examples in this section, all of the transformation tools work with image objects, as well.

Scaling

In Web design, the size of an object frequently needs adjustment. Sometimes a button is too large for the current navigation bar or the client wants the "On Sale" notice to be much bigger. Other times a graphic just looks better at a particular size. Regardless of the reason, Fireworks gives you a quick way to resize an object—either up or down—through the Scale tool.

The Scale tool is the first of three transformation tools in the Toolbox that become active when an object is selected. Choose the Scale tool (or use the keyboard shortcut, Q) and the standard selection highlight is replaced with a transforming highlight, as shown in Figure 9-1. There are eight sizing handles—one on each corner and one in the middle of each side—and a centerpoint on the transforming highlight. You can drag any of the sizing handles to a new position in order to resize the selected object. Dragging any corner handle scales the object proportionately.

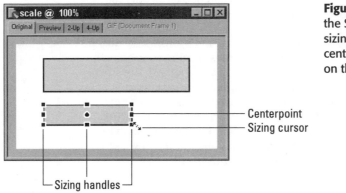

Figure 9-1: Choose the Scale tool and sizing handles and a centerpoint appears on the selected object.

To resize an object using the Scale tool, follow these steps:

1. Select the object you want to resize.

2. Choose the Scale tool from the Toolbox or use the keyboard shortcut, Q. Alternatively, you can use the menu command, Modify ⇨ Transform ⇨ Scale. Sizing handles and a centerpoint appear on the selected object.

3. Position your pointer over any sizing handle until it changes into a two-headed arrow.

4. Click and drag the sizing handle in the direction you want the object to grow or shrink. To scale an object while maintaining the current proportions, click and drag a corner sizing handle.

5. To cancel a resizing operation and return the object to its original dimensions, press Esc.

6. To accept a rescaled object, double-click anywhere on the document. You can also complete the resizing by selecting the Transform button in the Options panel, if it's visible.

You can also move or rotate an object when any of the transform tools are selected. When the pointer is positioned within the selected object and it becomes a four-headed arrow, click and drag the object to a new position. If the pointer is outside of the selected object's bounding box, the pointer turns into a rotate symbol; clicking and dragging when this occurs rotates the object around its centerpoint.

The transform tools all have two options available through the Options panel. By default, when you resize an object, the stroke, fill, and effect settings are resized, as well. If you disable the Scale Attributes option, these settings are reapplied without being recalculated. Why might you want to do this? Although the results can be unpredictable, interesting variations can occur, such as the variations in Figure 9-2.

Tip   In my experiments with the Scale Attributes option, the most interesting effects occurred when my object was filled with a gradient and the Scale Attributes option was turned off.

The other option in the transform tools Options panel is Auto-crop Images. When this option is enabled, Fireworks automatically removes transparent pixels around image objects before resizing them.

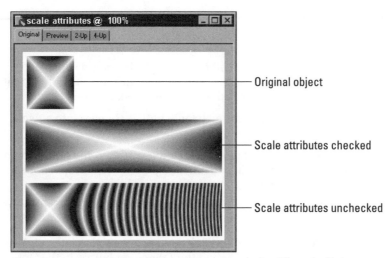

Original object

Scale attributes checked

Scale attributes unchecked

Figure 9-2: Most of the time you want your stroke, fill, and effects to rescale along with your image, but turning off the Scale Attributes option can lead to some interesting effects.

Skewing

The Skew tool is used to move one side of an object while the opposing side remains stationary. Select the Skew tool by clicking and holding the Scale tool until you can choose the Skew tool from the flyout or by pressing the keyboard shortcut Q twice. Selecting the Skew tool causes transform handles to appear on the selected object, just like selecting the Scale tool. The Skew handles work somewhat differently, though:

✦ Drag any middle Skew handle in order to slant that side of the object.

✦ Drag any corner Skew handle in order to slant that side and the opposing side in the opposite direction.

Skewing a corner is a useful technique for giving an object a dynamic appearance, as can be seen in Figure 9-3.

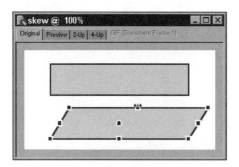

Figure 9-3: Skew an object along one side by dragging the middle handle.

New Feature Skewing an object in conjunction with Fireworks 3's new Motion Blur effect can enhance the feeling of action even further.

Completing a Skew operation is handled the same as completing a scaling operation: press Esc to cancel or double-click anywhere to accept the new shape.

Distorting

With both the Scale and Skew tools, entire sides move when one of the transform handles is adjusted. The Distort tool (the third tool on the transform flyout) removes this restrictions. When the Distort tool is selected, you can adjust the bounding box surrounding the selected object by dragging the handles in any direction. The object is then redrawn to fit within the confines of the new bounding box shape, as in Figure 9-4.

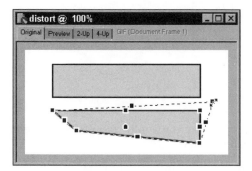

Figure 9-4: Use the Distort tool to reshape an image or an object by altering its bounding box.

The Distort tool is useful for warping flat objects — especially images — into novel shapes or for fitting an object into the shape of another object.

Tip Use the Distort tool to flip an image horizontally or vertically by dragging a middle handle across the opposite side. This technique won't automatically size the image to match the original size, as do the Flip Horizontal or Flip Vertical commands, but you can control the sizing.

Rotating

Rotating is available with any of the transform tools: Scale, Skew, or Distort. Moving your mouse cursor just outside of the bounding box causes the Rotate cursor to appear. As you can see in Figure 9-5, an object rotates around its centerpoint and can rotate a full 360 degrees.

To rotate any object, follow these steps:

Rotate cursor   Centerpoint

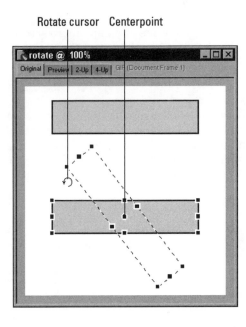

Figure 9-5: An Object rotates around its centerpoint when the Rotate cursor drags the object.

1. Select any one of the transform tools from the Toolbox or choose the equivalent tool from the Modify ⇨ Transform menu.

2. Move your pointer outside of the bounding box. The pointer turns into a Rotator cursor.

3. Click and drag in any direction to rotate the object.

4. To cancel the rotation and return to the original object, press Esc.

5. To accept the transformation, double-click anywhere or click the Transform button in the Options panel.

An object's centerpoint is placed in the middle of the transform bounding box by default. To change the rotation axis, click and drag the centerpoint to a new location — the centerpoint can remain within the object's bounding box or be placed outside of it. If the centerpoint is placed outside of the object, the radius used connects the centerpoint and the nearest corner handle, as shown in Figure 9-6.

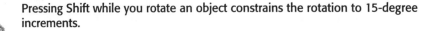

Tip   Pressing Shift while you rotate an object constrains the rotation to 15-degree increments.

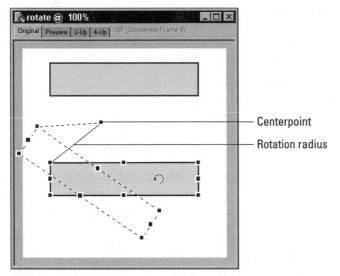

Figure 9-6: Rotate an object around a different axis by dragging the centerpoint to a new location, even outside of the object's bounding box.

Transforming Objects Numerically

Transforming an object interactively by clicking and dragging works well for many situations, but sometimes it's preferable to specify your new measurement or rotation precisely. For those exacting occasions, turn to Fireworks' Numeric Transform feature. With Numeric Transform, you can scale any object up or down by a percentage, set a specific pixel size, or rotate to an exact degree.

To use Numeric Transform, follow these steps:

1. Select the object you want to change.
2. Choose Modify ➪ Transform ➪ Numeric Transform or use the keyboard shortcut, Ctrl+Shift+T (Command+Shift+T). The Numeric Transform dialog box, shown in Figure 9-7, appears.

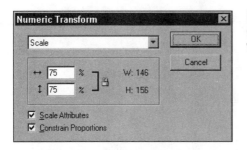

Figure 9-7: The Numeric Transform dialog box gives you exacting control when scaling or rotating an object.

3. Check Scale Attributes to reapply the object's attributes after the transformation.

4. Check Constrain proportions to preserver the object's aspect ratio.

5. To scale an object proportionately:

    • Choose Scale from the Option list.

    • Enter a new percentage value in either the height or width text boxes.

Tip If the height and width boxes are "locked" and you'd like to unlock them, uncheck Constrain Proportions.

6. To resize an object to a specific pixel size:

    • Choose Resize from the Option list.

    • Enter the pixel dimensions in either the width or height text boxes.

7. To rotate an object by a specific number of degrees:

    • Choose Rotate from the Option list.

    • Enter a degree value in the text box or drag the knob to select a rotation degree.

8. Choose OK when you're done.

Fireworks Technique: Creating Perspective

Though Fireworks is hardly a 3D modeling program, you can quickly generate perspective views using several of its transform and other tools. If you've ever taken Drawing 101, you understand the basic principles of perspective: the particular view you're illustrating has a vanishing point where the imaginary lines of the drawing meet on the horizon. The vanishing point concept is most simply applied by using a special property of the Skew tool.

To give an object the illusion of perspective, follow these steps:

1. Select the image you wish to modify.

2. Choose the Skew tool from the toolbox or press the keyboard shortcut, Q, twice.

3. Choose the direction of perspective:

   • To make the image appear as if it is along a left wall, vertically drag the top or bottom left corner away from the image.

   • To make the image appear as if it is along a right wall, vertically drag the top or bottom right corner away from the image.

   • To make the image appear as if it is on the floor, horizontally drag the left or right bottom corner away from the image.

   • To make the image appear as if it is on the ceiling, horizontally drag the left or right top corner away from the image.

4. To intensify the perspective, repeat Step 3 with the opposite corner, dragging in the opposite direction. For example, in Figure 9-8, I dragged the right bottom corner away from the image and the left bottom corner into the image to exaggerate the effect.

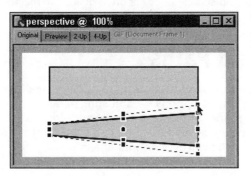

Figure 9-8: Make a flat figure appear to have perspective by using the Skew tool.

Applying textures to a rectangle fill is a good way to start building a perspective background. I've found it's better to break up the textures into small rectangles, rather than use one large rectangle. The room depicted in Figure 9-9 uses a series of rectangles with a Wood-Light Pattern fill, which are then grouped and skewed together to gain the perspective feel. By duplicating and flipping this skewed group, I'm able to quickly build the other sides of the room.

Cross-Reference   Texture fills are discussed at length in Chapter 11.

Figure 9-9: When using a Pattern for perspective, try smaller rectangles of the same Pattern, grouped and skewed together.

Tip

Dragging a corner with the Skew tool always moves the top opposite sides equally. This operation makes an object's vanishing point appear to be evenly spaced between the sides of an image, which is not always the case. You can also use the Distort tool to drag one corner unevenly. But use the Distort tool with caution — or perhaps with the Grid visible; there's no way to snap a dragged corner when using the Distort tool, and straight lines are often difficult to maintain.

Managing Points and Paths

Sometimes transforming an object in its entirety is more than you really want or need to do. Fireworks offers numerous options for adjusting paths on a point-by-point basis. You can easily move, add, or delete points. In addition, paths can be joined, either to themselves — changing an open path to a closed path — or to another path. Naturally, joined paths can also be split at any point.

Moving points with the Subselection tool

Much path work on the point level is handled through the Subselection tool. Similar to the Pointer tool in that it is used for selecting and dragging, the Subselection tool works on the components of the path, rather than on the path itself.

The Subselection tool is located directly to the right of the Pointer in the Toolbox; it can also be chosen through its keyboard shortcut, A. When you select a path with the Subselection tool, all the points that create the path appear, not just the path that becomes visible when the Pointer is used. Each point on a path initially resembles a small filled-in square. When you approach a point with the Subselection tool, the white pointer changes into a single white arrowhead, indicating that a point is available for selection, as shown in Figure 9-10. Clicking on that point selects it and changes the solid square to a hollow square.

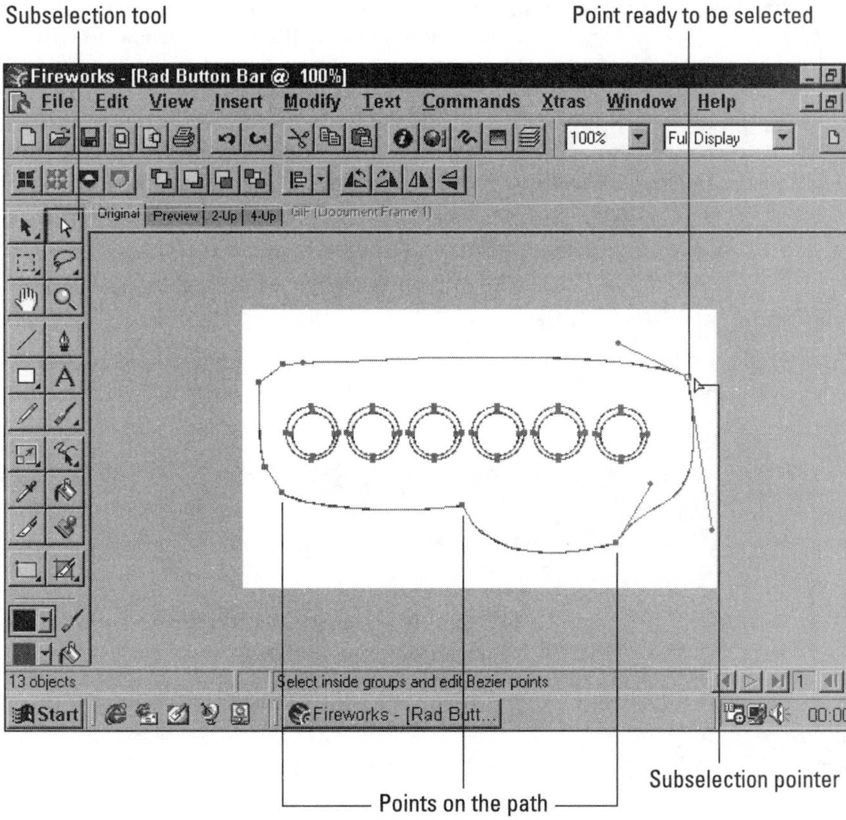

Subselection tool   Point ready to be selected

Subselection pointer

Points on the path

Figure 9-10: Adjust paths on the point level with the Subselection tool.

Tip If no Bézier control handles are visible from a point on a path, you can use the Subselection tool in combination with the Alt (Option) key in order to drag them out.

Clicking and dragging any point causes the path to move with it. You can completely reshape any path by using the Subselection tool.

Adding and removing points

It's easy to add or delete points on a path. Why would you want to increase the number of points? Most commonly, the object you're working on has a line that you need to extend in a different direction, and the Bézier curves create too smooth a transition. The reasoning behind removing points is just the reverse: you have a sharp break where you'd prefer a smooth curve. You'll also find that drawing any path with a freeform tool, such as the Brush or Pencil, creates many points. Not that there is really any increased overhead, such as file size, associated with additional points; it's just easier to work with an object that has fewer points.

To add a point on a path, follow these steps:

1. Choose the Pen tool from the toolbox or use its keyboard shortcut, P.

2. Press and hold Ctrl (Command) to temporarily switch to the Subselection tool.

3. Select the path that you want to work on.

4. Release Ctrl (Command).

5. Position your pointer over the area on the path where you want to add a point. A small caret (^) is added to the Pen tool pointer, as shown in Figure 9-11.

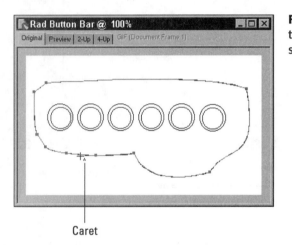

Caret

Figure 9-11: Add points with the Pen tool by clicking on a selected line.

6. To add a single point, click once.

7. To add a point with Bézier control handles, click and drag.

8. Continue adding points by repeating Steps 5-7.

9. When you're finished adding points, select another tool.

To delete points from a path, follow these steps:

1. Choose the Subselection tool from the Toolbox.

2. Select the path from which you want to delete points.

3. Move the pointer over the point you want to delete. A small X is added to the pointer when you are over a point on the path.

4. Click once to select the point.

5. Press Backspace (Delete) to remove the point.

Tip
> To delete multiple points, press Ctrl (Command) to temporarily use the Pointer tool and drag a selection rectangle around the points that you want to remove. Alternatively, hold down Shift while selecting points to keep adding to your selection. Press Backspace (Delete) to remove the points.

Closing an open path

Whether by accident ("Drat, I thought I closed that path") or design ("I like the simpleness of the open path"), sometimes you need to convert an open path to a closed path. Luckily, the Pen tool makes this a simple operation.

Tip
> If your path is almost closed — the end points are right next to each other — you can also select both points with the Subselection tool and choose Modify ⇨ Join, or you can use the key shortcut Ctrl+J (Command+J) to close your path.

To close an open path, follow these steps:

1. Select the path you want to close.

2. Choose the Pen tool from the toolbox.

3. Position your pointer over one endpoint of the path. An X is added to the lower right of the Pen cursor when it is over an existing endpoint.

4. Click once on the endpoint. A small arrow replaces the X at the lower right of the Pen cursor, as shown in Figure 9-12.

Pen tool cursor

Figure 9-12: Use the Pen tool to close any open path.

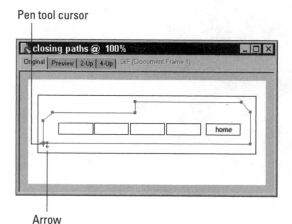

Arrow

5. Continue the path with the Pen. With each plotted point, any stroke or effects attributes are applied to the extended path.

6. To close the path, position the Pen over the remaining endpoint. A solid square appears on the lower right of the Pen cursor.

7. Click once to close the path.

Tip   If your stroke varies its thickness or opacity by speed or pressure, the section of the path that was completed with the Pen may look odd. This is because the Pen recognizes neither speed nor pressure. However, you can use the Path Scrubber tools, discussed later in this chapter, to increase or reduce these types of effects.

Working with multiple paths

Any path can be joined with another path with a simple command. Initially, this capability may appear to fall into the "Yeah, so what?" category; but once you realize that paths don't have to overlap, touch, or even be near each other, the design possibilities open considerably. Joining a number of simple shapes is an easy way to make one complex shape. For example, joining empty circles with an object effectively cuts holes in the object, as shown in Figure 9-13. Note that the joined object has the attributes — stroke, fill, effect, etc. — of the original object that was lowest in the stacking order (in other words, closest to the canvas.)

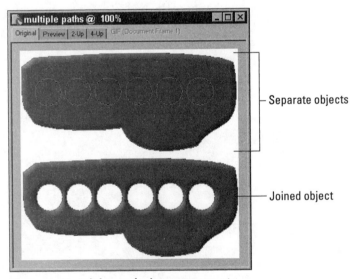

Figure 9-13: Joining paths is an easy way to create complex objects.

To join two or more paths, follow these steps:

1. Select each path you'd like to join with the Pointer tool.

2. Choose Modify ⇨ Join or Ctrl+J (Command+J).

   Windows users can also select the Join button on the Modify toolbar.

Once you've joined paths, they will stay that way until they are split. To split joined paths, choose Modify ⇨ Split or use the keyboard shortcut, Ctrl+Shift+J (Command+Shift+J). In Windows, you can also select the Split button on the Modify toolbar.

Editing Paths

So far in this chapter, most of the path editing tools have been fairly extreme; delete, distort, rescale, rotate — these terms don't promise much degree of subtlety. Fireworks does offer several other tools, however, that can redraw portions of a path or reshape an area with a varying amount of pressure. And for those times that require a precise, almost surgical removal of path segments, Fireworks offers a Knife tool that performs as sharply as any real blade.

Redrawing a path

If you've ever drawn a shape that was perfect except for one little area of it, you'll greatly appreciate the Redraw Path tool. As the name implies, this tool enables you to redraw any portion of a completed path, in effect throwing away the portion of the original path that you're replacing.

The Redraw Path tool, found in the flyout under the Brush, is a freehand drawing tool. When you're redoing a segment of a path, you initially select any part of the path to start redrawing and then reconnect to the original path. Fireworks erases the portion of the original path that is between the beginning and the ending points of your redrawn section and connects your new path to the old path.

To redraw a portion of a path, follow these steps:

1. Select the path you want to redraw.

2. Choose the Redraw Path tool from the flyout under the Brush tool. Alternatively, you can press the keyboard shortcut, B, twice.

3. Move the pointer over the area of the path where you want to start redrawing. Fireworks displays a small caret (^) in the lower right of the pointer when you are in position over the path.

4. Click and drag out your new path.

5. Position your pointer over the original path in the spot where you want to connect the new and old paths, and then release the mouse button. Fireworks removes the old path segment and connects the new path segment.

The Redraw Path tool isn't just for correcting mistakes, though. Figure 9-14 shows how the Redraw Path tool can be used to make a portion of a geometric shape more organic-looking.

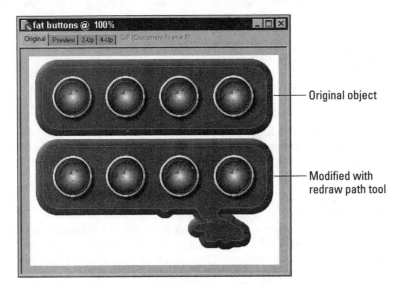

Figure 9-14: The Redraw Path tool can easily alter a standard shape into something unique.

> **Tip**   Pressing Shift while using the Redraw Path tool constrains your replacement path to lines in increments of 45 degrees.

Freeform and Reshape Area

Looking for a cool tool to give your objects that unique twist? Look no further than Freeform and Reshape Area. Rather than add or delete points like other tools, these reshaping features let you sculpt a path, pulling and pushing a line like so much stretchable clay.

Although similar, there are a couple of key differences between the two tools:

✦ **Freeform:** Both pushes and pulls a segment of a selected path.

✦ **Reshape Area:** Only pushes a path, but controls the degree it pushes through the strength field in the Tool Options. Moreover, this tool can reshape an entire object, as well as just a segment.

Pushing a path into a new shape

To push a path into a new shape with the Freeform tool, follow these steps:

1. Select the path you want to alter.

2. Choose the Freeform tool from the Toolbox or use it's keyboard shortcut, F.

3. Position your cursor slightly off the path that you want to push. This could to either side of an open path, or inside or outside of a closed path.

> **Note**
>
> Positioning your cursor slightly off a path enables the Freeform push cursor. Positioning your cursor directly on a path enables the Freeform pull cursor, covered later in this chapter.

The cursor changes into a circle, as shown in Figure 9-15. Think of the circle as an object that you will use to push against the stroke.

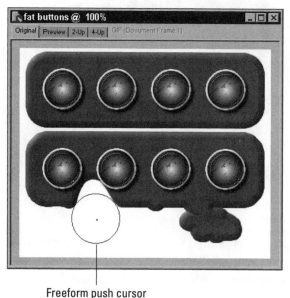

Freeform push cursor

Figure 9-15: Round out your paths with the Freeform tool's push mode.

4. Click and drag the ball cursor into the path, pushing it into a new shape.

Caution   Pushing a closed path too fast or too far results in an overlapping path line with unpredictable results.

5. Release the mouse button when you're satisfied with the shape.

Pulling a path segment into a new shape

To pull a segment of a path into a new shape, follow these steps:

1. Select the path you want to alter.

2. Choose the Freeform tool from the Toolbox or use its keyboard shortcut, F.

3. Position your cursor directly over the segment of the path that you want to pull. An S-curve is added to the lower right of the Freeform cursor, as shown in Figure 9-16.

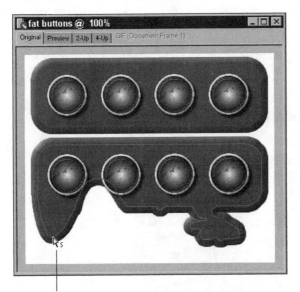

Figure 9-16: The Freeform tool is used to pull out a segment of a path.

Freeform pull cursor

4. Click and drag in the direction that you want to pull the segment. You can pull the path away from or into the object.

5. Release the mouse button in order to complete the pull.

Fireworks adds as few pixels as possible when you are pulling with the Freeform tool. Pulling is like pinching just the one point of the path and dragging it away from the rest of the shape. By contrast, the push mode of the Freeform tool is more like using a ball to reshape the path. The size of the ball with which you push is determined through the Freeform Tool Options panel.

Freeform Tool Options panel

To alter the size of the ball used with Freeform push mode, double-click the Freeform tool to view its Tool Options panel, shown in Figure 9-17, and enter a new value in the Size text box or use the slider to choose a new pixel size. The Size option ranges from 1 to 500 pixels.

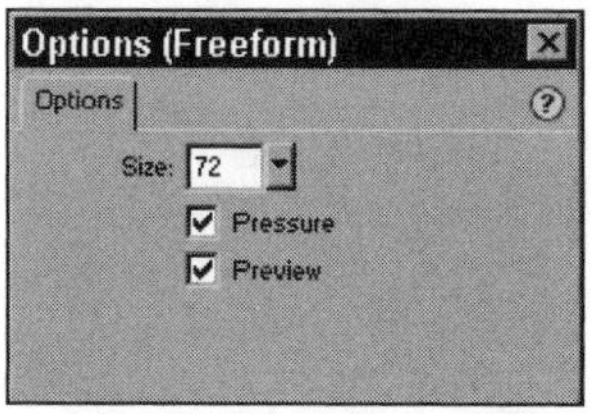

Figure 9-17: The Freeform tool's Tool Options panel allows you to set options, such as the size of the push cursor.

The Options panel offers two other options for the Freeform tool. The Preview option draws the stroke and fill, if any, while you use the Freeform tool. Although this can be a bit processor-intensive, I enable it whenever I'm using Freeform on an object with a wide stroke, such as an Airbrush, because the final effect can be so different from just the path. When the Preview option is not on, you'll see both the old outline and the new one while you are using the tool; when you stop drawing, the old outline vanishes.

The other option, Pressure, is generally useful only if you're using a pressure-sensitive graphics tablet. When enabled, a medium amount of pressure specifies a push cursor the size set in the Tool Options panel; lighter amounts of pressure reduce the size, and greater amounts increase it.

Altering a path object with one operation

Though the Reshape Area tool, when set to a small size, achieves similar effects to the Freeform tool, that's not what makes it special. The Reshape Area tool is best when used to warp or to reshape an entire image. Take Figure 9-18, for example. I start with a star created with the Polygon tool and then apply the Reshape Area tool, set to a size on the Options panel larger than the star. By dragging the Reshape Area tool over the star, I transform the entire standard shape—not just one segment—into something unique.

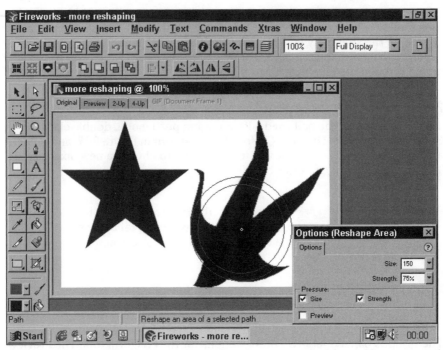

Figure 9-18: The Reshape Area tool can alter an entire path object with one operation.

To use the Reshape Area tool, follow these steps:

1. Select the path you want to alter.

2. Choose the Reshape Area tool from the flyout underneath the Freeform tool, or press the keyboard shortcut, F, twice.

Tip   Each time you press F, you toggle between the Freeform and Reshape Area tools.

3. Position your pointer over the object that you want to reshape.

4. Click and drag in the desired direction.

5. Release the mouse button when you're satisfied with the resulting object.

Like the Freeform tool, the Size is set on the Tool Options panel; you'll also find Pressure and Preview options that function in the same manner as those for the Freeform tool. In addition, the Reshape Area tool has a Strength option. The Strength value determines the strength of the Reshape Area tool's gravitational-like pull. Strength is percentage based; at 100 percent, you'll get the maximum effect from the tool. If you're using a pressure-sensitive graphics tablet, you can alter both the size and the strength of the Reshape Area tool while drawing with your stylus.

Tip Don't have a graphics tablet yet? To simulate a lighter stylus touch, use either 1 or the left arrow key; pressing 2 or the right arrow key simulates increasing the pressure on a graphics pad.

Path Scrubber

The Path Scrubber tools are fairly subtle compared to the other tools covered in this chapter. If you've experimented with strokes such as Airbrush, you've noticed how the stroke can change according to how fast or, with a graphics tablet, how much pressure you use when you draw. The Path Scrubber tools alter these variables, after you've completed the path. One Path Scrubber tool increases the interactive effect, and one lessens it, as shown in Figure 9-19.

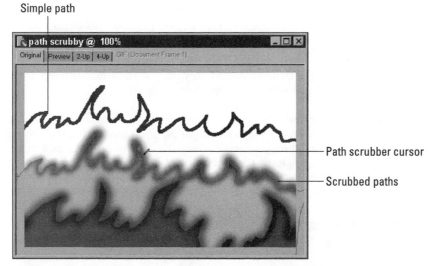

Simple path

path scrubby @ 100%

Original | Preview | 2-Up | 4-Up | GIF (Document Frame 1)

Path scrubber cursor

Scrubbed paths

Figure 9-19: The Path Scrubber tools can turn a simple path into one that looks like it was created with a pressure-sensitive pen and tablet.

To use the Path Scrubber tools, follow these steps:

1. Apply a stroke to your path that uses speed- or pressure-sensitive effects, such as Air Brush.

2. If you want to increase the pressure effect, choose the Path Scrubber Plus tool; if you want to decrease the pressure effect, choose the Path Scrubber Minus tool. Both are in the flyout underneath the Freeform tool. You can also select them by pressing the keyboard shortcut, U, twice.

3. Trace over the portion of the path where you want to adjust the speed or pressure effect.

Options panel

When Fireworks draws a path, both speed and pressure data are gathered. The Path Scrubber tools can work with either the speed or pressure information, or both; moreover, they can do it at a variable rate. The Options panel for these tools have all the controls you'll need:

✦ **Rate:** The relative strength of the tool. Pick a value from 10 (the most effect) to 1 (the least effect).

✦ **Pressure:** Enabling this option directs the Path Scrubber tools to adjust the path according to the simulated pressure of the stroke.

✦ **Speed:** Enabling this option directs the Path Scrubber tools to adjust the path according to the simulated speed of the stroke.

Knife

One of my favorite — and most useful — design tools is my X-ACTO knife. The ability to finely trim the tightest curves has saved me many times. The computer equivalent of this excellent implement is the Knife tool. The Knife tool is used only with paths, just as its counterpart, the Eraser, is only used with bitmap images. Basically, the Knife tool divides one path into two separate paths.

The Knife cuts paths by drawing a line where you want the separation to take place. You can use the Knife tool on open or closed paths, or on any path-based object. With an open path, you need only intersect the path once in order to make the cut once; with a closed path, you have to draw a line all the way across the object with the Knife, as shown in Figure 9-20.

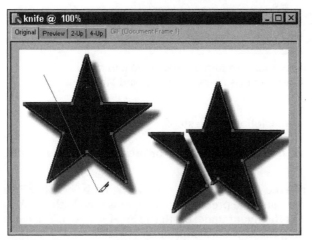

Figure 9-20: The Knife stroke on the left cut the object into two pieces, which can then be pulled apart, as shown on the right.

To use the Knife, follow these steps:

1. Select the path you plan to divide.

2. Choose the Knife tool from the Toolbox or use the keyboard shortcut, E.

3. Draw a line through the path with the Knife tool. Fireworks separates the path, although this is not always immediately obvious because both new paths are still selected.

4. To move one of the newly divided paths, choose the Pointer tool and click once on the canvas away from any object. The split paths are deselected.

5. Select either portion of the original path. Only one part is now selected and can be deleted, moved, or otherwise modified.

The Knife tool is also great for making specific shapes, such as arcs. Just draw a standard circle and then use the Knife to slice off a portion of it. Like many tools, pressing Shift constrains the Knife to angles with increments of 45 degrees.

 Caution Although the Tool Options panel shows various selections for the Eraser/Knife tool, all the parameters are only useful for the bitmap-oriented Eraser. Changing the options does not affect the Knife tool.

Path Operations

The more you work in vector-based drawing programs such as Fireworks, the sooner you begin to look for new and novel shapes. Face it, no matter how many points you put on that star, it's still a star. Whereas you can warp and reshape any existing object using the various tools described elsewhere in this chapter, it's often far easier to create a compound shape composed of two or more basic shapes.

You can find all the commands that merge paths — Union, Intersect, Punch, and Crop — under the Modify ⇨ Combine menu option. You'll find the stroke commands — Simplify, Expand Stroke, and Inset Path — under Modify ⇨ Alter Path.

When you combine multiple paths, the stroke, fill, and effects settings of the bottom object in the stacking order — the one closest to the canvas — are applied to the new combined object.

Union

The Union command enables you to combine two or more objects into one merged object. One technique that helps me decide whether Union is the proper command to use is that time-honored artist's tool, squinting. After I've positioned objects with which to form my new shape, I lean back from the monitor and squint so that I can see just the outline of the new shape. That's precisely what Union does — it combines the shapes into an overall outline and removes any overlapping areas.

The technique for using Union, like all of the Combine commands, is straightforward. Just position your objects, select them all, and then choose Modify ➪ Combine ➪ Union. Occasionally, you'll have to adjust the individual paths to get them just right. For example, when I created the martini glass in Figure 9-21, I united three objects: a triangle, a rectangle, and a custom Pen-drawn shape for the base. After my first attempt, I realized that the rectangle and the base didn't quite match, so I chose Edit ➪ Undo — okay, I actually used the shortcut, Ctrl+Z (Command+Z) — and adjusted the base. Then, after reselecting them and reissuing the command, I was ready to pour.

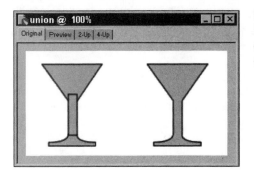

Figure 9-21: Three objects on the left were combined with the Union command to form the new object on the right.

Intersect

Whereas Union throws away the overlapping parts of combined paths, Intersect keeps only the overlapping areas from all selected paths. Believe it or not, the key word in the previous sentence is *all* — if even one object doesn't overlap at least some part of all of the other selected objects, the Intersect operation erases all of your objects. That caveat out of the way, you'll find Intersect to be a useful command. I mean, how else could you create the perfect pizza slice, as I did in Figure 9-22? After the two objects on the left were selected, I chose Modify ➪ Combine ➪ Intersect. Pizza's ready!

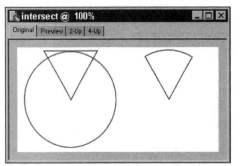

Figure 9-22: Combining a circle and a triangle with the Intersect command creates the perfect pizza slice.

Punch

Remember the paper punch you had in school? That little handheld device that took a round bite out of whatever you could get between its jaws? The Punch command is the same concept, except you define the punch shape to be anything you want. When two path objects overlap, the shape on top is punched out of the shape on the bottom. You can see the Punch command illustrated in Figure 9-23, as I continue the food metaphors with the creation of a donut of sorts. After making sure that my two circles were centered on each other, I selected them both and chose Modify ➪ Combine ➪ Punch.

Figure 9-23: The Punch command removes the shape of the top object from the bottom object.

Tip   What happens when you apply the Punch command to more than two selected objects? The top object is still used as the punch pattern—and all of the objects are affected, but not joined.

Crop

Plainly put, Crop is the opposite of Punch. With Punch, the top object is cut out of any other selected object. With Crop, the bottom object forms the clipping path for the top object. To round out our food-like illustrations of the Combine commands, Figure 9-24 disposes of all but the last bite of a cookie. I created the shapes of the remains, joined the shapes into a single object, and selected that object and the cookie, and then chose Modify ➪ Combine ➪ Crop. Almost all gone in one bite.

Simplify

Freeform drawing tools are terrific for quickly sketching out a specific shape. But, quite often, the computer representation of your flowing strokes turns out pretty blocky. The Simplify command is designed to reduce the number of points used in a path while maintaining the overall shape of the object.

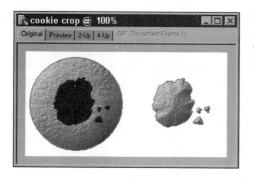

Figure 9-24: With the Crop command, the shape of the original top object provides the shape of the resulting object.

If you choose Modify ⇨ Alter Path ⇨ Simplify, the Simplify dialog box opens and enables you to specify the number of pixels affected. The range is from 1 to 100; a relatively low value of 12 was used to dramatic effect in Figure 9-25. The original hand-drawn fellow on the left has too many points; trimming them down by hand would be arduous. After I applied the Simplify command, a smoother, simpler object resulted. That's not necessarily the last step, though. Usually, you'll find yourself tweaking a simplified object's Bézier handles in order to get things just right.

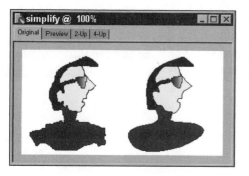

Figure 9-25: After the Simplify command is applied to the original hand-drawn paths, the result is the smoother and simpler gentleman on the right.

Expand stroke

Though you can accomplish much with an open path through the Stroke panel, sometimes you need a Fill, as well. The Expand Stroke command offers an easy way to convert any path — open or closed — into a larger closed path by enclosing the existing path and then deleting it.

When you apply this command by choosing Modify ⇨ Alter Paths ⇨ Expand Stroke, the Expand Stroke dialog box appears, as shown in Figure 9-26. As you can see, it offers quite a few options that enable you to control exactly what kind of path to use to expand the stroke. The options include the following:

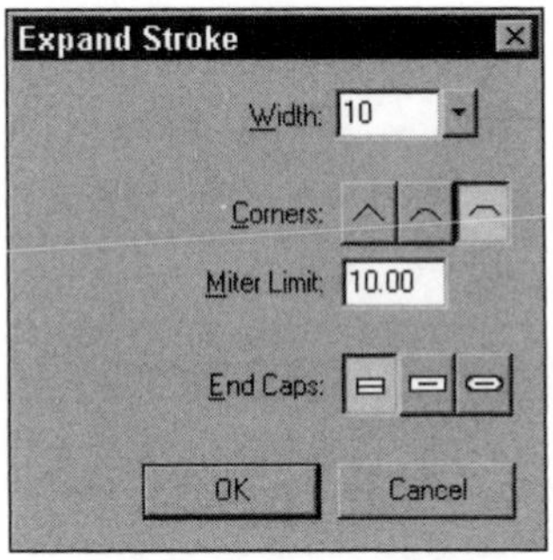

Figure 9-26: Choose your options in the Expand Stroke dialog box in order to make a wide range of Expanded strokes.

✦ **Width:** Determines the final width of the expanded stroke. The range is from 1 to 99 pixels.

✦ **Corners:** Choose from three types of corners. From left to right, the buttons represent

- **Miter:** With a miter corner, the outside edges of the path extend until they touch in a sharp corner. Because miter corners can become quite long, you can limit their length with the Miter Limit option, which is explained in this list.

- **Round:** The corner is rounded equally from both sides of the path approaching the corner. Round corners and round end caps are often used together.

- **Bevel:** The corner is cut off at the center of the meeting paths, rather than on the outside edge, as with the miter corner. This results in a truncated corner.

✦ **Miter Limit:** The number of pixels the miter corner can extend before being cut off. The Miter Limit works only with miter corners.

✦ **End Caps:** Choose among the following three End Cap types for closing off the expanded path:

- **Butt Cap:** The Butt Cap creates a right-angle End Cap where the end is perpendicular to the last point of the stroke.

- **Square Cap:** Similar to the Round Cap, the Square Cap attaches a square to the end of the path, extending it the same radius as half the set width.

- **Round Cap:** A Round Cap attaches a semicircle to the end of the path, extending it the same radius as half the set width.

Figure 9-27 shows the three different End Cap types, as well as an example of what it looks like to change an object that consists of strokes and fills into an object made up entirely of fills. Once you've expanded the strokes, set the stroke to None and apply a fill to the whole object. Note that the third and fourth face use the hair from the first face.

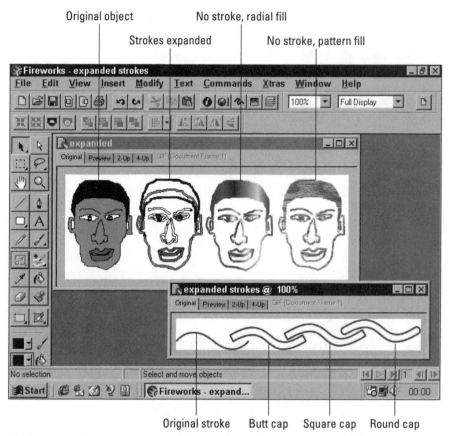

Figure 9-27: The Expand Stroke command can change strokes to fills.

Inset path

Whereas Expand Stroke applies strokes on both sides of a selected path, Inset Path only applies strokes on one side. The Inset dialog box is identical to the Expand Stroke dialog box except for the addition of Inside and Outside options. You'll get the most predictable results with Inset Path if you apply it to closed paths, but you can use it with any kind of path except straight lines.

Often, a plain and boring object can be replaced with an interesting variation just by applying the Inset Path command, as shown in Figure 9-28.

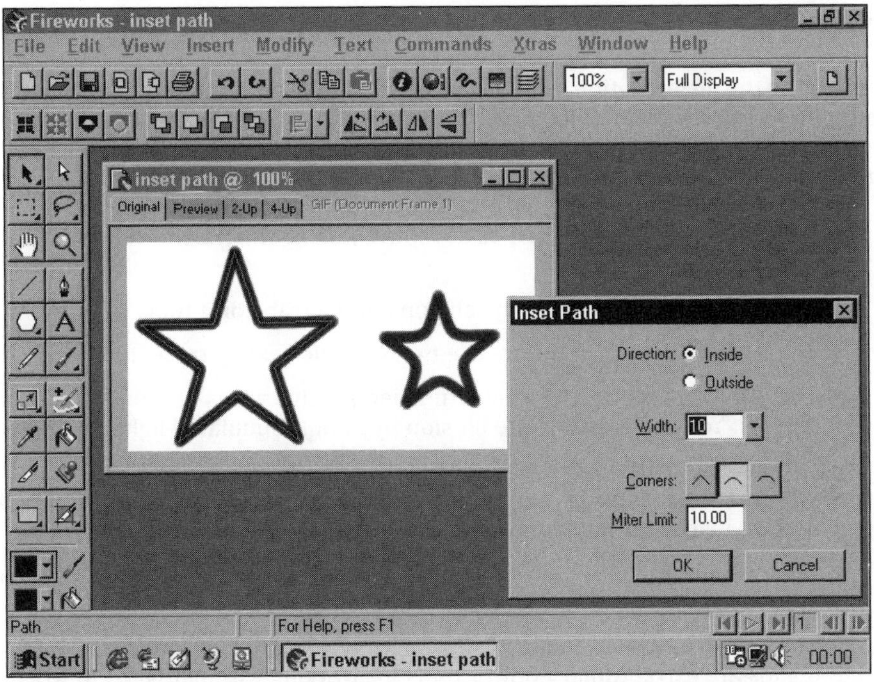

Figure 9-28: Create variations of an object with the Inset Path command.

One of my favorite applications of the Inset Path command is to create concentric shapes, each one within the next.

To use the Inset Path command to create concentric shapes, follow these steps:

1. Select the closed path to which you want to add concentric shapes.

2. Choose Edit ➪ Clone. Because Inset Path erases the original path, you must apply the command to a clone of the original path.

3. Choose Modify ➪ Alter Path ➪ Inset Path. The Inset dialog box appears.

4. Choose the Direction, Width, and Corner option. If you choose the Miter Corner, you can enter a Miter Limit. Click OK when you're done. The new path is drawn and the old path is deleted.

5. Repeat Steps 2-4 for as many concentric shapes as desired, keeping the same values in the Inset dialog box in order to create equidistant shapes.

After you've created your basic shapes, you can go in and vary the stroke width or other settings in order to create interesting effects.

Summary

Mastering the manipulation of paths is essential in order to achieve the most possible with Fireworks. Path objects can be distorted, resized, rotated, and adjusted in many subtle ways in order to create the basic shapes you need for unique Web graphics. When altering Fireworks objects, keep these points in mind:

✦ Objects can be manipulated as a whole by using the transform tools: Scale, Skew, and Distort.

✦ You can rotate an object using any one of the transform tools.

✦ For precise sizing or rotation, use the Numeric Transform feature.

✦ The Skew tool is great for simulating perspective views — especially of image objects. You can enhance the illusion by adding simulated light and shadow effects.

✦ Whereas the Pointer is used to move an entire path, the Subselection tool is used to maneuver individual points — and their Bézier control handles.

✦ Once you draw a path, you can edit it in numerous ways by using tools such as Freeform, Redraw Path, Redraw Area, and Path Scrubber.

✦ The Union, Intersect, Punch, Crop, Simplify, Expand Path, and Inset Path commands are extraordinary power tools for working with paths in Fireworks.

In the next chapter, you'll see how to add text to your Web graphics in Fireworks.

✦   ✦   ✦

Composing with Text

In This Chapter

Composing with the Text Editor

Inserting text files

Applying strokes and fills to text

Changing from text to paths

Flowing text on a path

Masking images with text

Text has a special place in Web graphics. Though the vast majority of text — paragraphs, lists, and tables of information — is a product of the HTML page viewed through a browser, graphic-based text is generally used to create logos, fancy headings, and other decorative elements that aren't possible with basic HTML. In addition, text is an integral part of a key Web element: navigation. Many navigation buttons use text, either alone or in combination with symbols, to quickly convey meaning.

Before Fireworks, a recurring nightmare for Web designers involved modifying a text graphic. Whether it was a typo or a client change-of-mind that forced the revision, the designer was stuck having to redo an entire graphic because any text, once applied, was just another bunch of pixels. Fireworks changed all that with the introduction of editable text. Now, if a client's logo changes because of a $7-billion merger or you just forgot to put the period at the end of *Inc.*, text modifications are just a double-click away.

A few programs have since followed Macromedia's lead, but Fireworks still leads the way. We'll look at basic things like choosing fonts and aligning text, as well as more advanced features like attaching text to a path. We'll also explore a technique that enables you to combine images with text using Fireworks Mask Groups.

Using the Text Editor

In Fireworks, all text creation and most modification takes place in the Text Editor. The Text Editor, shown in Figure 10-1, is a separate window with a full range of text controls and its own preview pane. After you create the text, a *text object* appears in the current Fireworks document, surrounded by a bounding box. The text object has many, but not all of the properties of a path object—you can, for example, use the transform tools such as Skew, but you can't use Reshape Area to warp the text as you can a path. On the other hand, text objects have features unlike any other object, such as the capability to be aligned to a path, such as a circle. If necessary, it's possible to convert a text object to a path object or an image object, but the text can no longer be edited.

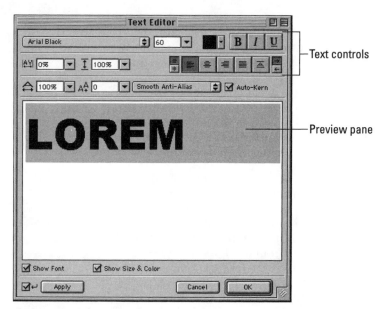

Figure 10-1: The Text Editor is used to compose and edit text in Fireworks.

The Text tool in the Toolbox is your initial gateway into the Text Editor. The Text tool can be used two ways:

✦ Click once on the canvas with the Text tool to set a starting point for your text. If necessary, the text flows to the edge of the current document and expands downward toward the bottom of the document.

✦ Drag out a rectangular text region with the Text tool. The text created in the Text Editor wraps on the horizontal boundaries of the established region and, if necessary, expands downward.

The general steps for inserting text into a Fireworks document are:

1. Select the Text tool from the Toolbox or use the keyboard shortcut, T.

2. Set the text area by:

- Clicking once on the document where you'd like the text to start

- Dragging out a text area for the text to fit into

Either method opens the Text Editor.

3. From the Text Editor, choose the text characteristic such as font, size, color, and alignment.

4. Click in the Preview pane and input the text. If Auto-Apply is enabled, Fireworks updates the text object in the document after each keystroke.

5. Click OK when you're done.

Tip

Pressing Enter (Return) when your cursor is in the Preview pane adds a line break, as you might expect. Unfortunately, the OK button in the Text Editor is highlighted, and that may tempt you to hit Enter (Return) to dismiss the Text Editor dialog box. Press the other Enter on the numeric keypad to dismiss the Text Editor.

Once the text object is onscreen, you move it as you would any other Fireworks object, by clicking and dragging with the Pointer tool. To adjust the shape of the text object, drag any of the six handles that become available when you select the object.

Note

Dragging a text object's handles doesn't resize the text itself, but instead changes the outside boundaries of the text object, after which, the text reflows through its new boundaries. A text object can only be vertically resized to fit the current text it contains. If you want your text object to take up more vertical room, select it and choose a larger font size from the Text ➪ Size menu.

When you need to edit an existing text object, there are several ways to open the Text Editor. You can select the text object as you would any other Fireworks object and then choose Text ➪ Editor. Alternatively, once the text object is selected, you can press the keyboard shortcut, Ctrl+Shift+E (Command+Shift+E). You can also choose the Text tool from the toolbox and hover it over an existing text object; when the I-beam cursor gains a small, right-pointing triangle, click once to open the Text Editor. Finally, the most efficient method (and certainly my most often-used one) is to double-click the text object with the Pointer or Subselection tool.

Previewing on the fly

Fireworks features real-time text updating in the document for each change made in the Text Editor. Any edit — either to the text itself in the Preview pane or through the text controls — is instantly reflected in the text object, as shown in Figure 10-2. This simplifies both the creation phase, when you're trying to find the right overall look, and the tweaking phase, as you make incremental adjustments.

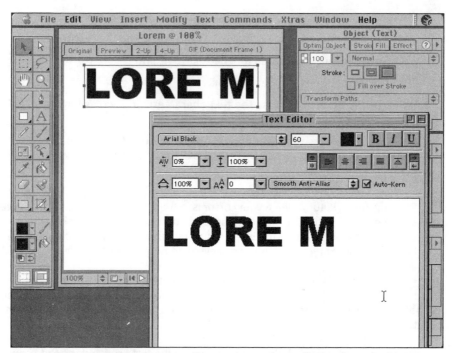

Figure 10-2: Updates in the Text Editor are instantly applied to the text object in the document in Fireworks. A space added between the *E* and the *M* in the Text Editor shows up immediately on the canvas.

Choosing basic font characteristics

Within the Text Editor, you have full control over the look and style of your text. The Text Editor offers two methods of working, just like a word-processing program. To set your options, use either one of the following techniques:

✦ Set the font attributes prior to entering text into the Preview pane.

✦ Select the text you want to modify in the Preview pane — all or a portion — and then alter the attributes.

The core characteristics are all found at the top of the Text Editor, as shown in Figure 10-3.

Text size slider   Text styles

Font list   Text size box   Color well

Figure 10-3: Select your font typeface, size, color, and style from the top of the Text Editor.

The basic attributes are very straightforward to establish:

✦ **Font:** To choose a typeface, select a name from the Font list. The Font list displays all the available TrueType or Type 1 fonts on your system.

> **Tip**
>
> Windows users can also select the Font list itself and either use the cursor keys to move up or down the list one font at a time, or type the first letter of a font's name to jump to that part of the list.

✦ **Size:** Choose the text size using the Text Size slider or by entering a value directly in the Text Size box. Size is the height of a font in points. Fireworks accepts sizes from 4 to 1,000 points, although the slider only goes from 8 to 128.

Caution You can also adjust text size by using the Scale tool on your text object, just as you would resize any other object. Although the text remains editable, its point size in the Text Editor doesn't change as you resize it. This can become confusing when you attempt to edit a huge text object and find that it says it's 10pt in the Text Editor.

✦ **Color:** Initially, the Text Editor applies the color specified in the Fill color well. However, you can easily choose a new text fill color by selecting the option arrow next to the color well in the Text Editor. The standard pop-up color picker is displayed with the current swatch set. Each character in your text object can have its own color.

✦ **Style:** Choose from Bold, Italic, and Underline styles for your text; each style button is a toggle and any or all can be applied to one text object.

Tip The Underline style is useful for mimicking hyperlinks in design mock-ups you might create for client approval, before actually making any HTML.

All of the basic attributes are applicable on a letter-by-letter basis. You can — although it's inadvisable for aesthetic reasons — change every letter's font, size, color, or style. Ransom notes were never easier.

Adjusting text spacing

All adjustments to how text is located within the text object occurs in the Text Editor only. Fireworks includes five text-spacing controls, as shown in Figure 10-4.

Kerning

Kerning determines how close letters appear to each other. The default value of 0 percent uses the standard font spacing. Increasing the Kerning slider (1 percent to 100 percent) moves letters further apart, whereas decreasing it (-1 percent to -100 percent) moves letters closer together, or overlaps them. Alter the kerning between two letters by placing the cursor between the letters in the Preview pane of the Text Editor and moving the Kerning slider or entering a new value. To change the kerning for a range of letters or the entire text in the Preview pane, select the letters before changing the kerning value.

Note The Preview pane does not show changes in the kerning. However, if you have the Auto-Apply option checked, you can see the effect of kerning on your text object in the document itself after each change.

Auto Kern

Many fonts define the spacing for *kerning pairs,* like the letters "WA" or "ov," which fit together, to make text more legible. Some fonts come with as many as 500 kerning pairs defined. Fireworks applies the kerning pair information whenever the Auto Kern option is enabled. The Auto Kern option affects the entire text object.

Horizontal Scale   Baseline shift

Kerning   Leading   Auto Kern checkbox

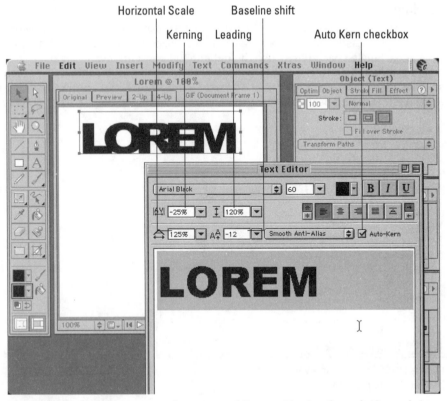

Figure 10-4: Control your text character and line positioning through Fireworks' text-spacing controls.

The effect of kerning pairs is most noticeable in the larger font sizes. The top text object in Figure 10-5 has Auto Kern enabled, which is the default. The bottom object is identical except that the Auto Kern option has been unchecked. Note the differences in the overall length of the word as well as how the first A fits between the W and the V. Leave Auto Kern checked unless you have a specific reason not to do so.

Auto kerning on

Auto kerning off

Figure 10-5: The Auto Kern option uses a font's built-in spacing for better kerning, as shown in the top text object.

Leading

Leading (pronounced *ledding*) is the printer's term for line spacing. In Fireworks, leading is expressed as a percentage of the font size and only affects text with multiple lines. Single-spaced lines use the default 100 percent; a value of 200 percent would give you a double-spaced paragraph. Leading values less than 90 percent or so will cause lines to touch or overlap (see Figure 10-6). Unless you're creating a special effect, you'll probably want to keep your leading at 90 percent or higher.

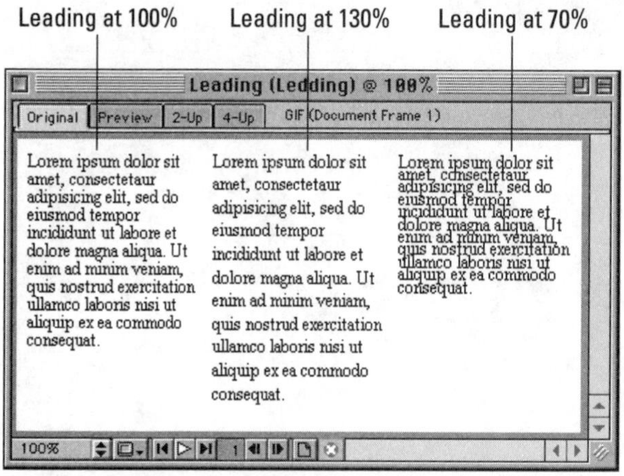

Leading at 100%   Leading at 130%   Leading at 70%

Figure 10-6: The Leading value controls the space between multiple lines of text.

Horizontal Scale

You can alter the relative width of any text through the Horizontal Scale control. The range of the Horizontal Scale slider is from 50 percent to 300 percent, but you can specify another value through the text box. The effect of the Horizontal Scale can be seen in Figure 10-7 where the same text is presented at 200 percent, 100 percent, 50 percent, and 25 percent. Horizontal Scale does not display in the Preview pane.

Note   Don't confuse kerning and Horizontal Scale. Kerning is the space between individual characters; Horizontal Scale affects the size of the whole text object as one.

Baseline Shift

If you're building a Web site where chemical formulas are a key element, you'll be happy to discover the Baseline Shift control. Normally, all text is rendered along the same baseline so that the bottoms of most letters are aligned. The Baseline Shift control enables you to place letters or words above or below the normal baseline. Fireworks specifies the Baseline Shift value in points: negative values go below the baseline, and positive values go above. For a standard subscript letter, such as the 2 in H_2O, use a negative value about half the size of the current font (see Figure 10-8). Likewise, for a superscript, choose a positive value; again, about half the current font size.

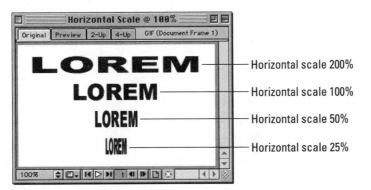

Horizontal scale 200%
Horizontal scale 100%
Horizontal scale 50%
Horizontal scale 25%

Figure 10-7: Change the width of a text object by adjusting the Horizontal Scale slider in the Text Editor.

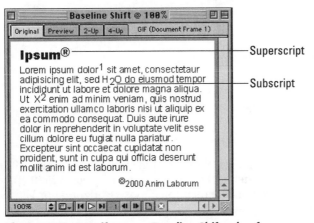

Superscript
Subscript

Figure 10-8: Specify a new Baseline Shift value for subscript characters like the 2 in H_2O, and superscript characters such as the ® and the footnote-style 1.

Aligning text

All text objects, when selected in the Fireworks document, are surrounded by a bounding box. The bounding box sets the position of the text through its upper-left corner coordinates, but it also determines the limits for the text block. Most importantly, all alignment for the text is relative to the bounding box.

Different alignment options can be applied to different text in the same text object, as long as each piece of text is on its own line. Figure 10-9 illustrates this capability with each of the five horizontal alignment options in one paragraph, as well as showing whole paragraphs of each option.

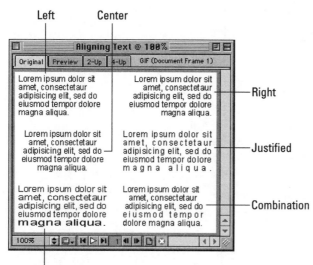

Figure 10-9: Fireworks offers many text alignment options.

The Text Editor contains controls for specifying text alignment (see Figure 10-10). Text can be either Horizontal (the default) or Vertical, and run left to right (the default) or right to left. Depending on whether you choose Horizontal or Vertical, the remaining alignment buttons change.

When Horizontal is selected, the alignment choices are:

✦ **Left Alignment:** Text is aligned to the left edge of the bounding box.

✦ **Right Alignment:** Text is aligned to the right edge of the bounding box.

✦ **Center Alignment:** Text is centered between the left and right edges of the bounding box.

✦ **Justified Alignment:** Text is evenly spaced so that the letters of each line touch both the left and right edges of the bounding box; the letters, however, remain the size specified in the Font size.

✦ **Stretched Alignment:** Text is expanded horizontally so that the letters of each line touch both the left and right edges of the bounding box.

✦ **Text Flows Left to Right:** Text is rendered across the screen, from left to right.

✦ **Text Flows Right to Left:** Text is rendered across the screen, from right to left.

Tip

The middle sizing handles on a text object's bounding box are always adjustable. This is a very useful feature, because you can quickly center text in a document by dragging the middle sizing handles to either edge of the canvas and choosing the Center alignment option in the Text Editor.

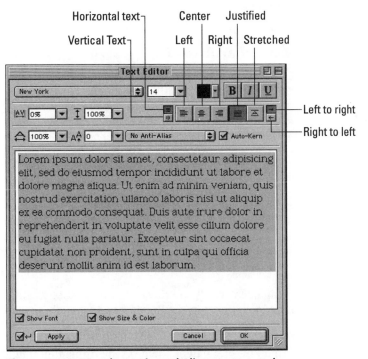

Figure 10-10: Use the Horizontal Alignment controls to align text left, center, right, justified, or stretched.

When Vertical Text is chosen, the alignment options change to:

✦ **Top Alignment:** Text is aligned to the top of the bounding box.

✦ **Center Alignment:** Text is centered between the top and bottom of the bounding box.

✦ **Bottom Alignment:** Text is aligned to the bottom of the bounding box.

✦ **Justified Alignment:** Text is evenly spaced so that the letters of each line touch both the top and bottom edges of the bounding box; however, the letters remain the size specified in the Font size.

✦ **Stretched Alignment:** Text is expanded vertically so that the letters of each line touch both the top and bottom edges of the bounding box.

✦ **Text Flows Down and Up:** Text is rendered down the screen, starting from the top of the bounding box.

✦ **Text Flows Up and Down:** Text is rendered up the screen, starting from the bottom of the bounding box.

Enabling Text Editor options

The final element found in the Text Editor are the options: two for the Text Editor itself and three for the final product. To get the closest approximation possible in the Preview pane, enable both the Show Font and Show Size & Color options. The Show Font option displays the text in the current selected typeface; when the Show Font option is turned off, the Preview pane shows text in a sans-serif font, such as Arial or Helvetica. The Size & Color option — no surprises here — let you see your text in the current size and color. Without this option enabled, you'll see text at approximately 24 points and black.

The three other options, Anti-Alias, Auto Kern, and Apply, are applicable to the text object. The Anti-Alias option smoothes the text by providing an anti-aliased edge to the fill for the text object. Auto Kern, as discussed in the previous section on text spacing, uses a font's kerning pairs. Apply enables any changes made in the Text Editor to be automatically updated and viewed in the document's text object.

In my way of working, only occasionally do these features actually become optional. If I have a large block of text in the Preview pane, I might disable the Size & Color option, but I almost never turn off the Font option. Only when I'm trying to achieve a special effect would I even consider disabling either Anti-Alias or Auto Kern. And I've noticed that I'm totally dependent on the Apply function for constant feedback as I work.

Re-Editing Text

The Text Editor is perhaps the most commonly used method for editing text in Fireworks, but it's not the only one. To make a global change to a text object, such as altering the typeface or size, you can use a menu command. Although you do sacrifice the full range of features, menus can be much faster than using the Text Editor, especially if you take advantage of the keyboard shortcuts.

In all, four menu items under the Text heading can be applied to a selected text object:

  ✦ **Font:** Lists the fonts available on your system, in alphabetical order. To access a font not shown in the list for lack of room, choose Text ➪ Fonts ➪ More Fonts to open a small dialog box that enables you to access all of the fonts in your system.

  ✦ **Size:** To quickly change your selected text object to a set size, choose Text ➪ Size and then one of the dozen point sizes: 8, 9, 10, 12, 14, 18, 24, 36, 48, 72, 96, and 120. Choose Other to enter a different size than those available.

New Feature Fireworks 3 now offers more precise control of text sizing for those who prefer to use the menus to set sizing. Choose Text ➪ Size ➪ Other to view the Text Size dialog box and enter a custom size.

  ✦ **Style:** In addition to the options available through the Text Editor (Bold, Italic, and Underline), the Text ➪ Style menu enables you to remove all styles with one command, Text ➪ Style ➪ Plain. You can also use the keyboard shortcut, Ctrl+Alt+Shift+P (Command+Option+Shift+P).

  ✦ **Align:** The Text ➪ Align menu is broken up into two groups, one for horizontal text and one for vertical text. Choosing an alignment from one group automatically alters the orientation of the text, if necessary. For example, if you apply Text ➪ Align ➪ Bottom to a horizontal text object, the text object converts to a vertical text object and aligns the text to the bottom, simultaneously.

To be completely thorough, there is one other command in the Text menu that could be listed in this category, Text ➪ Editor, which opens the Text Editor for the selected text object. Alternatively, you can use the keyboard shortcut, Ctrl+Shift+E (Command+Shift+E).

Importing Text

Almost all of the text that's used in Web graphics is relatively short; longer paragraphs are generally part of the HTML file rendered by the browser. There are numerous reasons why text on the Web is generally not in graphic form, although first and foremost—as with many aspects of the Web—is file size. Download times for a page of graphic text is considerably longer than for that of HTML text.

However, in the for-every-rule-there's-an-exception category, occasionally blocks of text have to be rendered as a graphic. Some clients insist on an absolute fidelity to their traditional printed material across all platforms. The only way to keep these types of clients happy—even at the expense of a longer download—is to render the text as a graphic. In these cases, you'll have the potential for taking advantage of one of Fireworks' least-known features: text import.

In addition to the numerous graphic file types supported by Fireworks, you can also open ASCII and Rich Text Format (RTF) files. ASCII (American Standard Code for Information Interchange) files are the lowest common denominator of all text files and contain no formatting whatsoever. RTF files, on the other hand, convey a good deal of basic formatting, such as typeface, size, styles (bold, italic, and underline), and alignment.

Although you can copy short passages of text from another program and paste it in Fireworks' Text Editor, for a large block of text, you're better off importing it.

To import a text file, follow these steps:

1. Be sure the file you want to import is saved in either ASCII or RTF format.

2. Choose File ➪ Import or use the keyboard shortcut, Ctrl+R (Command+R). The Import dialog box displays.

3. If you're working in Windows, choose either ASCII Text (*.txt) or RTF Text (*.rtf) from the Files of Type option list.

4. Navigate to your ASCII or RTF file, select it, and click Open. After the Import dialog box closes, the Insert cursor appears.

5. Place the imported text in your document in one of two ways:

   • Position the cursor where you'd like the upper-left corner of the text object to start and click once.

   • Click and drag out the bounding box for the text file.

   The text flows into the new text object.

Caution The click-and-drag method for creating a text object is currently somewhat limited. Rather than have the full freedom to draw whatever shape you desire, the rectangle is constrained to a 4:1 ratio of vertical to horizontal space. In other words, the initial text object will always be four times as wide as it is tall. More importantly, Fireworks renders the text to fit within this bounding box, regardless of its previous font size.

Transforming Text

You really start to feel the power of Fireworks once you begin adding strokes, textured gradient fills, and multiple effects to a block of text — and you're still able to edit it. You can even use any of the transform tools — Scale, Skew, or Distort — to warp the text completely, and it's still editable.

There's no real shortcut to mastering text in your images. You really can only get a sense of what's possible by working, experimenting, trying — in essence, playing. In the following sections, you'll find some avenues to begin your text explorations.

Adding strokes

When you first create a text object, only the basic fill color is applied. However, this doesn't mean you can't add a stroke to your text — any combination of stroke settings is fair game. You do have to be a bit careful, though. Some of the preset strokes, such as Basic Airbrush, are quite hefty and can completely obscure all but text in the larger font sizes. However, modifying a stroke size (or color, softness, or texture) is quite easy and you can generally adjust the presets to find a workable setting.

One use for text with an added stroke is to create outlined text. Almost all fonts are presented with solid, filled-in letters. In Fireworks, however, you can make almost any font an outline font, with a fairly straightforward procedure:

1. Select a text object.

2. Open the Stroke panel by choosing Window ➪ Stroke or clicking the Stroke panel's tab if it's docked behind another.

3. Change the stroke category from None to any of those available in the Category option list.

Tip   Try Basic or Pencil strokes for simple outlines; experiment with Airbrush or Random strokes for more unusual results.

4. Select any desired preset from the Type option list and modify its settings as needed.

5. Open the Fill panel by choosing Window ➪ Fill or clicking the Fill tab.

6. Set the fill category to None in the Category option list. The solid fill disappears and the remaining stroke outlines the text.

The results of these steps are shown in Figure 10-11.

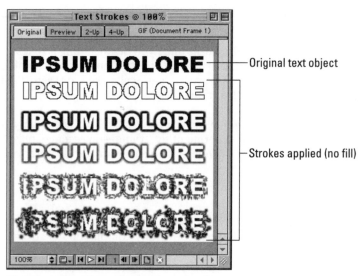

Original text object

Strokes applied (no fill)

Figure 10-11: Fireworks' Strokes can turn almost any font into an outline version.

Another technique for adjusting the look of a stroke on text is to alter the stroke's orientation. With most path objects, an applied stroke is centered on the path. With text objects, however, the default is to place the stroke on the outside of the path. Change the orientation of the stroke on the Object panel with the text object selected. By altering the stroke orientation, you can get three completely different graphic looks, as shown in Figure 10-12.

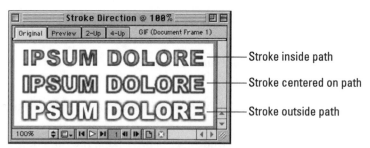

Stroke inside path

Stroke centered on path

Stroke outside path

Figure 10-12: The only difference between these three variations is the orientation of the stroke.

Cross-Reference To find out more about strokes, turn to Chapter 8.

Enhancing fills

Although the default method of displaying text already uses a colored fill, it's just the tip of what's possible with Fireworks text. Any type of fill that can be devised — solid color, Web dither, gradient, or textured — is applicable to text objects. Moreover, you can alter the edges of a fill to give either a softer or harder textual appearance.

Applying a fill to text is very straightforward. Just select the text object and choose your fill from the Fill panel. Fireworks treats the entire text object as a single unit so gradients and Patterns flow across all the separate letters and words. You can, however, adjust the way the fill is distributed by adjusting the gradient and Pattern controls, as described in these steps:

1. Select your text object.

2. Choose Window ➪ Fill or click on the Fill tab, if visible. The Fill panel opens.

3. Choose a gradient or Pattern fill.

4. If Auto-Apply is not enabled, select Apply. The gradient or Pattern fill is applied to the text object.

5. Select the Paint Bucket tool. The gradient editing handles appear on the filled text object, as shown in Figure 10-13.

6. To adjust the centerpoint of the gradient, click and drag the round starting handle.

7. To adjust the direction of the gradient, click and drag the square ending handle. Some gradients, such as Ellipse, Rectangle, and Starburst, have a third handle, which can be moved to adjust the width and skew of the gradient.

8. Click any tool other than the Paint Bucket to leave the Edit Gradient mode.

Cross-Reference Want to know more about fills? Turn to Chapter 11.

Using the transform tools

Each of the three transform tools — Scale, Skew, and Distort — can be applied to any text object. This means that text can be resized, rotated, slanted, and even pulled out of shape and can still be edited in the Text Editor. In this regard, text objects act just like path objects: the same sizing handles appear and even the Flip Horizontal/Vertical or Numeric Transform commands can be used, as in Figure 10-14.

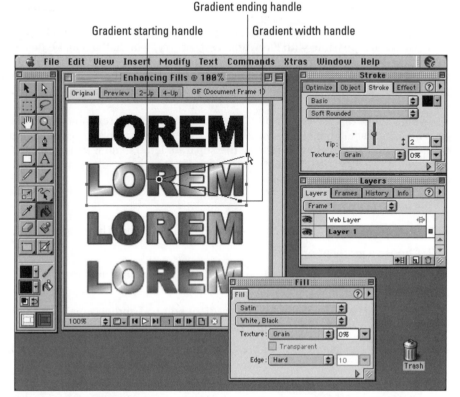

Figure 10-13: Alter the way a gradient moves across your text by moving the Gradient Fill handles.

Keep a few points in mind about transforming text:

✦ Before using the Skew tool on a text object, narrow the bounding box on either side of the text object as much as possible. Skew affects all portions of a text object and excess area will probably give you an undesirable effect.

✦ As with a regular path object, both Skew and Distort are useful for providing perspective effects with text. Adding an effect to text, such as inner bevel or drop shadow, also helps the effect.

✦ Text can be transformed in one of two ways: as a path object or as a pixel image. These options are available on the Object panel when the text object is selected. The Transform as Path option (the default) results in smoother, less jagged text than the Transform as Pixels option; however, in some instances, you may prefer the more ragged look.

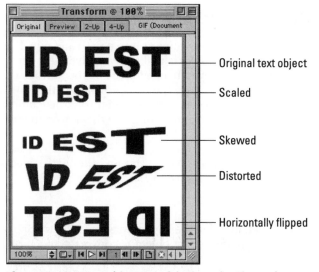

Figure 10-14: Text objects are fair game for Fireworks transform tools. Text, as always, remains editable.

Converting text to paths

So if editability of text is such a big deal, why would you ever want to give it up? Once you convert text to a path, you can combine it with other path objects by using commands on the Modify ⇨ Combine submenu . You might also want to alter a letter's shape, but to do that, you need to convert it to a path in order to gain access to its underlying points. You might find an interesting graphic hiding in a dingbats font and want to use it as a clipart foundation for a new drawing. In any case, select your text and choose Text ⇨ Convert to Paths.

> **Tip**   Before I convert a text object to a path object, I always, always, always make a copy of it and keep the copy on a hidden layer or unused frame. It's a good backup for when things go wrong, and an additional design element for an unforeseen creative moment ten or twenty steps down the line.

Converting text to an image

Not only can you convert text to paths, you can also convert it to an image. Just select the text object and choose Modify ⇨ Merge Images. As with the path conversion, text converted to pixels is no longer editable through the Text Editor.

Fireworks Technique: Cookie-Cutter Text

One of my favorite things to do with text is to convert it to a path and punch it through other path objects. The resulting objects make great guinea pigs for experimentation with Xtras or Fireworks 3's newly enhanced Live Effects. Buttons created this way are easy to turn into rollovers, because the text — or rather, the hole that the text punches out — is transparent. You can make these buttons glow different colors by placing them over different backgrounds, or place them over an image so the image shows through.

In any case, to use a former text object as a cookie cutter on other path objects, follow these steps, which are illustrated in Figure 10-15:

1. Create a text object.

2. Choose Text ➪ Convert to Paths or use the keyboard shortcut, Ctrl+Shift+P (Command+Shift+P). Each letter in the text object is converted to a path and then grouped.

3. Select your text path object and choose Modify ➪ Ungroup and then Modify ➪ Join or use the key shortcuts Ctrl+U (Command+U) and Ctrl+J (Command+J), respectively. This ungroups the individual letters and then joins them all into one composite path.

4. Create a path object — such as a rectangle — to punch your text through. Make sure that it has a fill of some sort.

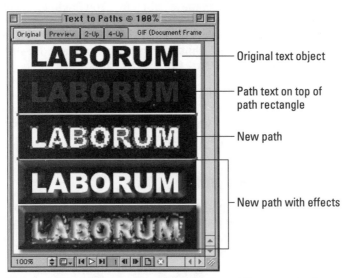

Figure 10-15: Text is converted to a path and then punched through another path object, cookie-cutter style.

5. Place the your text path object on top of your path object, aligning the text path object carefully where you want it to punch through.

You may have to select your text paths and choose Modify ⇨ Arrange ⇨ Bring to Front to bring it higher in the stacking order than your path object. Alternatively, you could send the path object to the back.

6. Select both objects and choose Modify ⇨ Combine ⇨ Punch.

Your two objects are combined into a new path object with the same fill, stroke and other properties of the bottom object. Experiment with different fills, strokes, and effects, or place your new object on top of other objects that will show through.

Fireworks Technique: A Font Safety Net

Ideally, source files such as Fireworks documents would never go anywhere without the fonts that were used to create them. Of course, this is not always the case. You may archive a document, find a need for it a year later and then upon opening it, discover that you no longer have one or more of the fonts you originally used. You might send a document to someone and forget to send the fonts, or need to open a Fireworks document on another platform where your fonts won't work without conversion. Suddenly, a careful design is thrown into disarray because the substituted fonts don't have the same spacing or characteristics.

One simple way to provide a little insurance against the above situations is to make backup image layers of all the text in a Fireworks document before you archive it. Then, if you open the document later without the correct fonts, you can hide the editable text layer(s) and show the image text layer(s). At the very least, the design is preserved and can be recreated. If all you wanted to do was modify a graphic element slightly and then publish, you might save a significant amount of time because your safety-net text is in place.

This technique assumes you've followed the common practice of giving text objects their own layers—with names like Logo, Headline, Body Text, and so on. If not, then you can select all of your text objects manually and copy them to a separate layer and then see the following instructions from step 4 on. Be careful to preserve the correct stacking order, if necessary. Combining objects on one layer may bring them in front of other objects they were previously behind.

To create backup image layers of the editable text in a Fireworks document, follow these steps:

1. Select a text layer in the Layers panel and drag it to the New Layer button (it looks like a pad of paper). Fireworks makes a copy of the layer and appends a 1 to the new layer's name.

Caution   Leave the copied layer where it is in the stacking order. You want it to shadow the original layer as closely as possible.

  2. Repeat step 1 until you have copies of all of your text layers.

  3. Choose Single Layer Editing from the Layers panel pop-up menu so that you can work on one layer at a time. With Single Layer Editing checked, choosing a layer from the Layers panel effectively locks all other layers.

  4. Select a copied text layer from the Layers panel and choose Edit ➪ Select All to select all of the text objects on that layer.

  5. Choose Modify ➪ Merge Images to convert the text objects to an image.

  6. Repeat steps 4 and 5 until you have converted all of your copied text layers to images.

  7. Hide your copied text layers by clicking the eye icon next to each layer in the Layers panel.

Your document is now ready to travel font-free, while still leaving the graphic elements editable.

Text on a Path

For the most part, text is either strictly horizontal or vertical. The Text on a Path command, however, enables you to flow text in the shape of any path — whether the path is a circle, rectangle, or freeform shape.

The basic procedure is pretty simple: first, create each part — a text object and a path — and then combine them. Because paths can come in so many shapes, Fireworks offers a number of different controls and options to help you get what you want. Amazingly enough, text remains editable even after it's been attached to a path.

To align text on a path, follow these steps:

  1. Draw or create any path object.

  2. If necessary, create a text object.

  3. Select both the path and the text object.

  4. Choose Text ➪ Attach to Path or use the keyboard shortcut, Ctrl+Shift+Y (Command+Shift+Y). The text flows along the path and the attributes of the path (stroke, fill, and effect) disappear, as shown in Figure 10-16.

  5. To edit the text, double-click it to open the Text Editor.

  6. To separate the text from the path, choose Text ➪ Detach from Path.

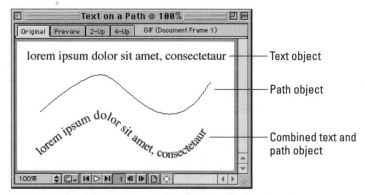

Figure 10-16: The two separate objects — text and path —
are combined in one with the Attach to Path command.

Several variables affect exactly how the text flows along the path. First, the alignment of the text itself can have an effect:

✦ **Left Aligned:** The text starts at the beginning of the path.

✦ **Centered:** The text is centered between the beginning and end of the path.

✦ **Right Aligned:** The text ends at the end of the path.

✦ **Justified:** All the characters are evenly spaced along the path with additional spacing, if necessary.

✦ **Stretched:** All the characters are stretched to fit along the path with standard spacing.

It's pretty easy to guess where a linear path starts and ends, but how about a circle? If you remember the discussion on using the Ellipse tool in Chapter 5, you might recall I mentioned that circle paths generally start at about 9 o'clock and travel in a clockwise direction, around the outside of the circle. To cause the text to begin its flow in a different area, you have three options:

✦ Rotate the text attached to the path using one of the transform tools.

✦ Choose Modify ➪ Transform ➪ Numeric Transform and select Rotate from the option list before choosing the angle of rotation.

✦ Enter an Offset value in the Objects panel.

The Offset value moves the text the specified number of pixels in the direction of the path. Because circle diameters vary, trial and error is the best method for using the Offset value. The Offset option also accepts negative numbers to move the text in the opposite direction of the path.

To flow the text along the inside of the circle, choose Text ➪ Reverse Direction (see Figure 10-17). With an Offset value at 0, the text will begin at 6 o'clock and flow counter-clockwise.

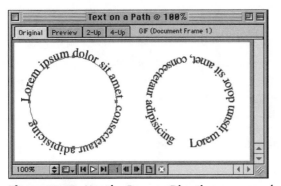

Figure 10-17: Use the Reverse Direction command in combination with Offset to properly place your text in a circle.

The final aspect that you can control with regard to attaching text to a path is the text's orientation to the path. You can find the options, shown in Figure 10-18, under Text ➪ Orientation:

✦ **Rotate around Path:** Each letter in the text object is positioned perpendicularly to its place on the path (the default).

✦ **Vertical:** Each letter of the text object remains straight relative to the document as the letters travel along the path.

✦ **Skew Vertical:** Rotates the letters along the path, but slants them vertically.

✦ **Skew Horizontal:** Keeps the letters straight on the path and slants them horizontally according to the angle of the curve.

After looking at the Skew Horizontal example in Figure 10-18, you might be wondering why this option was included. One of the reasons why it looks so unappealing is that the skew changes when the underlying path changes its angles. When Skew Horizontal is applied to a path with no or fewer curves, you can achieve a more pleasing effect, as shown in Figure 10-19.

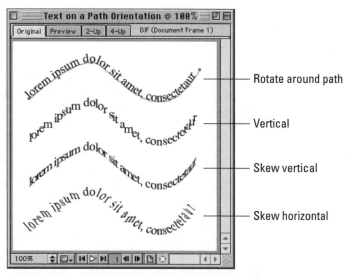

Figure 10-18: Achieve different effects by changing the orientation of the text to its attached path.

Figure 10-19: The horizontal skew orientation looks best when it's applied to a path with few or no curves.

Fireworks Technique: Masking Images with Text

What do you get when you combine images and text so that the text becomes the image? A graphic worth a thousand and one words? Actually, I think the technique of masking images is often worth far more. Moreover, its relative ease of creation in Fireworks makes it especially valuable.

A mask group is two or more objects grouped together where the bottom object is visible only through the top object. Take a look at Figure 10-20 and you'll see immediately what I mean. Because color is often so vital to a mask group's effect — and because I think it's cool — I've also included the image in the color insert.

Text   Image

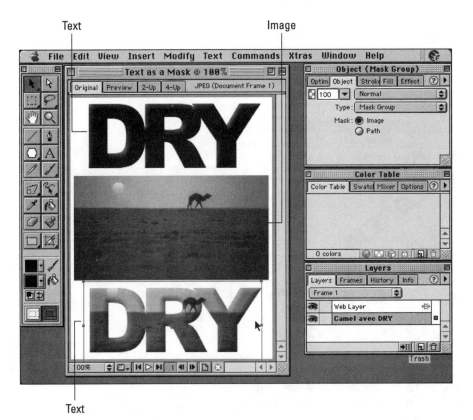

Text

Figure 10-20: Combine imagery and text through a mask group. Note the bevel Live Effect on the text, which remains after grouping.

To mask an image with text, follow these steps:

1. Create an image and a text object, or move existing image and text objects into the same document.

2. Position the text object over the image in its approximate final place.

3. Select both objects.

4. Choose Modify ➪ Mask Group ➪ Mask to Image or use the key shortcut Ctrl+Shift+G (Command+Shift+G). The image is now only visible through the text.

5. Use the Subselection tool to select and modify the placement of the image, if necessary.

> **Tip**
> You can still edit the text used in a Mask Group — you just have to ungroup it and select it by itself. When you're finished with your edits, apply the Mask Group command again.

The basic technique for masking an image with text is the same as using any other object as a mask. I've found, however, that manipulating the text into the proper shape beforehand creates a more successful mask. I try to start with a fairly wide font so that much of the image comes through and then apply the Horizontal Scale and/or Kerning controls in the Text Editor to get the largest possible type. For example, the font used in Figure 10-20 is the very thick Arial Black, with a –12 percent Kerning value so that the characters touch and don't break up the image.

Summary

Text and images are codependents on the Web. It's nearly impossible to have one without the other, but the text-handling features of Fireworks make for a smooth integration. Gaining a complete understanding of creating and editing Fireworks' text objects is essential for strong Web design. Keep these considerations in mind as you work with text in Fireworks:

✦ Text is always editable for files saved in Fireworks native format. You can apply a stroke, fill, or effect, and you can transform text repeatedly — and you'll still be able to edit all the text, all the time.

✦ Text in Fireworks is represented in the document as a text object. Text objects are created through the Text Editor or can be imported from ASCII or RTF files.

✦ The Text Editor is the major text interface and contains all the controls necessary for assigning attributes such as typeface, size, color, spacing, and alignment to text.

✦ In Fireworks, alterations made in the Text Editor are instantly visible in the document.

✦ Text can accept the full range of strokes, fills, and effects available in Fireworks. The transform tools — Scale, Skew, and Distort — also work with text objects.

✦ Converting a text object into a series of paths allows you to combine those paths with other path objects for interesting effects.

✦ Fireworks has a very full-featured Align Text with Path command that enables you to flow text around a circle, down a curving slope, or tracing any path you desire. Moreover, you can adjust the spacing of the text through the Alignment and Offset features.

✦ You can easily combine text and images by using the Fireworks Mask Group command.

In the next chapter, you'll get into the center of Fireworks objects as we examine fills and textures.

✦   ✦   ✦

Achieving Effects

In This Part

Chapter 11
Fills and Textures

Chapter 12
Live Effects and Xtras

Chapter 13
Arranging and
Compositing Objects

Fills and Textures

✦ ✦ ✦ ✦

In This Chapter

Understanding fills

Choosing a fill type

Extending color range with Web Dither

Modifying a Gradient fill

Fireworks technique: making transparent gradients

Enhancing your graphics with Patterns

Fireworks technique: developing seamless Patterns

Texturizing your Web graphics

Filling parts of an image with the Paint Bucket

✦ ✦ ✦ ✦

Fills and strokes are pretty much equal partners in Fireworks graphics. A fill gives substance to the inside of an object, just as a stroke does the outside. Fills in Fireworks come in many flavors — solid colors, gradations of color, and image patterns — and, like strokes, they are astoundingly flexible and almost infinitely variable. Moreover, fills in objects are always editable, which means changing from a flat color to a repeating pattern takes only a click or two.

After touring the standard fills included with Fireworks, this chapter begins to explore all the many ways you can customize and enhance fills. In addition to the techniques for editing gradients and Patterns and the many variations obtainable through the addition of textures, you'll see how you can add custom gradients, Patterns, and textures.

Using Built-in Fills

As with strokes and the Stroke panel, fills are generally applied and modified from the Fill panel, shown in Figure 11-1. You can display the Fill panel by choosing Window ➪ Fill, clicking on the Fill tab if visible, or using the keyboard shortcut, Ctrl+Alt+F (Command+Option+F).

There are five primary fill categories:

- ✦ **None:** No fill.
- ✦ **Solid:** Specifies a flat color fill, selectable from the pop-up color picker or by using the Eyedropper.
- ✦ **Web Dither:** Extends the Web-safe color range by using a repeating pattern of two Web-safe colors that simulates an unsafe color.

✦ **Pattern:** Applies a full-color image as a repeating pattern.

✦ **Gradient:** Inserts one of 11 gradient patterns blending two or more colors. The Gradient category is not separately listed, but implied through the listing of the gradient patterns.

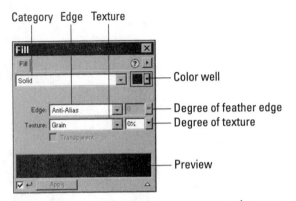

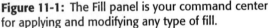

Figure 11-1: The Fill panel is your command center for applying and modifying any type of fill.

Each of the different categories offers a slightly different Fill panel. If you choose Solid, for example, no additional presets are presented; if you select Pattern, an option list with all the available Patterns appears. All fill types (except for None) have some similarities: the standard color well is present in all categories, as is the Edge option list.

The Edge option acts exactly like the one found in the Stroke panel, with three choices: Hard Edge, Anti-Alias, and Feather. Choosing a Hard Edge fill uses just the fill specified with no enhancements; Anti-Alias blends the edge a bit, softening away the jaggies, if any; and Feather blends the edge the number of pixels specified through the Amount of Feather slider.

Textures work with fills in the same fashion as they do with strokes, but because they're so much more visible, you'll find a special section later in this chapter that delves deeper into their use.

Turning off an object's fill

Just as important as adding a fill is knowing how to remove the fill. In Fireworks, there are two methods you can use. One is to choose None from the Category option list on the Fill panel. The other is to choose the No Color button from the pop-up color picker in the Toolbox, shown in Figure 11-2. Selecting the No Color button eliminates any type of fill, regardless of whether it's a solid, gradient, or pattern.

Toolbox

Figure 11-2: The color picker in the Toolbox is unique in that it has a No Color button for completely removing a Fill.

No color button

Solid

A Solid fill is a basic, monochrome fill, sometimes called a *flat fill*. The color used in the Solid fill type is selected from the Fill color well — whether it's the one on the Fill panel, the Toolbox, or the Mixer. The Fill color well uses the standard Fireworks pop-up color picker, shown in Figure 11-3. The color picker displays the swatches active in the Swatches panel, which, by default, is the Web-safe, 216-color palette.

System palette button

Eyedropper

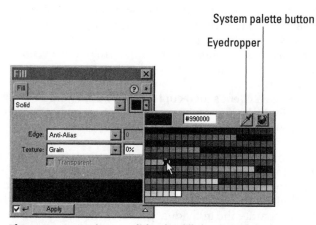

Figure 11-3: Assign a solid color fill through the Fill color well.

To apply a solid color to an object, follow these steps:

1. Select the object.

2. Access the Fill color well in one of these three ways:

   • Choose Window ➪ Fill to open the Fill panel and select the color well.

   • Select the Fill color well, as marked by the Paint Bucket, in the Toolbox (refer back to Figure 11-2).

   • Choose Window ➪ Mixer to display the Mixer and select the Fill color well, as marked by the Paint Bucket.

   Any of the these methods display the pop-up color picker.

3. To choose a color from the current swatch set, select any of the visible swatches.

4. To choose a color found onscreen, select the Eyedropper tool and click that color.

5. To access the operating system color picker(s), select the Palette button and select one of the colors in that dialog box.

Solid fills can be adjusted in several ways. You can select different edge options (Hard, Anti-Aliased, or Feather) from the Edge option list on the Fill panel; if you choose Feather, the Amount of Feather slider becomes available. In addition, a texture chosen from the Texture option list on the Fill panel may be applied. Remember, though, for a texture to be visible, you have to increase the Amount of texture past zero percent.

Web Dither

Color is one of the most frustrating elements of Web design. Most Web designers use a palette of 216 Web-safe colors that the major browsers display correctly on both Macintosh and Windows computers set to 256 colors (8-bit color). The most obvious limitation is the relatively small number of colors: 216 out of a visible palette of millions of colors. Another limitation is the distance between colors; each Web-safe color is a large jump from its nearest Web-safe neighbor. These limitations become particularly acute when a client's logo contains colors that aren't available in the Web-safe palette. Luckily, Fireworks offers you a way to increase the Web-safe color variations to over 45,000: the Web Dither fill.

To understand how to use the Web Dither fill, you'll need a little more background in computer color. *Dithering* refers to the process where two or more pixels of different colors are positioned to create a pattern which, to the human eye, appears to be a third color. This technique works because a small pattern of pixels tends to blend visually; the eye can't separate the individual pixels. Dithering was originally used to overcome the 256 color restriction of early computer monitors. If you convert a photograph with millions of colors to a GIF with only 256 colors, you'll notice dithered areas where the computer graphics program is attempting to simulate the unavailable colors. For flat-color graphics, though, relying on dithering forces the designer to give up a lot of control. You don't know what you're going to get until you export.

Hybrid-Safe Colors were developed initially by Don Barnett and Bruce Heavin and later popularized by Web designer Lynda Weinman. A Hybrid-Safe color consists of two Web-safe colors in an alternating 2 × 2 pattern. Fireworks has adopted this technique and renamed it Web Dither. Not only does this feature now give you a total of 46,656 (216 × 216) Web-safe colors, but it also enables you to make any solid fill semitransparent, opening up a whole new area of graphic design.

When you choose the Web Dither category from the Fill panel, you'll notice a new set of options becomes available, as shown in Figure 11-4. Instead of one color well, there are now three. The top color well represents the current Fill color, whereas the other two color wells are used to create the dither pattern. If the current Fill color is already Web safe, both dither colors will be identical. If the Fill color is not Web safe, Fireworks creates the closest match possible by dithering two Web-safe colors.

To apply a Web Dither fill, follow these steps:

1. Select your object.

2. Open the Fill panel by choosing Window ⇨ Fill, clicking on the Fill tab (if visible), or using the key shortcut Ctrl+Alt+F (Command+Option+F).

3. Select the arrow button next to the topmost color well to display the pop-up color picker.

Figure 11-4: The Web Dither fill greatly expands the range of possible Web-safe colors that can be used.

4. Pick a color that is not Web-safe in one of these ways:

   • To select a color from the swatch in your active palette, choose the color from the pop-up color picker. The active color must not be from the Web 216 Palette for this method.

- To select a color from an image onscreen, choose the Eyedropper from the pop-up color picker and sample the desired color.

- To select a color using your system's color picker, choose the Palette button from the pop-up color picker.

Tip

If you can't find an unsafe color, go outside of Fireworks with the eyedropper and sample one elsewhere on your display. Windows users should select the eyedropper and then hold down the mouse button while still over Fireworks. Keep the mouse button down as you hover the mouse over the color you want to sample, and release the mouse button to sample it.

Fireworks creates the closest color match possible by dithering your original color, as shown in Figure 11-5.

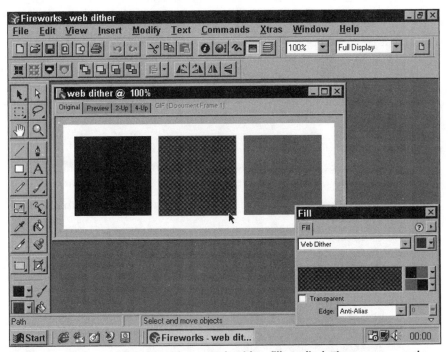

Figure 11-5: The middle square has a Web Dither fill applied. The squares on the left and right are the Web-safe colors used in the Web Dither, shown for example.

The Web Dither fill is terrific for finding absolute must-have colors — like those used for a logo — in a Web environment. When working from print materials, you can sample the color for the Web Dither fill.

Tip Though the Web Dither does give you a huge range of colors to choose from, that doesn't mean all of the color combinations are useful. If you choose two highly contrasting colors for the dither color wells, the dithered pattern appears to be dotted. It's usually best to select the desired color for the Fill color well by using the Eyedropper or any other method and let Fireworks create the dither pattern for you.

Fireworks takes the Web Dither fill further by including a Transparent option. When you enable the Transparent option, Fireworks sets the first dither color well to None while snapping the second dither color well to the nearest Web-safe color. The dither pattern now alternates a transparent pixel with a Web-safe colored pixel, and the resulting fill pattern is semitransparent.

Tip When you export a figure using a Transparent Web Dither fill, be sure to select either the Index or Alpha Transparency option.

Managing Gradients

A *gradient* is a blend of two or more colors. Gradients are used to add a touch of 3D or to provide a unique coloration to a graphic. A gradient is composed of two parts: a *color ramp,* which defines the colors used and their relative positioning, and a *gradient pattern,* which describes the shape of the gradient.

Fireworks includes 11 different types of gradient patterns and 13 preset color combinations. As you might have guessed, that just scratches the surface of what's possible with gradients because, like many features in Fireworks, gradients are completely editable.

Applying a Gradient fill

A Gradient fill is applied in a slightly different manner than a Solid or Pattern fill. To apply a Gradient fill, follow these steps:

1. Select your object.

2. Choose Window ➪ Fill or click the Fill tab to bring the Fill panel to the front.

3. From the Category option list, choose one of the gradient options below the divider. When the selected gradient is initially applied, the current Brush and the Fill colors are used to create the blend and a Preset option list appears in the Fill panel, as shown in Figure 11-6.

Figure 11-6: Select a gradient pattern and preset color combination from the Fill panel.

4. Choose a color combination from the Preset option list.

5. Change the fill edge or add a texture, if desired.

Rather than describe the standard gradients in words, it's much easier to grasp the differences visually, as demonstrated in Figure 11-7.

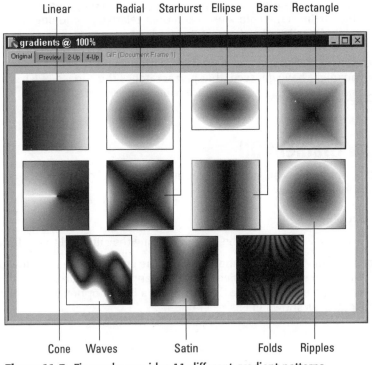

Figure 11-7: Fireworks provides 11 different gradient patterns.

Altering gradients

Fireworks' built-in gradient patterns and preset colors offer a good number of possibilities, but the real power of gradients comes in their customizability. You can modify gradients in two major ways:

✦ Every gradient pattern's center, width, and skew (if any) are all adjustable. With this facility, you can reshape the gradient's appearance with any object.

✦ The color ramp used to create the progression of colors in a gradient is completely flexible. Existing colors can be changed, deleted, or moved, and new colors can be added anywhere in the gradation.

You can save the custom color ramp information as a new preset, much like a custom stroke. However, a modified gradient pattern cannot be saved, either as a gradient or style. Unfortunately, there's no way to transfer a modified gradient pattern other than copying and pasting the actual object.

Modifying the gradient pattern

The key to unlocking—and customizing—the gradient pattern is the Paint Bucket tool. The Paint Bucket is generally used to fill any selected areas of an image object or any path objects with the current Fill panel settings. However, if the Paint Bucket is chosen when a Gradient or Pattern fill is in use, the gradient controls appear. All gradients have a starting point and an ending point, and four (Ellipse, Rectangle, Starburst, and Ripples) use two controls to adjust the size and skew of the pattern. The gradient controls are placed differently for each gradient pattern, as is evident in Figure 11-8.

To modify a gradient pattern, follow these steps:

1. Select the object with the Gradient fill.

2. Select the Paint Bucket tool from the Toolbox, or use the keyboard shortcut, Ctrl+K (Command+K). The gradient controls appear.

3. To move the starting point for the gradient, drag the circular handle to another position.

4. To rotate the direction of the gradient, move the cursor over the length of any control handle until the Rotate cursor appears and then drag the handles to a new location. As you rotate the gradient, Fireworks uses the gradient's starting point as a center axis.

5. To change the size of any gradient, drag the square handle straight to another position.

6. To alter the skew of an Ellipse, Rectangle, Starburst, or Ripples gradient, drag either square handle in the desired direction.

Control handles

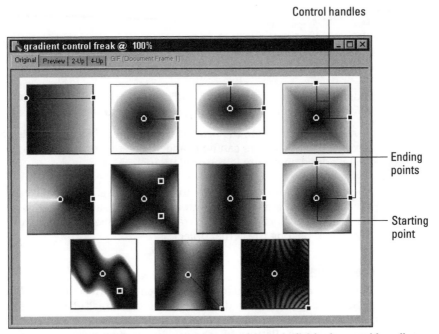

Ending points

Starting point

Figure 11-8: Each of the 11 standard gradients have individual control handles.

You're not limited to keeping the gradient controls within the selected object. Any gradient control—beginning, ending, or sizing/skewing handle—can be moved away from the object. In fact, some of my nicest gradient patterns resulted from placing the controls completely outside of the object. Experiment and think "outside the box."

Caution   Remember, there's no way to copy a modified gradient pattern from one object to another—much less one image to another—outside of copying and pasting the object itself. To mimic an effect on two widely different objects, you have to duplicate the placement of the gradient controls by hand.

Editing gradient colors

If you cycle through the preset gradient color combinations, you'll notice that some presets have as few as two colors and others have as many as six. To see how the color preset is structured, choose the Edit Gradient command from the Fill panel pop-up menu. The Edit Gradient dialog box, shown in Figure 11-9, is divided into three main areas: the color ramp, the color wells, and the preview pane.

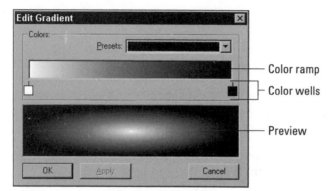

Figure 11-9: Modify the colors used in a gradient through the Edit Gradient dialog box.

The color ramp shows the current color combination as it blends from one key color to another. The key colors are displayed in the color wells, located beneath the color ramp. The preview pane shows how the color combination would be applied to the active gradient pattern. You can either modify a preset gradient or adjust a gradient created from the Fill and Brush colors.

To edit a gradient, follow these steps:

1. Choose Window ➪ Fill or use the key shortcut Ctrl+Alt+F (Command+Option+F) to display the Fill panel.

2. Choose Edit Gradient from the Fill panel pop-up menu. The Edit Gradient dialog box appears.

3. If you'd like to modify a preset gradient, choose one from the Preset option list.

4. To adjust the rate of change between colors, drag the color wells into new positions. One color well can be dragged on the far side of another color well.

5. To remove a color well completely, drag the color well away from the color ramp toward the preview pane.

6. To add a new color well, click anywhere directly below the color ramp. The added color well displays the color directly above it in the color ramp.

7. To select a new color for a color well, double-click the color well. The standard pop-up color picker appears. Select any of the available swatches or use the Eyedropper tool to sample an onscreen color, including one from another color well. The Palette button on the pop-up color picker can be used to access the system color picker(s).

8. Click OK when you're done.

Although there's no real limit to the number of colors you can add to an edited gradient, it's not practical to add more than two dozen or so. With so many colors, the color wells begin to overlap and it becomes increasingly difficult to select the correct one to modify.

Saving and renaming

Once you've modified an existing gradient, you need to save it in order to recall it. In Fireworks, you can store an altered gradient two ways:

✦ Use the Save Gradient command, found on the Fill panel pop-up menu, to store the gradient color combination in the current document.

✦ Create a new Style and save just the Fill type.

Examining Fill panel options

The Fill panel pop-up menu offers several gradient management options:

✦ **Save Gradient As:** Stores the current gradient under a new name within the active document.

✦ **Edit Gradient:** Displays the Edit Gradient dialog box.

✦ **Rename Gradient:** Relabels the current gradient.

✦ **Delete Gradient:** Removes the current gradient, custom or standard, from the Gradient panel.

Storing a modified gradient

To store a modified gradient, follow these steps:

1. Choose Save Gradient As from the Fill panel pop-up menu. The Save Gradient As dialog box appears.

2. Enter a unique name for the gradient. If you choose a name already in use, Fireworks asks if you want to replace the existing gradient.

3. After entering a new name, choose Save. The new gradient name is displayed alphabetically in the Preset option list of any gradient.

Using the gradient in another document

It's important to understand that any new or modified gradients are stored only within the document in which they're used. To use the gradient in another document, follow these steps:

1. Open the document containing the gradient you want to use.

2. Select an object using the new gradient.

3. Open the new document in which you want to use the new gradient.

4. Copy the selected object to the new document either by using Edit ➪ Copy and Edit ➪ Paste or by dragging and dropping the object from one document to the other. The new gradient setting is added to the Fill panel when the object containing the gradient is arrives in the new document.

5. If desired, delete the copied object from the new document.

There are several other ways to achieve the same effect of transferring gradients from one document to another:

✦ Use Insert ➪ Image to insert a document containing one or more custom gradients. After you've clicked once to place the document, choose Undo. The graphics will vanish, but all custom gradients will be incorporated into the Gradients panel.

✦ Copy the path with the custom gradient in one document and just paste the attributes to a path in the new document by selecting that path and choosing Edit ➪ Paste Attributes.

Using the Styles feature

Perhaps the best way to be sure your custom gradients are available is to save them as Styles and store them in the Styles panel. To create a new Style using a custom gradient, follow these steps:

1. Select an object that uses the custom gradient.

2. If necessary, choose Window ➪ Styles, use the keyboard shortcut, Ctrl+Alt+J (Command+Option+J), or click the Style tab, if visible. The Style panel is displayed.

3. On the Style panel, select the New Style button.

4. In the Edit Style dialog box, enter a descriptive name for your gradient in the Name text box and deselect all checkboxes except Fill Type.

5. Click OK when you're done. A new Style is entered in the Style panel.

Any Style added in the just-described fashion is always available for any Fireworks document. To apply the gradient, just highlight any Fireworks object and select the new Style. Your custom gradient is then added to the Fill panel.

Cross-Reference To find out more about using Styles, see Chapter 16.

Fireworks Technique: Making Transparent Gradients

Although you can pick any available color in the spectrum for a gradient color well, you can't pick "no color." In other words, there's no way to create a gradient that uses transparency in the Edit Gradient dialog box. However, there is a fairly straightforward and flexible technique you can apply to get the desired effect of having any Fireworks object — path or image — fade away.

Almost all of Fireworks' transparency effects take advantage of the Mask Group feature — and the transparent gradient is no exception. A Mask Group combines a regular object with an object with a black-to-white Gradient fill and makes the black parts transparent and the white, opaque. Because there is a gradual blend from black to white, you get a smooth transition from transparent to opaque.

Note   Technically speaking, a Mask Group uses the alpha channel of the top object as a transparency mask for the other objects.

To create a transparent gradient, follow these steps:

1. Create or insert an object or image that you want to make partially transparent.

2. Draw a second masking object that completely encompasses the original object. If you are masking a path object, rather than an image object, you can clone the original.

3. Open the Fill panel.

4. With the masking object selected, choose a gradient pattern, such as Linear or Radial.

5. From the Preset option list, choose Black, White.

6. If necessary, reposition the masking object over the original object, making sure that the masking object is in front of the original object.

7. Select both objects by drawing a selection around them with the Pointer tool.

8. Choose Modify ⇨ Mask Group ⇨ Mask to Image or use the keyboard shortcut, Ctrl+Shift+G (Command+Shift+G).

As you can see in Figure 11-10, where I combined the top two objects to make the mask group below them, the transparent background shows through quite well. In fact, it may show through a bit too well. I often find that I need to adjust the standard Black and White gradient preset so that there is more black than white. I do this by choosing Edit Gradient in the Fill panel pop-up menu and sliding the black color well closer to the white one. To edit the gradient in this fashion, it's best to first select the Mask Group and then choose the Paint Bucket tool to expose the gradient control handles. When the gradient controls are active, you can use the Edit Gradient feature and immediately apply it—otherwise, you must first ungroup the Mask Group and reselect just the Gradient fill.

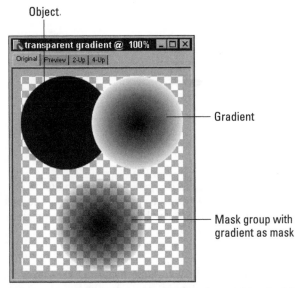

Figure 11-10: A gradient-filled object is combined with another object to make a Mask Group that enables a fade to transparency.

Using Patterns

Simply put, a Pattern fill uses a repeating image to fill an object. Patterns are often used to provide a real-world surface, such as bricks or wood paneling, to a computer-generated drawing. More abstract Patterns are also used to vary the look of a graphic. Fireworks includes 14 standard Patterns with an additional 70 available in the Goodies/Patterns folder of the Fireworks CD-ROM. Not surprisingly, you can also add your own images to be used as a Pattern.

Cross-Reference   Fireworks' built-in Patterns are detailed in the color insert.

The Pattern fill is one of the primary categories found on the Fill panel. When you select the Pattern option, a second option list, Fill Name, appears with all the available Patterns. As you move down the Fill Name option list, a small preview of the Pattern is displayed next to each highlighted file, as shown in Figure 11-11.

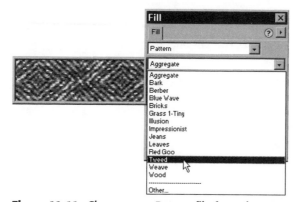

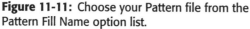

Figure 11-11: Choose your Pattern file from the Pattern Fill Name option list.

The only Fireworks requirement for a Pattern fill image is that the image be in PNG format. However, not all images are well suited to making Patterns; the best Patterns are those that repeat seamlessly so that the boundaries of the original file cannot be detected. All of the standard Fireworks files fill this requirement, as is clearly visible in the color insert.

Like any other fill, Pattern fills can be applied to any shape object. The other fill attributes — edge and texture — are also applicable.

Adding new Patterns

There are two ways to add Patterns to the Pattern Name option list so that they are available every time you use Fireworks:

  ✦ Save or export a file in PNG format to the Fireworks 3/Settings/Patterns folder.

  ✦ Through the Fireworks Preferences dialog box, assign an additional folder for Patterns.

As PNG is Fireworks' native format, it's quite easy to store any file as a Pattern just by saving it. Pattern images are usually full-color (whereas textures are displayed in grayscale), but that's not a hard-and-fast rule. Likewise, Patterns are generally 128 pixels square, but that's just a convention, not a requirement; one of the Patterns found on the Fireworks CD, Light Panel, is 12 pixels wide by 334 pixels high.

Once you've saved a file in your Patterns folder and restarted Fireworks, the new Pattern is listed along with the other Patterns. As shown with my new Patterns in Figure 11-12, they even preview in the same way.

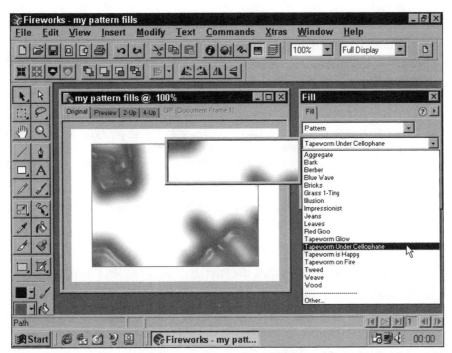

Figure 11-12: My own Tapeworm Patterns are available from the Pattern Name option list after saving them in the Fireworks 3/Settings/Patterns folder and restarting Fireworks.

Assigning an external Patterns folder is a very easy way to add a whole group of folders at one time, as well as a good way to share resources in a networked environment. To assign an additional Patterns folder, follow these steps:

1. Choose File ➪ Preferences. The Preferences dialog box opens.

2. Select the Folders tab (choose Folders from the option list on the Macintosh).

3. In the Additional Materials section, choose the Browse button next to the Patterns option. A navigation dialog box appears.

4. Locate the external folder that contains the PNG files you want to access as Patterns. Click OK when you've selected the folder. The Patterns checkbox is now enabled on the Preferences dialog box.

5. Click OK to accept the changes and close Preferences.

6. Relaunch Fireworks to make the additional Patterns available for use.

Tip Want quick access to the 70 Patterns on the Fireworks CD? Assign your external Patterns folder in Preferences to the Goodies/Patterns folder and restart Fireworks. When Fireworks opens, if the CD is present, the additional Patterns are integrated into the Fill panel list—and you can remove the CD after Fireworks has finished loading and the Patterns will still be available. If the CD is not available, Fireworks loads normally, but the additional Patterns are not incorporated.

Adding Patterns to a document

Adding commonly-used Patterns to your default list in Fireworks is great, but what if you want to quickly grab an image file and use it as a Pattern without the hassle of moving it into Fireworks' Patterns folder first? What if you want to use that Pattern within just one document and nowhere else? Fireworks 3 now allows you to work with Patterns in a more flexible manner: on a document by document basis.

New Feature

Fireworks 3 allows you to quickly access any PNG file on your computer and use it as a Pattern from wherever it is – without restarting Fireworks. In addition, Patterns that are applied in this way are saved with the current document, so that they're available whenever – and wherever – you open that document.

To access an external PNG image as a Pattern in the current document, follow these steps:

1. Select the object you'd like to apply the Pattern to.
2. Choose Window ➪ Fill or click the Fill tab to view the Fill Panel.
3. Choose Pattern from the Fill panel category list.
4. From the Pattern Name option list, choose Other to display an Open dialog box.
5. Navigate to the PNG file you'd like to use as a Pattern and select it. Click OK when you're done.

Fireworks adds your new Pattern to the Pattern Name option list and applies it to your selected object. The Pattern will be accessible from the Pattern Name option list only within the current document. When you save the document, the Pattern is saved within the document.

Tip

The fact that the Pattern is saved within the document makes it portable. If you share work with someone at another location, adding the custom Patterns you use to your document automatically makes them available to that coworker when they receive the document.

Altering Patterns

Patterns can be adjusted in the same manner as gradients. After a Pattern fill has been applied to an object, selecting the Paint Bucket tool causes the control handles to appear, as shown in Figure 11-13. The same types of vector controls are available:

✦ Adjust the center of the Pattern fill by dragging the round starting point.
✦ Rotate the Pattern fill by moving the cursor over the length of any control handle until the Rotate cursor appears, then drag the handles to a new angle.

✦ Change the size of any Pattern by dragging either square handle straight to another position.

✦ Alter the skew of any Pattern by dragging either square handle in the desired direction.

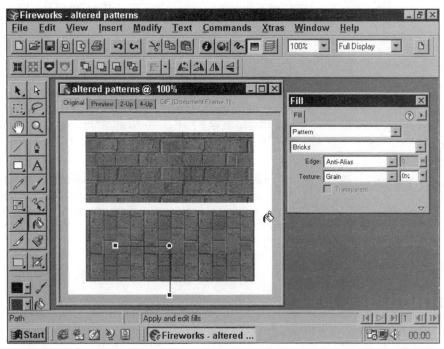

Figure 11-13: Both rectangles were filled with the standard Bricks Pattern and then the control handles of the bottom rectangle were rotated 90 degrees to change the Pattern direction.

Unlike gradients, all Patterns have two control handles in addition to the starting point of the fill. The handles are always perpendicular to one another and presented in the same ratio as the height to the width.

Caution When rotating an object, the Pattern or gradient fill does not rotate with it. Instead, you'll need to use the Pattern or gradient control handles to change the angle of the fill.

Fireworks Technique: Creating Seamless Patterns

The biggest problem with creating new Pattern fills is making them appear seamless. When Fireworks tries to fill an object larger than the size of the Pattern file, it repeats or tiles the image until the object is completely filled. If an image is used with even the smallest border, the repeating pattern is immediately noticeable; in most cases, this is not the desired effect. Several methods eliminate the appearance of seams.

The first, and simplest, technique is to avoid placing graphic elements near the edge of your Pattern image. This enables the canvas — or background color — to blend smoothly from one instance of a Pattern into another. For example, the image shown in Figure 11-14 could be made into a Pattern without showing any seams.

Figure 11-14: An image that has the same color all around its outside border can easily be made into a Pattern, because areas of identical color will appear seamless when they touch.

Many images, of course, rely on a visually full background where the canvas color is completely covered. To convert this type of graphic into a Pattern, a fair amount of image editing is necessary to make the edges disappear. Luckily, Fireworks contains enough graphic editing power to make this procedure feasible.

A tiled Pattern places images next to every side of the original image. To remove any indication of a boundary, you need to simulate a tiled Pattern and then blend the images so that no edges show. The following steps detail the procedure I use to smooth Pattern edges in Fireworks.

Note   Throughout this technique, I refer to the menu syntax for the command, like Edit ➪ Copy. Naturally, you should feel free to use whatever keyboard shortcuts you're familiar with.

1. Open the image you'd like to convert to a Pattern.

2. Select a portion of the image to use as the basis for your Pattern.

It's quite common to use just a part of a scanned image or other graphic as a Pattern. The best technique I've found for this is to determine how large you want your Pattern to be (128 × 128 pixels is a good size), and then use the Fixed Size feature of the Marquee tool available through the Options panel to set those dimensions. This lets you work with a preset Marquee and move it into position more easily.

3. Choose Edit ➪ Copy to copy the selected area.

4. Choose File ➪ New to create a new document. The document should be at least three times the size of your selected image. Because mine is 128 pixels square, 384 × 384 pixels would be my minimum size.

5. To guide placement, choose View ➪ Grid Options ➪ Edit Grid to set the size of the grid the same as your image, and enable the Show Grid and Snap to Grid options.

6. Choose Edit ➪ Paste to paste the copied area in the upper-left corner of the document, as shown in Figure 11-15.

Figure 11-15: After setting the grid to help with alignment, the first image is pasted down.

7. Copy the image with the Alt+drag (Option+drag) method. Place the copy of the image to the right of the original.

8. Repeat Step 7 twice more, but place the two new image copies below the two already in place, as shown in Figure 11-16.

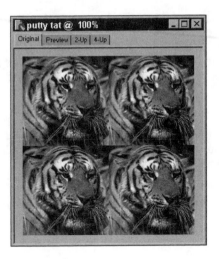

Figure 11-16: With all four copies in place, the edges are plainly visible.

9. Turn off both the grid (choose View ➪ Grid) and the Snap to Grid options (choose View ➪ Grid Options ➪ Snap to Grid).

10. Select all four copies of the image and choose Modify ➪ Merge Images. This step is necessary because the core of this technique uses the Rubber Stamp tool, which only works with image objects. By selecting all copies, the four separate image objects have been merged into one.

11. Select the Rubber Stamp tool from the Toolbox.

The next step is the core of this procedure and, as such, requires a bit of finesse and trial-and-error to get it right. You might want to save the document at this stage just so you can restart the process without having to start completely over.

12. Working on the vertical seam between the copies on the left and the right, click the Rubber Stamp origin point down one side a few pixels to the side, near the edge. Drag over the edge in a left-to-right motion (or from right to left, depending on which side the Rubber Stamp origin is located), extending the side of one image into the side of another.

Follow this procedure down the vertical seam. Occasionally you might need to switch directions and origin point to vary the blurring. Press Alt to reset the origin point of the Rubber Stamp tool. If necessary, set the Rubber Stamp options to the softest possible edge on the Options panel.

13. After you've blurred the vertical seam, repeat the process for the horizontal seam, changing the direction of the Rubber Stamp as needed.

When you're done blurring both the vertical and horizontal edges, the resulting image should appear to be a seamless Pattern, as shown in Figure 11-17. After this step, it's time to copy the portion of the image used to make the Pattern.

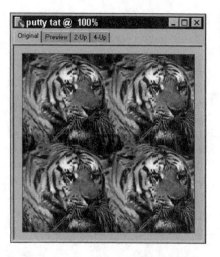

Figure 11-17: After the edges are blurred, it's hard to tell where one image stops and the other starts.

14. Choose View ➪ Grid Options ➪ Edit Grid and reset the grid to half of its former size, enabling both the view and the snap options as well. Using a half-sized grid lets you easily grab the center of the current image. My original grid was 128 × 128 pixels, so my new one for this step is 64 × 64.

15. Choose the Marquee tool from the Toolbox. The Marquee's Options should still be set to the Fixed Size option, using your original dimensions.

16. Use the Marquee to select the central portion of the overall image, as shown in Figure 11-18. Notice that the selection takes a part of all four images, previously separate.

17. Choose Edit ➪ Copy to copy the selection.

18. Choose File ➪ New to create a new document. Fireworks automatically sizes the new document to match the graphic on the Clipboard.

19. Choose Edit ➪ Paste to paste the selection. This is your finished Pattern file (see Figure 11-19).

20. Choose File ➪ Save and store the image in the Fireworks 3/Settings/Patterns folder.

21. Restart Fireworks.

Tip If you don't want to restart Fireworks, you don't have to, but you'll have to use the Other option from the Pattern Name option list to select your Pattern file for use.

22. Test your Pattern by drawing out a closed path and filling it with your new Pattern.

23. If necessary, open the just-saved Pattern file and edit to remove any noticeable edges.

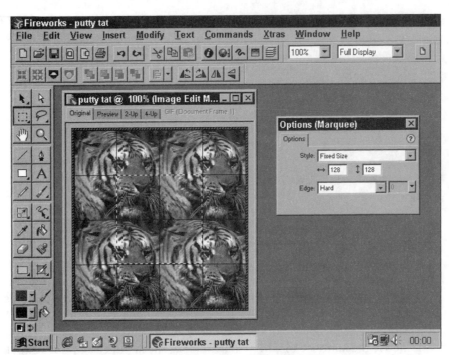

Figure 11-18: The combination of the grid and the Fixed Size marquee selection make it easy to select part of all four original images.

Figure 11-19: The final Pattern uses the center of four adjacent images so that its edges will meet seamlessly when patterned.

There are numerous other ways to blur the line between your edges, but the Rubber Stamp tool works in many situations. Although it does take a bit of practice to get the hang of the tool and this technique, the results are definitely worth it.

Cross-Reference   For more information on the Rubber Stamp tool and its options, see Chapter 6.

Adding Texture to Your Fills

A common complaint about computer graphics in general is that their appearance is too artificial. If you take a quick look around the real world, very few surfaces are a flat color — most have some degree of texture. Fireworks simulates this reality by enabling any fill (or stroke, for that matter) to combine with a texture. In Fireworks, a texture is a repeating image that can be applied on a percentage basis.

Like Fireworks patterns, textures are PNG images designed to be repeated, and are stored in a specific folder. But that's pretty much where the similarity with patterns ends. Whereas a pattern replaces any other fill, a texture is used in addition to the chosen fill. A texture is, in effect, another object, which is blended on top of the original object. As you increase the degree of a texture through the Fill panel slider, you are actually increasing the opacity of the texture. When the amount of texture is at 100 percent, the texture is totally opaque and the textured effect is at its maximum.

Another difference between pattern and texture is color: patterns can be any range of color, whereas textures are displayed in grayscale. The reason for this is purely functional: if textures included color, the color of the original fill or stroke would be altered. One consequence of the grayscale property is that flat white fills are almost totally unaffected by textures.

Tip   Generally, textures work better with darker colors, which permit more range of contrast.

Fireworks provides a wide range of textures: 26 included with the program and 21 more on the Fireworks CD-ROM. Each texture is chosen from an option list on the Fill panel and, like patterns, a preview is displayed for each texture. Next to the Texture option list is a slider that controls the chosen texture's degree of intensity. The higher the amount of texture, the more pronounced the texture's effect on the fill, as shown in Figure 11-20.

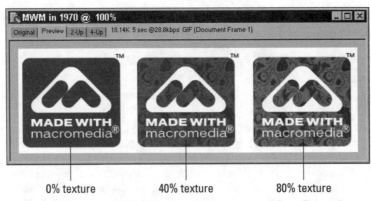

0% texture   40% texture   80% texture

Figure 11-20: Increasing the amount of texture on the Fill panel makes the texture more visible.

There's one other property of textures: transparency. If your textured object is on top of other objects, enabling the Transparent option lets the background objects show through the light portions of the texture. The higher the degree of texture, the more transparent an object becomes.

Extending Textures to Strokes and Images

Textures aren't limited to enhancing fills. You can just as easily apply them to strokes and, with just a little more work, images as well. Sometimes a stroke is used to define a filled object and it's best not to extend the texture onto the stroke. Certain images, however, benefit from a continuation of the texture from fill to stroke.

Take, for example, the following figure. I created a very simple texture of alternating lines that is applied to the stroke (a big airbrush) in the top example. Because the same set of textures are available from both the Fill and Stroke panel, it's easy to duplicate settings from one panel to the other, so in the middle example, a fill has been added and the same lines texture applied to it. The bottom example has had some Live Effects added, but the lines still show through and bring the stroke and fill together.

Applying a texture to an image requires an additional step. Strokes and fills cannot be applied directly to an image. The technique then is to create a path object that completely covers the image and apply the texture to that path object. Blend it into the image either by altering the opacity of the path object, and/or its blending mode (both of these controls are in the Object panel) or by using the path object as a mask for the image. As is often the case with Fireworks, a little experimentation can lead to some very interesting results.

Adding new textures

New textures are accessed exactly the same way that new patterns are added:

✦ Save or export a file in PNG format to the Fireworks 3/Settings/Textures folder.

✦ Through the Preferences dialog box, assign an additional folder for textures.

Textures files work best when they enable a repeating pattern without visible edges and, as mentioned previously, all textures are shown in grayscale.

Converting a color image to grayscale

Although you don't have to convert images to grayscale before saving them as textures — Fireworks simply displays color textures as grayscale, anyway — converting them allows you to get a better sense of how the texture will ultimately look, and also gives you a chance to alter the overall brightness and contrast to achieve the best looking texture.

Until Fireworks 3, if you wanted to convert a color image to grayscale, you had to apply an Xtra to it or export it with a grayscale palette, resulting in all path objects being converted to images. Now, in Fireworks 3, one of the included Commands converts to grayscale for you.

New Feature   Fireworks 3 includes a Convert to Grayscale Command that makes converting a color image to grayscale a one-step process, and it works on path or image objects, retaining editability.

To convert a color path or image object to grayscale using the Convert to Grayscale Command, follow these steps:

1. Select the object you want to convert.

2. Choose Commands ⇨ Creative ⇨ Convert to Grayscale. Fireworks converts your object to grayscale.

Assigning an additional textures folder

If you have an entire group of textures you want to add at one time, you can assign an additional folder for Fireworks to include in the texture list. To assign an additional Textures folder, follow these steps:

1. Choose File ⇨ Preferences. The Preferences dialog box opens.

2. Select the Folders tab (choose Folders from the option list on a Macintosh).

3. In the Additional Materials section, choose the Browse button next to the Textures option. A navigation dialog box appears.

4. Locate the external folder that contains the PNG files you want to access as textures. Click OK when you've selected the folder. The Textures checkbox is now enabled on the Preferences dialog box.

5. Click OK to accept the changes and close Preferences.

6. Restart Fireworks to make the additional textures available.

Can't get enough textures? You'll find 50 additional ones in the CD-ROM of this book in the Textures folder.

Adding textures to a document

Like patterns, textures can be opened one at a time and used with your current document, allowing easy access to textures stored anywhere on your computer. Textures opened in this way are saved within the current document.

Fireworks 3 allows you to use any PNG file, from anywhere on your computer, as a texture. Previously, textures had to be placed in the Textures folder, and were only available after restarting Fireworks.

To access an external PNG image as a texture in the current document, follow these steps:

1. Choose Window ➪ Fill or click the Fill tab to view the Fill Panel.

2. Choose Solid, Pattern or a gradient from the Fill panel category list in order to view the Texture Name option list.

3. From the Texture Name option list, choose Other to display an Open dialog box.

4. Navigate to and select the PNG file you'd like to use as a texture. It can be a color or a grayscale image, but the result will always be a grayscale texture. Click OK when you're done.

Fireworks adds your new texture to the Texture option list.

Filling with the Paint Bucket Tool

The Paint Bucket tool is used to fill a selected area with the current Fill panel settings — whether those settings involve a solid color, a gradient, or a pattern. The Paint Bucket can be used to fill both path objects and image objects. There is a difference, however; the Paint Bucket fills all of a path object completely, whereas it only fills the selected portion of an image object, or a range of like, adjacent colors if there is no selection, as shown in Figure 11-21.

Path objects   Image objects

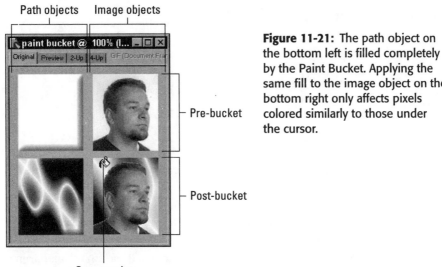

Pre-bucket

Post-bucket

Cursor point

Figure 11-21: The path object on the bottom left is filled completely by the Paint Bucket. Applying the same fill to the image object on the bottom right only affects pixels colored similarly to those under the cursor.

With path objects, nothing is simpler than using the Paint Bucket. Just choose the Paint Bucket tool (or use the keyboard shortcut, K) and then click the object once to apply the current Fill panel settings. If the Fill panel is set to None, the current fill color — seen on the Toolbox and Mixer — is used to give the object a Solid fill.

Caution   Fireworks doesn't distinguish between open and closed paths when the Paint Bucket is used. If the Paint Bucket is used on an open path, such as an S-curve, an invisible line is drawn from the beginning to the ending point and the fill is applied.

Image objects are a different story with regard to the Paint Bucket. If you click an image object with the Paint Bucket without selecting an area using one of the selection tools (Marquee, Ellipse Marquee, Lasso, Polygon Lasso, or Magic Wand), one of three things will happen:

✦ The current Fill settings will be applied to the selected pixel and the neighboring pixels that fall within the Tolerance range set in the Options panel.

✦ The entire image object will be filled with the current Fill settings, if the Fill Selection Only object is selected from the Options panel and the Expand to Fill Document option from Preferences is not enabled.

✦ The entire document will be filled with the current Fill settings, if the Fill Selection Only object is selected from the Options panel and the Expand to Fill Document option from Preferences is enabled.

As you can see, the Options panel, shown in Figure 11-22, becomes very important when you apply the Paint Bucket tool to image objects.

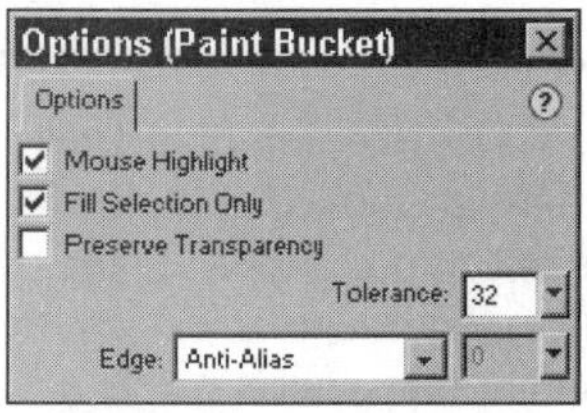

Figure 11-22: The Options panel for the Paint Bucket tool has a major effect on how image objects are filled.

The available options are

✦ **Mouse Highlight:** Highlights a selectable area when passed over with the pointer.

✦ **Fill Selection Only:** Disregards color tolerance settings and fills a selected area, or if no area is selected, either the image object or document according to the Expand to Fill Document setting.

✦ **Preserve Transparency:** Only colors existing pixels, so that transparent pixels stay transparent.

New Feature

In Fireworks 3, the Paintbrush tool can now be set to ignore transparent areas and color existing pixels only.

✦ **Tolerance:** Sets the range of colors to be filled when Fill Selection Only is not enabled. The Tolerance slider accepts values from 0 (where no additional colors are filled) to 255 (where all additional colors are filled).

✦ **Edge:** Determines the type of edge on the fill — Hard, Anti-Aliased, or Feather. If Feather is selected, the Amount of Feather slider becomes available, which sets the degree to which the fill is blended into surrounding pixels.

Tip

Once you've made a selection in an image object, you don't have to click in the selected area with the Paint Bucket to change it. Clicking anywhere in the document automatically fills the selected area.

Summary

Fills are one of Fireworks' basic building blocks. Without fills, objects would appear to have outlines only and it would be difficult, if not impossible, to arrange objects on top of one another. As you begin to work with fills, keep these points in mind:

✦ Fills can be applied to any Fireworks object: path or image.

✦ Access all the fill settings through the Fill panel. The Fill color well can also be found on the Toolbox and the Mixer.

✦ There are five options for fills: None, Solid, Web Dither, Pattern, and Gradient.

✦ The Web Dither fill visually blends two Web-safe colors to make a third color outside the limited Web-safe palette.

✦ You can modify a Gradient or Pattern fill by selecting the filled object with the Paint Bucket tool and adjusting the control handles.

✦ New gradient color combinations can be saved in each document and reused or stored in a Style.

✦ A Pattern fill can be made from any repeating image, stored in PNG format, or can now be stored within a document in Fireworks 3.

✦ Textures can bring a touch of realism to an otherwise flat graphic, and can also be stored within documents in Fireworks 3.

✦ The Paint Bucket options control whether the entire image object is filled or just a selection is filled.

In the next chapter, you'll learn about the razzle-dazzle side of Fireworks: Live Effects and Xtras.

✦   ✦   ✦

Live Effects and Xtras

✦ ✦ ✦ ✦

In This Chapter

Understanding
Fireworks Effects

Using the Effect panel

Working with
Live Effects

Fireworks technique:
creating perspective
shadows

Managing Live
Effects

Applying Xtras

Using Photoshop-
compatible plug-in
filters

Third-party filters

✦ ✦ ✦ ✦

Many Fireworks graphics are based on three separate but interlocking features: strokes, fills, and effects. Not everyone would put effects — the capability to quickly add a drop shadow or bevel a button — on the same level as strokes and fills, but most Web designers would. Effects are pretty close to essential on the Internet. Not only are the look and feel of many Web sites dependent on various effects, but much of their functionality, especially when techniques like button rollovers are concerned, demands it.

Live Effects are a Fireworks innovation. For the first time, designers could edit common effects without having to build the graphic from the ground up. But what makes Live Effects truly "Live" is Fireworks' capability to automatically reapply the effects to any altered graphic — whether the image was reshaped, resized, or whatever. Fireworks 3 continues the innovative trend by introducing the capability to use many standard Photoshop-compatible filters as Live Effects. Now, effects that used to require objects to be flattened into bitmaps are just as easily applied, edited, or removed as Fireworks' own classic bevels and glows.

Later in the chapter, we'll look at how you can apply Xtras and what you can apply them to. You'll work with the Xtras that are included with Fireworks and examine some of the techniques that you can use to apply them creatively. You'll also see how you can add more Xtras to Fireworks, including ones that you may already have as part of another application. Finally, this chapter reviews two very popular third-party image filter packages: Eye Candy and Kai's Power Tools.

Understanding Fireworks Effects

With Fireworks 3, Macromedia has extended the always-editable promise of Fireworks to include many Photoshop-compatible image filters, blurring the line between the two types of Fireworks effects: Live Effects and Xtras. While the Xtras menu contains the definitive list of the image filters to which Fireworks has access, many image filters are also available in live versions from the Effect panel.

New Feature   Using Photoshop-compatible image filters in Fireworks 2 meant dipping into the Xtras menu and abandoning editability. With Fireworks 3, many image filters are also available in the Effect panel and can be used with as much freedom as any other Live Effect. Apply them to path objects, remove them, or edit their settings at any time.

If there's a new feature in Fireworks 3 that excites me, this is it. New kinds of creative experimentation are now possible with many of the same image filters that you may have used for years in previous versions of Fireworks or in Photoshop. Rearranging the order that filters are applied without having to start from scratch or easily saving favorite combinations of filters is truly liberating. Exciting new combinations of effects are made possible just because they're so easy to mix, match, and experiment with.

The Effect panel

The Effect panel, shown in Figure 12-1, is a powerful tool that centralizes almost all of the effects in Fireworks, with the exception of some third-party image filters, which remain only accessible from the Xtras menu. The Effect panel fundamentally offers you access to two lists: the Effect Category option list, which contains all of the Live Effects with which you have access; and the Effects list, which contains only the Live Effects that are currently applied to a selection.

The Effect Category option list is divided into five distinct parts:

✦ **None:** Choosing this option removes all of the effects from the selection.

✦ **Use Defaults** loads the classic Inner Bevel, Outer Bevel, Drop Shadow, and Glow Live Effects into the Effects list. Check them to enable them for your selection.

✦ Effects combinations that you save. This section is not visible until you save your first combination.

✦ Included Live Effects, such as bevels, blurs, and glows.

✦ Third-party Photoshop-compatible image filters, including the Eye Candy LE filters from Alien Skin Software that are bundled with Fireworks 3.

Not all third-party image filters can be used as Live Effects. Those that can't simply don't show up in the Effect Category option list and can only be accessed in the Xtras menu.

Effect category option list

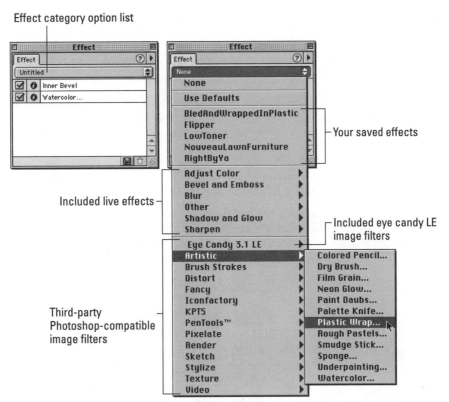

Your saved effects

Included live effects

Included eye candy LE image filters

Third-party Photoshop-compatible image filters

Figure 12-1: The Effect panel with its Effect Category option list is a central access point for almost all of the effects available in Fireworks.

Applying Live Effects

Live Effects can only be applied to objects selected in object edit mode. If you'd like to apply a Live Effect to a pixel selection, you have two choices:

✦ Select an area with the pixel selection tools and copy it to the clipboard. Exit Image Edit Mode. If you're in Windows, exit by pressing the "stop" button in the Status bar. Or, if you're on a Macintosh, exit the Image Edit Mode by pressing the "stop" button at the bottom of the document window. Next, paste the selection as a new image object. The new image object is placed exactly where your pixel selection was located. Apply the Live Effect to your new image object. If you like, you can then group the new image object and the original image object from which the pixel selection was taken.

✦ Some Live Effects are also available from the Xtras menu and can be applied to a pixel selection from there, although this doesn't maintain editability.

Although each effect has its own unique settings, they are all applied in basically the same fashion:

1. Select an object or objects in object edit mode. Fireworks can simultaneously apply the same effect to multiple objects.

Tip

If you are currently in Image Edit Mode, enter object mode by clicking the "stop" button in the Status bar on Windows, or, if you are on a Macintosh, click the "stop" button on the bottom of the document window.

2. Choose Window ➪ Effect to open the Effect panel. Alternatively, you could use the keyboard shortcut Ctrl+Alt+E in Windows (Command+Option+E on a Macintosh), or click the Effect tab, if it is visible.

3. Select your effect from the Effect Category option list. If the effect has editable settings — most do — Fireworks displays either a headless dialog box (Figure 12-2) or a regular dialog box, depending on the effect.

Apply effect checkbox   Info button   Pop-up menu

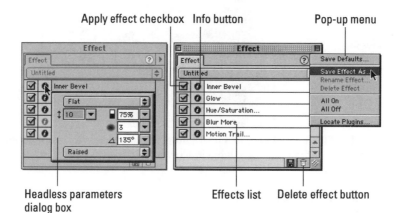

Headless parameters
dialog box

Effects list   Delete effect button

Figure 12-2: The Effect panel offers a high level of control over the way effects are applied, edited, and removed.

4. Modify the settings in the dialog box to achieve the desired effect. After you're done, click anywhere outside a headless dialog box or click OK in a regular dialog box, or press Enter (Return) in either.

The effect is applied to all selected objects.

Once an effect is applied, it is added to the Effects list in the Effect panel, and Fireworks keeps it alive throughout any other changes that the object may undergo. Fireworks actually recalculates the required pixel effects and reapplies the effect after a change is made for path, image, or text objects. To my mind, the capability to make completely editable vector artwork (Figure 12-3) look like bitmaps that have undergone numerous image filter modifications is a superb addition to the Web designer's toolbox.

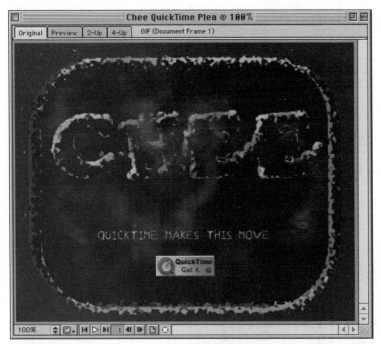

Figure 12-3: Fireworks' always-editable Live Effects make these path objects look like bitmaps that have been extensively modified with image filters.

Cross-Reference   For another look at Figure 12-3, turn to the color insert.

To edit the parameters for an applied effect, select the object and click the Info button next to the effect that you want to modify in the Effects list. Fireworks displays the effect's dialog box. Edit the parameters and dismiss the dialog box by clicking OK or by clicking outside the dialog box it if it is headless.

As good as Fireworks effects look, sometimes objects look better with no effects. To remove all effects from an object, select the object and then, from the Effect panel, choose None from the Effect Category option list. To temporarily disable a single effect, deselect the checkbox next to that effect in the Effects list. To temporarily disable all effects, choose All Off from the Effect panel pop-up menu. Of course, choosing All On from the pop-up menu enables all applied effects. To remove a single effect permanently, select the effect in the Effects list and click the Delete Effect button, which looks like a trash can and is located at the bottom of the Effect panel.

The Xtras menu

Many bitmap-editing applications offer you a dedicated menu that contains Photoshop-compatible plug-in image filters. Fireworks is no exception, and the Xtras menu, shown in Figure 12-4, is it. When you launch Fireworks, it populates the Xtras menu with all of the image filters it has access to. Generally, these are installed in Fireworks Xtras folder (Fireworks 3/Settings/Xtras) or in the Photoshop plug-ins folder specified in your Fireworks preferences.

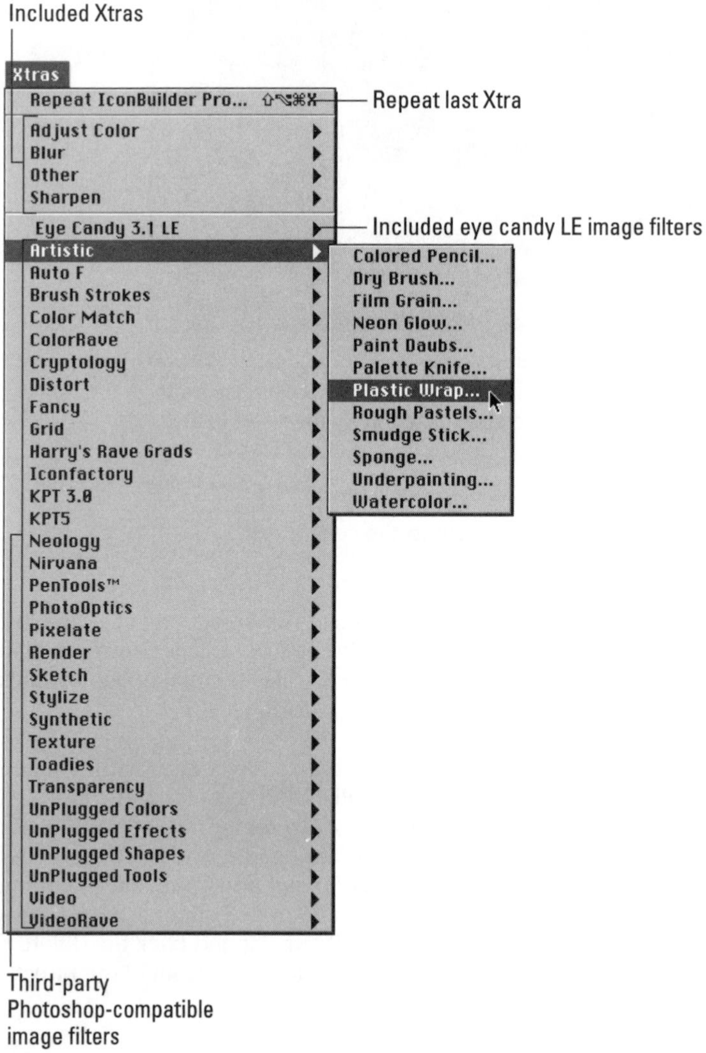

Included Xtras

Xtras		
Repeat IconBuilder Pro... ⇧⌥⌘X	— Repeat last Xtra	
Adjust Color ▶		
Blur ▶		
Other ▶		
Sharpen ▶		
Eye Candy 3.1 LE ▶	— Included eye candy LE image filters	
Artistic ▶	Colored Pencil...	
Auto F ▶	Dry Brush...	
Brush Strokes ▶	Film Grain...	
Color Match ▶	Neon Glow...	
ColorRave ▶	Paint Daubs...	
Cryptology ▶	Palette Knife...	
Distort ▶	Plastic Wrap...	
Fancy ▶	Rough Pastels...	
Grid ▶	Smudge Stick...	
Harry's Rave Grads ▶	Sponge...	
Iconfactory ▶	Underpainting...	
KPT 3.0 ▶	Watercolor...	
KPT5 ▶		
Neology ▶		
Nirvana ▶		
PenTools™ ▶		
PhotoOptics ▶		
Pixelate ▶		
Render ▶		
Sketch ▶		
Stylize ▶		
Synthetic ▶		
Texture ▶		
Toadies ▶		
Transparency ▶		
UnPlugged Colors ▶		
UnPlugged Effects ▶		
UnPlugged Shapes ▶		
UnPlugged Tools ▶		
Video ▶		
VideoRave ▶		

Third-party
Photoshop-compatible
image filters

Figure 12-4: The Xtras menu contains built-in Fireworks image filters, as well as any third-party, Photoshop-compatible image filters you've added.

> **Tip**   Image filters are called "filters" because every pixel in the image is evaluated—filtered—and either modified or not according to the settings and the effect that's being applied. I'll use the terms Xtras and filters interchangeably throughout this chapter.

In a nutshell, the difference between the effects contained in the Xtras menu and the ones in the Effect panel are that the ones in the Xtras menu are not live. Xtras can only be applied to bitmap image objects; applying them to a text or path object flattens the object into an image object. Once an Xtra is applied, there is no way to remove the effect except with the Undo command or the History panel.

The Xtras menu is divided into three sections. From top to bottom, they are the following:

✦ A single menu command that identifies and repeats the last-used filter

✦ Image filters that are included with Fireworks itself

> **Caution**   One exception is the DitherBox filter that's included with Photoshop 5. It finds its way onto the Other menu if you make it available to Fireworks.

✦ Third-party, Photoshop-compatible image filters

Plug-in image filters automatically organize themselves into submenus.

Working with Included Live Effects

Fireworks is shipped with a range of useful Live Effects built-in, contained in the following submenus of the Effect panel's Effect Category option list:

✦ **Adjust Color:** Auto Levels, Brightness/Contrast, Curves, Hue/Saturation, Invert, Levels

✦ **Bevel and Emboss:** Inner Bevel, Inset Emboss, Outer Bevel, and Raised Emboss

✦ **Blur:** Including Blur, Blur More, and Gaussian Blur

✦ **Other:** The unclassifiable Convert to Alpha and Find Edges

✦ **Shadow and Glow:** Drop Shadow, Glow, Inner Glow, Inner Shadow

✦ **Sharpen:** Including Sharpen, Sharpen More, and Unsharp Mask

Table 12-1 details the Live Effects that are included with Fireworks, and what each one does.

Table 12-1
Included Live Effects

Live Effect	Description
Auto Levels	Automatically produces an image with the maximum tonal range.
Brightness/Contrast	Adjusts the brightness and/or contrast of all the pixels in an image.
Curves	Enables you to adjust the level of a particular color in an image, without affecting other colors.
Hue/Saturation	Adjusts the color in an image.
Invert	Changes the color of each pixel to its mathematical inverse. Creates a photo-negative-type effect.
Levels	Enables you to adjust the tonal range of all of the pixels in an image.
Inner Bevel	Adds a three-dimensional look to an object by beveling its inside edge.
Inset Emboss	Simulates an object in relief against its background.
Outer Bevel	Frames the selected object with a three-dimensional, rounded rectangle.
Raised Emboss	Simulates an object raised from its background.
Blur	Blurs pixels together to create an unfocused effect.
Blur More	Same as Blur but across a slightly larger radius, for a more pronounced blur.
Gaussian Blur	Same as Blur More but with a Gaussian bell curve and a dialog box that enables you to specify the blur radius.
Convert to Alpha	Converts an image into a grayscale image that's suitable for use as an alpha mask. White pixels are colored transparent.
Find Edges	Detects the outlines of forms and converts them to solid lines.
Drop Shadow	Shadows the object against the background to make it stand out more effectively.
Glow	Puts a halo or soft glow around an object.
Inner Glow	Puts a glow within the inner edge of an object.
Inner Shadow	Puts a shadow within the inner edge of an object.
Sharpen	Sharpens by finding edges and increasing the contrast between adjacent pixels.
Sharpen More	Same as Sharpen but across a larger radius.
Unsharp Mask	Same as Sharpen More but with control over which pixels are sharpened (and which are left "unsharp") according to the image's grayscale mask.

Cross-Reference For more about mask groups, see Chapter 13.

Adjusting color

The Adjust Color submenu of the Effect Category option list contains powerful tools for adjusting the tonal range and color correcting, or for adding special effects to objects. Traditionally, these tools have only been available in a destructive form: you adjust an image's tonal range and if you find out later you went a little too dark or light, you had to start with an earlier iteration of a document and redo your work. Introducing these tools to Fireworks users as Live Effects provides a dramatic increase in workflow flexibility.

New Feature The Adjust Color Live Effects replace the PhotoOptics filters included with Fireworks 2, while adding the capability to live color correct image or path objects.

Adjusting tonal range

Ideally, a photographic image would have a fairly even ratio of dark tones, midtones, and light tones. Too many dark pixels hides detail; too many light pixels and your image appears washed out. Too many midtones — darks aren't dark enough and lights aren't light enough — and your image appears bland, like the Before image in Figure 12-5. Fireworks offers you a few different methods for adjusting the tonal range of images. Which one you choose to use depends on how bad the damage is.

Brightness/Contrast

For images that are only a little too dark or light, or lacking slightly in contrast, slight adjustments made with the Brightness/Contrast effect may be all you need. Fireworks can provide visual feedback by previewing your adjustments in the document window.

To use the Brightness/Contrast filter, follow these steps:

1. Select the image you'd like to modify in object mode.

2. If the Effect panel is not currently visible, choose Window ⇨ Effect to display it, or use the key shortcut Ctrl+Alt+E (Command+Option+E).

3. Choose Adjust Color ⇨ Brightness/Contrast. Fireworks displays the Brightness/Contrast dialog box, as shown in Figure 12-6.

4. Check Preview to view your changes as you make them in the document window.

5. Use the Brightness and/or Contrast sliders to adjust the settings. Values for the sliders range from -100 to 100. Click OK when you're done.

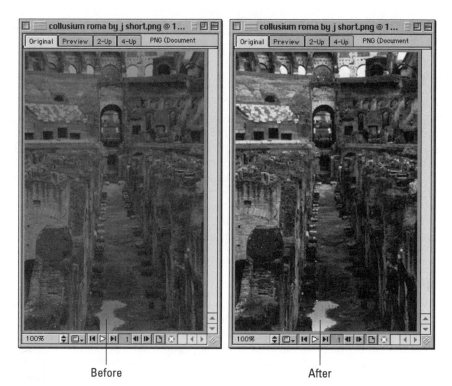

Before   After

Figure 12-5: Before and after increasing an image's tonal range to add contrast. Dark pixels are darkened and light pixels are lightened.

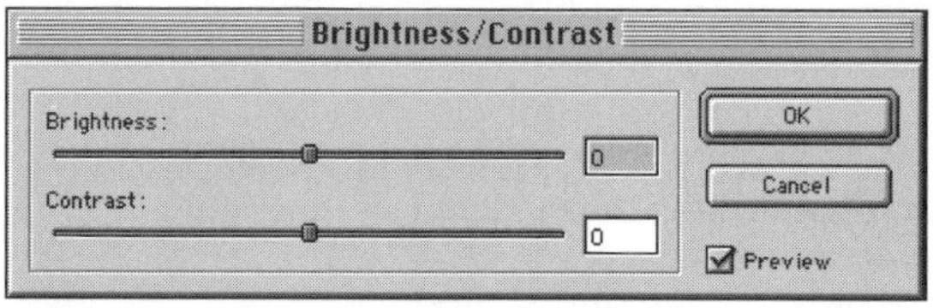

Figure 12-6: Adjust an image's brightness or contrast with the controls in the Brightness/Contrast dialog box.

Levels and Auto Levels

For images that need more adjustment than is possible with Brightness/Contrast, Fireworks offers the Levels and Auto Levels filters. Auto Levels works just like Levels, except that you skip the Levels dialog box entirely, and Fireworks maps the darkest pixels in your image to black and the lightest ones to white. For many images, you may find that Auto Levels does the trick in record time. If not, you can take matters into your own hands with Levels.

Cross-Reference See the Auto Levels filter demonstrated in the color insert.

The Levels dialog box introduces a special set of three eyedropper tools, shown in Figure 12-7, that are also available in the Curves dialog box, which we'll look at in the next section. The trio of eyedroppers, one for highlights, one for midtones, and one for shadows, enable you to remap the highlights, midtones, or shadows of an image to new levels by pointing to a pixel with the desired level. For example, if your image is too dark, use the Shadow eyedropper and select a pixel that is a little lighter than the darkest pixels. Fireworks substitutes the tones of the newly selected "shadow" pixels for the darkest pixels in your image, lightening the image. The highlights and midtones eyedroppers work in a similar fashion, providing target levels for highlights and midtones, respectively.

 Tip Clicking Auto in the Levels dialog box is just like using the Auto Levels filter.

Shadow eyedropper

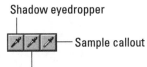 — Sample callout

Midtone eyedropper

Figure 12-7: These special Eyedropper tools enable you specify a new highlight, midtone, or shadow level by pointing to pixels.

Note Identify the three eyedroppers by the ink they seem to contain. The highlight eyedropper has white ink, while the midtone eyedropper has gray ink, and the shadow eyedropper has black.

The Levels dialog box also includes a Histogram — essentially a chart — that reports the levels of dark, middle, and light tones in your image, giving you a quick graphical representation of what might need to be fixed. The horizontal axis is dark to light, from left to right. The vertical axis is a level from 0 to 255.

To apply the Levels filter and modify the tonal range of an image, follow these steps:

1. Select the image you'd like to modify in object mode.

2. If the Effect panel is not currently visible, choose Window ⇨ Effect to display it, or use the key shortcut Ctrl+Alt+E (Command+Option+E).

3. Choose Adjust Color ⇨ Levels. Fireworks displays the Levels dialog box, as shown in Figure 12-8.

4. Check the Preview checkbox to view your changes as you make them in the document window.

5. Select which channels you'd like to modify from the Channels option list: just Red, just Green, just Blue, or RGB to modify all three.

Histogram   Midtone input level box

Shadow input level box   Highlight input level box

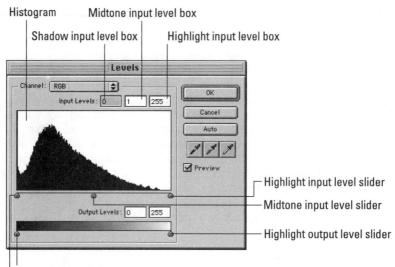

Highlight input level slider

Midtone input level slider

Highlight output level slider

Shadow output level slider

Shadow input level slider

Figure 12-8: The Levels dialog box displays a Histogram of the light, midtone, and dark tones in your image.

Tip

Modifying just the Red channel in a RGB image is similar to adjusting a color by increasing or decreasing the R value in the Color Mixer panel when it's set to RGB or Hexadecimal.

6. Modify the highlights and shadows in your image with the Highlight, Midtone, and Shadow Input Levels sliders or enter new values directly in the Highlight and Shadow Input Levels boxes. Highlights and shadows are specified from 0 to 255, while midtones are specified with 1.0 being neutral or 50 percent gray.

Note

The Shadow value can't be higher than the Highlight value, and the Highlight value can't be lower than the shadow Value.

7. Use the Highlights and Shadows Output Levels sliders to adjust your image's overall contrast.

8. If desired, use the Highlight, Midtone, or Shadow eyedropper to select a target level for highlights, midtones, or shadows, respectively, from your image.

9. Click OK when you're satisfied with the changes you've made.

The changes you've made are applied to the selected object.

Cross-Reference

Turn to the color insert to see a demonstration of the Levels filter.

Curves

The Curves filter essentially serves the same purpose as the Levels filter, but it presents the information to you in a different way. Whereas the Levels filter enables you to adjust the individual levels of light, mid, and dark tones in an image, the Curves filter focuses on the levels of individual colors. You can adjust the level of red, for example, without affecting the balance of light to dark in an image.

The Curves dialog box contains a grid. The horizontal axis is the original brightness values, which are also shown in the Input box. The vertical axis displays the new brightness values, which are also shown in the Output box. The values that are represented are 0 to 255, with 0 being complete shadow. The line plotted on the grid always starts out as a perfect diagonal, indicating that no changes have been made (the Input and Output values are the same).

As mentioned previously, the Curves dialog box also contains a trio of eyedropper tools just like the Levels dialog box. The Curves dialog box also contains an Auto button, which yields the same result here as it does in the Levels box: the darkest pixels in your image are mapped to black and the lightest to white, just as if you'd used the Auto Levels filter.

To use the Curves filter, follow these steps:

1. Select the image you'd like to modify in object mode.

2. Choose Window ➪ Effect or use the key shortcut Ctrl+Alt+E (Command+ Option+E) to display the Effect panel, if it's not already visible.

3. Choose Adjust Color ➪ Curves. Fireworks displays the Curves dialog box, as shown in Figure 12-9.

4. Check the Preview checkbox to view your changes as you make them in the document window.

5. Select which channels you'd like to modify from the Channels option list: just Red, just Green, just Blue, or RGB to modify all three.

6. Click a point on the grid's diagonal line, and drag it to a new position to adjust the curve. Changing the curve changes the Input and Output values.

7. To delete a point from the curve, select it and drag it out of the grid.

Caution   You can't delete the curve's endpoints.

8. If desired, use the Highlight, Midtone, or Shadow eyedropper to select a target level for highlights, midtones, or shadows, respectively, from your image.

9. Click OK when you're satisfied with the changes you've made.

Fireworks applies the changes you've made to the selected object.

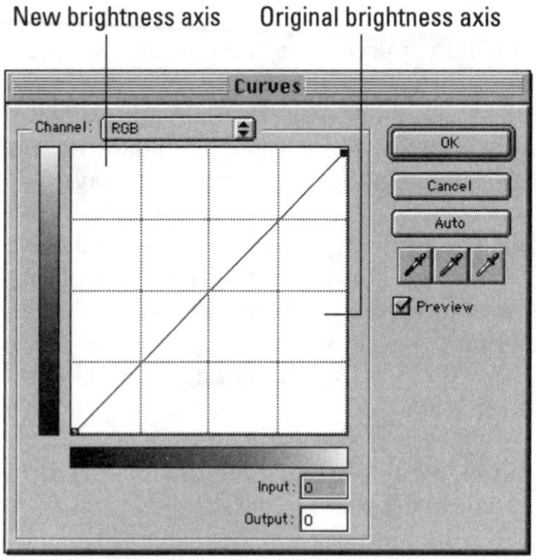

New brightness axis   Original brightness axis

Figure 12-9: The Curves dialog box enables you to graphically alter a color curve.

Cross-Reference   See the color insert to compare the effects of the Curves filter.

Hue/Saturation

The Hue/Saturation filter is similar to specifying colors using the HSL (Hue, Saturation, and Lightness) color model. If you're familiar with the concept of a color wheel, adjusting the hue is like moving around the color wheel, selecting a new color. Adjusting the saturation is like moving across the radius of the color wheel, selecting a more or less pure version of the same color.

Tip   Find examples of color wheels in your operating system's color picker(s), accessed by clicking the Palette button on the Fireworks pop-up color picker. Mac users can choose to view different color methods, including an HLS picker.

To adjust the hue or saturation of an image with the Hue/Saturation filter, follow these steps:

1. Select the image you'd like to modify in object mode.

2. Choose Window ➪ Effect or use the key shortcut Ctrl+Alt+E (Command+Option+E) to display the Effect panel, if it's not already visible.

3. Choose Adjust Color ➪ Hue/Saturation. Fireworks displays the Hue/Saturation dialog box, as shown in Figure 12-10.

4. Check the Preview checkbox to view your changes in the document window as you make them.

5. Choose Colorize to add color to a grayscale image or change an RGB image into a two-tone image.

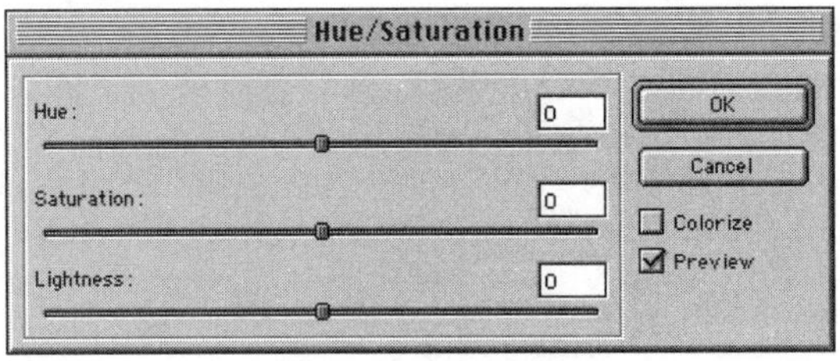

Figure 12-10: The Hue/ Saturation dialog box offers Hue, Saturation, and Lightness sliders.

Note If you choose Colorize, the range of the Hue slider changes from -180 through 180, to 0 through 360; and the range of the Saturation slider changes from -100 through 100, to 0 through 100.

6. Adjust the purity of the colors with the Saturation slider.

7. Adjust the color of the image with the Hue slider.

8. Adjust the lightness of the colors with the Lightness slider.

9. When you're satisfied with the changes you've made, click OK.

The changes you've made are applied to the selected object.

Cross-Reference See the Hue/Saturation filter in action in the color insert.

Three dimensions with Bevel and Emboss

The Bevel and Emboss effects are Fireworks' key to 3D. Both types of effects simulate light coming from a specific direction, illuminating an object that seems to be raised out of or sunken into the background.

Bevel effects

The bevel effects are similar in terms of user interface, available attributes, and preset options. In fact, they only differ in two key areas:

✦ As the names imply, the Inner Bevel creates its edges inside the selected object, whereas the Outer Bevel makes its edges around the outside of the selected object.

✦ The Outer Bevel effect has one attribute that the Inner Bevel does not: color. The Inner Bevel uses the object's color to convert the inside of the graphic to a bevel, whereas the Outer Bevel applies the chosen color to the new outside edge.

When you select either Inner Bevel or Outer Bevel from the Effect Category option list, Fireworks displays their headless dialog boxes so that you can adjust their parameters, as shown in Figure 12-11.

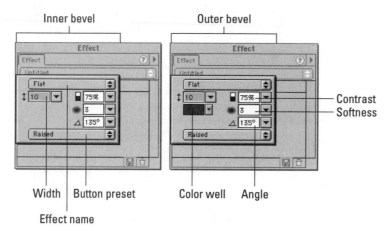

Figure 12-11: The Outer Bevel's headless dialog box is the same as the one for Inner Bevel, except for the addition of a color well.

Table 12-2 explains how to control aspects of bevel effects.

Table 12-2 Bevel Effects	
Bevel effect	**Description**
Effect name	Seven different types of bevel effects are accessible through the Effect name option list. Each type of effect alters the number, shape, or degree of the bevel.
Width	Sets the thickness of the beveled side. The Width slider has a range from 0 to 10 pixels, although you can enter a higher number directly in the text box.
Contrast	Determines the difference in relative brightness of the lit and shadowed sides, where 100 percent provides the greatest contrast and 0 percent provides no contrast.
Softness	Sets the sharpness of the edges used to create the bevel, where 0 is the sharpest and 10 is the softest. Values above 10 have no effect.
Angle	Provides the angle for the simulated light on the beveled surface. Drag the knob control to a new angle or enter it directly in the text box.
Button Preset	Offers four preset configurations, primarily used for creating rollover buttons.
Color	Available for Outer Bevel, this standard color well is used to determine the color of the surrounding border.

Caution Though the bevel effects can be applied to any object, if the object's edge is feathered too much, you won't be able to see the effect. To combine a feathered edge with a bevel, set the Amount of Feather to less than the width of the bevel.

Each of the bevel effects has the same types of edges. Compare the Inner Bevel and Outer Bevel effects in Figure 12-12, and you'll see the similarities among the seven types for both effects. Found under the Effect name option list, these types vary primarily in the shape of the bevel itself. Looking at each of the bevel shapes from the side makes it easier to differentiate between the possible shapes.

Inner bevel   Side views

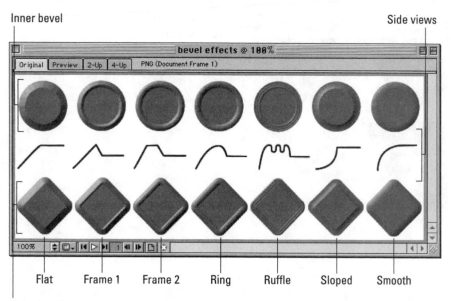

Flat   Frame 1   Frame 2   Ring   Ruffle   Sloped   Smooth

Outer bevel

Figure 12-12: Inner Bevel effects are all contained within the original path of the object, while Outer Bevel effects create edges outside the original path. The side views make it easier to tell the types of effects apart.

Bevel effect Button presets

Bevel effects are terrific for creating buttons for all purposes: navigation, forms, links, and so on. One of the most common applications of such buttons involves *rollovers*. Rollover is the generally used name (another is *mouseover*) for the effect when a user moves the pointer over a button and it changes in some way. Both bevel effects provide four presets under the Button preset option list—Raised, Highlight, Inset, and Inverted—which can be employed for rollovers.

Unlike Stroke or Fill panel presets, the bevel Button presets do not actually change the panel attributes, but rather internally change the lighting angle and lighten the object (Figure 12-13). The Raised and Highlight presets use the same lighting angle, derived from the Angle value, but Highlight is about 25 percent lighter. The Inset and Inverted presets, on the other hand, reverse the angle of the lighting — and, of this pair, Inverted is the lighter one.

Raised   Highlight

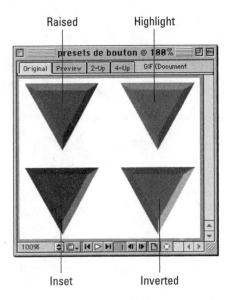
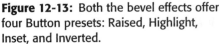

Figure 12-13: Both the bevel effects offer four Button presets: Raised, Highlight, Inset, and Inverted.

Inset   Inverted

> **Tip**   To take the fullest advantage of the bevel effect Button presets in creating rollovers, set your lighting angle first with the Effect panel Angle knob. Then duplicate the image and apply the different Button presets to each copy.

Embossing

If you've ever seen a company's Articles of Incorporation or other official papers, you've probably encountered embossing. An embossing seal is used to press the company name right into the paper — so that it can be both read and felt. Fireworks' emboss effects provide a similar service, with a great deal more flexibility, of course.

Both emboss effects replace an object's fill with the canvas color or the color of background objects, and then add highlights and shadows. Inset Emboss and Raised Emboss each reverse the placement of these highlights and effects in order to make the embossed object appear to be pushed into or out of the background, respectively, as shown in Figure 12-14.

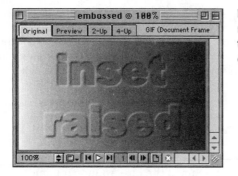

Figure 12-14: The two emboss effects make an object appear to be part of the background – either pushed into or out of it.

The Emboss effects are applied like any other Live Effect, with the options presented in a headless dialog, shown in Figure 12-15.

Width

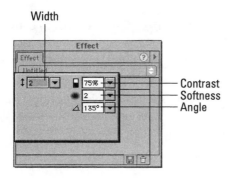

Contrast
Softness
Angle

Figure 12-15: Adjust the parameters of either the Inset Emboss or Raised Emboss effects through their identical headless dialog boxes.

Following are the adjustable emboss parameters:

✦ **Width:** Determines the thickness of the embossed edges. As with other effects, the slider's range is from 0 to 30, but higher values can be entered directly into the associated text box.

✦ **Contrast:** Contrast controls the relative lightness of the highlights to the darkness of the shadows.

✦ **Softness:** Sets the sharpness of the embossed edges; higher numbers make the edges fuzzier.

✦ **Angle:** Establishes the direction of the embossed edges.

Adding depth with blurring

Sometimes, what should be the focal point of your image can get lost among other elements of the composition. This is especially true when you're compositing multiple objects or really laying the filters on thick. Adding a little blur to the background area of an image can cause the foreground to stand out, immediately drawing the viewer's eye to it.

To add depth to the background area of an image, follow these steps:

1. Use one of the Marquee selection tools to create a pixel selection around the part of your image that you want to remain in the foreground. You might create a circle to focus attention within that circle or use the Magic Wand to create a complex selection, such as around a person's head or face.

Note   Fireworks automatically enters Image Edit mode when you use one of the Marquee selection tools.

2. Choose Edit ➪ Copy or use the key shortcut Ctrl+C (Command+C) to copy your pixel selection to the clipboard.

3. Choose Modify ➪ Exit Image Edit or click the Exit Image Edit ("stop") button to enter object mode.

4. Choose Window ➪ Effect or click the Effect tab, if it is visible. The Effect panel opens.

5. From the Effect Category option list, choose Blur ➪ Gaussian Blur.

   Fireworks displays the Gaussian Blur dialog box.

Note   Some Live Effects have an ellipsis after their menu command, which indicates that choosing that command will open a dialog box in which you can specify settings. Xtras without the ellipsis either don't have any parameters for you to change, or display their parameters in a headless dialog box.

6. Adjust the Blur Radius slider to specify the intensity of the effect. The more blur you add, the more depth you add to your image. Generally, a blur radius of between 1 or 2 creates a depth effect without destroying the edges of the elements in the image. Click OK when you're done.

7. Choose Edit ➪ Paste or the keyboard shortcut Ctrl+V (Command+V) to paste your original—unblurred—foreground selection back into your document as a new image object.

Tip   You may want to select both your background and foreground image objects and choose Modify ➪ Group to make them into a group.

The area that was within your original pixel selection now seems to stand out and draws the eye at first glance (see Figure 12-16). In addition, an overall feeling of depth has been created. Elements in the background seem to be a little further away.

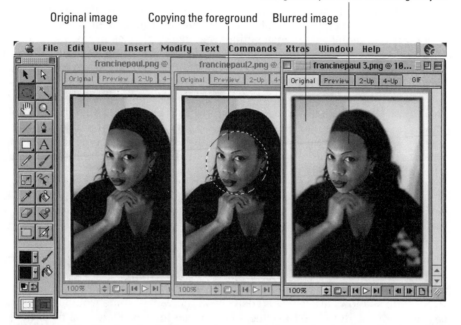

Figure 12-16: Blurring the background seems to give an image extra depth and makes the foreground stand out. Notice how your eye is immediately drawn to the subject's face.

The Blur and Blur More effects work similarly to the Gaussian Blur effect, except that they don't have parameters. Blur provides a slight blurring effect, and Blur More—well, you get the idea.

Holdover effects

The two effects on the Other submenu of the Effect panels Effect Category option list are holdovers all the way from Fireworks 1. The Convert to Alpha filter is unnecessary now that Fireworks has mask groups, but you may find creative uses for it. Applying it converts the selection to grayscale and sets white to transparent. The Find Edges filter detects the outlines of forms and converts them to solid lines. This can be useful for special effects, or for creating masks.

Shadow and Glow

The shadow and glow effects help to create depth and softness in your Fireworks documents.

Drop and inner shadows

I remember the overwhelming sense of pride I felt after I made my first drop shadow in an early version of Photoshop. Of course, it had taken me all afternoon to follow two different sets of instructions and involved masking layers, Gaussian blurs, nudged layers, and who remembers what else. My pride was quickly deflated when I tried out my new drop-shadowed image against a color background — and found a completely undesired halo of white pixels around my graphic.

All of that effort and anxiety is out the window with Fireworks. Applying a drop shadow to an object can be a simple, two-step process: select the object and then choose Drop Shadow from the Effect panel. Best of all, you can position the drop shadow against any colored background; Fireworks adjusts the blending of shadow to background, eliminating the unwanted halo effect.

Note   I'm not trying to defame Photoshop, which is a fine application. It's only fair to acknowledge that newer versions also have a Drop Shadow effect that's easily applied and is easily imported into Fireworks 3, with editability intact.

A drop shadow is a monochrome copy of an image, offset so that it appears behind the image to one side. Drop shadows are usually presented in a shade of gray (although they can be any color) and can be either faded on the edge or hard edged. Drop shadows are used extensively on the Web — some would say that they're overused. However, the effect of giving flat images dimension by adding a shadow behind it is so compelling and downright useful that I think drop shadows will be around for a long time.

In addition to Drop Shadow, Fireworks also offers an Inner Shadow effect. Both effects are essentially the same — and even use the same headless dialog box for setting parameters — except for the location of the shadow. Inner Shadow places the shadow within your object, as though it is recessed and the shadow is being cast by the edges of whatever it's recessed into.

To apply a Drop Shadow or Inner Shadow to any object in Fireworks, follow these steps:

1. Select the object. Drop shadows work well on most any object: open or closed paths, geometric shapes, image objects, text objects, and more.

2. Choose Window ➪ Effect or click the Effect tab, if it is visible. The Effect panel opens.

3. Choose either Drop Shadow or Inner Shadow from the Effect Category option list. The initial parameters — which are the same for both effects — are displayed in a headless dialog box, as shown in Figure 12-17.

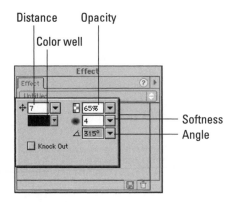

Figure 12-17: The default Drop Shadow effect offers a classic soft shadow, slightly cast to the right, but you can modify it in the headless parameters dialog box.

4. To make the shadow appear farther away or closer, change the Distance slider or enter a value directly in the associated text box.

Tip The Distance slider has a range from 0 to 100 pixels, but you can enter a higher number in the text box to make the shadow appear even farther away. The text box also accepts negative numbers, which cause the shadow to be cast in the opposite direction of the Angle setting.

5. To change the shadow color from the default black, pick a color from the Color well.

6. To change the transparency of the shadow, alter the Opacity slider or text box. Opacity is given in a percentage value; 100 percent is completely opaque and 0 percent is completely transparent (and therefore invisible).

7. To make the edge of the shadow softer or harder, move the Softness slider or enter a value in its text box. The Softness slider goes from 0 to 30, but you can enter a higher value directly in the text box.

8. To change the direction of the shadow, drag the Angle knob to a new location or enter a degree (0 to 360) directly in the text box.

9. To display just the shadow and make the object disappear, choose the Knock Out option.

I find myself using a hard-edged shadow almost as much as I do the soft-edge versions, particularly in graphics, where file size is paramount. Any image with a blended edge is larger than the same image with a solid edge because more pixels are necessary to create the faded look — typically half again as many. When file size is key — and you like the look of a solid drop shadow — bring the Softness slider all the way down to zero.

I do find softer shadows particularly effective, however, when one shadow overlaps another. A good way to enhance the three dimensionality of your Web graphics is to place one object with a shadow over another object, also with a shadow.

Using the Knock Out option

The Knock Out option offered in the shadow effects deserves special mention. The phrase knock out is an old printer's term referring to the practice of dropping the color out of certain type to let background show through. Obviously if you eliminated the color from an ordinary bit of type — without an outline or other surrounding element — the type would seem to disappear. A shadow is perfect for surrounding knocked out type because of the way the mind has of filling in the details that are missing from the actual image. Selecting the Knock Out option removes both the fill and stroke color of the object and leaves just the shadow, as shown in Figure 12-18.

Figure 12-18: Use a Drop Shadow effect with Knock Out checked to highlight text or other objects with just the shadow.

> **Tip**
>
> In the introduction to this section, I noted how it's easy in Fireworks to avoid the so-called halo effect that occurs when you move a drop shadow built against one background to another. In Fireworks, there are really two ways to do this. If you don't need the object or its shadow to be transparent, change the canvas color to the background color of your Web page and export the image normally. To avoid the halo effect, but maintain a transparent image, make the background color transparent during export.

Glow

Whereas a shadow is only visible on one or two sides of an object, the glow effects — Glow and Inner Glow — create a border all around the object. The glow's color is user selectable, as is its width, opacity, and softness.

To apply a glow, follow these steps:

1. Select the desired object.

2. Choose Window ➪ Effect or click the Effect tab, if it is visible. The Effect panel opens.

3. Choose either Glow or Inner Glow from the Shadow and Glow submenu on the Effect Category option list. Fireworks displays the glow parameters in a head-less dialog box, which is identical to the drop-shadow dialog box, shown pre-viously in Figure 12-17, except for the lack of a Knock Out option.

4. Set the other options — Width, Color, Opacity, and Softness — as desired.

All of the Glow effect parameters are the same as those found on the shadow effects.

Tip   One effect you can create with Glow that's not immediately obvious is a border. Apply Glow effect to an object and set the Softness to 0 and the Opacity to 100 percent. Voila, a border.

Sharpening to bring out detail

Sharpening an image can bring out depth that's not there by finding the edges of objects and creating more contrast between pixels on either side of that edge. It can especially help to fix a bad scan, or bring out detail after you go overboard with special effects Xtras.

To sharpen an image a little bit, select it and choose Sharpen ➪ Sharpen or Sharpen ➪ Sharpen More from the Effect Category option list in the Effect panel.

To sharpen an image with control over individual settings, follow these steps:

1. Select an object.

2. Choose Window ➪ Effect or click the Effect tab, if it is visible. Alternatively, use the key shortcut Ctrl+Alt+E (Command+Option+E). The Effect panel opens.

3. From the Effect Category option list, choose Sharpen ➪ Unsharp Mask.

   Fireworks displays the Unsharp Mask dialog box, as shown in Figure 12-19.

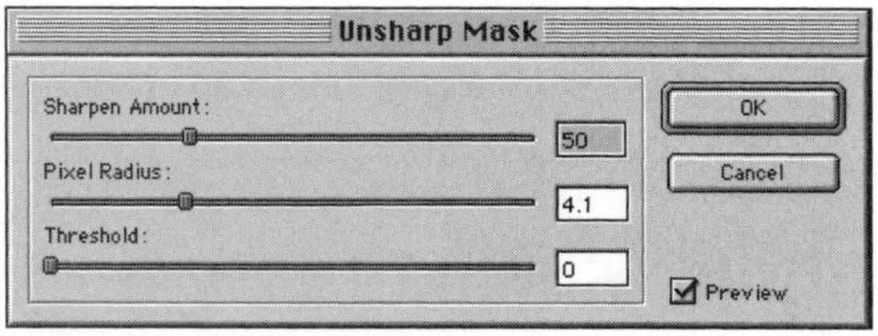

Figure 12-19: Specify the parameters for Unsharp Mask in the Unsharp Mask dialog box.

4. Moving the Sharpen Amount slider specifies the intensity of the effect. You might start with this slider at about midway and increase or decrease it later, after setting other options.

5. Move the Pixel Radius slider to control how many pixels are evaluated simultaneously. A larger radius value results in a more pronounced effect because the differences among a larger group of pixels typically are greater.

6. Move the Threshold slider to determine which pixels are affected. Only pixels that have a grayscale value higher than the threshold value are affected. A lower threshold affects more pixels. Click OK when you're done.

Your image should now have a crisper, sharper look (see Figure 12-20).

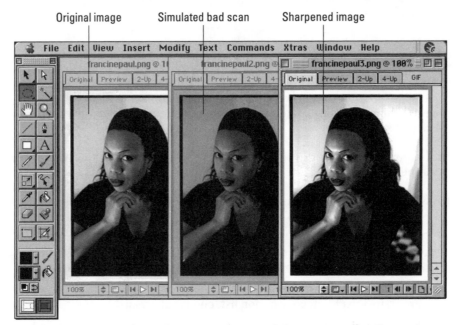

Figure 12-20: Sharpening an image may seem to bring out extra detail.

Tip   Sometimes, a sharpened image will seem too harsh. Adding a touch of blur with the Blur Live Effect or applying the Auto Levels filter may help to remedy this.

Fireworks Technique: Making Perspective Shadows

Fireworks is flexible enough to enable you to extend its Live Effects to create many of your own effects. One such possibility is perspective shadows. Unlike drop shadows, perspective shadows are not flat carbon copies of the selected object, but rather shadows that appear to exist in a three-dimensional world. In addition, perspective shadows can appear in front, behind, or to the side of the object.

Alien Skin's Eye Candy filters, covered later in this chapter, include a perspective shadow effect that's worth investigating if you have the Eye Candy package.

This perspective shadow technique takes advantage of Fireworks' facility with path objects and its capability to adjust gradients and edges. With this technique, you can add perspective shadows to text, image, or path objects. An image object that received this treatment is shown in Figure 12-21.

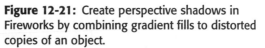

Figure 12-21: Create perspective shadows in Fireworks by combining gradient fills to distorted copies of an object.

To create a perspective shadow, follow these steps:

1. Duplicate the outline of the original object to create a new shadow object. Depending on the type of object, this first step is either very simple, very time-consuming, or something in-between. Here are techniques for working with the three basic types of objects:

   • **Path objects:** By far the easiest of the three, simply choose Edit ➪ Clone to copy any path object. Cloning is a better choice than Duplicating because it's easier to align the shadow and its source later.

   • **Text objects:** Although it's not absolutely necessary, I've found it sometimes easier to work with text as a path for my shadow object than with regular text. In my experience, distorting path objects gets more predictable results than distorting text. Therefore, I first Clone the text and then choose Text ➪ Convert to Paths. Finally, to reduce the gradients of the separate letters to one, choose Modify ➪ Combine ➪ Union.

- **Image objects:** Image objects can be simple rectangles or irregular shapes. If your object is rectangular or another geometric shape, use the Rectangle, Ellipse, or Polygon to create a same-size copy of the object. Otherwise, the best tool I found for this particular job is the Pen. For outlining an image, I use the Pen primarily in its straight-line mode, clicking from one point to the next, although occasionally when I need to copy a curve, I can with the Pen's Bézier curve feature. The outline doesn't have to be exact, although the more details you include, the more realistic your shadow will be.

2. If necessary, flip the shadow object. Depending on your hypothetical light source, you'll want to flip the shadow object vertically so that the perspective shadow falls in front of the original object.

3. If necessary, move the shadow object into position.

   You won't need to move the shadow object if the perspective shadow falls behind the original object. However, for perspective shadows in front, you do need to move the shadow object so that the bases of each object meet. While it's entirely possible to use the mouse to drag the shadow object into position, I often find myself using the cursor keys to move the selected shadow object in one direction. Pressing Shift+Arrow key moves the object in ten-pixel increments and the regular arrow keys, one pixel.

4. Send the shadow object behind the original object.

   Whether you choose Modify ⇨ Arrange ⇨ Send Backward or Modify ⇨ Arrange ⇨ Send to the Back depends on what other objects are in the document and how you want the shadow to relate to them. But even if the perspective shadow falls in front of the source object, you'll want to put it behind to mask the meeting point.

5. Distort the shadow object.

   Here's where the real artistry — and numerous attempts — enter the picture. Select the shadow object and choose the Skew tool from the Toolbox to slant the shadow in one direction; again, the direction depends on where the apparent "light" for the shadow is coming from. Next, while the Skew tool is still active, switch to the Scale tool. (By pressing the keyboard shortcut Q, twice, you don't have to move the mouse.) You can now easily resize the same bounding box. Choose the middle horizontal sizing handle on the edge farthest away from the original object. Now you can drag that handle to either shorten or lengthen the shadow.

6. Optionally, fill the shadow object with a gradient.

   You may be satisfied with the shadow as it stands now, but adding and adjusting a gradient will add more depth and realism to the image. From the Fill panel, choose the Linear gradient with a Black, White preset color combination.

7. Adjust the gradient of the shadow object.

As applied, the Linear gradient just goes left to right. If you need it to flow at a different angle (and you probably will), choose the Paint Bucket tool while the shadow object is selected to activate the gradient controls. Reposition and angle the gradient so that the starting point is at the juncture of the source and shadow object, and the ending point is just beyond the end of the shadow. This enables the shadow to gently fade away.

8. If desired, slightly feather the edge of the shadow object.

To my eye, shadows look a bit more realistic if they're not so hard edged. I like to set my Fill panel Edge option list to Feather and set the Amount of Feather relatively low, about three or four pixels. You may have to adjust the shadow object a bit to hide the feathered edge where it touches the original object.

Many enhancements can be added to this technique. For example, you could add an object for the shadow to fall over by bending or pulling the shadow object with the Reshape Path or Reshape Area tools, or the shadow itself could be not so realistic to make a point. Computer graphics make it oh-so-tempting to turn anyone's shadow into a horned devil or winged angel. Play with perspective — you'll be glad you did.

Managing Live Effects

Like strokes and fills, custom configurations of Live Effects can be saved with each document. These custom effects can then later be applied to other objects in the same document or, if the object is copied to another document, other graphics. As with strokes and fills, management of custom effects is easily handled through the pop-up menu.

The Effect panel pop-up menu commands are

- ✦ **Save Defaults:** Stores the effects settings of the currently selected object as defaults for those effects.

- ✦ **Save Effect As:** Stores the current effect settings under a unique name in the Effect name option list.

- ✦ **Rename Effect:** Renames any custom or standard effect.

- ✦ **Delete Effect:** Removes any custom or standard effect. If you remove a standard effect, it will be restored when Fireworks is restarted or when you access another document.

- ✦ **All On** and **All Off:** Turns all applied effects on or off, respectively. This is the same as checking or unchecking all of the checkboxes in the Effects list.

- ✦ **Locate Plugins:** A shortcut to specifying a folder of Photoshop-compatible plug-ins for Fireworks to use. This is the same as modifying the Photoshop Plug-Ins option in the Folders area of Fireworks preferences. Fireworks must be restarted for this to take effect.

Storing a customized effect

Creating your own effects is a tremendous time-saver and an enjoyable creative exercise, as well. With Fireworks 3, saved effects can include Photoshop-compatible image filters that are being used as Live Effects, as well as the classic Live Effects, such as bevels and shadows. This leads to the creation of complex and creative effects, like the ones shown in Figure 12-22, that combine Fireworks default effects with some that are borrowed from Photoshop 5.5.

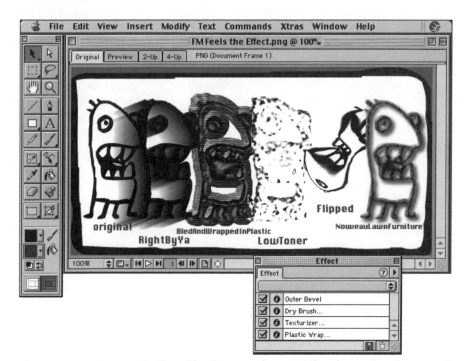

Figure 12-22: A range of effects like these can be created and stored under sometimes goofy names for instant recall.

To store a customized effect, follow these steps:

1. Apply effects to an object until you create a combination that you'd like to save.

2. Choose Save Effect As from the Effect panel pop-up menu. The Save Effect As dialog box appears.

3. Enter a unique name for the effect. If you choose a name already in use, Fireworks asks if you want to replace the existing effect.

4. After entering a new name, click Save. The new effect name is displayed alphabetically in the user area of the Effect Category option list.

Cross-Reference See some saved effects in greater detail in the color insert.

Missing effects

Now that you can include all kinds of third-party filters in your saved effects, the downside is that documents that use those effects depend upon them being available. If you try to open a document from a colleague, for example, who used effects that you don't have on your system, Fireworks displays the Missing Effects dialog box(Figure 12-23), warning you that certain effects are unavailable. Obviously, the remedy is to install the correct effects, but you can edit the document in the meantime.

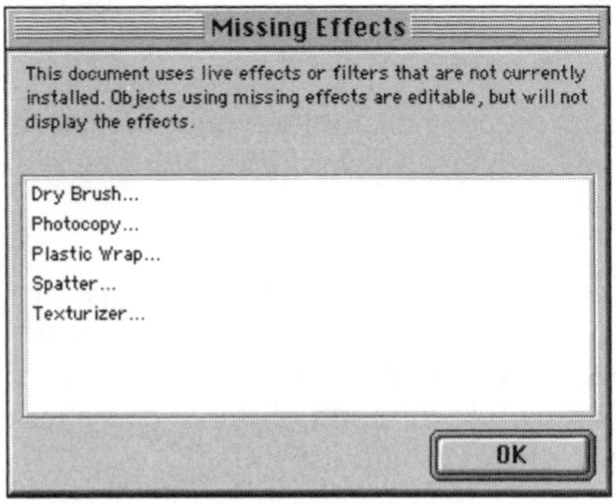

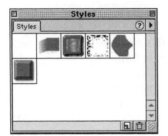

Figure 12-23: Fireworks displays the Missing Effects dialog box when you open a document that uses filters that are not available.

Saving effects in Styles

Another way to save and recall custom effects is to save them as Styles. As well as saving fills, strokes, and text properties, Styles remember Live Effects settings, even image filters used as Live Effects. If you save only the effect setting, you can apply that effect setting with one click. This also provides a graphical thumbnail of the effect, visible in the Styles panel, as shown in Figure 12-24.

Figure 12-24: The saved effects from Figure 12-22, saved as Styles, display a thumbnail of what the effect looks like.

To create a new Style using a custom effect, follow these steps:

1. Select an object that uses the custom effect.

2. If necessary, choose Window ➭ Styles, use the keyboard shortcut Ctrl+Alt+J (Command+Option+J), or click the Style tab, if it is visible. The Style panel is displayed.

3. On the Style panel, select the New Style button.

4. In the Edit Style dialog box, enter a descriptive name for your effect in the Name text box and deselect all checkboxes except Effect.

5. Click OK when you're done. A new Style is entered in the Style panel.

Any Style added in the just-described fashion is always available for any Fireworks document. To apply the effect, just highlight any Fireworks object and select the new Style.

If you export your new Style, it won't work properly on another machine that doesn't have the same effects installed. If you only use Fireworks' default Live Effects, you can avoid this problem, of course.

As well as being useful for complex combinations of effects, saving simple effects can save you much time, as well. I often find myself choosing the same simple drop shadow or using the same 4-pixel flat Inner Bevel on almost every standard 88 × 31 pixel micrbutton that I create. An effects-only Style for each of the above shaves a small amount of time and trouble out of my day over and over again.

To find out more about the powerful Styles feature, see Chapter 16.

Xtras, Read All About Them

In Fireworks 3, many of the items in the Xtras menu are also available in the Effect panel. Choosing them from the Xtras menu has a few key differences, though:

✦ A filter in the Xtras menu can be applied to any kind of selection in Fireworks, in either Image Edit mode or object mode, whereas items from the Effect panel can only be applied in object mode.

✦ Unlike the Effect panel, applying a filter from the Xtras menu flattens text and path objects into image objects, reducing their editability.

Before you choose a filter from the Xtras menu, you have to decide what you want to modify with that Xtra and select it in the appropriate way. All the Xtras that are included with Fireworks will work on any type of selection, but some third-party Xtras work better on pixel selections within image objects, or even require such a selection to run.

Path objects

As mentioned previously, applying an Xtra to a path object or path object group flattens it into an image object. The vector information is thrown away and you lose the advantages, such as scalability and editability, that path objects provide. Try using Live Effects on your path objects to achieve the look that you want before you apply Xtras. Once your path object becomes an image object, there's no going back, except by using the Undo command or the History panel.

Tip   Sometimes, though, you can get the best of both worlds. If you're using an Xtra that draws outside the selection (for example, the Eye Candy Fire filter, which draws flames around your image), you can apply the Xtra to a copy of your object and then place the resulting, filtered image behind your original object and group them. Later, you can still color and use Live Effects on your path object. If you resize it, you should throw away the filtered image and reapply the saved settings of the filter to a new copy of your object. If you're applying an Xtra that alters within the selection, try applying the Xtra to a copy of your object and then using the copy as an alpha mask for your original. Some interesting effects can be created this way, without being stuck in Image Edit mode.

When you do apply an Xtra to a path object, Fireworks warns you that doing so will convert it to an image object. You can disable this warning by checking the "don't show again" check box. I recommend that you leave it unchecked for a little while, until you get used to this conversion. If you accidentally convert a path object to an image object and then save your file, your vector information may be gone for good.

To apply an Xtra to a path object, select it with the mouse in object mode and then choose the Xtra from the Xtras menu.

Image objects

Applying an Xtra to an image object couldn't be easier. The only thing to keep in mind is that some Xtras draw outside the selection, to create effects such as motion trails and drop shadows. If your image object is the same size as the canvas, the effect will either be invisible, because it's off the canvas, or, with some Xtras, won't even be drawn. Before applying one of these filters, resize the canvas to give them a little room.

To apply an Xtra to an image object, select it with the mouse in object mode and then choose the Xtra from the Xtras menu.

Pixel selections in an image object

Many filters work best when applied to a pixel selection within an image object because they create a difference between the area inside the selection and the area outside the selection. Often, complex pixel selections, such as those made with the

Magic Wand or the Polygon Lasso, work better than simple rectangular or circular selections. The extra complexity creates areas where some filters create things, such as bevels, shadows, or textures.

Note　Creating a pixel selection doesn't necessarily mean that you've limited an Xtra to drawing only inside the selection. Although most will stay inside, some draw outside the selection to create their effect. Your selection marks a focal point for whatever filter you're applying.

To apply an Xtra to a pixel selection within an image object, use one of the Marquee selection tools from the Toolbox to draw your selection in Image Edit mode, and then choose an Xtra from the Xtras menu.

Cross-Reference　For more on creating selections within image objects, see Chapter 6.

False pixel selections

Some filters will ignore your pixel selections and apply their effect to an entire image object. If you find that a particular filter exhibits this behavior, you can work around it by creating a "false pixel selection," by copying your pixel selection to the Clipboard and pasting it as a new image object.

Tip　All the filters in Kai's Power Tools 5, detailed later in this chapter, apply their effects to your entire image object and require that you use a false pixel selection to limit them to a portion of your image.

To create a false pixel selection, follow these steps:

1. Choose Modify ⇨ Image Object or the key shortcut Ctrl+E (Command+E) to enter Image Edit mode.

2. Create a selection around the area to which you want to apply the Xtra by using one of the Marquee selection tools from the Toolbox.

3. Copy the selection to the Clipboard by choosing either Edit ⇨ Copy or the keyboard shortcut Ctrl+C (Command+C).

4. Paste the selection back into the document by choosing either Edit ⇨ Paste or the keyboard shortcut Ctrl+V (Command+V).

   The selection is pasted as a new image object, on top of the area it was copied from. Even though it now has a square marquee selection, the image object is, in fact, the same size and shape as what you originally copied to the Clipboard.

5. Apply an Xtra to the new image object by choosing the Xtra from the Xtras menu.

The filter affects only the new image object.

6. Either choose Modify ➪ Exit Image Edit, use the keyboard shortcut Ctrl+ Shift+D (Command+Shift+D), or press the stop button in the status bar to return to object mode.

The original image object and the new one that you created and then filtered are merged into one. The net result is that only the area of your original pixel selection is modified.

Multiple objects

In addition to individual objects, you can apply Xtras to a selection or group of multiple objects. If your selection or group contains any path objects, they will be converted to image objects, just as they would be if you were applying the Xtra to them individually. When applying Xtras to multiple objects, keep the following in mind:

✦ If you apply an Xtra to a selection of objects in object mode, the Xtra runs multiple times, applying to each object in turn. If you select three objects, for example, the Xtra runs three times in a row, once on each object. If you select Cancel in any of the filter's dialog boxes, it cancels the entire operation, and none of your objects will be altered.

✦ If you apply an Xtra to a group of objects, they will act as if they are one object. After you apply the Xtra, the objects actually are one image object, and you can't separate them. To make a selection of objects into a group, select multiple objects and choose Modify ➪ Group or use the keyboard shortcut Ctrl+G (Command+G).

 Caution The exceptions to the preceding list are the Adjust Color, Blur, Other, and Sharpen Xtras that come with Fireworks (all of those above the line in the Xtras menu). They act on a selection of objects as if they are already grouped.

The differences in the way groups and selections are handled by Xtras is actually quite handy. Imagine that you have created five objects that are going to be five buttons in a navigation interface. If you want to apply an Xtra with the exact same settings to all of them, group them and apply the Xtra. If, however, you want to apply the same Xtra to all of them, but tweak the settings for each — to add a slightly different texture to each one, for example — just select them and apply the Xtra.

Tip Many Xtras start with the same settings as when you last used them. When applying an extra to a selection of objects, the second time the Xtra starts, it will have the same settings that you used on the first object, making it easier to apply a similar effect across a selection of objects. You can also save settings in some Xtras.

Using Third-Party, Photoshop-Compatible Filters

So far, you've seen what you can do with the Live Effects and Xtras that are included with Fireworks, but that's just the tip of the iceberg. Many third-party, Photoshop-compatible, plug-in filters are available.

Caution Fireworks supports Photoshop-compatible filters, but some developers target their filters directly at Photoshop itself, creating filters that don't work in other applications. Check the Disabled plugins file in your Fireworks Xtras folder for a list of filters that are known to be incompatible. Just because a filter is not on that list doesn't mean that it's guaranteed to work with Fireworks, though. Whenever possible, ask the software publisher about Fireworks compatibility before purchasing filters.

Installing third-party filter packages

Most filter packages come with installers that are just like the installers provided with full applications, such as Fireworks. Before you install a package, close Fireworks. You have to restart Fireworks before you use the filters, anyway. When the installer's instructions ask you to locate your Photoshop Plug-Ins folder, specify your Fireworks Xtras folder. If the package did not come with an installer, you have to copy the filters to your Xtras folder yourself.

Note On Windows machines, the Fireworks Xtras folder is usually at C:\Program Files\ Macromedia\Fireworks 3\Settings\Xtras. On Macintosh machines, it is typically located at Macintosh HD:Applications:Fireworks 3:Settings:Xtras.

After the installation is complete, start Fireworks. You should see a new option under the Xtras menu, and — if Fireworks can use the filters as Live Effects — on the Effect Category option list in the Effect panel. This will be a whole new submenu, which usually has multiple filters available. Sometimes, new effects will hide themselves on menus you already have. If you have a Distort submenu, for example (some of Photoshop 5's filters create this), and you install a filter that also wants to live in a Distort submenu, it may not be apparent that you've gained a filter until you open the Distort submenu.

Tip Where can you get more filters? A good place to start is Adobe Plug-in Source's Photoshop Plug-ins page, at ⟨http://www.pluginsource.com/photoshop/⟩, where you can find a variety of offerings available for purchase and download. Another site I like is PlugIn Com HQ, at ⟨http://pico.i-us.com⟩, where you can find filter enthusiasts and many free filters and links.

Using filters with multiple applications

If you use another image-editing application in addition to Fireworks, you may have a whole host of filters on your computer that can also be used in Fireworks. Sharing filters among numerous applications can instantly add many features to all of them and can also speed up your workflow because you don't have to leave an application to apply a particular effect.

Aside from Fireworks, here are some other applications that use Photoshop-compatible filters:

✦ Adobe Photoshop and Illustrator

✦ Macromedia FreeHand and Director

✦ Corel Photo-Paint and CorelDRAW

I have about six or seven applications that use filters, so I keep all of my filters in one folder, independent of all the applications, and then I have all the applications use that folder as their plug-ins folder. The alternative would be to install filters numerous times into the plug-ins folder of each and every application. If you have multiple applications that use standard filters, you might want to do the same thing.

You may have only one other application that uses standard filters, perhaps Photoshop itself. If this is the case, you can tell Fireworks to use that application's plug-ins folder in addition to using Fireworks' own Xtras folder.

To specify an additional filters folder, follow these steps:

1. Choose File ⇨ Preferences.

   Fireworks displays the Preferences dialog box.

2. Choose the Folders tab (Folders option on Macintosh), as shown in Figure 12-25.

3. Check the Photoshop Plug-Ins check box.

4. Click the Browse button to the right of the Photoshop Plug-Ins check box.

   Fireworks displays the Browse for Folder dialog box.

5. Select the folder that contains the filters you want to use. Click OK when you're done.

6. Restart Fireworks to see the changes to the Xtras menu and to use your newly available filters.

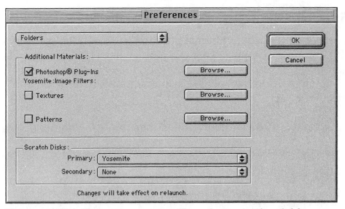

Figure 12-25: Fireworks can use filters from another folder on your computer, such as Photoshop's Plug-Ins folder.

Using Shortcuts (Aliases) to plug-in folders

Another method for specifying an additional plug-in folder or folders is to place shortcuts (aliases) to those folders into Fireworks' Xtras folder. As well as being an intuitive way to specify where filters are located, this also has the advantage of enabling you to specify more than one additional folder (see Figure 12-26).

To create a shortcut to a folder of filters on Windows, select the folder right-click it, and then drag it into your Fireworks Xtras folder. When you drop it, choose Make Shortcut from the contextual menu that appears. On the Mac, hold down Command+ Option while you drag the folder into your Fireworks Xtras folder and an alias to the plug-ins folder will be created.

Alien Skin Eye Candy

Eye Candy is a popular filter collection that you can purchase and install as Xtras in Fireworks. Fireworks even includes two of the filters as Eye Candy LE. Even if you don't (yet) have the full Eye Candy 3.1 package, this section introduces you to the kinds of things that are possible with filters in general, and this section may help you evaluate other, similar packages for their quality and creative potential.

> **Tip**   Alien Skin has optimized Eye Candy for use as Live Effects in Fireworks. If you already have the Eye Candy package, make sure to download the updater patch. Visit Alien Skin on the Web at <http://www.alienskin.com> or go direct to Eye Candy at <http://www.eyecandy.com>.

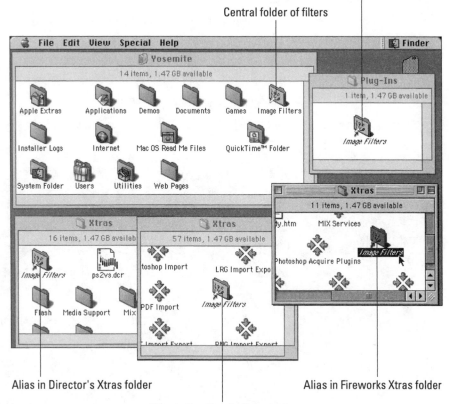

Figure 12-26: Place shortcuts (aliases) to folders that contain filters into Fireworks Xtras folder to enable Fireworks to access the filters.

The theme here is classic effects done right: beveling, drop shadows, smoke, motion trails, distortion. The Eye Candy filters are a great foundation for any filter collection because they're the kind of blue-collar, hard-working, tried-and-true effects that are used again and again in the kinds of tasks that the working Web artist does every day.

Following are some of the features you'll find in Eye Candy:

✦ Many presets for each filter enable you to start using them quickly. In addition, you can save your own settings to the preset list for later recall.

✦ A dynamic preview capability enables you to zoom in or out on your image for precise, detailed modifications.

✦ All Eye Candy filters share common interface features, which cuts down the learning curve (see Figure 12-27).

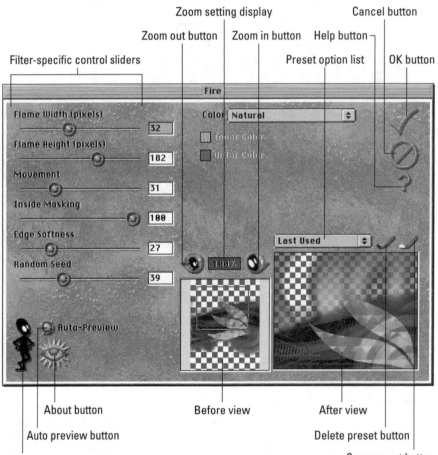

Figure 12-27: The Eye Candy filters are famous for their dynamic interface and easy-to-use presets. Figure 12-27 shows the Fire filter igniting the Fireworks logo.

Table 12-3 details each of the filters that make up Eye Candy 3.1 and explains what they do.

Caution   Many Eye Candy filters draw outside the selection and, therefore, rely heavily on having a pixel selection within an image object or having space around an image object against the canvas.

Table 12-3
Alien Skin Eye Candy 3.1

Filter	Description
Antimatter	Inverts brightness without affecting hue and saturation values. For example, dark red becomes light red, but is still red.
Carve	Makes a pixel selection appear carved or chiseled into the image.
Chrome	Applies a metallic effect that can be used to simulate chrome, silver, gold, and other metals.
Cutout	Makes a pixel selection appear as a hole in the image, including a shadow, so that it appears recessed.
Drop Shadow	Adds a drop shadow to a pixel selection or an object.
Fire	Creates a realistic flame effect rising from a pixel selection or object.
Fur	Applies randomly placed clumps of fur.
Glass	Superimposes a sheet of colored glass.
Glow	Adds a semitransparent glow around the outside edge of a pixel selection or object.
HSB Noise	Adds noise by varying hue, saturation, brightness, and transparency.
Inner Bevel	Makes a pixel selection or object appear embossed (raised up from the background). The effect is placed within the pixel selection or object.
Jiggle	Creates a bubbling, gelatinous, or shattered effect.
Motion Trail	Creates the illusion of motion by smearing a pixel selection or object outward in one direction.
Outer Bevel	Makes a pixel selection or object appear embossed (raised up from the background). The effect is placed outside the pixel selection or object.
Perspective Shadow	Adds a shadow to a pixel selection or object so that the light appears to come from above and in front, like standing in sunlight.
Smoke	Creates smoke coming from a pixel selection or object.
Squint	Unfocuses a pixel selection or object in a way similar to bad eyesight.
Star	Creates stars and other polygon shapes.
Swirl	Adds randomly placed whirlpools.
Water Drops	Adds randomly placed water drops.
Weave	Applies a woven effect.

Jiggle

Jiggle produces a unique distortion based on randomly placed bubbling. The patterns that it produce seem more random and organic—less computerized—than many distortion filters. A selection can seem like it's bubbling, gelatinous, or shattered.

To use Jiggle, select an image and follow these steps:

1. Choose Xtras ➪ Eye Candy 3.1 ➪ Jiggle.

The Jiggle dialog box appears (see Figure 12-28).

Original image   Jiggled image   Jiggled image as alpha mask

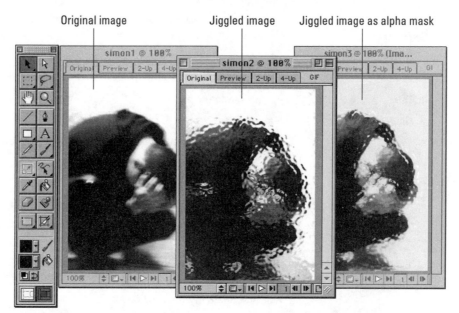

Figure 12-28: Jiggle is organic distortion in action, using the Bubbles type of movement. The third image (right) is the original image with the jiggled image as its alpha mask, and the canvas color changed to show through.

2. Adjust these controls to achieve the effect you desire:

- **Bubble Size slider:** Controls the frequency of the distortion. The lower the value, the more closely spaced the distortion.

- **Warp Amount:** Controls how much your selection is stretched.

- **Twist:** Controls the amount of twisting that occurs, measured in degrees.

- **Movement Type drop-down list:** Use to select the way you want the image jiggled. The three types of jiggling are Bubbles, which is a smooth, even distortion; Brownian Motion, which is a more ragged effect; and Turbulence, which creates sharper breaks in the image.

3. If you like, you can save your settings by using the Save Preset button. Click OK (the check mark) when you're done.

The effect is applied to your image.

Perspective Shadow

The ubiquitous drop shadow has its place, but a more realistic shadow that mimics the effects of the sun can be applied with Eye Candy's Perspective Shadow. The effect makes your selection appear to be standing up as the light comes from above and in front. The shadow is attached to the object rather than floating, which creates the three-dimensional perspective.

To use Perspective Shadow, select an image and follow these steps:

1. Choose Xtras ➪ Eye Candy 3.1 ➪ Perspective Shadow.

The Perspective Shadow dialog box appears.

2. Select any of these preset effects and/or adjust the controls, if necessary, to achieve the effect you desire:

- **Vanishing Point Direction:** Controls the direction in which the shadow falls behind your selection. The shadow always falls behind your selection.

- **Vanishing Point Distance:** Controls how far the vanishing point on the horizon is from your selection. Lower values are closer.

- **Shadow Length:** Controls the length of the shadow without affecting the tapering much. Lower values produce a shorter shadow.

- **Blur:** Controls how blurred the edges of the shadow will be. Higher values make the shadow blurrier and create the effect of a faraway light source.

- **Opacity:** Adjusts the overall transparency of the shadow.

- **Color:** Changes the color of the shadow.

3. If you like, you can save your settings, using the Save Preset button. Click OK (the check mark) when you're done.

The effect is applied to your image, as shown in Figure 12-29.

Original object   Perspective shadowed object

Figure 12-29: Perspective Shadow puts a realistic 3D shadow at your disposal. The original is a path object. The other is an image object with the Perspective Shadow filter applied to it.

Kai's Power Tools 5

Kai's Power Tools 5 (KPT 5) stands out from the crowd with the extremity of the modifications you can make to your images. It's easy to end up with a completely unrecognizable image after applying just one Xtra. In fact, it takes some work to make sure your image stays recognizable.

Tip   The Kai in Kai's Power Tools is Kai Krause, who became a legend among graphic artists when he introduced the original Kai's Power Tools.

Some highlights of KPT 5 include the following:

✦ Complex masking and transparency options

✦ Complex three-dimensional lighting and environment options

✦ Interactive Preview windows

✦ Presets with thumbnail views

✦ Common interface elements shared by the entire set of filters (see Figure 12-30)

Filter-specific control panels

KPT preferences button

Filter preferences button

Preview window

KPT Web site link button

Credits button

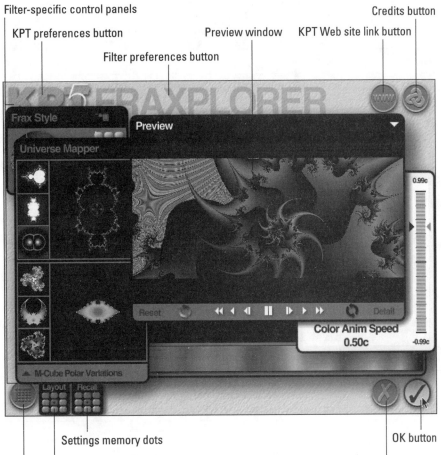

Settings memory dots

Interface layout memory dots

OK button

Cancel button

Presets button

Figure 12-30: The KPT 5 interface is a bit tricky at first, but it contains much functionality. This is FraxPlorer.

    The color insert shows what you can do with FraxPlorer.

Table 12-4 details KPT 5 filters.

    The KPT 5 package also includes Kai's Power Tools 3, with 19 completely separate and useful plug-ins, making the KPT 5 package an excellent value.

Table 12-4 Kai's Power Tools 5	
Filter	**Description**
Blurrrr	All the blur effects you could ever need, including spins, zooms, spirals, and motion blurs.
Noize	Typical and unusual noise effects, including transparent noise.
RadWarp	Creates or corrects a fish-eye lens effect. Sort of like a fun-house mirror on steroids.
Smoothie	Multiple ways to clean up dirty, jagged edges, quickly and easily.
Frax4D	Creates 3D or "4D" fractal sculptures. The "4D" ones look like really chewed-up versions of the 3D ones.
FraxFlame	Fractal effects that look like fire. Reminiscent of long-exposure photographs of fireworks.
FraxPlorer	An incredible Fractal Explorer with real-time fly-throughs, which are like fractal movies. Create amazing textures or backgrounds or just have fun playing.
FiberOptix	Adds true three-dimensional fibers onto images, including masks. You can make something hairy and then composite it easily.
Orb-It	Creates very detailed three-dimensional spheres. Make bubbles, raindrops, lenses, and distortions.
ShapeShifter	Makes three-dimensional shapes from masks, including environment maps and textures.

RadWarp

KPT RadWarp simulates a photographic effect called barrel roll. You can either add the fish-eye effect to create fantastic variations on an image or use the filter to "unfish-eye" an image with a slight, unwanted barrel roll.

Caution   All KPT 5 filters will affect your entire image object, even if you have created a selection. If you want to affect just a portion of an image object, see the workaround under "False pixel selections," earlier in this chapter.

To use RadWarp, select an image object and follow these steps:

1. Choose Xtras ➪ KPT 5 ➪ RadWarp.

   The RadWarp dialog box is displayed (see Figure 12-31).

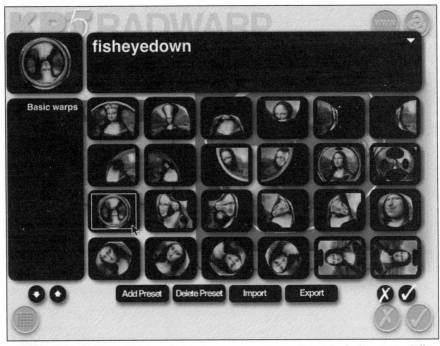

Figure 12-31: RadWarp is fun and can create extreme effects, including especially strange-looking faces.

Tip

By default, KPT 5 dialog boxes open up full screen, but you can snap the dialog boxes to a number of pixel sizes, if you prefer. Hold down Ctrl (Command) and press 1 for 640 × 480, 2 for 800 × 600, 3 for 1024 × 768, 4 for 1152 × 870, 5 for 1280 × 1024, and 0 for full screen. The panels are also set to Panel Auto Popup by default, which I found distracting. Click the name of the filter at the top of its dialog box to select the panel options. If your display has a low resolution, Panel Solo mode will save the day.

2. Adjust these controls to achieve the effect you desire:

- **Alpha slider:** Controls how much of a rounded distortion is added

- **Beta slider:** Controls how much of another type of slightly squarer distortion is added

- **X Center:** Controls where the horizontal center of the warping effect is located

- **Y Center:** Controls where the vertical center of the warping effect is located

Tip   You can also modify *X* and *Y* Center by dragging your mouse in the real-time Preview window.

Rotation rotates the image.

3. Click OK (the check mark) to apply the effect.

The effect is applied to your image.

ShapeShifter

When you're working with path objects in Fireworks, you can use Live Effects to apply amazing three-dimensional effects. If you've ever tried to get the same effect with an image object using Live Effects, you were probably quite disappointed. KPT 5's ShapeShifter filter enables you to make those image objects compete with your path objects.

To use ShapeShifter, select an image and follow these steps:

1. Choose Xtras ➪ KPT 5 ➪ ShapeShifter.

The ShapeShifter dialog box is displayed (see Figure 12-32).

Figure 12-32: Using ShapeShifter gives your image objects that three-dimensional look so that they can compete with Live Effects on path objects.

2. In the Main Shape panel, click the thumbnail preview to import a mask. The mask specifies how the three-dimensional shape is added to your image. Adjust the Bevel Scale and Height to determine how much of a three-dimensional effect you're going to create. Select from the three bevel modes.

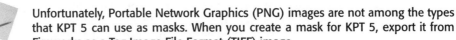

Note Unfortunately, Portable Network Graphics (PNG) images are not among the types that KPT 5 can use as masks. When you create a mask for KPT 5, export it from Fireworks as a Tag Image File Format (TIFF) image.

3. In the 3D Lighting panel, add light sources by clicking the plus (+) button. Drag light sources to different locations to affect the highlights and shadows on your image.

4. In the Bump Map panel, add a three-dimensional texture to your image and set the scale and height. Scale zooms in on the texture. Height specifies how thee-dimensional the bump map will be.

5. In the Glow panel, add a colored glow to your image, if you want to. You can choose to offset it from the image and also vary the transparency.

Tip Click the eye icon on the Glow panel to show or hide the glow, just like the eye icons in the Fireworks Layers panel.

6. In the Shadow panel, add a shadow to your image, if you want to. Just like glow, you can offset the shadow by varying degrees, choose colors, and specify transparency.

7. In the Top Mask panel, you can import another mask to create an emboss effect on top of your three-dimensional object, as if you had stamped out a shape in the top.

8. In the Environment Map panel, load an image to be used as an environment map. This image will be reflected by your three-dimensional shape as if it were the sky being reflected on a quiet lake. This adds much depth and character to your image.

Tip You can also alter the settings by dragging your mouse across the Preview window.

9. Click OK (the check mark) to apply the effect.

The effect is applied to your image.

Summary

Effects may be the icing on the cake, but then what's cake without icing? Seriously, effects play an important role in Web graphics, particularly when it comes to creating buttons with variations that can be used for rollovers. Fireworks makes the hardest effect easy by providing five standard effects and numerous preset looks. When you first begin applying effects to your graphics, consider these points:

✦ Filters and effects applied from the Effect panel remain editable. Filters applied from the Xtras menu flatten text and path objects.

✦ Fireworks applies Live Effects, which are recalculated every time a graphic is altered.

✦ All Fireworks effects are specified through the Effect panel, which changes to offer different attributes according to the effect chosen.

✦ The Inner Bevel and Outer Bevel effects are similar but result in completely different looks. The Inner Bevel effect uses the object's color to create an edge within the object itself, whereas the Outer Bevel effect uses a separate color chosen by the designer to make a border around the outside of the object.

✦ The Drop Shadow sets off any path, text, or image object with a shadow behind the figure — large or small, subtle or bold, your choice.

✦ Emboss removes the fill and stroke from any selected object and builds edges from the underlying canvas or objects to make it appear as if the object is emerging from the background or sinking into it.

✦ Fireworks Glow effect creates a soft glow around an object.

✦ Using a combination of other Fireworks tools and commands, any object can have a perspective shadow.

✦ In Fireworks, you can easily apply multiple effects.

✦ Custom effects combinations can be saved and quickly recalled, or saved as part of a Fireworks Style.

✦ You can share filters among multiple, compatible applications, to have access to them wherever you're working.

In the next chapter, you'll learn how Fireworks is used to arrange and composite different objects.

✦   ✦   ✦

Arranging and Compositing Objects

♦　♦　♦　♦

In This Chapter

Using layers

Aligning and
distributing objects

Layout assistance

Grouping objects

Mask groups
and transparency

Opacity and
blending

Simulating a
light source with
blending modes

Feathering selections

Applied compositing

♦　♦　♦　♦

Fireworks differs dramatically from other bitmap-editing
applications in that the component parts of your document are often independent vector objects and are always
editable. One of the best aspects of this creative power is
that it enables you to easily composite, layer, and blend
objects and then return to them later and undo or change
any aspect of your work. Even advanced operations, such
as alpha masking, leave the masked image — and the mask
itself — intact and editable.

> **Tip** *Compositing* is the process of combining multiple images
> into one image, usually by feathering, blending, masking,
> and altering the transparency of the images.

This chapter looks at the various ways to combine, group,
arrange, align, blend, and generally lay out multiple objects
within Fireworks.

Using Layers

Layers are a powerful Fireworks feature that enable you to
organize your document into separate divisions that you can
work with individually or hide from view when convenient.
Think of an artist drawing on separate transparencies instead
of one sheet of paper. He or she could take one transparency
out of the stack and draw only the background elements of
the drawing and then take another transparency and put
related foreground elements on that. Another could have
text elements and another a signature. Restacking the
transparencies produces a finished drawing.

Caution

The concept of layers can differ from program to program. Layers in Fireworks may not work exactly as you expect if you're used to another application. Layers in Fireworks, for example, work more like the layers in most vector-drawing programs than like the layers in Photoshop.

The Layers panel (see Figure 13-1) is the central control center for using layers. To show or hide the Layers panel, choose Window ➪ Layers or use the key shortcut Ctrl+Alt+L in Windows (Command+Option+L on a Macintosh). The Layers panel enables you to see at a glance how many layers you have in your document, which ones are locked or hidden, and even whether a selection exists on the current layer.

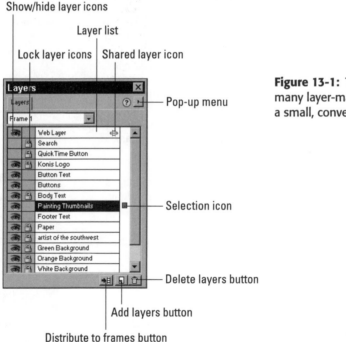

Figure 13-1: The Layers panel packs many layer-manipulation options into a small, convenient space.

Working with layers

When you create a new document in Fireworks, it initially has two layers:

✦ **Web Layer:** A special layer just for hotspots and slices

✦ **Layer 1:** A regular layer on which all of the objects you create will reside until you create another layer

Adding a layer

Each new layer that you add to your document is named "Layer," by default, and is given the next available number. You can change the names of layers, however, to help you remember what sort of objects are on each layer. For example, you might name a layer with background elements "Background," or name a layer with text elements "Text."

To add a new layer to your document, do one of the following:

✦ Click the Add Layer button on the Layers panel.

✦ Hold down Alt (Option) and click the layer list in the Layers panel.

✦ Choose New Layer from the Layers panel pop-up menu, shown in Figure 13-2.

✦ Choose Insert ➪ Layer.

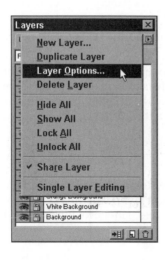

Figure 13-2: The Layers panel pop-up menu contains many commands for working with layers.

The new layer appears at the top of the layers list (but underneath the Web Layer). To change the name of a layer, double-click its name in the layer list and type a new name in the Layer Options dialog box.

You can also add a new layer by duplicating one that already exists. When you duplicate a layer, all the objects on that layer are also duplicated.

Duplicating a layer and then hiding the duplicate is a quick way to make a backup of all the objects on a layer before you perform extensive edits. If the edits don't go well, you can always delete them and show the "backup" layer, taking you back to square one.

To duplicate a layer, drag the layer to the New Layer button (blank piece of paper) in the Layers panel, or select a layer and choose Duplicate Layer from the Layers panel pop-up menu.

Deleting a layer

When you delete a layer, all the objects on that layer are also deleted. If you delete a layer accidentally, choose Edit ⇨ Undo right away to get it back.

To delete a layer, do one of the following:

✦ Drag a layer from the layer list in the Layers panel to the Delete Layer button (trash can) on the Layers panel.

✦ Select a layer from the layer list in the Layers panel and click the Delete Layer button.

✦ Select a layer from the layer list in the Layers panel and choose Delete Layer from the Layers panel pop-up menu.

Changing stacking order

Once you have more than one layer in your document, you may want to change the stacking order at some point. To change the stacking order of layers in your document, you simply have to click and drag a layer higher or lower in the layer list in the Layers panel. This moves all the objects on that layer either ahead or behind objects on other layers.

Moving objects between layers

When you want to move objects from one layer to another, you might be inclined to cut them to the Clipboard, change the current layer, and then paste the objects into the new layer. That works fine, but the Layers panel provides you with a quicker method.

Whenever you select an object or objects on the canvas, a small blue box appears in the layer list next to the layer that the selected objects are located on. Drag this box up or down to another layer, and the objects are moved there.

To move objects to another layer, follow these steps:

1. Select the objects. Fireworks displays a selection icon (blue square) next to the current layer's name in the layer list of the Layers panel.

2. Drag the selection icon to the target layer.

Layer-by-layer editing

To work on one layer at a time, you can lock or hide the layers that you don't want to affect, or you can choose Single Layer Editing from the Layers panel pop-up menu. In Fireworks, working on all the layers simultaneously is the default. You have to ask specifically to work on only one layer at a time. This is the opposite of the way that Photoshop and some other applications handle layers.

To show or hide a layer, click within the far-left column of the Layers panel, next to the layer that you want to show or hide. When the eye icon is visible, the layer is visible. When the eye icon is not showing, the layer is hidden and all the objects on that layer are invisible in the document window.

Tip   When a layer is hidden, it also is locked, and the objects on that layer cannot be selected, edited, or changed. After you hide a layer, you don't need to lock it as well.

To lock a layer, click within the second column of the Layers panel, next to the layer you want to lock. When a layer is locked, a padlock icon appears in that column, and none of the objects on that layer can be selected or edited in the document window, although they are still visible.

The Layers panel pop-up menu features commands for hiding or showing all layers simultaneously, or locking or unlocking all layers simultaneously. Alternatively, you can hold down Alt (Option) and click in the Show/hide or Layer lock column to affect all layers at once.

To enter Single Layer Editing mode, choose Single Layer Editing from the Layers panel pop-up menu. When you're in Single Layer Editing mode, you can select or edit only the objects on the current layer, although you can still see objects on other layers. As you select each layer from the layers list in the Layers panel, the other layers automatically act as if they are locked. When working with a complex document, this is an easy way to limit the scope of your edits.

Giving your layers descriptive names before using Single Layer Editing mode really speeds up your editing. If your layers are named Background, Text, and so forth, you can quickly select a layer, based on which objects you want to edit, without worrying about accidentally altering objects on other layers.

Tip   Two of the commands in the new Command Menu also enable you to quickly work on a single layer without using Single Layer Editing mode. Choose Commands ⇨ Document ⇨ Hide Other Layers to hide all but the current layer. Choose Commands ⇨ Document ⇨ Lock Other Layers to lock all but the current layer.

The Web Layer

All Fireworks documents have a Web Layer on which you can draw "Web objects," such as hotspots and slice guides. You can move the Web Layer in the stacking order by dragging it up or down the layer list in the Layers panel, but you can't delete the Web Layer. The Web Layer is always shared across all frames.

Cross-Reference   For more information about using the Web Layer, see Chapter 20 and Chapter 21. For more details about sharing layers across frames, and about frames in general, see Chapter 23.

In addition to creating hotspots in the traditional way with Fireworks, with the hotspot tool you can create hotspots out of regular objects by using the Layers panel. This is a handy way to quickly add hotspots to objects if you want the hotspots to be the same size as the objects.

To create hotspots out of objects, follow these steps:

1. Select in the document window the object or objects that you want to make into hotspots.

   Fireworks displays a selection icon (a blue box) in the far-right column of the Layers panel, next to the layer that the selected objects are located on.

2. Drag the selection icon and drop it in the same column, next to the Web Layer.

   If you have multiple objects selected, Fireworks asks whether you want to create one hotspot or multiple hotspots. Choosing to create one hotspot combines the shapes into one.

   The hotspots are created on the Web Layer, and your original objects are unaffected.

Hiding selected objects

Not only can you hide layers, but you can also hide selected objects within a layer to get them out of the way. You can even close a document and then reopen it, and the objects will remain hidden.

To hide one or more objects, select them and choose View ➪ Hide Selection. To show the objects again, choose View ➪ Show All.

Aligning and Distributing Objects

One of the most basic layout techniques is aligning and distributing objects. If you've ever used any kind of drawing or publishing application, then you're familiar with the concept. When you're not in Image Edit mode in Fireworks, every object on the canvas "floats" and can be easily aligned with another.

Using a theoretical rectangle

When you're aligning a selection, imagine a rectangle around your selection (see Figure 13-3). The rectangle is described by the objects themselves. The top of the rectangle is the topmost point on the topmost object, the left side of the rectangle is the far-left point on the farthest-left object in the selection, and so on. This theoretical rectangle is what you align objects to, and what you distribute them across.

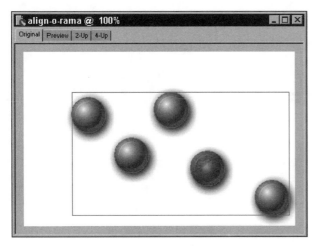

Figure 13-3: Imagine a theoretical rectangle around your selection. This is what the objects align to.

When you left-align the objects, all the objects move left until they bump into the left border of the theoretical rectangle. Similarly, if you align to the bottom, all the objects move down until they hit the bottom border of the rectangle.

Note

Alignment in Fireworks has nothing to do with aligning to a page or to the canvas, as in many other applications. In Fireworks, objects are aligned and distributed within a selection. If you try to align only one object, the alignment commands are unavailable.

To align a selection of objects to the selection's left, right, top, or bottom, select the objects that you want to align and choose the appropriate alignment command:

✦ **Left alignment:** To align all objects to the far-left point of the farthest-left object, choose either Modify ➪ Align ➪ Align Left or the keyboard shortcut Ctrl+Alt+1 (Command+Option+1).

✦ **Right alignment:** To align all objects to the far-right point of the farthest-right object, choose either Modify ➪ Align ➪ Align Right or the keyboard shortcut Ctrl+Alt+3 (Command+Option+3).

✦ **Top alignment:** To align all objects to the topmost point of the topmost object, choose either Modify ➪ Align ➪ Align Top or the keyboard shortcut Ctrl+Alt+4 (Command+Option+4) (see Figure 13-4).

✦ **Bottom alignment:** To align all objects to the bottommost point of the bottommost object, choose either Modify ➪ Align ➪ Align Bottom or the keyboard shortcut Ctrl+Alt+6 (Command+Option+6).

In addition to the traditional left, right, top, and bottom alignment, Fireworks has these two special alignment commands:

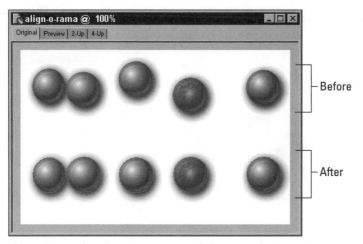

Figure 13-4: The Align Top command aligns a selection of objects to the top of the topmost object in the selection.

✦ **Vertical center alignment:** To align all objects to a theoretical vertical center line, choose either Modify ➪ Align ➪ Center Vertical or the keyboard shortcut Ctrl+Alt+2 (Command+Option+2).

Caution   Remember that the center in question is not the center of the canvas, but the center of the selection.

✦ **Horizontal center alignment:** To align all objects to a theoretical horizontal center line, choose either Modify ➪ Align ➪ Center Horizontal or the keyboard shortcut Ctrl+Alt+5 (Command+Option+5).

You can also distribute objects across the selection, which is handy when you have a few objects, such as a row of buttons, that you want to space evenly. To distribute a selection of objects across the selection, select the objects that you want to distribute and choose the appropriate distribute command:

✦ **Even horizontal distribution:** To space your objects evenly from left to right, choose either Modify ➪ Align ➪ Distribute Widths or the keyboard shortcut Ctrl+Alt+7 (Command+Option+7) (see Figure 13-5).

✦ **Even vertical distribution:** To space your objects evenly from top to bottom, choose either Modify ➪ Align ➪ Distribute Heights or the keyboard shortcut Ctrl+Alt+9 (Command+Option+9).

Aligning to the canvas

Prior to Fireworks 3, if you wanted to align a single object to the canvas, you had to create a rectangle the size of the canvas, align your single object to the rectangle, and then delete the rectangle. This gets the job done, but doing it more than once in a while is a pain in the neck, to say the least.

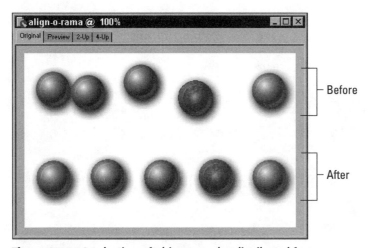

Figure 13-5: A selection of objects can be distributed from left to right with the Distribute Widths command.

New Feature

Align objects to the center of the canvas with Fireworks' new Command menu.

Fireworks 3 now includes a Command that aligns selected objects to the canvas in one easy step. Simply make a selection and choose Commands ⇨ Document ⇨ Center in Document, and your selected objects snap right to the absolute (horizontal and vertical) center of the canvas.

Layout Assistance

Fireworks provides a variety of ways to precisely lay out objects on the canvas. Rulers enable you to place guides at precise locations and snap objects to those guides as you move them around. Or, you can choose to lay a grid over your document to help you align things correctly.

Using rulers

Rulers are a standard feature of pretty much every drawing or graphics application. In fact, rulers (the kind that you hold in your hand) are a standard feature of traditional, paper-based layouts, as well. Rulers enable you to keep track of the size of your objects and their placement on the canvas with much more precision than the naked eye alone.

To toggle the visibility of the rulers, choose either View ⇨ Rulers or the keyboard shortcut Ctrl+Alt+R (Command+Option+R). The rulers appear within your document, running along the top and left borders (see Figure 13-6).

Zero-point marker

Zero-point cursor

Vertical ruler   Horizontal ruler

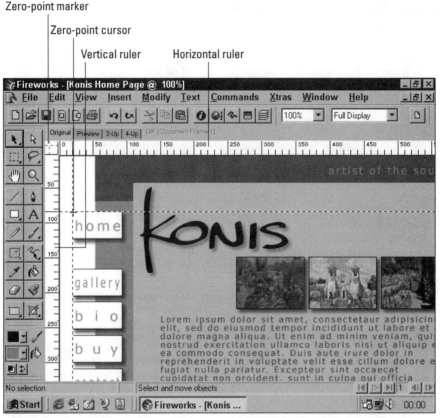

Figure 13-6: Rulers enable you to keep track of the size of your objects and their relationship to each other. Dragging the Zero-Point cursor from the Zero-Point marker to the top-left object you're aligning simplifies the math involved in aligning objects.

Tip   You can see your mouse pointer's position on the canvas in the rulers as they track your mouse. This is helpful when you want to draw a new object at a precise position on the canvas.

By default, the ruler's *zero-point*—the point where the horizontal and vertical rulers meet—is set to 0 pixels, but you can set it to another location in your document by dragging the zero-point marker to a new location and releasing it. The zero-point marker is in the upper-left corner of the document window when the rulers are visible. If all objects in your document are going to be at least 20 pixels from the top and 20 pixels from the left, moving the zero-point to 20 × 20 pixels (see Figure 13-7) simplifies the math that you have to do later as you align objects. To set the zero-point back to zero again, double-click the zero-point marker.

Working with guides

Guides are simply lines that you can position to mark important points in your documents, such as a margin or center point. Guides don't print or export, and they exist above the layers of your document. They are a design-time tool intended to make laying out objects easier. For example, if your layout calls for many objects to be placed at 20 pixels from the top, then creating a horizontal guide at that position enables you easily to see where that point is located so that you can place objects there.

Creating guides

Adding a new guide to your document is a simple, mouse-only affair. Simply clicking and dragging the horizontal ruler into your document creates a new horizontal guide that you can drop anywhere.

A horizontal guide runs parallel to the horizontal ruler, so you drag from the horizontal ruler to make a horizontal guide. Sometimes, this can be a bit confusing because you'll tend to drop a horizontal guide after checking its position on the vertical ruler. In other words, you might place a horizontal guide at 20 pixels from the top according to the vertical ruler. If you find yourself trying to create horizontal guides by dragging from the vertical ruler, think of the guides as clones of the rulers from which you drag them — horizontal for horizontal, vertical for vertical.

To add a new guide to your document, follow these steps:

1. If the rulers aren't visible, choose either View ➪ Rulers or the keyboard shortcut Ctrl+Alt+R (Command+Option+R) to show them.

2. Drag from the horizontal ruler to create a new horizontal guide. Drag from the vertical ruler to create a new vertical guide (see Figure 13-7). When you reach the position where you want to place your guide, simply drop it in place by releasing the mouse button.

Locking or hiding guides

After you create quite a few guides, you may find that they get in the way. Because they aren't on a layer, you can't just lock or hide their layer to make them invisible or not editable. Carefully placing a guide in the correct spot and then dragging it somewhere else accidentally goes a long way toward negating the primary time-saving aspect of using guides.

To show or hide guides, choose either View ➪ Guides or the keyboard shortcut Ctrl+Semicolon (Command+Semicolon). Hiding guides periodically gives you a better sense of what your final image will look like.

To lock all of your guides so that they can't be moved, choose either View ➪ Guide Options ➪ Lock Guides or the keyboard shortcut Ctrl+Alt+Semicolon (Command+Option+Semicolon).

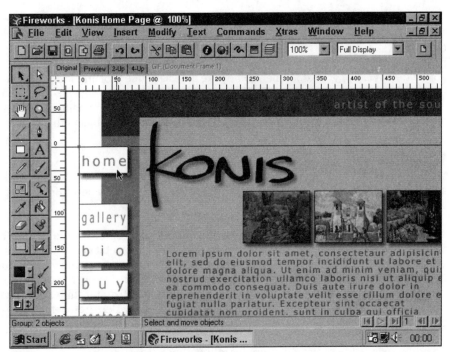

Figure 13-7: Drag from the vertical ruler to create a vertical guide. Drop it when it's in the right place.

Snapping to guides

Snapping objects to guides really uses guides to their full potential. With a little planning, you can create guides at important points in your document so that your layout comes together almost automatically as you move objects around the canvas.

To toggle whether objects snap to the nearest guide, choose either View ➪ Guide Options ➪ Snap to Guides or the keyboard shortcut Ctrl+Shift+Semicolon (Command+Shift+Semicolon).

Guide colors

If your document contains a lot of green objects, the default green color of the guides may be hard to see. Guides can be any color. Choosing a color that contrasts sharply with the color scheme of your document makes guides easier to see and also has the effect of separating them from your document so that you can see your layout through the guides without having to hide the guides all the time.

To change the color that guides are displayed in, follow these steps:

1. Choose either View ➪ Guide Options ➪ Edit Guides or the keyboard shortcut Ctrl+Alt+Shift+G (Command+Option+Shift+G).

   Fireworks displays the Guides (Grids and Guides) dialog box (see Figure 13-8).

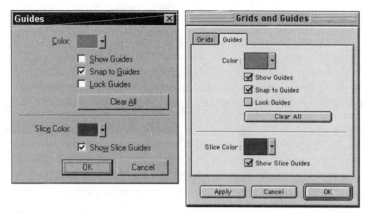

Figure 13-8: Change the color that guides are displayed in (and other options) by using the Guides (Grids and Guides) dialog box.

Note   On the Macintosh, instead of a Guides dialog and a Grids dialog, the single Grids and Guides dialog box offers a Grids tab and a Guides tab that selects between Grids and Guides views.

   2. Use the guides color picker to specify the color you'd like the guides to be displayed in and then click OK.

For convenience, all the guide options have been collected into the Guides (Grids and Guides) dialog box. You can check or uncheck Show Guides to toggle the visibility of the guides; check Snap to Guides to cause objects to snap to the guides; or check Lock Guides to lock them. Options for slice guides are also available here.

Clearing guides

Removing a single guide from your document is a drag-and-drop affair, just like adding one. Simply grab the guide with your mouse and drag it out of your document. You can drag it out to the left, right, top, or bottom, and it will disappear from you document.

You can also clear all the guides out of your document simultaneously by using the Guides (Grids and Guides) dialog box. To clear all guides, follow these steps:

   1. Choose either View ➪ Guide Options ➪ Edit Guides or the keyboard shortcut Ctrl+Alt+Shift+G (Command+Option+Shift+G).

     Fireworks displays the Guides (Grids and Guides) dialog box (refer to Figure 13-8).

   2. Click the Clear All button to remove all the guides from your document. Click OK when you're done.

Note   The Clear All button removes ruler guides, but not slice guides.

The grid

The *grid* is a quick way to achieve more precise layouts. Usually, you'll want objects to align in a fairly regular pattern. The grid makes it easy to see the relationship between the elements of your layout by splitting the document into smaller, more manageable sections. Grid lines don't export or print, and they aren't on a layer. They're simply a visual aid at design time.

To show or hide the grid, choose either View ➪ Grid or the keyboard shortcut Ctrl+Apostrophe (Command+Apostrophe).

> **Caution**
> The apostrophe, or single quote, is on the same key as the double quotes, next to the Enter (Return) key, and not the reverse-quote on the tilde key below Escape.

Snap to Grid

You can choose to have objects snap to the grid automatically, just like you did earlier with guides. When this feature is enabled, you'll notice that objects are attracted to the grid lines like magnets. Because all of your objects are snapping to the same grid, you can get more precise layouts without any extra effort.

To make objects snap to the grid, choose either View ➪ Grid Options ➪ Snap to Grid or the keyboard shortcut Ctrl+Shift+Apostrophe (Command+Shift+Apostrophe).

Grid color and frequency

Again, just like guides, you can change the color of the grid to make it stand out from your document. The default color for each new document is black.

If you're creating a navigation bar with numerous buttons that are 100 pixels wide and 50 pixels tall, set the grid so that it also is 100 pixels wide and 50 pixels tall, so that you can easily see where each button should sit. Enable Snap to Grid, and your layout will come together automatically. The default grid frequency for new documents is 36 × 36 pixels.

To modify the grid, follow these steps:

1. Choose either View ➪ Grid Options ➪ Edit Grid or the keyboard shortcut Ctrl+Alt+G (Command+Option+G).

   Fireworks displays the Edit Grid (Grids and Guides) dialog box (see Figure 13-9).

2. Use the grid color picker to specify the color in which you want the grid to be displayed.

   For convenience, you can also toggle the visibility of the grid or enable Snap to Grid while you're in the Edit Grid (Grids and Guides) dialog box.

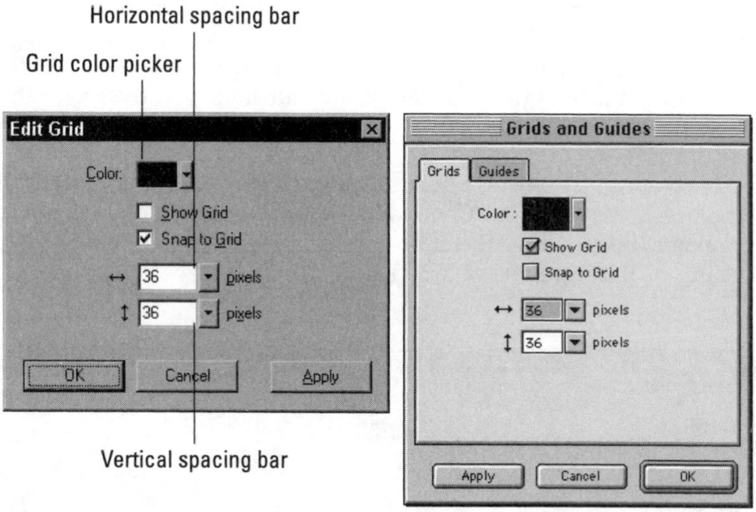

Horizontal spacing bar

Grid color picker

Vertical spacing bar

Figure 13-9: Set grid options in the Edit Grid (Grids and Guides) dialog box.

3. In the horizontal spacing box, enter the horizontal spacing that you want the grid to have. This is the space, in pixels, between vertical grid lines.

4. Enter in the vertical spacing box the vertical spacing that you want the grid to have. This is the space, in pixels, between horizontal grid lines.

5. Click Apply to see the results of your modifications without exiting the Edit Grid (Grids and Guides) dialog box. Click OK when you're done.

Grouping Objects

When you group objects, you basically create an object that consists of other objects. You can treat a group as if it's a single object, apply Live Effects, alter blending modes, and more.

Objects in a group maintain their positions and stacking order relative to each other. They retain their effects settings until you modify the whole group. If half the objects in a group have a drop shadow, and you apply a drop shadow to the whole group, then all of the objects will have a drop shadow. Fireworks is smart enough to apply that drop shadow to the whole group, as if all members were one object. You can also select and modify the component objects of a group individually, without ungrouping them.

Grouping objects is a good way to keep a complex drawing under control. For example, you might build a logo out of path and text objects and then group together the objects so that you can manipulate and lay out the logo as one object. Group together any objects that you don't need to manipulate individually so that you can manipulate them all at the same time.

To group two or more objects, select them and choose either Modify ➪ Group or the keyboard shortcut Ctrl+G (Command+G). Your grouped objects now behave as if they are one object. A Live Effect or opacity setting applied to a group affects the whole group, as if it were one object (see Figure 13-10).

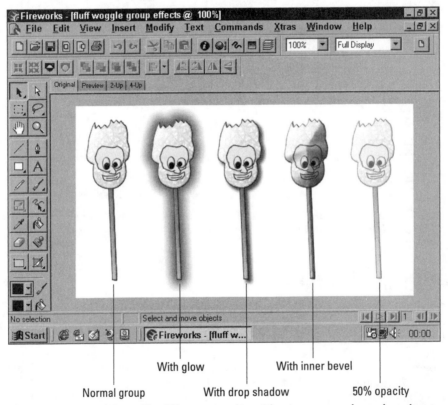

With glow

With inner bevel

Normal group

With drop shadow

50% opacity

Figure 13-10: Applying a Live Effect or opacity setting to a group shows how it acts like one object.

After you make a group, you can ungroup it at any time. To ungroup a group, select it and choose either Modify ➪ Ungroup or the keyboard shortcut Ctrl+U (Command+U).

Caution If you have applied Live Effects, opacity settings, or blending modes to a group, they are lost when you ungroup it.

Subselecting and superselecting

To modify individual objects within a group, you can either ungroup them or use the Subselection tool to subselect only the objects you want to work with. If you move a subselected object to another layer, it is removed from the group. To select all the component objects within a group, choose Edit ➪ Subselect. To select the parent group of an object, choose Edit ➪ Superselect.

Fireworks actually has three types of groups: the plain groups discussed here; mask groups, which are discussed next; and Symbols, which are covered in Chapter 24. You can use all the techniques, such as subselecting and superselecting, on any kind of group.

Mask groups

In a nutshell, *mask groups* are groups in which the luminance of the topmost object is used as an alpha mask for the entire group. The group then has the size and shape of the mask and the advanced alpha transparency of a 32-bit Portable Network Graphics (PNG) image.

An important thing to notice about mask groups is that both the mask and the object are always editable, and they can be ungrouped anytime. Also note that mask groups can be made from two or more path objects, two or more image objects, or a mixture of path and image objects. This flexibility and the ease with which mask groups can be created and edited really takes the mystery out of alpha masking and makes it a much more creative process.

If you've ever created a transparent Graphics Interchange Format (GIF) with a light-colored background and then placed that GIF in a Web page with a dark background, you've seen a graphic (no pun intended) example of the challenges of compositing transparent images. The edges of your image, where they meet the transparent color, are antialiased to either a light color or a dark color. Artifacts are visible when the image is placed over the opposite-colored background.

The 8-bit alpha mask used in Fireworks and the PNG image format solves this problem, enabling you to composite transparent objects without worrying about the color of the objects on which you're placing them, because transparency is specified for each and every pixel (see Figure 13-11).

Typically, your Fireworks images have three 8-bit channels — one for red, one for green, and one for blue — resulting in a 24-bit RGB image. When you add one more 8-bit grayscale channel to describe the levels of transparency, you get a 32-bit image (see Table 13-1).

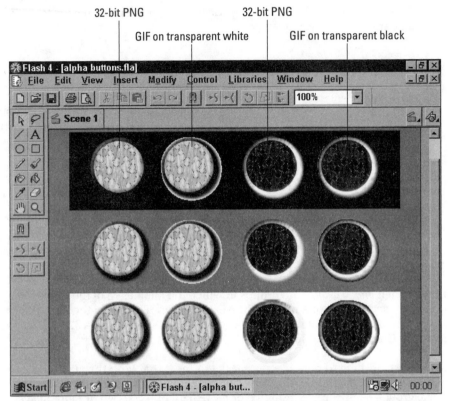

Figure 13-11: The 32-bit PNG images in the first and third columns can be placed against any background color. The second column is a GIF, with white transparent. A GIF with black transparent is in the final column. White or black rings become apparent as the GIF is moved onto a background other than the one it was created for.

Table 13-1
Channels and Bit Depth

Image	Channels	Bit Depth
Grayscale	1 grayscale	8-bit
True Color	1 red, 1 green, 1 blue	24-bit
True Color with Alpha Mask	1 red, 1 green, 1 blue, 1 grayscale (as mask)	32-bit

Each pixel of the alpha mask has a value between 0 and 255, to indicate the amount of transparency, which ranges from completely opaque (black, or 0) to completely transparent (white, or 255). The grays in between can be thought of as shades of transparency. Fireworks uses the value of each pixel of the mask to determine the transparency level for the underlying pixel of the mask group, which in turn determines how to blend that pixel with the background pixel it sits on.

If you haven't worked with 32-bit PNG images yet and are used to the limited transparency options inherent in the GIF format, the ease with which alpha transparency allows you to composite transparent objects will thrill you.

Caution   Currently, there aren't any Web browsers available that support the PNG alpha channel. Alpha transparency is still useful for working within Fireworks and exporting transparency to other applications, such as Macromedia Director and Flash. Incidentally, both Director and Flash can import your Fireworks PNG files—no need to export as a regular PNG.

To create a mask group, follow these steps:

1. Choose an object to mask, as shown in Figure 13-12.

Figure 13-12: The image of the Fireworks display doesn't blend into the striped background.

2. Create an object to act as a mask for your original object, as shown in Figure 13-13. The size of the mask will specify the size of the resulting mask group. Where the mask is white, the resulting mask group will be transparent; where the mask is black, the mask group is opaque. Shades of gray in the mask vary the transparency of the group, according to how light or dark they are.

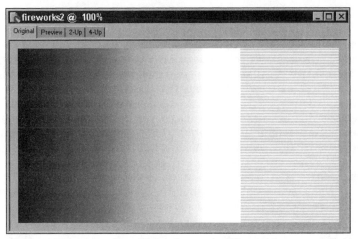

Figure 13-13: A gradient fill for the mask will provide a smooth transparent fade for the mask group.

3. Select the object and the mask and choose Modify ⇨ Mask Group ⇨ Mask to Image or the keyboard shortcut Ctrl+Shift+G (Command+Shift+G).

> **Tip**
>
> If you use an image as a mask and the transparency is the inverse of what you want, the Invert Live Effect—found in the Effect panel—can quickly invert your mask and set things straight.

Your objects are grouped, with the top object converted to grayscale and used as an alpha mask, as shown in Figure 13-14.

Figure 13-14: The mask group blends into the background because the mask's fade from black to white is translated into a transparency fade from opaque to transparent.

Masking to paths

If you've ever cropped an image and then later found that you cropped off too much, you'll appreciate being able to mask to a path in Fireworks. Instead of using the luminance of the top object and altering transparency, when you create a mask group by masking to a path, the resulting object is the size and shape of the top-most object (the mask), but it is essentially a window through which you can see the other objects in the mask group. If you want to see more of those objects, simply expand the size of the mask.

To mask to a path in Fireworks, select two or more objects and choose Modify ➪ Mask Group ➪ Mask to Path.

Tip   Double-click a mask group at any time to open the mask group Object inspector, and you'll find controls that enable you to alter whether the mask group is masking to an image or a path. You'll also find an option list that enables you to turn a mask group into a regular group — and vice versa.

Mask group image cropping

Often, when you are working with an image object in Fireworks, you'll want to crop the image to a smaller size. Although you could use the crop tool to crop out a section or make a pixel selection and copy out that area, those techniques are destructive. You alter the image object permanently. For example, if later you want to add back 100 pixels, or add 10 pixels all around the image so that you can feather the edges, you're out of luck. That information has been thrown away.

Mask groups provide a way around this, though. To crop an image nondestructively with mask groups, follow these steps:

1. To enter Object mode (if you aren't there already), either choose Modify ➪ Exit Image Edit, use the keyboard shortcut Ctrl+Shift+D (Command+Shift+D), or click the stop button in the status bar.

2. Draw a shape (not a selection, but an actual shape in Object mode) on top of the image that you're going to crop. This can be a rectangle, circle, or polygon. Anything inside the shape will be kept, and anything outside the shape will be hidden.

3. Fill the shape with black.

4. Select the shape and your image by holding down the Shift key and clicking one after the other with the mouse. Choose Modify ➪ Mask Group ➪ Mask to Image.

A mask group is created, and your image is now the same size and shape as the black shape that you drew on top of it. Click the mask group handle in the center of your mask group and drag it to move the underlying image around without affecting the mask. Once again, an object remains editable in Fireworks. Double-click the handle to select the image so that you can alter its properties. Apply an Xtra to it, if you like.

Now, select the entire mask group again by deselecting it and clicking it again, but not on its handle. You can alter the mask's fill, stroke, or Live Effects. Apply an inner bevel, change its color (which also changes the transparency of the whole group), or apply an interesting stroke to affect the edges of the group.

Mask group suggestions

Mask groups are a creative and powerful tool that you can experiment with again and again. Here are some suggestions to try:

✦ Apply Live Effects or Styles to path objects, and then use them as masks.

✦ Make a mask group that includes another mask group.

✦ Alter the Stroke settings of a mask.

✦ Use a text object as a mask.

✦ Apply texture fills to masks.

✦ Apply Xtras to masks.

Fireworks technique: quick photo edges

Fireworks Live Effects can create some nice border effects when applied to an image object in Object mode, but modifying a path object and using it as an alpha mask for an image gives you fine-control over your image's shape and transparency.

One application of alpha masks in Fireworks is to quickly give an image any one of an almost unlimited supply of interesting borders. Remember that the group will also be cropped to the size of the visible elements — although they won't actually be altered and remain editable — so this is a great way to bring together a group of differently sized objects.

To create an image border, open an image in Fireworks and follow these steps:

1. To enter Object mode (if you aren't there already), either choose Modify ➪ Exit Image Edit, use the keyboard shortcut Ctrl+Shift+D (Command+Shift+D), or click the stop button in the status bar.

2. Use the drawing tools to draw a rectangle on top of your image but make the rectangle a bit smaller than the image itself (see Figure 13-15). The area outside the rectangle will be thrown away.

3. Color the rectangle black by selecting it and choosing black from the fill color well at the bottom of the toolbox.

   The next time that you use this technique, experiment by giving your shape various gradient fills or textures. Remember, any black area will be completely visible in your final image, whereas any white area will be thrown away. The darker the areas in between these extremes, the more transparent they become.

Figure 13-15: Use a rectangle to block out the area of your photograph that you want to keep.

4. Select the rectangle and feather its edges by choosing Modify ⇨ Edge ⇨ Feather.

   The next time that you use this technique, stop at this point to experiment with applying Live Effects, Styles, Xtras, or various strokes to your shape, instead of feathering it. If you have Photoshop 5's filters installed, the Distort, Brush Strokes, Sketch, and Stylize filters are good choices. If you use Alien Skin's Eye Candy, the Jiggle feature is a great choice, too.

5. Select both the object and your image by holding down Shift and clicking each one with the mouse. If they are the only two objects in the document, you can quickly select them both by choosing either Edit ⇨ Select All or the keyboard shortcut Ctrl+A (Command+A).

6. Choose either Modify ⇨ Mask Group ⇨ Mask to Image or the keyboard shortcut Ctrl+Shift+G (Command+Shift+G) to make them into a mask group.

Your image now has a feathered edge (see Figure 13-16). Many different photo edge effects can be created with this technique simply by modifying the mask in different ways. You can use a circle instead of a rectangle or combine shapes to create complex masks.

Eye candy jiggle Xtra mask

Original image

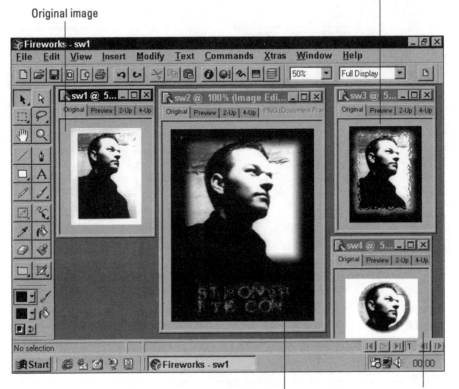

Feathered edge mask — Photoshop torn edges Xtra mask

Figure 13-16: A photo edge effect created by applying Live Effects to a path object and using it as an alpha mask for an image. The image on the left was created with this technique.

Opacity and Blending

The primary tools in compositing images are opacity and blending. Altering these properties can literally merge two images together. You can make one image show through the other by giving the first image a lower opacity setting, or you can use a blending mode to make them steal colors from each other. An image object or pixel selection that appears to float above a background can be seamlessly integrated in just a few short steps.

Tip   Feathering objects before compositing them often provides good results. With a softer edge, removing the borderline between the two images is easier. Experiment with blending Fireworks Strokes, texture fills, and effects.

After you select an object in Fireworks, you can use the Object inspector (see Figure 13-17) to control various aspects of that object's properties. Opacity and blending modes are front and center for all objects, and are the only options for images.

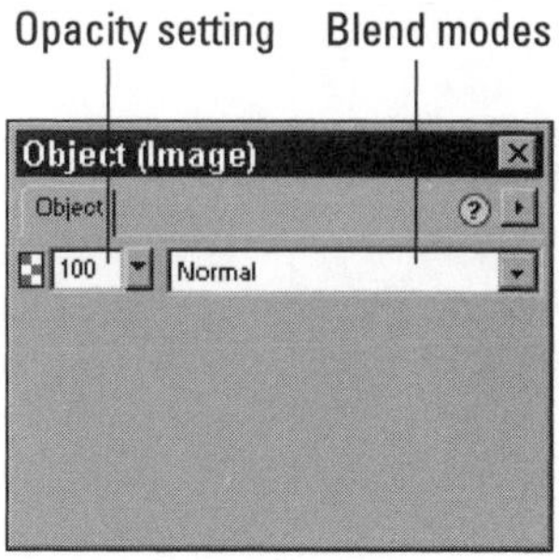

Opacity setting   Blend modes

Figure 13-17: The Object inspector contains the opacity and blending settings for a selected object.

Controlling opacity

As you make an object more transparent, more of the background shows through. This can go a long way toward integrating two images.

Controlling opacity in Fireworks is easy. Select an object, open the Object inspector by choosing either Window ➪ Object or the keyboard shortcut Ctrl+I (Command+I), and then slide the opacity slider. A setting of 100 equals no transparency, completely opaque. A setting of 1, with the slider all the way down, brings an object as close to invisible as possible in Fireworks (see Figure 13-18). If you do want to make an image completely invisible, you can type a zero in the opacity box and press Enter (Return).

Caution

If you specify an opacity setting without an object selected, you will set a default opacity for objects that you create from that point on. If you accidentally set it to 10 percent or less, you might not even be able to see some of the objects that you draw. If this happens, you'll know where to go to change it back. Deselect all objects with Edit ➪ Deselect and move the opacity slider in the Object inspector back to 100.

Using blending modes

Blending modes manipulate the color of pixels in a foreground image and the color of pixels beneath them in the background image in a variety of ways to blend the two together. Before you start using blending modes, here's the terminology that you need to know:

✦ **Blend color:** The color of the selected object, typically a foreground object

✦ **Base color:** The color beneath the selected object, typically a background object

✦ **Result color:** The color resulting from the blend of the blend color and base color

100% opacity   75% opacity   50% opacity   25% opacity   10% opacity

Figure 13-18: Vary the opacity level of your object by using the Object inspector. The fellow on the left is 100 percent opaque. On the extreme right, he's 10 percent opaque.

For the sake of simplicity, this discussion primarily uses foreground, background, and result.

As you've seen already, Fireworks enables you to alter the opacity of an object at any time with the opacity menu in the Object inspector. The opacity of an object also effects the way it blends.

A blending mode applies to an object or to an entire group. If you give an object a certain blending mode and then group it, the blending mode disappears because the object is given the group's blending mode instead (although ungrouping will restore the individual object's blending mode). If you're working extensively with blending modes, instead of grouping your objects, you might want to use layers to separate and organize your objects. This also enables you to stack blending modes for interesting effects, as objects on each layer blend into objects on the layer below.

Depending on what kind of object you have selected, the blending modes work in one of the following ways:

✦ **Object mode:** The blending mode affects the selected object.

✦ **Image Edit mode:** If you have a marquee selection drawn, the blending mode affects the selection of pixels. If you don't have a marquee selection drawn, the blending mode affects the strokes and fills that you draw from then on. You draw with blending modes.

Select an object and modify its blending mode setting in the Object inspector. If no object is selected, modifying the blending mode creates a new default blending mode for objects that you create from that point on.

Investigating the modes

Blending modes can be confusing and strangely mathematical. The best way to start understanding them is to compare their results, which is what Figure 13-19 does.

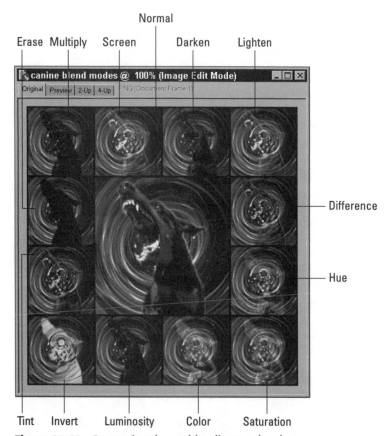

Figure 13-19: Comparing the 12 blending modes that Fireworks offers, with the unaltered image in the center.

Cross-Reference   The dogs in Figure 13-19 can be seen in full color in the color insert.

Twelve mysterious blending modes can seem like much at first, but most modes have an opposite partner or other related modes. After you understand one mode of a group, you're well on your way to understanding them all.

References to the foreground or background color refer to the color at the pixel level, not at the object level. Individual pixels of the foreground and background objects are compared.

Multiply and Screen

Multiply mode multiplies the foreground color with the background color. It can give your blended image a deeper, richer tone. The result color is always darker. If the foreground or background color is black, the result will be black; if one of them is white, Multiply has no effect.

Screen mode is basically the opposite of Multiply. The result color is a ghostly, faded blend. It works by inverting the foreground color and then multiplying it with the background color. Whereas Multiply always results in a darker color, Screen always results in a lighter one. If either the foreground or background is white, the result color will be white. If either is black, Screen has no effect.

Darken, Lighten, and Difference

Darken compares the foreground and background colors and keeps the darkest one, whereas *Lighten* does the opposite; the foreground and background color is compared and only the lightest is kept.

Difference compares the foreground color and the background color, and it subtracts the darker color from the lighter color. It can result in some surprising color choices.

Hue, Saturation, Color, and Luminosity

Hue combines the hue value of the foreground color with the luminance and saturation of the background color. Essentially, you get the foreground color, but as dark or light as the background.

Saturation combines the saturation of the foreground color with the luminance and hue of the background color.

Color combines the hue and saturation of the foreground color with the luminance of the background color. Grays are preserved, so this is a good way to add color to a black-and-white photograph or to tint color photographs.

Luminosity combines the luminance of the foreground color with the hue and saturation of the background color.

Invert and Tint

Invert and Tint don't bother with the foreground color at all. With *Invert*, the foreground object's colors are replaced with inverted background colors. With *Tint*, gray is added to the background color to create the result.

Erase

Removes all background color pixels, leaving the canvas color.

Fireworks technique: simulating a light source with blending modes

One key to creating a good three-dimensional look is providing a simulated light source. Blending an object that uses a black-and-white gradient fill into another object mimics the interplay of light and shadows. In other words, the image has a controllable light to dark range added. This enables you to adjust the "lighting" so that it looks appropriate with your particular graphic.

To use blending modes to simulate light and shadow and create objects like those shown in Figure 13-20, follow these steps:

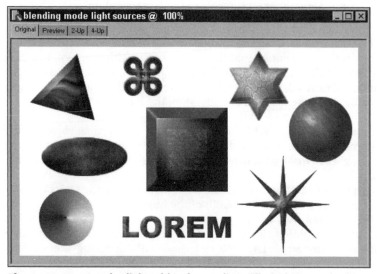

Figure 13-20: Get the lights: blend a gradient filled object and adjust the gradient to simulate a light source.

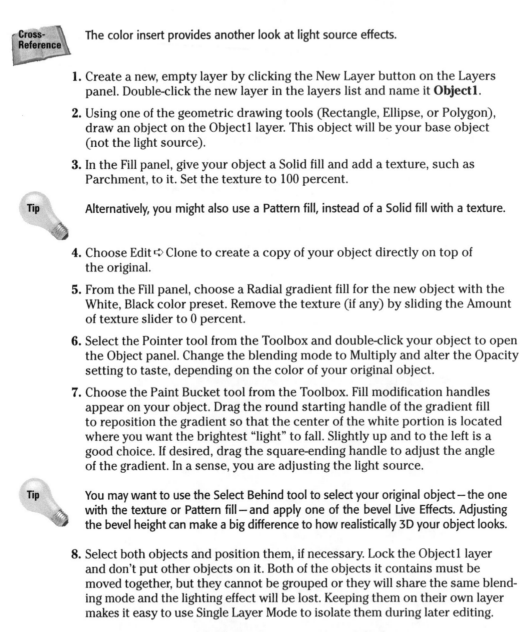

The color insert provides another look at light source effects.

1. Create a new, empty layer by clicking the New Layer button on the Layers panel. Double-click the new layer in the layers list and name it **Object1**.

2. Using one of the geometric drawing tools (Rectangle, Ellipse, or Polygon), draw an object on the Object1 layer. This object will be your base object (not the light source).

3. In the Fill panel, give your object a Solid fill and add a texture, such as Parchment, to it. Set the texture to 100 percent.

Tip Alternatively, you might also use a Pattern fill, instead of a Solid fill with a texture.

4. Choose Edit ➪ Clone to create a copy of your object directly on top of the original.

5. From the Fill panel, choose a Radial gradient fill for the new object with the White, Black color preset. Remove the texture (if any) by sliding the Amount of texture slider to 0 percent.

6. Select the Pointer tool from the Toolbox and double-click your object to open the Object panel. Change the blending mode to Multiply and alter the Opacity setting to taste, depending on the color of your original object.

7. Choose the Paint Bucket tool from the Toolbox. Fill modification handles appear on your object. Drag the round starting handle of the gradient fill to reposition the gradient so that the center of the white portion is located where you want the brightest "light" to fall. Slightly up and to the left is a good choice. If desired, drag the square-ending handle to adjust the angle of the gradient. In a sense, you are adjusting the light source.

Tip You may want to use the Select Behind tool to select your original object—the one with the texture or Pattern fill—and apply one of the bevel Live Effects. Adjusting the bevel height can make a big difference to how realistically 3D your object looks.

8. Select both objects and position them, if necessary. Lock the Object1 layer and don't put other objects on it. Both of the objects it contains must be moved together, but they cannot be grouped or they will share the same blending mode and the lighting effect will be lost. Keeping them on their own layer makes it easy to use Single Layer Mode to isolate them during later editing.

I used the Radial gradient in the previous example, but you can get some really great effects (such as a starburst of light) by applying different gradient types. Moreover, you can adjust the subtlety of the lighting by editing the gradient and toning down the pure white to a more muted gray. Feel free to experiment with different blending modes, as well.

Cross-Reference For more about gradients, see Chapter 11.

Fireworks Technique: Feathering Selections

A common image-editing task is to remove a subject from one image and place that subject in another document against another background. Feathering your selection can make this process much more forgiving, hiding ragged edges and stray background pixels that come along for the ride.

To copy a foreground image from one document and place it into another, follow these steps:

1. Open your source and target documents in Fireworks. The source document should have a foreground element. The target document should contain a suitable background.

2. In the source document, use the Lasso or Polygon Lasso tools to make a pixel selection (see Figure 13-21). Select your foreground element as accurately as possible.

Figure 13-21: Copying a feathered pixel selection into another document.

3. Choose Edit ➪ Feather, enter **10** in the Feather Selection dialog box and then click OK. This feathers your selection, which will hide any rough edges.

4. Choose either Edit ➪ Copy or the keyboard shortcut Ctrl+C (Command+C) to copy the pixel selection to the Clipboard.

5. Switch to your target document. To enter Object mode (if you aren't there already) choose Modify ➪ Exit Image Edit, use the keyboard shortcut Ctrl+Shift+D (Command+Shift+D), or click the stop button in the status bar (on the bottom border of the document window on the Mac).

6. Choose either Edit ➪ Paste or the keyboard shortcut Ctrl+V (Command+V) to paste the pixel selection from the Clipboard into your document as a new image object.

7. Move the subject around until it's placed where you want it to be located.

Fireworks Technique: Applied Compositing

Presenting separate elements as an integrated image often means applying a few different compositing techniques. In the following example, we'll use mask groups, opacity, blending modes, and layering along with texture fills and drop shadows to unify seven or eight separate objects into one final, composited image.

If you want to take a look at the final result of the techniques in this section before you start, turn to the color insert.

Starting from the bottom of the stacking order, the first step is a canvas color; in this case, it's black, as shown in Figure 13-22. Only a small portion of the canvas will show along the bottom of the final image. The background object has a mesh texture fill, which will show through other elements later and provide a feeling of depth. It also has a red drop shadow effect that softens the transition between it and the canvas. Avoiding straight lines and obvious borders — or hiding them — helps to make separate objects appear to be one.

The next layer up contains a red and black pattern. In order to blend it with the background object, I want to use an alpha mask to make the red and black pattern fade from opaque at the top to fully transparent at the bottom. This can be achieved by combining it into a mask group, with the mask shown in Figure 13-23. Where the mask is black, the underlying object will be opaque; where it's white, the object will be completely transparent. Shades of gray provide varying degrees of transparency.

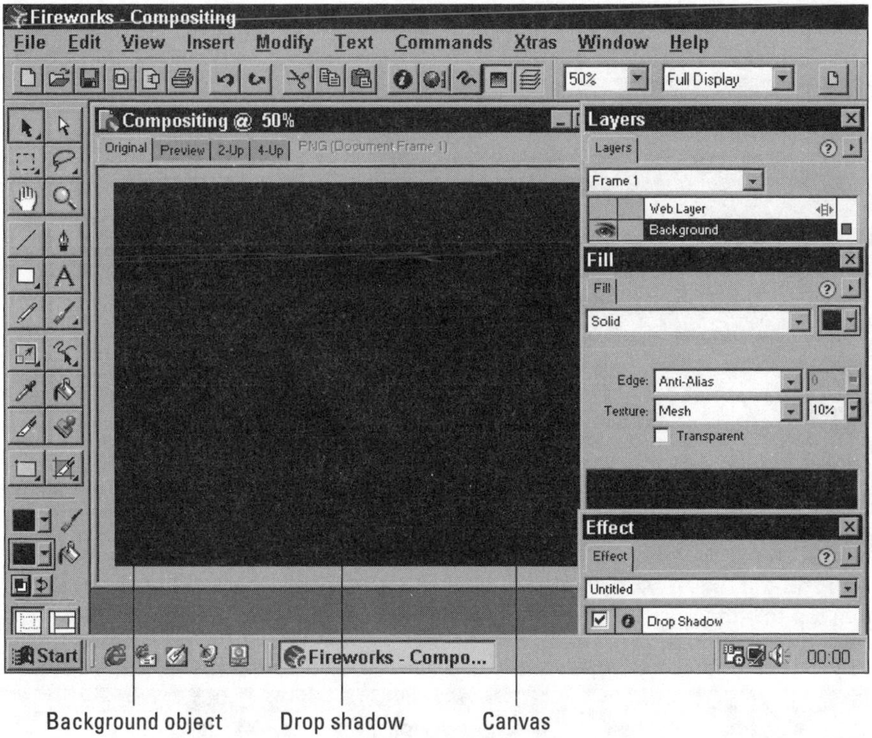

Background object   Drop shadow   Canvas

Figure 13-22: The background object's texture will show through objects above it, while its drop shadow blends it into the canvas.

Combining the mask and object into the mask group shown in Figure 13-24 is as simple as selecting them both and choosing Modify ➪ Mask Group ➪ Mask to Image. The background object is now showing through the mask group. All of the objects appear to be part of the same presentation, rather than distinct objects.

The three separate variations on the Fireworks logo in Figure 13-25 are on separate layers. The Big Crinkley Logo has holes in it where the background shows through, and its bevel effect raises it off the canvas and provides a feeling of depth. The Real Logo — quickly purloined from the Fireworks Web site or somewhere similar — looks a little ragged, but will be mostly covered by the Hand-Drawn Logo so that only its colors show through. The drop shadow and inner bevel applied to the Hand-Drawn Logo adds more depth and provides a nice transition between it and the Real Logo beneath it.

Object   Mask

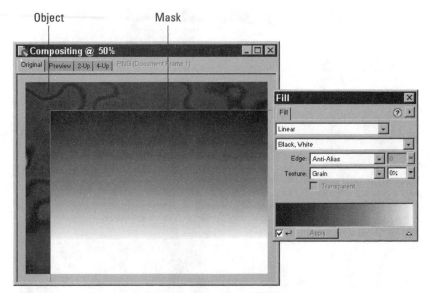

Figure 13-23: This mask will make the red and black pattern appear to fade away from top to bottom by defining its alpha transparency as part of a mask group.

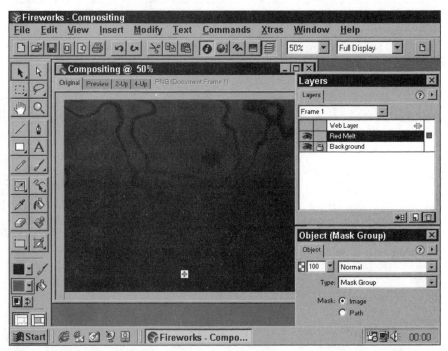

Figure 13-24: The variable transparency of the mask group allows the textured background object to show through.

Big Crinkley Logo   Hand-Drawn Logo with effects

Stacked objects

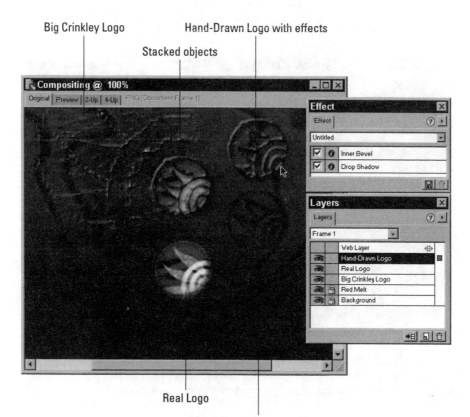

Real Logo

Hand-Drawn Logo no effects

Figure 13-25: These foreground elements stack nicely because of their transparent holes and their drop shadow and bevel effects.

The leathery look of the bottom half of the document seems like a good place to put some text. In Figure 13-26, you can see that my chosen typeface — Heavy Rotation — is structured to look as if it's been pressed into something. A 50 percent opacity setting for the text object allows some of the underlying texture to show through and adds to the inset look of the text. Changing the text object's blending mode to Screen completes the illusion; inverting the foreground color and multiplying it with the background color to blend them.

The final product — completed using mask groups, opacity settings, blending modes, and layers along with texture fills and effects, such as drop shadows — is shown in Figure 13-27.

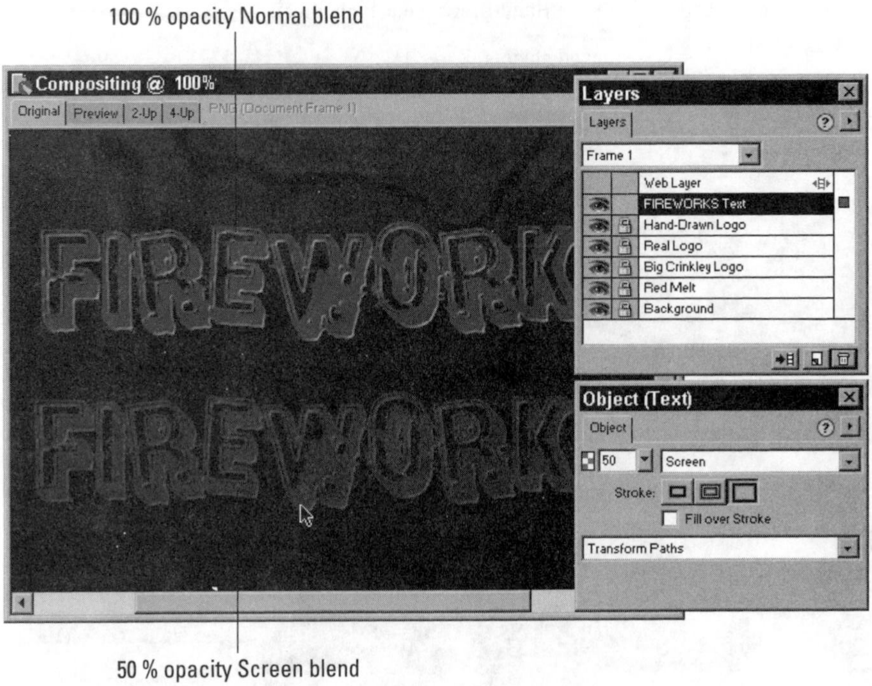

100 % opacity Normal blend

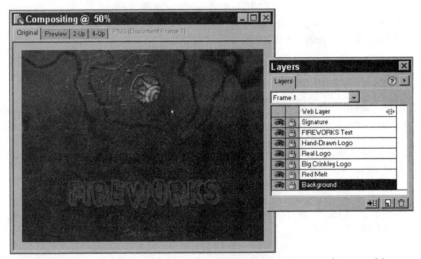

50 % opacity Screen blend

Figure 13-26: The opacity setting and blending modes in the Object panel help to sink this text object into the underlying texture of the background.

Figure 13-27: A number of compositing techniques were used to combine multiple objects into this integrated image.

Summary

Fireworks gives you lots of options for combining many types of objects to create more complex objects or special effects. When you're arranging or compositing objects in Fireworks, keep these points in mind:

✦ Layers can be used to organize objects in your document into separate groups, for easier selection and editing.

✦ The Layers panel is your control center for working with layers.

✦ You can choose to work with individual layers in a variety of ways, including hiding, showing, and locking layers.

✦ The ruler, grid, and guides are all available to help you precisely position objects on the canvas.

✦ Objects can be grouped, and a group behaves as if its one object.

✦ Mask groups give you amazing control over alpha transparency.

✦ Blending modes enable you to blend objects quickly and easily.

✦ Many compositing techniques can be utilized together to integrate many Fireworks objects into a seamless image.

The next chapter looks at capturing and importing images into Fireworks.

✦   ✦   ✦

Coordinating Workflow

P A R T

IV

◆ ◆ ◆ ◆

In This Part

Chapter 14
Capturing and
Importing

Chapter 15
Exporting and
Optimizing

Chapter 16
Working with
Fireworks Styles

Chapter 17
Using Symbols and
Libraries

Chapter 18
Updating and
Maintaining Web
Graphics

Chapter 19
Enhancing Workflow
with Commands and
the History Panel

◆ ◆ ◆ ◆

Capturing and Importing

In This Chapter

Scanning

Working with digital cameras and camcorders

Incorporating objects from other applications

Importing bitmap and Photoshop files

Importing vector art

Working with clip art

Screen captures

Opening animations

How easily you can move information from one application to another has a great effect on your workflow and productivity. In addition to creating objects from scratch in Fireworks, you can also quickly and easily include elements created in a traditional drawing program, such as Macromedia FreeHand, stock photos from a clip-art collection, or photographic prints directly from a page scanner or digital camera.

From a design perspective, incorporating elements from a wide variety of sources can give your documents depth and contrast, and make them more interesting and pleasing to the eye. Simple vector shapes can be combined and contrasted with detailed photographs and organic bitmap textures. After these elements are incorporated into Fireworks, they're fair game for Fireworks' unique drawing tools and comprehensive export features.

This chapter begins with a discussion of the issues involved in accessing image capture hardware, such as a scanner or digital camera within Fireworks. You'll look briefly at screen captures and explore how you can drag and drop, or copy and paste from other applications. You'll look at importing bitmap and vector art files. Finally, you'll examine some of the issues involved in importing animations.

Image Capture Introductions

Acquiring an image from a hardware device, such as a page scanner or digital camera, is an almost magical process — unless your hardware and software aren't talking to each other. In Fireworks, getting this conversation started involves an industry standard called *TWAIN*. TWAIN is a fully cross-platform method that enables scanners, digital cameras, and other devices to acquire images. On a Macintosh, Fireworks also supports Photoshop Acquire plug-ins. If your scanner or digital camera uses a Photoshop Acquire plug-in, see "Installing Photoshop Acquire Plug-ins," later in this chapter.

Note   What does TWAIN stand for? It's rumored to be an acronym for "Technology Without An Interesting Name." It might also have started as a play on bringing software and hardware together, as in "ne'er the twain shall meet." For its part, the TWAIN Working Group that created the standard claims that it's just a name and has no meaning at all. For more information about TWAIN, visit the TWAIN Working Group on the Web at www.twain.org.

TWAIN-compliant devices

When you start Fireworks, if a TWAIN module or Photoshop Acquire Plug-in (Mac only) is available, a Scan command will be added to the File menu, as shown in Figure 14-1. If you have multiple TWAIN-compliant devices connected to your computer, you can select any one of them from within Fireworks.

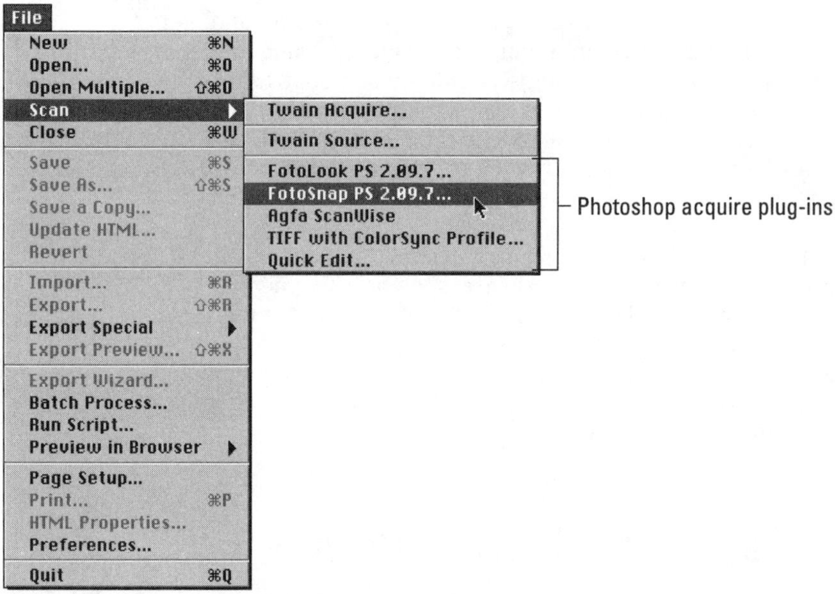

Figure 14-1: Fireworks adds a Scan submenu to the File menu if a TWAIN module or Photoshop Acquire Plug-in is available.

Note   If you have a scanner or digital camera and the Scan submenu is not available, verify that your capture hardware is correctly installed and that its software is current. If necessary, consult the device's documentation for details.

To select a TWAIN source in Fireworks, follow these steps:

1. Choose File ➪ Scan ➪ Twain Source.

Fireworks displays the Select a source dialog box (see Figure 14-2).

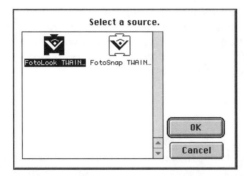

Figure 14-2: In Fireworks, select a TWAIN source from which to capture images in the Select a source dialog box.

2. Choose the TWAIN-compliant device from which you want Fireworks to acquire an image. Click OK when you're done.

Caution

If you haven't purchased a scanner or digital camera yet, but are planning to do so, visit the Fireworks Web site by choosing Help ➪ Fireworks Product Web Site and refer to the Fireworks TechNotes for a list of hardware that has been tested and found to work well with Fireworks.

Installing Photoshop Acquire Plug-ins (Macintosh only)

On a Macintosh, Photoshop Acquire Plug-ins provide another way to interface with a scanner or digital camera. Many devices — especially those that aren't TWAIN-compliant — generally come with a Photoshop Acquire Plug-in. To use one in Fireworks, you must do one of the following:

✦ Install the Photoshop Acquire Plug-in into your Fireworks 3/Settings/Xtras folder.

✦ Install the Photoshop Acquire Plug-in into your Photoshop Plug-Ins folder or another folder on your computer. Then, in Fireworks, choose File ➪ Preferences, select the Folders tab (option list), check Photoshop Plug-Ins, and then browse to and select the folder that contains the Acquire plug-in.

Caution   You can also refer Fireworks to plug-ins that are located in an external folder by placing a shortcut (alias) to that folder in Fireworks 3/Settings/Xtras.

After following either of these methods, Fireworks will add a Scan submenu to the File menu. Select your Photoshop Acquire plug-in from that menu to initiate a scan.

Caution   Some Photoshop Acquire plug-ins may not function correctly with Fireworks because they are generally marketed and tested first and foremost for use with Photoshop. If your Acquire plug-in doesn't work, check the manufacturer's Web site for an updated version that may be compatible with Fireworks or investigate whether your hardware device is TWAIN-compliant.

Page Scanning

A *page scanner* enables you to capture printed documents—from drawings to artwork to photographs. You can scan an image and use it in your Fireworks document unaltered, or you can transform it a little or a lot with Fireworks' drawing tools, effects, and Xtras, and then export it for publishing on the Web.

Note   Scanning for print publishing requires a different approach than scanning for online publishing. For the print publisher, the online image is part of the process and not an end in itself. Because Fireworks is almost exclusively a Web-publishing tool, this book looks at things from the perspective of the online publisher.

Scanning an image is the procedure of literally converting an image from a printed image to an online image (one that's viewed on a computer). Most of the confusion in scanning comes from mixing up print and online concepts, especially when it comes to resolution. *Resolution* basically means "the number of dots," which is important to scanning because print and online images fundamentally consist entirely of dots.

Resolution is measured differently for printed images than it is for online images. Printed resolution is a measure of how many dots are in an inch of the image, which is expressed as *dots per inch*, or *dpi*. An example is 300 dpi. Online resolution is a measure of how many dots are in the entire image, measured in X pixels by Y pixels. An example is 640×480 pixels. If you select an image in Fireworks and choose Modify ⇨ Image Size, Fireworks displays the Image Size dialog box (see Figure 14-3), which clearly shows the relationship between online and printed resolution. If you specify 100 dpi, a 500×400 pixel image will have a print size of 5×4 inches.

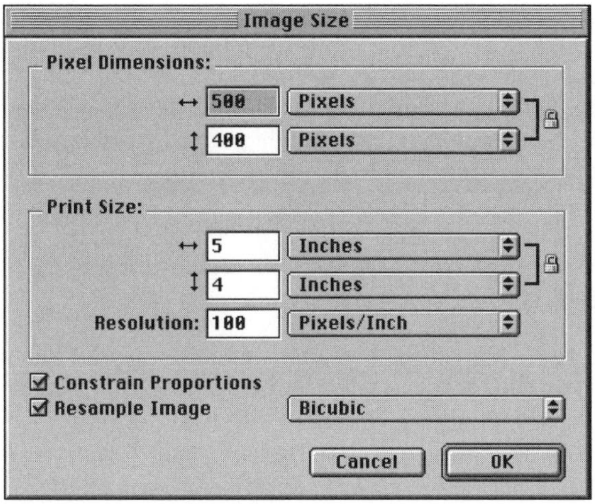

Figure 14-3: Fireworks' Image Size dialog box shows the relationship between an image's online resolution (pixel size) and print resolution.

The following list describes some of the resolutions that you'll encounter as you scan:

✦ **The resolution of the printed image, in dpi:** The upper limit of detail that the printed image contains.

✦ **The scan resolution, in dpi:** Before you scan an image, you must specify a scan resolution, which specifies how the scanner should translate the printed image, measured in inches, into an online image, measured in pixels. A scan resolution of 100 dpi tells the scanner to split each inch of the printed image into 100 parts, and make those 100 parts into 100 pixels of online image. You'll look more closely at scan resolution later in the chapter.

✦ **The scanner's maximum optical resolution, in dpi:** The upper limit of the scanner's ability to look at something it's scanning. A scanner with a maximum optical resolution of 300 dpi can split an inch of your printed image into 300 parts. Detail finer than that cannot be captured with that scanner.

✦ **The scanner's interpolated resolution, in dpi:** The upper limit of the scanner's ability to guess at details it can't see. A 300-dpi scanner that is asked to scan at a resolution of 600 dpi will guess at what the missing pixels should be. This is similar to resampling an online image to a higher resolution and generally should be avoided.

✦ **The online image's resolution, in pixels:** Because each pixel of an online image is represented by one screen-pixel location, an online image's resolution is the same as its size. A 640-x- 480-pixel image has a resolution of 640 × 480 pixels.

✦ **The display resolution, in pixels:** A computer display might have a resolution of 800 × 600 pixels or 1024 × 768 pixels. How big the display is in inches is unknown and, therefore, unimportant.

Note   A common misconception is that computer displays have a standard resolution of 72 dpi. Early Macintosh displays did have a 72-dpi resolution, and it became a standard because Macs dominated the publishing industry, and they all had the same size and type display. These days, computer displays come in a wide variety of sizes and resolutions. A 19-inch display with a resolution of 640 × 480 pixels has a drastically different number of dots per inch than a 14-inch display with a resolution of 1024 × 768 pixels.

The Scanning Process

When you initiate a scan in Fireworks, a dialog box that's specific to your scanner or Acquire plug-in is displayed so that you can specify the settings that you want for the particular scan. Some scanners offer a choice of different interfaces. One interface may be a quick and simple dialog box with few options, while another interface may contain an almost bewildering array of options for the advanced user. Some scanners also offer a supplementary wizard-based interface, such as the one shown in Figure 14-4, allowing you to specify options in plain English. For example, instead of choosing a specific descreen setting—to compensate for the patterns inherent in some types of printing—you might only have to specify that your original is from a magazine or newspaper. The software then chooses the correct setting for you.

Figure 14-4: Agfa's ScanWise is tailored for beginners and allows them to choose scanning options in plain English.

Chances are that you'll want to learn to use your scanner's advanced interface so that you can exert a greater degree of control over the settings that you use and, therefore, get the best results. The most important of these settings are the scan resolution and the color depth. We'll look at them closely, and then look briefly at some of the other options you might be presented with.

Selecting a scan resolution

In simple terms, the *scan resolution* that you choose determines the size of the resulting online image—and that's all. Table 14-1 shows the relationship between the size of the original, printed image and the size of the resulting, online image at various scan resolutions.

Table 14-1 Scan Results at Various Scan Resolutions		
Printed Image Size (inches)	*Scan Resolution (dpi)*	*Online Image Size (pixels)*
5 × 7	10 dpi	50 × 70
5 × 7	20 dpi	100 × 140
5 × 7	50 dpi	250 × 350
5 × 7	100 dpi	500 × 700
5 × 7	150 dpi	750 × 1,050
5 × 7	200 dpi	1,000 × 1,400
5 × 7	300 dpi	1,500 × 2,100

Note that each of these three important pieces of information are measured in different ways:

✦ **Printed image:** Measured in inches. In print publishing, the inch is the constant. If you create an 8.5-x-11-inch page layout and print it at different print resolutions, it will still be an 8.5-x-11-inch page layout, but it will have a different number of dots on each page.

✦ **Scan resolution:** Measured in dots per inch. This is the translation of the printed image (in inches) to the online image (in dots, or pixels). How many pixels of online image do you want for each inch of printed image? Fifty? That's a scan resolution of 50 dpi.

✦ **Online image:** Measured in pixels. In online publishing, the pixel, or dot, is the constant. If you create a 640-x-480-pixel image and view it at different screen resolutions, it will still be a 640-x-480-pixel image, but it will be a different size in inches on each screen.

Determining the ideal resolution

To determine an ideal scan resolution, follow these steps:

1. Decide how wide you want your online image to be, in pixels.

2. Divide that number by the width of the printed image, in inches.

   The result is your scan resolution in dots per inch.

Caution   If you're not sure how big you want the final image to be, overestimate rather than underestimate. Making an image smaller later in the process is not as detrimental to its quality as trying to make it larger. A scan resolution of 100 dpi is a good place to start because it makes the translation from inches to pixels easy to calculate. A 3-x-5-inch printed image will be 300 × 500 pixels after scanning. If 300 × 500 ends up being too big or too small, adjust the scan resolution from there.

Running out of printed resolution

When selecting a scan resolution, keep in mind the resolution of the printed image that you're scanning. At the point when the scan resolution is equal to either the resolution of the printed image or the maximum optical resolution of your scanner, increasing the scan resolution stops capturing more detail. For example

✦ If your printed image was printed at 200 dpi, a scan resolution of 300 dpi will not add detail that isn't already there. Scan the image at 200 dpi and resample it to a larger size in Fireworks, if necessary.

✦ If your scanner's best optical resolution is 300 dpi, you won't be able to capture more than 300 dots for each inch of the printed image. Many scanners allow you to choose a higher scan resolution than they can really achieve, and then the scanner "interpolates," or fills in, the missing information with a best guess. This is equivalent to scanning the image at your scanner's maximum optical resolution and resampling it in Fireworks, if necessary.

Choosing a color depth

Choose a *color depth* based on the type of document you are scanning. Typically, a scanner has three main color settings for you to choose from: line art, grayscale, and color. You may also be able to specify bit depth for grayscale and color scans. Higher bit depths scan a higher number of colors and are more accurate, but also result in a larger file size.

Line art

Line art refers to black-and-white images that don't contain shades of gray. This might include cartoons, blueprints, or diagrams. Line art is scanned with 1-bit color depth. In other words, each pixel is either on or off; black or white.

Grayscale images

Grayscale images contain actual shades of gray. Typically, a grayscale setting will be 8-bit, meaning that your image will have 256 different shades of gray. This is the best setting for black-and-white photographs.

Color images

The *color setting* is obviously used for scanning any sort of color image. Typically, this is 24-bit color, but some scanners have a 36-bit setting. Twenty-four-bit color means that each pixel can be any one of 16.7 million colors. A 36-bit scanner can record 68.7 billion colors. Scan at your scanner's best setting and then remove extra colors when you export your image as a Graphics Interchange Format (GIF), a Joint Photographic Experts Group (JPEG), or a Portable Network Graphics (PNG) for use on the Web.

Cross-Reference

For more about color depth, see Chapter 7.

Setting other options

Consult the documentation that came with your scanner for specific information on other options or features that your scanner has.

Here are some of the options you may encounter:

✦ **Preview window:** A window in which you can see a thumbnail of the original before you perform the actual scan. You can usually draw a border in this window to limit the scan to the portion of the scanner window. Some scanning interfaces will draw a best guess selection themselves, which you can adjust as required.

✦ **Brightness and Contrast:** Adjust these only if your original is exceptionally bright or dark, or lacking in contrast.

✦ **Image enhancements:** For example, dust, scratch, or moiré removal.

✦ **Orientation:** You may be able to specify that the scanner flip the image vertically or horizontally.

✦ **Settings** for different types of original documents, such as transparencies and slides.

✦ **Gamma correction:** Most Macs are set to a gamma correction of 1.8, while most Windows machines use 2.2.

✦ **Descreen:** A descreen setting enables you to scan newspaper or magazine clippings with better results.

Figure 14-5 illustrates these options.

Scanning bed   Scan area

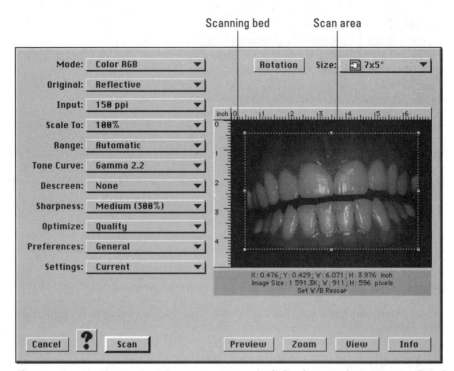

Figure 14-5: Setting options in a page scanner's dialog box. Each scanner or digital camera has its own unique interface. Note the selection limiting the scan area to a portion of the scanning bed.

Scanning directly into Fireworks

To scan directly into Fireworks, follow these steps:

1. Place the original document onto your scanner's scanning bed.

2. If you're using a TWAIN source and have multiple TWAIN-compliant devices, choose File ➪ Scan ➪ Twain Source and select the appropriate device.

3. If you're using TWAIN, choose File ➪ Scan ➪ TWAIN Acquire. If you're using a Photoshop Acquire plug-in (Macintosh only), choose File ➪ Scan and the name of that plug-in.

   Your scanner's options dialog box appears.

4. In the scanner's options dialog box, adjust the settings for the scan, specifying resolution, color depth, and other settings, as required. Consult your scanner's documentation for specific information about the options you're presented with. Click OK after you're done.

The device begins scanning and then sends the image to Fireworks. When the scan is completed, the image appears as a new document in Fireworks.

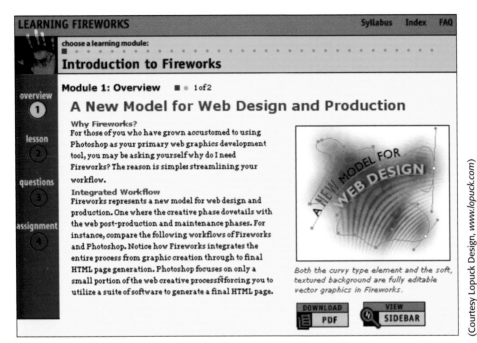

(Courtesy Lopuck Design, www.lopuck.com)

Fireworks is capable of graphics ranging from a simple, clear navigation system to a wonderfully layered and sophisticated graphic, shown here in a site design by Lisa Lopuck.

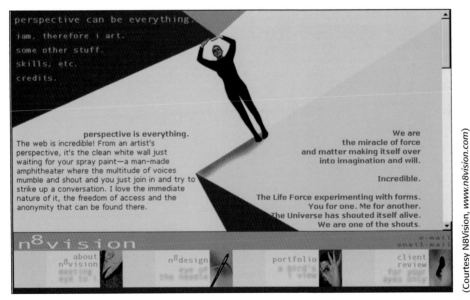

(Courtesy N8Vision, www.n8vision.com)

Fireworks handles object-oriented shapes, photo-realistic graphics, and straightforward text with equal ease, as illustrated in this Web page by Donna Casey. Each navigation element swaps a monochromatic image with a full-color image when a cursor passes over it, while the blurred text becomes crystal clear.

The power to integrate many different types of images and objects is yours with Fireworks. In this example, the flower — a 32-bit PNG with alpha transparency — overlays a feather-edged image. The shooting star was created with Fireworks tools and then multiplied using Symbols and Instances. The type was grouped with a gradient to form a mask group.

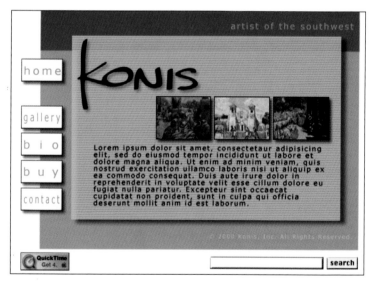

You can work on individual images in Fireworks, just as you might in a traditional image editor, such as Photoshop, but you can also design complete Web sites within one Fireworks document, as shown here. Building in one document means you can export everything with one command and easily share elements and effects.

In 32-bit color, an image contains four channels: 8 bits of red, 8 bits of green, and 8 bits of blue that together cover the range of colors the eye can see, as well as an 8-bit grayscale alpha channel that describes a transparency mask. Here, an image with a feathered edge is placed on a white background. The alpha mask ensures the feathered edges have a variable transparency, with more of the white background showing through at the extreme edges of the image. This image could also be placed against a black background, or any color, and the transparency of the feathered edges would still be apparent.

The image from the preceding color plate loses its alpha channel – and thus its transparency – when shown in 24-bit color.

The image from the preceding color plate suffers when it's reduced to 8-bit color, which doesn't allow for the fine gradations necessary to accurately represent a photographic image. The obvious lines in the color changes in the sky are called *banding*.

Reducing the number of colors further – in this case, to only four – can sometimes produce an attractive effect, but it obviously doesn't describe the original landscape as accurately.

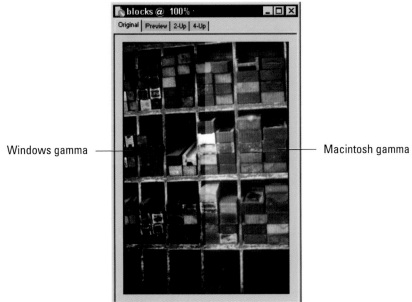

Windows gamma —————

————— Macintosh gamma

This image was created in Windows and looks good at Windows' standard gamma correction setting of 2.2.

Macintosh gamma —————

————— Windows gamma

Choosing View ⇨ Macintosh Gamma in Windows provides a look at what this image would look like on a Mac, with the standard Mac gamma correction setting of 1.8.

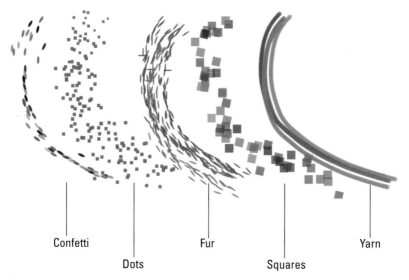

Confetti

Dots

Fur

Squares

Yarn

The Random Strokes category takes advantage of Fireworks' stroke capability by randomizing size, opacity, hue, and other characteristics.

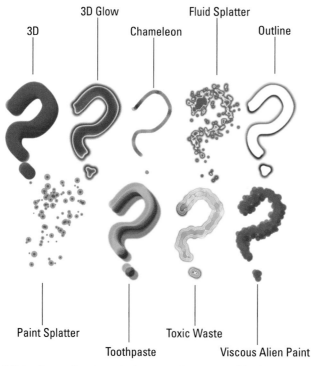

3D

3D Glow

Chameleon

Fluid Splatter

Outline

Paint Splatter

Toothpaste

Toxic Waste

Viscous Alien Paint

Wild color and style variations are the norm with the distinctive Unnatural category of Fireworks Strokes.

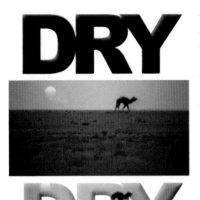

This desert vignette was manipulated to place the camel on the horizon and then combined into a mask group with a text object. The text object is on top, so it becomes the mask. Black areas in the mask make the underlying image opaque. White, or empty areas, make the underlying image transparent. Shades of gray apply a varying amount of transparency. Note the bevel effect on the text, which remains for the mask group.

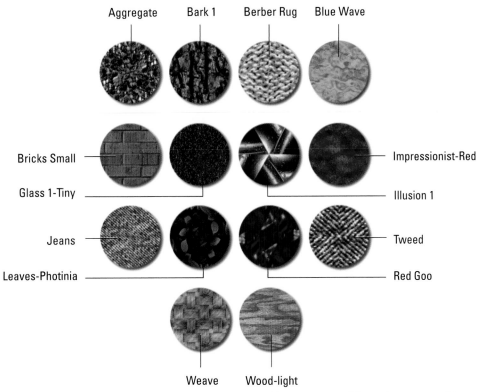

Aggregate Bark 1 Berber Rug Blue Wave

Bricks Small

Glass 1-Tiny

Impressionist-Red

Illusion 1

Jeans

Leaves-Photinia

Tweed

Red Goo

Weave Wood-light

These standard Fireworks Patterns are always available for Pattern fills, and you can add your own, too.

QUICKTIME MAKES THIS MOVE

QuickTime
Get 4.

It may be hard to believe, but the only image object here is the QuickTime button. Fireworks Live Effects add incredible depth to path objects without compromising edibility. The red in the background is actually five or six squiggly lines drawn with the Brush tool and then treated with the Outer Bevel Live Effect and the following three Photoshop plug-ins (used as Live Effects, though): Dry Brush, Texturizer, and Plastic Wrap. The distressed border is thanks to Outer Bevel, Cutout, and the Photoshop plug-ins Spatter and Photocopy.

The sunset in this unaltered image looks fine, but the farmhouse near the bottom is too dark. Applying the Auto Levels filter to the farmhouse and the nearby details will bring them out by removing some shadow.

Here, the Lasso tool is used to select just the pixels that need to be adjusted. A feather of two pixels is applied to the selection with Edit ⇨ Feather. The feathered selection helps to hide the border between altered and unaltered pixels.

Once the Auto Levels filter is applied to the pixel selection by choosing Xtras ⇨ Adjust Color ⇨ Auto Levels, the area that was selected has its own complete tonal range and is not so shadow heavy.

Adjusting the Midtone Input Level Slider in the Levels dialog box enables you to brighten the whole image. Compare this color plate to the unaltered image.

This image is flat looking because the shadows and highlights are too close together in value.

The Curves filter enables you to make fine adjustments to an image's tonal range until the image has dark shadows and bright highlights. Good results can often be achieved by just moving a single point on the Curves filter's graph.

This unaltered image contains little color variation. If you use it in a page design that includes a very different range of colors, the Hue/Saturation filter can be used to modify the overall color of the image to match the design, as shown in the following color plates.

The overall color of an image can be altered with the Hue slider in the Hue/Saturation dialog box. Here, the overall green caste of the image in the preceding color plate is changed to purple.

Increasing the Saturation value increases the amount of color in the image.

Moving too far from the original settings with the Hue/Saturation filter can result in a posterization effect, where areas of color become flat, edges stand out, and the overall tonal range is adversely affected.

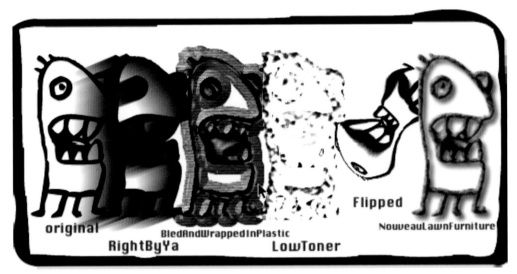

Using Photoshop filters as always editable Live Effects provides a wonderful degree of creative freedom. And once you find that perfect effect, it's easy to save it under your made-up name (like the ones in this image) and apply it to all kinds of objects. These are path objects.

Kai's Power Tools is an example of a third-party, Photoshop-compatible filter set that doesn't limit you to making slight changes to your images. FraxPlorer enables you to turn pretty much any image into a remarkable fractal study.

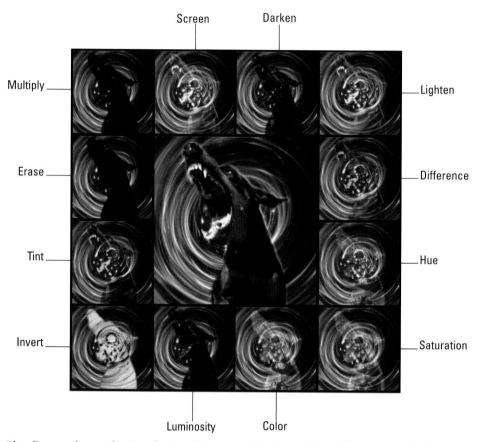

Screen   Darken

Multiply —   — Lighten

Erase —   — Difference

Tint —   — Hue

Invert —   — Saturation

Luminosity   Color

Blending modes are best understood by comparing the various effects. Here, the dog is blended against the whirlpool pattern; the Normal blending mode is shown in the center image.

Each of these objects is actually two objects: the obvious one and a not-so-obvious, gradient-filled one that is blended on top to provide the "lighting" across the fills. This is especially obvious in the center object, where the pattern fill has a "light" shining across it. Fireworks provides some three-dimensional lighting on the edges of objects with its bevel effects; continuing the lighting effect across the fill enhances the realism of these simple, path-based objects. Of course, these are all completely editable.

Compositing multiple objects – and multiple types of objects –
is easy in Fireworks, where everything is editable all the time. The
black textured background shows through the gooey red layer
(an image object), thanks to a mask group. The Fireworks logo
is a combination of an image object and a hand-drawn path
object that hover above the other objects, thanks to a Drop
Shadow Live Effect. Blending modes and opacity settings enable
the texture to show through the (editable) text object, making
it seem to be stamped out of the underlying layers.

The buttons in this figure are
Symbols, so they only need to
be made once, stored in the
Library, and from there inserted
into documents. Each Button
Symbol has unique text and URL
properties. The watermarking in
the background is provided by
Fireworks strokes and took
about 15 seconds to create.

Compositing multiple objects – and multiple types of objects – is easy in Fireworks, where everything is editable all the time. The black textured background shows through the gooey red layer (an image object), thanks to a mask group. The Fireworks logo is a combination of an image object and a hand-drawn path object that hover above the other objects, thanks to a Drop Shadow Live Effect. Blending modes and opacity settings enable the texture to show through the (editable) text object, making it seem to be stamped out of the underlying layers.

A simple story line is easiest to convey within the limited space and time you are given with a banner ad. Confining the motion to a small r egion, using a highly compressible, flat color background, and limiting the number of colors all contributed to keeping this banner ad under 12K. This ad is built standard-size: 468 x 60 pixels.

The Eye Candy LE Motion Trail image filter included with Fireworks 3 is great for creating the effect of fast motion without adding extra frames or increasing bandwidth. Here, the flying saucer travels more than half the width of the ad in just three frames, and obviously stops.

Digital Cameras

Increasingly, images are staying completely digital. The advantages of creating images for the Web using a digital camera are obvious: no film or printing expenses, nearly instant access to the photographs, no loss of quality as photos are printed and then scanned. Whether you consider yourself a great photographer or not, graphics professionals are increasingly called upon to get behind the camera, even if only to grab a couple of quick snapshots for the company Intranet.

Some of the same considerations that apply to scanning also apply to using images from a digital camera. You use TWAIN or a Photoshop Acquire plug-in to interface with the camera, and you are presented with a dialog box full of options that help you transfer the images from the camera into Fireworks.

Cameras differ from scanners in that you don't have to worry about print resolution because no printing is involved. Resolution is specified—just like online images—in terms of width by height in pixels. Generally, you'll want to use the camera at its highest resolution in order to get the best quality image and leave yourself the most editing options in Fireworks. A larger image can be made smaller without losing quality, but the reverse is not true. For the most part, though, images on the Web tend to be smaller, rather than larger, and photos from even a basic digital camera are often 640 × 480 pixels or larger, plenty big enough for most Web applications.

Capturing images directly in Fireworks

To capture images from a digital camera directly into Fireworks, follow these steps:

1. Take some pictures.

If your camera supports it, create pictures in a lossless file format, rather than a lossy format, such as JPEG. JPEG images should—whenever possible—be considered a final product only. They will display noticeable artifacting when exported from Fireworks.

2. Connect the camera to your computer according to the camera's documentation. Cameras that connect with a universal serial bus (USB) can be hot plugged into a Windows or Macintosh machine and accessed immediately. If your camera uses a legacy interface, you will have to shut down your computer before making connections.

3. If you're using TWAIN and you have multiple TWAIN-compliant devices, choose File ⇨ Scan ⇨ Twain Source and select the appropriate device.

4. If you're using TWAIN, choose File ⇨ Scan ⇨ TWAIN Acquire to initiate the image capture. If you are using a Photoshop Acquire plug-in, choose File ⇨ Scan and the name of that plug-in, instead.

   Your camera begins transferring thumbnails of the images that it contains to its interface software, as shown in Figure 14-6.

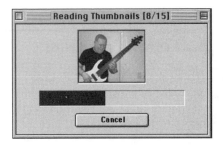

Figure 14-6: Digital cameras often transfer thumbnails of their images first.

Once the camera's interface software has all the thumbnails, it displays a dialog box where you can specify options and choose images that you can transfer into Fireworks, as shown in Figure 14-7.

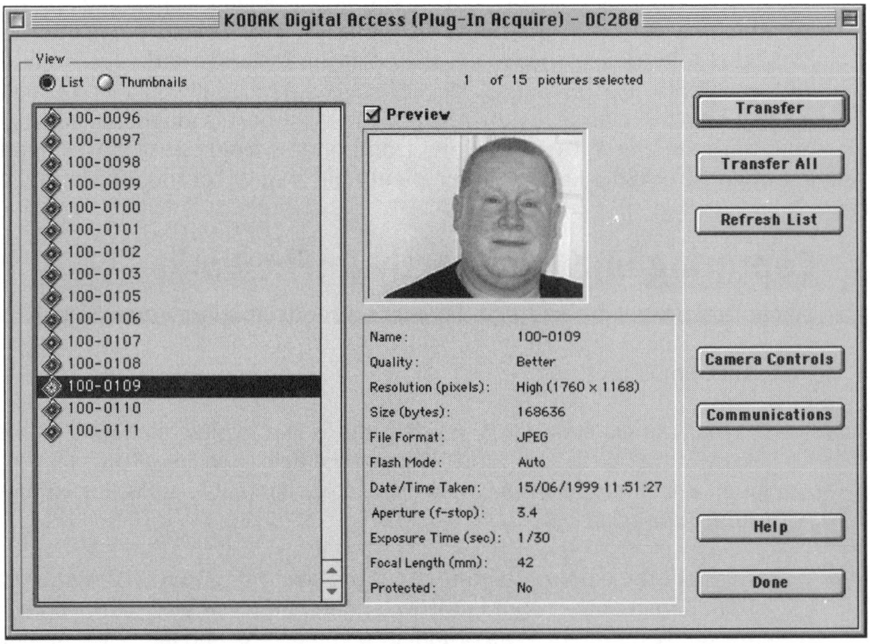

Figure 14-7: Pick and choose which images to transfer into Fireworks with the camera's dialog box.

5. In the camera's dialog box, choose which image or images you want to transfer into Fireworks. Consult your camera's documentation for specific information about the options with which you're presented. Click OK when you're done.

Digital Camcorders

Many digital camcorders offer a still photo mode, making them an alternative to regular, digital still cameras. This mode captures one frame at the camera's highest resolution and typically writes this image onto seven seconds of tape, creating a much better image than a single freeze-frame of video. An advantage to using a camcorder rather than a camera is that a camcorder can typically store 500 still images on an hour-long, digital video tape with one battery charge, while most still cameras max out well below 100 photos and eat batteries with a vengeance.

Digital camcorders can also transfer their images to a computer or another camcorder at high speeds, using an IEEE 1394 interface, often called FireWire or i.Link. FireWire interfaces are standard on all Macintosh computers except the iBook, and they are included on many Windows machines from Sony, Compaq and other manufacturers. FireWire interfaces can also be added to most computers with an add-in card. Connecting the camcorder simply involves hot plugging the camcorder and the computer together with the correct cable. Most camcorders have a 4-pin IEEE 1394 connector, while most computers offer a 6-pin connector. No special converter is required, though, just an inexpensive cable with a 4-pin connector on one end and a 6-pin connector on the other end.

Although you can't transfer images from a digital camcorder directly into Fireworks like you can with a scanner or still camera, many camcorders and FireWire interfaces include the necessary software. Typically, the output from the camera is presented in real time in an onscreen window. This preview enables you to pick and choose which images you'd like to transfer from tape to an image file on disk. In VideoShop, shown in Figure 14-8, this means clicking the little camera button while a particular image is displayed.

Figure 14-8: Auditioning still photos from a digital camcorder in VideoShop.

Once an image is stored as an image file on your hard disk—usually as a TIFF, PICT or BMP—it can easily be opened in Fireworks. Because the images are always stored digitally, there is no loss of quality as they move from tape to disk.

Caution   Make sure to use still video mode when capturing still images with a digital camcorder. Still frames of a moving video are only half of an interlaced image and will make poor quality photographs.

Inserting Objects from Other Applications

So far, we've covered how you can import a document from external hardware or a screen capture, but what if the elements that you want to include are sitting right there on your computer screen, but within another application? Fireworks has two methods for directly inserting elements from other applications: copy and paste, and drag and drop.

Copy and paste

The simplest and most widely used method for moving information from one application to another is with the system clipboard and the commands Cut, Copy, and Paste.

You can paste the following formats into Fireworks:

✦ Bitmap images

✦ Vector art from Macromedia FreeHand or Adobe Illustrator (Windows only)

Caution   For some reason, pasting vector art into Fireworks on a Macintosh converts the objects to bitmap images. Use drag and drop, detailed later in this chapter, to transfer vector art, instead.

✦ ASCII text

To copy from another application and paste into Fireworks, follow these steps:

1. In the source application, select the object(s) or pixel area that you want to copy.

2. Choose Edit ➪ Copy or the keyboard shortcut Ctrl+C in Windows (Command+C on a Macintosh).

   Your selection is copied to the clipboard.

3. In Fireworks, choose either Edit ➪ Paste or the keyboard shortcut Ctrl+V (Command+V).

4. If your source selection has a different print resolution than your Fireworks document, Fireworks displays a dialog box, shown in Figure 14-9, and offers to resample the pasted image to match the target document. Choose Resample to maintain the pasted object's original width and height, adding or subtracting pixels as necessary. Choose Don't Resample to keep all the original pixels, which may make the relative size of the pasted image larger or smaller than expected.

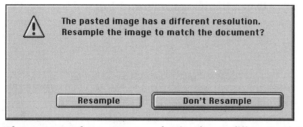

Figure 14-9: If your source selection has a different print resolution than your target document, Fireworks offers to resample the selection for you.

Your selection is inserted into the active document, centered on the canvas.

Caution

If you're pasting into Fireworks and you want to fill a new, empty canvas, copy from the source application and then create a new Fireworks document. Fireworks will offer to make the new document the same dimensions as the clipboard.

Drag and drop

You can drag and drop objects into Fireworks from any application that supports OLE (object linking and embedding) drag and drop on Windows, or Macintosh drag and drop on a Macintosh. Dropped objects are rendered as images, unless they're vector art from Macromedia FreeHand or Adobe Illustrator. Following are other applications that support drag and drop:

✦ Macromedia Flash

✦ Netscape Navigator

✦ Adobe Photoshop

✦ Microsoft Word

If you're not sure whether a specific application supports drag and drop, try it to find out. As you drag and drop, you can tell whether it's working in Windows if your mouse cursor changes when you hover above a target application. Similarly, on the

Mac, sounds provide feedback when things become "droppable." The target application on the Macintosh may also provide some visual indication.

To drag and drop an object into Fireworks from another application, follow these steps:

1. Make sure that you have a Fireworks document open to drop objects into.

2. Position the source application and Fireworks side by side so that you have a clear path to drag between them (see Figure 14-10).

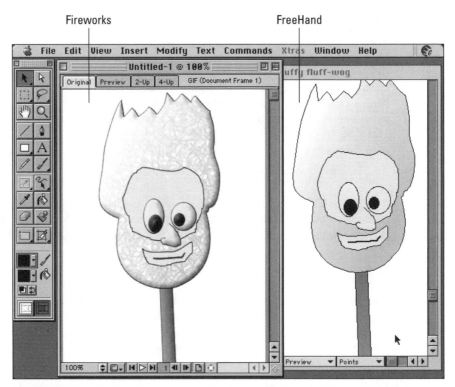

Figure 14-10: This FreeHand vector object instantly became a Fireworks vector object after being dragged and dropped, and then it quickly fell victim to the Inner Bevel Live Effect and a Fiber texture fill.

3. In the source application, select the object(s) that you want to drag and drop into Fireworks.

4. Click the selected object(s) and hold down the mouse button in order to "pick up" the objects.

5. While keeping the mouse button down, position the mouse cursor over the target Fireworks document.

6. Release the mouse button to drop the object(s) into Fireworks.

The object(s) appear centered on your Fireworks canvas and are now part of your Fireworks document.

You can also drag and drop between two open Fireworks documents.

Importing External Files

Sharing objects between applications on your computer is fine, but sometimes you'll want to import whole files into Fireworks. This is as easy as opening Fireworks' own PNG files. The process is slightly different depending upon whether you're importing bitmap image files or vector art.

As well as using File ⇨Import, you can quickly import entire files into Fireworks by dragging them from Explorer on Windows or the Finder on Macintosh and then dropping them into a Fireworks document window.

Bitmap image files

Imported bitmap image files appear as image objects in Fireworks. Table 14-2 details the bitmap image file formats that Fireworks understands.

<table>
<tr><td colspan="4" align="center">Table 14-2
Bitmap Image Files Fireworks Can Import</td></tr>
<tr><td>**Format**</td><td>**Filename Extension**</td><td>**Macintosh Type Code**</td><td>**Notes**</td></tr>
<tr><td>Fireworks File Format</td><td>.png</td><td>PNGf</td><td>A PNG file with Fireworks-only information, such as vectors, added.</td></tr>
<tr><td>Fireworks 2.0</td><td>.png</td><td>PNGf</td><td>Converted to Fireworks 3 when opened, but can optionally be saved again as Fireworks 2 for later editing in Fireworks 2.</td></tr>
<tr><td>Fireworks 1.0</td><td>.png</td><td>PNGf</td><td>The Background is placed on its own layer.</td></tr>
</table>

Continued

Table 14-2 *(continued)*			
Format	*Filename Extension*	*Macintosh Type Code*	*Notes*
Portable Network Graphic	.png	PNGf	Standard PNG documents that don't have extra Fireworks information.
Photoshop Document	.psd	8BPS	Version 3.0 or later only. Layers, editable text, and Layer Effects are preserved.
GIF	.gif	GIFf	Graphics Interchange File Format. Static or animated. Each frame of an animated GIF is placed on its own frame in Fireworks.
JPEG	.jpg, .jpeg, .jpe, .jfif	JPEG	Avoid importing JPEG images due to their lossy compression scheme and low quality.
xRes	.lrg	LRG	The default format of Macromedia's defunct xRes application.
Targa	.tga	TPIC	Common Unix image format.
TIFF	.tif or .tiff	TIFF	Tag Image File Format. High-quality lossless compression similar to PNG.
Microsoft Bitmap	.bmp	BMP	Default image format for Windows 3.0 and later.
PICT (Macintosh only)	.pict, .pic, .pct, .p	PICT	Default image format for Mac OS 1-9. Combination vector-bitmap format. Fireworks renders any vector as a bitmap.

Importing a bitmap image into an existing document

To import a bitmap image into an existing Fireworks document, follow these steps:

1. Choose File ➪ Import or use the keyboard shortcut Ctrl+R (Command+R). Alternatively, you can use the command Insert ➪ Image.

Fireworks displays the Import File dialog box (Figure 14-11).

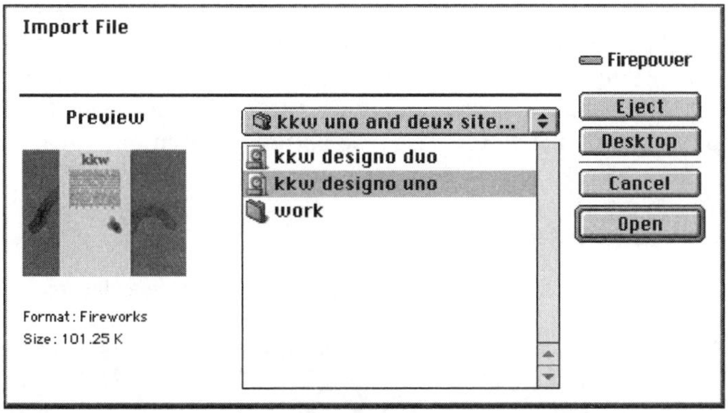

Import File

⊂⊃ Firepower

Preview

⊞ kkw uno and deux site... ⬍

Eject
Desktop
Cancel
Open

🔲 kkw designo duo
🔲 kkw designo uno
🔲 work

Format: Fireworks
Size: 101.25 K

Figure 14-11: The Import File dialog box shows you previews as you navigate and then choose a file to import into Fireworks.

2. In the Import File dialog box, select your file and click Import after you finish.

3. Hover your mouse cursor over the Fireworks document window into which you would like to import.

The cursor changes to the import cursor, which looks like a right angle.

4. Position the import cursor where you want the upper-left corner of the imported image to be located and then do one of the following:

  • If you want to insert the image at its original size, click once.

  • If you want to insert the image so that it fits a specific area in your document, click and drag a box that delineates that specific area. Fireworks will resize the image to fit that area while maintaining the image's aspect ratio.

The chosen image is inserted into the document as a new image object.

Bringing in Photoshop files

Most of the bitmap files that Fireworks can import are fairly interchangeable; importing a PNG or TIFF image results in a single image object inside Fireworks. Photoshop documents are a bit different, though, because they contain layer information. Therefore, they can contain multiple image objects. Photoshop files also contain unique attributes, such as editable text and layer effects.

New
Feature

When importing Photoshop documents, Fireworks 3 now converts Photoshop 5's Layer Effects to Fireworks Live Effects and maintains editable text.

Layer Effects are similar to many of Fireworks Live Effects, creating editable bevels, drop shadows and glows. In fact, when you import a Photoshop document into Fireworks, all Layer Effects are converted directly into their corresponding Live Effects and remain editable, as shown in Figure 14-12. Also note that the layers of the Photoshop document are intact. The translation is remarkably accurate.

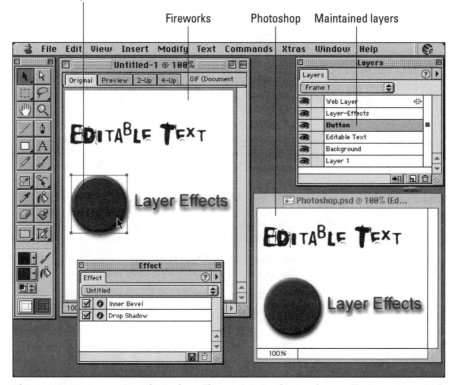

Figure 14-12: Importing Photoshop files maintains layers, layer effects — converted to Live Effects — and editable text.

To import a Photoshop document into an existing Fireworks document, follow these steps:

1. Choose File ➪ Import or use the keyboard shortcut Ctrl+R (Command+R). Alternatively, you can use the command Insert ➪ Image.

   Fireworks displays the Import File dialog box.

2. In the Import File dialog box, select your Photoshop file and then click Import after you're done.

Fireworks displays the Photoshop File Options dialog box (Figure 14-13).

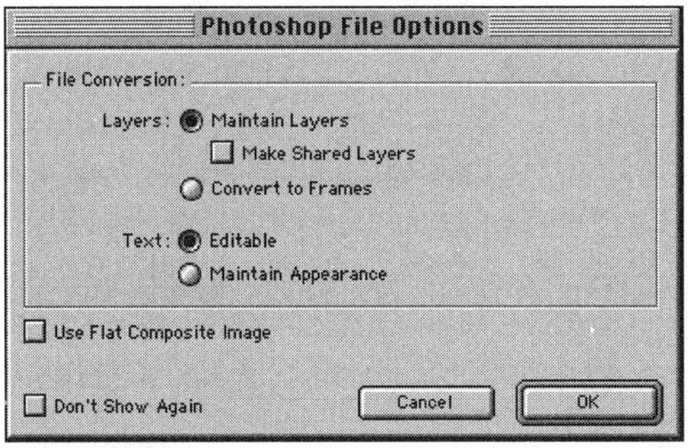

Figure 14-13: The Photoshop File Options dialog box allows you to makes some choices about how you import a Photoshop file.

3. Under Layers, choose Maintain Layers in order to distribute the layers of the Photoshop document to Fireworks layers; check Make Shared Layers in order to share the Fireworks layers across frames. To distribute Photoshop layers to Fireworks frames instead, choose Convert to Frames.

4. Under Text, choose Editable to convert Photoshop editable text to Fireworks text objects. Choose Maintain Appearance to flatten editable text into Fireworks image objects. You might want to flatten text when you know you won't need to edit it so that the appearance will be even closer to the original Photoshop document. You might also choose this option if you know you don't have the correct typefaces installed.

Caution   If the text in your Photoshop documents is not on Photoshop Text Layers — in other words, it's not even editable in Photoshop — it will not be editable in Fireworks.

5. Check Use Flat Composite Image to ignore all the special attributes of the Photoshop document and import it as a single flat image, as though it were a TIFF. This provides the maximum similarity to the original Photoshop image, and is a good choice if you're only using Fireworks to optimize and export your Photoshop document.

6. Check Don't Show Again to skip this dialog box when importing Photoshop documents, in which case these options will be taken from your Fireworks Import preferences.

Caution   Choose File ⇨ Preferences and then the Import tab (list option on Macintosh) in order to modify your Import Preferences.

7. Hover your mouse cursor over the Fireworks document window into which you would like to import.

   The cursor changes to the import cursor, which looks like a right angle.

8. Position the import cursor where you want the upper-left corner of the imported image to be located, and then do one of the following:

   • If you want to insert the image at its original size, click once.

   • If you want to insert the image so that it fits a specific area in your document, click and drag a box that delineates that specific area. Fireworks will resize the image to fit that area while maintaining the image's aspect ratio.

The Photoshop document is inserted into your Fireworks document.

Caution   Fireworks can import Photoshop documents version 3, 4, and 5. Photoshop was a Macintosh-only application before version 3, and the file format was also different. Photoshop 2.5 or earlier documents have a Macintosh Type of "8BIM," rather than the newer format's "8BPS," and they typically don't have a filename extension. Open them in Photoshop 3 or higher versions and save in the newer format before importing into Fireworks.

Although Fireworks can't directly import the native file formats of applications other than Photoshop, many other bitmap-editing applications, such as Painter, can export as Photoshop documents. These can then be imported into Fireworks with layers intact.

Caution   Corel Photo-Paint is a popular Photoshop alternative that can save images as Photoshop documents and retain layer information. Unfortunately, Fireworks imports Photo-Paint-created Photoshop documents as flat images.

Vector art files

If you prefer to do your drawing in a traditional vector graphics drawing program, Fireworks is the ideal place to finish up your work and prepare it for the Web. Vector objects remain vector objects, just as if you had created them in Fireworks itself.

Table 14-3 details the vector file types that Fireworks can import.

These file types cover the most common vector drawing tools. One vector art file format that is notable for its absence is Macromedia's own open vector standard, Shockwave Flash (.swf). Moving objects between Flash and Fireworks involves exporting from Flash as an Illustrator document and then importing into Fireworks. Another fairly common format that Fireworks can't import is a Windows Meta File (.wmf), which is commonly used for vector graphics clip-art collections for Windows users. To open these files, first open them in another application and export them as one of the file types in Table 14-3.

Table 14-3
Vector Graphics File Types Fireworks Can Import

Format	Filename Extension	Macintosh Type Code	Notes
FreeHand Document	.fh7 or .fh8	AGD3	The vector-based format of FreeHand 7 or 8.
Illustrator 7 Document	.ai	uMsk	Adobe Illustrator 7's vector-based default format.
CorelDRAW 8 Document	.cdr	CDR8	CorelDRAW's vector-based format must have been saved without CorelDRAW's built-in bitmap or object compression in order to be openable in Fireworks.

Importing a vector art file

To import a vector art file from Macromedia FreeHand, Adobe Illustrator, or CorelDRAW into an existing Fireworks document, follow these steps:

1. Choose either File ➪ Import or use the keyboard shortcut Ctrl+R (Command+R).

   Fireworks displays the standard Import dialog box.

2. In the Import dialog box, select your CorelDRAW document and click Open after you're done.

   Fireworks displays the Vector File Options dialog box (see Figure 14-14), with suggested settings appropriate to the document you are importing.

3. In the Vector File Options dialog box, change the dimensions or resolution of the vector art, if necessary. Change the dimensions with the Scale, Width, or Height boxes. Change the resolution with the Resolution box.

4. Under File Conversion, select what to do with pages from the Page Import option list. You can choose to open a single page by choosing Open a Page and putting the page number in the Page box. You can also choose Open Pages as Frames to distribute all the pages in the file to frames in Fireworks.

5. Under File Conversion, select what to do with layers from the Layers Import option list. Choose Ignore Layers to flatten the layers. Choose Remember Layers to keep them as they are. Choose Open Layers as Frames in order to distribute all the layers in the file to frames in Fireworks.

6. To include invisible and background layers, select the appropriate check boxes.

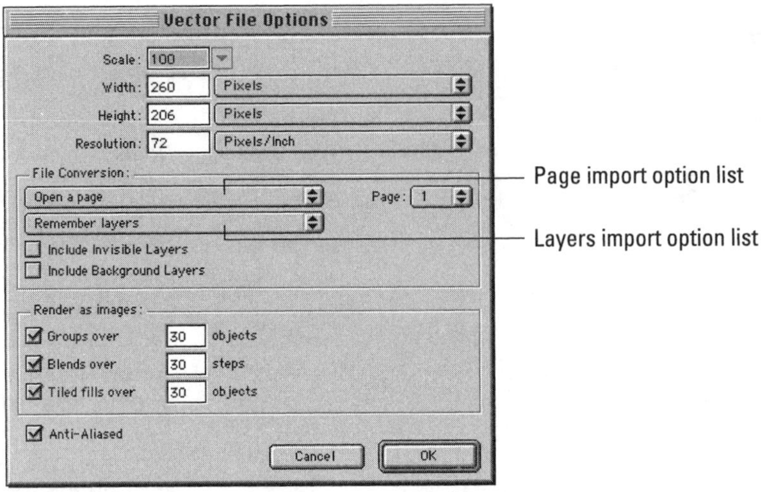

Figure 14-14: The Vector File Options dialog box
allows you to specify how your vector file is imported.

7. Under Render as Images, select how you want to handle complex vector objects. Deselect all the boxes to maintain vector information under all circumstances.

8. Select Anti-Aliased to apply antialiasing to your imported vector art. Click OK after you're done.

9. Hover your mouse cursor over the Fireworks document window into which you would like to import.

   The cursor changes to the import cursor, which looks like a right angle.

10. Position the import cursor where you want the upper-left corner of the imported vector art to be located and then do one of the following:

    • If you want to insert the vector art at its original size, click once.

    • If you want to insert the vector art so that it fits a specific area in your document, click and drag a box describing that specific area. Fireworks will resize the image to fit that area while maintaining the image's aspect ratio.

The vector information is inserted into the document as a new vector object.

Working with clip art

In a commercial or production environment, the constraints of deadlines often preclude creating documents completely from scratch. Besides, there's no need to keep reinventing the wheel. Often, things like icons and buttons can be quickly based on existing clip-art images, which are easily modified in Fireworks to suit a particular project.

Fireworks includes an extensive collection of clip art on its CD-ROM; almost 2,000 separate Fireworks documents. Thankfully, these documents are also referenced by an Extensis Portfolio database file called "Fireworks 3 Clipart.fdb". This document opens in the free Extensis Portfolio browser — also included on the CD-ROM and shown in Figure 14-15 — displaying thumbnails for each and every clip-art document. Use the Portfolio Browser to search or browse for a particular document. Double-click a thumbnail in order to view it at full size; right-click (Control-click) a thumbnail and choose Edit Original from the context menu in order to open it in Fireworks for editing. Once the thumbnail has been opened in Fireworks, you can drag and drop elements into other Fireworks documents.

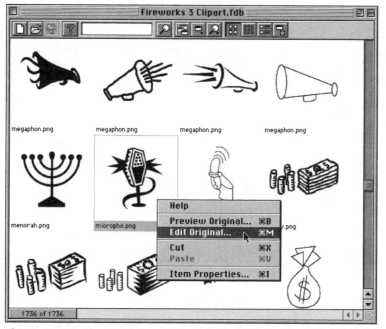

Figure 14-15: Choose to preview or edit an image with a quick right-click (Control-click) on its thumbnail in the Portfolio Browser. Double-clicking a thumbnail also previews it.

Caution

Look in the Goodies folder on your Fireworks CD-ROM and find the Fireworks clip art in the Clipart folder and the Extensis Portfolio Browser inside the Portfolio Browser folder.

Clip-art collections are also commonly included with vector drawing tools, such as FreeHand and CorelDRAW. In fact, Corel is famous for including extensive collections of clip art with their products; often 10,000 items or more. Clip art in FreeHand, CorelDRAW and Illustrator formats is easily imported into Fireworks.

Many stand-alone clip art collections are also available, either on CD-ROM or on the Web. Be careful to choose collections in formats that Fireworks can import and favor collections of vector images because they provide maximum flexibility in Fireworks.

Extensis also offers a full version of Portfolio that enables you to organize your own files into Portfolio databases (available at <http://www.extensis.com>). On a Macintosh, iView Multimedia from Script Software—find it at <http://www.scriptsoftware.com>—is an excellent shareware alternative, providing similar functionality at one-eighth the price.

Text files

Obviously, Fireworks can work with a multitude of image formats, but Fireworks is also adept at handling text and can import two types of text files: Rich Text Format (RTF) and ASCII. Either kind of text file is imported by choosing File ➪ Import and navigating to and selecting the file.

RTF is native to Microsoft Word; therefore, RTF files contain formatting, such as typefaces, and italicized or bold text. Many word-processing applications other than Word can also save RTF files. If you need to preserve text formatting, use an RTF file.

ASCII text files are plain text without formatting, but they can be read with few or no translation problems by any application that handles text. If you want to move blocks of text from another application into Fireworks and you're not worried about preserving formatting, ASCII text files are good choice.

For more about importing and using text in Fireworks, see Chapter 10.

Common problems

The fact that Fireworks can import a particular document doesn't mean that the transition from the original file to the Fireworks document will be seamless. Converting data between different applications may involve some compromises along the way.

Missing fonts

Ideally, documents would never leave home without their font suitcases (or font files on Windows). Unfortunately, this is not always the case. When you open or import a document that relies on a typeface that's not available on your system, Fireworks warns you by displaying the Missing Fonts dialog box(Figure 14-16).

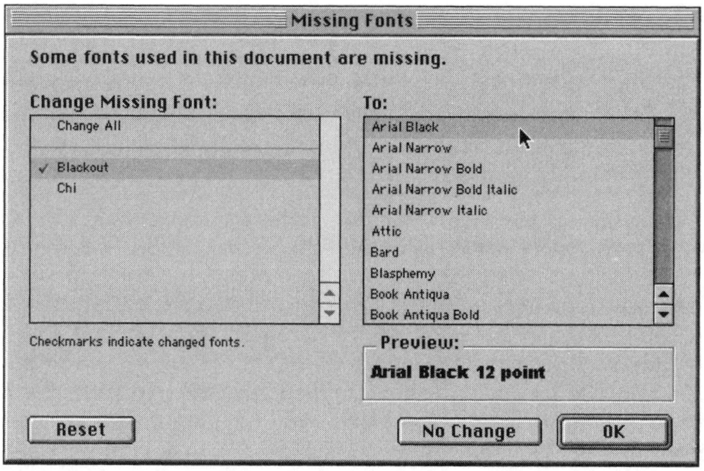

Figure 14-16: The Missing Fonts dialog box enables you to substitute new fonts for fonts that are missing from your system.

To replace a missing font, select its name from the Change Missing Font box and select a font to replace it from the To box. Repeat this process for every font listed in the Missing Font box. Click Reset to restore the original state of the Missing Fonts dialog box at anytime. Click No Change to open your document without making any substitutions. Click OK after you're done.

If you choose No Change, you can edit and even save the document while leaving the font information intact for a future time when the document can be opened with the correct fonts available.

Caution   If your document uses Type 1 (PostScript) fonts, make sure to install or enable Adobe Type Manager before opening the document.

Font spacing

In general, you can expect many of the print-related features of your vector documents to be unsatisfactorily translated. These include the following:

✦ Postscript strokes, fills, and effects

✦ Fine letter spacing, leading, and kerning

Rendering text as paths before saving a vector document for Fireworks import generally leads to better results, although the text will not be editable in Fireworks. If you want to keep text editable throughout your workflow, leave any fine text positioning or even text creation until you're in Fireworks.

Sharing files across platforms

Almost all of the documents that Fireworks can open or import are cross-platform. On the surface, this would seem to suggest that you can ignore any cross-platform issues, but what it really means is that you're likely to be working with files from the "other" platform at some point. While there are no insurmountable issues, keeping a few points in mind can quickly save the day—and your deadline.

Importing Macintosh files into Fireworks for Windows

Files don't need to have filename extensions on a Macintosh, but they do on Windows. Although most Mac users understand this and add the correct filename extensions before "shipping out" a document, occasionally you may find yourself trying to import a file that does not have an extension into Fireworks for Windows. If you know what kind of file it is, add the correct filename extension; if you don't, you'll probably have to ask the Mac user who sent you the file, or take a few best guesses. Without the correct filename extension, Fireworks for Windows will not import a file.

You may also receive a file with a four-character filename extension rather than with the three-character extension that Windows favors. For example, you receive a file with .jpeg as its filename extension rather than .jpg. Windows sometimes treats these as the same file type and sometimes it doesn't. Fireworks for Windows will import JPEG's with the extensions .jpg, .jpeg, or .jpe; but not with the less-common extension .jfif.

Fireworks for Windows cannot import Macintosh PICT files (.pict, .pct, .pic or .p), although they can be imported and exported by Fireworks for Macintosh.

Importing Windows files into Fireworks for Macintosh

When you move documents to a Macintosh system from a Windows system, the Mac OS typically adds the correct Macintosh Creator and File Type codes based on filename extensions. Even if a particular file type is not listed in your File Exchange preferences—in which case it appears with a blank icon—after you have chosen File ⇨ Import, Fireworks for Macintosh will go the extra mile and import it on faith, as long as it has the correct filename extension.

You can also manually "bless" files with Creator and File Type codes by using certain utilities, such as File Buddy, FinderPop, or Snitch. Adding the Fireworks Creator code MKBY to a file will cause it to open in Fireworks after it is double-clicked.

Screen Capture

Capturing all or part of your computer screen to the clipboard or to a file has applications above and beyond creating illustrations for computer books. There are sometimes workflow advantages to screen captures at design time. Two applications may refuse to maintain the proper formatting if you copy and paste between them, but a capture of one will paste or import easily into the other. If you are presented with an esoteric file format — a specialty of Web design clients — you may find that you can open the file in a viewer but not convert it to a file format that Fireworks can use. A quick screen capture will have you pasting or importing that image into Fireworks in no time.

In addition, a screen capture of a browser window dropped into an e-mail is a good way to send a client quick design proofs of a site that is not yet live or to build a portfolio page of your Web-design work. Screen captures of a browser window might also make good link icons for a Web page, if appropriately resized.

Built-in screenshot tools

Screen capture tools are built right into Windows and Mac OS. Windows provides just enough functionality to get the job done, while Mac OS provides a few extra features over and above the call of duty.

Windows

What Windows lacks in screen-capture functionality it probably makes up for in utility: everything is centered around the easy-to-remember PrintScreen key, which is sometimes marked Prt Scrn, or similarly. Pressing PrintScreen copies an image of the entire screen to the clipboard. Pressing Alt+PrintScreen copies just the active window or dialog box to the clipboard. From there, paste the contents of the clipboard into Fireworks.

Caution

When you choose File ⇨New, Fireworks offers to create a document with the same dimensions as the clipboard. Take your screen capture before you create a new document in order to automatically size the canvas correctly.

Mac OS

On a Macintosh, you can capture the whole screen, a single window or dialog box, or a selected portion of the screen to either a picture file (PICT) or the clipboard.

To make a screen capture on the Macintosh and save it as a picture file in the root folder of your startup disk, press and hold Shift+Command and then do one of the following:

✦ Press 3 to capture the entire screen.

✦ Press 4 and then draw a selection with the mouse to capture only the contents of that selection.

✦ Enable Caps Lock, press 4, and then click on a window or dialog box in order to capture only that window or dialog box.

To place a screen capture on the clipboard instead of saving it to a file, follow the above instructions, but hold down Control in addition to Shift+Command.

If you captured to the clipboard, paste your capture into Fireworks. If you captured to a file, open your startup disk and then drag the picture file(s) onto the Fireworks icon. Alternatively, you can choose File ➪ Open or File ➪ Import in Fireworks, navigate to the picture file(s), and then open them.

Specialized applications

Numerous third-party applications provide additional screen-capture features, such as on-the-fly palette changes, capturing individual menus or individual "child" windows in Windows, or a choice of file formats, sometimes including movie files. One such application for the Macintosh is Ambrosia Software's Snapz Pro, shown in Figure 14-17. Snapz Pro was used to create all of the screen captures in this book. There are also many screen-capture applications available for Windows. Most screen-capture tools fit perfectly into the Shareware or Freeware application categories and can be found on Web sites that feature those listings.

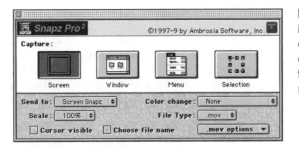

Figure 14-17: Snapz Pro for Macintosh offers many different screen-capture options and a variety of file formats, including QuickTime movies.

Opening Animations

Opening an animated GIF by choosing File ➪ Open works just as you might expect; the animated GIF is opened and the individual frames are available on — what else — Fireworks frames. You can then modify the GIF, if you like, and optimize and export it for the Web.

Cross-Reference   For more information about animation in Fireworks, see Chapter 23. For more information on exporting, see Chapter 15.

However, if you import an animated GIF into an existing animation, you may be in for a surprise. Only the first frame of the animated GIF will be imported. If you want to import one animation into another, the workaround is to open both animations in Fireworks and then copy and paste objects from one to the other until you have the combined animation that you require.

Importing multiple files as a new animation

Most animation programs can export their animations as a series of individual documents, one frame of animation to one document. If your animation is ten frames long, you export ten files, each with a similar filename and numbered 1-10. You can open these files as an animation in Fireworks by using the Open Multiple command with Open as Animation checked. Each document becomes a frame in Fireworks, and you have an animation again.

Imagine that you've created an exciting, full-color animation with your favorite three-dimensional animation program, and you want to change it into an animated GIF for use on the Web. Unfortunately, this three-dimensional animation program is not too Web-savvy, and the GIFs it creates are always dithered and contain a full 256-color palette. You could create a much more optimized GIF if you could only create it in Fireworks. The way to achieve this is to export your animation as a series of high-quality PNG or TIFF bitmaps and then import that series into Fireworks.

Importing a group of files as a new animation will render them as images, even if they are vector art documents or Fireworks PNG files with vector information. For a workaround using Macromedia Flash as an example, see "Importing Flash animations," later in this chapter.

To open a group of independent documents as one animation, follow these steps:

1. Choose either File ➪ Open Multiple or the keyboard shortcut Ctrl+Shift+O (Command+Shift+O).

   Fireworks displays the Open Multiple Files dialog box (see Figure 14-18).

2. In the Files of Type option list, choose the type of files you will be opening.

3. Navigate to a file from your animation series and click the Add button to add it to the Open list, or click the Add All button to add all the files in a particular folder to the Open list.

If the files you are importing are numbered — movie01.png, movie02.png, for example — Fireworks will distribute them to frames in the correct order. If the files are not numbered, add them to the list of files to be opened in the correct order.

4. Repeat step 3 as many times as necessary to add all of the files in your animation series to the Open list.

5. Select the Open as Animation check box. Click Done.

A new Fireworks document is created, and your files are now frames in that document.

Test your animation by setting it to play by using either the VCR-style controls in the Fireworks status bar in Windows or by using the bottom of each document window on a Mac. Adjust frame timing in the Frames panel.

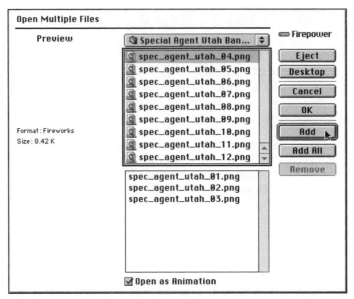

Figure 14-18: Files become frames when you import an animation series using File ➪ Open Multiple with Open as Animation checked.

Importing Flash animations

Macromedia Flash has more sophisticated animation tools than Fireworks, but its animated GIF export features pale in comparison to Fireworks.

If you want to use Fireworks tools on the vector elements of your Flash animation, you have to go a little further to import your Flash animation as vectors. Ideally, you would export from Flash as an Adobe Illustrator Sequence, import into Fireworks using the File ➪ Open Multiple, and then check Open as Animation. Unfortunately, Open as Animation always renders vectors as image objects. A workaround is to turn your Flash movie into a multilayer Adobe Illustrator document, where each layer is actually a frame of your movie, and then convert the layers to frames while importing into Fireworks. While this example uses Flash, if you use another vector animation application the principles might still apply.

Caution   If you're not worried about retaining vector information, you can export from Flash as a PNG sequence and then import the file into Fireworks by using Open Multiple with Open as Animation checked.

To import a Flash animation into Fireworks while retaining vector information, follow these steps:

1. Export your movie from Flash as a Flash SWF movie.

2. Create a new Flash document and import the SWF movie into it.

You have effectively flattened the layers of your Flash movie, leaving you with a single-layer, frame-by-frame animation.

3. Export your movie from Flash as an Adobe Illustrator Sequence.

4. Create a new Flash document and import the Adobe Illustrator Sequence into it. Select all the files in the sequence by individually Ctrl+clicking (Command+clicking) each file until they are all selected. Click OK after you're done.

   You have effectively converted the frames of your Flash movie to layers. Frame 1 is now Layer 1, Frame 2 is Layer 2, and so on.

5. Export your movie from Flash as an Adobe Illustrator file.

   This is the file you will import into Fireworks. Flash can export seven vector file types, and Fireworks can import three vector file types, but Adobe Illustrator is the only vector file type that they have in common.

Caution   Choose Adobe Illustrator, not Adobe Illustrator Sequence.

6. In Fireworks, choose either File ➪ Open or the keyboard shortcut Ctrl+O (Command+O).

   Fireworks displays the Open dialog box.

7. Choose the Adobe Illustrator file that you created in Step 5. Click OK after you're done.

   Fireworks displays the Vector File Options dialog box.

8. Under File Conversion, select Convert Layers to Frames in the Layers Import option list so that each layer of your Adobe Illustrator file is placed in a Fireworks frame.

9. Under Render as Images, deselect Groups Over and Tiled Fills Over. Click OK after you're done.

Fireworks imports the file, and your Flash animation is now a Fireworks animation, complete with vector information. Objects are editable and are ready to be manipulated with Fireworks' tools and exported as an animated GIF.

Summary

Elements can be incorporated into Fireworks documents from external sources. When you're importing elements into Fireworks, keep these points in mind:

✦ You can acquire images directly into Fireworks from TWAIN-compliant hardware devices, such as page scanners and digital cameras. On a Macintosh, you can also use Photoshop Acquire plug-ins.

✦ Resolution—the number of dots—is the most important thing to understand about scanning.

✦ You can copy and paste, or drag and drop elements from other applications into Fireworks.

✦ Fireworks imports Photoshop 5 files with editable text and layer effects intact.

✦ Fireworks includes an extensive collection of clip art, as well as the Portfolio Browser for accessing it.

✦ Screen captures are a simple but effective tool.

✦ Animated GIFs should be opened instead of imported. Opening them gets you an animated GIF, whereas importing them gets you only the first frame of an animation.

✦ A series of files can be imported as an animation. Extra steps are necessary to maintain vector information.

In the next chapter, we'll look at exporting your images from Fireworks.

✦   ✦   ✦

Exporting and Optimizing

♦ ♦ ♦ ♦

In This Chapter

Introducing export
fundamentals

Optimizing indexed
color

Working with
photographic images

Using Export Preview

Summoning Export
Wizards

Other export features

♦ ♦ ♦ ♦

The cross-platform, almost universal access of the Web is achieved with limitations. Although there are many different image file formats, browsers are currently limited to displaying only three of them: GIF, JPEG, and PNG. What's more, only GIF and JPEG enjoy truly wide acceptance. Bandwidth is severely limited for the mass market: while an increasing number of Web surfers enjoy the speed of a DSL or cable modem, the vast majority still view the Internet through a 56K dial-up modem.

These limitations make optimizing and exporting graphics a necessity and not just a nicety. Your work in Fireworks has to be exported in the correct format and with the smallest file size possible. Macromedia realized the importance of export features when it created Fireworks; much of the program centers around making the best-looking graphic, with the smallest file size, in an accepted format. The features covered in this chapter rank among the best available with advanced controls, such as lossy GIF and color locking. Fireworks takes the limitations of the Web and turns them into an art form.

This chapter covers the fundamentals of exporting and optimizing your graphics. For more specific information on exporting graphics with hotspots and slices, see Part V. You'll find details on exporting animations in Chapter 23.

Exploring Optimization Features

Although it's possible to use a graphic stored in Fireworks native format, PNG, in a Web page, this really isn't practical, nor is it the intention of the program for you to do so. Every graphic produced in Fireworks should really be stored in two files: a Fireworks-format PNG master file, and an exported format to be published on the Web. Think of the Fireworks

PNG file as an original, and the exported file as a photocopy ready for wide circulation. Working hand-in-hand with selecting an appropriate file type is the other main goal of exporting: *optimization*. Optimization is the process of producing the best-looking, smallest possible file. An optimized image loads faster, without sacrificing perceived quality.

Optimizing and exporting in Fireworks is focused around the preview tabs of the document window, the Optimize and Color Table panels, and the Frames panel for animations. Adjusting settings in these panels is a necessary precursor to choosing File ➯ Export to create your exported image file. Once you've made these settings, they are saved with your Fireworks PNG file for next time. Export settings are as much a part of a document as the kinds of fills or strokes you used.

New Feature   Fireworks 3 introduces a whole new paradigm by bringing optimization and export features into the workspace itself. One of the most dramatic of Fireworks 3's new features, moving to in-place previews has affected many components of the Fireworks interface, removing the necessity to access a separate Export Preview dialog box to see how your work will look on the Web.

The hardest part of optimizing is finding a balance between image quality and file size. Fireworks takes a lot of the guesswork out of this task by providing up to four comparison views of different formats at various color resolutions or compressions. Optimizing every image that goes out on your Web page is important, because the smaller your files, the shorter the loading time of your Web pages — and the quicker visitors can view your work.

You'll explore individual export features in much greater depth throughout this chapter, but for now, here's an overview of the typical procedure to use when optimizing a file:

1. Create your image with optimization in the back of your mind at all times; scale and crop images as small as possible, and create large areas of flat color or horizontal stripes of color to make the smallest GIFs.

2. Select a file format in the Optimize panel, based on the type of image you're working on. Choose an indexed color format such as GIF for illustrations and flat-color artwork, or a continuous-tone, True Color format such as JPEG for photographic images.

3. For indexed color images, reduce the number of colors as much as possible, using the setting in the Optimize panel in concert with the Color Table panel. Reducing the number of colors is the primary method of reducing the file size of indexed color images. The fewer colors used, the smaller the file.

4. For the JPEG format, use the Quality slider in the Optimize panel to choose the lowest acceptable quality in order to achieve the smallest file size.

5. Select any additional format-specific options in the Optimize panel, such as Interlaced GIF or JPEG Smoothing.

6. Choose File ➪ Export to export your document and create the optimized file.

Optimize panel

The Optimize panel is the main control center for your image optimization efforts in Fireworks, containing nearly all of the controls you use to set export options. Choose an export file format and modify settings unique to that format. The Optimize panel's settings affect your entire Fireworks document, except when you have an individual slice object selected, in which case the settings are just for that slice.

New Feature The Optimize panel is completely new for Fireworks 3, bringing features formerly found only in the Export Preview dialog box right into the workspace.

If the Optimize panel (Figure 15-1) is not visible, choose Window ➪ Optimize to view it. Many factors contribute to image optimization, but the format of an image plays perhaps the most important role. In Fireworks, all format selections are made in the Optimize panel's Export File Format option list. Selecting a particular format displays the available options, such as Bit Depth or Quality, for that format. Choosing GIF, for example, makes the transparency controls available, while choosing JPEG removes the transparency controls and displays the Quality slider.

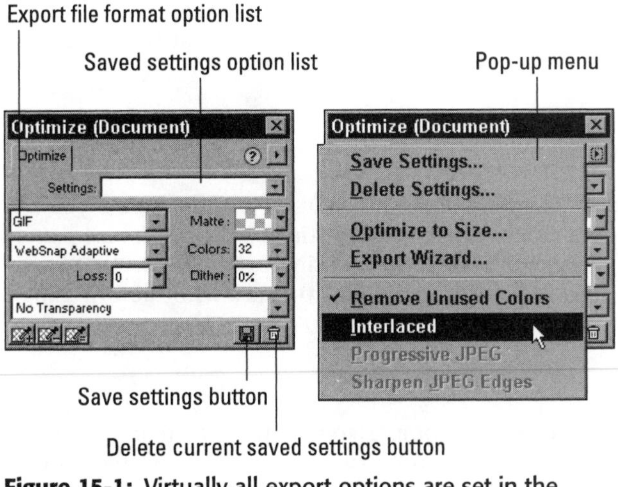

Export file format option list

Saved settings option list   Pop-up menu

Save settings button

Delete current saved settings button

Figure 15-1: Virtually all export options are set in the new Optimize panel.

The Optimize panel also allows you to save its settings as a preset at any time. Your preset is added to the default presets on the Saved Settings option list. Choosing a preset and then adjusting any setting (except Matte) creates a custom setting. To save a custom export setting, click the Save Settings button (the disk icon) on the bottom of the Optimize panel. A simple Preset Name dialog box appears for you to enter a unique name for the setting. After you enter the name and click OK, the setting is added to the preset list and is always available. To delete the current saved setting, click the Delete Current Saved Settings button (the Trash icon).

Note   We'll look more closely at the features of the Optimize panel as we work with specific export formats later in this chapter.

Color Table panel

The Color Table panel comes alive when you optimize an indexed color image such as a GIF or 8-bit PNG. These formats carry their own limited palette of colors with them, and limiting the size of this palette is the primary way to limit the file size of indexed color images. The Color Table provides easy access to this palette, and enables you to add, remove, and lock specific colors and more.

New Feature   Previously available only in the Export Preview dialog box, the Color Table panel displays the export palette in the workspace.

If it's not already visible, view the Color Table panel, shown in Figure 15-2, by choosing Window ⇨ Color Table. Choosing the Rebuild Color Table command from the Color Table's pop-up menu displays swatches of the current document's export palette. The number of colors in your document is displayed at the bottom of the Color Table.

Workspace preview

The Preview tab of the document window, shown in Figure 15-3, offers you an optimized view of your document according to the settings in the Optimize panel. The Preview tab provides a view so similar to the working Original view that I sometimes find myself grabbing a tool and getting back to work without switching away from Preview.

Multiple previews

Fireworks' ability to offer side-by-side comparisons of the effects of different export settings on an image is often crucial to optimizing a graphic. This chapter has noted several times that an optimized graphic is one that strikes a balance between the best appearance and the smallest file size. That balance can be directly judged through Fireworks' multiple previews.

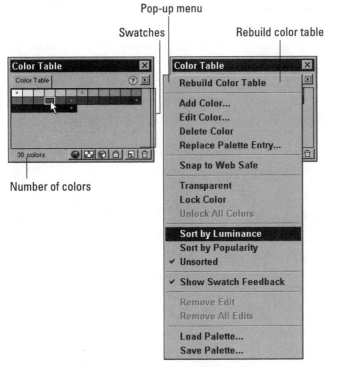

Figure 15-2: The Color Table panel displays the export palette for 8-bit indexed color images.

Previewing Cross-Platform Gamma

As well as seeing what your work will look like once it's exported, Fireworks can also give you an idea of what your work will look like on both the Windows and Macintosh platforms. Windows machines use a gamma correction setting of 2.2, while most Macs use 1.8. The difference in gamma corrections settings — which regulate how dark or light the display looks — means that the same image will look brighter on a Mac than on Windows.

At any time during a Fireworks session — not just when you're looking at one of the preview tabs of the document window — a Windows user can choose View ⇨ Macintosh Gamma or a Mac user can choose View ⇨ Windows Gamma to toggle the document window to simulate the other platform. Viewing your images at both gamma settings enables you to avoid a surprise when seeing your work on the opposite platform.

Figure 15-3: An optimized preview of your work is never more than a click away, thanks to the document window's in-place previews.

The 2-Up and 4-Up tabs show you both sides of the export equation: how the image looks, and the file size. The file size is given in both kilobytes and its approximate download time with a 28.8 Kbps modem. While the visual representation of your document is an obvious benefit, the file size information that accompanies a preview is just as important. Every adjustment you make in the Optimize panel is reflected in a recalculated and updated file size estimate. The file size is shown in both kilobytes and the approximate length of time the exported image will take to download.

Note
If your image contains multiple frames, the file size shown is for the current frame only, unless the chosen format is Animated GIF. Images with rollovers, for example, use multiple frames, and each frame is exported as a separate image. To find the total "weight" of a multiple-framed image, you must add all the frames together.

Each of the document window's three preview tabs offers its own kind of multiple preview.

Preview tab

A somewhat hidden multiple preview can be accessed by choosing Window ➪ New Window to create a second document window for your current document. Then select the Preview tab in the new window, as shown in Figure 15-4. With one document window set to Original and one set to Preview, your work in the Original window is immediately reflected in the Preview window.

Original tab   Preview tab

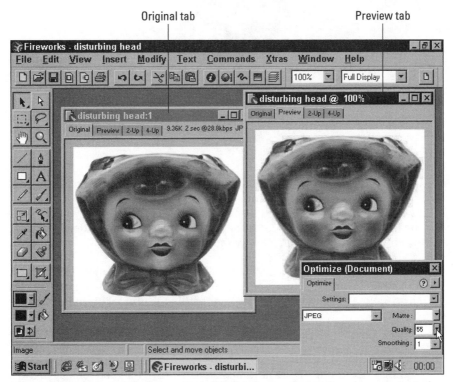

Figure 15-4: Choose Window ➪ New Window to create another document window and set one to Original and one to Preview.

2-Up tab

The 2-Up tab splits the document window vertically and provides two views of your image. The left pane displays your original image, while the right displays the optimized version, according to the settings in the Optimize panel. On Windows, the document window expands to give you more than a half-and-half view (Figure 15-5); on the Mac, the document window is split evenly. On either platform, you can stretch the document window to get a complete side-by-side view.

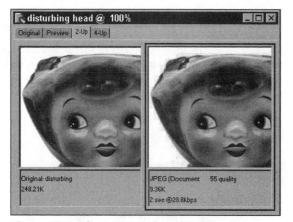

Figure 15-5: The 2-Up preview shows you one original and one optimized view of your document.

4-Up tab

The 4-Up tab (Figure 15-6) offers four views, each approximately one quarter of the document window, arranged in a square. The upper left view is your original document, while the other three panes display optimized views. When you select a view with the mouse, Fireworks indicates the selected view with a border. Changes you make to the Optimize panel affect only the selected view.

I find that the 4-Up view is especially useful when optimizing an image for JPEG export. The JPEG format is finicky; reducing the quality to 70 percent might make one image look terrible, while another might still look great with the quality dialed all the way down to 50 percent. Achieving the perfect JPEG quality setting for a particular image is often best accomplished by viewing it at three different settings at once.

Tip   You may have to resize the document window to get a good look at your document, especially if your document is on the small size. A portion of each preview pane is given over to the file size report, and this can be most of the window for a 200 × 200 or smaller document.

Panning

If the image is too big to view all at once in the preview area, you can use the Hand tool to pan the image. When you select an image in a preview area with the Hand, the cursor becomes a hand, and you can drag the other parts of the image into view. The panning capability of the Hand tool is especially valuable when viewing multiple settings. Panning one of the multiple views causes all the other views to pan as well, as shown in Figure 15-7. This feature makes direct comparison very straightforward.

Selected pane

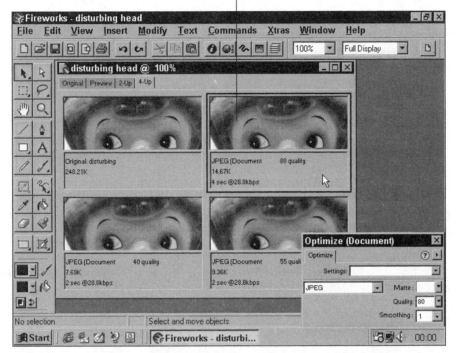

Figure 15-6: In the 4-Up preview, you have to select a pane to be the focus of your work in the Optimize panel. Here the upper-right pane is selected.

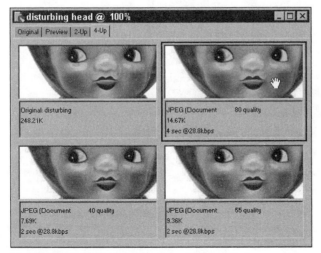

Figure 15-7: With multiple views, if you pan in one view, the other view pans, too.

Caution Panning a preview window with the Pointer tool instead of the Hand actually moves your image object across the canvas, rather than just panning the view.

Zooming

One of the export features in Fireworks is *color locking;* you can lock the color of any pixel in the preview by selecting it and then clicking the Lock Color button on the Color Table. How do you identify just the right pixel? You zoom in, naturally. The Zoom tool and the document window view controls work exactly the same way in the preview views as they do in the original view of the document window. To magnify a view, either select the Zoom tool and click the image, or choose a magnification from the view controls option list. To reduce the magnification of the view, press Alt (Option) while clicking with the Zoom tool — or choose a lower magnification.

Tip Keep in mind that your Web graphics will almost *always* be viewed at 100 percent. Although you might be tempted to make a decision on which file format to use based on a magnified view, the magnified view is largely irrelevant to how the graphics are ultimately viewed.

If you have two or four multiple views enabled, changing the magnification of one view changes the magnification for all of them, as shown in Figure 15-8.

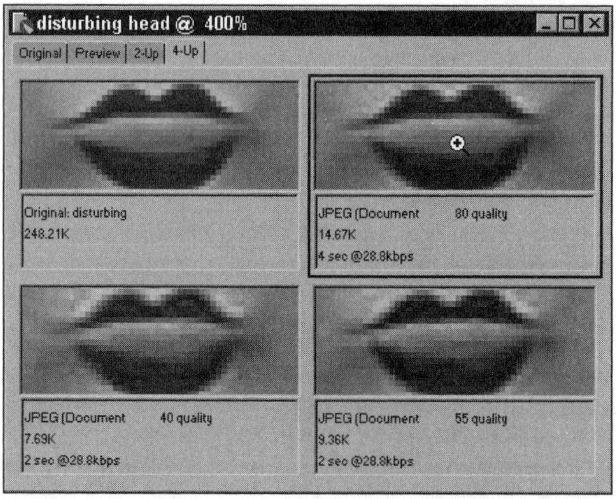

Figure 15-8: When you zoom in on one view, the accompanying views also zoom in.

Tip To pan in for a close-up view without having to switch away from the Zoom tool, press and hold down the spacebar to temporarily switch to the Hand tool.

Frame controls

The VCR-like controls can be used no matter which document window tab you are currently viewing. When optimizing in one of the preview tabs, the frame controls can be used to quickly call up a specific frame for optimization, or to play the frames in sequence. On the Mac, the VCR controls are attached to the bottom of each document window; on Windows, they're attached to the bottom of the Fireworks window, and affect whichever document window has focus.

The controls, from left to right, are as follows:

✦ **Go to First Frame:** Displays the first frame of the image.

✦ **Play/Stop:** Plays all the frames in sequence. When the frames are playing, the button image changes to a square and, if pressed, stops the playback.

✦ **Go to Last Frame:** Displays the last frame of the image.

✦ **Frame Counter:** Displays the current frame number of the image. The frame can be changed by using the Frame Counter slider.

✦ **Previous Frame:** Displays the frame before the current one.

✦ **Next Frame:** Displays the frame after the current one.

In addition to being useful for viewing the separate frames of an animation, I often use the VCR controls to step through the frames of a rollover. Remember that each frame in an image is a separate file and thus can be optimized individually.

Cross-Reference In addition to the VCR controls, the Frames panel also contains frame-timing controls. Explore these animation and export features in Part VI.

Exporting Indexed Color

Images that have large areas of flat color (typically illustrations, as opposed to photographic images) and that can get by with only a limited number of colors are exported in an indexed color format. Indexed color formats have a maximum of 256 different colors, also known as 8-bit color. Which 256 colors a particular image file contains is maintained in a color index inside the file, hence the name *indexed color*.

A key feature of indexed color files is that their index can be reduced to only the specific colors actually used in the image. Reducing the number of colors has a major impact on file size. In fact, this is the primary method for optimizing indexed color files. Fireworks' Color Table panel provides a comprehensive access point to this index.

When an indexed color graphic needs to create the impression of more than 256 colors, dithering can be used. A dithered color is made from a pattern of two or more colored pixels that, because the eye cannot differentiate the individual pixels, blend into the new color.

The indexed color formats that Fireworks exports are detailed in Table 15-1.

Table 15-1 Indexed Color Export Formats	
Format	**Description**
GIF	Graphics Interchange Format. The overwhelmingly most popular indexed color format for the Web. Excellent Web browser support; small file sizes; 1-bit transparency.
Animated GIF	Same as GIF, except that it contains multiple images that are shown one after the other, usually rapidly, like a film or flipbook.
PNG 8	Portable Network Graphic. Offers similar features to GIF, but transparency is not supported by Web browsers.
TIFF 8	Tag Image File Format. Not suitable for the Web, but common for print work.
BMP 8	Microsoft Bitmap image. The native graphics format of Microsoft Windows. Not suitable for the Web, but a good way to share images between Windows applications.
PICT 8 (Macintosh only)	Macintosh Picture. The native graphics format of Mac OS. Vectors are not supported by Fireworks. Not suitable for the Web, but a good way to share image files between Mac applications.

Of all the formats, only GIF and PNG 8 can be used on the Web. GIF is easily the most popular and the most suitable on today's Web, because of overwhelming browser support. While PNG is a superior format in many ways, its transparency features have yet to find support in a wide range of browsers.

Both GIF and PNG support transparency, but again, PNG suffers for lack of browser support. This feature is extremely valuable on the Web, because it enables you to create graphics that appear nonrectangular, or create the illusion that one image is in front of another. Both GIF and PNG files can optionally be interlaced. An interlaced image appears to be developing on the page as it downloads.

The process of exporting any indexed color image is very similar, no matter which format you choose, except that GIF has more options. Because it has the most options, and because it's easily the most popular, we'll focus on the GIF format throughout this section. Once you can export a GIF, it's easy to apply that knowledge to exporting any of the other indexed color formats, because when you switch from GIF to another format in the Optimize panel, Fireworks removes the controls that are no longer applicable, while those that are left function in the same way.

Color palette

A *palette* is the group of colors actually used in the image. Fireworks offers nine preset palettes in the Optimize panel's Indexed Palette option list, plus the Custom setting that refers to a deviation from one of the preset palettes. After you customize a palette, you can store it as a preset and add it to the Indexed Palette option list.

Each of the nine different palettes (available to all indexed formats, not just GIF) accesses a different group of colors. The WebSnap Adaptive and Web 216 palettes are the choices generally made for Internet graphics, although other palettes are appropriate in some situations. The following are the nine preset palettes:

✦ **Adaptive:** Looks at all the colors in the image and finds a maximum of 256 of the most suitable colors; it's called an *adaptive* palette because, instead of a fixed set of colors, it is the best 256 colors adapted to the image. If possible, Fireworks assigns Web-safe colors initially and then assigns any remaining non-Web-safe colors. The Adaptive palette can contain a mixture of Web-safe and non-Web-safe colors.

✦ **WebSnap Adaptive (listed as Web Adaptive on the Mac):** Similar to the Adaptive palette insofar as both are custom palettes in which colors are chosen to match the originals as closely as possible. After selecting the initial matching Web-safe colors, all remaining colors are examined according to their hexadecimal values. Any colors close to a Web-safe color (plus or minus seven values from a Web-safe color) are "snapped to" that color. Although this palette does not ensure that all colors are Web-safe, a greater percentage of colors will be Web-safe.

Note — Exactly how does Fireworks decide which colors are within range for the use of WebSnap Adaptive? The plus or minus seven value range is calculated by using the RGB model. For example, suppose that one of the colors is R-100, G-100, B-105 — a medium gray. With the WebSnap Adaptive palette, that color snaps to the R-102, G-102, B-102, because the difference between the two colors is seven or less (R-2, G-2, B-3 = 7). If, however, the color was just slightly different, say R-99, G-100, B-105, the difference would be outside the snap range and the actual color would be used.

✦ **Web 216:** All colors in the image are converted to their nearest equivalent in the Web-safe range.

✦ **Exact:** Uses colors that match the exact original RGB values. Useful only for images with less than 256 colors; for images with more colors, Fireworks alerts you that you should use the Adaptive palette.

✦ **Macintosh:** Matches the system palette used by the Macintosh operating system when the display is set to 256 colors.

✦ **Windows:** Matches the system palette used by the Windows operating system when the display is set to 256 colors.

✦ **Grayscale:** Converts the image to a grayscale graphic with a maximum of 256 shades of gray.

✦ **Black & White:** Reduces the image to a two-tone image; the Dither option is automatically set to 100 percent when you choose this palette, but this setting can be modified.

✦ **Uniform:** A mathematical progression of colors across the spectrum are chosen. This palette has little application on the Web, although I have been able to get the occasional posterization effect out of it by reducing the number of colors severely and reducing the 100 percent Dither setting that is automatically applied.

✦ **Custom:** Whenever a stored palette is loaded or a modification is made to one of the standard palettes, Fireworks labels the palette Custom. Such changes are made through the pop-up menu found on the Options panel.

Given all of these options, what's the recommended path to take? Probably the best course is to build your graphic in Fireworks by using the Web Safe palette, and then export them by using the WebSnap Adaptive palette. This choice ensures that your image remains the truest to its original colors while looking the best for Web viewers whose color depth is set to 24-bit or higher, and still looking good on lower-end systems that are capable of showing only 256 colors.

Keep in mind that even if you use all Web-safe colors in your graphic, the final result won't necessarily be completely within that palette. Fireworks generates other colors to antialias, to create drop shadows, and to produce glows, and the colors generated may not be Web-safe. This is why either the Adaptive palette or WebSnap Adaptive palette often offers the truest representation of your image across browsers.

Number of colors

One of the quickest ways to cut down an image's file size is to reduce the number of colors. Recall that GIF is referred to as an *8-bit format;* this means that the maximum number of colors is 256, or 8 bit planes of information — higher-math lovers will remember that 256 is equal to 2^8 (2 raised to the 8th power). Each bit plane used permits exponentially more colors and reserves a certain amount of memory (but also increases the file size). This is why the Number of Colors option list contains powers of 2, 4, 8, 16, 32, 64, 128, and 256.

Color Table panel

For complete control of individual colors, the controls on the Color Table panel enable you to add, edit, and delete individual colors, as well as store and load palettes. Fireworks enables you to select a color from the swatches and then lock it, snap it to its closest Web-safe neighbor, or convert it to transparent by clicking one of the Color Table panel's buttons, or choosing a command from its pop-up menu.

Locking one or more colors in your graphic ensures that the most important colors — whether they're important for branding, a visual design, or both — can be maintained. After a color is locked, it does not change, regardless of the palette chosen. For example, you could preview your image by using the Web 216 palette, lock all the colors, and then switch to an Adaptive palette to broaden the color range, but keep the basic colors Web-safe. Web-safe colors are displayed in the swatches with a diamond symbol in them, and locked colors are identified by a square in the lower-right corner of the swatch, as shown in Figure 15-9.

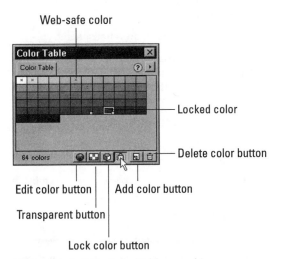

Figure 15-9: The Color Table panel is your window into an image's color index.

Tip   Clicking a pixel in the preview with the Pointer tool selects its color in the Color Table panel.

The Color Table panel's pop-up menu commands are detailed in Table 15-2, along with whether they are also represented by a button.

Table 15-2 Color Table Panel Pop-Up Commands		
Command	**Button**	**Description**
Rebuild Color Table	No	Rebuilds the color table swatches according to the settings in the Optimize panel.
Add Color	Yes	Allows you to insert an additional color into the current palette by choosing it from the system color picker(s).
Edit Color	Yes	Opens the system color picker(s) to permit a new color to be chosen to replace the selected color.
Delete Color	Yes	Removes the selected color(s).
Replace Palette Entry	No	Swaps the selected color for the color chosen through the system color picker(s).
Snap to Web Safe	Yes	Converts the selected color(s) to the closest color in the Web-safe palette.
Transparent	Yes	Makes the selected color(s) transparent.
Lock Color	Yes	Maintains the current color during any overall palette transformations, such as bit-depth reduction or palette changes. The color, however, can still be edited directly.
Unlock All Colors	No	Allows all colors to be changed.
Sort by Luminance	No	Sorts the current palette swatch set from brightest to darkest.
Sort by Popularity	No	Sorts the current palette swatch set from most pixels used to least pixels used.
Unsorted	No	Restores the default swatch arrangement.
Remove Edit	No	Reverts the swatch to its original color.
Remove All Edits	No	Restores the current palette to its original state.
Load Palette	No	Allows a palette to be loaded from a Adobe Color Table (ACT) file or from a GIF.
Save Palette	No	Stores the current palette as a Color Table file.

Tip All of these commands are also available from the shortcut menu that appears when you right-click (Control+click) an individual swatch.

Sort by popularity

The Sort by Popularity command is available from the Color Table's pop-up menu, and is very helpful when it's time to trim file size down by cutting colors. By default, the swatches are displayed in an unsorted order. After you choose Sort by Popularity from the pop-up menu, the most-used color is displayed first, in the upper-left corner, and the least-used color is shown last, in the lower-right corner. This makes it easy to select for deletion the colors that are least likely to be missed. You can Shift+click two colors to select them and the range between them, or Ctrl+click (Command+click) to select multiple swatches that are not adjacent to each other.

Matte

When a photograph is framed, the framer often mounts the image on a matte, which provides a different, contrasting background to make the photograph stand out. Fireworks uses the matte idea to allow the Web designer to export images with varying canvas colors — without changing the canvas. One of the biggest problems with GIF transparency are the unwanted "halos" that result from creating a drop shadow or other gradation against a different background. The traditional method of handling this problem is to change your canvas color in the graphics program to match the background color on the Web page. This solution works well for one-off-type graphics, but many Web designers find that they need to use the same graphic in many different situations, against many different backgrounds. The Matte feature enables you to keep one master graphic and export as many specific instances — against as many different mattes or canvases — as necessary, as shown in Figure 15-10.

Choosing a matte color is very straightforward: Simply click the Matte arrow button to display the standard pop-up color picker. From there, choose one of the swatches or sample a color by using the Eyedropper tool. To return a matte color to transparent, click the No Color button in the pop-up color picker.

Lossy GIF compression

Recall that the GIF format uses lossless compression; so what's this Loss option in the Optimize panel all about? The so-called Lossy GIF is not a new format at all, but rather a method for optimizing an image so that when it's actually saved as a GIF it will have a smaller file size.

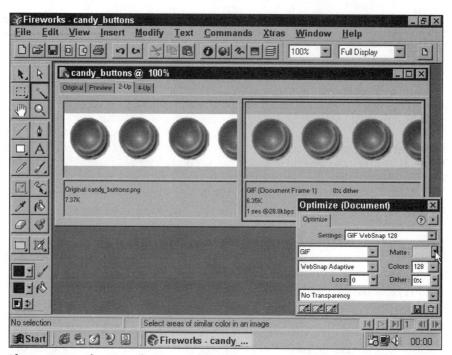

Figure 15-10: The Matte feature enables you to export your image against different canvas colors, without having to modify the original image.

New Feature

Fireworks 3 enables you to create even smaller GIF images in many cases with a Loss setting in the Optimize panel. This setting optimizes repeating patterns of pixels in an image to make it more attractive to the peculiarities of the GIF format's compression scheme.

The Loss option works to make your GIF smaller by finding similar repeating patterns of pixels and making them identical. The identical patterns compress better when you export your document as a GIF image, as shown in Figure 15-11. The Loss slider goes from 0 to 100, with a higher number meaning that more pixels are evaluated and made into similar patterns.

I find that the Loss option works for some images and not for others. Sometimes it will actually increase the resulting file size until you really get into a high Loss setting. For those times when it trims a particular image down to a much lower weight, you'll be happy to have this tool in your export toolkit.

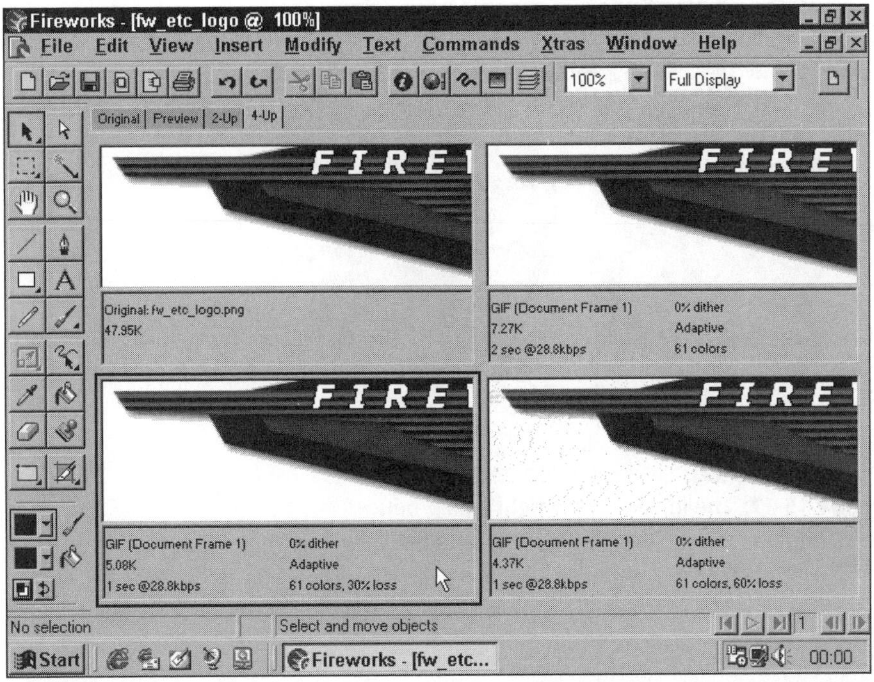

Figure 15-11: In the lower-left pane, the lossy compression at 30 percent is starting to become visible. In the lower-right pane, at 60 percent, it's unacceptably so.

Dither

One way—although not necessarily the best way—to break up areas of flat color caused by the lower color capabilities of GIF is to use the Dither option. When the Dither option is enabled, Fireworks simulates new colors by using a pattern of existing colors—exactly how the Web Dither fill is created. However, because dithering is not restricted to a single area, but instead is spread throughout the graphic, the dithering can be significantly more noticeable—dithering makes the image appear "dotty," as shown in Figure 15-12, and usually increases your file size. The degree of dithering is set by changing the Dither Amount slider or by entering the amount directly in the text box.

Transparency

One of the main reasons GIF is often selected as a format over JPEG is GIF's ability to specify any one color—and thus certain apparent areas—of the graphic transparent. As mentioned previously, transparency is the key to making nonrectangular-shaped graphics, and the Fireworks transparency controls (Figure 15-13) are the key to making transparency.

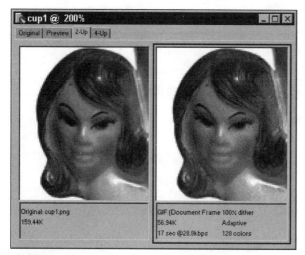

Figure 15-12: The image on the right was produced with dithering at 100 percent, causing the solid color to be heavily dotted.

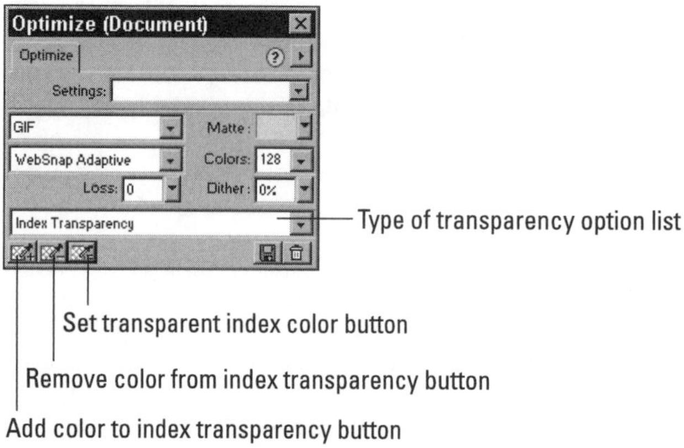

Type of transparency option list

Set transparent index color button

Remove color from index transparency button

Add color to index transparency button

Figure 15-13: Part of the power of the GIF format is the ability to make any color transparent.

The transparency controls in detail are as follows:

✦ **Type of Transparency option list:** Choose either No Transparency, Index Transparency, or Alpha Transparency to specify the transparency type. By default, the canvas color is initially made transparent.

✦ **Add Color to Index Transparency button:** Enables you to choose additional colors to make transparent, either from the swatch set or sampled directly from the previewed image.

✦ **Remove Color from Index Transparency button:** Converts transparent colors to their original color, either from the swatch set or sampled directly from the previewed image.

✦ **Set Transparent Index Color button:** Select to choose a single color to be transparent, either from the swatch set or sampled directly from the previewed image.

When a color is made transparent, its swatch and pixels in the Preview image are replaced with a gray-and-white checkerboard pattern, as shown in Figure 15-14. You can choose as many colors as you'd like to make transparent.

Figure 15-14: Part of the power of the GIF format is the ability to make any color transparent.

To make portions of your GIF image transparent, follow these steps:

1. Select a document window preview tab to view a preview of your document.

2. If the Optimize panel is not visible, choose Window ➪ Optimize to view it.

3. If necessary, select GIF from the Optimize panel's Export Format option list.

4. To make the canvas color transparent, select Index Transparency from the Type of Transparency option list.

5. To make a color other than the canvas transparent, click the Set Transparent Index Color button and sample a color either from a swatch or from the preview image.

Tip If you want to select a small area in your image for transparency, use the Zoom tool to magnify that selection before choosing the color.

6. To make more colors transparent, click the Add Color to Index Transparency button and sample the colors either from the swatch or from the Preview image.

7. To restore a transparent color to its original color, click the Remove Color from Index Transparency button and select the color either from a swatch or from the Preview image.

8. For even greater control, select a color or colors from the Color Table panel and click the Transparent button.

As noted in the Transparency option list description, two different types are available: Index and Alpha Transparency. Index Transparency allows you to make any color totally transparent — think of it as an On/Off switch; the color is either transparent or it isn't. Alpha Transparency, on the other hand, allows degrees of transparency — you can create tints and shades of a color. You'll find out more details about Alpha Transparency in the PNG section, later in this chapter.

Index Transparency is generally used for the GIF format, because, technically, only the PNG format truly supports Alpha Transparency. However, the Fireworks engineers have left Alpha Transparency enabled for GIFs, to achieve a slightly different effect. When Alpha Transparency is chosen, a new color register is created for the canvas and then made transparent. How is this different from converting the canvas color to transparent, as occurs with Index Transparency? If you've ever created an image where part of the graphic is the same color as the background — the white of a person's eyes is also the white of a canvas — you'll quickly understand and appreciate this feature. Basically, Alpha Transparency, as applied in Fireworks' GIF format, leaves your palette alone and just makes the canvas transparent, as shown in Figure 15-15.

Figure 15-15: The Alpha Transparency feature enabled me to make the white background of this image transparent without also making the white areas within the subject transparent.

> **Note**
>
> If you don't notice a new color register being added when you select Alpha Transparency, check to see whether the Optimized option is enabled. If it is, Fireworks may combine other colors to keep the same number of colors.

Remove unused colors

The Remove Unused Colors option — which is enabled by default — is a Fireworks-only feature that causes the program to discard duplicate and unused colors from a palette. This can seriously reduce your file size, particularly when choosing one of the fixed palettes, such as Web 216 or either of the operating system palettes. Find the Remove Unused Colors option on the Optimize panel's pop-up menu.

Interlaced

The Interlaced option on the Optimize panel's pop-up menu enables a GIF property that displays a file as it downloads. The file is shown in progressively finer detail as more information is transferred from the server to the browser. Although a graphic exported with the Interlaced option won't download any faster, it provides a visual cue to Web page visitors that something is happening. Interlacing graphics is a matter of taste; some Web designers don't design a page without them; others are vehemently opposed to their use.

Saved settings

Four of the six presets in the Saved Settings option list in the Optimize panel relate to the GIF format:

✦ **GIF Web 216:** Sets the GIF format using the Web 216 palette. The Optimized and Dither options are enabled.

✦ **GIF WebSnap 256:** Sets the GIF format using the WebSnap Adaptive palette and a maximum of 256 colors. The Optimized option is enabled.

✦ **GIF WebSnap 128:** Sets the GIF format using the WebSnap Adaptive palette and a maximum of 128 colors. The Optimized option is enabled.

✦ **GIF Adaptive 256:** Sets the GIF format using the Adaptive palette and a maximum of 256 colors. The Optimized option is enabled.

Use these settings as they are when exporting GIFs, or use them as a starting point for your own optimizations.

Fireworks technique: creating GIF-friendly images

Before you even get to the Optimize panel, an image can be made more GIF-friendly by paying attention to the patterns of pixels that make up the image, and understanding how the GIF format compresses pixels. Taking a little time to create more GIF-friendly images can be an even more effective means of reducing export file size than the obvious methods offered by Fireworks' export tools.

The easiest way to create a GIF-friendly document is to include large areas of flat color. Any changes from pixel to pixel are less compressible than large similar areas. A small experiment shows just how much the GIF format loves flat color. Create a new document, 400 × 400 pixels, and choose a canvas color. Click on the Preview tab of the document window and note the tiny export file size of about 600 bytes, or 0.6K (you may have to stretch the document window to see the file size). Switch back to the Original tab and use the Pencil tool to draw a large *X* through your document, touching each corner. Go back to Preview and note that your file size has increased to about 1.74K — or almost triple — all for that skinny, penciled X.

The next best thing to large areas of flat color in the GIF format is horizontal lines. GIF compresses pixels from left to right, so a horizontal line of identically-colored pixels is very compressible. Without compression, a line of red pixels might be expressed as "red pixel, red pixel, red pixel, red pixel, red pixel." You can see that expressing just five pixels takes a lot of explaining. With GIF compression, that same line might be "red pixel × 5." That's a dramatic savings in and of itself, but "red pixel × 300" is an even more dramatic savings than spelling out each pixel in turn. It's obvious that paying a little attention to using horizontal lines in your designs can minimize GIF file size.

The simplest way to put more horizontal lines into your images is to replace complex, chaotic texture fills such as Fiber with a simpler, horizontal lines texture, as shown in Figure 15-16. The two documents are identical except that the one on the left uses a 50% Fiber texture fill in the circle, and the one on the right uses a 50% Lines texture fill. Other export settings are the same, but the one with the Lines texture is one quarter of the weight.

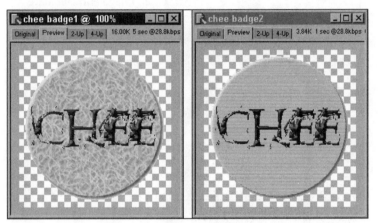

Figure 15-16: Replacing a Fiber fill with an alternating lines texture reduced the export file size from 16K to less than 4K (note the export file sizes next to the preview tabs) because of the compressibility of long horizontal lines of similar pixels in the GIF format.

Look in the Textures folder and find the Lines texture used in Figure 15-16, as well as multiple variations of horizontal lines textures.

Another way to make an image more GIF-friendly is to reduce areas of stray pixels. Sometimes an area of otherwise flat color will have some randomly-placed pixels of colors one or two shades away. When viewed at 100%, these pixels may not be obvious, but their random nature is reducing the GIF-compressibility of your image. Zooming in and cleaning up those stray pixels is optimization-time well spent.

Tip One way to end up with lots of stray pixels is to work from a JPEG original. Sometimes an image goes through a few hands before it ends up in yours. I've had clients submit flat-color artwork such as illustrations or logos — obvious candidates for GIF export — as JPEGs, in spite of my protestations. What's worse, they've lost the original PNG or TIFF files. As good as the JPEG format can be for photographic images, it mangles areas of flat color, creating lots of unsightly and uncompressible stray pixels. Use this technique to reduce or eliminate stray pixels and reclaim the image for the GIF format.

You can use the Pencil tool to clean up areas of stray pixels, as shown in Figure 15-17. Drawing the predominant flat color over the strays creates more areas of flat horizontal lines, often dramatically reducing export file size.

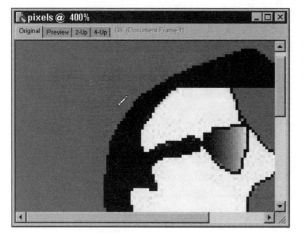

Figure 15-17: Zoom in on an image and eliminate stray pixels to create bigger areas of flat color that compress better upon GIF export.

To zap stray pixels, follow these steps:

1. Choose the Pencil tool from the toolbox.
2. Select the eyedropper from the Stroke color well on the toolbox, and sample a predominant flat color from your image.
3. Use the Pencil tool to color over stray pixels that are adjacent to that flat color, converting them to the flat color.
4. Repeat steps 2 and 3 until you have flattened as many areas of stray pixels as possible.

Tip While you're zoomed in on your image, Choose Window ➪ New Window to create a new, 100% window to monitor how your changes are affecting your image at its true size.

Exporting Photographic Images

Photographic images are most often displayed in 24-bit True Color, in a format such as JPEG, rather than the limited palette of an indexed color image, such as a GIF. Photographic images contain subtle gradations that are not easily reproduced in fewer colors and yet are dithered quite serviceably by the browser if the client machine is running in a 256-color video mode.

What's more, the JPEG format excels at compressing the smooth tones of a photographic images down to unbelievably small file sizes without an appreciable loss of quality. The fact that the JPEG format is so good at the things the GIF format fails miserably at is part of the reason for their enduring, successful partnership as the king and queen of Web graphics formats.

The True Color formats that Fireworks exports are detailed in Table 15-3:

Table 15-3 True Color Export Formats	
Format	**Description**
JPEG	Joint Photographic Experts Group image file format. Used for almost all of the true color images on the Web. Uses lossy compression to achieve maximum reduction in file size.
PNG 24, PNG 32	Portable Network Graphic. Offers lossless compression that results in larger file sizes than JPEG—often much larger—but maintains pristine quality.
TIFF 24, TIFF 32	Tag Image File Format. Print artists commonly use 24- and 32-bit TIFFs, although they are not suitable for the Web.
BMP 24	Microsoft Bitmap image. The native graphics format of Microsoft Windows. Not suitable for the Web, but a good way to share images between Windows applications.
PICT 24 (Macintosh only)	Macintosh Picture. The native graphics format of Mac OS. Vectors are not supported by Fireworks. Not suitable for the Web, but a good way to share image files between Mac applications.

Of all the formats in Table 15-3, only JPEG and PNG 24 can be used on the Web. PNG 32's alpha mask is ignored by browsers, rendering it the same as PNG 24. If you want to display an image with the highest quality, regardless of file size, then PNG 24 is a good choice. If bandwidth is an issue at all — and it's very rare that it isn't — then JPEG is the better choice, providing excellent quality photographic images in a much smaller file size than PNG.

To alter the bit depth for an exported image, choose a lower bit-depth export format from the Optimize panel's Export Format option list. Instead of PNG 32, for example, choose PNG 24. While a change from 24-bit to 8-bit means lowering the maximum number of colors supported, a change from 32-bit to 24-bit supports the same colors, but removes the alpha mask. The upper 8-bits of a 32-bit image are always an alpha channel — an 8-bit grayscale image that defines the image's transparency.

For more about alpha masks, see Chapter 13.

JPEG

Whereas GIFs generally are made smaller by lowering the number of colors used, JPEGs use a sliding scale that creates smaller file sizes by eliminating pixels. This sliding scale is built on a *lossy* algorithm, so-called because the lower the scale, the more pixels are lost. The JPEG algorithm is a very good one and you can significantly reduce the file size by lowering the JPEG Quality setting.

Other characteristics of the JPEG format include:

✦ JPEG images are capable of displaying over 16 million colors. This wide color range, also referred to as *24-bit,* enables the subtle shades of a photograph to be depicted easily.

✦ Although JPEG images can display almost any color, none of the colors can be made transparent. Consequently, any image that requires transparency in a Web browser must be stored as a GIF.

✦ For JPEG images to be viewed as they are downloaded, they must be stored as Progressive JPEGs, which appear to develop onscreen, like an interlaced GIF. Progressive JPEGs have a slightly better compression engine and can produce smaller file sizes.

Internet Explorer doesn't fully support Progressive JPEGs. They are displayed just as if they were not Progressive, though, so there's no harm in using them.

Quality

The major method for altering a JPEG's file size is by changing the Quality value. In Fireworks, the Quality value is gauged as a percentage, and the slider goes from 0 percent to 100 percent. Higher values mean less compression, and lower values mean that more pixels are discarded. Trying to reduce a JPEG's file size by lowering the Quality slider is always worthwhile; you can also enter a value directly in the text box. The JPEG compression algorithm is so good that almost every continuous-tone image can be reduced in file size without significant loss of quality, as shown in Figure 15-18. On the other hand, increasing a JPEG's Quality value from its initial setting is never helpful. Whereas JPEG is very good at losing pixels to reduce file size, adding pixels to increase quality never works — you'll only increase the file's size and download time.

Figure 15-18: Each of these three previews uses a different JPEG quality value; only when the quality is lowered significantly does the image become unacceptable.

Tip   With the JPEG image-compression algorithm, the initial elements of an image that are "compressed away" are least noticeable. Subtle variations in brightness and hue are the first to disappear. With additional compression, the image grows darker and less varied in its color range.

A good technique for comparing JPEG images in Fireworks is to use the 4-Up preview option. The upper-left pane shows your original document, so that you always have an image on which to base your comparisons. In another view, reduce the

Quality to about 75 percent or so. If that image is acceptable, reduce the Quality setting to 50 percent in another view. By then, you'll probably start to get some unwanted artifacts, so use the fourth window to try a setting midway between the last acceptable and the unacceptable Quality settings, such as 65 percent. Be sure to view your images at 100 percent magnification. That's how your Web audience will see them, so you should too.

Tip Don't forget that you can stretch the document window to a larger size to increase the size of the multiple preview panes.

Sharpening edges

Graphics on the Web are often a montage of photographs, illustrations, and text. Although JPEG is the right choice for a continuous tone image, such as a photograph, it can make text that overlays a photograph appear fuzzy, because JPEG is far better at compressing gradations than it is at compressing images with hard edges and abrupt color changes. To overcome these obstacles, use Fireworks' Sharpen JPEG Edges option, which can be found on the Optimize panel's pop-up menu.

As the name implies, Sharpen JPEG Edges restores some of the hard-edge transitions that are lost during JPEG compression. This is especially noticeable on text and simple graphics, such as rectangles, superimposed on photographs. The other point to notice about Sharpen is that it can significantly increase your file size: in Figure 15-19, the unsharpened image on the lower left is 15.77K, whereas the Sharpen-enabled version on the lower right at a whopping 25% less Quality is only a few K smaller at 12.45K. The Sharpen JPEG Edges option is another tool whose use requires that you always keep an eye on the balance between image quality and file size, but it is very useful for certain images.

Smoothing

The more that a JPEG file is compressed, the "blockier" it becomes. As the compression increases, the JPEG algorithm throws out more and more similar pixels — after a certain point, the transitions and gradations are lost and areas become flat color blocks.

Fireworks' Smoothing feature slightly blurs the overall image so that any stray pixels resulting from the compression are less noticeable. The Smoothing scale in the Optimize panel runs from zero to eight. Smoothing offers two benefits: it reduces the blockiness that is sometimes evident with JPEG compression and also slightly decreases file size.

Just as images with lots of straight lines or text benefit from the Sharpen JPEG Edges setting, Smoothing works best for images with lots of curves and generally smooth shapes.

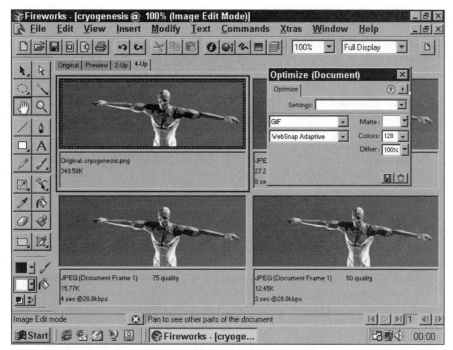

Figure 15-19: The lower-left preview could only be reduced to 75% Quality before it became unacceptably blurry. With the Sharpen JPEG Edges option enabled for the lower-right preview, it could be further reduced to 50% Quality while still maintaining the blocky look of the subject.

Progressive

To most, Progressive JPEG is seen only as an incremental display option for JPEGs, much like Interlaced for the GIF format. The Progressive JPEG option on the Optimize panel's pop-up menu is more than that though: it actually enables a different compression algorithm — a second generation one — that many times offers lower file sizes at the equivalent quality of the original JPEG compression. The Progressive JPEG format was developed by Netscape, but has won the support of recent browser versions from Microsoft, as well.

> **Note**   Although Internet Explorer displays Progressive JPEG images, it displays them without the progressive look of developing as they download. They seem to the user to be regular JPEG images.

In practice, I find that enabling the Progressive JPEG option often gives me a smaller file size, but not always. For me, choosing this option generally depends on whether the client prefers to see the images slowly develop as they download or prefers them to download completely and appear as a finished image.

PNG 32 and 24

As a Web format, PNG is still in its infancy—well, maybe early childhood—as far as general browser acceptance is concerned. The PNG format holds great promise for Web graphics. Combining the best of both worlds, PNG has lossless compression, like GIF, and is capable of millions of colors, like JPEG. Moreover, PNG offers an interlace scheme that appears much more quickly than either GIF or JPEG, as well as transparency support that is far superior to both other formats.

One valuable aspect of the PNG format makes the display of PNG pictures appear more uniform across various computer platforms. Generally, graphics made on a PC look brighter on a Macintosh, and Mac-made images seem darker on a PC. PNG includes *gamma correction* capabilities that alter the image depending on the computer used by the viewer.

Until recently, the various browsers supported PNG only through plug-ins. After PNG was endorsed as a new Web graphic format by the World Wide Web Consortium (W3C), both Netscape and Microsoft 4.0 browser versions added native, inline support of the new format. Perhaps most importantly, however, Macromedia's Dreamweaver was among the first Web-authoring tools to offer native PNG support. Inserted PNG images preview in the document window just like GIFs and JPEGs do. Then, Fireworks was introduced, which not only allows you to export PNG image, but uses PNG as its own format.

Although support for PNG is growing steadily, browser support currently is not widespread enough to warrant a total switch-over to the PNG format. PNG is capable of many more features, such as Alpha Transparency, that are not fully in use by any major browser. Interestingly enough, Fireworks is way ahead of most other graphic programs in its support of PNG. Greg Roelofs, one of the developers of the PNG format and the keeper of the PNG home page at http://www.libpng.org/pub/png/>, calls Fireworks, "the best PNG-supporting image editor available."

Unlike an Index Transparency color, which is either completely transparent or completely opaque, an Alpha Transparent color can be partially transparent—in fact, the transparency can use as many as 256 gradations. This allows a 32-bit image to be easily composited with other images, meaning that although PNG is not yet the best choice for the browser, it is an excellent choice for creating graphics for use in multimedia presentations such as Shockwave or Flash movies, where animated objects are often stacked on top of each other, or composited with different backgrounds. Director and Flash are also both happy to import your actual Fireworks PNG files, Fireworks header and all.

Caution   The Fireworks native PNG format is considered an extended PNG format, because of the additional effects, text, and other data included in the header of each file. Other programs capable of generally displaying PNG files may show the basic Fireworks image, but won't be able to edit it in the same way. To display a file in PNG format on a Web page, it's best to specify PNG as the format when you export so that your PNG image lacks extra Fireworks information and is as small as possible.

Other formats

The issues that are involved in exporting a PNG 24 or PNG 32 image are the same as those for exporting a TIFF, BMP, or PICT (Macintosh only) image from Fireworks. Generally, this export is straightforward, involving only the Matte setting.

Working in the Export Preview

As convenient as it is to optimize and preview images in Fireworks' workspace, you may sometimes find that you want to access all of the export features in one centralized location. Fireworks' Export Preview dialog box (Figure 15-20) is just the place, and offers some extra export options that are unavailable in the workspace, to boot.

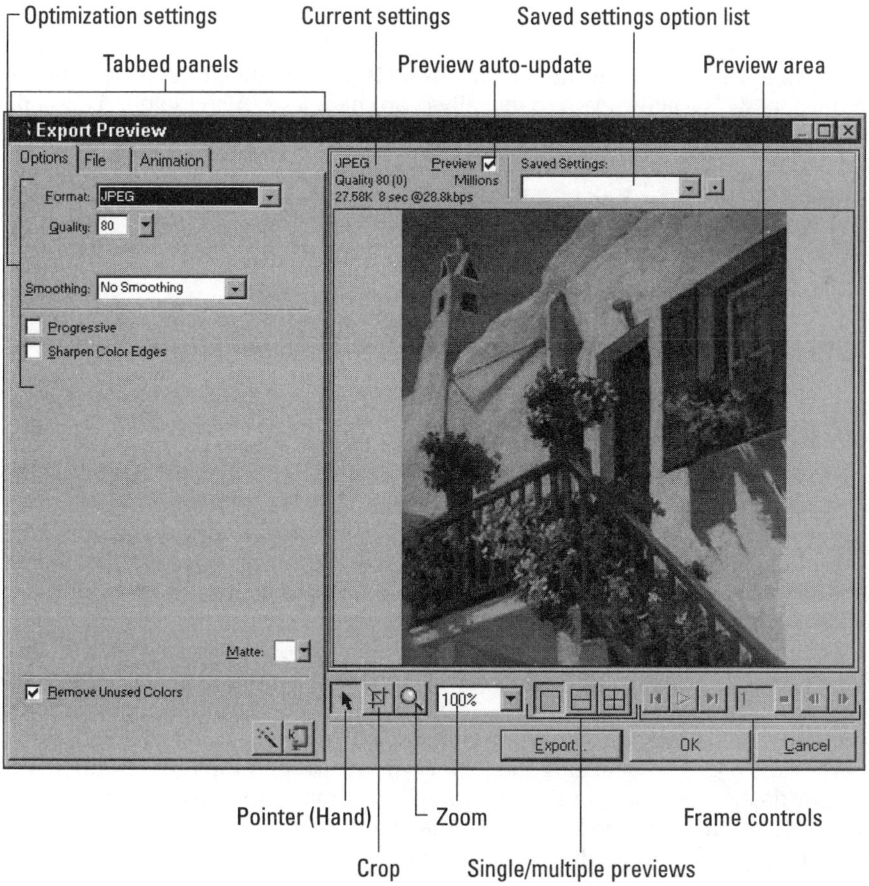

Figure 15-20: The Export Preview dialog box centralizes Fireworks export features, and offers a few special features of its own.

The three tabbed panels in the Export Preview dialog box are as follows:

✦ **Options:** The primary panel for optimizing your image. The file format, bit-depth, compression, transparency, and other preferences are selected here. All color control — such as locking, editing, and deleting colors — is handled here, as well. The controls here are analogous to those found in the Optimize and Color Table panels.

✦ **File:** Controls two aspects of an exported file — scale and numeric cropping. The exported image can be resized either by a percentage or to a precise pixel measurement. The image can be cropped by entering X and Y coordinates for the upper-left corner, and width and height dimensions of the new area. In Fireworks, the exported image can also be cropped visually in the Preview area.

✦ **Animation:** Contains all the settings for running an animated GIF, including the frame delay, disposal method, and looping preferences. Many of these options are also available in the Frames panel when you're optimizing in the workspace.

The always-visible Preview area provides a visual reference to compare different settings, and also allows you to visually crop the image. Also included are a panning tool (the Pointer), a Zoom tool (the magnifying glass), and a VCR-like control for playing an animation or other multiframe file. You may experience some *déjà vu* as you look around the Export Preview dialog box. Many of the controls are the same or very similar to those you use when optimizing in the workspace, and with good reason. There's no need to learn the Export Preview dialog box from scratch.

As previously mentioned, the Export Preview dialog box does contain some additional, unique export features, such as cropping and scaling exported images.

Cropping

The Export Area tool found on the Toolbox as part of the Pointer flyout might seem a logical place to define an export area within the document window, but using the Export Area tool is only a first step to exporting an image with the Export Preview dialog box. In other words, although the Export Area tool is used in the document window, it's not part of the document window's in-place preview or export.

You can export a cropped version of a document by outlining an area with the Export Area tool and double-clicking that area to open the Export Preview dialog box, or you can simply open the Export Preview dialog box directly and then crop your image in its preview. When you initiate a cropping session in the Export Preview dialog box by clicking the Export Area button in the Preview area, the familiar dashed cropping outline surrounds the image, as shown in Figure 15-21. The eight handles are used to narrow the exported area. The original image is not permanently cropped or altered in any way.

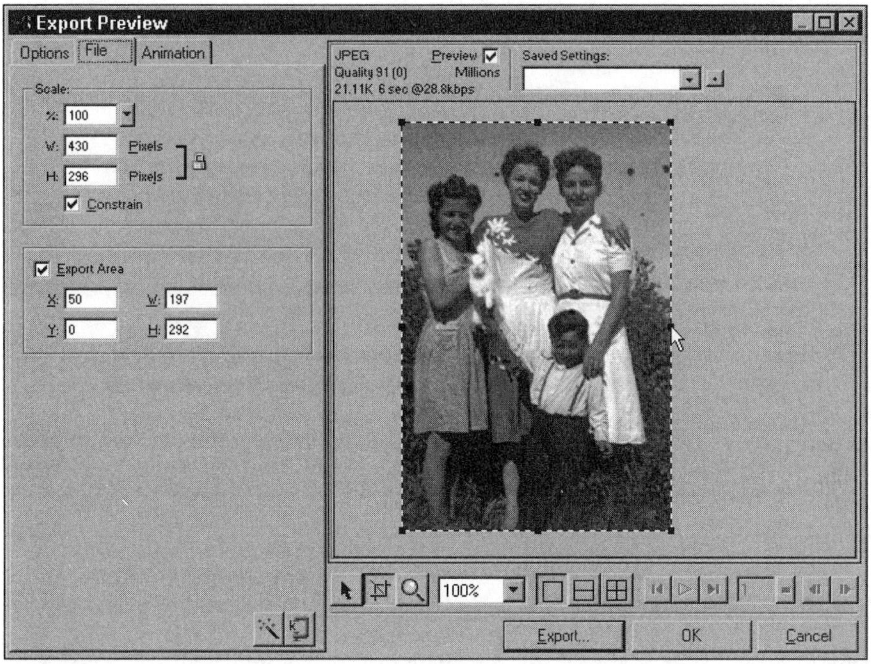

Figure 15-21: In Fireworks, you can crop visually right in the Export Preview dialog box.

> **Note**
>
> Unlike the regular Crop tool in the document window, the Export Area tool can't be used to expand the boundaries of the canvas.

If the File panel is displayed in the Export Preview while you're cropping, the X and Y coordinates of the upper-left corner of your exported area, as well as the width and height dimensions, are visible. The numeric cropping information is updated each time after a cropping handle is dragged to a new position. Alternatively, you can adjust the visual cropping precisely by entering values in the appropriate Export Area text boxes.

> **Tip**
>
> You can also crop an image by selecting an area in the document window with the Export Area tool (the camera on the flyout under the Pointer tool) and double-clicking the area. The Export Preview opens and you can export your cropped image without affecting the original.

To crop an image visually, follow these steps:

1. Choose either the Export Area tool beneath the Preview window(s) or the Export Area option on the File panel. An outline with cropping handles appears around the image.

2. Drag the handles to a new position so that only the area you want to export is displayed.

3. Choose any other tool (Pointer or Zoom), or click either the Set Defaults or the Next button to accept the new cropped area.

To crop an image numerically, follow these steps:

1. From the File panel, select the Export Area option.

2. Select a new upper-left coordinate by entering new values in the X and/or Y text boxes, and press Tab to accept the changed value.

3. Select a new image size by entering new values in the W (Width) and H (Height) text boxes, and press Tab to accept the changed value.

Both cropping methods — visual and numeric — work together as well as separately. While viewing the File panel, select the Export Area tool and crop the image visually. When you release the mouse button, the numeric values automatically update. Similarly, change the numeric values, and the visual display is redrawn.

Scaling exported images

It might seem redundant to note that "Web graphics come in all shapes and sizes" — except it's also true to say that the *same* Web graphic often comes in different shapes and sizes. Reusing graphic elements is a very key design strategy in product branding in most media, and the technique is especially useful on the Web. Fireworks makes it very easy to export resized or cropped graphics from a master file, through the Export Preview dialog box.

Scaling controls can be found under the File tab in the Export Preview dialog box. You can resize a graphic by specifying either a percentage or an exact pixel size. By default, all rescaling is constrained to the original height-to-width ratio — however, you can disable the Constrain option to alter one dimension separately from the other.

To resize an image, follow these steps:

1. From the Export Preview dialog box, select the File panel.

2. To rescale an image by percentage, use the % slider or enter a value directly into the % text box.

    The % slider's range is from 1 percent to 200 percent, but you can enter any value in the text box.

3. To resize an image to an exact dimension, enter a figure in the W (Width) and/or H (Height) text box.

If the Constrain option is selected, enter a value in just one of the dimension text boxes and press Tab. The other dimension will be calculated for you according to the image's original height-to-width ratio.

4. To alter the height-to-width ratio, deselect Constrain and perform Step 3.

Tip   One of my favorite image optimization techniques is to scale an image to 50 percent of its size upon export and then place it in an HTML page at double size; doubling the width and height attributes of the img tag. The effects of this are usually noticeable, but often not objectionable, especially for flat color images. One thing's for sure: there's no faster way to halve the weight of an exported document. Experiment with this technique and see if it works for you.

Using the Export Wizards

Fireworks' export options are very full-featured and can certainly be overwhelming if you're new to Web graphics. If you're not even sure how best to begin optimizing your image, let one of Fireworks' Export Wizards guide you. In addition to the original Export Wizard, which is very helpful for selecting the appropriate file format, Fireworks introduces the Export to Size Wizard, to meet those absolute file-size limits.

If you are ready to export but don't know where to start, bring up Fireworks' Export Wizard, which not only helps you to determine the correct file format best suited to the graphic's purpose, but it also provides you with an alternative in certain cases. For this reason, seasoned Web designers can also use the Export Wizard to get quickly to a jumping-off place for further optimization.

Regardless of the selection that the Export Wizard makes for you, it always presents you with a visual display through the Export Preview dialog box, covered extensively earlier in this chapter. Feel free to either accept the recommendations of the Export Wizard as is — and click the Next button to complete the operation — or tweak the settings first before you proceed.

The Export Wizard has three primary uses:

✦ To help you select an export format.

✦ To offer suggestions to optimize your image after you select an export format.

✦ To recommend export modes that will reduce a graphic to a specified file size.

To use the Export Wizard to select an export format, follow these steps:

1. Choose File ➪ Export Wizard.

   The initial screen of the Export Wizard appears, as shown in Figure 15-22.

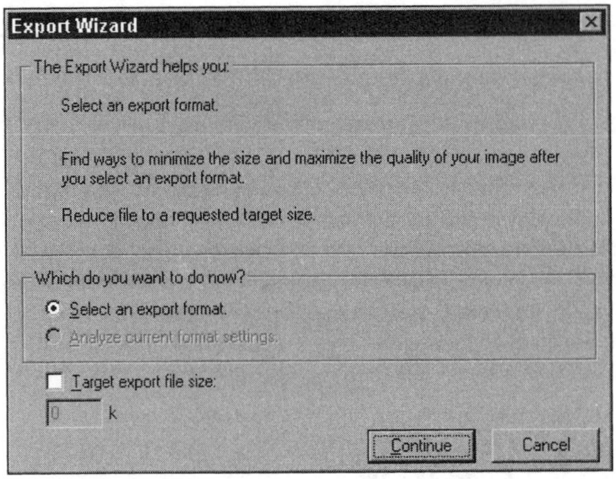

Export Wizard   ☒

The Export Wizard helps you:

　　Select an export format.

　　Find ways to minimize the size and maximize the quality of your image after
　　you select an export format.

　　Reduce file to a requested target size.

Which do you want to do now?
　⦿ Select an export format.
　○ Analyze current format settings.

☐ Target export file size:
　　0　　k

　　　　　　　　　　　　　　　[Continue]　　[Cancel]

Figure 15-22: The Export Wizard provides a good
launchpad for export selections.

2. With the "Select an export format" option selected, click Continue.

3. The next screen of the Export Wizard appears and offers four choices for the
graphic's ultimate destination:

- **The Web:** Restricts the export options to the most popular Web formats,
GIF and JPEG.

- **An image-editing application:** Selects the best format for continuing
to edit the image in another program, such as Photoshop. Generally,
Fireworks selects the TIFF format.

- **Desktop publishing application:** Selects the best print format, typically
TIFF.

- **Dreamweaver:** The same as The Web option, restricts the export
options to the most popular Web formats, GIF and JPEG.

Note　If your graphic uses frames, the Export Wizard asks instead whether your file is to
be exported as an Animated GIF, a JavaScript button rollover, or a single image file.

4. Click Continue after you make your choice.

Fireworks presents its analysis of your image, with suggestions on how to narrow the selection further, if more than one export choice is recommended.

Caution　If you select Animated GIF as your destination for your multiframe image, you
must select the resulting Preview window to display the details in the Options
panel.

5. Click Exit to open the Export Preview dialog box and complete the export
operation.

If you choose either The Web or Dreamweaver for your graphic's export destination, Fireworks presents you with two options for comparison: a GIF and a JPEG. The file in the upper Preview window is the smallest file size. Fireworks is fairly conservative in this aspect of the Export Wizard and does not attempt to seriously reduce the file size at the cost of image quality.

If you'd like to limit the file size while selecting an export format, select the "Target export file size" option on the Export Wizard's first screen. After you enable this option, you need to enter a file size value in the adjacent text box. File size is always measured in kilobytes. After you enter a file size, click Continue for Fireworks to calculate the results.

When Fireworks attempts to fit a graphic into a particular file size, it exports the image up to 12 times to find the best size with the least compression. Although it's usually very fast, this process can take several minutes to complete with a large graphic. Again, for graphics intended for the Web, Fireworks presents two choices — both at, or under, your specified target size.

In addition to specifying a file size through the Export Wizard, you can choose the Export to File Size Wizard by clicking the button on the Options panel of the Export Preview dialog box. The Export to File Size Wizard opens a simple dialog box that asks for the specified file size. The major difference between this wizard and the Export File Size option on the Export Wizard is that the Export to File Size Wizard works only with the current format — no alternative choices are offered. Consequently, the Export to File Size Wizard is faster, but it's intended more for the intermediate-to-advanced user who understands the differences between file formats.

Additional Export Options

The vast majority of the time graphics are exported from Fireworks by using the in-place workspace preview and the Optimize panel. However, Fireworks also offers several extra export options, including:

✦ Export all layers separately.

✦ Export all frames separately.

✦ Export all slice objects separately.

All the preceding items can be exported as one of the following:

✦ A separate graphics file

✦ A Cascading Style Sheet (CSS) layer for use in Dynamic-HTML-capable browsers

✦ Image Well format, used in Lotus Domino

✦ Vector artwork in Flash SWF or Adobe Illustrator formats

All of these additional export methods are grouped under the File ➪ Export Special submenu. In fact, even though six separate commands exist, each command displays the same dialog box (Figure 15-23) with different options set.

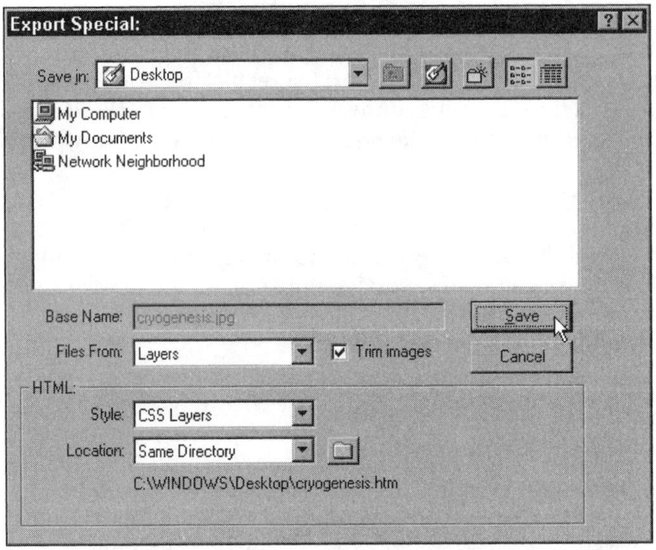

Figure 15-23: The Export Special dialog box handles a variety of individual export situations.

> **Tip**   Regardless of which Export Special operation you undertake, the current settings in the Optimize panel determine the file format and other settings.

Exporting single slices

The File ➪ Export Special ➪ Selected Slice command is useful for exporting a single slice as a file.

To export a single slice, follow these steps:

1. Select the slice that you want to export.

2. Choose Window ➪ Optimize to view the Optimize panel if it is not already visible.

3. Specify export settings in the Optimize panel. These settings affect only the selected slice.

4. Choose File ➪ Export Special ➪ Selected Slice.

   The Export Special dialog box appears.

5. Navigate to a folder to export your slice, and specify a filename.

6. Click Save when you're done.

Your selected slice is exported as an individual image file.

Exporting files

Occasionally, you need to break up the component parts of your graphic — layers, frames, and slice objects — for use as a separate file. Perhaps you need to reuse some of these elements in another part of the Web site, or maybe you want to process the files in another application before reintegrating them in Fireworks. Whatever the reason, Fireworks provides a fairly straightforward method for generating separate graphic files for almost any situation.

Because each component is potentially stored as an individual file, Fireworks must assign a unique filename for each file. Each of the components uses a slightly different naming scheme. Both frames and slice objects combine a *base name,* selected in the Export Special dialog box, with a generated extension. Frames add _Fnn as a suffix, where *nn* is a number starting with 01 and incrementing for each frame. For example, exporting separate files from a graphic with three frames with the Base Name of myFrame would result in three files: myFrame01, myFrame02, and myFrame03.

Files created from slice objects, on the other hand, are named according to the current Auto-Naming scheme found in the Document Properties dialog box. By default, slice objects use an extension based on their row and column position in a completed table, such as mySlice_r1_c1 for a slice with the base name of mySlice found in row 1, column 1 of a table. You can override these automatic names by deselecting the Auto-Name Slices option in the Objects panel and entering a unique slice name. The Export Special command then uses those unique names.

Fireworks layers do not require a base name and suffix combination — instead, each file created from a layer takes its filename from the actual layer names used in Fireworks. By default, Fireworks names new layers sequentially (Layer 1, Layer 2, Layer 3, and so on). However, you can personalize a layer by double-clicking its name or by choosing the Layer Options command from the Layers panel pop-up menu.

To export a Fireworks element as a separate file, follow these steps:

1. Specify format and optimization settings in the Optimize panel.

2. Choose File ⇨ Export Special ⇨ Layers/Frames to Files.

The Export Special dialog box appears.

3. Select the Fireworks component (Layers, Slice Objects, or Frames) to export from the Files From option list.

4. Select the Trim images option to export the individual components on the smallest-sized canvas necessary.

    If Trim images is not selected, each exported file will be the same dimensions as the original image.

5. For frames and slice objects, select a new Base Name, if desired.

6. Make sure that the HTML Style option is set to None.

7. Browse to the desired folder to store the images.

8. Click Save when you're ready.

Tip   You can control which frames or layers are exported by turning off their visibility in their respective panels. The visibility is controlled by the Eye symbol in the far-left column, next to each item name. If the frame or layer is not visible when the Export Special command is run, it's not exported.

Exporting as CSS layers

The term *layers* is used quite often in the Web graphics field. To the Photoshop user, a "layer" is a division capable of holding a single graphic element. In Fireworks, a "layer" can hold any number of objects and is a useful organizational tool. In Dynamic HTML and in Web-authoring tools such as Dreamweaver, a "layer" is a type of container that can be precisely positioned, hidden, or displayed — or flown across the screen. These types of layers are created by using a standard known as Cascading Style Sheets (CSS). Fireworks enables you to save any of its components while generating the HTML required for putting those components in a separate CSS layer. This facility enables you to achieve effects such as the "flying" buttons in Figure 15-24.

To export Fireworks components as CSS layers, follow these steps:

1. Specify format and optimization settings in the Optimize panel.

2. Choose File ⇨ Export Special ⇨ CSS Layers.

    The Export Special dialog box appears.

3. Select the Fireworks component (Layers, Slice Objects, or Frames) to export from the Files From option list.

4. Select the Trim images option to export the individual components on the smallest-sized canvas necessary.

    If Trim images is not selected, each exported file will be the same dimensions as the original image.

5. For frames and slice objects, select a new Base Name, if desired.

6. Make sure that the HTML Style option is set to CSS Layers.

7. Determine where the HTML file should be stored by selecting an option from the Location option list: Same Directory, One Level Up, or Custom.

   Selecting Custom (or clicking the Browse button) opens the standard Save As dialog box, which can be used for selecting a new folder and filename.

8. Browse to the desired folder to store the images.

9. Click Save when you're ready.

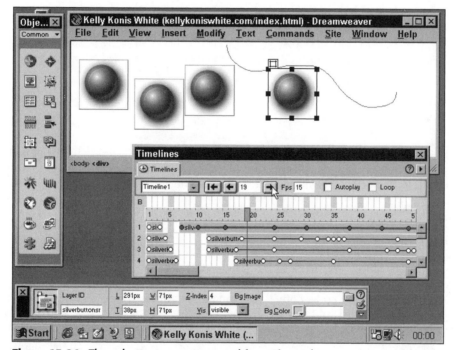

Figure 15-24: These buttons were exported from Fireworks as separate CSS layers and then animated here in Dreamweaver to fly into place.

After you complete the export process, you'll have both the separate images and the HTML necessary to place each image in its own CSS layer. To use the layers on your Web page, you need to incorporate the generated code into your own Web page. You can accomplish this with any Web-authoring tool that allows you to access the HTML directly. If you look at the HTML in a text editor such as Windows' Notepad or the Mac's SimpleText, the code looks like this in the `<body>` section of the document:

```
<! ---------- BEGIN COPYING THE CODE HERE ---------->

<div id="silverbuttonsr1c1" style="position:absolute; left:2px;
top:5px;width:71px; height:70px;z-index:1;
visibility:visible"><img name="silver_buttons_r1_c1"
```

```
src="images/silver_buttons_r1_c1.png" width="71" height="70"
border="0"></div>
<div id="silverbuttonsr1c2" style="position:absolute;
left:77px; top:4px;width:71px; height:71px;z-index:2;
visibility:visible"><img name="silver_buttons_r1_c2"
src="images/silver_buttons_r1_c2.png" width="71" height="71"
border="0"></div>
<div id="silverbuttonsr1c3" style="position:absolute;
left:152px; top:4px;width:71px; height:71px;z-index:3;
visibility:visible"><img name="silver_buttons_r1_c3"
src="images/silver_buttons_r1_c3.png" width="71" height="71"
border="0"></div>
<div id="silverbuttonsr1c4" style="position:absolute;
left:481px; top:69px;width:71px; height:71px;z-index:4;
visibility:visible"><img name="silver_buttons_r1_c4"
src="images/silver_buttons_r1_c4.png" width="71" height="71"
border="0"></div>

<! ---------- STOP COPYING THE CODE HERE ---------->
```

Although the code can appear quite overwhelming initially, only the plain-English phrases that bracket it are important for incorporating the code. In your favorite HTML or text editor, select the code from the line

```
<! ---------- BEGIN COPYING THE CODE HERE ---------->
```

and end your selection with the line

```
<! ---------- STOP COPYING THE CODE HERE ---------->
```

After you select the code, copy it and then open your working HTML page and paste the Clipboard contents anywhere in the <body> section. Now, you can continue to manipulate the layers however you like in your Web-authoring program.

Note Dreamweaver users don't have to use the HTML Source window or any other text tool to copy and paste the Fireworks code. In Dreamweaver, just find the Invisible Element symbols that enclose the layer code — you'll see a Dreamweaver HTML comment symbol on either side of the layer symbols. Select all of these symbols and then copy and paste into your working document. You must have Invisible Elements enabled for this technique to work.

Exporting as Image Wells

Image Wells are used by Lotus Domino Designer R5 to create rollover effects. Just as Fireworks uses frames to separate the different rollover states — up, over, down, and overdown — Domino Designer uses Image Wells. An Image Well is a single graphic with separate frames, side by side, separated by a single pixel, as the example in Figure 15-25 shows.

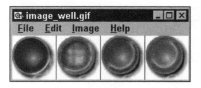

Figure 15-25: The final output of an Image Well export is used in Lotus Domino Designer R5.

Note Image Wells are similar to the four state rollovers in Fireworks, but not exactly the same. The last two states — over and overdown — are reversed. Fireworks, however, understands this difference and exports your Image Well in the correct format.

This feature is best used to convert your existing multiframe images to Image Wells for use as rollovers. To export a graphic as an Image Well, follow these steps:

1. Specify format and optimization settings in the Optimize panel.
2. Choose File ➪ Export Special ➪ Lotus Domino Image Well.

   The Export Special dialog box appears.
3. Select Slice Objects to export from the Files From option list.

   Trim images is not relevant for Image Wells and is ignored.
4. Select a new Base Name, if desired.
5. Make sure that the HTML Style is set to Image Well.
6. Browse to the desired folder to store the images.
7. Click Save when you're ready.

Fireworks saves your document as an Image Well, in the image format specified in the Optimize panel.

Exporting vectors

The last two options under Export Special export the vector shapes in your document as either a Flash SWF file or an Adobe Illustrator document.

New Feature Fireworks 3 satisfies the many user requests for exportable vector shapes and now exports as either a Flash SWF or an Adobe Illustrator document. Drawings you make in Fireworks can now be repurposed in a Flash movie or in print.

It's important to keep in mind that while Fireworks works with vector lines, it uses vector lines only as a substructure or "skeleton" for bitmaps and bitmap-based effects such as bevels and drop shadows. Exporting this vector skeleton is a useful feature, but the exported objects will often bear only a passing resemblance to their Fireworks-native counterparts, as shown in Figure 15-26.

Figure 15-26: The object in Fireworks (left) is a vector shape, but much of its look comes from Live Effects and a texture fill. After export, in the Flash player, the object is reduced to just its vector lines.

To export vector shapes from Fireworks, follow these steps:

1. To export as a Flash SWF file, choose File ➪ Export Special ➪ Flash SWF. Alternatively, to export as an Illustrator 7 document, choose File ➪ Export Special ➪ Illustrator 7.

   Fireworks displays the Export Special dialog box.

Note Although this dialog box is called Export Special, it is different from the Export Special dialog box that is used for all other Export Special operations.

2. To set specific export options, such as maintaining editable text, click the Setup button.

   Fireworks displays the options dialog for the vector type you are exporting, as shown in Figure 15-27.

3. If you are exporting as Flash SWF, set the appropriate options:

   • Set the Objects radio buttons to Paths to export paths, or to Maintain Appearance to export as JPEG bitmaps. If you choose Maintain Appearance, set the JPEG Quality slider to specify the quality of the JPEGs.

   • Choose to maintain text or convert text to paths with the Text radio buttons.

   • Export all frames or a range of frames with the Frames option.

   • Set a target frame rate in the Frame Rate box.

   Click OK when you're done.

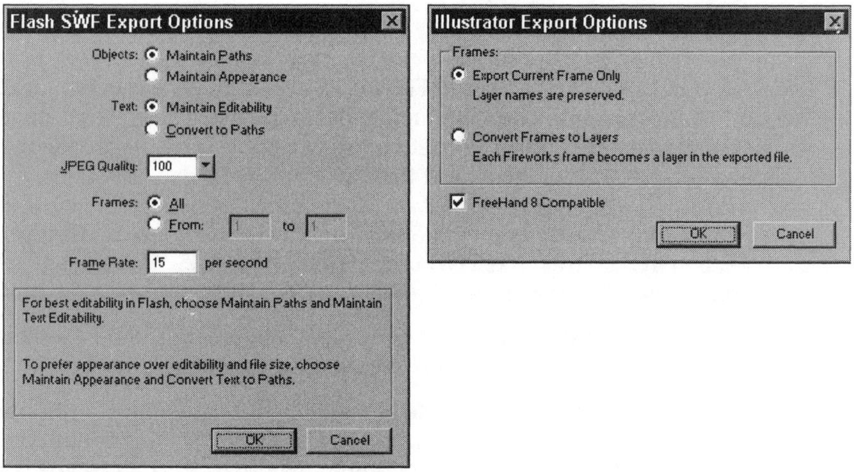

Figure 15-27: Specify export options for a vector format in the Flash SWF Export Options dialog box (left), or the Illustrator Export Options dialog box, depending on which export format you choose.

4. If you are exporting Illustrator 7, set the appropriate options:

   • Choose to export the current frame only, or to export Fireworks frames as Illustrator layers.

   • If you are going to import your file into Macromedia FreeHand, make sure the FreeHand 8 Compatible checkbox is checked.

   Click OK when you're done.

5. In the Export Special dialog box, navigate to a folder to save your exported file, and specify a filename. Click Save when you're done.

Your document's vector shapes are exported.

If you have the standalone Flash Player, double-clicking your Flash SWF file will open it for viewing. If not, you can drop the SWF file onto a browser equipped with the Flash Player plug-in to view it. A Flash SWF file can also be placed in a Web page, or imported into Flash for further editing.

If you exported as an Illustrator 7 document, open this document with Illustrator, FreeHand, Flash, or another vector art application.

Summary

Every graphic created or edited in Fireworks is eventually exported for use on the Web or in another application. Reducing file size is a key facet of making Web graphics, so Fireworks offers a wide variety of export options. Keep the following points in mind as you optimize and export images:

✦ Maintaining at least two versions of any file is considered a best practice: one version in the Fireworks PNG format and a second version in whatever format you've exported for use on the Web.

✦ The primary goal of an export operation is to create the best-looking image with the smallest file size. This is called optimizing a graphic.

✦ Fireworks now provides access to optimization and export options directly in the workspace, through the Optimize, Color Table, and Frames panels, and with the multiple tabs of the document window. Alternately, you can choose to use the Export Preview dialog box, which is opened by choosing Window ➪ Export Preview.

✦ Fireworks offers up to four comparison views of an image being exported, so that you can quickly judge appearance alongside the displayed file size and approximate download time.

✦ The two major formats for the Web — GIF and JPEG — are each best used for different types of images. The GIF format is good for graphics with flat color, for which transparency is important, such as logos. The JPEG format works best with continuous-tone images, such as photographs.

✦ Another format, PNG, is gaining acceptance on the Web, but still doesn't have enough support to warrant widespread usage. The PNG format has many advantages, such as full alpha transparency and gamma correction, to ameliorate image differences on different platforms.

✦ Images can be easily — and precisely — scaled and cropped during the export operation, right in the Export Preview dialog box.

✦ Fireworks advanced color control allows you to lock or replace any color in an indexed palette.

✦ Fireworks offers expert export guidance in the form of Wizards: the Export Wizard and the Export to Size Wizard.

✦ In addition to the standard image export, Fireworks can also export components of an image, such as layers, frames, or slice objects, in several different ways. Fireworks can even export just the vector shapes of your Fireworks objects as Flash SWF or Illustrator documents.

In the next chapter, you'll see how to maintain a consistent look and feel for your Web graphics through Fireworks Styles.

✦   ✦   ✦

Working with Fireworks Styles

In This Chapter

Introducing styles

Working with the
Styles panel

Making your
own styles

Maintaining a
styles library

Fireworks technique:
isolating patterns or
textures from styles

Although not obvious to the beginning designer, Web graphics is as much repetition as it is creation. After you establish a particular look and feel, that theme — the palette, fonts, effects, and more — are often carried through Web page after Web page. Several reasons exist for this repetition:

+ Consistency of approach is one of the fundamental tenets of design work.

+ For commercial sites, a consistent look and feel often ties in with the particular marketing message or branding that is being pursued.

+ With regard to the Internet, repetition of graphic elements aids visitors in the navigation of a Web site: if navigation buttons look the same from page to page, the user can quickly learn how to move around the site — even on their first visit.

However, no matter how many reasons exist declaring that repetition is good, it can also be mind-numbing drudgery. Fireworks comes to every Web designer's rescue with a marvelous time- and work-saver known as *styles*. By using styles, you can easily apply the overall look and feel to any selected object. A single style can contain a variety of user-definable settings, and styles are always available as you move from document to document. Moreover, Macromedia designed styles to be very portable — you can import and export them as a group. This facility enables you, as a working Web designer, to keep different style files for different clients. Styles are, without a doubt, a major boost in Web productivity.

Understanding Styles

A Fireworks object is potentially composed of several separate formatting choices: a path, a stroke, a fill, and one or more Live Effects. Each of those elements can be broken down further; for example, a stroke consists of a particular stroke type set to a specific color. Duplicating all the individual settings, one by one, that are necessary to establish a custom look would be extremely time-intensive and error-prone. Although you can copy an object to the clipboard and then paste its formatting onto another object, this requires that you first have a suitable object available to copy. Rather than keep example objects around just in case you want to recreate their look, Fireworks allows you to separate the appearance of an object from the object itself, and save that appearance as a style.

Fireworks provides a very novel, graphical method of maintaining and presenting styles: the Styles panel, shown in Figure 16-1. Acting like a formatting library, the Styles panel enables you to create, import, export, delete, and otherwise manage styles.

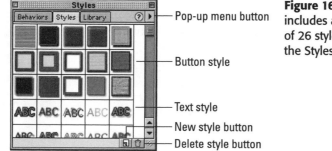

Pop-up menu button

Button style

Text style

New style button

Delete style button

Figure 16-1: Fireworks includes a default palette of 26 styles, available through the Styles panel.

Styles are visually divided in the Styles panel with two different types of icons: button styles and text styles. The only difference between the two is that a text style contains additional information: a typeface, size, and style, or any combination of the three. Button styles are depicted as squares and text styles are displayed as the letters ABC, but both preview the appearance that their style contains. Fireworks comes with 15 button styles and 11 text styles in its built-in default collection (which can be restored at any time) and over 300 more styles are available on the Fireworks CD-ROM, or on the Web at www.macromedia.com/software/ fireworks/download/styles). If you think the default styles are a little bland for your taste, be sure to check out the wide variety of additional styles.

You'll find even more styles, sorted in two different ways. In the Settings/Styles folder, you'll find all of the styles, ready to be copied to your own Fireworks 3/Settings/Styles folder and then imported into the Styles panel. Additionally, in the Styles folder, you'll find the styles grouped by author, sometimes with a ReadMe file describing the styles.

Even though the Styles panel is divided between the button and text style types, both can be applied to any Fireworks object. In other words, button styles can be applied to text objects, and text styles can be applied to path objects. Any unusable style information (such as font color for a path object) is disregarded. You might think of button styles as styles, and text styles as "styles-plus"; the extra information they contain doesn't stop them from being a perfectly good choice for a button or other graphic.

Caution The term *styles* is commonly used in computer programs. Unlike the styles you'd typically find in a word processor, Fireworks styles maintain no link between the original style and the applied objects. If you edit a style, any objects that the style was previously applied to remain unaffected.

Applying Styles

To apply a style, you must first access the Styles panel, which can be opened in any one of several ways:

+ Choose Window ➭ Styles.

+ Use the keyboard shortcut, Ctrl+Alt+J (Command+Option+J).

+ Click the Styles tab, if the Styles panel is docked behind another, visible panel.

Once the Styles panel is available, actually applying the style is very straightforward: simply select the object you want to apply the style to and then click on a style from the Styles panel. If you don't like the results, you can select another style. You can even duplicate the object and apply several styles, to select the best option, as shown in Figure 16-2.

Caution Applying one style overrides another style only if both styles affect the same settings. Styles that contain every possible setting can be mixed and matched freely because they will always override the previously-applied style. However, applying multiple styles that contain only a few of the possible settings — just a fill and stroke color, or just an effect, for example — will lead to your object having a mix of those styles. Suppose that you apply a style that only contains a green fill and then apply another style that only contains a drop shadow effect. Your object will now have a green fill and a drop shadow.

After you apply a style, the object remains completely independent of the style, and all the settings on the various panels — Stroke, Fill, Effects, and Text — can be adjusted to customize the object. Regardless of what changes you make to a styled object, the style itself is unaltered.

Figure 16-2: Applying different styles to the same object gives you a wide range of choices.

Creating New Styles

Although using the standard styles — or any of those included on the Fireworks CD-ROM — is a good way to establish a consistent look and feel quickly, you may not be able to find the exact style that you want. The real power in Fireworks styles comes from the ability to create, save, and use your own styles. The look of any object — the stroke, fill, effect, or text settings — can be converted to a style and easily used over and over again, by you or a colleague.

Now in Fireworks 3, the enhanced Effects panel has led to an enhanced side effect for Fireworks styles. Styles can now contain Xtras and even Photoshop Plug-in settings.

New Feature   Xtras and Photoshop-compatible plug-ins that appear in the Effects panel's list are saved in the Effects setting of styles that you create. In addition to the traditional Live Effects that previously could be included in a style in Fireworks 2, you now have access to an almost unlimited palette of plug-in image filters. The settings that are applied to an object remain completely editable at all times.

Imagine you've created an object — a button, say — with a finely-tuned stroke setting, a perfect fill color, and five complex effects modifications with a mix of Fireworks' built-in drop shadows and bevels and third-party Photoshop plug-ins such as Kai Power Tools or Alien Skin's Eye Candy. The entire process might take five minutes to recreate, but instead of doing so, select your object and create a style from it. Image or path objects can look incredibly textured and fussed-over in the time it takes to apply a style. It's worth noting again that these effects remain completely editable on each new object they're applied to.

Cross-Reference

For more about Fireworks 3's enhanced Live Effects and Xtras, see Chapter 12.

To create a new style, follow these steps:

1. Select the object upon which you want to base the style.

Tip

If you want to base your new style on a style you already have, apply the style to your object, modify the object's formatting accordingly, and then continue with step 2.

2. If the Styles panel is hidden, choose Window ⇨ Styles to view it, or use the key shortcut Ctrl+Alt+J (Command+Option+J), or click the Styles panel's tab if it is docked behind another, visible window.

3. Click the New Styles button (the pad of paper) at the bottom of the Styles panel. The Edit Style dialog box appears, as shown in Figure 16-3.

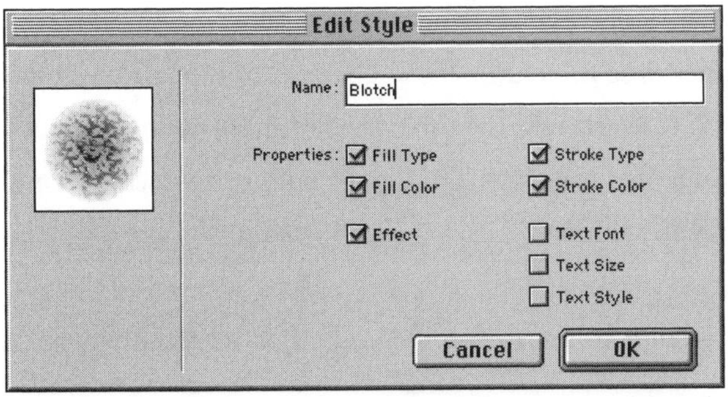

Figure 16-3: Create a new style by selecting available options in the Edit Style dialog box.

4. Enter a unique name for your new style in the Name text box.

Caution

Fireworks automatically names new styles Style 1, Style 2, Style 3, and so on, which it considers to be different than the Style 01, Style 02, Style 03, and so on with which its built-in styles are named. You can rename your new style by deleting the suggested name and entering your own choice. Be aware, however, that Fireworks does not check for conflicting names, so you can easily end up with two or more styles with the same name. I find it's best to make very descriptive names for the styles I create, so that they're easy to recall later, and harder to duplicate accidentally. If you hover your mouse over a style's icon in the Styles panel, Fireworks will show you the style's name at the bottom of the panel.

5. Select which of the available style settings you want to save with your style. Available settings are the following:

- **Fill Type:** Stores the Fill category (Solid, Gradient, Web Dither, or Pattern), the name of the gradient or Pattern, the edge settings (including the Amount of Feather, if applicable), and all the texture settings (name, degree, and transparency).

- **Fill Color:** Stores the Fill colors for Solid fills. For Gradient, Web Dither, and Pattern fills, the colors are stored with the Fill Type option.

- **Stroke Type:** Stores the category, name of stroke, all stroke stamp information (even if customized through the Edit Stroke command), the edge softness, the stroke size, and the texture settings (name and amount of texture).

- **Stroke Color:** Stores the selection in the current object's Stroke color well.

- **Effect:** Stores all the settings for an object's Live Effect, whether single (Inner Bevel, Outer Bevel, Drop Shadow, Glow, or Emboss) or multiple.

- **Text Font:** Stores the name of the current font for a text object.

- **Text Size:** Stores the size of the current font for a text object.

- **Text Style:** Stores the style (bold, italic, and/or underline) for a text object.

6. Click OK when you're done.

For all the information that styles are capable of retaining, you should note that the following few items are *not* stored (although you might expect them to be):

✦ While a style remembers gradients, Fireworks styles do not retain any gradient settings pertaining to modified Gradient Control handles, accessed through the Paint Bucket tool.

✦ None of the Text Style settings store any information on text spacing (kerning, leading, horizontal scale, or baseline shift), text alignment (horizontal, vertical, left, center, right, stretched, or direction), or anti-alias.

You should remember two points when you are creating and applying new styles. First, if a style does not affect a particular setting, that setting is left as is on the selected object. Second, a Stroke, Fill, or Effect set to None is as valid a setting as any other. For example, if the object on which you base your new style does not include a fill, but you've selected Fill Type on the Edit Style dialog box, any object to which this style is applied — whether it has a fill or not — will have the fill removed.

Managing Styles

Every time that you add a style, it stays available for every document opened in Fireworks. If you really become adept at using styles, you'll quickly begin to have a massive collection of styles — truly too much of a good thing. Fireworks offers several commands, mostly grouped under the Styles panel's pop-up menu, for managing your styles.

Tip   Before you start selecting styles in order to delete or modify them, make sure that you don't have any objects in your document selected, or selecting a style will apply that style to the object. Click the mouse in an empty area of the canvas, or choose Edit ➪ Deselect, or use the key shortcut Ctrl+D (Command+D).

You've seen how you can create a style by selecting the New Style button from the bottom of the Styles panel. Its obvious companion is the Delete Style button (the trash can) right next to it. To remove any unwanted style, select its icon in the Styles panel and choose the Delete Style button.

Tip   You can select multiple styles at the same time. Hold down Ctrl (Command) while you select Styles to add one at a time. Hold down Shift to select a range of adjacent styles; Fireworks will select the two styles you click on and every style along the shortest route between them. This selection method is more like a spreadsheet than a word processor. To select a row of styles, hold down Shift and click on the first and last in the row. To add another row to your selection, keep holding Shift and click on the last style in the second row. To add part of a row to your selection, switch to holding down Ctrl (Command) and add the final styles one by one. The same technique applies to selecting columns.

A total of seven commands are available in the Styles panel's pop-up menu, shown in Figure 16-4:

✦ **New Style:** Creates a new style based on the selected object. This command is identical to the New Style button.

✦ **Edit Style:** Opens the Edit Style dialog box, enabling you to select or deselect the setting options.

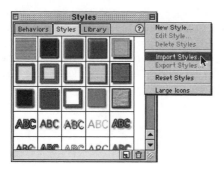

Figure 16-4: Manage your styles through the commands in the Styles panel's pop-up menu.

Tip   You can also access the Edit Style dialog box by double-clicking a style's icon in the Styles panel.

✦ **Delete Styles:** Removes a selected style or styles.

✦ **Import Styles:** Loads a new set of styles after the currently selected one. Styles must be stored in the Fireworks Styles format, and can't be imported from a Fireworks document, for example.

✦ **Export Styles:** Stores the currently selected style or styles in the Fireworks Styles format.

✦ **Resets Styles:** Removes any styles you have added to the Styles panel and reloads the default configuration of styles.

✦ **Large Icons:** Toggles between regular and large-sized icons. When checked, icons are displayed twice their normal size.

Earlier in this chapter we looked at how to create and delete styles; the New Style and Delete Styles commands work in the same way as their respective buttons. Editing an existing style is also a familiar process. Choose Edit Style, and you are presented with the same options in the Edit Styles dialog box as when you create a new one. Just make any changes, click OK, and your revised style is ready to use.

Tip   The Edit Style command is also a good way to check what formatting options a particular style affects before applying it. Double-click the style or select it and choose Edit Style from the pop-up menu to see which formatting options are checked.

The Export Styles command opens a dialog box, shown in Figure 16-5. Fireworks offers to save your new file in its Styles folder under the name "Custom Styles.stl," but you can change the name to anything else and store the file wherever you want (as long as you can find it later). If you use a Macintosh, the .stl filename extension is not necessary, but leaving it on keeps your style files cross-platform-ready, and will enable you to share your styles with Windows users or use them yourself on a Windows machine.

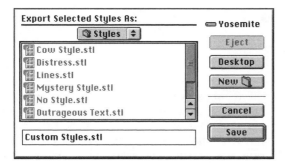

Figure 16-5: Export a collection of styles and save them as a Fireworks style file with the filename extension .stl.

The Import Styles command opens a standard Open dialog box. Choose a style file and click Open to import it.

Tip Mac users: if you receive a Fireworks Style file from a Windows-using friend or download it unarchived from the Internet, it may not have a Mac OS Creator or Type and will appear with a blank icon. As long as it still has its .stl filename extension, though, Fireworks will recognize it and allow you to import and use it. If you like, you can use the File Exchange Control Panel or a utility such as File Buddy or FinderPop to give the file the proper creator of *MKBY* (Fireworks, of course) and type of *STYf,* which will restore its icon.

As noted previously, when you import a set of Fireworks Styles, all styles are inserted after the currently selected style. For this reason, I typically find it best to select the last currently-loaded style before importing. You also can create a spacer or two — create a style from a plain object with no fill, stroke, or effects. The style icon will appear blank and acts to separate your imported styles from the standard ones.

On the CD-ROM You'll find a style file called No Style.stl in the Settings/Styles folder which contains just one style that applies a Fill, Stroke, and Effect of none. This makes a handy spacer and a quick, easy way to unformat an object before applying another style. You could also save this as the first or last style in your exported Style files to provide an easy-to-see start or finish.

The final two Styles panel commands, Reset Styles and Large Icons, are fairly self-explanatory. Reset Styles removes all styles currently in the Styles panel and reloads the standard set of styles in their place. Because this is a fairly drastic measure, Fireworks asks for confirmation before proceeding. Selecting Large Icons displays the style icons at twice their standard size — they enlarge from 36 pixels square to 72. This feature is sometimes useful when trying to differentiate between two similar styles.

Fireworks Technique: Isolating Patterns and Textures from Styles

A close look at some of the styles that come with Fireworks — both the defaults and the extras found on the Fireworks CD-ROM — reveals several exciting Patterns and textures. On the CD you'll find a style — quite innocently named Style 37, and contained within text1-201.stl — that has an intriguing spotted Pattern, shown in Figure 16-6. A quick check of the Fill panel reveals that a texture, called (appropriately) cow, is in use as part of the style. However, no such file exists in the Textures folder; so, where did it come from? The texture is actually embedded in the style.

> **Note**   Style 37 was one of Fireworks 2's default styles, and was previously known as Style 51. The default styles in Fireworks 3 are a lot fewer and a little less interesting. Now, more than ever, it's a good idea to dig into the extra styles on the Fireworks CD-ROM.

Donna Casey, a Web designer whose work can be seen at www.n8vision.com, uncovered a technique for extracting the embedded textures and Patterns that you may find in a style. Why would you do this? You might find that the Pattern and/or texture is, to your eye, better when combined with a different stroke or effects setting — or you might want to incorporate just the Pattern or texture in an image. Two methods are available to approach this problem. First, you could edit the style, removing all the options except for Fill Type. This is, at best, a partial solution. The Pattern/texture is still encased in the other pertinent settings; textures, for example, could be part of a Solid, Pattern, or Gradient Fill. To completely separate the texture or Pattern and then save it, follow these steps:

1. Draw a fairly large rectangle or square, approximately 500 × 500 pixels.

   The goal is to make the object large enough so that the pattern clearly repeats.

2. From the Styles panel, select the style whose texture or fill you want to isolate.

   The style is applied to the object.

3. From the Stroke panel, choose None in the Stroke category.

4. In the Effect panel, select None in the Effect category.

5. To retrieve a texture, make the following changes to the Fill panel:

   • Set the Fill category to Solid.

   • Set the Fill color to black.

   • Set the Amount of texture to 100%

6. To retrieve a Pattern, set the Amount of texture to 0%.

7. Choose the Crop tool from the Toolbox.

Figure 16-6: Examining the cow texture from Style 37. Works fine on a plain circle and also specifies 170pt Arial Black when applied to text.

8. Crop the object to encompass the repeating pattern.

   This is, by far, the hardest part; you might take several attempts to get it just right. A good idea is to save the file before you begin to crop the object. With most textures, the repeating pattern will actually be smaller than it might first appear.

9. When you finish cropping, save the file either in the Settings/Patterns or Settings/Textures folder.

10. Restart Fireworks to refresh the Pattern and texture lists.

Tip   You can also use your new Pattern or texture without restarting Fireworks by choosing Other from the Pattern or texture list in the Fill panel and selecting your newly-saved file.

Your new extricated Pattern or texture should now be available to you in the Stroke and Fill panels.

Summary

Styles are a major production boost, allowing you to easily build up a library of formatting choices and add a consistent look and feel to all of your graphics on a client-by-client or site-by-site basis. Styles are also a significant work-saver — rather than having to add individually all of the characteristics that compose a particular look, you can add them all with one click of the Styles panel. The main points with regard to styles are:

✦ Styles are accessible through the Styles panel.

✦ A style may contain almost all the information for reproducing a graphic's stroke, fill, effect, and text settings.

✦ Unlike some other programs, such as Macromedia FreeHand, Fireworks styles do not retain a link to objects that use them.

✦ Any newly created style is available to all documents until the style is removed from the Styles panel.

✦ Styles can be edited, imported, exported, and otherwise managed through the commands found in the Styles panel's pop-up menu.

✦ A style can be "reverse engineered" to isolate the Pattern or texture that it contains.

In the next chapter, you find out how to use Symbols and Libraries to cut down on even more repetitive work.

✦   ✦   ✦

Using Symbols and Libraries

✦   ✦   ✦   ✦

In This Chapter

Understanding
Symbols

Creating and
modifying Symbols

Modifying Instances

Working with Buttons

Managing Libraries

✦   ✦   ✦   ✦

Many Fireworks features are specifically designed to prevent duplication of effort on the part of the busy Web artist. Perhaps none more so than the Symbols. In a nutshell, a *Symbol* is an object that's been designated as a master copy and stored in a Symbol Library. Copies of a Symbol, called *Instances*, retain a link to their Symbol so that they can be modified as a group. Editing the Symbol causes its Instances to inherit the changes.

New Feature
Fireworks 3 greatly simplifies working with Symbols by organizing them into Libraries, which are easily accessed from the Library panel. Gone are the days of wondering which Instance is a Symbol and which is an Instance. In Fireworks 3, only Instances are allowed in the document window, while Symbols remain in the Library panel.

This chapter begins with a discussion of the basics of using Symbols, Instances, and Libraries in Fireworks. Later, you'll discover how to make, modify, and manage Symbols, Instances, and Libraries.

Understanding Symbols and Instances

Symbols in Fireworks are like templates for single objects. The Symbol itself is like a rubber stamp that you dip in ink. You can "stamp out" virtually unlimited copies of any Symbol, called *Instances*. Instances are copies of Symbols that retain a link to their parent Symbol. Editing the Symbol causes its Instances to inherit many of the changes, such as fill and stroke settings. On the other hand, Instances have some independent properties of their own: you can apply the Transform tools to them, add Live Effects, or alter opacity settings on an individual basis, as shown in Figure 17-1. From a design perspective, Symbols and Instances enable you to maintain a common look without losing a feeling of variety.

Unmodified instance

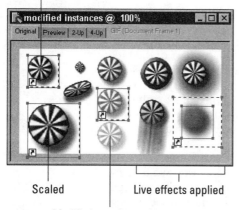

Scaled   Live effects applied

Modified opacity settings

Figure 17-1: These are all Instances of the same Symbol, with modifications made to scale, skew, opacity, and with Live Effects.

Symbols themselves are always stored in a *Library*, accessible through the Library panel, shown in Figure 17-2. Converting an object to a Symbol places it in the Library and leaves a copy behind — an Instance — in the document window. The Library panel provides a range of functions for managing and modifying Symbols and Libraries, but its most basic function is as a way to make Instances. Dragging a Symbol from the Library and dropping it in the document window makes a new Instance, much like making a shortcut to a file in Windows, or a file alias on the Mac. In fact, Instances even have the little arrow badge that Windows shortcuts and Mac aliases share.

An advantage of Instances that's not so obvious is that they are simplified renderings of their parent Symbol. Where a Symbol might be a complex path object with an intricate stroke and gradient fill, an Instance of it is just a simple bitmap image object. Using many Instances rather than of using independent objects, as shown in Figure 17-3, improves your computer's performance because Fireworks draws bitmap images instead of the more-complex path objects over and over again.

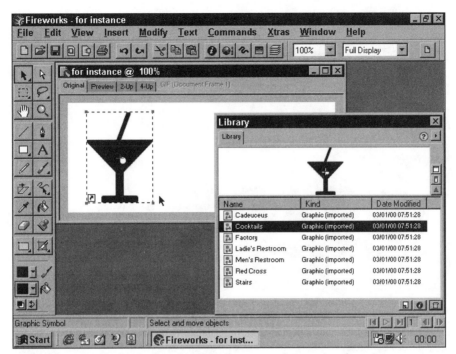

Figure 17-2: Symbols are stored in the Library panel. Dragging them into a document creates an Instance, identified by the arrow badge in its bounding box.

Fireworks has these two types of Symbols:

✦ **Graphic Symbols:** You might think of a Graphic Symbol as a basic, vanilla Symbol. Generally, when we refer to a Symbol, we're talking about a Graphic Symbol. An Instance of a Graphic Symbol acts pretty much the same way as any Fireworks object. You can place it anywhere on the canvas, move it to another layer, and modify many of its properties.

✦ **Button Symbols:** Button Symbols are *Symbols-Plus*. A button Symbol has multiple frames that contain the different states of the button, such as Up, Over, and Down. Instances of Button Symbols carry their own slice object with them, which can have a URL or Behavior attached. In a sense, a Button Symbol is a combination of all the separate Fireworks objects you'd need to use to make a button, wrapped up into a tidy package that's easy to edit and reuse.

The steps you take to create and modify the two types of Symbols are slightly different, as each type of Symbol has its own editor, but they are also similar in many ways. Button Instances share the same properties with their parent Symbols as Graphic Instances.

Original path drawing

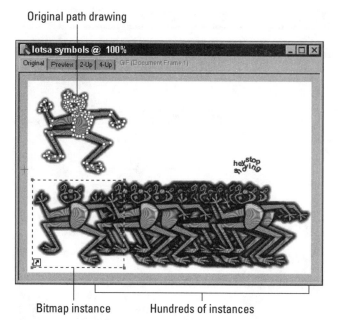

Bitmap instance   Hundreds of instances

Figure 17-3: Instances are simplified, bitmap versions of their parent Symbols. You can use numerous Instances without adversely affecting Fireworks' performance.

Instances also enable advanced animation building because Fireworks can tween two or more of them and automatically create intermediate steps, simplifying and speeding up the animation process. Tweening a scaled-down Instance with a scaled-up one, for example, causes Fireworks to connect them with stair steps of new Instances, which are then easily distributed to frames to create an animation of a single object growing or shrinking.

Find out more about tweening Instances in Chapter 23.

Introducing the Library Panel

The *Library panel*, shown in Figure 17-4, is a central place to access and manage a Symbol Library. Every Symbol in the current document is displayed in the Symbol list in the Library panel, and they are identified as either a Graphic Symbol or Button Symbol by a distinctive icon. Like most other Fireworks panels, the Library panel has a pop-up menu and can be docked with other panels. To display the Library panel, choose Window ➪ Library.

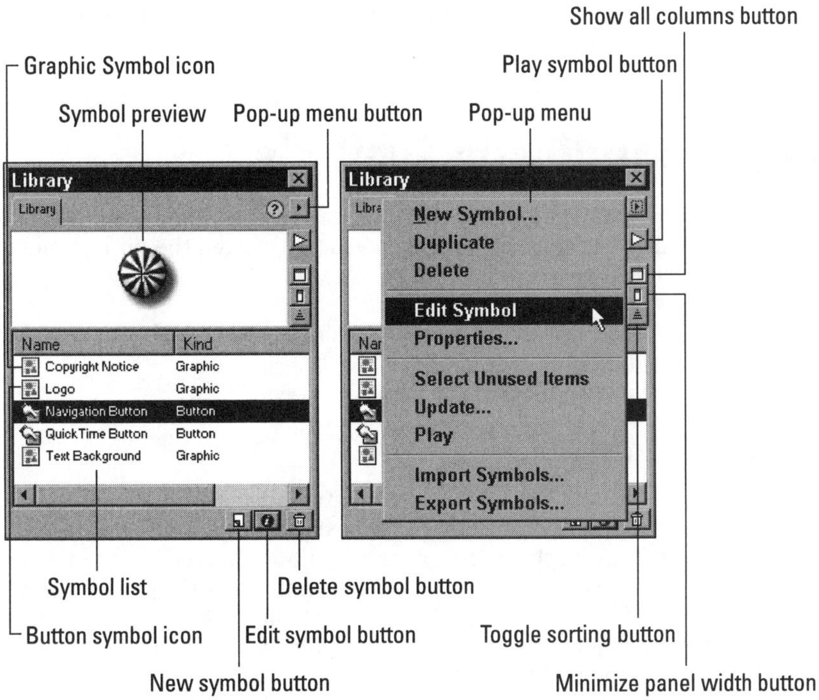

Figure 17-4: The Library panel is a central place to store and manage Symbol Libraries.

Following are the main features of the Library panel to keep in mind:

✦ **Symbol list:** As you create or import Symbols, they are added to the Symbol list automatically. Initially, when you create a new document, the Library panel is completely empty. The Symbol list is divided into columns that detail different properties of the Symbols it contains, similar to the columns you see in a Windows or Macintosh folder that is set to List view. Double-clicking a Symbol's entry in the Symbol list opens the Symbol Properties dialog box for that Symbol, enabling you to rename the Symbol or convert it from a Button to a Graphic Symbol, or vice versa.

✦ **Symbol preview:** Selecting a Symbol from the Symbol list displays a preview of the Symbol. Dragging the Symbol's preview into a document creates an Instance of the Symbol in the document. Double-clicking the Symbol preview opens the Symbol for editing.

✦ **Pop-up menu:** The Pop-up menu contains commands for creating and managing Symbols.

We'll look more closely at the Library panel as we use it throughout this chapter to create, edit, and manage Symbols.

Making and Modifying Symbols

Most of the time, you create and manage Symbols using the commands in the Insert menu, although similar commands are also available through the pop-up menu on the Library panel, which we'll look at in detail later in this chapter.

New Feature In Fireworks 3, the commands for creating Symbols have moved from the Edit menu to the Insert menu.

Creating a Symbol

Obviously, the first step in using Symbols is to actually make one. Fireworks provides three routes to a new Symbol: convert an existing object into a Symbol, create a Symbol from scratch, or duplicate an existing Symbol. Converting an existing object is probably the most common method of creating a new Symbol. Fireworks even betrays this bias for converting existing objects in the key shortcuts it uses: plain F8 to convert an object, and Ctrl+F8 in Windows (Command+F8 on a Macintosh) to create a Symbol from scratch.

 Caution Mac users: if you have mapped the keyboard's function keys in the Keyboard Control Panel to start programs or perform other tasks, function key shortcuts in Fireworks are superceded by those mappings. Use the menu commands in Fireworks instead or disable the mappings in the Keyboard Control Panel.

Converting an object

Almost any object can be converted into a Symbol, whether it is a path object or an image object, or even a group.

Note Although you can convert an Instance into a Symbol, doing so breaks the link to its original parent Symbol.

To convert an object into a Symbol, follow these steps:

1. Select the object you'd like to convert to a Symbol.

2. Choose Insert ⇨ Convert to Symbol or use the key shortcut F8. Fireworks displays the Symbol Properties dialog box (Figure 17-5).

3. In the Name box, change "Symbol" to a unique name for your Symbol.

4. By default, Fireworks offers to create a Graphic Symbol. Leave the Type radio buttons set to Graphic. Click OK when you're done.

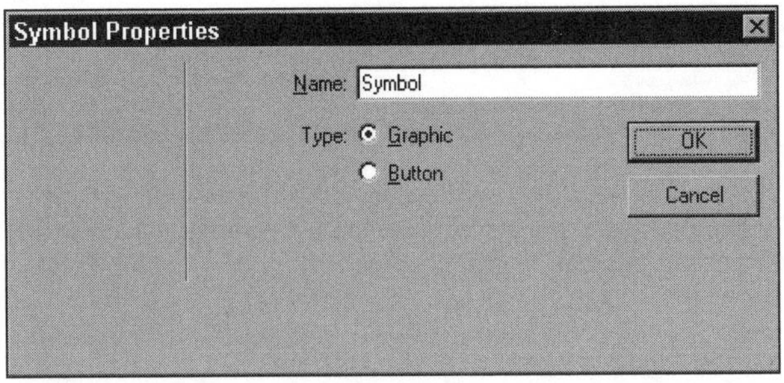

Figure 17-5: Give a Symbol a name in the Symbol Properties dialog box and decide whether it will be a Graphic or a Button Symbol.

Note

Button Symbols are covered later in this chapter.

Fireworks places your original object into the Library panel and leaves an Instance behind in its place in the document. You can identify the Instance by its arrow badge.

Creating a Symbol from scratch

When you have the presence of mind to know that an object should be a Symbol right from the start, you can make one entirely from scratch. You may also want to create a Symbol that's a combination of different objects. In this case, you can create a new Symbol and then copy and paste different elements from the document window into your new Symbol.

To create a brand-new Symbol, follow these steps:

1. Choose Insert ➪ New Symbol or use the key shortcut Ctrl+F8 (Command+F8). Alternatively, you can choose New Symbol from the pop-up menu on the Library panel. Fireworks displays the Symbol Properties dialog box.

2. Change "Symbol" in the Name box to a unique name for your Symbol.

3. Leave the Type radio buttons set to Graphic to create a Graphic Symbol. Click OK when you're done.

4. Fireworks displays the Symbol Editor (Figure 17-6).

5. Create your new Symbol in the Symbol Editor, just as you would in the document window, using any combination of Fireworks tools and floating panels, such as Live Effects. You can copy and paste between the Symbol Editor and the document window, as well.

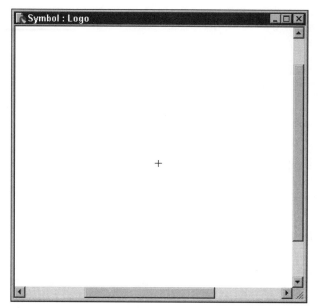

Figure 17-6: The Symbol Editor is like a special document window for creating or editing Graphic Symbols.

Tip   Your new Symbol will be easy to edit and modify later, so don't worry about making it absolutely perfect.

6. Close the Symbol Editor when you're done by clicking its close box, located on the upper-right corner of the box in Windows and on the upper-left corner on a Mac.

Your new Symbol appears in the Library panel, and an Instance is placed in the document window.

Duplicating an existing Symbol

The final way to create a new Symbol is to duplicate an existing one.

To duplicate a Symbol, follow these steps:

1. Choose Windows ➪ Library to view the Library panel, if it is not already visible.

2. Select a Symbol to duplicate from the Symbol list.

3. Choose Duplicate from the Library panel pop-up menu.

Fireworks duplicates the selected Symbol, adding a number after its name to distinguish it from the original.

 Tip To rename a Symbol, double-click its name in the Symbol list and change its name in the Symbol Properties dialog box.

Modifying Symbols

Symbols are easily edited in the Symbol Editor. When you're done editing a Symbol and have closed the Symbol Editor, the changes that you've made are applied to the Symbol and to all of its Instances. Editing a Symbol, then, is also editing all of its Instances.

To modify an existing Symbol, follow these steps:

1. Choose Window ➪ Library to view the Library panel, if it isn't already visible.

2. Select the Symbol you want to edit from the Symbol list.

3. Double-click the Symbol preview to open the Symbol in the Symbol Editor. Alternatively, you can choose Edit Symbol from the Library panel's pop-up menu.

4. Modify the Symbol in the Symbol Editor. When you're done, close the Symbol Editor by clicking its close box, located on the upper-right corner in Windows and on the upper-left corner on a Mac.

   Your edits are applied to the Symbol and to all of its Instances.

Symbol-editing shortcuts

Fireworks also provides these two shortcuts for editing Symbols:

✦ If you have an Instance selected in the document window and you just want to edit its parent Symbol, choose Modify ➪ Symbol ➪ Edit Symbol to view the Instance's parent Symbol in the Symbol Editor.

✦ If you are editing a Symbol's properties in the Symbol Properties dialog box (detailed in the next section), you can click the Edit button to open the Symbol in the Symbol Editor.

When using either of these shortcuts, closing the Symbol Editor applies your changes to all of the Symbol's Instances.

Tip If you take a wrong turn with your edits in the Symbol Editor, you can close the Symbol Editor — which applies your changes — and then choose Edit ➪ Undo to undo those changes.

Modifying Symbol properties

In addition to modifying the Symbol itself, you can also modify a Symbol's properties, changing its name or converting it from a Graphic Symbol to a Button Symbol, or vice versa.

To edit a Symbol's properties, follow these steps:

1. Choose Window ➪ Library to view the Library panel, if it isn't already visible.

2. Open the Symbol Properties dialog box by doing one of the following:

    • Double-click a Symbol's name in the Symbol list

    • Select the Symbol in the Symbol list and choose Properties from the pop-up menu.

    Fireworks displays the Symbol Properties dialog box, shown in Figure 17-7.

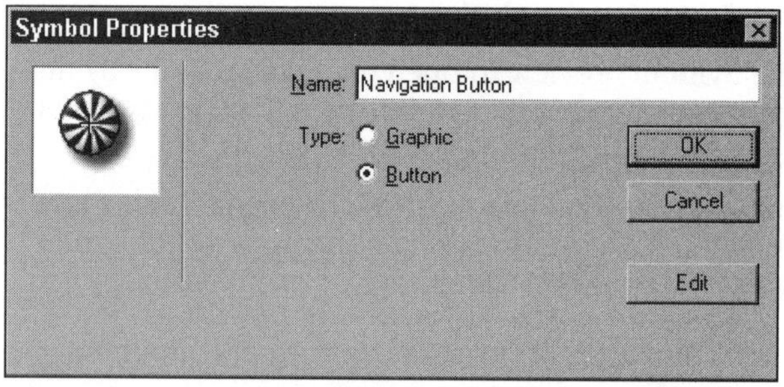

Figure 17-7: The Symbol Properties dialog box displays a thumbnail of an existing Symbol and enables you to rename a Symbol or convert its Type.

3. Modify the Symbol's properties in the Symbol Properties dialog box and click OK when you're done.

Fireworks applies your changes to the Symbol. If you converted the Symbol's Type, all of its Instances also take on that change. For example, if you converted a Symbol from a Graphic Symbol to a Button Symbol, all of its Instances become buttons.

Deleting a Symbol

Deleting a Symbol is an easy affair, but keep in mind that if the Symbol has Instances, they will be deleted, too.

To delete a Symbol, follow these steps:

1. If the Library panel is not visible, choose Window ⇨ Library to display it.

2. Select the Symbol you want to delete in the Symbol list.

3. Choose Delete from the Library panel pop-up menu. If the Symbol doesn't have any Instances, it is deleted immediately without confirmation. If the Symbol does have Instances, Fireworks displays the Delete Symbol dialog box, shown in Figure 17-8.

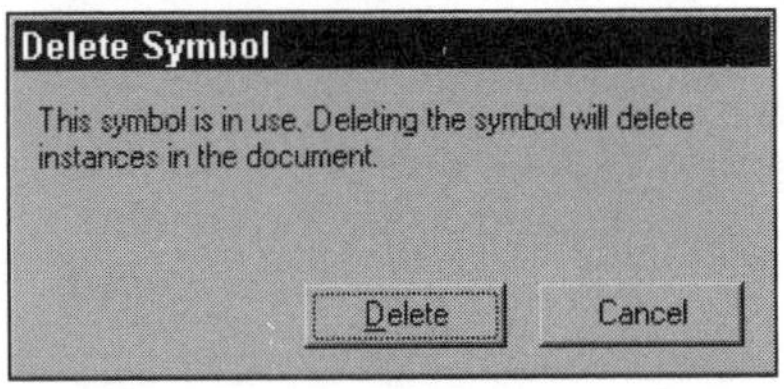

Figure 17-8: The Delete Symbol dialog box confirms that you really want to delete a Symbol.

4. Click the Delete button in the Delete Symbol dialog box to delete the Symbol.

The Symbol and its Instances are removed from your document.

Creating Instances

Creating an Instance is a common task that can be accomplished with one of two simple methods:

✦ Drag and drop a Symbol from the Library panel onto the canvas. You can drag it from either the Symbol preview or from the Symbol list.

Tip   You can create Instances of multiple Symbols in one step by selecting a group of Symbols from the Symbol list and dragging them all onto the canvas.

✦ Duplicate an Instance in the document window. A copy of an Instance is also an Instance. Any of the methods that you're used to using to duplicate objects in Fireworks also work to duplicate Instances:

• Select the Instance and choose Edit ⇨ Duplicate or Edit ⇨ Clone

• Copy the Instance to the clipboard and Paste back a copy

• Hold down the Alt (Option) key, and drag an Instance to create a copy

The new Instance can be identified as another Instance by the arrow icon in the lower-left corner of its bounding box.

Modifying Instances

Modifying a Symbol passes changes on to all of its Instances, but modifications can also be made to individual Instances. Fireworks treats Instances like groups, allowing you to apply similar transformations. The relationship between transformations applied to a Symbol and transformations applied to an Instance is the same as making transformations to individual objects and then grouping them and applying a transformation to the group. In fact, you can observe the group-like behavior of an Instance by breaking the link with its Symbol. What you're left with is a group.

Although you can apply an Xtra to an Instance, this breaks the link and turns it into an image object.

Applying modifications to an Instance has no effect on any other Instance or on the parent Symbol. Scale one Instance, for example, and its parent Symbol and other Instances of that Symbol are unaffected. In other words, the link goes one way, only from Symbol to Instance.

You can apply these transformations to Instances:

✦ **Shape transformations:** Adjust the width, height, skew, distortion, and rotation; or flip the Instance vertically or horizontally. Anything on the Modify ➪ Transform submenu is fair game.

✦ **Opacity:** Alter the opacity setting in the Object panel.

✦ **Blending mode:** Alter the blending mode in the Object panel.

For more about opacity and blending modes, see Chapter 13.

✦ **Live Effects:** Apply Live Effects from the Effect panel. The effects that are applied to the Symbol are flattened in the Instance, so even though an Instance may appear to have Live Effects, there are actually no Live Effects applied until you add them to an individual Instance.

For more about Live Effects, see Chapter 12.

Breaking links

If you want to break the link between an Instance and its parent Symbol, select the Instance and choose Modify ➪ Symbol ➪ Break Link. The link is broken and your Instance is now a regular group, even if the Symbol only contained one object. To separate the group, choose Modify ➪ Ungroup.

Deleting Instances

Deleting an Instance works just like deleting any Fireworks object and has no effect on the parent Symbol or any other Instance. To delete an Instance, select it and press Delete.

Working with Buttons

Button Symbols enable you to encapsulate up to four button states, such as Up, Over, and Down, along with a slice object containing a URL or a Behavior into a single object that can be thought of as a button.

New Feature

The addition of Button Symbols to Fireworks 3 recognizes the fact that Web artists can often spend an inordinate amount of time creating, editing, and managing similar navigation buttons.

Button Instances can be placed onto the canvas again and again, and the link and Button Text independently changed for each one. In addition, Behaviors are applied to the Button Symbol itself, meaning that you only have to build one rollover for an entire Web site of rollover buttons.

Cross-Reference

Behaviors are covered in Chapter 21.

Making and Modifying Button Symbols

The Fireworks Button Editor is a special Symbol Editor window with tabs for each state of a button that makes it easy to make or modify a Button Symbol.

New Feature

Fireworks 3 includes a valuable new tool for building and previewing rollover buttons: the Button Editor. A tabbed window enables you to assemble objects and link them together to create a two-, three- or four-state button Symbol.

To create a Button Symbol, follow these steps:

1. Choose Insert ➪ New Button.

   Fireworks displays the Button Editor, as shown in Figure 17-9.

2. Create the Up state of your button in the Up tab of the Button Editor.

3. Select the Button Editor's Over tab and create the over state of your button. To start with the Up state and modify it to be an Over state, click Copy Up Graphic. Fireworks copies the Up state to the Over tab, ready for editing.

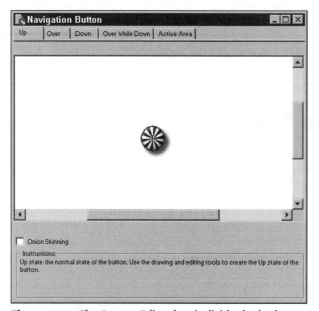

Figure 17-9: The Button Editor has individual tabs for each state of a button.

Tip   At any time, you can view all of the tabs in the Button Editor at once, by checking the Onion Skinning box.

4. If you want to include a Down state in your button, select the Down tab and create the Down state of your button. Fireworks automatically checks Include Down State when you start building a down button. Again, you can click Copy Over Graphic to copy the previous state to this tab for modification.

5. Check Show Down State Upon Load to display the Down state when a page loads, when your button is exported as a Nav Bar.

6. To add an Over While Down state to your button, switch to the Over While Down tab and either create a new state or copy the previous one—click Copy Down Graphic—and modify it to create the Over While Down state.

7. Switch to the Active Area tab. Fireworks automatically creates a slice in the Active Area tab that encompasses the area of your button. Adjust the size of the slice if necessary.

8. Click the Link Wizard button to access the Link Wizard. Move from tab to tab in the Link Wizard dialog box and set defaults for each Button Instance that will later be created from this Button Symbol.

Cross-Reference The Link Wizard is detailed later in this chapter.

9. Close the Button Editor when you're done.

Your new Button Symbol is added to the Library panel and an Instance is placed in the document window.

To modify a Button Symbol, double-click its Symbol preview in the Library panel, double-click one of its Instances in the document window, or select it in the Symbol list and choose Edit Symbol from the Library panel's pop-up menu.

Converting existing objects into Button Symbols

Converting an existing object into a Button Symbol is a quick way to get a button started. Since each state of a multistate button is usually a variation on the first state, converting an existing object into a Button Symbol and then modifying it slightly in the Button Editor to create Over, Down, and Over While Down states is an excellent strategy.

To convert an object into a button, select it and choose Insert ⇨ Convert to Symbol. Choose Button from the Type setting in the Symbol Properties dialog box, give your button a unique name in the Name box, and click OK. Fireworks converts your object into a Button Symbol, creating a slice object on top of the it in the document window, as shown in Figure 17-10.

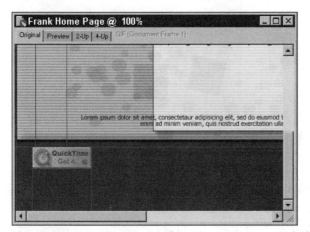

Figure 17-10: Converting an object into a Button Symbol also covers it with a slice object.

Add more states to your button by editing it in the Library panel.

Converting Button Symbols into Graphic Symbols

If you convert a Button Symbol into a Graphic Symbol by editing its properties in the Symbol Properties dialog box, the slice object that makes up the Active Area of the button will remain with the Symbol. To remove it, edit your Symbol in the Symbol Editor and manually delete the slice object.

Using Button Instances

In addition to the standard, modifiable Instance properties, such as opacity and Live Effects, Button Instances have two additional editable properties: their Button Text and the links that are applied to their slice objects (Figure 17-11). Both of these are modified by selecting the Button Instance and viewing the Object panel. This allows you to assign each Button Instance a separate URL and some unique text.

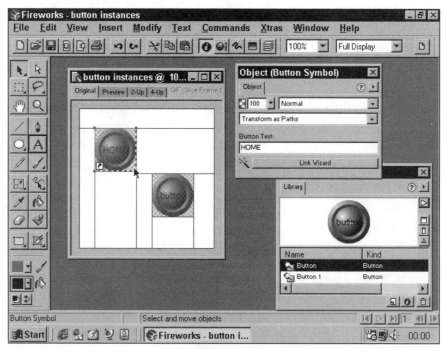

Figure 17-11: Modify the Button Text and the URL for each Button Instance in the Object panel to truly turn each Instance into a separate button.

To modify the Button Text, type new text into the Button Text box in the Object panel and press Enter (Return). Fireworks prompts you with a dialog box asking if you'd like to apply the edited text to just the current button, or to all of the buttons in the document. The Text in your Button Instance is modified to reflect the new text, but retains its original formatting.

Note You can only modify Button Text if your Button Symbol contains a text object. If it doesn't, the Button Text area of the Object panel is grayed out.

To modify a button's link, click the Link Wizard button to access the Link Wizard, detailed next.

The Link Wizard

The Link Wizard enables you to modify the properties of a Button Instance that would normally be applied to a regular slice object. The tabbed dialog box, accessed from the Button Instance Object panel, walks you through the steps required to edit all of the link properties of the selected Button Instance.

The Link Wizard offers these four tabs:

✦ **Export Defaults:** Export settings for the button, such as GIF WebSnap 128. An Edit button also enables you to create additional export settings.

✦ **Link:** A URL, alternate text, and a Status Bar message — displayed when the user hovers their mouse — for the button (Figure 17-12).

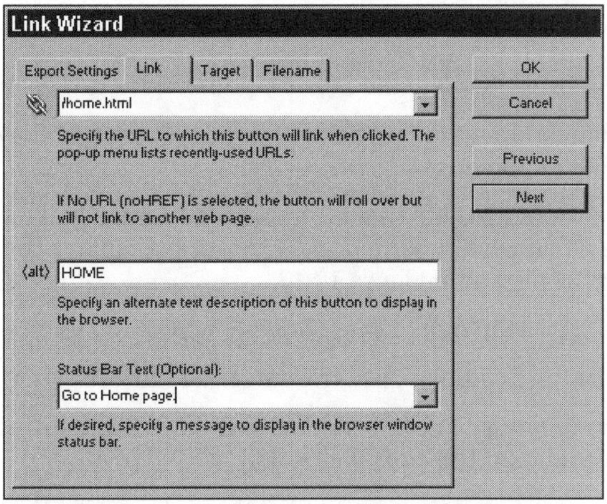

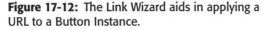

Figure 17-12: The Link Wizard aids in applying a URL to a Button Instance.

✦ **Target:** A target window or frame for the hyperlink to open in.

✦ **Filename:** A filename for this buttons slice, or leave Auto-Name Slices checked to have Fireworks name the slice.

After you select a Button Instance in your document, you will be able to access the Link Wizard for that button and apply the appropriate settings.

Tip   The Link Wizard can also be accessed from the Active Area tab of the Button Editor, enabling you to set defaults for the Symbol and, consequently, for each new Button Instance.

Managing Libraries

If you've worked with Macromedia Flash, you'll be happy to see the Library make it into a Fireworks release. Making and managing buttons is a common task in both programs, and having a central place to store buttons and an easy way to reuse them — drag and drop from the Library panel to a document — saves time and work again and again.

Libraries exist in one of two places: within a document by default or as a standalone PNG file that you create by exporting a Library.

Importing a Library

Libraries can be imported from other Fireworks documents or from Library-only PNG files that are created by exporting a Library from Fireworks.

To import a Library into the current document, follow these steps:

1. Choose Window ➪ Library to view the Library panel, if it's not visible.

2. From the Library panel pop-up menu, choose Import Symbols. Fireworks displays an Open File dialog box.

3. Navigate to the Fireworks PNG file that contains the Library you'd like to import and choose Open when you're done. Fireworks displays the Import Symbols dialog box, as shown in Figure 17-13.

4. Choose Symbols to import in one of the following ways:

   • To import all of the Symbols, click the select all button.

   • To import a contiguous list of Symbols, hold down Shift and click the first and last Symbol in the contiguous list.

   • To pick and choose Symbols from the list, hold down Ctrl (Command) and, in turn, click each Symbol you want to import.

Tip   To quickly import a single Symbol, double-click its name in the Import Symbols dialog box.

5. When you've made your selection, click Import to import the Symbols into the current document.

Fireworks imports the Symbols and makes them available in the Symbol list.

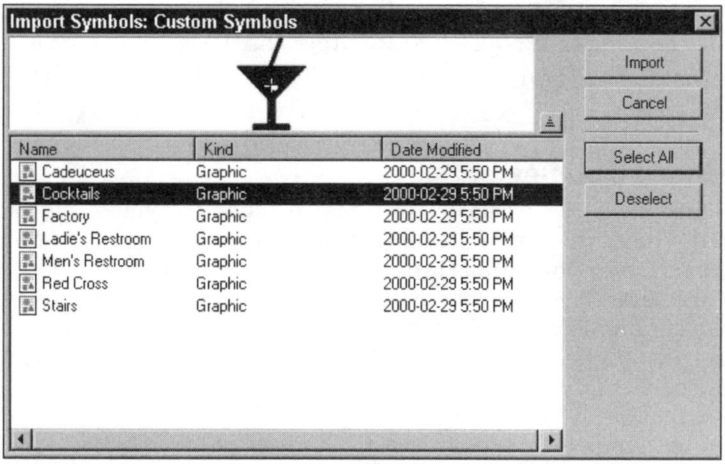

Figure 17-13: Fireworks displays the Import Symbols dialog box when you import a Library.

Accessing often-used Libraries

Choose a library from the Insert ➪ Libraries submenu to begin importing it. This submenu reflects the contents of Fireworks' Libraries folder, shown in Figure 17-14. Placing a Library PNG file into this folder and restarting Fireworks makes the new Library available from the Insert ➪ Libraries submenu. If you frequently access the same sets of Libraries, this can be a real timesaver.

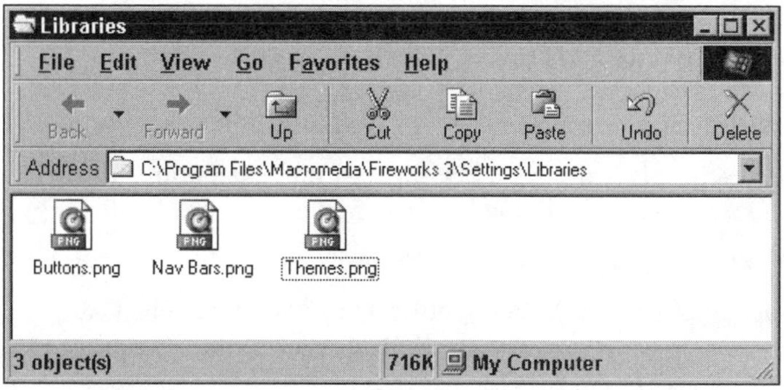

Figure 17-14: Place often-used Libraries into Fireworks' Libraries folder for easy import.

Tip

In Windows, the Libraries folder is usually found at C:\Program Files\ Macromedia\Fireworks 3\Settings\Libraries. On a Mac, it is usually at Macintosh HD:Applications:Fireworks 3:Settings:Libraries.

You can also import a Library from the Insert ➪ Libraries submenu without restarting Fireworks by choosing Insert ➪ Libraries ➪ Other and navigating to the Library PNG file anywhere on your computer. Fireworks imports the Library into the current document.

Updating imported Libraries

Fireworks remembers where it originally acquired an imported Symbol and can update imported Symbols from that original source. This enables you, for example, to maintain a single Library of buttons for a Web site and to import that Library into multiple documents. If you need to modify a button later, modify it in the Library and then click update in each of the documents that uses that Library. In one step for each document, any number of documents can be updated from a single edit of the master Library.

To update imported Symbols from their original sources, choose Update from the Library panel pop-up menu.

Caution   If you try to edit an imported Symbol, Fireworks notifies you that this will break the link to the original Symbol. In effect, you are creating a new Symbol based on that Symbol by editing it.

Exporting and sharing Libraries

Although you can import Libraries directly from any Fireworks document that contains Symbols, exporting a group of Symbols as a standalone Library — which is still a standard Fireworks PNG file — is a good way to share Symbols with colleagues or to create archives of Symbols for later use.

To export Symbols as a standalone Library, follow these steps:

1. Choose Window ➪ Library to view the Library panel, if it is not visible.

2. Choose Export Symbols from the Library panel pop-up menu. Fireworks displays the Export Symbols dialog box, as shown in Figure 17-15.

3. Choose Symbols to export in one of the following ways:

    • To export all of the Symbols in your document, click Select All.

    • To export a contiguous list of Symbols, hold down Shift and click the first and last Symbol in the contiguous list.

    • To pick and choose Symbols from the list, hold down Ctrl (Command) and click each Symbol you want to export.

4. When you've made your selection, click Export. Fireworks displays the Export Symbols As dialog box.

5. Navigate to a folder where you'd like to save your Symbols file and provide a filename. Click Save when you're done.

The exported file contains your exported Symbols, and it can be imported into another document or shared with others.

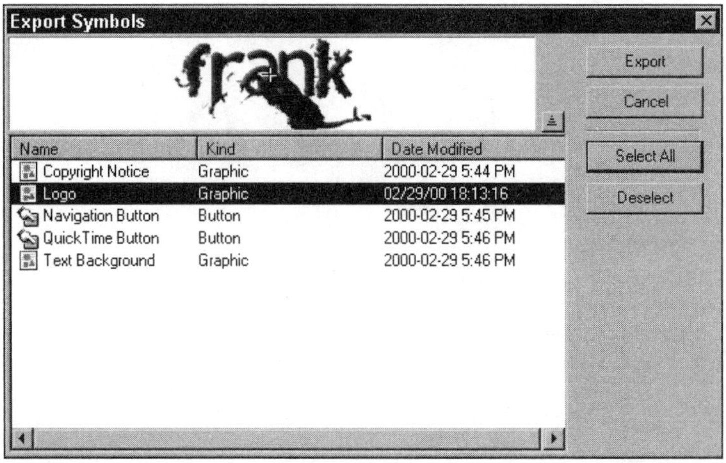

Figure 17-15: Fireworks displays the Export Symbols dialog box, enabling you to choose which Symbols you'd like to export.

Summary

Symbols and Libraries can greatly simplify many of the most common tasks of the Web artist. Keep these things in mind:

✦ Fireworks has two kinds of Symbols: Graphic and Button.

✦ Symbols are kept in the Library panel. Dragging a Symbol from the Library panel onto the canvas creates an Instance of the Symbol.

✦ Symbols can contain any object except Instances.

✦ Every copy that you make of an Instance is another Instance.

✦ Some properties of Instances, such as Live Effects, and some transformations, such as scale and skew, can be modified independently of the parent Symbol or other Instances. Some properties, such as fill and stroke, can be modified only on the Symbol and are then inherited by its Instances.

✦ Symbols are stored in Libraries, which can be exported from and imported into the current document using the Library panel.

In the next chapter, we'll look at how to update and maintain your graphics in Fireworks.

✦   ✦   ✦

Updating and Maintaining Web Graphics

✦ ✦ ✦ ✦

In This Chapter

Viewing your graphics in a browser

Managing links in Fireworks

Updating a site with Find and Replace

Batch processing automation

Reusing Scriptlets

✦ ✦ ✦ ✦

I'm sure you've heard the expression, "1 percent inspiration and 99 percent perspiration." In my experience, Web graphics is more balanced—half the time you're creating a new work, and the other half you're revising something that you've already done. Updating Web pages is a continual, seemingly never-ending process, and although some of the work involves importing new text, quite often the graphics need to be altered, as well. No product can completely turn such a chore into a joyful, creative pleasure, but at least Fireworks helps you to get the job done in the most efficient manner possible.

Web-graphic maintenance is at the core of Fireworks' "everything editable, all the time" philosophy. When Fireworks first arrived, Web designers everywhere were thrilled with the ease with which changes to images could be made. Fireworks has since extended that ease-of-use philosophy to include production tasks such as updating URLs and replacing colors. This chapter explores all the production enhancement techniques—from previewing your graphics directly in a browser to optimizing entire folders of images at one time.

Preview in Browser

It's amazing to me how many so-called Web-graphics programs don't let you easily see your work through its intended medium: the browser. Fireworks enables you to preview in not one, but two browsers at the press of a keyboard shortcut. Not only do you quickly get to see how the browsers are interpreting your graphics, but you can also test any rollovers or other Behaviors you may have included in Fireworks.

Web designers, like most Internet users, tend to work with a particular version of Navigator or Internet Explorer most of the time. But, unlike ordinary Web surfers, Web designers must be able to view work under various conditions in order to ensure consistency across platforms and browser versions. As of this writing, Netscape and Microsoft share the browser market fairly evenly. One company is usually ahead of the other in terms of new versions — and with them, new features — so the ability to preview in more than one browser is essential.

Tip   Fireworks shows that it's truly a tool for Web designers by permitting work to be previewed in both a primary and secondary browser. This makes quickly viewing your graphics — and even comparing their appearance in two different browsers — straightforward. I even use the Preview in Browser feature to display different versions of the same graphic side by side, without having to make additional copies in Fireworks.

Before you can use the Preview in Browser feature, you have to tell Fireworks which two browsers you'd like to use. Although you don't have to define both a primary and a secondary browser, it's a good idea (if you have two browsers on your system). To set the browsers, follow these steps:

1. Choose File ➪ Preview in Browser ➪ Set Primary Browser.

    The Locate Browser dialog box appears, as shown in Figure 18-1.

2. In the Locate Browser dialog box, navigate to the browser directory to locate the application itself. Table 18-1 shows typical locations for browser application files, although you may have chosen a different location if you installed the browser yourself. If you're using a Macintosh, you may also have moved it after installation, or if the browser doesn't have an installation program (Internet Explorer or iCab, for example), then it will be wherever you left it.

Table 18-1
Typical Browser Locations

Browser	Windows Location	Macintosh Location
HotJava	`C:\HotJava\hotjava.exe`	**Macintosh HD:**`HotJava:hotjava`
Internet Explorer 4.x	`C:\Program Files\ Internet Explorer\ Iexplore.exe`	**Macintosh HD:**`Internet: Microsoft Internet Applications:Internet Explorer 4.01 Folder: Internet Explorer 4.01`
Internet Explorer 5.x	`C:\Program Files\ Internet Explorer\ IEXPLORE.exe`	**No default location. (Drag and drop the IE folder from a CD or disk image to a hard drive.)**

Browser	Windows Location	Macintosh Location

Navigator 4.x	`C:\Program Files\`
	`Netscape\Navigator\`
	`netscape.exe`
		Macintosh `HD:Internet:`
		`Netscape Navigator:`
		`Netscape Navigator`

Communicator 4.x	`C:\Program Files\`
	`Netscape\Programs\`
	`netscape.exe`
		Macintosh `HD:Internet:`
		`Netscape Communicator:`
		`Programs:Netscape`
		`Navigator`

Opera	`C:\Program Files\` `Opera\Opera.exe`	n/a

Tip Although the Web TV Viewer for Macintosh or Windows is a great way to get an idea of what your work will look like on Web TV, the application itself can't receive a URL from another application, and so it can't be used as a Primary or Secondary browser in Fireworks. Preview in a regular browser instead and then copy and paste the file:\\ URL from there to the Web TV Viewer. If you don't have the Web TV Viewer, it's free at <`http://developer.webtv.net`>.

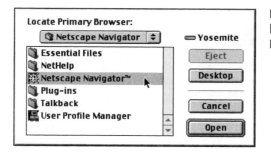

Figure 18-1: Declare your primary browser through the Locate Primary Browser dialog box.

3. Click Open after you locate the browser.

4. To define the secondary browser, choose File ➪ Preview in Browser ➪ Set Secondary Browser and repeat Steps 2 and 3.

After you define your browsers, they're immediately available for use. If you selected Netscape Navigator as your Primary browser and you want to view a graphic in a browser, select the browser and then choose File ➪ Preview in Browser ➪ Preview in Browser Name (. I heartily recommend memorizing the keyboard shortcuts for this command: to preview in your primary browser, press F12; to preview in your secondary browser, press Shift+F12.

Caution Each time you preview in Internet Explorer for Windows, an entirely new instance of Internet Explorer is launched, which can heavily tax your system's resources. Whenever possible, close Internet Explorer for Windows before previewing again.

Working with a client who depends on a different browser or a browser version different than the one you normally use isn't an unusual circumstance. It's a good idea to install as many different browsers—and different browsers versions—as possible.

Caution

Internet Explorer (IE) for Windows only allows you to have one version installed at a time. The (sort of) exception to this is if you install IE 5 over IE 4 and select the "Compatibility Mode" custom install option. You can continue to launch IE 4 as before, and you'll get an IE 4/5 hybrid that mimics most—but not all—of IE 4's unique quirks and formatting. Installing IE 4 on a version of Windows that comes with IE 5 preinstalled is not possible. If possible, keep multiple Windows systems or multiple Windows partitions with a different version of IE on each.

Previewing early and often in multiple browsers helps to avoid surprises caused by browser incompatibilities or bugs.

Tip

Macintosh users might want to investigate an IBM PC-compatible emulator, such as Connectix Virtual PC. Because you can create multiple "hard drives" with multiple and varied installations of the different flavors of Windows and Internet Explorer, it's possible to maintain every Windows and Macintosh Web browser on one machine. It's even possible to install Linux and OS/2 into Virtual PC and run browsers there, too.

Managing Links with the URL Panel

To me, links are the lifeblood of the Web. Without the ability to jump from one section, page, or site to another, the Internet would be a very linear medium—and nowhere near as popular. Before Fireworks, the normal course of Web graphics production kept the images and the links completely separate until the final Web page was assembled. However, because Fireworks extends its graphic capabilities into HTML and JavaScript code through Behaviors and hotspots, links can actually be incorporated during the creation phase.

A link is more technically known as a *URL* (generally pronounced as if it were spelled out, U-R-L). URL is short for Uniform Resource Locator and is best thought of as the Web's address system. Every Web page on the Internet has a URL. Web design deals with two kinds of URLs: absolute and relative. An *absolute URL* is the exact address that allows a Web page to be accessed from anywhere on the Internet, such as `http://www.idest.com/fireworks/index.htm#book`.

In the preceding example, the URL is divided into five main parts:

✦ **Method:** The method specifies the protocol used to address the server. Web servers use *HTTP* (HyperText Transfer Protocol). Other methods include *FTP* (File Transfer Protocol), for transmitting files; News, for accessing newsgroup servers; and Mailto, for sending e-mail.

✦ **Domain:** The domain name (in this example, `www.idest.com`) is registered with an Internet authority, such as Network Solutions, so that the server to which the domain name refers can be found. The *IP* (Internet Protocol) address (for example, 199.227.52.143) can be used in place of a domain name.

✦ **Path:** Depending on exactly where on the server the Web page is located, the path can be a single folder, as it is in this example (`fireworks`), or many folders, in which case each folder is separated by a forward slash (/).

✦ **Page:** The name of the Web page itself is the name under which it is stored — in the example the name is `index.htm`. The file extension used depends on the type of server and the authoring system. Most typically, Web pages end in either .html or .htm; however, you'll also see extensions such as .shtml, .asp, .cfm, and .taf, just to mention a few.

✦ **Named anchor:** A portion of the page marked with an HTML tag, called an anchor (in the URL example it is `#book`). With named anchors, you can quickly move from one section of a long document to another, all on a single page.

All but the target portion is mandatory for an absolute URL. The other type of URL, a *relative URL*, however, can use as little as just the page, or even just the named anchor. Whatever the link is, its location is relative to the current page. For example, if you need to link to another Web page in the same folder as the current one, the link would look something like this example:

```
contact.html
```

On the other hand, if you need to link to a page that is stored in a subfolder of the current page, the relative link would resemble the following:

```
old_news/pr98.htm
```

The more that your site structure is developed — blank Web pages and empty folders created — before working in Fireworks, the more you can take advantage of the program's URL tools.

Accessing the URL History list

In Fireworks, links are attached to either of the two types of Web object: a hotspot or a slice. You can assign a link to a selected Web object either through the Object panel or the URL panel. The Object panel, shown in Figure 18-2, enables you to assign a link in one of two ways:

✦ Enter the link directly into the Current URL text box.

✦ If you choose to type your new link into the Current URL text box, double-check your text to avoid any mistakes. Computers are literal when it comes to URLs, and thus every element — names, punctuation, and even case (uppercase or lowercase) on some servers — must match.

✦ Select the from the Current URL option list.

Current URL box

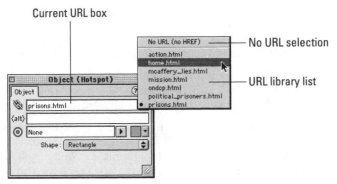

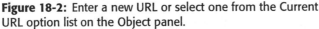

No URL selection

URL library list

Figure 18-2: Enter a new URL or select one from the Current URL option list on the Object panel.

The Current URL option list is divided into two parts: the No URL selection and the URL History list. Choose the No URL (noHREF) selection when your slice or hotspot does not have a link assigned; this is the default selection for Web objects. The URL History is a list of links that have been added to the current document. Every time that you manually enter a new link in the Current URL text box, it is stored as part of the URL History.

If your URL History list is filled with links that are no longer used, a command that is available through the URL panel pop-up menu, Clear History, can remove all but the links actually used in the document. Another command, Add History to Library, can save your document links so that they can be retrieved independently of the document.

Adding URLs to the URL Library

The URL Library represents a more permanent list of links than those found in the URL History. URL Libraries can be stored, edited, and reloaded to work with any document. This facility makes building all the graphics involving rollovers and image maps — anything that needs a URL — far easier on the site level. From a Web graphics production perspective, a different URL Library can be maintained for each site or client, which further simplifies your workflow.

Although you can access what's in the URL Library from the Object panel for a selected Web object, all management of the Library is handled through the URL panel, shown in Figure 18-3. To open the URL panel, choose Window ➪ URL or press the keyboard shortcut, Ctrl+Alt+U in Windows (Command+Option+U on a Macintosh). Alternatively, if the URL panel is docked with another panel, click the URL panel's tab to bring it forward.

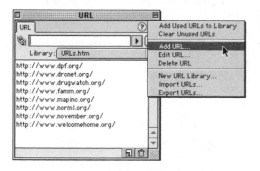

Figure 18-3: Use the URL panel to build, access, and store URL Libraries.

The URL Library is stored in an HTML file format used for browser bookmark files; the default Library is called URLs.htm. However, you can add URLs to the Library in several ways, almost all of which are commands available in the URL panel's pop-up menu. The commands are shown in Figure 18-4 and in the following list:

✦ **Add History to Library:** Enables you to save the current document's URL History as part of the URL Library.

✦ **Add URL:** Adds a single URL directly to the Library.

✦ **Import URLs:** Inserts URLs found within any HTML file, including Bookmark pages.

✦ **Add to Library button:** Adds the URL in the History text box of the URL to the Library.

Figure 18-4: Most URL Library commands are accessible through the URL panel's pop-up menu.

Combining the document's URL History with the current URL Library is a one-step process — just choose the Add History to Library command from the pop-up menu. Fireworks automatically integrates the two lists of links, alphabetically. If any links appear in both lists, Fireworks eliminates the duplicates.

To add a single URL to the Library, choose the Add URL command from the pop-up menu. The New URL dialog box appears. Enter the new link directly in the large text area and click OK when you're done. The new link is added to the Library list.

Tip You can also click the New URL button located at the bottom of the URL Panel to add a new link.

The Import URLs command is a wonderful work-saver and is extremely flexible. Because you can import the links from any HTML file, you can quickly bring in all the links from a site just by importing a Web site's home page.

Tip You can also import Netscape Bookmark files because Netscape stores bookmarks as plain HTML pages. This is handy if you're creating a links page that will contain sites you've already been to while surfing the Web. Windows users can find their Netscape Bookmarks.html file at `<C:\Program Files\Netscape\Netscape Users\Username\Bookmarks.html>` while Macintosh users will find theirs at `<Macintosh HD:System Folder:Preferences:Netscape Users:Username: Bookmarks.html>`.

To import links from an HTML page, follow these steps:

1. From the URL panel pop-up menu, choose Import URLs.

   The standard Open dialog box appears.

2. Locate the HTML page containing the links you want to incorporate into a Library; click Open after you find the HTML page.

   Any link, relative or absolute, found on the selected HTML page is integrated with the current URL Library.

As you'll see in the next section, you can also create, edit, delete, store, and load URL Libraries through the URL panel.

Managing URL Libraries

URL Libraries are extremely flexible in Fireworks. New Libraries can be created with a single command, and existing Libraries can be edited, deleted, loaded, or stored.

From time to time, a Web page will move to a new location on the Web. If you have the page's URL in your URL Library, you'll have to change it. To do so, follow these steps:

1. Select the URL you want to change from the URL panel list.

2. From the URL panel's pop-up menu, choose Edit URL.

   The Edit URL dialog box, shown in Figure 18-5, appears.

Figure 18-5: Update your URL Library links with the Edit URL command and the Edit URL dialog box.

3. Enter the new URL in the text area. To also update any existing links in the current document, select the Change All Occurrences in Document checkbox. Click OK when you're done.

The URL is modified in the Library.

Following are the two ways to remove a URL from the Library:

✦ Select the unwanted URL and then click the Delete URL button in the lower-right corner of the URL panel.

✦ Select the URL and then select Delete URL from the URL panel pop-up menu.

By default, Fireworks starts with one URL Library, URLs.htm. You can add others by following these steps:

1. Choose the New URL Library command from the URL panel pop-up menu.

The New URL Library dialog box, shown in Figure 18-6, appears.

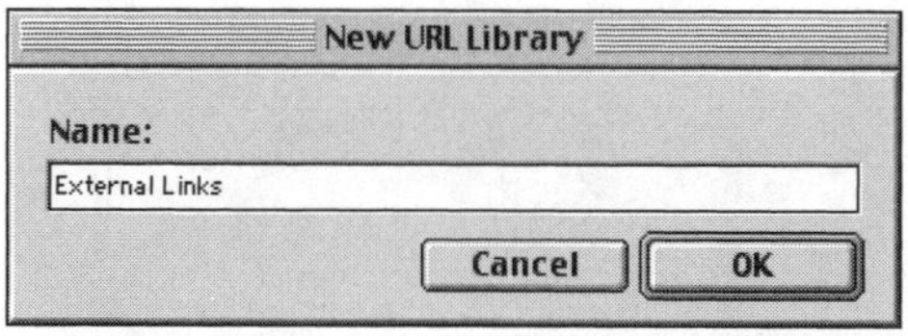

Figure 18-6: Organize a new Library for each client through the New URL Library command.

2. Enter a unique name for the new library.

If you don't include a .htm or .html file extension, Fireworks automatically appends one.

Fireworks creates a new file in the Fireworks 3/Settings/URL Libraries folder. This file is updated when Fireworks closes; you don't need to save your URL Library in a separate operation.

Tip   While Fireworks makes creating a new Library a breeze, removing an unwanted Library is a little more hands-on. No command is available to delete a Library, so you have to open the Fireworks 3/Settings/URL Libraries folder and delete the HTML file using Windows Explorer or the Macintosh Finder. The deleted Library will disappear from the URLs list when Fireworks is restarted.

If Fireworks automatically stores the URL Libraries that you create, why would you need an Export command? The Export URLs command, found in the pop-up menu, enables you to save the URL Library as an HTML file in another directory. The HTML file, as shown in Figure 18-7, is a straightforward list of links. If your URL Library is complete, you could use the exported Library file as the basis for a text-only home page to go along with the graphical one you're making in Fireworks.

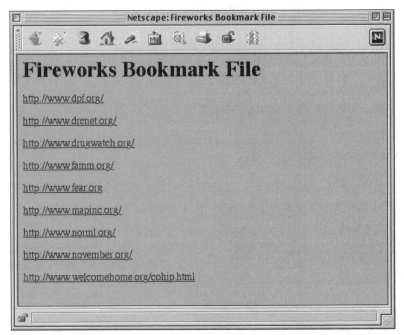

Figure 18-7: Exporting a URL Library results in a list of links in HTML format.

Caution   On the Macintosh, even if you name your exported file with an .html filename extension, Fireworks will still save it with an .htm filename extension.

Updating Graphics with Find and Replace

Fireworks has always been great about allowing you to alter any aspect of your graphic at any time; before Fireworks, you had to make every change by hand. Graphics for a Web site often have a great deal of overlap—a consistent color scheme, the same typeface, even the same URLs embedded in image maps and buttons. Replacing a misspelled client name in one graphic is one thing, replacing them in all the graphics, site-wide, is another.

Fireworks offers a robust Find and Replace feature that automates the onerous chore of modifying text, fonts, colors, and URLs. Through the new Find and Replace panel, you can direct your updates to the current selection, frame, document, or to a selection of documents. The Find and Replace options for text and URLs include a powerful wildcard capability known as Regular Expressions. You can also track your changes through Fireworks' Project Log.

Outside of batch processing and Scriptlets, all automated modifications in Fireworks are handled through the Find and Replace panel, shown in Figure 18-8, which displays different options depending on which attribute is being altered. The five attributes and their options are the following:

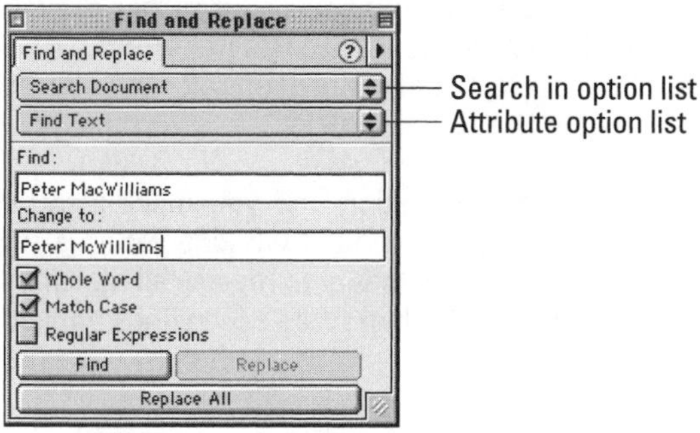

Search in option list
Attribute option list

Figure 18-8: Use the Find and Replace panel to automate changes to text, fonts, URLs, and even color.

✦ **Text:** Any text object in a Fireworks file can be modified under Find and Replace. The text search can include anything from a single character to full sentences. Options include Whole Word, which ensures that the text to be found is not within another word; Match Case, which seeks out the exact text entered and replaces it verbatim; and Regular Expressions, a system of wildcard matching discussed in detail later in this chapter.

✦ **Font:** Every text object must use a particular font with a set style (or lack of one), in a particular size. Fireworks' Find and Replace feature enables you to update all of these characteristics, either separately or combined. You can even search for a font in a range of sizes and convert all occurrences to one size.

✦ **Color:** In a Fireworks object, color is just another attribute that can be searched for and replaced, if necessary. You can find and replace a specific color from the pop-up color picker displaying the current swatch set (which can be selected in the Mixer panel) or from your operating system color picker(s). You can also use the Eyedropper tool to sample a color. Color can be altered in strokes, fills, effects, strokes and fills, or all four.

Caution   Some restrictions apply to replacing color by using the Find and Replace command. Bitmap or text objects can't be accessed. You can, however, replace the colors of any part of a graphic by using the Edit Color command in the Export Preview dialog box.

✦ **URL:** The URL Find and Replace panel is similar to the Find and Replace panel for text. Any link can be altered in any way; you can even use the Find and Replace feature to remove all links. The Whole Word, Match Case, and Regular Expressions options are available for the URL, attribute just as they are for the Text attribute of Find and Replace.

✦ **Find Non-Web 216:** This option searches for non-Websafe colors and changes them to their nearest Websafe color. You can apply it to fills and/or strokes, effects, or every object.

Regardless of the specific attribute, with each Find and Replace operation, you have the option of making changes on a case-by-case basis or all at once. Click Find Next to locate the next item fulfilling the search criteria and then click either Replace, to make a change to the selected item, or Find Next, to locate the next item without making a change. You can also click Replace All at any time to make the alterations within your search scope to all matches in the document(s).

Tip   What if you're running a Find and Replace operation and you make a mistake, such as clicking Replace All instead of Replace? If you're working within a single document, you can use Edit ➪ Undo or the History panel to reverse all the changes and start over. This method has no effect on Find and Replace actions applied to multiple files.

With all attributes, the scope of the search is defined by the value set in the Search In option list, which includes the following possible options:

✦ **Selection:** You can modify only the currently selected object or objects.

✦ **Frame:** Limits the search to the current selected frame of the active document.

✦ **Document:** Allows the search to be applied to the entire active document.

✦ **Project Log:** Limits the search to files listed in the Project Log. Use of the Project Log is covered in detail later in this chapter.

✦ **Files:** Carries out the Find and Replace operation on any accessible file or files. Selecting the Files option displays the Open Multiple dialog box, in which files are added to the selection list either individually or by the folder.

Tip   If you need to adjust the selected files for a Multi-File Find and Replace operation, reopening the Open Multiple dialog box involves a small trick. Temporarily choose a different Search In option, such as Document or Frame, and then select Files again. The Open Multiple dialog box will reopen.

While all the Search In options have their place, Fireworks' Multi-File capability really gives the Find and Replace feature its power. Naturally, such increased power also brings increased risk for making a mistake. To offset that risk, Fireworks offers two backup options. To set the backup options, choose Replace Options from the Find and Replace panel's pop-up menu. The Replace Options dialog box (Figure 18-9) appears. If the first option, Save and Close Files, is selected, Fireworks closes each file after it makes a replacement; if the option is not selected, the files are left open. The Backup Original Files drop-down list box includes three choices:

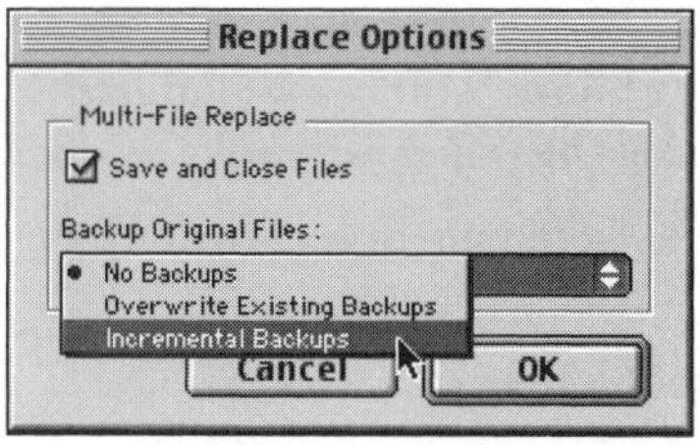

Figure 18-9: Choose your backup options from the Replace Options dialog box.

✦ **No Backups:** The target files are overwritten and no backups are saved.

✦ **Overwrite Existing Backups:** The target files are copied to a subfolder called Original Files, and the Find and Replace operation is performed on the files in their original location. Each time you perform another Find and Replace operation, the existing backup in the Original Files folder is overwritten with a newer backup. In a sense, this is like having an Undo feature with only one Undo. The Original Files folder always contains files that are one step older than the last Find and Replace operation.

✦ **Incremental Backups:** If you don't want to risk losing any changes, choose this option. Each time you perform a Find and Replace, the target files are copied to the Original Files folder, but rather than overwriting the other files there, they are renamed incrementally. For example, the first time a file named Star.png is changed, the source file is saved in the Original File subfolder as Star.png. The next time you use Find and Replace, the copy of Star.png in the Original Files folder is renamed Star-1.png and the target file is copied there as Star.png. The most recent version always retains the original name, and the oldest version ends with the highest number. This essentially gives you an unlimited Undo for Find and Replace (except for running out of hard drive space).

You could use the Incremental Backups option as a type of version control, but the downside is that this choice stores *all* the files. Your choice may depend on how much free hard drive space you have and/or how big your target files are. If you have 10GB of hard drive space, go ahead and use Incremental Backups. After you've finished your work session, you can easily go into the original files folder and delete (Trash) anything with a number higher than three, so that you're saving only the last few versions.

Searching and replacing text

I recently had a client come to me with every Web designer's major nightmare — a name change. Not only did every logo need to be altered, but much of the Web site incorporated the name as a graphic background. I was faced with days upon days of pure drudgery — until I realized that I could use Find and Replace to automate the process. I was able to make the revisions in a few short hours, much of the time quite amazed at how quickly the job was getting done.

To find and replace text, follow these steps:

1. If the Find and Replace panel is not visible, choose Window ➪ Find and Replace or, if it is visible, click its tab to bring the panel forward.

2. Choose the scope of the search operation by selecting one of the choices from the Search In option list.

3. Make sure that the Attribute selection is set to Text.

4. Enter in the Find text box the text that you want to find.

5. If you intend to change the text, enter its replacement in the Change To text box.

6. Select any options desired: Whole Word, Match Case, or Regular Expressions.

7. To make changes on a case-by-case basis, first click Find Next and then click either Replace, to change the text, or Find Next again, to move to the next matched text.

8. To change all the text at once, click Replace All.

   If no changes are made, Fireworks reports that the search is complete. Otherwise, Fireworks informs you of how many occurrences it changed.

Although the Find and Replace Text operation may be the most straightforward of all the attributes, you still need to be aware of some issues:

✦ Text objects expand to make room for new words, but if you add a lot of text, you may find objects hanging off canvas. Left-aligned text expands to the right, right-aligned text expands to the left, centered text expands in both directions.

✦ During Multi-File Find and Replace operations, if one of the selected documents is open in Fireworks, the document must be activated before any changes can be made.

Searching with Regular Expressions

The serious power in the Find and Replace feature is the Regular Expressions option. I've referred to Regular Expressions as being similar to wildcards in other programs, but the Fireworks capabilities are really far, far more extensive.

Regular Expressions are best described as a text pattern-matching system. If you can identify any pattern in your text, you can manipulate it with Regular Expressions. For example, suppose that you're building a navigation bar in which the buttons are all contact names that are listed in a Lastname, Firstname format. With Regular Expressions, you could match the pattern and reformat the entire list, placing the Firstname before the Lastname, without the comma—all in one Find and Replace operation.

You can apply Regular Expressions to either the text or URL attributes by selecting the Regular Expressions option. When you enable this option, Fireworks processes the text entered in both the Find and Change To text boxes differently, looking for special key characters, such as backslash and asterisk.

The most basic Regular Expression is the text itself. If you enable the Regular Expressions option and then enter "th" in the Find What text box, Fireworks will locate every example of "th" in the text and/or source. Although this capability by itself has little use, it's important to remember this functionality as you begin to build your patterns.

Wildcard characters

Initially, it's helpful to be able to use what traditionally are known as *wildcards*: characters that match different types of characters. The wildcards in Regular Expressions all represent single characters only, as described in Table 18-2. In other words, no single Regular Expression represents all the characters, like the asterisk does when used in DOS file searches. However, such a condition can be represented with a slightly more complex Regular Expression (described later in this section).

Table 18-2
Regular Expressions Wildcard Characters

Character	Matches	Example
.	Any single character.	**w.d** matches **wide** but not world.
\w	Any alphanumeric character, including the underscore.	**w\wd** matches **wide** and **world**.
\W	Any nonalphanumeric character	**jboy\Widest.com** matches **jboy@ idest.com** and **jboy$idest.com**.
\d	Any numeric character 0-9.	**y\dk** matches **Y2K**.
\D	Any nonnumeric character.	**\D2\D** matches **Y2K** and **H2O**.
\s	Any white-space character, including space, tab, form feed, or line feed.	**\smedia** matches **media** but not Macromedia.
\S	Any nonwhite-space character.	**\Smedia** matches Macro**media** but not media.

Caution   Be careful with the \S wildcard. In Fireworks, it actually matches one more character than it should; for instance **\Sworks** actually matches Fir**eworks**, instead of just Fire**works**.

The backslash character (\) is used to escape special characters so that they can be included in a search. For example, if you want to look for an asterisk, you need to specify it like this: *****. Likewise, when trying to find the backslash character, precede it with another backslash character: ****.

Matching character positions and repeating characters

With Regular Expressions, you not only can match the type of character, but also match its position in the text. This feature enables you to perform operations on characters at the beginning, end, or middle of the word or line. Using Regular Expressions also enables you to find instances in which a character is repeated either an unspecified or specified number of times. Combined, these features broaden the scope of the patterns that can be found.

Table 18-3 details the options available for matching by text placement and character repetition.

Table 18-3
Regular Expressions Character Positions

Character	Matches	Example
^	Beginning of a line.	**^c** matches "**C**all me Ishmael".
$	End of a line.	d$ matches the final *d* in "Be afraid. Be very afrai**d**".
\b	A word boundary, such as a space or carriage return.	**\btext** matches **text**book but not SimpleText.
\B	A nonword boundary inside a word.	**\Btext** matches Simple**Text** but not textbook.
*	The preceding character zero or more times.	**b*c** matches **BBC** and **c**old.
+	The preceding character one or more times.	**b+c** matches **BBC** but not cold.
?	The preceding character zero or one time.	**st?un** matches **stun** and **sun** but not strung.
{n}	Exactly *n* instances of the preceding character.	**e{2}** matches **ree**d and each pair of two e's in Aie**ee**e**ee**e**ee**!, but nothing in the word red.
{n,m}	At least *n* and at most *m*.	C{2,4} matches #**CC**00FF and #**CCCC**00, but not the full string #CCCCCC.

Matching character ranges

Beyond single characters or repetitions of single characters, Regular Expressions incorporates the ability to find or exclude ranges of characters. This feature is particularly useful when you're working with groups of names or titles. Ranges are specified *in set brackets*. A match is made when any one of the characters within the set brackets is found, not necessarily all of the characters.

Table 18-4 describes how to match character ranges with Regular Expressions.

Table 18-4
Regular Expressions Character Ranges

Character	Matches	Example
[abc]	Any one of the characters a, b, or c.	[lmrt] matches the *l* and *m*'s in **lemm**ings and the *r*'s and *t* in **r**oad**t**rip.
[^abc]	Any character except a, b, or c.	[^etc] matches each of the letters in **GIFs**, but not **etc** in the phrase "GIFs etc".
[a-z]	Any character in the range from a to z.	[l-p] matches *l* and *o* in **lo**wery and *m*, *n*, *o*, and *p* in **pointm**an.
x|y	Either x or y.	**boy|girl** matches both **boy** and **girl**.

Using grouping with regular expressions

Grouping is perhaps the single most powerful concept in Regular Expressions. With it, any matched text pattern is easily manipulated — for example, a list of names like this:

```
Schmidt, John Jacob Jingleheimer
Kirk, James T.
Fishman, Cara
```

could be rearranged so that the last name comes last and the comma is removed, like this:

```
John Jacob Jingleheimer Schmidt
James T. Kirk
Cara Fishman
```

Grouping is handled primarily with parentheses. To indicate a group, enclose it in parentheses in the Find text field. Regular Expressions can manage up to nine grouped patterns. Each grouped pattern is designated by a dollar sign ($) in front of a number, (1 to 9) in the Change To text field, like this: **$3**.

To switch the series of names as previously described, enter the following in the Find text box:

```
(/w+),/s(.+)
```

In Regular Expressions speak, this translates into "(Pattern 1 matches any alpha-numeric character, one or more times) followed by a comma, a space, and (Pattern 2 matches any character — including white spaces — one or more times)." In the Change To text field, enter

```
$2 $1
```

This configuration places the second matching pattern before the first, with just a space in between.

Caution   Remember that the dollar sign is also used after a character or pattern to indicate the last character in a line.

Table 18-5 shows how Regular Expressions uses grouping.

	Table 18-5	
	Regular Expressions Grouping	
Character	*Matches*	*Example*
(*p*)	Any pattern *p*.	(**/d**).(**/d**) matches two patterns, the first before a period and the second after a period, such as in a filename with an extension.
$1, $2...$9	The *n*th pattern noted with parentheses.	The replacement pattern **$1's extension is .$2** would manipulate the pattern described in the preceding example so that Chapter07.txt and Image12.gif would become **Chapter07's extension is .txt** and **Image12's extension is .gif**.

Altering font characteristics

Choosing the Font attribute in the Find and Replace panel enables you to search based on any or all of three different font characteristics:

✦ **Font:** Choose Any Font or select from a list of installed fonts.

✦ **Style:** Choose Any Style or choose standard options, such as Plain, Bold, Italic, or Underline. You can also choose combinations, such as BoldItalic or ItalicUnderline.

✦ **Size:** Use the Min and Max boxes to target a range of font sizes or set them both to the same value to find only one size.

The real power of the Font Find and Replace is that you can search on one criteria, such as Size, and if a match exists, you can change another criteria, such as Font. This flexibility enables you to, for example, search all graphics in a site and, if the font size is between 8 and 12, change the font from Times to Helvetica, without changing the original size (leave the Change to size box empty). This might cover all of the "body text" in your document in one shot.

To change the font characteristic with Find and Replace, follow these steps:

Note We'll start at the top of the Find and Replace box and work down as we go.

1. If the Find and Replace panel is not showing, choose Window ➪ Find and Replace or, if it is visible, click its tab to bring the panel forward.

2. Choose the scope of the search operation by selecting Search Document, Search Selection, and so on, from the Search In option list.

3. Select Font from the Attribute option list to specify a Font Find and Replace.

   The Find and Replace panel displays the Font options, as shown in Figure 18-10.

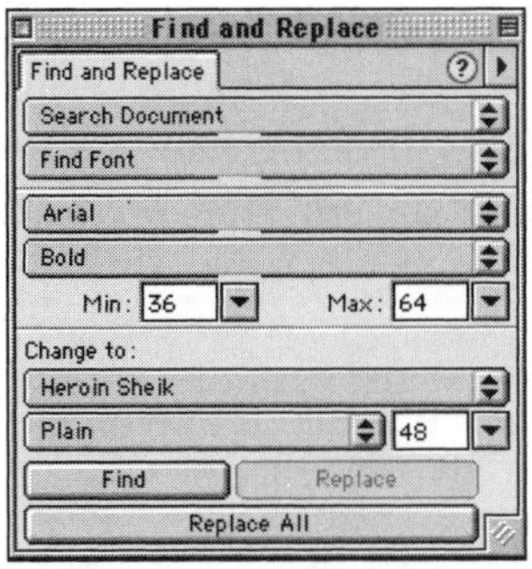

Figure 18-10: Change font size, typeface, or style when the Font attribute is selected from the Find and Replace panel.

4. To search for a specific typeface, change Any Font to an installed font by choosing the font from the list.

5. To search for a specific font style, change Any Style to one of the other options on the list, such as Plain or Bold.

6. To search for a specific range of font sizes, set the minimum point size in the Min box and the maximum point size in the Max box; to search for a single point size, set the Min and Max text boxes to the same value.

Tip The Min and Max boxes also have pop-up sliders to adjust their values.

7. To change target objects to a specific font, change Same Font to another installed font by choosing a font from the list.

8. To change target objects to a specific style, change Same Style to another option, such as Italic.

9. To change target objects to a specific size, enter a value in the Size text box or use the slider to select a value.

10. Click the Find button to find the first target object and then click Replace to replace it, or click the Replace All button to make all of the changes in one step.

Changing colors throughout a site

A color can be as important to a brand as a logo — for example, IBM blue. Web graphics often use a specific color scheme to make a marketing point or to assist with navigation. Previously, updating graphics to incorporate a color change could be an extraordinarily tedious chore. In Fireworks, you can search for and replace colors just as easily as you can text — and, in some cases, even more easily.

Fireworks applies color to its path objects via three primary components: strokes, fills, and effects. When the Color attribute is selected in the Find and Replace panel, you can change colors associated with any single one of these components, associated with both strokes and fills, or associated with all four. To search and replace a color, follow these steps:

1. If the Find and Replace panel is not showing, choose Window ➪ Find and Replace or, if it is visible, click its tab to bring the panel forward.

2. Choose the scope of the search operation by selecting one of the choices from the Search In option list.

3. From the Attribute option list, select Color.

   The Find and Replace panel displays the Color options, as shown in Figure 18-11.

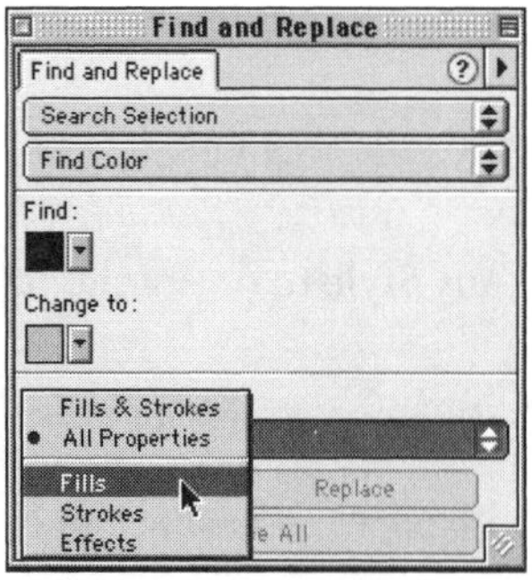

Figure 18-11: Update all the colors across a site with the Find and Replace panel's Color attribute.

4. In the Find pop-up color picker, select the color to search for.

You can select one of the available swatches, use the Eyedropper tool, or select the Palette icon to open the system color picker(s).

5. From the Apply To option list, set which component of Fireworks the search should be limited to.

6. In the Change To pop-up color picker, select the color to replace the color being searched for.

7. Click the Find and Replace buttons to make changes on a case-by-case basis or click the Replace All button to make global changes.

Snapping colors to Websafe

Replacing colors with their nearest Websafe equivalent is unfortunately a reality of today's Web. Until the vast majority of computer users have 32-bit color hardware (and know how to enable it), sticking to Websafe colors gives you the best chance of your work looking similar for the majority of your audience.

New Feature

Fireworks 3 adds a new tool to your Find and Replace toolbox: Find Non-Web 216. Now you can apply a Websafe palette to objects in a selection, an entire document, or even a group of documents.

Find Non-Web 216 is similar to the Color Find and Replace. The same caveats apply, but in this case, Fireworks chooses the colors. To search for non-Websafe colors and replace them with Websafe colors, follow these steps:

1. If the Find and Replace panel is not showing, choose Window ⇨ Find and Replace or click its tab to bring the panel forward, if it's docked behind another.

2. Choose the scope of the search by selecting one of the choices from the Search In option list.

3. From the Attribute option list, select Find Non-Web 216.

   The Find and Replace panel displays the Find Non-Web 216 options, as shown in Figure 18-12.

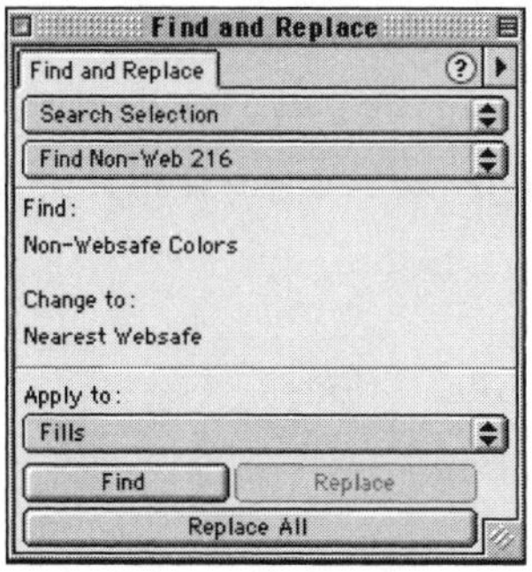

Figure 18-12: Search for non-Websafe colors in a selection, a document, or across multiple files and snap them to their nearest Websafe color.

4. From the Apply To option list, set which component of Fireworks the search should be limited to.

5. Click the Find and Replace buttons to make changes on a case-by-case basis or click the Replace All button to make global changes.

Updating URLs

After you spend any amount of time designing for the Web, you'll appreciate how active the Web is. Sites are constantly in motion, with new pages being added and old ones deleted or moved. Because Fireworks graphics are tied so directly to the Web through the URLs embedded in hotspots and slices that Fireworks creates, you need a way to modify the links quickly, if necessary. The URL attribute of the Find and Replace panel fulfills that need.

The URL attribute works much the same way that the Text attribute does — in fact, the interfaces for the two are identical, as you can see in Figure 18-13. A link to be searched for is entered in the Find text box and the new link is entered in the Change To text box. The same three options (Whole Word, Match Case, and Regular Expressions) apply. With URLs, however, a whole word is not designated by a space, but rather by a separator — either a period, a forward slash, or a colon.

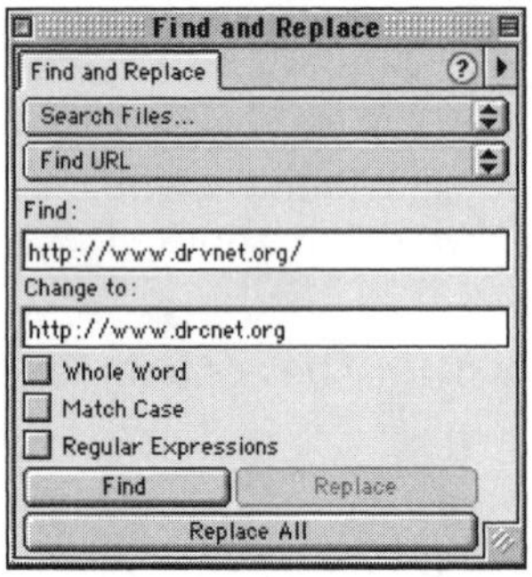

Figure 18-13: Update your links with the URL attribute of the Find and Replace panel.

To search and replace links embedded in Fireworks graphics, follow these steps:

1. If the Find and Replace panel is not showing, choose Window ➪ Find and Replace or, if it is visible, click its tab to bring the panel forward.

2. Choose the scope of the search operation by selecting one of the choices from the Search In option list.

3. From the Attribute option list, select URL.

   The Find and Replace panel displays the URL options.

4. Enter the link to be found in the Find text box.

5. If you intend to change the link, enter its replacement in the Change To text box.

6. Select any options desired: Whole Word, Match Case, or Regular Expressions.

7. To make changes on a case-by-case basis, first click Find Next and then click either Replace, to change the link; or Find Next again, to move to the next matched URL.

8. To change all the URLs at once, click Replace All.

As noted earlier in the chapter, the URL attribute can take advantage of Fireworks' Regular Expressions features when the Regular Expressions option is selected. The pattern-matching features of Regular Expressions go far beyond any simple wildcard character. For example, suppose that you have to convert from absolute to relative an entire site's worth of links inside of graphics, where all the links are within the same folder. This would require changing files from `http://www.idest. com/fireworks/main.htm` to just `main.htm`. Moreover, suppose that you have links to files from both Windows and Macintosh designers, so that some files end in .htm and others in .html. With Fireworks' Regular Expressions option enabled, here's what you'd enter in the Find text box:

```
(.+)/(/b.*/.html?)
```

Translated from Regular Expressions language, this means "(Pattern 1 contains all characters) before a forward slash and (Pattern 2, which can be any single word followed by a period and then either htm or html)."

To change these patterns to just the filename, enter **$2** by itself into the Change To text box. This returns just the results of pattern 2, without any other characters.

Working with the Project Log

One of the dangers of working with a find-and-replace feature as powerful as Fireworks' Find and Replace is that unwanted changes can be made inadvertently. This is especially true when the Multi-File Search & Replace option is used — Fireworks can open, modify, and close a file so quickly that you won't know what happened. You won't know, that is, unless you enable the Project Log option to track all changes.

With the Project Log option turned on, all Multi-File changes are noted. The Project Log, shown in Figure 18-14, lists the filename, the frame in which the change was made, and the date and time that the modification took place. Moreover, you can immediately check the alteration by double-clicking the filename in the Project Log in order to open the file in Fireworks.

Figure 18-14: Keep track of all your Multi-File Find and Replace operations through the Project Log.

You enable the Project Log to note search-and-replace changes by selecting the Add Files to Project Log command found in the pop-up menu on the Find and Replace panel. Once selected, any file altered when the search scope is set to Files is listed by name, frame number, date and time. To verify a change — or to reverse it — open the file from the Project Log by double-clicking its name or selecting it, and then clicking the Open button.

The Project Log panel's pop-up menu offers some additional functionality with the following four commands:

✦ **Export Again:** Because all Find and Replace operations are conducted only on source files, after you alter a file, you usually need to re-export it. The Export Again command repeats the last export and overwrites the previously exported file.

✦ **Add Files to Log:** You don't have to run a Find and Replace procedure on a file to include it in the Project Log. By selecting the Add Files to Log command, you can select which additional files are listed in the Project Log. This is a handy way of having your working files close at hand, but not opened until they're necessary.

✦ **Clear Selection:** Removes the currently selected listing from the Project Log.

✦ **Clear All:** Removes all entries from the Project Log.

The Project Log has yet another use: all files or selected files in the Project Log can be processed together with Fireworks Batch Processing feature, discussed in the next section.

Tip   To get a separate hard copy of the Project Log, detailing all the changes in a session, open the `Project_Log.htm` file found in the Fireworks Settings folder and then print the page from your browser. The `Project_Log.htm` file is updated with every change.

Batch Processing Graphics Files

The unfortunate truth is that producing graphics for the Web involves about as much mindless repetition as it does creative expression. The more you can automate the processes, the more time you'll have to experiment and create. Fireworks has seriously enhanced its batch-processing capabilities, making it easier than ever to optimize, scale, and export large numbers of images.

The Batch Processing dialog box, shown in Figure 18-15, is the automation control center.

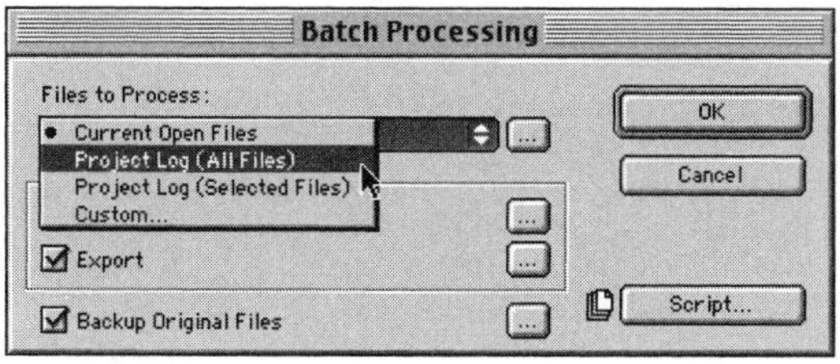

Figure 18-15: Select your automation options from the Batch Processing dialog box.

Basic procedure

Following is the basic procedure for running an automated session:

1. Choose File ➪ Batch Process to open the Batch Processing dialog box.

2. Determine which files are to be affected from these choices in the Files to Process option list:

    Current Open Files: All the files currently open in Fireworks, whether active or not, are processed.

    Project Log (All Files): All the files listed in the Project Log, whether open or not, are processed.

    Project Log (Selected Files): Only the selected files in the Project Log are processed. Multiple individual files can be selected by Ctrl+clicking (Command+clicking), and a range of files can be selected by Shift+clicking.

    Custom: A selection of files chosen through the Open Multiple dialog box is processed. The Custom option can also be selected by clicking the ellipsis (...) button next to the Files to Process option list.

3. If you want a Find and Replace operation to be part of the batch process, click the Find and Replace ellipsis (...) button.

    This opens the Batch Replace dialog box (Figure 18-16), with options similar to the Find and Replace panel. Selecting the Update Project Log option adds to the Project Log any files that are processed.

4. If you want to include an Export operation, click the Export ellipsis (...) button, which displays the Batch Export dialog box (Figure 18-17), with the following options:

Select a preset setting from the Export Settings drop-down list or click the ellipsis button to access the Export Preview dialog box, which offers additional Export options.

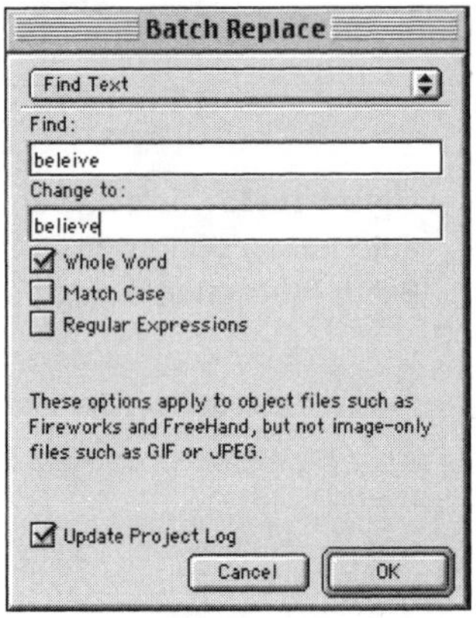

Figure 18-16: The Batch Replace dialog box changes according to which Attribute — Text, Font, Color, URL or Non-Web 216 — you choose. Here, the Text attribute is selected.

To differentiate your exported files from the originals, you can add a custom prefix or suffix from the File Name option list.

The Scaling options are No Scaling, Scale to Size (specific pixel measurements), Scale to Fit Area (while maintaining the proper aspect ratio within a maximum width and height), and Scale to Percentage. A common use of this Batch Process feature is to create thumbnails.

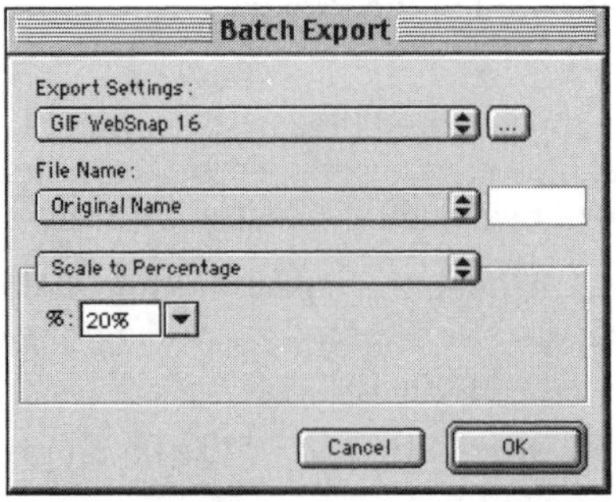

Figure 18-17: The Batch Export dialog box optimizes, scales, and renames groups of files with ease.

5. Select the backup options from the Save Backups dialog box. If used, backups can overwrite existing files or save each one incrementally, as described earlier in the "Updating Graphics with Find and Replace" section.

6. After setting all other criteria, you can save the Batch Process operation as a Scriptlet (discussed in the next section) by clicking the Script button.

7. Clicking OK in the Batch Processing dialog box initiates the procedure. A Batch Progress dialog box reports how many files have been processed and how many are remaining. When finished, the total number of affected files is displayed.

Running Scriptlets

Scriptlets are Fireworks script files, written in JavaScript. You can generate Scriptlets by using the Batch Processing dialog box, by hand coding them, or by using a combination of both options. The simple, yet powerful, idea behind Scriptlets is that they are reusable.

After you save a Scriptlet, with an identifying .jsf filename extension, you can run it in any of these ways from the Batch Process dialog box:

✦ Double-click the Scriptlet icon.

✦ Choose File ➪ Run Script and select the Scriptlet.

✦ Drag the Scriptlet icon onto the Fireworks application, onto a shortcut or onto an alias of it.

✦ Drag the Scriptlet icon into the Fireworks window (Windows only).

All Scriptlets run immediately. Fireworks includes many custom JavaScript "hooks" so that you can take advantage of the functions that are accessible through Scriptlets.

Cross-Reference For more detailed information on Scriptlets, see Part VII.

Summary

The term production can't be overemphasized in Web graphics production. Much of a Web designer's job is devoted to updating and editing existing graphics. Fireworks offers a number of workflow solutions to reduce the workload:

✦ Graphics can be previewed immediately — with or without rollovers — and directly in the primary and secondary browsers of your choice.

✦ Links used in Fireworks Web objects, such as rollovers and hotspots, are coordinated through the URL panel, which maintains both the current document's links (URL History) and an independently stored set of links (URL Library).

✦ The links from any HTML file can be imported into a separate URL Library.

✦ The Find and Replace panel enables you to update text, font attributes, colors, and URLs, and it even snaps colors to Websafe in the current document, frame, selection, or a series of selected documents.

✦ Export operations — including optimization and scaling of images — can be automated through Fireworks' Batch Processing features. Find and Replace operations and automatic backups can be batch processed, as well.

✦ A batch processing session can be saved as a special JavaScript file known as a Scriptlet. Scriptlets can be customized or run, as is, any time they are needed.

In the next chapter, you'll work with Fireworks' new Commands menu and History panel.

✦   ✦   ✦

Automating Workflow with Commands and the History Panel

◆ ◆ ◆ ◆

In This Chapter

Running built-in
Commands

Increasing productivity
with the History panel

Commands
without coding

Managing the
Commands menu

◆ ◆ ◆ ◆

Although Fireworks 2 exposed quite a bit of the program's functionality to enthusiastic JavaScript coders, those without JavaScript experience or without a knack for coding were left a little out in the cold. Fireworks 3 remedies this in a big, big way with the addition of the History panel.

New Feature   The History panel and the Commands menu are new additions to Fireworks 3.

In a nutshell, the *History panel* is a combination super-Undo tool and macro recorder. Actions you take while working in Fireworks are recorded in the History panel automatically. While the obvious side effect of this is the capability to step back through those actions as though rolling back time, the truly exciting consequence is that you can save those steps as Commands and replay them again and again. Constantly resizing buttons to 40 × 40 pixels to satisfy corporate guidelines? Do it once, save it as a Command, and make it a one-step process forever after.

In this chapter, we'll look at the Commands menu's built-in default Commands, as well as how to add to the menu's contents with the History panel. We'll also run through the History panel's other raison d'être: Undo central. Finally, we'll touch on the kind of housekeeping you can do to keep the Commands menu from scrolling off your screen as you fill it with workflow shortcuts.

Tip   The History panel is sometimes — but not always — referred to as the History Palette in Macromedia's Fireworks documentation and in the Fireworks JavaScript API. The term palette is properly reserved for color palettes in Fireworks 3, though, and the actual nomenclature is History panel.

Running Built-in Commands

Although storing your own Commands is perhaps the primary purpose for the Commands menu, the menu arrives from the factory with a group of built-in Commands that enable you to take Fireworks extensibility for a test drive. After a couple of turns around the block, I found myself amazed that these kinds of features can be added to Fireworks using JavaScript, and in some cases without even writing a line of code! The built-in Commands, shown in Figure 19-1 and detailed throughout this section, are useful additions to the Fireworks toolkit.

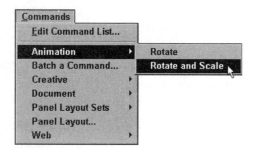

Figure 19-1: The Commands menu contains a range of Commands — organized into submenus — that demonstrate Fireworks' extensibility.

Animation

Two quick animation tricks are contained in the Commands ⇨ Animation submenu, providing a quick way to start an animation:

✦ Commands ⇨ Animation ⇨ Rotate creates a multiframe animation from a selected object or objects by creating frames and distributing rotated versions of your objects across those frames.

✦ Commands ⇨ Animation ⇨ Rotate and Scale works just like Rotate, except that your objects scale as they rotate, which makes them appear to zoom away from the viewer.

Tip   To have your object(s) zoom toward the viewer, use the Reverse All Frames Command, detailed later in this section.

To use the Animation Commands, follow these steps:

1. Select an object or objects.

2. Choose Commands ⇨ Animation ⇨ Rotate or Commands ⇨ Animation ⇨ Rotate and Scale.

Fireworks displays a dialog box explaining the chosen Command, as shown in Figure 19-2.

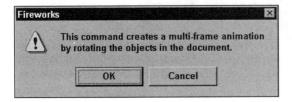

Figure 19-2: Confirm that you want an instant animation created.

3. Click OK to create the animation.

Fireworks creates an animation from your selected object(s), adding 12 frames to your document in the process.

Cross-Reference

Although the animation Commands always create 12 frames, you can modify this number using the extensibility techniques in Chapter 26.

Batch a Command

Using Batch a Command enables you to apply a single Command to all open documents, a group of files defined in the Project Log panel, or a group of files selected from a disk.

To use Batch a Command, follow these steps:

1. Prepare a group of target files with one of the following methods:

- Open two or more documents in Fireworks.
- Add two or more documents to the Project Log panel.
- Select one or more files in the Project Log panel.

Alternatively, you can wait and choose your target files later.

2. Choose Commands ⇨ Batch a Command.

3. Fireworks displays an Open dialog box, focused on your Commands folder.

Note

The Commands folder is covered in detail later in this chapter.

4. Choose a Command (.jsf) file to apply to multiple files. Click Open when you're done.

Caution Don't try to batch Batch a Command (its filename is `Batch a Command....jsf`) or you'll get an error dialog that explains "You may not run this Command on itself."

Fireworks displays the Files to Process dialog box, as shown in Figure 19-3.

Figure 19-3: Choose a Command to batch.

5. Choose an option from the Files to Process option list and click the ellipsis button to execute that option:

   • Current Open Files applies the chosen Command to all of the documents you currently have open in Fireworks.

Tip This is the only option that is Undoable.

   • Project Log (All Files) applies the chosen Command to all of the files listed in the Project Log panel.

   • Project Log (Selected Files) applies the chosen Command to files that are selected in the Project Log panel.

Note If there are no files listed in the Project Log, choosing either of the Project Log options is the same as choosing Custom.

   • Custom opens the Open Multiple dialog box, enabling you to create a list of files by navigating to each one in turn and adding it to a list or by adding whole folders of files.

6. Click Open to start executing the chosen Command on your selected files.

   Fireworks displays the Batch Processing dialog box.

7. When the batch processing is complete, Fireworks displays the message "Batch processing complete." Click OK to dismiss the Batch Processing dialog box.

Cross-Reference For more about the Project Log and batch processing in general, see Chapter 18.

Creative

Two of the three Commands in the Creative submenu convert the palette of selected objects:

   ✦ Commands ➪ Creative ➪ Convert to Grayscale simply converts any object to a grayscale palette, which is 256 shades of gray.

✦ Commands ➪ Creative ➪ Convert to Sepia Tone is similar to Convert to Grayscale, but the resulting image has a sepia tint.

Tip   If you have to export a photographic image as a Graphics Interchange Format (GIF) — in order to create a transparent portion or to include it in an animated GIF, for example — converting it to grayscale or sepia first often leads to much better results than dithering the True Color image. Grayscale and sepia both contain 256 shades or less, just like the GIF format.

The final Creative Command, Create Picture Frame, wins the award for truth in advertising.

To create a picture frame around your document, follow these steps:

1. Choose Commands ➪ Creative ➪ Create Picture Frame.

Fireworks displays a JavaScript dialog box.

2. Enter a width for the picture frame in pixels. Click OK when you're done.

Fireworks expands the canvas to make room and creates a picture frame around your document, with the specified pixel width, a three-dimensional look, and a saucy faux-wood texture, as shown in Figure 19-4.

Figure 19-4: Place an instant picture frame around a document with the Create Picture Frame Command.

> **Tip** If pixel veneer doesn't do it for you, select the picture frame and alter its settings in the Fill panel.

Document

The Commands ➪ Document submenu contains five Commands that operate on the canvas, layers, or frames of your document.

Center in Document

The inclusion of the Center in Document Command in Fireworks 3 may have ignited a celebration amongst Fireworks users. As powerful as Fireworks' object-to-object align commands are, there are definitely times when you just want to center an object or objects smack in the middle of the canvas. In the past, you had to create a dummy object the same size as the canvas just to align other objects to it.

To use the Center in Document Command, select an object or objects and choose Commands ➪ Document ➪ Center in Document. Fireworks aligns your selected object(s) in the absolute center of the canvas.

Toggling layers

Two Commands provide straightforward shortcuts to focusing in on only the current layer:

✦ Commands ➪ Document ➪ Hide Other Layers hides all layers except the current layer.

✦ Commands ➪ Document ➪ Lock Other Layers locks all layers except the current layer.

Reversing frames

Occasionally, you may find that you've imported a rollover button upside down so that the initial state is not in Frame 1 in Fireworks. This often occurs when FreeHand layers are converted into Fireworks frames. Reversing frames is also a common way to save time and work while creating animations. Fireworks provides two Commands to reverse the order of frames in a document.

✦ Commands ➪ Document ➪ Reverse All Frames simply reverses the order of all of the frames in your document. The first frame becomes the last frame, the last frame becomes the first frame.

✦ Commands ➪ Document ➪ Reverse Frame Range works in the same way as Reverse All Frames except that it prompts you for a starting and ending frame and then reverses just that frame range.

Fireworks technique: completing an animation

When working on an animation, it's common to build one half of an animation sequence, such as a sun rising, and then reverse the already built frames to create the other half of the animation, such as the sun setting. Fireworks Reverse All Frames Command provides an easy way to accomplish this in record time.

1. Create the first half of your animation, such as the previously mentioned sunrise, or an animated object flying onto the canvas.

2. Choose File ➪ Save a Copy to save a copy of your document.

3. Choose Commands ➪ Document ➪ Reverse All Frames to reverse the frames of your animation, essentially running it backward.

4. Choose Add Frames from the Frames panel pop-up menu.

   Fireworks displays the Add Frames dialog box.

5. In the Number box, type in the same number of frames as you document currently contains. For example, if your document has 10 frames, enter **10** to create 10 new frames so that you end up with 20 frames.

6. Under Insert New Frames, select At the Beginning and click OK when you're done.

   Fireworks creates the new frames at the beginning of your document and selects Frame 1.

7. Choose File ➪ Import. Navigate to and select the copy of your document that you created in step 2. Click Import to import it.

8. Place the L-shaped import cursor at the top left of the canvas in order to line up the imported document with the current document. Click once to complete the import operation.

Your original animation—running forward—fills up the empty frames and provides the beginning of the animation. The reversed frames provide the end of the cycle so that the animation completes itself.

 Cross-Reference Find out more about animation in Fireworks in Chapters 23 and 24.

Panel Layout Sets

Panel Layout Sets are saved configurations of Fireworks' floating panels. Saved sets are added to the Commands ➪ Panel Layout Sets submenu automatically for easy recall of any particular organization of floating panels.

Tip

Panel Layout Sets are a welcome solution when you change to a lower display resolution and all of your floating panels are out of the visible area. Recalling a saved set restores Fireworks to working order.

Fireworks provides two built-in Panel Layout Sets, each specifically optimized for a different screen resolution:

✦ Commands ➪ Panel Layout Sets ➪ 1024 × 768 places four docked groups of floating panels along the right side of the display. All panels are onscreen, and the Optimize, Color Table, Layers, and Behaviors panels are placed in front.

✦ Commands ➪ Panel Layout Sets ➪ 800 × 600 creates a reversed L-shape of floating panels, as shown in Figure 19-5, with all panels onscreen and docked into four groups. The Optimize, Color Table, Layers, and Library panels are placed in front.

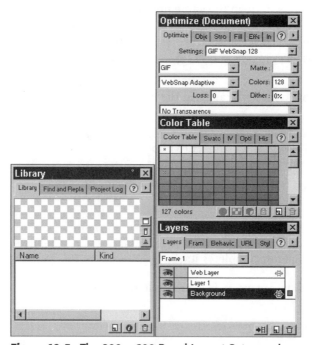

Figure 19-5: The 800 × 600 Panel Layout Set organizes panels into a reversed L-shape in one step.

 Tip

Although the Commands are named for specific display resolutions, running one of them at a different resolution often leads to satisfactory results.

Panel Layout

The Panel Layout Command enables you to easily save your own Panel Layout. Aside from saving your One True Favorite panel setup for posterity, you might save configurations that are optimized for certain tasks, such as a drawing layout that places the Object, Info, Fill, and Stroke panels front and center, or an optimization layout that pops up the Optimize, Color Table, and Frames panels.

To create your own Panel Layout Set, follow these steps:

1. Create a panel layout worth saving by toggling the visibility of particular panels and/or adjusting their positions.

2. Choose Commands ➪ Panel Layout.

   Fireworks displays a JavaScript dialog box asking for a name for your new Panel Layout, as shown in Figure 19-6.

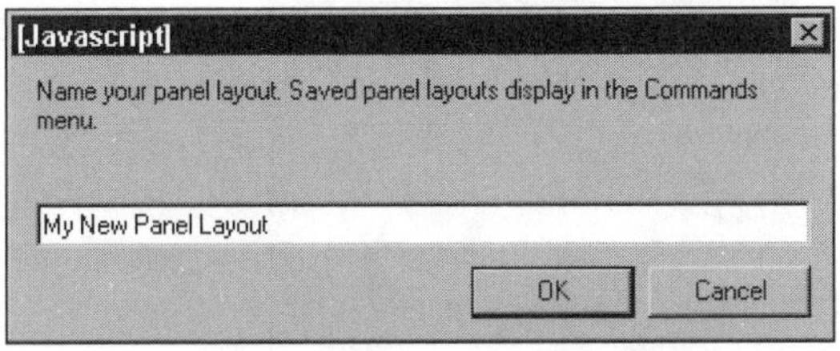

Figure 19-6: Name your Panel Layout before saving it.

3. Enter a name for your Panel Layout in the dialog box. Click OK when you're done.

Fireworks saves your panel configuration as a new Panel Layout and adds it to the Panel Layout Sets submenu in the Commands menu.

Caution   Creating a new Panel Layout with the same name as an existing one overwrites the original without asking for confirmation. It's possible to have both entries briefly coexist on the Panel Layout Sets submenu, but your original Command file will still be lost.

Web

The Web submenu of the Commands menu has two entries that enhance Fireworks' export features.

Create Shared Palette

The Create Shared Palette Command looks at a folder full of images and creates a common color table file (.act) from them.

To create a shared palette from a folder of images, follow these steps:

1. Choose Commands ➪ Web ➪ Create Shared Palette.

Fireworks displays a confirmation dialog box that explains the Command.

2. Click OK to confirm that you want to continue with the Create Shared Palette Command.

Fireworks displays the Select Folder dialog box (Figure 19-7).

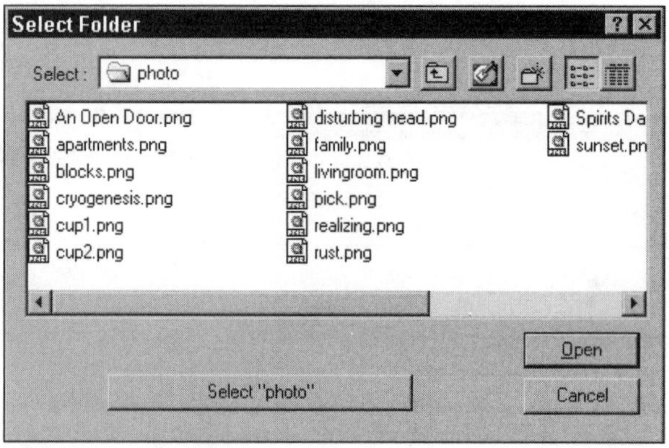

Figure 19-7: Select a folder of images and Fireworks creates a shared palette from them.

3. Navigate to a folder of images and click the select button to create a shared palette from the images.

Fireworks displays a JavaScript dialog box.

4. Enter the maximum number of colors for the shared palette and click OK.

Fireworks displays a "processing Command script" dialog box while the images are processing, and then it displays a Save dialog box when it's done.

5. Navigate to a folder and specify a filename for the palette file. Click Save when you're done.

Fireworks saves the shared palette as a color table file, with the filename extension .act. This file can be opened with the Fireworks Color Table panel or imported into Photoshop.

Tip   Mac users: Fireworks saves the palette file with a Fireworks Creator code (MKBY), but Fireworks doesn't provide an icon for a color table file type (8BCT). If you also have Photoshop, applying a Photoshop Creator code (8BIM) to the file with AppleScript or a utility, such as File Buddy, will apply an icon to it, as well.

Set Alt Tags

The HTML img tag that's used for inserting images into Web pages can have an alt attribute that displays text to users who have images turned off in their browser or are using a text-only browser. You can set alt text in the Object panel while a hotspot or slice object is selected, but Fireworks' Set Alt Tags Command enables you to set them all to the same text string in one step. You might set all buttons to say "button," for example.

When you choose Commands ⇨ Web ⇨ Set Alt Tags, Fireworks displays a dialog box, as shown in Figure 19-8. Enter your alt text and click OK after you're done. Leaving the text field empty and clicking OK is the same as clicking Cancel.

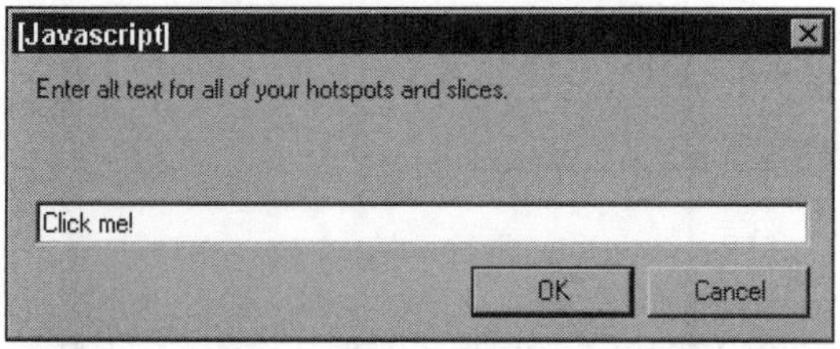

Figure 19-8: Provide alt tags for all of the Web objects in your document in one step.

Enhancing Productivity with the History Panel

The History panel not only enables you to Undo actions, but it also enables you to save steps as Commands, which you can then repeat. This productivity enhancements can be quite remarkable. If you're used to a History panel from Photoshop, you know that it's hard to do without it once you're hooked.

Tip   Macromedia's Dreamweaver also gained a History panel in version 3.

Super Undo and Redo

Fireworks has long had multiple Undo, enabling busy Web artists to Ctrl+Z in Windows (Command+Z on a Macintosh) or Edit ⇨ Undo their way step-by-step back through their previous actions. With the History panel, Fireworks' Undo feature gains a friendly front-end that makes jumping back one or ten steps a simple, intuitive affair.

The History panel contains a special slider, called an Undo Marker, that enables you to point to any of your previous steps in order to return your document to the state it was in right before that step. Figure 19-9 displays the History panel with the Undo Marker.

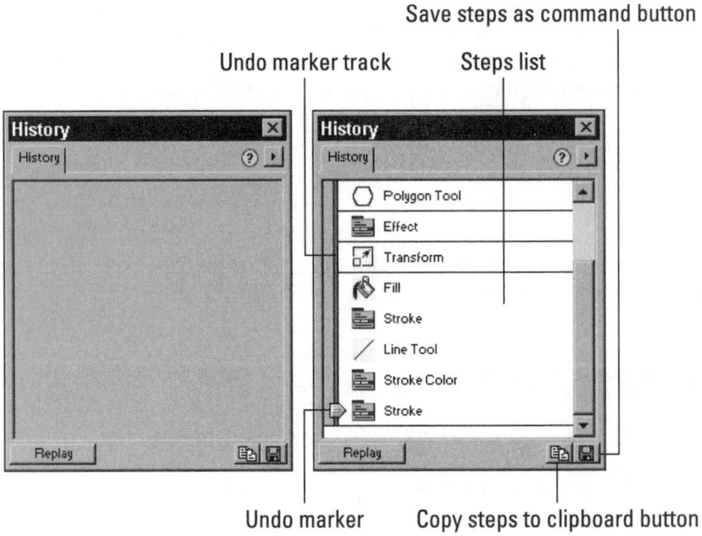

Figure 19-9: The History panel is empty when you create a new document (left), but from that point on it records your every move.

To undo steps in the History panel, try one of the following methods:

✦ Drag the Undo Marker up the History panel until it is next to the last step that you want to undo.

✦ Click the Undo Marker track next to the last step that you want to undo. The Undo Marker slides directly to that point.

Undone steps are grayed out in the History panel, and your document changes to reflect the steps that have been undone.

The logical companion to Undo is, of course, Redo. Once you have undone a step or steps, reversing the procedure applies those actions again.

To redo undone steps with the History panel, try one of the following methods:

✦ Drag the Undo Marker down the History panel until it is next to the last step that you want to redo.

✦ Click the Undo Marker track next to the last step that you want to redo. The Undo Marker slides directly to that point.

By default, Fireworks records 20 unique steps in the History panel, after which, the oldest step is discarded to make room for the newest step.

To change the number of unique steps the History panel can record, follow these steps:

1. Choose File ⇨ Preferences.

   Fireworks displays the Preferences dialog box.

2. If necessary, click the General tab in Windows or choose the General option from the option list on a Mac.

3. Change the number of steps in the Undo Steps box to the number of steps that you want the History panel to record.

Caution The number of Undo steps that Fireworks for Macintosh can provide is limited by the amount of RAM to which it has access. Fireworks for Windows is limited to a maximum of 100 steps, regardless of how much RAM is available.

Clearing steps from the History panel can free memory and disk space, although you lose the ability to work with the steps you are deleting. For example, you will be unable to perform Undo or Redo on deleted steps. To clear all steps from the History panel, choose Clear History from the History panel pop-up menu.

Commands without coding

Building Commands with the History panel is a tremendous timesaver, and a lot of fun, to boot. Creating Commands with the History panel emphasizes the minimalist, easy-to-use interface of the History panel.

The simplest way to create a Command is just to replay a step or a series of steps from the History panel by using the Replay button. Select a step in the History panel by clicking it and then click the Replay button to reapply that step to whatever is currently selected on the canvas.

For example, imagine that you colored an object a certain blue and then later decided that a few other objects should also share that same blue color. Click the Fill Color step in the History panel that represents the application of that blue fill (Figure 19-10) and the Replay button is now a Fill With Blue button. Select objects on the canvas and hit Replay to color them blue. Multiple contiguous steps can be selected in the History panel by holding down Shift while clicking the first and last steps in a series. Multiple noncontiguous steps can be selected by holding down Ctrl+clicking (Command+clicking).

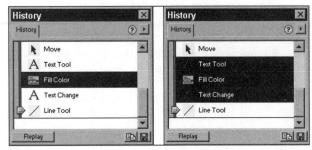

Figure 19-10: With the Fill Color step selected (left), the Replay button becomes a Command that applies a fill to selected objects on the canvas. Hold down Shift to select multiple steps and apply them to selected objects with the Replay button.

But what if you decide that blue fill is so useful that you'll need it again and again? The Fill Color step moves further up the History panel as you continue your work and will eventually be removed to make space for newer steps. To keep your Fill With Blue Command for later use, simply press the History panel's Save Steps as Command button, which looks like a floppy disk. Saving a step or steps as a Command adds the Command to the Commands menu for later use.

To save History panel steps as a Command, follow these steps:

1. Perform an action or a consecutive series of actions that you'd like to save as a Command. Following are examples of steps you could perform before saving them:

   • Create a standard copyright/legal footer for your Web site, with associated text formatting and precise canvas placement.

   • Create a circle object, duplicate it five times, select all six objects, align them horizontally, and distribute them to widths, creating a basic button bar that can be easily built upon or modified.

2. If you want to save just one step as a Command, click that step in the History panel to select it. To save multiple steps, hold down Shift and click the first and the last step in the series that you want to save. Ctrl+click (Command+click) noncontiguous steps to select them.

   The selected steps are colored a dark selection color.

3. Click the Save Steps as Command button in the History panel.

   Fireworks displays the Save Command dialog box, as shown in Figure 19-11.

4. Enter a name for your new Command. Click OK after you're done.

Your steps are saved as a Command and added to the Commands menu in alphabetical order. To apply your Command, choose Commands ⇨ and the name of your new Command.

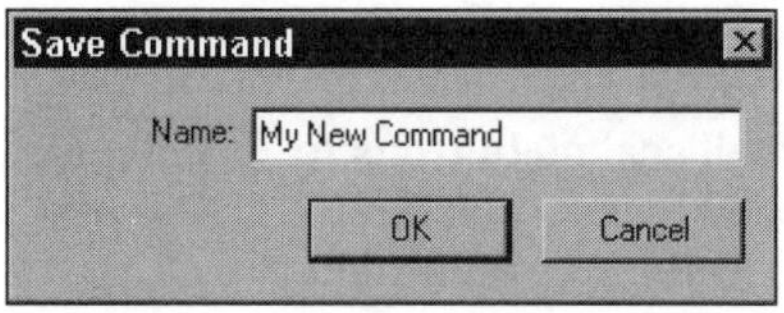

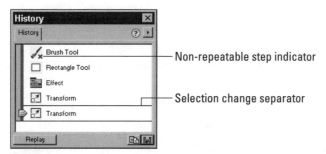

Figure 19-11: Enter a name for your new Command in the Save Command dialog box.

Save as Command limitations

There are two caveats to saving steps as Commands:

✦ Some actions, such as drawing a shape with the Brush tool, are nonrepeatable. Fireworks marks these steps with a red *X*, as shown in Figure 19-12.

Figure 19-12: Items with a red *X* next to them are nonrepeatable. A separator line indicates a change in selection, which can lead to unpredictable results.

✦ Fireworks places a separator in the History panel (also shown in Figure 19-12) when you change your selection. Replaying steps across a separator can have unpredictable results because some objects can't be modified in the same way as other objects.

When you attempt to save steps that include either of these potential problems, Fireworks notifies you with a dialog box, indicating that there may be a problem and allowing you the opportunity to continue or cancel.

Fireworks technique: quick menu command shortcuts

Fireworks offers the user a lot of editing choices and power with many menu commands that have numerous options. This creative flexibility is, of course, a wonderful feature, but there have been times I wished for a few simpler commands, such as Modify ⇨ Reduce Image to 25%. Once you've opened up the Image Size dialog box and almost laboriously chosen Percentage and entered **25%** for the 20th time in a particular session, you start to think there must be a better way. And with Fireworks 3's History panel, there is.

The History panel not only enables you to create a complex series of steps and make intricate Commands, but it's also useful as a way to make one step Commands that simply use common settings. If you find yourself scaling buttons to 30 × 30 pixels all the time, or changing the canvas size to 300 × 200 pixels constantly, create new scaling and canvas-changing Commands with those settings built right in.

To save a Fireworks menu command as a modified Command with your own built-in settings, follow these steps:

1. Open a Fireworks document. As long as you don't save the document after creating your Command, this can be almost any document. Simply use it as a guinea pig in your Command-building session.

2. Perform a simple, one-step transformation on your document. Some ideas:

   • Choose Modify ➪ Image Size and reduce the image's size to 50%, or another percentage (or a pixel size) that you commonly change images to.

   • Import a commonly used file, such as a logo.

3. Select the single step in the History panel that represents the Command you just gave Fireworks.

4. Click the Save Steps as Command button in the History panel.

   Fireworks displays the Save Command dialog box.

5. Enter a name for your new Command. Click OK after you're done.

Your step is saved as a Command and added to the Commands menu in alphabetical order.

Copying steps to the clipboard

As previously mentioned, the ability to turn steps in the History panel into Commands on the clipboard without writing a line of code is a major productivity enhancement, but the History panel also has a trick or two for those of us who don't mind getting into a little JavaScript once in a while.

The Copy Steps to Clipboard button copies the History panel's selected steps to the clipboard as plain text JavaScript statements, ready for pasting into any text editor. Copy Steps to Clipboard provides a way for even the experienced JavaScript coder to get a Command or Scriptlet roughed out in record time.

Once the steps are pasted into a text editor, they can be modified and added to until you have created a complex Command. The Fireworks application programming interface (API) contains a host of entries that make it possible to build complex Commands or Scriptlets that access almost any feature of Fireworks.

The Fireworks API is covered in Chapter 26.

To use Copy Steps to Clipboard to start building a Command or Scriptlet visually, follow these steps:

1. Create a series of steps that you'd like to save.

2. Select the steps in the History panel.

3. Click the Copy Steps to Clipboard button to copy your steps to the system clipboard as JavaScript statements.

4. Launch or switch to your favorite text editor, such as Notepad in Windows or SimpleText on a Mac. Create a new document or open an existing one, if necessary.

5. Choose Edit ⇨ Paste within the text editor to paste your JavaScript code, as shown in Figure 19-13.

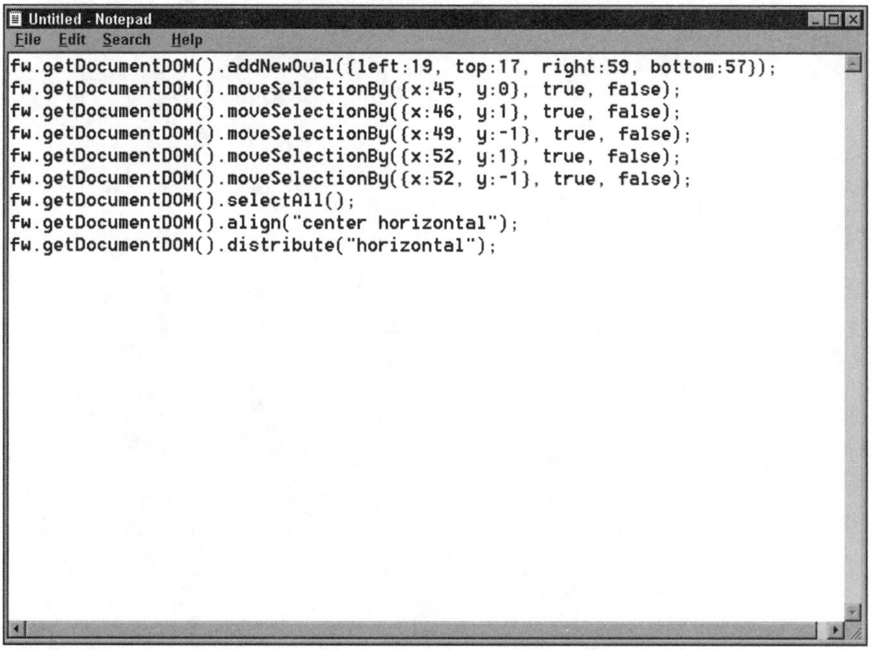

```
Untitled - Notepad
File  Edit  Search  Help
fw.getDocumentDOM().addNewOval({left:19, top:17, right:59, bottom:57});
fw.getDocumentDOM().moveSelectionBy({x:45, y:0}, true, false);
fw.getDocumentDOM().moveSelectionBy({x:46, y:1}, true, false);
fw.getDocumentDOM().moveSelectionBy({x:49, y:-1}, true, false);
fw.getDocumentDOM().moveSelectionBy({x:52, y:1}, true, false);
fw.getDocumentDOM().moveSelectionBy({x:52, y:-1}, true, false);
fw.getDocumentDOM().selectAll();
fw.getDocumentDOM().align("center horizontal");
fw.getDocumentDOM().distribute("horizontal");
```

Figure 19-13: History panel steps that are copied to the clipboard arrive in your text editor as JavaScript.

Feel free to modify the pasted JavaScript or even to repeat steps 1-5 above to add more code to your project.

Cross-Reference Chapter 26 has all the details on the Fireworks JavaScript API.

Using Commands in Commands

After you've applied a Command, the action is recorded in the History panel as a step called Command Script. It might not be immediately obvious, but steps that apply Commands can themselves be selected and saved as part of a Command (see the figure), thus, creating meta-Commands: Commands that combine a number of Commands into one.

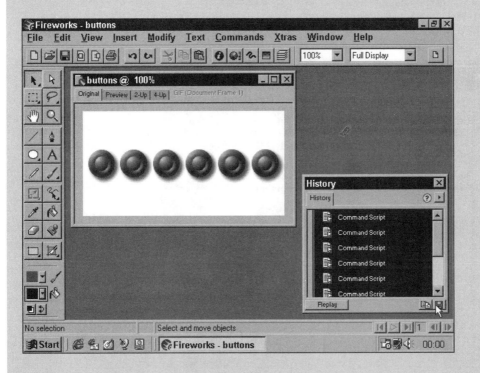

The button bar in the accompanying figure was built almost entirely by running Commands that I had previously saved. One Command applied a drop shadow and inner bevel, while still another Command applied a radial gradient fill and offset the fill to provide a lighting effect. Selecting the steps that applied the Commands and saving them creates a complex sequence of actions that can be applied in the future with just one step. There is one small caveat, though: the new Command is dependent on the original Commands being installed and available so that it can run them.

Managing the Commands Menu

The Commands menu is all about enhancing productivity, and as such, maintaining a neat and tidy Commands menu is an important part of the process. It doesn't take too much experimentation with the Copy Steps as Command button to realize that you can fill up your Commands menu with useful — okay, and sometimes not so useful — new Fireworks Commands.

Organizing installed Commands

Fireworks offers a couple of methods for organizing your Commands. The Edit Command List Command provides a visual interface for renaming or deleting installed Commands.

Editing the Commands menu

To edit your Commands menu with the Edit Command List Command, follow these steps:

1. Choose Commands ⇨ Edit Command List.

   Fireworks displays the Edit Command List dialog box, as shown in Figure 19-14.

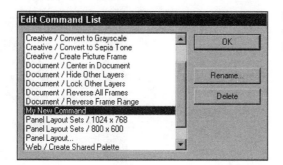

Figure 19-14: Rename or remove Commands in the Edit Command List dialog box.

2. Select a Command to modify and apply one of the following:

   • Click Delete to delete the Command from the Command menu.

Caution

Deleting a Command in the Edit Command List dialog box removes the Command's Scriptlet from your computer and cannot be undone. What's more, Fireworks offers no confirmation or warning dialog box after you press Delete.

   • Click Rename. Fireworks displays the Save Command dialog box. Enter a new name for the Command and click OK to rename it.

3. Click OK in the Edit Command List dialog box after you're done.

The Commands folder

In addition to removing or renaming Commands in the workspace, you can get "under the hood" and organize or add Commands in Fireworks' Commands folder.

The Commands folder is typically found in these locations:

✦ **On Windows machines at** `C:\Program Files\Macromedia\Fireworks 3 \Settings\Commands`.

✦ **On a Mac at** `Macintosh HD:Applications:Fireworks 3:Settings:Commands`.

The hierarchy of your Fireworks Commands folder determines the hierarchy of your Commands menu. In other words, a folder inside the Commands folder becomes a submenu in the Commands menu so that the Animation folder is shown as an animation submenu (Figure 19-15).

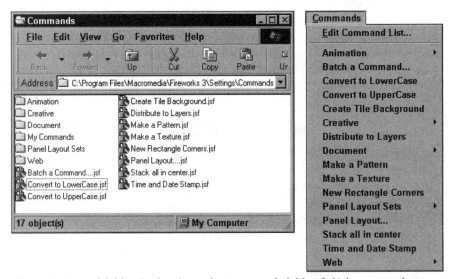

Figure 19-15: Subfolders in the Fireworks Commands folder (left) become submenus in the Fireworks Commands menu.

Create new subfolders in the Commands folder in order to better organize your Commands. Placing folders within those subfolders has no effect; the hierarchy can only be one deep. Changes take effect immediately in Fireworks, without relaunching, making it easy to experiment with new arrangements.

At 1,024-x-768-pixel display resolution, Fireworks for Macintosh allows you about 45 Command menu entries (commands and submenus) before it begins scrolling the menu. When it's maximized, Fireworks for Windows can contain about 30

Command menu items at a 1,024-x-768-pixel display resolution before the menu scrolls. I find scrolling menus to be a real productivity hit. Aside from the fact that you can't see all of the entries, they are sometimes hard to navigate, especially on Windows, where the menu itself does not stay fixed to the menu bar when it gets too long, and it interferes with the Taskbar at the bottom of the display. Keeping your Commands menu organized into a smaller number of subfolders is worth the effort.

Adding more Commands

One of the key points of Fireworks new Commands menu is that it's extensible. Items can be easily created and added to it. In addition to the default Commands included with Fireworks 3, since the program's release Macromedia has created nine more Commands that have been made available on the Fireworks Web site.

Note Obtain the Commands from the Fireworks Support Center at `<http://www.macromedia.com/support/fireworks>`.

Adding the Commands to Fireworks is as simple as dropping the .jsf files themselves into Fireworks Commands folder.

Tip Once you add a Scriptlet to Fireworks' Commands folder, it appears right away in the Commands menu, without restarting Fireworks.

The new Commands:

✦ **Convert to Lowercase:** Converts text in selected objects to lowercase

✦ **Convert to Uppercase:** Converts text in selected objects to uppercase

✦ **Distribute to layers:** Cuts your selection to the clipboard and then pastes each object back onto its own new layer

✦ **Make a Pattern:** Creates a Pattern file out of your selection

✦ **Make a Texture:** Creates a texture file out of your selection

Cross-Reference Textures and Patterns are covered in Chapter 11.

✦ **New Rectangle Corners:** Enables you to select a rectangle or rectangles and then specify a new corner value for them, as shown in Figure 19-16

✦ **Stack all in center:** Stacks all selected objects in the center of the document

✦ **Time and Date Stamp:** Adds the current time and date as a text object

✦ **Create Tile Background:** Converts the current selection to a tiled background on its own layer

Figure 19-16: The New Rectangle Corners Command jazzes up your old boxes with new corner settings (right), so you don't have to draw them again.

Creative shortcuts, such as Make a Pattern; convenience shortcuts, such as Convert to Lowercase; and a lifesaver, such as New Rectangle Corners, are example of the wide range of what's possible with Fireworks' enhanced extensibility

Find even more Commands to enhance your productivity in Fireworks.

Summary

The Commands menu and the History panel are powerful productivity features and welcome additions to Fireworks. Keep these points about them in mind:

✦ Fireworks' extensible Commands menu already contains useful Commands right out of the box.

✦ The History panel offers precise control over multiple Undo and Redo.

✦ Steps in the History panel can be replayed, saved as a Command, or copied to the clipboard as JavaScript code for later editing.

✦ New Commands can be added to Fireworks by dropping them in the Fireworks 3/Settings/Commands folder, the structure which represents the Commands menu.

In the next chapter, you'll explore image maps and slices in Fireworks.

✦   ✦   ✦

Entering the Web

In This Part

Chapter 20
Mastering Image
Maps and Slices

Chapter 21
Activating Fireworks
with Behaviors

Chapter 22
Integration with
Dreamweaver

Mastering Image Maps and Slices

In This Chapter

Working with
Web objects

Assigning hotspots
in image maps

Inserting exported
code into a
Web page

Dividing an image
with slices

Exporting slices
to HTML

Animating a slice

Have you ever encountered a Web page in which all the image links are broken? All you see amidst the text is a bunch of rectangles with the browser's icon for "No graphic found." That's what a Web page really is to a browser: text and rectangles. You can use GIF transparency to disguise the box-like shape of an image file, but that won't limit the image link to the just the visible area. For that, you need to use image maps or slices, which also enable you to create the effect of intertwined irregularly-shaped image links, such as a yin yang symbol.

Fireworks excels in its support of image maps and slices. Collectively known as *Web objects* in Fireworks, both slices and image maps (or their individual parts, referred to as *hotspots*), serve several functions. In addition to helping designers break out of the rectangularity of the Web, Web objects add interactivity through links and a bit of flair through rollovers and other Behaviors. Although you could design a site full of Web graphics without ever coming near hotspots or slices, fully understanding their uses and limitations significantly increases your Web design repertoire.

This chapter covers the basics of setting up hotspots and slices, and includes some techniques for incorporating them into your Web pages. For detailed information on building rollovers and using other Fireworks Behaviors, see Chapter 21.

Understanding Image Maps and Hotspots

To understand how an image map works, you need go no further than an actual map of almost any country in the world. Divisions between regions, territories, or states are usually geographic and rarely rectangular. To best translate any such map to the Web, you'd make each region (territory or state) a separate clickable area (see Figure 20-1). This is exactly the type of job for which an image map is intended.

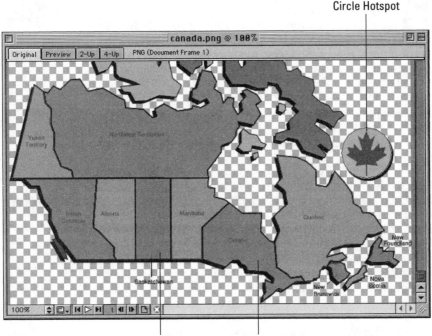

Circle Hotspot

Rectangle Hotspot   Polygon Hotspot

Figure 20-1: The simplest example of an image map is one made from a real map.

Each separately defined area of an image map is referred to as a hotspot. Hotspots come in three basic shapes: rectangles, circles, and polygons. Rectangles can be rectangles or squares, and circles can be circles or ovals; every other shape is a polygon. After you define an area of an image map, you can name it and assign a URL to it. Hotspots can also be used to trigger other events, such as rollovers or the display of messages. Hotspots are not visible on the graphic when viewed through the browser. Hotspots themselves are not actually part of the final image; to be used, the hotspot information is translated into HTML code, which is embedded in the Web page.

The following are the two different kinds of image maps:

✦ **Server-side**: All the map data is kept in a file on the server. When the user clicks a particular hotspot on the image, the server compares the coordinates of the clicked spot with its image-map data. If the coordinates match, the server loads the corresponding link. The key advantage to a server-side image map is that it works with any image-capable browser. One disadvantage is that it consumes more of the server's processing resources and tends to be slower than the client-side version. Another problem is that various server-side image map implementations exist. Probably the most popular one was developed by the National Center for Supercomputing Applications, and is known as the NCSA protocol; Fireworks outputs NCSA server-side image-map code.

✦ **Client-side**: All the map data that is downloaded to the browser is kept in the Web page. The comparison process is the same as with server-side image maps, but it requires a browser that is image-map savvy. Originally, only server-side image maps were possible. Not until Netscape Navigator 2 was released did the client-side version become an option. Microsoft began supporting client-side image maps in Internet Explorer 3.

You can pretty safely assume that most users visiting your site can handle client-side image maps. That widespread availability plus the ease of access from the designer's point of view — no need to transfer files to the server simply to test the image map — has made server-side image maps all but obsolete. Nonetheless, it's good to know that Fireworks can output either (or both) varieties, should the need arise.

To set the type of code that Fireworks outputs, choose File ➪ HTML Properties to open the HTML Properties dialog box, shown in Figure 20-2. Choose the image map type through the Map Type option list: Client-side, Server-side (NCSA), or Both. Client-side is the default choice. Additionally, you can set the Background URL — the link used for an image if an area outside of any defined hotspots is selected — and the Alternate Image Description. Text entered in the Alternate Image Description text box appears while the image is loading or if the image is not available.

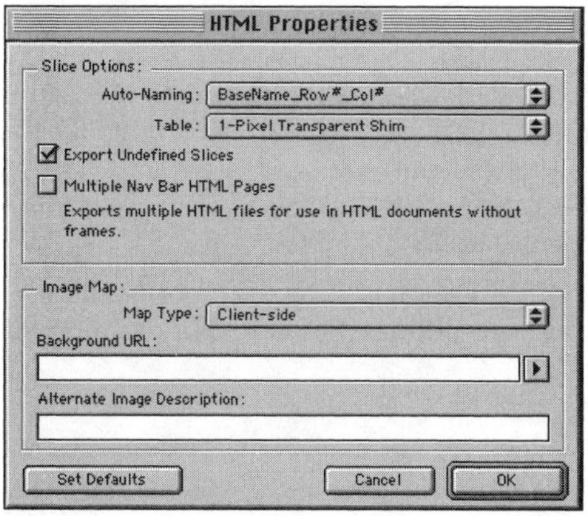

Figure 20-2: Select the image map server type and more through the HTML Properties dialog box.

Caution   Any text entered in the Alternate Image Description text box is used for every Web object in the document — hotspots and slices alike. Use the Alt tag text box in the Object panel to set the alternate text for individual Web objects.

Because image maps and hotspots are HTML constructs and not data embedded in your graphics file, you need to export both the image and the code from Fireworks — and insert them both in your Web page. As you'll see later in this chapter, Fireworks handles this dual export quite effortlessly and gives you many options for incorporating graphics and code however you like.

Using the Hotspot Tools

In Fireworks, the Hotspot tools are immediately accessible in the bottom-left area of the Toolbox. The following are the three basic Hotspot tools, corresponding to the three basic hotspot shapes:

✦ **Rectangle**: Use to draw rectangular or square hotspots. You can't round the corner of a rectangle, as you can with the standard Rectangle tool, although the keyboard modifiers work the same.

✦ **Circle**: Use to draw elliptical or circular hotspots. Again, the keyboard modifiers, Shift and Alt (Option), function the same as they do with the regular Ellipse tool.

✦ **Polygon**: Use to draw irregular-shaped hotspots. It functions similarly to the Polygon Lasso and uses a series of points, plotted one at a time, to make the hotspot shape.

When drawn, the hotspot appears as a shape overlaying the other graphics, as shown in Figure 20-3. Fireworks keeps all hotspots — and slices, for that matter — on the *Web Layer*, which is always shared across all frames and can be both hidden and locked and moved up or down in the stacking order like other layers. Hotspots are displayed initially with the same color, but each hotspot can be assigned its own color, if desired, through the Object panel.

Rectangular hotspot

As noted previously, all the Hotspot tools work in a similar fashion to corresponding standard tools. However, a few key differences exist. To create a rectangular hotspot, follow these steps:

1. Select the Rectangular Hotspot tool from the Toolbox.

2. Click once to select your originating corner and drag to the opposite corner to form the rectangle. As you drag your pointer, Fireworks draws a preview outline of the hotspot.

Polygon hotspot tool   Circle hotspot

Polygon hotspot

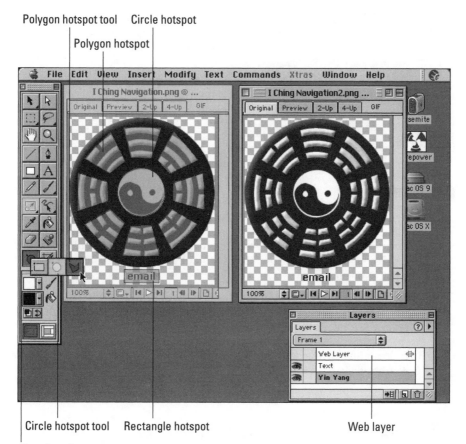

Circle hotspot tool   Rectangle hotspot   Web layer

Sample callout

Figure 20-3: Use the three Hotspot tools to draw Hotspots on the Web Layer.

> **Tip**
>
> To create a square hotspot, press Shift while you drag out your shape. To draw your hotspot from the center instead of from the corner, press Alt (Option) when dragging out the shape. You can also combine the two modifier keys to create a square drawn from the center.

3. Release the mouse button when the rectangle is the desired size and shape.

   Fireworks creates the hotspot with a colored fill, as shown in Figure 20-4.

Figure 20-4: Use the Rectangular Hotspot tool to create square or rectangular hotspots.

Circle hotspot

To draw an elliptical or circular hotspot, follow these steps:

1. Select the Circle Hotspot tool from the Toolbox. If it's not visible, click and hold the visible Hotspot tool until the flyout appears, and then click the Circle Hotspot button.

2. Click once to select the origin point and then drag to the opposite corner to create the circle or ellipse. As you drag your pointer, Fireworks draws a preview outline of the form.

Tip: Hold down Shift while drawing to create a perfect circle, and/or hold down Alt (Option) to draw from the center.

3. Release the mouse button when the circle or ellipse is the desired size and shape.

   Fireworks creates the hotspot, as shown in Figure 20-5.

Figure 20-5: Use the Circle Hotspot tool to create circular and elliptical hotspots.

Tip: Precisely matching the size and shape of an elliptical object with a corresponding hotspot is fairly difficult. After you create hotspot objects, however, you can move them with the pointer, resize them with the transform tools, or adjust them numerically through the Info panel. If the oval you're creating a hotspot for is a separate object — as opposed to a region of a larger object — the easiest method by far is to select the object and choose Insert ➪ Hotspot, which commands Fireworks to make the hotspot for you.

Polygon hotspot

To draw a polygon hotspot, follow these steps:

1. Select the Polygon Hotspot tool from the Toolbox. If it's not visible, click and hold whichever Hotspot tool is visible until the flyout appears, and then click the Polygon Hotspot button.

2. Click the starting point for your hotspot and move the mouse to the next point on the outline surrounding the desired area, and then click again.

   Fireworks connects each point that you set down with a straight line, as shown in Figure 20-6.

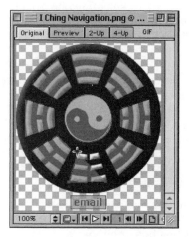

Figure 20-6: Fireworks fills in the polygon hotspot as you select each point.

3. Repeat Step 2 until you've outlined the entire area.

   As you create more points, Fireworks fills in the polygon with the default hotspot color.

4. To finish creating the hotspot, click your original starting point to close the polygon.

   Fireworks creates the hotspot with a colored fill.

Assigning links to hotspots

The Object panel does much more for hotspots than choose their color. In fact, the Object panel (Figure 20-7) could easily be regarded as the fourth Hotspot tool. To be truly useful, hotspots must be assigned a link and other HTML options — all of which are handled in Fireworks through the Object panel.

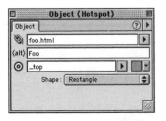

Figure 20-7: Use the Object panel for a selected hotspot to enter essential Web data, such as the linked URL.

The Object panel options for a hotspot include:

✦ **Current URL:** Use this text box to both assign and display the link associated with the selected hotspot. You can either enter a new link by typing directly into the text field or choose an existing link by selecting one from the option drop-down list. The option list can be divided into as many as three parts: the No URL (noHREF) choice; the URL History list for the current document; and the current URL Library.

 For more information on using the URL History and URL Library to manage your links as well as links in general, see Chapter 18.

✦ **Alt tag:** Alternate image text entered here is shown when either the image can't be found by the server or the user's mouse is hovering over the image. In the latter case, the text appears in a tooltip attached to the pointer. Fireworks includes both the standard alt attribute and the title attribute required by Internet Explorer in the generated HTML.

✦ **Link Target:** The target defines where the Web page requested by a link appears. Targets are commonly used with HTML framesets. You can enter a named frame directly in the Target text box or choose one of the following target keywords:

• **_blank** opens the link into a new browser window and keeps the current window available.

• **_parent** opens the link into the parent frameset of the current frame, if any.

• **_self** opens the link into the current frame, replacing its contents (this keyword is the default).

• **_top** opens the link into the outermost frameset of the current Web page, replacing all frames.

✦ **Color:** When created, all hotspots are filled with the same semitransparent color. You can, however, alter an individual hotspot's color by selecting a new one from the pop-up color picker.

✦ **Shape:** Displays the current hotspot shape. This shape is initially derived from the tool used to create the hotspot, and is used to determine a portion of the HTML code. You can change the shape by selecting a different one from the option drop-down list, although this can radically alter your hotspot.

Cross-Reference

If you're entering links directly into the Current URL text box, be careful of your spelling. Web servers are very sensitive to typos — even whether you use upper or lower case letters in some instances. You can save yourself a great deal of painstaking typing by using Fireworks' Import URL feature, located in the URL panel and covered in Chapter 18, to import links from any HTML file.

Converting an object to a hotspot

As one who has played connect-the-dots one too many times while trying to create a star-shaped hotspot, I heartily embrace Fireworks' object-to-hotspot converter. Instead of attempting to outline an object with any of the hotspot drawing tools, select the object and choose Insert ➪ Hotspot. A hotspot precisely matching the shape of the object is created on the Web Layer, ready for linking. This command works for rectangular, elliptical, and irregular shapes, whether they are path, image, or text objects.

Note

If you select multiple objects before using the Insert ➪ Hotspot command, Fireworks asks whether you want to create one hotspot or multiple hotspots. Choosing to create one hotspot combines the Web Layer shapes into one rectangular hotspot encompassing all the selections.

Exporting Image Map Code

When an image map is translated into HTML, it appears in two key parts. The first part is the image tag, `<img>`, which holds the information for the overall graphic. The `<img>` attributes include `src` (the filename of the graphic), the dimensions of the image, and a connection to the map data, `usemap`. The `usemap` attribute is set to the name of the second image map element, the `<map>` tag. For every hotspot in the image map, a corresponding `<area>` tag exists within the `<map>` ... `</map>` tag pair. The following code is for an image map with five hotspots:

```
<img name="sloth" src="sloth.gif" width="300" height="125"¬
 border="0" usemap="#m_sloth">
<map name="m_sloth">
<area shape="rect" coords="14,18,68,46" href="sloth.html">
<area shape="rect" coords="68,18,122,46" href="envy.html">
<area shape="rect" coords="122,18,176,46" href="greed.html">
<area shape="rect" coords="176,18,230,46" href="lust.html">
<area shape="rect" coords="230,18,284,46" href="ties.html">
</map>
```

Fireworks handles outputting all of this code for you—and in several different styles for various authoring tools, as well. All that you're responsible for is incorporating the code in your Web page.

Choosing an HTML style

The HTML code for an image map is generated by Fireworks when you export your image. During the export process, you can select from various HTML styles that dictate how the code is output. Choosing an HTML style that matches your Web-authoring program makes incorporating the Fireworks-generated code easier. The standard HTML styles included in Fireworks are:

✦ **Generic**: The basic code, useful in hand-coded Web pages and the majority of Web-authoring tools that work with standard HTML.

✦ **Dreamweaver 2 or 3**: Code stylized for Dreamweaver 2 or 3. For image maps, no real difference exists between the Generic and the Dreamweaver 2 or 3 code.

✦ **Dreamweaver 3 Library**: HTML to be used in a Dreamweaver 3 Library has additional code marking it as a Library item. This code must be saved in the site's Library folder, and the file is given the filename extension .lbi.

✦ **GoLive**: Code optimized for use with Adobe's GoLive HTML editor.

✦ **FrontPage**: FrontPage uses a series of *webbots* to format its code; Fireworks includes the code necessary for an image map webbot, as well as instructional code that displays when the document is opened in FrontPage.

 You can find additional HTML templates in the HTML Templates folder on the CD-ROM accompanying this book. To use, just copy the desired folder with its files to the Fireworks/Settings/HTML Settings directory—you don't need to relaunch Fireworks.

To export an image map, follow these steps:

1. Optimize your image as needed in the Optimize panel.

2. Choose File ➪ Export to begin the exporting process.

   The Export dialog box, shown in Figure 20-8 is displayed.

3. Choose a folder and provide a filename to save your exported file under.

4. For image maps that do not use slices, make sure the Slicing option list is set to No Slicing.

5. In the HTML area of the Export dialog box, select the desired type of HTML output from the Style option list.

Tip Fireworks remembers your last Style setting.

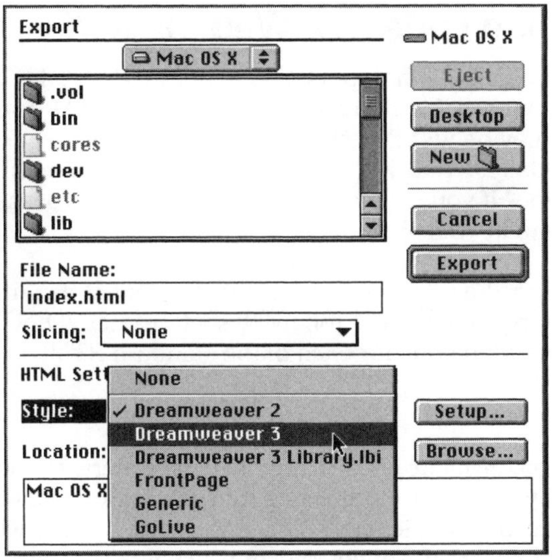

Figure 20-8: Choose the type of image map output from the HTML Style option list.

6. If you've chosen the Dreamweaver 3 Library HTML style, the Locate Site Library Directory opens for you to identify the Library folder of your site.

7. Choose the desired location for your HTML code:

   • To output the code to the same folder as the images, select Same Directory from the Location option list.

   • To output the code in the parent folder of the images, select One Level Up from the Location option list.

   • To place the code in another folder, click the folder icon and select the path from the standard dialog box. Alternatively, you can open the dialog box by selecting Custom from the Location option list.

Note Although the dialog box for the custom folder is titled Locate Site Library Directory, you don't have to choose the Library template to use the dialog box.

   • To output the code to the clipboard — ready to paste into place in your HTML editor — choose Copy to Clipboard.

New Feature You can choose to export your code to the clipboard and paste it into your HTML editor with Fireworks 3.

8. To alter any of the image map settings previously set, click Setup to reopen the HTML Properties dialog box and adjust your settings.

9. After you make your selections, click Export to complete the export.

10. If you copied the HTML to the clipboard, paste it into an HTML editor.

Inserting image map code in a Web page

After you create the graphic, link the hotspots, and generate the code, how do you integrate all of that material within an existing Web page? Although the thought of touching code may be just this side of horrifying for many graphic designers, for most situations it's really not that bad—and for some, it's an absolute breeze. Bottom line? If you can cut and paste in a word processor, you can insert an image map in your Web page.

Although the process is much the same for most of the different style outputs, some variations exist in the procedure. The following sections detail how to integrate the Fireworks-generated code for each of the standard HTML styles.

Generic

The Generic HTML code is, as the name implies, used in most general situations. If you're building Web pages by hand—using a text editor such as Notepad in Windows or SimpleText on the Macintosh—the Generic HTML style is for you. Likewise, if you're using a Web-authoring program, but not one for which Fireworks has a specific template, such as Dreamweaver or GoLive, you should use Generic HTML.

The general procedure for incorporating a Generic image map is fairly straightforward:

1. Open the Generic code in a text editor or in the text editor portion of your Web-authoring tool.

2. Select and copy to the Clipboard the section in the `<body>` tag that starts with

    `<!---------- BEGIN COPYING THE HTML ---------->`

    and ends with

    `<!---------- STOP COPYING THE HTML HERE ---------->`

3. Open your existing Web page in a text editor or in the text editor portion of your Web-authoring tool.

4. In the `<body>` section of your Web page, insert the code where you want the image to appear.

Caution   Be sure that you insert the code between the `<body>` and `</body>` tags, and not between the `<head>` and `</head>` tags.

5. Preview the page in a browser and adjust the placement of the `<img>` tag, if necessary.

It's not essential that the `<img>` part of the image map code and the `<map>` section appear side by side, as long as they are in the same document.

Note If the image map is to form the basis of your document—and you don't have another existing page to use—you don't have to delete or move any code whatsoever. Just add HTML elements around the image map as you build your new page. If you'd like, you can remove the HTML comments, but, frankly, they don't add much weight to a page, so removing them really isn't necessary.

Dreamweaver 2 or 3

You can incorporate the standard Dreamweaver HTML code into a Web page in two ways. The first is similar to the procedure used for including Generic code: cut the code from the Fireworks-generated page and paste it into the Dreamweaver page through the HTML Source window. As long as you make sure to insert the code in the <body> section of the document, and not the <head> section, you won't have any problems.

The other method takes advantage of Dreamweaver's Invisible Elements to completely avoid opening the HTML Source window. To incorporate Dreamweaver-style HTML visually, follow these steps:

1. In Dreamweaver, open the Fireworks-generated HTML page which was created with the Dreamweaver style option.

2. Make sure that View ➪ Invisible Elements is enabled.

    Notice a Comment symbol on one side of the image, followed by a Map symbol and another Comment symbol on the other side, as shown in Figure 20-9.

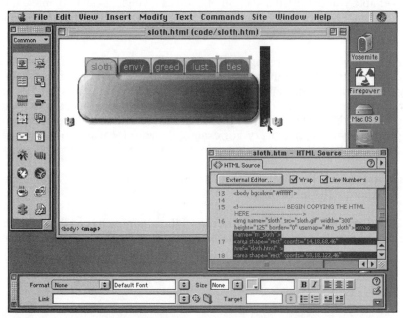

Figure 20-9: With Dreamweaver's Invisible Elements feature, you can copy and paste visual icons instead of chunks of code in the HTML Source window.

3. Select the image, press Shift, and click the Map symbol on the right of the image.

Note

If you want to transfer all the comments as well, click the first Comment symbol, press Shift, and then click the last Comment symbol.

4. Choose either Edit ⇨ Copy or use the keyboard shortcut Ctrl+C (Command+C).

5. Open the existing Web page to which you want to add the image map.

6. Place the cursor where you want the image map to appear.

7. Choose either Edit ⇨ Paste or use the keyboard shortcut Ctrl+V (Command+V).

The image map — and its code — is inserted into the Dreamweaver document.

Note

If for some reason you don't see either the Comment symbols or the Map symbol in Dreamweaver's document window, select Edit ⇨ Preferences in Dreamweaver and, from the Invisible Elements panel, make sure that the Comments and Client-side Image Map options are selected.

Dreamweaver 3 Library

Library Items are a powerful Dreamweaver feature that enable a section of a Web page to be updated once, after which Dreamweaver automatically updates all pages on which the section appears. Originally intended to replace page elements that are often repeated, such as a copyright line or logo, Dreamweaver Library items also enable you to regard a section of code as a single, easy to manage unit. If, as a designer, you're familiar with Encapsulated PostScript, think of Dreamweaver Libraries as Encapsulated HTML.

For a Library item to be recognized as such, it must be stored in a special folder for each local site. When you choose the Dreamweaver 3 Library option from the HTML Style list during export, Fireworks prompts you to locate your site's Library folder. If you've never created a Library item for the current site before, you need to make a new folder. The folder must be placed in the local site root and must be named, appropriately enough, Library. For example, if your local site root is located in a folder called Web Pages, the Library folder must be created at Web Pages/Library.

After you export the HTML file as a Dreamweaver Library item, follow these steps to incorporate the image map:

1. In Dreamweaver, choose Window ⇨ Library or click the Library button from the Launcher palette. Alternatively, you can use the keyboard shortcut, F6.

The current site's Library palette displays, as shown in Figure 20-10

Caution Mac users: if you have mapped the keyboard's function keys in the Keyboard Control Panel to start programs or perform other tasks, function key shortcuts in Fireworks are superceded by those mappings. Use the menu commands instead, or disable the mappings in the Keyboard Control Panel.

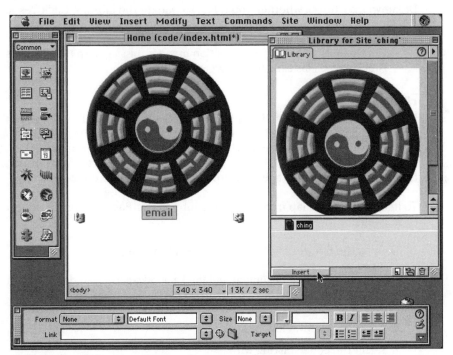

Figure 20-10: After you export an image map from Fireworks as a Dreamweaver Library item, it is available from Dreamweaver's Library palette.

2. Place your cursor in the document window where you want the image map to appear.

3. In the Library palette, select your exported image map from the list window.

The preview pane of the Library palette displays the selected list items.

4. Click the Insert button or, alternatively, drag the item from either the preview pane or the list window and drop it in the document window.

The image map and all the necessary code are inserted into the Dreamweaver page.

If you ever need to edit the image map, you first need to select it and then click Open from Dreamweaver's Property Inspector. A new HTML page appears with just the Library item on it. From there, you can choose the image and select either Edit from the Property Inspector or Optimize Image in Fireworks from the Commands menu. After you edit the image, closing the Library document window prompts Dreamweaver to ask whether you'd like to update the Library. Click Yes to update the Library items; click No to postpone the update.

Note The Optimize Image in Fireworks Command is missing from Dreamweaver if Fireworks was installed before Dreamweaver.

FrontPage

Microsoft's FrontPage is an introductory Web-authoring tool that uses proprietary code for many of its special effects, including image maps. Fireworks outputs code to match the FrontPage format when you select FrontPage from the HTML Style option list during export. The exported image map is inserted into an HTML page that instructs the FrontPage user how to incorporate the code.

To insert an image map from Fireworks into a FrontPage document, follow these steps:

1. Open the Fireworks-generated page in FrontPage.

Caution Both the FrontPage document and the Fireworks-generated document must be in the same folder.

2. Select the HTML View.

3. Select the code starting with

   ```
   <!---------- BEGIN COPYING THE HTML ---------->
   ```

   and ending with

   ```
   <!---------- STOP COPYING THE HTML HERE ---------->
   ```

4. Choose Edit ➪ Copy.

5. Open the document into which the image map is to be inserted.

6. While still in HTML View, choose Edit ➪ Paste to insert the code into the document.

GoLive

HTML code can be easily selected and then copied and pasted in GoLive's HTML Source Editor, or dragged and dropped between HTML Outline windows (Figure 20-11). The HTML Outline windows make it easy to move individual tags between documents, because the img or map tag can be easily collapsed to a single line. As well as the img and map tags, code exported with the GoLive style contains a cssscriptdict tag that tells GoLive how to edit the image map. Make sure to copy all three tags to the new document, placing the img and map tags into the body tag and the cssscriptdict tag into the head tag. HTML code exported with the GoLive option is very plain, with just a single "exported by Fireworks" comment.

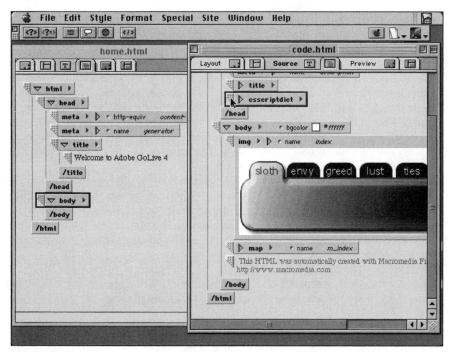

Figure 20-11: GoLive's HTML Outline view is a good way to drag and drop the img, map, and cssscriptdict tags from your exported code to another document.

To insert an image map from Fireworks into a GoLive document, follow these steps:

1. In GoLive, open the Fireworks-generated HTML page which was created with the GoLive style option.

2. Switch to the HTML Outline view for both your source and target documents.

3. Select the img tag in the exported Fireworks code and drag it into place in your target document. Do the same for the map tag, placing both tags within the body tag in your target document.

4. Select the cssscriptdict tag from the head of your source document and drag it into the head of your target document.

Note   If you want to transfer the "created by Fireworks" comments as well, select it in the source document and drag it to the target document.

Understanding Slices

If image maps enable you to target areas of a graphic for links, why not use them for everything? The primary drawback to an image map is also one of its key characteristics: an image map is a single file. As such, image maps of any size — and they tend to be sizable, to take advantage of multiple hotspots — take a long time to download and can be frustrating for the Web page visitor. Moreover, with one file, you're locked into one graphic format with a single palette. What if your image map contains a photographic image in one color with lots of flat color in the rest of the graphic? You'd be forced to export the entire file as a JPEG, to make the photo look good, and the file size would be much higher than if you exported the image as a GIF. And forget about including animations or special effects such as rollovers — duplicating frames of a large graphic would make the file huge.

An alternative approach to image maps is a technique known as slicing. Slicing takes a large image and literally carves it into multiple smaller graphics, which are reassembled in an HTML table for viewing. Each separate image is referred to as a slice and the whole process is often just called *slices*. Here are some of the key features of slices:

 ✦ **Incremental download**: On most servers, each slice appears as it's downloaded, which makes the whole image appear to be loading faster.

 ✦ **Linking without image maps**: Each slice can have its own link, although all such links are rectangular.

 ✦ **Mixed file formats**: Each slice can be optimized separately, reducing the overall file size of the image while enhancing the quality. This technique means that you not only can have a JPEG and GIF side by side, but can also export one slice as a JPEG at 100 percent and another slice as a JPEG at 30 percent.

 ✦ **Update image areas**: If your graphic includes an area that must be updated frequently, such as a headline or a date, you can simply alter the single image in the slice and leave the rest of the image untouched.

 ✦ **Embedded rollovers**: One of the chief uses of slices, especially in Fireworks, is to create rollovers (also known as *mouseovers*). With slices, you can have a series of rollovers, as with a navigation bar, all tied together in one graphic. You can also use one slice to trigger a rollover in another part of the image.

 ✦ **Embedded animation**: With a GIF animation in one slice, you can achieve special effects, such as a flashing neon sign in a large graphic, without doubling or tripling your file size.

The key, fact-of-life, limitation to slices is their shape: all slices are rectangular. Not only are images that make up each individual slice always rectangular, but the table cells into which the slices must fit are too. To create any illusion of nonrectangular shapes, you must use GIF or PNG files with transparency. An additional restriction is that slices cannot overlap.

When deciding whether or not to slice an image, keep in mind that slices depend on HTML tables to hold them together in the browser. Tables, in turn, have some of their own limitations. For example, you can't place two tables side by side on a Web page; the code won't allow it. However, you can nest one table inside another, to achieve a similar effect.

Because slices are tied to HTML tables, special care must be taken to ensure that all browsers treat the tables identically. Under some situations, tables viewed in some browsers can "collapse" and lose all their width and height information that is necessary to appear as a single graphic. The workaround for this problem is to use very small (one pixel) transparent images called *shims*. Fireworks automatically generates the shims if you like, or outputs the code for the sliced image without them. Shims are covered in detail later in this chapter.

Cross-Reference This chapter covers the basics of creating slices. For information on how to use slices to build rollovers, see Chapter 21.

Slicing Images in Fireworks

Slices and hotspots are created in a similar manner — generally, you draw a slice area on top of an image. However, while hotspots can be any shape, including circular, slices are ultimately rectangular, although Fireworks aids in creating complex slices by enabling you to use the Polygon Slice tool to draw complex polygon-shaped slices, which Fireworks then converts into multiple rectangular slices upon export.

New Feature Fireworks 3 adds the Polygon Slice tool to your arsenal of image-slicing weapons. While slices are still ultimately rectangular once they reach the browser, Fireworks does the math to convert your polygon slices into multiple rectangular slices upon export.

The two Slice tools are located on the lower right of the Toolbox, on a flyout similar to the one used for the Hotspot tools.

As you draw slices with the Slice tools, Fireworks creates *slice guides*, which help you to keep the number of files exported to a minimum by aligning the slices. The fewer images you ultimately use, the faster your work will display in a browser and the less taxing the page will be for the browser to display.

Rectangle slices

To slice an image with the Rectangle Slice tool in Fireworks, follow these steps:

1. Select the Rectangle Slice tool from the Toolbox.

2. Click the image and draw out a rectangle the size and shape of the desired slice, as shown in Figure 20-12.

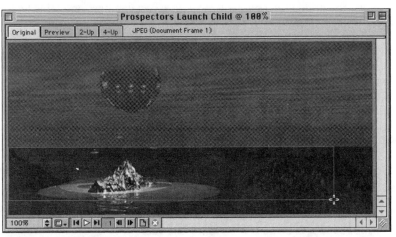

Figure 20-12: The Rectangle Slice tool divides a Fireworks document into straightforward rectangular slices that are exported as individual image files.

> **Tip**
>
> As with the regular Rectangle tool, the Alt (Option) key causes the Slice tool to draw from the center rather than from a corner, and the Shift key constrains the slice to a square.

3. Release the mouse when you're satisfied with the shape.

Fireworks creates the slice object and fills in the rectangle with the default, semitransparent slice color. If enabled, the slice guides appear.

After you draw the slice object, you can manipulate it much like any other object in Fireworks. You can use the four handles on the slice object to resize it — just drag one corner in the desired direction. Rectangular slices are constrained to rectangles, so moving just one point moves the entire side. In fact, you don't have to select the corner; it's just as effective to click and drag a slice object's side.

You can also use the transform tools, such as Scale, although any resulting nonrectangular shape is converted back into an encompassing rectangle. To move the slice object one pixel at a time, use the arrow keys.

An alternative to the Slice tool is to use the standard guides. In this technique, guides are dragged from the horizontal and vertical rulers to form the slicing grid. Then, during export, choose the Slice Along Guides option. This technique works well when your goal in slicing an image is to enable smaller portions of the image to appear quicker than a single large image could load. If you want to add a URL or a Behavior to a slice, you have to create slice objects.

Polygon slices

As previously mentioned, polygon slices exist only within Fireworks. When you export your document, Fireworks uses your polygon slices as a guide in creating more-complex rectangular slices. Polygon slices can be any shape — just like Polygon hotspots — as shown in Figure 20-13.

Figure 20-13: Outline nonrectangular areas with the Polygon Slice tool.

A side effect of this conversion is that polygon slices can often result in a large number of individual image files. This adds to the overhead of displaying the page in a browser. Each image file must be asked for by the browser and sent by the server, and each image must be rendered by the browser separately. Once you incorporate 10 or 15 images, the user may start to notice the difference in the perceived speed of the download.

To draw a polygon slice, follow these steps:

1. Select the Polygon Slice tool from the Toolbox. If it's not visible, click and hold the Rectangle Slice tool until the flyout appears, and then click the Polygon Slice button.

2. Click at the starting point for your Slice and move the mouse to the next point on the outline surrounding the desired area, and then click again.

   Fireworks connects each point that you set down with a straight line.

3. Repeat Step 2 until you've outlined the entire area.

   As you create more points, Fireworks fills in the polygon with the default Slice color.

4. To finish creating the slice, click your original starting point to close the polygon.

Fireworks creates the slice with a colored fill.

Working with slice guides

Before Fireworks, creating a sliced image by hand was very meticulous, eye-straining work. Each slice had to be measured and cut precisely to the pixel—if you were off even one pixel, the resulting image would either have gaps or over-lapping areas. You can approximate this level of frustration by disabling the slice guide features in Fireworks.

Unlike regular guides, you don't position slice guides by hand; they are automatically created as you draw out your slices. The slice guides effectively show you the table layout that would result from the existing slices. More importantly, the slice guides take advantage of the Snap to Guide feature and help you to avoid overlapping slices or sliced images with gaps.

Personally speaking, I find the slice guides very useful, and I highly recommend using them. Choose View ➪ Slice Guides to enable this feature. Slices automatically snap to the edge of a document, but to snap to the guides themselves, choose View ➪ Guide Options ➪ Snap to Guides.

The standard guides and the slice guides are drawn in two different colors. Occasionally, the slice guide color is too similar to that of the current image and you can't see where the guides are. To change the color of the slice guides, select View ➪ Guide Options ➪ Edit Guides to see the Guides (Grids and Guides) dialog box, shown in Figure 20-14. Select a new color from the Slice Color pop-up menu.

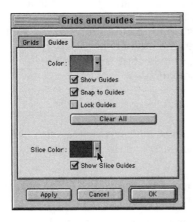

Figure 20-14: Choose a new slice guide color from the Guides (Grids and Guides) dialog box.

Note On Windows, the grid and guide options are displayed in separate Grids and Guides dialog boxes. On the Mac, a single Grids and Guides dialog box contains both sets of options, separated by tabs.

You can also enable the slice guide feature from the Guides (Grids and Guides) dialog box, by choosing Show Slice Guides, or turn on the Snap feature, by selecting Snap to Guides.

Note Unlike the regular guides, the slice guides can't be dragged to a new location; their position is controlled by the slices themselves. Therefore, the Lock Guides option on the Guides (Grids and Guides) dialog box applies only to standard guides.

Copying an image to a slice

Sometimes, making sure that you have all of a particular object can be very tricky — especially if that object has a drop shadow or glow effect. Incorrect placement of a slice could cut off part of the image. To avoid these problems, you can have Fireworks do all the work for you. Just as Fireworks can convert any object to a hotspot, any object can also be made into a slice.

To make an object into a slice, select the object and choose Insert ⇨ Slice. Fireworks draws the slice completely encompassing the selected object — special effects and all. If you select multiple objects, Fireworks asks whether you want to create slices for all the items together or separately.

Setting URLs in slices

To use a slice as a link, the slice must be assigned a URL. You can assign URLs to slices in two different locations: the Object panel or the URL panel. Slices have the same options on both panels as those covered earlier in this chapter for Hotspots.

To assign a link to a slice by using the Object panel, follow these steps:

1. Select the slice to which you want to assign a link.

2. Choose Window ⇨ Objects or the keyboard shortcut Ctrl+I (Command+I).

   The Object panel, shown in Figure 20-15, appears.

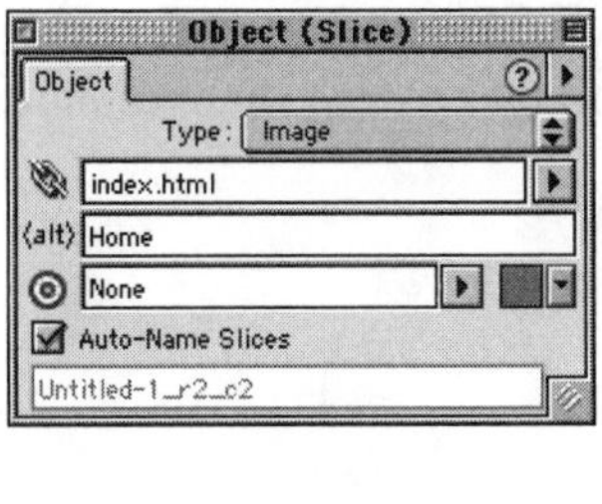

Figure 20-15: The Object panel enables you to assign a link to a slice.

3. Enter a link directly in the Current URL text box or select one from the option list. The option list shows both the URL History and the URL Library.

4. If desired, enter any alternative text in the Alt text field.

5. To set the target for the linked page to load into, choose one of the presets from the Target option list or enter a frame name.

6. To change the color of the selected slice object, pick a new one from the pop-up color picker.

7. To assign a custom name for the slice, deselect the Auto-Name Slices option and enter a new name in the Custom Base Name text box.

You can also set a different pattern for the Auto-Naming scheme in the HTML Properties dialog box, as described later in this chapter.

Text Slices

One little known, but useful feature of slices is the ability to create a Text Slice. A Text Slice displays HTML text in your image instead of part of the image, as shown in Figure 20-16.

Figure 20-16: Setting a slice's type to Text enables you to incorporate HTML text inside a sliced graphic.

To make a Text Slice, follow these steps:

1. Select the slice and display the Object panel.

2. From the Type option list, choose Text.

   The Object panel displays a text area.

3. Enter the desired text and/or HTML directly in the text area of the Object panel.

4. Select any other tool or object when you're done.

5. To edit the text, select the slice object and make your changes in the Object panel.

> **Tip**
>
> HTML tables used for slices typically have no borders or additional cell spacing or padding, so that all the images fit snugly next to each other. However, if you are using a Text Slice, this can be a problem, because the text fits too snugly to the image, with no surrounding margin. You can work around this problem by creating a slightly larger, but empty, Text Slice in front of the Text Slice with the content.

Slice options

Fireworks enables you to set several slice-specific options through the HTML Properties dialog box. The four options are:

- ✦ **Auto-Naming**: Choose from six options to set the Auto-Naming scheme for exported slices. The Auto-Naming choices are described next in this section.

- ✦ **Table Shims**: Fireworks enables you to use transparent shims, shims from the image itself, or no shims at all. A detailed discussion of shims follows later in this chapter.

- ✦ **Export Undefined Slices**: If this option is not selected, only those areas of the image explicitly covered by a slice are exported. For most situations, this option should remain selected.

- ✦ **Generate Rollover Demos**: If selected, this option creates an additional HTML file entitled *filename*_Demo (where *filename* is the basename selected during export), which runs the rollover but does not link to any other page.

Naming slices

Even with only two slices explicitly defined—depending on their placement—you can generate many slices for an image. For the slices to be inserted into a table, each slice has to have a unique filename. To save you the work of entering in name after name, Fireworks automatically names the slices. If desired, you can override the automatic naming on a slice-by-slice basis by unchecking the Auto-Name Slices option and entering a unique name in the associated text box. Although I like to name slices individually in a navigation bar so that I can easily find the image reference in the HTML code, I tend to let Fireworks automatically name most of my slices.

In Fireworks, you can choose from six different Auto-Naming schemes. For each pattern, a user-supplied basename is combined with a suffix or a prefix. The suffixes and prefixes are automatically generated according to the position of the slice in the table.

The Auto-Naming options and their examples are listed in Table 20-1, where the basename "logo" is used.

	Table 20-1 Auto-Naming Options	
Option	**Example**
Basename_Row#_Col#	logo_r01_c01 logo_r01_c02 logo_r02_c01
Basename_Alphabetical	logo_a logo_b logo_c
Basename_Numeric	logo_01 logo_02 logo_03
Row#_Col#_Basename	r01_c01_logo r01_c02_logo r02_c01_logo
Alphabetical_Basename	a_logo b_logo c_logo
Numeric_Basename	01_logo 02_logo 03_logo

Shims

Fireworks can create some extremely complex tables as a result of slicing; multiple column and row spans are quite normal. In some ways, such complex tables are like a house of cards — and certain browsers are a big wind, ready to knock them down. In some circumstances, the table cells appear to lose their carefully calculated widths and heights, and the table literally breaks apart to display the separate images.

To support such tables, Fireworks uses a series of *shims*. A shim is a very small (one pixel by one pixel) transparent GIF image placed in cells along the top and right of the HTML table. Fireworks takes advantage of how HTML works, to use just one image, shim.gif, which weighs just 43 bytes — or, in other words, .04K. The same image is used in each shim cell and sized appropriately in the code. HTML enables you to specify a different height and width for an image and then enables the browsers to handle the scale. Although this is generally a bad idea for most images — browsers don't use very sophisticated scaling algorithms — it works well for shims. The shims are almost invisible: those along the top row remain one pixel in height and those on the side remain one pixel in width. But, most importantly, shims do the job for which they were intended — a sliced table with shims maintains its shape and integrity regardless of the browser.

Despite all their intended good, transparent shims are not for every situation. Therefore, Fireworks offers a degree of user control over shim creation, through the Table Shims option of the HTML Properties dialog box. You can choose to use transparent shims, shims taken from the image itself, or no shims at all.

Why might you prefer shims from the image rather than transparent shims? Occasionally, a sliced table must be placed directly next to the top or side of the Web page or below another table or image. Even with just a one-pixel shim, the gap is sometimes noticeable. To avoid this problem, choose the Shims from Image option of the Table Shims option list. With this option selected, Fireworks uses a very thin slice of the image — again, a single pixel — along the top and right of the table so that any perceived gap is avoided. Using the Shims from Image option does have one downside: if a rollover or other effect where the image is swapped is applied to those shim edges, the shim does not get swapped as well.

If you're dead-set against using shims of any kind, in Fireworks you can select No Shims from the Table Shims option list. Use this feature only with caution and an awful lot of testing in various browsers.

Exporting Slices

When exporting an image map, you end up with an image and a snippet of HTML code. When exporting slices, you could get a whole lot of images and a bit more HTML. You need to realize that each sliced image ultimately means numerous files that must all be stored together. Fireworks offers two different slicing techniques and a variety of HTML styles from which to choose. The options you select are determined by how your slices were created and which Web-authoring tool you are using.

Exporting slices as different image types

Another advantage of slices over hotspots is that each slice can be a different image format, because each slice is an individual image file. This enables you to export one slice as a JPEG, one as a GIF, and another as a PNG, if you so desire.

Specifying the export format for a slice is easy: simply select the slice object in the document window and choose Window ➪ Optimize to view the Optimize panel. While a slice object is selected, the Optimize panel displays its individual export settings. Choose a format and optimization options. Then select another slice and modify its options, or deselect all slices to modify the export options for the whole document.

Tip   You can also use the command File ➪ Export Special ➪ Selected Slice to open the Export Preview dialog box for just the currently selected slice. Only the selected slice is displayed in the preview window of the Export Preview dialog box, and only the selected slice is exported.

Setting the Export options

After deciding on a path and filename for your images, you must select which slicing technique to use. In the Export dialog box, the options under Slicing are:

✦ **No Slicing**: When this option is chosen, the image is exported in one piece, regardless of the number of slice objects.

✦ **Use Slice Objects**: The exported slices are created from the slice objects on the image.

✦ **Slice Along Guides**: The standard guides are used to determine the slices.

For most situations, Use Slice Objects is the best choice. Slice objects are required for rollovers or any other Behavior, and they are very easy to create. The only reason to choose Slice Along Guides is to carve a large image into numerous smaller ones, without any attached Behaviors. To use Slice Along Guides, you must have set the standard guides into place, as detailed earlier in this chapter.

To export an image in slices, follow these steps:

1. Choose File ➪ Export.

   The Export dialog box appears.

2. Set the filename and path of the Export in the upper part of the dialog box.

3. Choose either Use Slice Objects or Slice Along Guides from the Slicing option list.

4. In the HTML area of the Export dialog box, select the desired type of HTML output from the Style option list.

5. If you chose the Dreamweaver 3 Library HTML style, the Locate Site Library Directory opens for you to identify the Library folder of your site.

6. Choose the desired location for your HTML code:

   • To output the code to the same folder as the images, select Same Directory from the Location option list.

   • To output the code in the parent folder of the images, select One Level Up from the Location option list.

   • To place the code in another folder, click the folder icon and select the path from the standard dialog box. Alternatively, you can open the dialog box by selecting Custom from the Location option list.

   • To output the code to the clipboard, choose Copy to Clipboard.

7. To alter any of the slice settings previously set, click Setup to reopen the HTML Properties dialog box and adjust your settings.

8. After you make your selections, click Export to complete the export.

9. If you copied the code to the clipboard, paste it into a document in your HTML editor.

Inserting slices in a Web page

As with image maps, Fireworks provides six HTML templates to choose from: Generic, Dreamweaver 2 or 3, Dreamweaver 3 Library, FrontPage, and GoLive. Each template generates an HTML file with the same name as set in the Base Name text box of the Export dialog box.

Inserting code from a simple sliced image is straightforward. From an HTML perspective, all the code is contained within one tag, `<table>`. Remember, in HTML, tags containing data use both a starting and ending tag; in the case of the tags for an HTML table, the starting tag is `<table>` and the ending tag is `</table>`. So, all the necessary code is between `<table>` and `</table>`, inclusive. Fireworks plainly marks this code with HTML comments showing where to begin copying and where to stop.

The techniques provided in this chapter for integrating slices in your Web pages are for simple sliced images, without rollovers or other Behaviors. To learn how to export slices with Behaviors, see Chapter 21.

Generic

Use the Generic template when you are hand coding your pages in a text editor or using a Web-authoring tool without a specific template.

Follow these steps to incorporate a Generic sliced image:

1. Open the Generic code in a text editor or in the text editor portion of your Web-authoring tool.

2. Select and copy to the Clipboard the section in the `<body>` tag that starts with

```
<!---------- BEGIN COPYING THE HTML ---------->
```

and ends with

```
<!---------- STOP COPYING THE HTML HERE ---------->
```

3. Open your existing Web page in a text editor or in the text editor portion of your Web-authoring tool.

4. In the `<body>` section of your Web page, insert the code where you want the image to appear.

5. Preview the page in a browser and adjust the placement of the `<img>` tag, if necessary.

Dreamweaver 2 or 3

Although you can use Dreamweaver's HTML Source window to integrate the Fireworks-generated code, you can also do it visually, thanks to Dreamweaver's Tag Selector.

To insert Fireworks-generated code for a sliced image into Dreamweaver, follow these steps:

1. In Dreamweaver, open the HTML page generated in Fireworks.

2. Click the exported image once.

   Because the image is now sliced into different sections, the entire image is not selected, just one slice.

3. On the bottom left of the document window, select the <table> tag from the Tag Selector, as shown in Figure 20-17.

   The entire sliced image and all the code is selected.

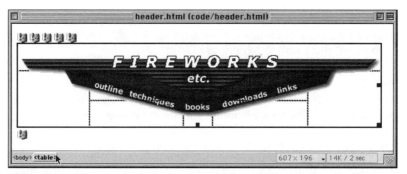

Figure 20-17: Use Dreamweaver's Tag Selector to choose the sliced image for cutting and pasting.

4. Choose either Edit ➪ Copy or the keyboard shortcut Ctrl+C (Command+C).

5. Open the existing Web page to which you want to add the sliced image.

6. Place the cursor where you want the sliced image to appear.

7. Choose either Edit ➪ Paste or the keyboard shortcut Ctrl+V (Command+V).

The sliced image and corresponding code is inserted into the document.

Dreamweaver 3 Library

The Dreamweaver 3 Library code template builds the same table as the Dreamweaver 3 template does, but it also marks the table as a Library item that can be inserted over and over again. As with the image map code, the sliced image code must be stored in a special folder called Library for each local site. If you've never created a Library item for the current site, you need to make a new folder in the local site root.

After you export the HTML file as a Dreamweaver Library item, follow these steps to incorporate the sliced image:

1. In Dreamweaver, choose Window ➪ Library or click the Library button from the Launcher. Alternatively, you can use the keyboard shortcut, F6.

   The current site's Library palette displays.

2. Place your cursor in the document window where you want the sliced image to appear.

3. In the Library palette, select your exported sliced image from the list window.

   The preview pane of the Library palette displays the selected list items.

4. Click the Add to Page button or, alternatively, drag and drop the item from either the preview pane or the list window.

The sliced image, and all the necessary code, is inserted into the Dreamweaver page.

FrontPage

Microsoft's FrontPage stores external code — including any JavaScript — in a structure (or webbot in FrontPage jargon) called HTML markup. Fireworks produces the proper structure through the FrontPage template so that the code can be seamlessly integrated.

To insert an image map from Fireworks into a FrontPage document, follow these steps:

1. Open the Fireworks-generated page in FrontPage.

Caution Both the FrontPage document and the Fireworks-generated document must be in the same folder.

2. Select the HTML View.

3. Select the code starting with

   ```
   <!---------- BEGIN COPYING THE HTML ---------->
   ```

   and ends with

   ```
   <!---------- STOP COPYING THE HTML HERE ---------->
   ```

4. Choose Edit ➪ Copy.

5. Open the document in which the sliced image is to be inserted.

6. While still in HTML View, choose Edit ➪ Paste to insert the code into the document.

GoLive

GoLive's HTML Outline view is an easy way to drag and drop HTML code between two documents. Code exported with the GoLive style also contains a cssscriptdict tag that tells GoLive how to edit the code. Make sure to copy the cssscriptdict tag as well as your plain HTML code.

To insert Fireworks-generated code for a sliced image into GoLive, follow these steps:

1. In GoLive, open the HTML page generated in Fireworks.

2. Switch to the HTML Outline view for both your source and target documents.

3. In the source document, select the `<table>` tag. This table contains all of your sliced images.

4. Drag and drop the table tag into place in your target document.

5. Select the cssscriptdict tag from the head of your source document and drag it into the head of your target document.

Fireworks Technique: Animating a Slice

Fireworks can build terrific animations — and with just a little technique, you can integrate any animation into a larger image through slices. Animations can be fairly heavy in terms of file size. If only a small section of an overall image is moving — such as a radar screen on a control panel — converting the entire image to an animation is prohibitive, due to the file size that would result. However, with slices, you can animate just the area that you need to animate, and keep the rest of the image static, thus dropping the size of the file dramatically.

To include an animation in Fireworks, follow these steps:

1. Build your animation in Fireworks as you would normally.

Explore Fireworks' animation features in Part VI.

2. If the animation is not already part of a larger image, go to Frame 1 in the Frame panel, choose Modify ➪ Canvas Size, and enlarge the canvas as desired.

3. Complete the graphics surrounding the animation.

4. Make a slice object from the animation either by choosing the animation and selecting Insert ➪ Slice or by using the Slice tool to draw a rectangle around the entire animation.

5. If it's not already visible, display the Object panel.

6. In the Object panel, set the link and any other desired options.

7. If it's not already visible, display the Optimize panel.

8. From the Export File Format option list, choose Animated GIF.

9. Specify other image optimization options as necessary.

Chapter 15 details Fireworks' image optimization options.

10. Repeat steps 4-9 for the static slices in your document, but choose formats other than animated GIF in the Optimize panel. Alternatively, deselect all slices and set an overall document export format in the Optimize panel. This format is used for any slices that are not explicitly set to another format.

11. When your document is ready for export, choose File ➪ Export.

The Export dialog box opens.

12. Set your path and filename in the upper portion of the dialog box.

13. Choose Use Slice Objects from the Slicing option list, and choose the desired HTML template from the Style option list.

14. Click Export when you're ready to export.

Your animation is exported as part of the overall image, as shown in the example in Figure 20-18.

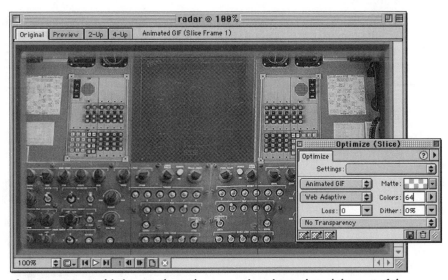

Figure 20-18: In this image, the radar screen is animated, and the rest of the graphic is static.

Summary

Fireworks Web objects — hotspots and slices — provide a gateway from graphic imagery to the Internet. By integrating Web objects with other graphic elements, the Web designer can seamlessly migrate from one medium to another, all the while maintaining editability. When working with Web objects, keep these points in mind:

✦ Fireworks supports two types of Web objects: hotspots and slices. A hotspot marks part of a larger graphic through code, whereas slices actually divide the larger image into smaller files.

✦ Hotspots come in three basic shapes: rectangle, circle, and polygon. Fireworks has a different tool for each type of hotspot. The term "hotspot" denotes an area of the overall image, called an image map.

✦ Any Fireworks object can be easily converted into a hotspot by selecting the image and choosing Insert ➪ Hotspot.

✦ When exporting image maps, be sure to get both parts of the code: the `<img>` tag containing the link to the source image, and the `<map>` code with the hotspot data.

✦ Fireworks makes slices in three ways: with the Rectangle or Polygon Slice tool, with the Insert ➪ Slice command, and with the standard guides.

✦ Enabling the Slice Guide option helps to reduce the number of slices to a minimum.

✦ Individual slices can be exported as different image types, even as animated GIFs, enabling you to mix animated and static slices.

In the next chapter, you learn how to assign Behaviors for interactive effects.

✦   ✦   ✦

Activating Fireworks with Behaviors

✦   ✦   ✦   ✦

In This Chapter

Using Behaviors

Creating rollover buttons

Using the URL panel

Exporting rollovers for the Web

Working with the Button Editor

Making disjointed rollovers

Creating external rollovers

Incorporating rollovers in slices

✦   ✦   ✦   ✦

From a user's perspective, the Web includes two types of images: graphics that you look at and graphics that you interact with. You can create the "look, but don't touch" variety of graphics with most any graphics program — Fireworks is among the few graphics programs that can output interactive graphics.

Although the result may be a complex combination of images and code, Fireworks uses *Behaviors* to simplify the process. With Fireworks Behaviors, you can create everything from simple rollovers — exchanging one image for another — to more complicated interactions, in which selecting a hotspot in one area may trigger a rollover in another, while simultaneously displaying a message in the status bar. And you can do it all in Fireworks without writing a line of code.

This chapter covers all the intricacies of using Behaviors and demonstrates some techniques that combine several Behaviors. You may never use each and every one of the Fireworks Behaviors, but once you start to use them, your Web pages will never be the same.

Understanding Behaviors

Before Fireworks, making your Web pages responsive to Web page visitors required in-depth programming skills or a Web-authoring program (such as Macromedia's Dreamweaver) that automated the process for you. The basic Web page, scripted in HTML, is fairly static; only forms allow any degree of user interaction. To activate your page, you have to use a more advanced language. Because of its integration into both major browsers,

JavaScript is the language of choice for this task for most Web programmers. Although JavaScript is not as difficult to use as, say, C++, the majority of Web designers don't have the time or the inclination to master it. Now that Fireworks permits Behaviors to be integrated into graphics, Web designers don't have to master a programming language.

A Behavior consists of two parts: an *event* and an *action*. An event is a trigger that starts an action, the way pushing Play on a VCR starts a videotape. Events on the Web are either user driven, such as moving a pointer over an image; or automatic, such as when a page finishes loading. Generally speaking, actions range from displaying a message to launching a whole new browser window.

Behaviors are said to be "attached" to a specific element on the Web page, such as a text link or an image; Behaviors in Fireworks are always attached to slices or hotspots. Several other products in the Macromedia family, including Dreamweaver and Director, use Behaviors in much the same way as Fireworks.

In one sense, Behaviors can be thought of as Encapsulated JavaScript. As a designer, you need only make a few key decisions, such as which two images to swap, and Fireworks handles the rest. Then, the code is written for you, in the HTML style of your choice. With Fireworks, you can output code that's tweaked for various Web-authoring programs, including Dreamweaver. Before you can export your images and associated Behavior code, however, you must assign the Behavior through the Behaviors panel.

Using the Behaviors Panel

The Behaviors panel is used to add and remove Behaviors. Although each Behavior has its own dialog box for selecting options and entering parameters, the Behaviors panel lists basic information for every Behavior assigned. You can assign multiple Behaviors — either the same Behavior or different ones — to any slice or hotspot; the number of Behaviors that can be attached to a single Web object has no practical limit.

Fireworks 3 includes four different Behaviors:

✦ **Simple Rollover:** Automatically swaps the image on Frame 1 with the image from Frame 2 when the user's mouse cursor rolls over the image. Optionally, the third and fourth frames can be swapped, as well.

✦ **Swap Image** (Swap Image Restore): Displays one image in place of another. The swapped image can be located on a different frame, in a different slice, or both. An external image can also be exchanged for the current or any other slice in the document. The Swap Image Restore Behavior is automatically applied to restore the swap to its original state.

✦ **Set Nav Bar Image:** (Nav Bar Over, Nav Bar Down, Nav Bar Restore): This is a group of Behaviors that specifies in which state of a navigation bar the selected slice should be.

✦ **Set Text of Status Bar:** Shows a message in the browser's status bar.

The Behaviors panel (see Figure 21-1) is the central control center for Behaviors. To show or hide the Behaviors panel, choose Window ➪ Behaviors, use the key shortcut Ctrl+Alt+H in Windows (Command+Option+H on a Macintosh) or click the Behaviors tab, if it is visible. The Behaviors panel enables you to select a hotspot or slice object and to add or to remove Behaviors. It also shows any Behaviors that have been previously added to the selected object. After you add a Behavior to a hotspot or slice object, selecting it again enables you to remove the Behavior or change its settings.

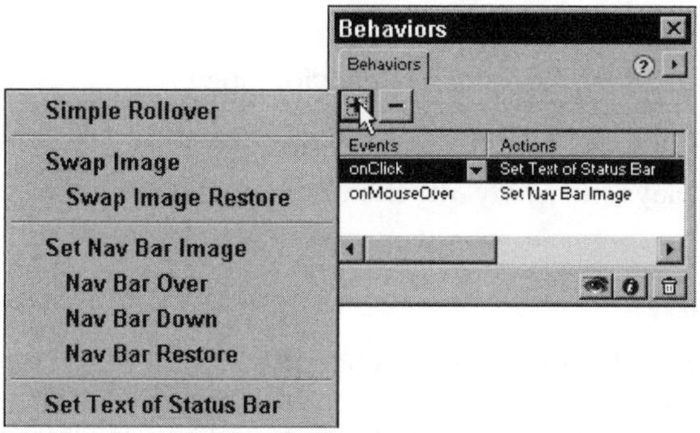

Figure 21-1: The Behaviors panel is the command center for attaching and removing Behaviors from hotspots and slices.

Adding new Behaviors

As noted previously, Behaviors are attached to Fireworks Web objects, either hotspots or slices. It's important to understand that hotspots are only capable of triggering events and are incapable of performing actions. Slices, on the other hand, can both trigger and receive events.

Practically, this means that hotspots by themselves can be used only in conjunction with the Set Text of Status Bar Behavior; all other Behaviors require slices in order to work. However, you can use hotspots to trigger an action that occurs in a slice, as explained later in the section "Working with hotspot rollovers."

Following is the general procedure for adding a Behavior to a Web object:

1. Select the hotspot or slice that you want to attach the Behavior to.

2. Choose either Window ➪ Behaviors or use the keyboard shortcut Ctrl+Alt+H (Command+Option+H) to open the Behaviors panel. Alternatively, if it is docked behind another panel, click the Behaviors panel's tab to bring it forward.

Note   If you have anything other than a Web object selected, Fireworks alerts you to this fact and gives you the option to create a Web object from the selected object. If nothing is selected when you try to add a Behavior, Fireworks asks you to choose a hotspot or slice first.

3. Click the Add Action button (the plus sign) and choose a Behavior from the drop-down list.

   A dialog box, which is specific to the chosen Behavior, opens.

4. Enter the desired options for the Behavior and click OK when you're done.

   The Behaviors panel displays the newly attached Behavior in the list window.

Modifying a Behavior

To modify a Behavior that you've already added to a hotspot or slice object, select a hotspot or slice object and double-click the Behavior's entry on the Behaviors list in the Behaviors panel. Fireworks displays the Behavior's dialog box, in which you can adjust the settings that you made when you added the Behavior.

In addition to modifying the Behavior's settings, you can select another event to trigger the Behavior. By default, Fireworks initially assigns the onMouseOver event for all events. Following is a list of available events:

✦ **onMouseOver:** A user's mouse cursor hovers over an image and triggers the Behavior.

✦ **onMouseOut:** When a user's mouse cursor moves away from an image, the Behavior is triggered.

✦ **onClick:** A user clicks an image and the Behavior is triggered.

✦ **onLoad:** When the Web page has finished loading, the Behavior is triggered.

When a Behavior is selected in the Behaviors list, the Event pop-up menu button (a down-pointing arrow) appears just to the right of the event. Click this button to choose a new event from the Event pop-up menu, as shown in Figure 21-2.

Figure 21-2: Click the Event pop-up button to choose another trigger for any selected Behavior.

Deleting a Behavior

When you delete a Behavior, all the settings that you have created are lost.

To delete a Behavior, follow these steps:

1. Select the hotspot or slice object from which you want to remove the Behavior.

2. Choose the Behavior that you want to remove from the Behaviors list in the Behaviors panel.

   The Behavior's event, action, and information are highlighted.

3. Click the Remove Action button (the minus sign) on the Behaviors panel.

The Behavior is removed from your hotspot or slice object, and its entry disappears from the Behaviors list.

Creating Rollovers

Perhaps the most common use of JavaScript on the Web is the rollover. *Rollovers* are images in a Web page that change appearance when a user rolls a mouse cursor over them.

Rollovers are popular because they're fairly simple to implement, are supported by many browsers, and are an effective way to heighten the feeling of interaction for Web site visitors.

How rollovers work

To understand how a rollover works, you need to grasp a fundamental HTML concept. Web pages do not contain images in themselves — they only contain links to images. With an image, the link is referred to its source and is specified in the

<img> tag in HTML as the src attribute. When a user's mouse pointer hovers over an image—or in some cases, clicks an image—the src attribute is changed to another image file. Because this happens quickly, it appears as if the image itself is changing.

Before the rollover effect, a typical <img> tag might read like the following:

```
<a href="home.html"><img src="button_regular.gif" height="100"
width="50" alt="home"></a>
```

After the rollover effect is applied, the effect is as if the code was the following code:

```
<a href="home.html"><img src="button_over.gif" height="100"
width="50" alt="home"></a>
```

As this code shows, the height, width, and alt text for the image doesn't change, nor does the link that the hyperlink is pointing to (in this example, home.html), as specified in the <a> tag. All that changes—and this can't be overemphasized—is the actual GIF (Graphics Interchange Format), JPEG (Joint Photographic Experts Group), or PNG (Portable Network Graphics) image file that's being used; the file referenced by the src attribute.

Caution   Because only the src attribute changes with a rollover, the original image and any swapped images must have the same dimensions. You can't swap a smaller image with a larger one, or vice versa. If you do, the browser applies the height and width dimensions of the original image, leading to a distorted image.

Note that any <img> tag can be modified, not just the <img> tag that is rolled over. This is the foundation for disjointed rollovers, as discussed later in this chapter.

Rollover states

Although a rollover actually switches one image for another, the illusion that most Web designers want is of a button changing into different modes, or *states*. Before the user triggers the rollover effect, the image is in the Up state. When the rollover is triggered, the image changes to an Over state because the cursor of the user's mouse is over the image. In Fireworks, the easiest and most typical method of creating the different states for a rollover is with frames.

A basic rollover uses just two states (and, thus, two Fireworks frames): Up and Over. Rollovers, though, can have up to four states, in which case they would be built across four Fireworks frames. Table 21-1 details the rollover states and their typical associated frames.

Table 21-1
Rollover States

Frame	State	Description
1	Up	The way the button looks when the user is not interacting with it; how it looks when the page first loads into the browser.
2	Over	The button's appearance when the user's mouse cursor is hovering over it.
3	Down	The button's appearance after it's pressed. The Down state of a rollover button depicts the button's state on the destination Web page. For example, the Down state is commonly used to show which button was clicked to view the current Web page.
4	Over Down	The way a button that's in its Down state looks when the user's mouse cursor hovers over it.

Creating rollover images

The first step in building a rollover is to create the separate rollover images that reside on the separate frames of a Fireworks document. I use either of two basic techniques to create images. Which technique I choose depends upon whether the rollovers are to be independently used, each in their own unique Fireworks document; or if they're part of a complete design in a larger document. Both techniques involve creating an initial button object, which is then duplicated and modified.

If your rollover buttons exist independently, use the following technique to create its images:

1. Create the initial button in Frame 1, as it should appear before being clicked by the user.

2. Click the button and choose Edit ➪ Clone to create a duplicate directly on top of the button.

3. If your are going to create a Down state for this button, repeat Step 2. If you are also going to create an Over Down state, repeat Step 2 so that you have a total of four objects stacked on top of each other in Frame 1.

4. Select all of your button states by drawing a selection around them with the mouse. Click the Distribute to Frames button (which resembles the small movie strip) in the Layers panel.

   Your objects are distributed to separate frames so that each button state is now in its own frame.

5. Frame 1 already contains a suitable Up state for your button. Go to Frame 2 and modify your button object slightly in order to create an interesting Over state for the button. You might add a Glow Live Effect to the Over state, or change the Fill or Stroke settings.

6. If you have Down and Over Down states, as well, modify them slightly on Frame 3 and Frame 4 so that each frame now contains a unique — but similar — button.

Tip   If the Over state of your button has a Live Effect bevel on it to give it a three-dimensional appearance, a good way to modify subsequent states is to click the button object and then modify the Button Preset settings of the bevel Live Effect (the bottom option list on the pop-up edit window) in order to create the impression of a three-dimensional button moving up and down. For example, the Up state could be set to Raised, the Over state to Highlighted, the Down state to Inset, and the Over Down state to Inverted.

If your rollovers are part of a larger document that contains many buttons or objects that you want to create rollovers for, use the following technique to create the images:

1. Create all of the initial objects in Frame 1 of your document.

2. From the options pop-up menu on the Frame panel, select Duplicate Frames.

   The Duplicate Frames dialog box appears.

3. In the Duplicate Frames dialog box, enter the number of frames that you want to add. In the Number text box, add one frame for each additional state used.

   For a simple rollover with just an Up and Over state, add one frame. For a rollover that also uses the Down and Over Down states, add three frames.

4. Make sure that the Insert New Frame After the Current Frame option is selected and click OK when you're done.

   The duplicate frames are inserted.

Tip   Another way to duplicate a frame is to drag its name to the New Frame button in the Frames panel (it looks like a pad of paper). Each time you do this, another duplicate frame is added after the one you dragged. Layers can also be duplicated in this fashion in the Layers panel.

5. In each new frame, modify the rollover objects slightly in order to create a different look in each frame.

Tip   You can modify many objects simultaneously — to make them all glow, for example — by selecting all of them at once and applying the changes through the Stroke, Fill, or Effects panel.

No matter which technique you use to create the separate rollover images, the best effect usually results from applying a degree of subtlety. If one button is too drastically different from another of its states, the underlying image swap becomes overt and the illusion of a single button being clicked or highlighted is lost. Instead, the user sees one image simply change into another. Small shifts in position or an incremental change in an effect seem to work best, as shown by the examples in Figure 21-3.

Figure 21-3: Subtle modifications to your original button image create convincing state changes. Here, three buttons are exploded in order to view (from left to right) their Up, Over, Over Down and Down states.

Tip   You can preview your soon-to-be rollover by clicking Play on the animation controls; the frames of your image are then shown one after the other.

Once your separate button images have been created, they are ready to have Behaviors applied to them and to be used as true buttons.

Applying the Simple Rollover Behavior

Fireworks 2 introduced a Simple Rollover Behavior that allowed you to quickly add a rollover to a Web object and additionally specify whether you wanted to include a Down Over state and a Down state (a four frame rollover). Fireworks 3 has taken the *simple* in Simple Rollover a step further: three and four frame rollovers are left to the other Behaviors, and Simple Rollover is now a no-dialog-box, no-options, classic Up-and-Over rollover effect.

The only difference between the Simple Rollover and Swap Image Behaviors is the interface and the number of options. The code you generate is the same compatible JavaScript you expect from Fireworks 3.

To apply the Simple Rollover Behavior, follow these steps:

1. Select a slice on the Web Layer of your document.

2. From the Behaviors panel, choose Simple Rollover from the Add Action pop-up menu in the Behaviors panel.

To preview your rollover, select the document window's Preview tab and roll the mouse over your button. You can also preview your rollover in your primary browser by pressing F12.

The Simple Rollover Behavior doesn't have any options that need to be specified. In fact, if you double-click the Behavior in the Behaviors list, Fireworks just explains the Behavior, as shown in Figure 21-4.

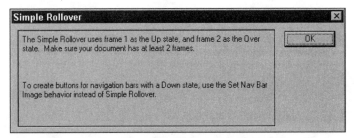

Figure 21-4: The "options dialog" for a Simple Rollover simply explains what a Simple Rollover is without offering any options; it's that simple.

Of course — as with any Behavior — you can still choose a different kind of event, such as onClick or onLoad, from the Behaviors panel Event list.

Cross-Reference   If you plan to use the rollover as a link, you first need to assign it a URL. For detailed information on how to add a link to a Web object, see Chapter 20.

Exporting Rollovers for the Web

Obviously, you can export images from Fireworks. When you create rollovers, the JavaScript code that controls the behavior of your images is exported within an HTML file. The JavaScript itself is compatible with Netscape Navigator 3 and above, and Microsoft Internet Explorer 4 and above. The Macintosh version of Internet Explorer 3 will also display your rollover effects, but in Internet Explorer 3 for Windows, your rollover effects will not be visible, although hyperlinks still work.

Starting with Fireworks 2, Macromedia has continually improved the HTML editor compatibility of Fireworks' exported JavaScript. In the first version of Fireworks, only one type of rollover code was generated; it worked in browsers, sure, but you had to edit it by hand if you opened it in a visual editor. Fireworks 2 introduced a flexible template system of outputting HTML, allowing you to pick the style of code that was best for your workflow or enabling you to create a template of your own to fine tune the settings even further. Fireworks 3 extends the familiar template system further with the addition of new and updated templates, and enhanced Dreamweaver integration.

Integrating a Fireworks-generated rollover into your Web page is a two-stage process.

✦ **Stage 1:** Export the code from Fireworks, either as an HTML file or as code copied to the clipboard.

✦ **Stage 2:** Insert the code into your Web page, using whatever HTML editor you prefer (even a plain text editor, such as NotePad or SimpleText, will work).

The most difficult part of the first stage is determining which HTML style to use. For the most part, this choice is governed by the Web-authoring tool that you are using to lay out the Web page onto which the rollover will be placed. The standard HTML styles included in Fireworks are the following:

✦ **Generic:** The basic functional code, useful in hand-coded Web pages and the majority of Web authoring tools that work with standard HTML.

✦ **Dreamweaver 2 or 3:** Code styled for Dreamweaver 2 or Dreamweaver 3. Dreamweaver-style rollover code generated by Fireworks appears as native Dreamweaver Behaviors when opened in Dreamweaver.

✦ **Dreamweaver 3 Library:** HTML to be used in a Dreamweaver 3 Library has additional code that marks it as a Library item. This code must be saved in the site's Library folder. If you're using Dreamweaver 3, choosing this style of HTML makes inserting the code into a Web page extremely easy.

✦ **FrontPage:** FrontPage uses a series of *webbots* — FrontPage-only code snippets — to create Web elements; Fireworks includes the code necessary for an image map webbot, so that it displays correctly when the document is opened in FrontPage.

✦ **GoLive:** Code styled for Adobe's GoLive, including special tags that make editing the code in GoLive easier.

You'll find additional HTML templates for exporting various code styles.

.htm or .html?

The code that Fireworks generates is saved in HTML files. By default, Fireworks uses the file-name extension .htm instead of the more-standard .html. If you prefer the .html extension — or want to have a choice of which to use each time you export code — an easy fix is at hand.

Fireworks HTML output templates are stored in the folder Fireworks 3/Settings/HTML Code. Each template lives within its own similarly named folder. The Dreamweaver 3 template files are within the Dreamweaver 3 folder, for example.

If you rename a copy of the Dreamweaver 3 folder to Dreamweaver 3.html and restart Fireworks, you'll gain the additional export option of Dreamweaver 3.html, which will be exactly the same as the Dreamweaver 3 option, except that a .html filename extension will be applied. Similarly, you can rename another copy to Dreamweaver 3.shtml in order to create an option for the .shtml filename ending. Of course this works with other templates, as well. If you don't want to use the .htm ending at all, just add .html onto the end of your original export template folders without making any copies.

Exporting the code from Fireworks

To export a rollover — and its code — from Fireworks, follow these steps:

1. Specify your image export settings in the Optimize panel.

2. Choose File ➪ Export.

   The Export dialog box, shown in Figure 21-5, appears.

3. Choose a target folder for your exported image file(s) and specify a filename.

4. Choose from among the following options in the Slicing option list:

   • Use Slice Objects slices your image according to the placement of Slice Objects.

   Tip This is the option you'll probably use most of the time.

   • Slice Along Guides slices your image along guides.

   • Slices: Current Frame is similar to Use Slice Objects, except that only images from the current frame are exported.

5. In the HTML area of the Export dialog box, select your preferred type of HTML output from the Style option list.

   If you chose the Dreamweaver Library HTML style, the Locate Site Library Directory opens so that you can identify your site's Library folder.

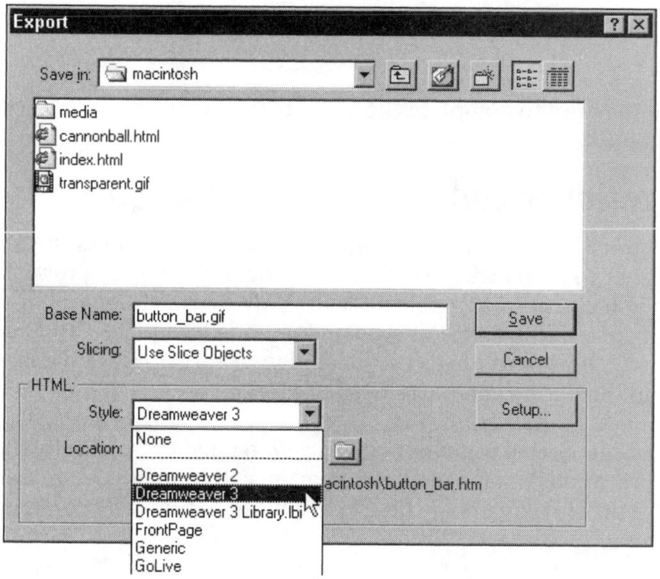

Figure 21-5: Choose the style of your HTML rollover code from the Export dialog box.

6. From the Location option list, choose the desired location for the HTML file in relation to your image file(s) from among the following options:

   • To output the code to the same folder as the images, select Same Directory from the Location option list.

   • To output the code in the parent folder of the image folder, select One Level Up from the Location option list.

   • To place the code in another folder, choose Custom and select the path from the standard dialog box. Alternatively, you can click the Browse button and choose the path.

   • To copy the code to the clipboard instead of creating an HTML file, choose Copy to Clipboard.

New Feature Fireworks 3 now enables you to copy exported HTML to the clipboard instead of creating an HTML file. If you typically open an exported HTML file and then copy and paste code from there to another HTML file, this feature saves you a couple of steps.

7. To alter any of the slice settings previously set, click Setup to reopen the HTML Properties dialog box and adjust your settings accordingly.

To review the possible slice settings, see Chapter 20.

8. When you're ready to complete the export, click Export.

Inserting rollover code in your Web page

After you select your HTML style, Fireworks automatically outputs the requested type of code, either to an HTML file or to the clipboard, according to which option you selected. If you chose to output the HTML code to the clipboard, open your target HTML file in your HTML editor and paste the code into place. If you chose to output to a file, you'll have to open that file and your target HTML file in a text or HTML editor and then copy and paste between them.

The process for transferring rollover code to a Web page is essentially the same as that for transferring image maps or sliced images, with one important exception; the code generated for rollovers — and all Behaviors — generally comes in these two parts:

✦ The event portion of a code, which contains the ⟨img⟩ tags and their triggers, is stored in the ⟨body⟩ section of a Web page.

✦ The action portion of a code — with all the JavaScript functions — is kept in the ⟨head⟩ section.

You must transfer both parts of the code in order for the rollover to function properly.

With Generic, Dreamweaver 2, Dreamweaver 3, and GoLive code, the process is similar. Cut or copy the code from both the ⟨body⟩ and the ⟨head⟩ sections of the Fireworks-generated document and paste it into your existing Web page. FrontPage does not separate the <head> and the <body> sections for rollovers in its code, so simply copy the one section of code from the source to the target page. With Dreamweaver Library-style code, the process is even simpler: include the code into your Web page using the Library palette, just as you would any Library item.

For Generic, Dreamweaver 2, Dreamweaver 3, FrontPage, and GoLive styles, follow these steps to insert Fireworks code into your Web page:

1. Open the Fireworks-generated source HTML file in a text or HTML editor.

2. Select and copy to the clipboard the section in the ⟨body⟩ tag that starts with

```
<!---------- BEGIN COPYING THE HTML HERE ---------->
```

and ends with

```
<!--------- STOP COPYING THE HTML HERE ---------->
```

Tip If you're using Dreamweaver, you don't have to open the HTML Source window or an external text editor in order to copy the code. Just make sure that View ➪ Invisible Elements is enabled and copy the icons that represent the code.

3. Open your existing, target Web page in a text or HTML editor.

4. In the `<body>` section of your Web page, insert the code where you want the image to appear.

If you're using the FrontPage template, your code transfer is complete; skip the rest of the steps. You can now view your rollover.

5. Return to the source HTML file and locate the `<head>` section.

6. Select and copy to the Clipboard the section in the `<body>` tag that starts with

```
<!------ BEGIN COPYING THE JAVASCRIPT SECTION HERE ------>
```

and ends with

```
<!------ STOP COPYING THE JAVASCRIPT HERE ------>
```

7. Switch to your existing Web page.

8. Paste the copied code in the `<head>` section of the document.

Tip Placing the JavaScript code after the `<title>` and any `<meta>` tags makes your page friendlier to the spider programs that add pages to Web search engines.

After you insert both sections of the rollover code, you can view your rollovers in any supported browser.

Preloading Rollover Images

When the HTML document that contains your rollovers is first displayed, the Up state of your rollovers is visible, along with the other image files on the Web page. Ideally, as the user interacts with your document, the other states of the rollovers will be instantly available from the browser cache instead of slowly available from the Web. Instantaneous reactions reinforce the illusion that an object is being modified—a button pushed, for example—. instead of one image being replaced with another. To make sure that the other states are available from the browser cache, Fireworks includes JavaScript with its HTML output that "preloads" the Over, Over Down, and Down image files.

The Dreamweaver Library feature enables a single repeating element to be inserted in multiple Web pages, which can then all be updated by modifying one item. Although Library items were available in the first version of Dreamweaver, Dreamweaver 2 added the ability to associate JavaScript code with any item, and this capability is retained in Dreamweaver 3, of course. This makes inserting Fireworks-generated Dreamweaver Library code extremely straightforward because Dreamweaver fills in the gaps later by generating the code functions that are required in the <head> tag. The only stipulation is that the rollover code must be stored in a special folder, called Library, for each local site during export. If you've never created a Library item for the current site, you need to make a new Library folder in the local site root.

After you export the HTML file as a Dreamweaver Library item, follow these steps to incorporate the rollover images and code:

1. In Dreamweaver, choose Window ➪ Library or use the keyboard shortcut F6.

Caution   Function key shortcuts may or may not be directly accessible on the Mac, depending upon the settings in the Keyboard Control Panel.

The current site's Library palette opens, displaying the exported Library item.

2. Place your cursor in the document window where you want the rollover to appear.

3. In the Library palette, select your exported rollover from the list.

The preview pane of the Library palette displays a preview of the selected item.

4. Click the Insert button, or you can drag the item from either the preview pane or the list window and drop it in your page.

The sliced image, and all the necessary code, is inserted into your Dreamweaver page.

Nav Bar Behavior

A *Nav Bar* is a way to turn a series of rollover buttons into a set of radio buttons. Each button is linked to the others, so that clicking one button and setting it to a Down state sets the other buttons to an Up state. Fireworks creates Nav Bars by using JavaScript cookies. In JavaScript, a *cookie* is a small bit of information written to the user's computer. Cookies generally are used by Web sites to record visitors' selections as they travel from one Web page to another, as with a shopping cart on an e-commerce site. Fireworks uses this same technology to keep track of which button in a group has been selected.

Nav Bars and cookies might seem like advanced topics, but if you've implemented a three- or four-frame Simple Rollover Behavior, you've already used them. Fireworks automatically creates a Nav Bar (named FwNavBar) for each Simple Rollover that uses a Down and/or Over Down state. You don't need to do anything else to get the toggle effect. However, if you use Swap Image to create your rollover or want to toggle just the two Up and Over states of a Simple Rollover, you need to apply the Nav Bar Behavior explicitly.

Creating a Nav Bar

To create a Nav Bar, follow these steps:

1. Create your rollover buttons, with appropriate states (Up, Over, Down, and Over Down) on the appropriate frames, one through four.

2. In Frame 1, draw a slice object over each rollover button.

3. Select each slice object, in turn, and turn it into a rollover by choosing Simple Rollover from the Add Action pop-up menu in the Behaviors panel.

   Your rollovers are now ready to be turned into a Nav Bar.

4. Select all the slice objects to be included in the Nav Bar.

5. Choose Set Nav Bar Image from the Add Action pop-up menu in the Behaviors panel.

   Fireworks displays the Set Nav Bar Image dialog box (see Figure 21-6).

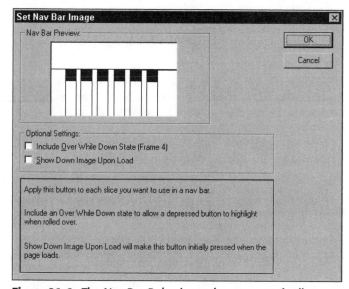

Figure 21-6: The Nav Bar Behavior makes any set of rollovers mutually exclusive; therefore, only one button can be selected at any time.

6. If you have included the Over Down state in your rollovers, check the Include Over While Down State box. Click OK when you're done.

7. If you want one of the buttons to appear in its Down state by default, first des-elect all the slices and then select the individual slice. Next, double-click the Set Nav Bar Image Behavior in the Behaviors panel and then check Show Down Image Upon Load. Click OK when you're done.

When you view your Nav Bar on the Preview tab of the document window or in a Web browser (Figure 21-7), the buttons change depending upon which one is clicked.

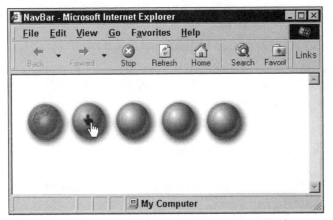

Figure 21-7: The second button in this Nav Bar is in the Down state. Only one button in a Nav Bar can be down at a time, creating the impression of a group of radio buttons.

Tip   The term *radio buttons* comes from tuning buttons on AM/FM radios. Only one station can be tuned in at a time, so only one button can be down at a time. Clicking a button causes all other buttons to pop up.

Building buttons in the Button Editor

The Fireworks Button Editor enables you to create or assemble a button Symbol that includes a two-, three- or four-state rollover. A special tabbed window—similar to the document window—walks you step-by-step through the process.

New Feature   Fireworks 3 includes a valuable new tool for building and previewing rollover but-tons: the Button Editor. A tabbed window enables you to assemble objects and link them together in order to create a two-, three- or four-state button Symbol.

To create a rollover button with the Button Editor, follow these steps:

1. Choose Insert ➪ New Button.

Fireworks displays the button editor (Figure 21-8).

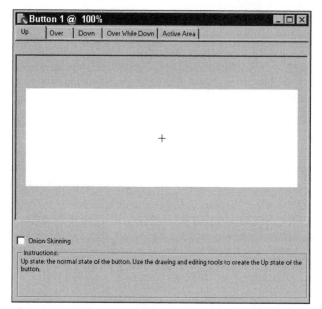

Figure 21-8: The Button Editor can display four button states—four Fireworks frames—plus a slice object on its five tabbed canvases.

2. Create the Up state of your button in the initial Up tab of the Button Editor.

3. Select the Button Editor's Over tab and create the over state of your button. Alternatively, to start with the Up state and modify it to be an Over state, click Copy Up Graphic. Fireworks copies the Up state to the Over tab, ready for editing.

At any time, you can check the Onion Skinning box to simultaneously view all of the tabs in the Button Editor, helping you to align your buttons correctly. You can also use the view controls to zoom in or out on your button, and you can choose a display option to view the buttons in Full or Draft display. Click the Play button at the top right of the Button Editor to cycle through the states of your button.

4. If you want to include a Down state in your button, select the Down tab and create the Down state of your button. Again, you have the option to click a button and copy the previous state to this tab for modification. Click Copy Over Graphic to do this.

5. If your button is exported as a Nav Bar, check Show Down State Upon Load to display the Down state when a page loads.

6. To add an Over While Down state to your button, switch to the Over While Down tab and either create a new state or copy the previous one — click Copy Down Graphic — and modify it to create the Over While Down state.

7. Switch to the Active Area tab. Fireworks automatically creates a slice in the Active Area tab that encompasses the area of your button, but you can adjust its size if necessary.

Tip   The slice on the Active Area tab is similar to the Hit area in Flash buttons.

8. To have Fireworks help with the process of adding a link to your button, click the Link Wizard button and move from tab to tab in the Link Wizard dialog box.

9. Close the Button Editor when you're done.

Your new Button Symbol is added to the Library panel, and a copy of it — an Instance — is placed in the document window, as shown in Figure 21-9. Switch to the Preview tab of the document window to preview your new button's rollover actions in the document window.

Figure 21-9: The Button Editor creates a new Button Symbol, which is added to the Library. An Instance of that Symbol is placed on the canvas.

For more about Symbols and Libraries, see Chapter 17.

Advanced Rollover Techniques

The Simple Rollover is quick and easy, and I use it quite often. However, sometimes a Web page needs more than just a Simple Rollover. Traditional rollovers can be extended with advanced techniques in order to create interesting effects or even more navigation help for your users. The underlying engine for the Simple Rollover, the Swap Image Behavior, is key to these advanced techniques.

Making disjointed rollovers

A *disjointed rollover* is one in which the user hovers their mouse cursor over one part of an image (the event area), and another part of the image (the target area) is exchanged for the contents of another frame. A typical use for a disjointed rollover is to display details of each button in a navigation bar in a common area. Creating a disjointed rollover generally involves outlining the event and target areas with slice objects, although it is possible to trigger a disjointed rollover from a hotspot.

To create a disjointed rollover, follow these steps:

1. Create a slice object over the event area (the part of your image that the mouse cursor needs to hover over in order to trigger the rollover).

2. Create a slice object over the target area (the part of the image that will seem to change).

3. Select the event area slice and choose Swap Image from the Add Action pop-up menu in the Behaviors panel.

   Fireworks displays the Swap Image dialog box (see Figure 21-10).

4. Choose the slice for the target area by choosing it from either the Target list of slice names or the Slice preview to the right of the Target list. Whichever you choose, the other is updated to reflect your choice.

5. Choose the Source for the swap by selecting a frame number from the Frame list. The area below the target slice on that frame will be used as the source for the image swap.

6. Check Restore Image onMouseOut to undo the swap again when the user moves their mouse cursor away from the event area. Click OK when you're done.

To swap more than one slice simultaneously, repeat the preceding steps to apply multiple Swap Image Behaviors to the same Web Layer object. Through this technique, your navigation button can roll over itself and display a disjointed rollover at the same time.

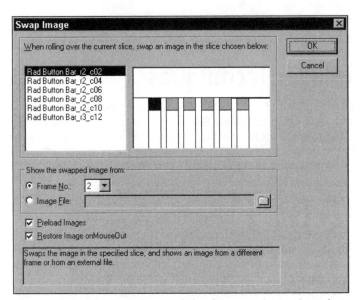

Figure 21-10: The Swap Image dialog box contains options that enable you to swap any slice in your document after any other slice is selected by the user.

Creating external rollovers

Instead of using an object in another frame as the Over state for a rollover, Fireworks can also use external GIF images (regular or animated), JPEG images, or PNG images. When the rollover is viewed in a Web browser, the external file is used as the source file for a rollover, instead of using an area of a frame within your Fireworks document. External rollovers enable you to easily include animated GIF images into an existing image.

Caution   You can't swap one image file format for another because of Web browser limitations. If you're going to export a slice as a GIF, make sure to use an external GIF or animated GIF only as the Over state. Similarly, if you're exporting a slice as a JPEG or a PNG, include only external JPEG images and PNG images, respectively, as the Over state.

Keep in mind that only the image source is changed (the `src` attribute of the `img` tag), so the browser will resize your external image to fit the size of the initial slice object it's being swapped for.

Tip   If you need to make a slice object the same size as an external image so that you can swap that sliced area of your image for an external file, select the slice object, choose either Modify ➪ Transform ➪ Numeric Transform or the keyboard shortcut Ctrl+Shift+T, choose Resize from the list in the Numeric Transform dialog box, and then enter the desired width and height.

To create an external rollover, follow these steps:

1. Select the slice to trigger the external rollover.

2. Choose Swap Image from the Add Action pop-up menu in the Behaviors panel.

   Fireworks displays the Swap Image dialog box.

3. To locate the external file through the standard Open dialog box, choose the Source for the swap by clicking the Folder icon.

4. Check Restore Image onMouseOut to undo the swap again when the user moves their mouse cursor away from the event area.

5. Click OK when you're done.

Working with hotspot rollovers

Hotspot rollovers enable you to create the effect of irregularly shaped rollovers. All images are rectangular boxes, so all image swaps involve swapping a rectangular area or slice. However, the image triggering the rollover does not have to be rectangular—any hotspot can be used. The key to the illusion of the hotspot rollover is Fireworks' ability to swap entire slices from different frames.

Figure 21-11 shows an image with slices that are far from rectangular, but the design requires that each area highlight independently when rolled over and link to different pages on the Web site. Hotspot rollovers swap the entire image, though, so each highlight can be any shape.

One limitation applies, though: because each hotspot swaps the entire image, the hotspots can't overlap, or the illusion of separate highlighted areas is lost. It's also a good idea to keep the overall image small because each added hotspot requires another copy of the whole image. A larger image could lead to a significant download time for the user.

Figure 21-11: This navigation system uses hotspots to trigger a rollover of the whole image in order to create the impression of irregularly shaped rollover buttons.

To create hotspot rollovers, follow these steps:

1. Create a hotspot for each active area with the Rectangle, Circle, or Polygon Hotspot tool.

2. Create a single slice that covers your whole image.

3. Select the slice and choose Modify ⇨ Arrange ⇨ Send to Back to send it behind your hotspots so that you can easily access the individual hotspots in order to apply Behaviors to them.

4. Duplicate your current frame until you have a separate frame for each active area. If you have made ten hotspots, make ten frames.

5. In each frame, modify a different active area so that it appears highlighted in some way. This will be the "Over" state for that area. The other areas in each frame are left in their default state.

Tip

Hiding the Web Layer—and your hotspots—makes it easier to see what you're doing when modifying your active areas. Hide the Web Layer by clicking the eye icon next to its name in the Layers panel.

6. Select a hotspot and fill in a URL for the hotspot in the Object panel.

7. With your hotspot still selected, open the Behaviors panel and apply a Swap Image Behavior to it. In the Swap Image dialog box, make sure you follow these steps:

   • Select the lone slice in the slice list.

   • Under "Show the swapped image from," set the Frame number to the corresponding highlighted frame for the selected hotspot. If the highlight for a hotspot is in Frame 3, set the hotspot to swap to Frame 3.

8. Repeat Steps 6 and 7 for each hotspot until all of your hotspots have a URL and a Behavior attached.

9. Export your image along with HTML code. In the Export dialog box, choose Use Slice Objects under the Slicing option.

Fireworks will export an HTML document along with an image file for each frame of your document. When displayed in a browser, the overall impression that's created is that of a single image with eccentrically shaped, individual rollovers.

Displaying a status bar message

You can provide the user with additional navigational assistance by supplying a message in the status bar. Status bar messages are often used with hotspots and image maps. They are limited by the width of the status bar area in the viewer's browser, which in the case of Internet Explorer 4 for Windows (but not 5) is very, very small. Even in other browsers, because browser window size can vary tremendously, lengthy messages are not recommended.

To add a status bar message to your document, follow these steps:

1. Select a slice object or hotspot and choose Set Text of Status Bar from the Add Action pop-up menu in the Behaviors panel.

   Fireworks displays the Set Text of Status Bar dialog box (see Figure 21-12).

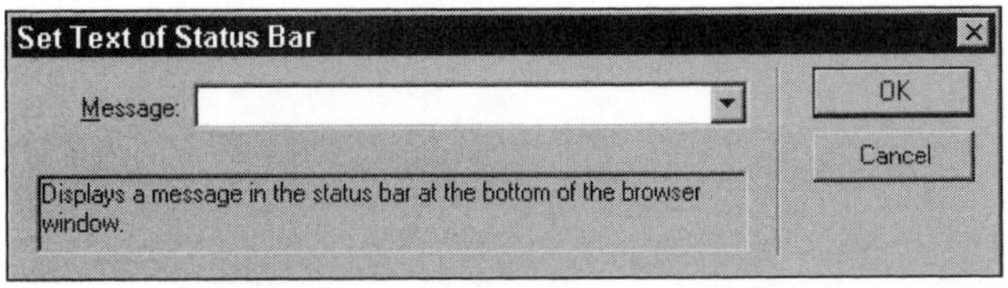

Figure 21-12: The Set Text of Status Bar dialog box enables you to add a status bar message to a slice or hotspot, which assist your users in navigating your site.

2. Type in the Message box the message that you want to display when the user activates this slice. Click OK when you're done.

3. Change the event from onMouseOver to onMouseOut, onClick or onLoad, if desired, by choosing that event from the event list.

Summary

Fireworks enables you to add dynamic JavaScript effects to your images, even if you don't know JavaScript, through the use of Fireworks Behaviors. When using Behaviors, keep these points in mind:

✦ The Behaviors panel is your control center for working with Behaviors.

✦ Behaviors are attached only to Web Layer objects (either hotspots or slices) and not to regular path or image objects on other layers.

✦ Rollovers can be rollover buttons, or they can be disjointed rollovers, in which the image that changes is not the same as the one that triggered the event.

✦ Fireworks includes a new Button Editor that simplifies the process of building a Button Symbol.

✦ Rollovers can be previewed in the document window by selecting the Preview tab.

✦ Fireworks can also show text in the browser's status bar through the Set Text of Status Bar Behavior.

In the next chapter, we'll look at integrating Fireworks with Dreamweaver.

✦   ✦   ✦

Integration with Dreamweaver

✦   ✦   ✦   ✦

In This Chapter

Setting up integration
features

Optimizing graphics
from within
Dreamweaver

Altering
Dreamweaver images
in Fireworks

Cross-program
Behaviors

Updating
Dreamweaver
Library items

Exporting CSS layers
into Dreamweaver

Creating a Web
photo album

Making hybrid
Commands

✦   ✦   ✦   ✦

Not all Web designers have the luxury — or the hardship — of just working on Web graphics. Many graphic artists create both the graphics and the layout for the Web pages on which they work. And those designers who only create imagery for the Internet must work closely with layout artists in order to incorporate their designs. No matter how you look at it, Fireworks is not — and was never intended to be — a standalone product. All graphics generated by Fireworks must be published on the Web by some other means.

Dreamweaver, the premier Web-authoring program from Macromedia, is the perfect partner for Fireworks. Both speak JavaScript Commands and Dreamweaver is happy to share Fireworks' Behaviors as its own. You can seamlessly optimize images with standard Fireworks controls from within Dreamweaver — without even opening Fireworks. This chapter delves into this and many other features, including Fireworks Commands that can be automatically issued from Dreamweaver.

On the CD-ROM If you don't have a copy of Dreamweaver 3, use the trial version included on the CD-ROM accompanying this book.

Integration Overview

As noted elsewhere in this book, Web graphics is as much about production and maintenance as it is about creation. The more efficiently you — or someone who works with you — can insert and update images into Web page layouts, the better the workflow. Because a Web page typically has numerous graphics, as well as text and other media, such as a Shockwave or QuickTime movie, a Web designer must be concerned with how all the elements work together. Not only must the overall design function well aesthetically, but the Web page as a whole must be practical—that is, the download time must be kept to a minimum. All of these concerns require a constant back-and-forth between graphics and layout programs.

New Feature Macromedia continues the tradition of Dreamweaver-Fireworks integration started with version 2 of each product by including even more integration in the third generation of each.

To take advantage of the additional benefits, the programs must be installed properly. In many cases, installation is a nonissue because Macromedia created a special combined installer program for users of Dreamweaver 3 Fireworks 3 Studio (Figure 22-1). This installer treats Dreamweaver 3 and Fireworks 3 as if they are one program and installs them both. Be sure to use this installer, rather than the separate installers that are included on the Dreamweaver 3 Fireworks 3 Studio CD-ROM.

Figure 22-1: Dreamweaver 3 Fireworks 3 Studio includes an extra installer that installs both Dreamweaver 3 and Fireworks 3 as if they were one program.

If you are not using Dreamweaver 3 Fireworks 3 Studio, and you installed Fireworks 3 after Dreamweaver 3, the installer will have added the required files to Dreamweaver to enable integration. However, if Fireworks was installed before Dreamweaver, you will need to install Fireworks again in order to add the Fireworks integration files to Dreamweaver. The integration files are detailed in Table 22-1.

Table 22-1 Integration Files Installed in Dreamweaver	
Files	**Location**
Set Nav Bar Image.htm Set Nav Bar Image.js	Dreamweaver 3/Configuration/Behaviors/Actions
Optimize Image in Fireworks.htm Optimize Image in Fireworks.js	Dreamweaver 3/Configuration/Commands
FWLaunch.dll (Windows) FWLaunch (Macintosh)	Dreamweaver 3/Configuration/JSExtensions

The Optimize in Fireworks Command opens a special version of the Export Preview dialog box directly in Dreamweaver, without launching the full version of Fireworks; the FWLaunch file makes this possible.

Optimizing Images with Fireworks

What's the most common modification needed for graphics being added to a layout? I don't know about everybody else, but I sure do an awful lot of resizing of images to get the right fit. To me, the term *resizing* encompasses rescaling an image, cropping it, *and* getting it to the smallest possible file size — all while maintaining the original image quality. The Optimize Image in Fireworks Command does just that, as well as enabling complete color and animation control. Best of all, you can do everything right from Dreamweaver in a standard Fireworks interface.

If you've never tried the Optimize Image Command, that last statement might give you pause. How can you optimize an image ". . . from Dreamweaver in a standard Fireworks interface"? Aren't we talking about two different programs? Well, yes, and — most excitedly — no. You definitely need both programs for the Command to work, but the full version of Fireworks does not have to be running. Instead, a special "light" version of Fireworks is launched, one that displays only the Export Preview dialog box, as shown in Figure 22-2.

The Optimize dialog box has all the features of Export Preview with one small change: an Update button sits in place of the Next button. In Fireworks, clicking Next from Export Preview opens the Export dialog box, in which you can select Slicing and HTML template options. The Command relies on your last settings saved from within Fireworks for these options.

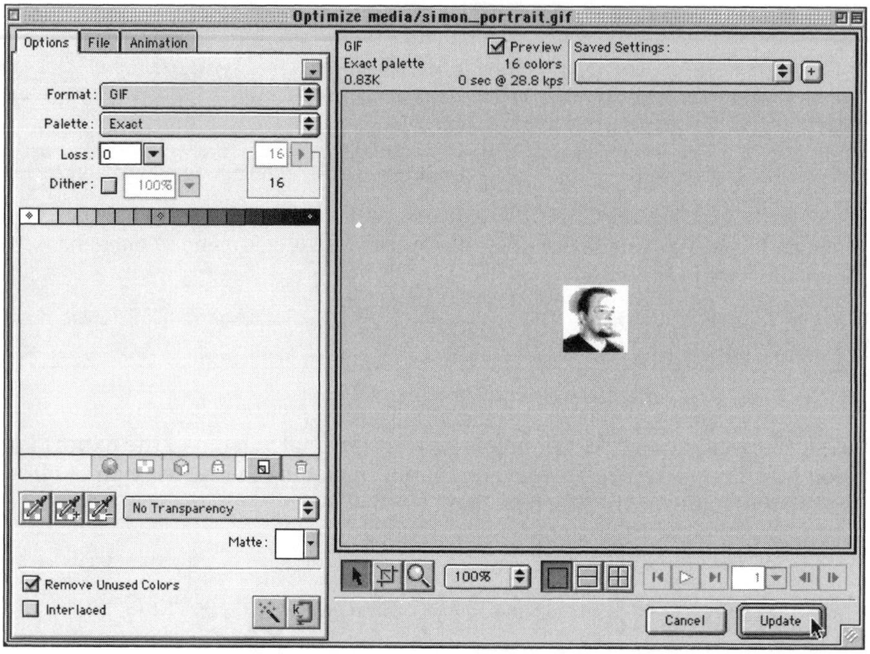

Figure 22-2: Choosing the Optimize Image in Fireworks Command opens a dialog box equivalent to the Export Preview dialog box, but without running Fireworks.

To optimize your image in Fireworks from within Dreamweaver, follow these steps:

1. In Dreamweaver, select the image you need to modify.

Caution   You must save the current page at least once before running the Optimize Image in Fireworks Command. The current state of the page doesn't need to have been saved, but a valid file must exist for the Command to work properly. If you haven't saved the file, Dreamweaver alerts you to this fact when you call the Optimize Image Command.

2. Choose Commands ⇨ Optimize Image in Fireworks.

3. If the selected image is not in PNG (Portable Network Graphics) format, you're given the opportunity to select whether you'd like to use a Fireworks source file instead of the lower-quality GIF (Graphics Interchange Format) or JPEG (Joint Photographic Experts Group), as shown in Figure 22-3.

4. Click No in the Find Source for Optimizing dialog box to continue and then optimize the GIF or JPEG image. Click Yes to have Dreamweaver automatically find the Fireworks source file, if possible. If not possible, you are prompted with a standard Open dialog box. Select the PNG format source file and click Open to continue.

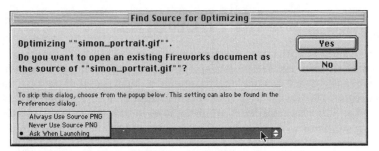

Figure 22-3: Choose whether to use a Fireworks PNG file as a source for the image, if one exists.

New Feature If you opt for the source file — and the image was originally created in Fireworks 3 — Dreamweaver reads the Design Note associated with the image to find the location of the source file and opens it. By setting the Always Use Source PNG option in the Find Source for Optimizing dialog box, you can skip the dialog and always open the source file. Should you change your mind about how you'd like to work, open Fireworks and select File ⇨ Preferences and then choose the desired option from the Editing panel.

After the selected file is located, if appropriate, the Optimize dialog box appears.

4. Make whatever modifications you want from the Options, File, and Animation tabs of the Optimize dialog box.

5. When you're finished, click the Update button.

If you're working with a Fireworks source file, the changes are saved to both the source file and the exported file; otherwise, only the exported file is altered.

If you changed the scale, size, or cropping of the image during optimization, you need to adjust the height and width values in the Dreamweaver Property inspector. To do this, click the Refresh button.

Caution If the image to be optimized is in PNG format — whether it be in the enhanced PNG format that Fireworks uses to store all of its additional editing information or in the bitmap PNG export — the Optimize Image in Fireworks Command saves it as a bitmap file. In other words, Fireworks native files lose their editability. As always, it's best to store your Fireworks source files in one directory and use your exported Web page files — in GIF, JPEG, or PNG format — from another.

Editing Images with Fireworks

For many purposes, optimizing an image is all you need to do—whether it's to crop one side slightly or to reduce the file size. Often, though, you need to go further, such as when the client has decided to change a department name on a navigation button. Without Fireworks-Dreamweaver integration, in a situation such as this you'd need to start your graphics program, load in the image, make the change, save the image, switch back to your Web-authoring tool, and reload the graphic. With Dreamweaver 3 and Fireworks 3, the process is greatly simplified. You need to only follow these steps:

1. Select an image in Dreamweaver and choose Edit from the Property inspector.

   The image is automatically loaded into Fireworks, which is started, if necessary.

2. Modify the image in Fireworks and click Update.

   The revised image is saved and automatically updated in Dreamweaver.

Setting Fireworks as the graphic editor in Dreamweaver

To take advantage of this enhanced connectivity, you first have to set Fireworks as your graphics editor in Dreamweaver's Preferences by following these steps:

1. In Dreamweaver, choose Edit ⇨ Preferences.

   The Preferences dialog box appears.

2. Select the External Editors category from the list on the left.

3. In the External Editors pane, shown in Figure 22-4, click the Image Editor Browse button to locate the main Fireworks program.

 Tip   The default location for Fireworks for Windows is C:\Program Files\Macromedia\ Fireworks 3\Fireworks.exe (the .exe filename extension may or may not be visible). On a Macintosh, Fireworks is usually found at Macintosh HD:Applications: Fireworks 3:Fireworks 3.

Now, whenever you want to edit a graphic, select the image and click the Edit button in the Property inspector. Fireworks will start up, if it's not already open. As with the Optimize Image in Fireworks Command, if the inserted image is a GIF or a JPEG, and not a PNG format, Fireworks asks whether you want to work with a separate source file. If you click Yes, you're given an opportunity to locate the file.

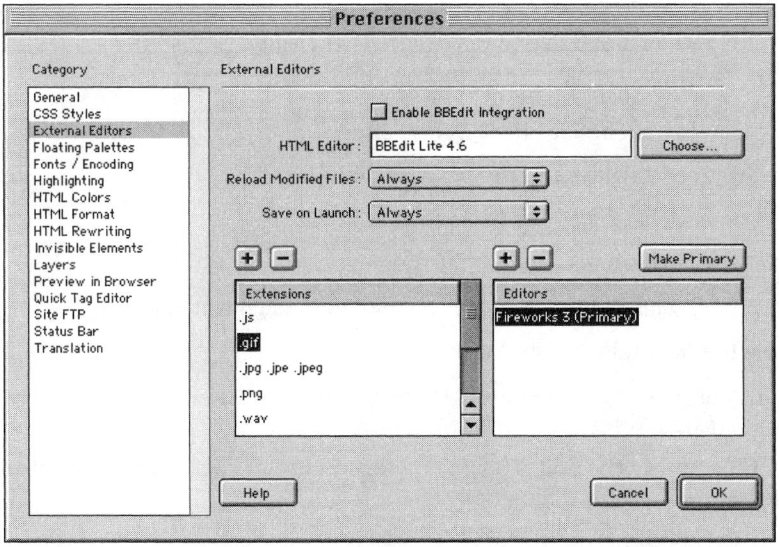

Figure 22-4: To quickly edit a graphic on a Dreamweaver page, make sure Fireworks is your default editor for common graphics files, such as GIF.

After you make your alterations to your file in Fireworks, choose either File ⇨ Update or the keyboard shortcut Ctrl+S in Windows (Command+S on a Macintosh). If you're working with a Fireworks source file, both the source file and the exported file are updated and saved.

Caution If you choose File ⇨ Update, make sure that your source file and exported file are the same dimensions. If your exported file is a cropped version of the source file, the complete source file is used as the basis for the export file, and any cropping information is discarded. To maintain the cropping, choose File ⇨ Export to re-export the file instead of saving it with File ⇨ Update.

Recognizing Design Notes from Fireworks

Both Dreamweaver and Fireworks are capable of saving Design Notes, an innovative method for sharing information between graphic designers who use Fireworks and Web designers using Dreamweaver. A *Design Note* is basically an external file that contains editable information about any element in Dreamweaver, such as HTML pages or graphics. Fireworks adds Design Notes to images that are exported into a Dreamweaver site, storing the location of the source file. This enables Dreamweaver to optimize or edit the source file of an included image without asking the user to locate the file.

From within Dreamweaver, you can read Fireworks Design Notes — or add your own information. However, you have to make sure that Design Notes are enabled for the current site. To enable Design Notes, follow these steps:

1. In Dreamweaver, choose Site ➪ Define Sites.

   Dreamweaver displays the Define Sites dialog box.

2. Select your current site and then click Edit.

   Dreamweaver displays the Edit Sites dialog box.

3. Select the Design Notes category to view the Design Notes panel.

4. Enable the Maintain Design Notes option.

5. If you want other team members to be able to view the Design Notes, select Upload Design Notes for Sharing.

6. Click OK to close the Edit Sites dialog box and then click Done in order to close the Define Sites dialog box.

To view or add Design Notes to a Fireworks (or any other) image, follow these steps:

1. Select the image file and right-click (Control-click) to display the context menu and choose Design Notes.

   The Design Notes dialog is displayed.

2. Select the All Info tab to see the path to the source file. The source file information is contained in a Design Note key called fw_source. It looks like this:

   ```
   fw_source=file:///D|/DW3 Bible/images/house.png
   ```

3. To add additional information to the Design Note, select the Add button and fill in the Name and Value fields.

Tip Tab out of the Value field to confirm your entry, rather than pressing Enter (Return).

Exporting Dreamweaver Code

In its first release, Fireworks was only capable of outputting its own style of HTML. Although it was the very model of efficient code, it didn't mesh too well with Dreamweaver. It worked just fine, but you couldn't modify it within Dreamweaver — you had to return to Fireworks to make any changes. Not exactly an optimum situation.

Fireworks speaks fluent Dreamweaver — and in two dialects and two versions, no less. For all export operations involving HTML output, including hotspots, slices, and Behaviors, Fireworks is capable of writing code either as Dreamweaver 3, Dreamweaver 3 Library or Dreamweaver 2.

The type of HTML output is set when exporting an image. In the Export dialog box, choose either Dreamweaver 2, Dreamweaver 3, or Dreamweaver 3 Library from the HTML Style option list, shown in Figure 22-5. The Fireworks and Dreamweaver engineers worked closely together to ensure that the code would match.

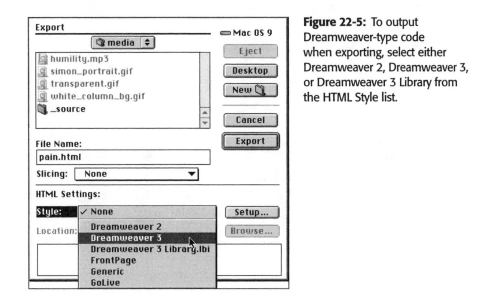

Figure 22-5: To output Dreamweaver-type code when exporting, select either Dreamweaver 2, Dreamweaver 3, or Dreamweaver 3 Library from the HTML Style list.

Cross-Reference   For precise details on how to export Dreamweaver-style code from Fireworks and insert it into your Dreamweaver pages, see Chapters 20 and 21.

Working with Dreamweaver Libraries

The export of Dreamweaver 3 Library code from Fireworks is a real time-saver. One of the most difficult tasks for graphic designers moving to the Web is handling code. With Generic, or even Dreamweaver 2 or Dreamweaver 3 output, all code must be cut and pasted from the Fireworks-generated page to the working Dreamweaver document. Although this is fairly straightforward in Dreamweaver (and Fireworks makes it as clear as possible with concise HTML comments marking the code to move), it still involves working in an environment in which many designers aren't comfortable: code.

Dreamweaver Libraries eliminate the need for designers to handle code when inserting any Fireworks output, including even the most complex Behaviors. What's a *Dreamweaver Library*? I like the explanation given to me by a Fireworks engineer, "Think of it as Encapsulated HTML." Designers routinely work with Encapsulated PostScript (EPS) files, and the metaphor fits. Like EPS files, a Dreamweaver Library item is capable of containing hundreds of lines of code, but the designer need only be concerned with one element — and a visual one, at that.

Dreamweaver's Insert Fireworks HTML

Dreamweaver gained a Fireworks logo in its Object palette with version 3, as shown in the following figure. The Insert Fireworks HTML Object enables you to browse to an HTML file that you exported from Fireworks and include it in your current Dreamweaver document.

I find the Insert Fireworks HTML Object handy for times when I'm exporting a lot of code from Fireworks. Rather than worry about where the code is going, I just export it all to one folder and later insert it into the right places within Dreamweaver.

After an item has been exported as a Dreamweaver 3 Library item, it's extremely easy to insert in your page by following these steps:

1. In Dreamweaver, open the document in which you want to insert the exported Fireworks code.

2. Choose Window ➪ Library or click the Library icon from the Dreamweaver Launcher.

   The Library palette opens.

3. Select the exported item from the list pane.

Tip I've found that I sometimes have to close the Library palette and reopen it before any newly added items from Fireworks will appear.

4. Insert the Library item on the page either by choosing Add to Page or by dragging and dropping the item from the list or preview pane.

The Library item is added to your page and initially selected.

Feel free to move the Fireworks-generated Library item anywhere on the page; if necessary, the code will move, as well.

A key feature of Dreamweaver Library items is their ability to be updated. Edit a single Library item, and Dreamweaver automatically updates all the Web pages using that item. This capability is a major time-saver. Unlike regular graphics, which can be modified at the click of the Edit button from Dreamweaver's Property inspector, Library item graphics first must be unlocked.

To edit a Library item, follow these steps:

1. In Dreamweaver, choose Window ⇨ Library to open the Library palette.

2. Select the Library item embedded in the page, either from the Web page or the Library palette.

3. From the Library palette (or from the Library Property inspector) click Open, as shown in Figure 22-6.

The Library item opens in its own Dreamweaver window.

4. Select the graphic and choose Edit from the Property inspector.

If the file is not in PNG format, Fireworks asks whether you prefer to edit an original source file and gives you the chance to locate it. The selected PNG file is opened in Fireworks.

5. Modify the file, as needed.

6. When you're done, select File ⇨ Update.

The altered file is automatically updated in the Dreamweaver Library file.

7. In Dreamweaver, choose File ⇨ Save.

Dreamweaver notes that your Library item has been modified and asks whether you'd like to update all the Web pages in your site that contain the item. Click Yes to update all Library items (including the one just modified) or No to postpone the updates.

8. Close the editing window by selecting File ⇨ Close.

If you opt to postpone the Library item update, you can do it at any time by selecting Modify ⇨ Library ⇨ Update Pages.

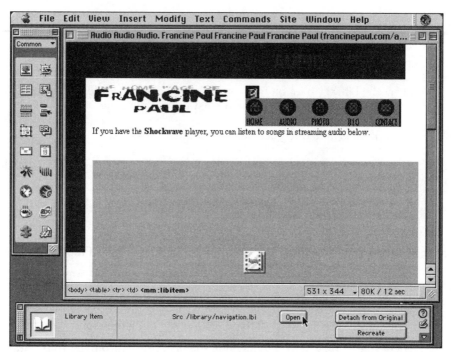

Figure 22-6: Select a Library Item and click Open in the Property Inspector in order to edit the item.

Fireworks technique: adding CSS layers to Dreamweaver

Fireworks 3 features another type of export that — although not strictly a Dreamweaver feature — fits so well in the Dreamweaver-Fireworks workflow that it's worth including in this chapter. Fireworks is capable of exporting images directly into Cascading Style Sheet (CSS) layers. A CSS layer is a free-floating structure that can be viewed in any version 4 or higher browser. CSS layers have several notable properties, including the following properties:

✦ **Position:** Layers — and, thus, the content they hold — can be precisely positioned. This makes layout far easier than with traditional HTML means.

✦ **Depth:** Layers can be stacked one upon another, and their depth can be changed, dynamically.

✦ **Visibility:** Layers can be hidden or revealed at will.

✦ **Movement:** Layers can be dynamically positioned and, thus, moved across the screen over time to create animation.

I've exported CSS layers to use in Dreamweaver with two different methods: exporting Fireworks layers and exporting Fireworks frames. Using Fireworks layers is useful for determining a precise layout of images against a background. For one project, eight separate artworks needed to be placed in the proper position against a background. To ease the workflow, I used the following technique:

1. In Fireworks, open the background graphic and lock it on the Layers panel.

2. Click the New Layer button on the Layers panel.

    A new layer is created.

Tip   If desired, give the layer a unique name; the layer names in Fireworks are used as the CSS layer names.

3. Choose Insert ⇨ Image to open a foreground image.

    Alternatively, you can cut and paste an object or image from an open file.

4. Position the image against the background.

5. Repeat Steps 2-4, creating a new layer for each object.

    Although each object is placed in its own layer, they appear as if side by side.

6. When all the images are properly placed, hide the layer the background is on by deselecting the appropriate eye symbol in the Layers panel.

7. Choose File ⇨ Export Special ⇨ CSS Layers.

    The Export Special dialog box appears.

8. Select Layers from the Files From option list as the type of Fireworks component to export.

9. Make sure the Trim Images option is not selected.

10. Make sure the HTML Style is set to CSS Layers.

11. Determine where the HTML file should be stored by selecting one of the following options from the Location option list: Same Directory, One Level Up, or Custom.

12. Click Save when you're ready.

    Each Fireworks layer is saved as a separate image, and the CSS layer information is written out in HTML.

13. In Dreamweaver, open the Fireworks-generated HTML page.

14. Select all of the CSS layers on the page by using one of the following methods:

    • From the Dreamweaver Layers palette, press Shift and select each layer.

    • In the Dreamweaver document window, press Shift and select each of the CSS layer symbols.

15. Choose Edit ➪ Copy to copy the selected layers.

16. Open the target Web page for the layers.

17. Choose Edit ➪ Paste to insert the layers.

The depth of the CSS layers is determined by the order of layers in Fireworks. In CSS layers, higher numbered layers are on top of lower numbered layers, just as a layer that is higher in the Layers panel's layer list is on top of those below it.those

The other method of using the CSS layer export feature of Fireworks, exporting Fireworks frames, comes in handy when you need to build complex Show-Hide Layer Behaviors in Dreamweaver. Often, the layers being alternately shown and hidden are in front of one another. You can take advantage of this positioning by setting up the separate objects as frames in Fireworks. Then, choose File ➪ Export Special ➪ CSS Layers and select Frames as the Files From selection in the Export Special dialog box. Deselect the Trim Images option if you want each image to maintain its relative place in the frames; enable the option if you want the upper-left corner of each image to match.

> **Tip**
>
> If you are displaying separately saved images, you can use the Open Multiple command with the Open as Animation option enabled in order to place each image automatically in its own frame. Then, choose File ➪ Export Special ➪ CSS Layers to output the frames as layers.

Using Fireworks Behaviors in Dreamweaver

Fireworks 3 started writing in Dreamweaver standard code so that its Behaviors would be recognized in Dreamweaver. What's the big deal about being recognized in Dreamweaver? If Dreamweaver can identify a Behavior as the same as its own, you can edit parameters in Dreamweaver that were defined in Fireworks. If you apply a Set Text of Status Bar Behavior in Fireworks and want to change the message in Dreamweaver, you can.

Fireworks 3 exports code for four categories of Behaviors: Simple Rollover, Swap Image, Set Nav Bar Image, and Set Text of Status Bar.

> **Note**
>
> Another Behavior is automatically inserted for all Fireworks Behaviors: Preload Images. As the name implies, the Preload Images Behavior makes sure that the browser has all images ready for smooth rollovers.

To modify a Fireworks-applied Behavior in Dreamweaver, you must first open the Dreamweaver Behavior inspector, shown in Figure 22-7, which looks quite similar to the Behaviors panel in Fireworks. Select an object or tag in Dreamweaver, and any applied Behaviors are listed in the Behavior inspector.

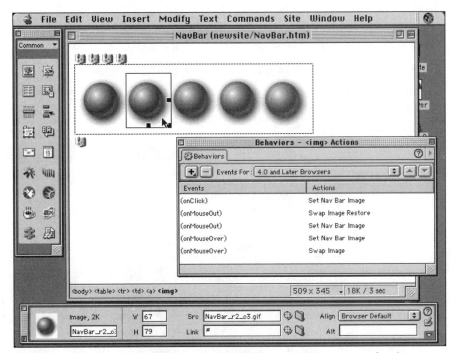

Figure 22-7: The Behavior inspector in Dreamweaver uses events and actions, just like the Behaviors panel in Fireworks.

Each of the Behaviors uses a different dialog box in Dreamweaver for modification; however, the overall procedure is the same. To modify any of the Fireworks-generated Behaviors in Dreamweaver, follow these steps:

1. In Dreamweaver, open the file incorporating your Fireworks-generated HTML code.

2. Choose Window ➪ Behaviors to open the Behavior inspector.

   Alternatively, you can click the Behavior button from the Launcher.

3. Select the image, object, or tag that the Behavior is assigned to.

   The Behavior's event(s) and action(s) are displayed in the Behavior inspector.

4. To change to a different triggering event, click the desired Behavior option arrow and choose another option from the drop-down list.

Tip   The list of available events changes depending upon the associated tag.

5. To cause one action to be triggered before another action with the same event (for example, two onClick events), click the action and use the Up and Down buttons in the Behavior inspector to move the Behavior.

6. Double-click the Behavior that you want to modify.

The appropriate dialog box appears, such as the one for the Set Nav Bar Image Behavior, shown in Figure 22-8.

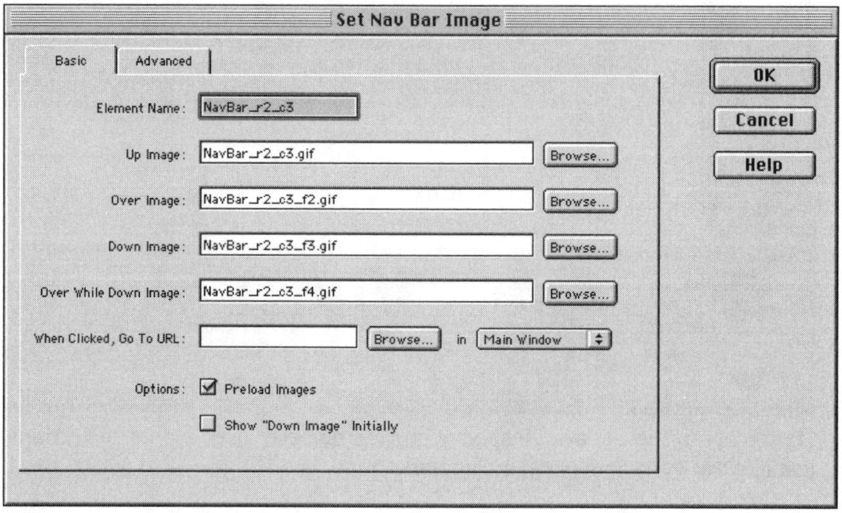

Figure 22-8: Make any necessary changes through the Dreamweaver-specific user interfaces for each Behavior.

7. Make any desired changes on the invoked dialog box.

8. Click OK when you're done.

The Set Nav Bar Image Behavior in Fireworks is translated into the following three separate Behaviors in Dreamweaver 3, each of which can be individually adjusted in Dreamweaver:

✦ **Set Nav Bar Image:** Controls the Down and highlighted Down state (typically, Frames 3 and 4 in a Fireworks rollover).

✦ **Swap Image:** Controls rollovers for Nav Bars.

✦ **Swap Image Restore:** Restores rollovers to their Up position when the user's mouse cursor leaves the image.

Fireworks Technique: Creating a Web Photo Album

Online catalogs and other sites often depend on images to help sell their products. Full-scale product shots can be large and time-consuming to download, so it's common for Web designers to display a thumbnail of the images instead. If the viewer wants to see more detail, a click on the thumbnail loads the full-size image. While it's not difficult to save a scaled-down version of an image in a graphics program and link the two in a Web layout program, creating page after page of such images is an overwhelming chore. An excellent example of Dreamweaver-Fireworks interoperability comes to the rescue: the Create Web Photo Album Command, which is included with Dreamweaver 3.

New Feature
Create Web Photo Album is a new Dreamweaver Command that takes the contents of any user-specified folder and creates thumbnail images using Fireworks. The graphics are placed in a Dreamweaver table, complete with links to a series of pages with the full-size image.

As long as you have both Dreamweaver 3 and Fireworks 3, the Web Photo Album Command can be used to create a presentation that enables a Web user to browse thumbnail images that can be clicked to access the full-size version. Although the Create Web Photo Album Command is a Dreamweaver Command, it uses Fireworks to do the image processing, such as scaling thumbnails and converting all full-size images to a common format.

To create a Web photo album with Dreamweaver and Fireworks, follow these steps:

1. Place all of the images that you intend to use into a single folder, anywhere on your computer. The Web photo Command will ask you to choose a single folder of images.

2. In Dreamweaver, choose Commands ⇨ Create Web Photo Album.

   Dreamweaver displays the Web Photo Album dialog box, as shown in Figure 22-9.

3. Enter a title for your Photo Album in the Photo Album Title box. The title will be displayed at the top of the page of thumbnails.

4. If desired, enter a subheading in the Subheading Info box. This appears directly below the title on the page of thumbnails.

5. If desired, enter a sub-subheading in the Other Info box. This appears below the Title and Subheading on the page of thumbnails.

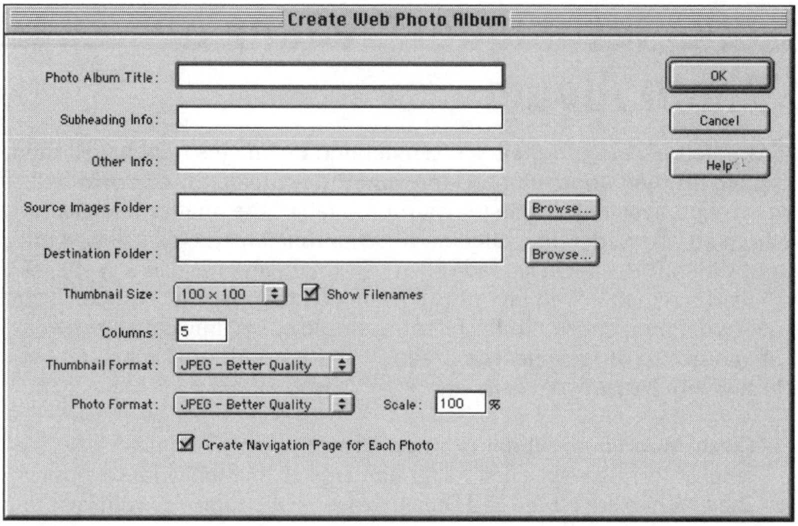

Figure 22-9: Choose from numerous options when building a Web Photo Album.

6. Click the Source Images Folder Browse button and select a folder containing the images to include in the photo album.

Image files from the folder will be included in the photo album if they have the following filename extensions:

- .gif
- .jpg or .jpeg

Caution Using JPEG images as source files is never recommended. JPEG compression makes files that are suitable for viewing, but not for importing and re-exporting.

- .png
- .tif or .tiff
- .psd

Caution Mac users: image files that don't have filename extensions are ignored by Fireworks and are not included in the photo album. Add appropriate filename extensions to any images that don't have them.

7. Click the Destination Folder Browse button and select or create a folder for all of the exported images and HTML.

8. Select a size for the thumbnail images from the Thumbnail Size option list.

Fireworks scales images proportionally to create thumbnails that fit within the specified pixel dimensions.

9. Check the Show Filenames checkbox to display the filenames of the original images below their thumbnails.

10. Enter the number of columns of thumbnails.

11. Select a format for the exported thumbnail images from the Format option list.

12. Select a format for the exported photo album images from the Photo Format option list.

13. If desired, enter a Scale percentage for the photo album images. A setting of 100% creates full-size images the same size as the original images.

Caution The scale setting is used for all of the photo album images.

14. If desired, check Create Navigation Page for Each Photo to create an individual Web page for each image in the photo album.

Note If you don't select Create Navigation Page for Each Photo, the thumbnail images are linked directly to the full-size images. This is a common way to create a Web photo album.

15. Click OK when you're done.

Fireworks is launched (if it's not already running). It creates a thumbnail and a full-size image for each of the imported image files in your photo album. Once the images are created, Dreamweaver creates the necessary HTML.

16. Dreamweaver displays an Album Complete dialog box. Click OK to end your photo album creation session.

Open your Web photo album in a browser, or integrate it into your Dreamweaver Web site.

Making Hybrid Commands

The scripting ability of Dreamweaver and Fireworks enables the Web artist to control either application with custom Commands. An exciting side effect of the enhanced control is that Dreamweaver can actually do the Fireworks scripting, making Fireworks a willing partner in executing Dreamweaver Commands.

 Tip Many Dreamweaver Commands are available for download on the Web. Some of these Commands, such as StyleBuilder and BulletBuilder, both created by Joseph Lowery, one of this book's authors, are hybrid Dreamweaver-Fireworks Commands. Visit Dreamweaver, etc. at `<http://www.idest.com/dreamweaver/>` for more Commands.

Here's how Dreamweaver is typically used to communicate with Fireworks:

1. The user runs a Command in Dreamweaver.

2. Dreamweaver opens a dialog box, as with other extensions.

3. After the user has filled in the dialog box and clicked OK, the Command is executed.

4. All user-supplied parameters are read and used to create a JavaScript Scriptlet or function, which serves as instructions for Fireworks.

5. If used, the Scriptlet is stored on the disk.

6. Fireworks is launched and instructed to run the Dreamweaver-created Scriptlet or function.

7. Fireworks processes the Scriptlet or function, while Dreamweaver tracks its progress via a cookie on the user's machine.

8. Once Fireworks is finished, a positive result is returned.

   The Fireworks application programming interface (API) includes several error codes for if problems, such as a full disk, are encountered.

9. While tracking Fireworks' progress, Dreamweaver sees the positive result and integrates the graphics by rewriting the DOM (Document Object Model) of the current page.

10. The dialog box is closed and the current page refreshed to correctly present the finished product.

To successfully control Fireworks, you'll need a complete understanding of the Fireworks DOM and it's extension capabilities. Macromedia provides documentation called Extending Fireworks, which is available on your Fireworks 3 CD-ROM, or from Fireworks Support Center at <http://www.macromedia.com/support/fireworks/>.

Cross-Reference The Fireworks API is detailed in Chapter 26. Also, See Chapter 19 for details on the History panel, which allows you to create Commands — or at least get them started — without coding.

On the Dreamweaver side of the API fence, you'll find seven useful methods in the FWLaunch JSExtension, detailed in Table 22-2.

Don't be afraid to experiment with Dreamweaver-Fireworks integration and with extensibility in general. Exciting possibilities await.

	Table 22-2	
	FWLaunch Methods	
Method	*Returns*	*Use*
bringDWToFront()	n/a	Brings the Dreamweaver window in front of any other running application.
bringFWToFront()	n/a	Brings the Fireworks window in front of any other running application.
execJsInFireworks (javascriptOrFileURL)	Result from the running of the Scriptlet in Fireworks. If the operation fails, returns an error code.*	Executes the supplied JavaScript function or Scriptlet.
mayLaunchFireworks()	Boolean	Determines if Fireworks may be launched.
optimizeInFireworks (fileURL, docURL, {targetWidth}, {targetHeight})	Result from the running of the Scriptlet in Fireworks. If the operation fails, returns an error code.*	Performs an Optimize in Fireworks operation, opening the Fireworks Export Preview dialog box.
validateFireworks	Boolean	Determines if the user has a (versionNumber) specific version of Fireworks

* Error codes: 1) The argument proves invalid; 2) File I/O error; 3) Improper version of Dreamweaver; 4) Improper version of Fireworks; 5) User cancelled operation

Summary

Fireworks and Dreamweaver integration is definitely a case of the whole being greater than the individual parts. Taken on their own merits, each program is a powerful Web tool, but together, they become a total Web graphics solution. As you begin to work with Fireworks and Dreamweaver together, consider these points:

✦ Dreamweaver 3 gains features when Fireworks 3 is installed.

✦ With the Optimize Image in Fireworks Command, you don't even have to leave Dreamweaver to rescale, crop, or store your graphics in another format.

✦ After designating Fireworks as your graphics editor in Dreamweaver, selected images can be edited and updated automatically.

✦ Fireworks 3 outputs Dreamweaver-compliant code, making modifications within Dreamweaver seamless.

✦ Fireworks images exported as a Dreamweaver 3 Library item can be inserted in a Web page without additional cutting and pasting.

✦ You can retain positioning set in Fireworks by exporting Fireworks layers as CSS layers through the Export Special command.

✦ Hybrid Dreamweaver-Fireworks Commands open up new possibilities for workflow automation.

In the next chapter, you'll learn about Fireworks' animation capabilities.

✦   ✦   ✦

Animation

In This Part

Chapter 23
Animation Techniques

Chapter 24
Animating
Banner Ads

Animation Techniques

Animation has become a prominent feature of the Web, and very few Web sites get by without at least a little of it. Animated GIF banner ads have proliferated from common to ubiquitous. Animated logos and buttons are an easy way to add spice to a site. Short, animated cartoons are increasingly popular as Web bandwidth increases.

This chapter looks briefly at some animation basics and then focuses on the Fireworks features that enable you to create animations. We'll work withGIF export features such as timing and looping. Next, we'll look at specific issues that you might confront when making animated banner ads, and then go through the process from start to finish.

Cross-Reference You'll find information on importing animations and importing multiple files as animations in Chapter 14.

Understanding Web Animation

Animation is a trick. Show me a rapid succession of similar images with slight changes in an element's location or properties, and I'll think that I see something moving. This movement can be very complex or very simple. The 24 frames per second of a motion picture aren't even required; in as little as 3 frames, an object can actually appear to be moving (loop 2 frames and an object just appears to flash).

Because Fireworks creates animated GIF images, this chapter focuses on that format. You'll find, though, that many of the ideas that go into creating good animated GIF images also apply when creating images in other Web animation formats.

♦   ♦   ♦   ♦

In This Chapter

Understanding Web animation

Managing frames

Animating objects

Using Onion Skinning

Using the VCR controls

Exporting your animated GIF

Tweening with Symbols and Instances

Fireworks technique: fading in and out

Animating Xtras

Tweening depth

♦   ♦   ♦   ♦

Bandwidth, bandwidth, bandwidth

Remember first and foremost that bandwidth is always an issue. Then, remember that bandwidth is always an issue. I'll end up harping on that again and again, because bandwidth affects everything. You must analyze each and every bold, creative move for its eventual effect on the overall *weight* of the resulting animated GIF file (the total file size). Throughout the entire process of creating an animation for display on the Web, you need to balance variables carefully, such as the number of colors you use, the number of frames, the timing of those frames, and how much area of your image is actually animated. If you want more colors, you may have to take out a few frames and settle for a less fluid animation. If you're animating complex shapes that don't compress well, you may have to get by with fewer colors.

The dial-up connection is the great equalizer. The Web is slow and generally static, and almost everybody knows it. If you can give your audience a quick, dynamic presentation, you'll score two times. Keep in mind the nature of GIF compression as you create your designs. Big blocks of cartoonish color and horizontal stripes compress much better than photographic images, vertical stripes, or gradients and dithers.

Making a statement

So, maybe you're not going to win an Oscar with your animation; that doesn't mean you shouldn't give it a reason for existing. Every part of your animation needs to be focused and necessary, because each little movement that you add you also purchase with a corresponding amount of bandwidth. A short, tight, and concise animation will be much more popular with your audience. This applies whether you're creating a complex cartoon with an intricate story line, a flashy, abstract design, or even an animated logo. If you decide before you start what you want to accomplish creatively, you increase your chances of ending up with a tight, presentable result.

Animated GIF images are good at some things, but not so good at others. Consider those limitations carefully and focus on creating a good animated GIF—not just a good animation that happens to be forced into the framework of an animated GIF. Logos, buttons, and simple frame-by-frame animations work best. You might find that thinking of an animated GIF image as a slide-show rather than a movie is helpful. Typically, you work with fewer frames than a movie uses, and with slow, simple, animated elements. I find that thinking of animated GIFs as little PowerPoint-style presentations reminds me of the limitations of the format. You can make a little movement go a long way. You can show that something's moving either by smoothly animating it, frame by frame, across the entire width of the image, or you can place it once on the left side of the canvas, followed by a blurred version in the center, and then display it again at the right side.

Tip Don't forget everything that you learned by watching Saturday morning cartoons or reading comic books. Techniques such as word balloons and lines that illustrate movement or action in still comics can help you get your message across without adding significantly to the frame count (and the file size). Instead of moving an element off the canvas in ten smooth frames, replace it with a puff of smoke and some lines that point to which way the element went. Study animations for tricks like that and make lean, mean animations that really make an impression and get your message across.

As usual on the Web, you're at the mercy of your users' browsers—and you don't even know which browsers they'll be using. However, generally, animated GIF images play back a little faster in Internet Explorer than in Navigator (and, naturally, play back faster on faster computers). Don't try to be too precise, attempting to measure the time between frames and worrying about it. Instead, embrace a little of the Web's anarchy and just try to find a good middle ground. Trust the timing settings in Fireworks and hope for the best.

Why animate a GIF?

Fireworks is the perfect place to create animated GIF images. Creating the illusion of animation means changing the objects on the canvas over time, and an always-editable object in Fireworks is easy to move, scale, or modify with effects. And when your animation is complete, Fireworks' unmatched image optimization enables you to create the lightest-weight animated GIF possible. (There's that bandwidth issue again.)

Tip Although you usually create animated GIF animations directly in Fireworks, you also can export an animation as a series of files, by using File ➪ Export Special ➪ Export as Files. These files—which can be other image formats such as PNG or JPEG—can then be modified in another application, or used in another animation format, such as an SMIL presentation in RealPlayer or an interactive Dynamic HTML (DHTML) slide-show.

The animated GIF has its share of limitations and gets its share of disrespect, especially when sized up feature for feature against some of the more "serious" animation formats used on the Web. Table 23-1 makes just such a comparison.

<table>
<tr><td colspan="6" align="center">Table 23-1
Comparing Web Animation Formats</td></tr>
<tr><td>*Format*</td><td>*Sound*</td><td>*Interactivity*</td><td>*Streaming*</td><td>*Transparency*</td><td>*Colors*</td></tr>
<tr><td>Animated GIF</td><td>No</td><td>No</td><td>No</td><td>Yes</td><td>256</td></tr>
<tr><td>Dynamic HTML</td><td>No</td><td>Yes</td><td>Yes</td><td>Yes</td><td>Millions</td></tr>
<tr><td>Java</td><td>Yes</td><td>Yes</td><td>Yes</td><td>No</td><td>Millions</td></tr>
</table>

Continued

Table 23-1 *(continued)*

Format	Sound	Interactivity	Streaming	Transparency	Colors
Flash	Yes	Yes	Yes	Sometimes	Millions
Shockwave	Yes	Yes	Yes	No	Millions
QuickTime	Yes	Yes	Yes	No	Millions
RealPlayer	Yes	Yes	Yes	No	Millions

Note Transparency refers to a transparent background when the animation is placed in a browser, not support within the editing environment or the animation format itself.

Based on this table, the animated GIF seems like a pretty poor choice. Other formats feature high levels of interactivity and automatically stream or simulate streaming with multiple component files. Some have video and many have sound. What's more, Flash gets a lot more done in a much smaller file size.

So, why is the animated GIF used so often? Why haven't designers dropped it in favor of one or more of these other, seemingly superior methods? Find the answers to these questions and more in Table 23-2, which details browser support for each format.

Table 23-2
Browser Support for Web Animation Formats

Format	Navigator 2/3 and IE 3	Navigator 4 and IE 4/5	Most Other Browsers
Animated GIF	Yes	Yes	Yes
Dynamic HTML	No	Yes	No
Java	Yes; user can disable	Yes; user can disable	No
Flash	With Plug-in	With Plug-in	No
Shockwave	With Plug-in	With Plug-in	No
QuickTime	With Plug-in	With Plug-in	No
RealPlayer	With Plug-in	With Plug-in	No

When you consider who can actually view your animation, the animated GIF doesn't look so bad after all. Other formats may be flashier, but the animated GIF is "old reliable." No matter which platform or browser, the animated GIF is always available.

The Fireworks Animation Toolkit

Animation in Fireworks focuses on these major tools:

✦ **Frames panel:** The heart of Fireworks' animation features, where you manipulate individual frames — like a director editing the frames of a film — adding, removing, reordering, and specifying timing for individual frames.

Tip   The Export Preview dialog box also duplicates some of the Frames panel controls, such as animation timing.

✦ **Layers panel:** Where you manage each frame's layers. Organize your animation by keeping objects on the same layer from frame to frame, or share a layer across every frame, so that backgrounds or static objects can be created once for the entire animation.

✦ **VCR-style controls:** Where you flip through frames or play your entire animation right in the document window.

✦ **Symbols and Instances:** Fireworks can create intermediate steps between two Instances of the same Symbol, quickly generating a complete animation.

Managing frames

What separates an animation from a regular Fireworks document is that the animation has multiple frames. The relationship between layers and frames can be hard to understand when you first start animating in Fireworks. However, understanding how they work — and work together — is essential.

Frames are like the frames of a traditional film strip (see Figure 23-1) that you might run through a movie projector. When you play your animation, only one frame is visible at a time. Frame 1 is shown first, and then Frame 2, Frame 3, and so on. When you add a frame to your document, you're extending the length of the film strip and making a longer movie. When you change the order of frames in the Frames panel, imagine that you're cutting a frame out of your film strip and splicing it back in at another point on the strip. If you move Frame 5 to the beginning of your movie, before Frame 1, all the frames are renumbered, so that what used to be Frame 5 is now Frame 1, what used to be Frame 1 becomes Frame 2, and so on.

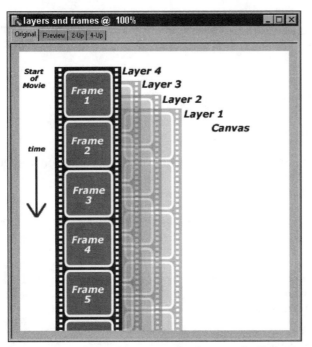

Figure 23-1: Think of frames as the frames of a film strip, and layers as a stack of film strips stuck together.

The layers in an animation are like separate film strips stacked together. When you play your animation, all the layers of Frame 1 are shown together, and then all the layers of Frame 2 are shown, and then Frame 3, and so on. Just like when you use layers in a static Fireworks document, layers provide a way to organize the order of objects and keep dissimilar objects separate from each other, for easier editing. When you add a layer to your document, you add a whole new film strip to the stack. Changing the order of layers in the Layers panel is like changing the order of that film strip in the stack of film strips.

Note When you add a frame to your movie, it automatically has the same layers as all the other frames. To continue the film-strip metaphor, adding a frame to one film strip in the stack adds it to all the film strips. When you add a layer to your movie, it is added to every frame. Adding a layer adds a whole new film strip, the same length as the others.

One very useful interaction between layers and frames is the ability to share a layer. When a layer is shared, its content is the same on every frame, and no matter which frame you are viewing when you edit the objects in that layer, the changes appear on every frame. This is handy for static elements, such as backgrounds. We'll take a closer look at this later.

You do the bulk of your animation work in the Frames panel (Figure 23-2), so you need to have it open all the time while creating an animation. From there, you can add, delete, reorder, or duplicate frames. You can view and edit a single frame, a group of frames, or all of your frames simultaneously. You can copy or move objects from frame to frame. You can specify the timing each frame will have in your animated GIF. As with the Layers panel, when a Frame contains a selection, a selection icon appears next to its name in the Frames panel.

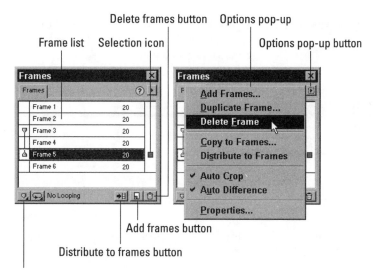

Figure 23-2: Manage Frames with the Frames panel and its handy options pop-up.

> **Tip** When working on animation, you might want to dock your Layers panel with your Frames panel, if it isn't already, so that you can easily move between the panels. If you're not short on screen real estate, you could even keep them side by side. Location doesn't matter, as long as they're both close at hand.

Adding frames

When you start creating an animation in Fireworks, your document has exactly one frame. Obviously, this has to change before you can simulate any kind of movement. At first, you might make a rough guess at how many frames your animation should contain, and then add that number of frames to your document. Later, you can add or remove frames as the need arises. Another approach is to start with just two frames: the first and the last. After you establish where your animation starts and finishes, filling in the intervening frames is often easier.

To add a frame to the end of the Frame list, click the Add Frames button (blank sheet of paper) at the bottom of the Frames panel, or choose Insert ➪ Frame.

To add one or more frames at a specific point in the Frame list, follow these steps:

1. Choose Add Frames from the Frames panel options pop-up.

   Fireworks displays the Add Frames dialog box (see Figure 23-3).

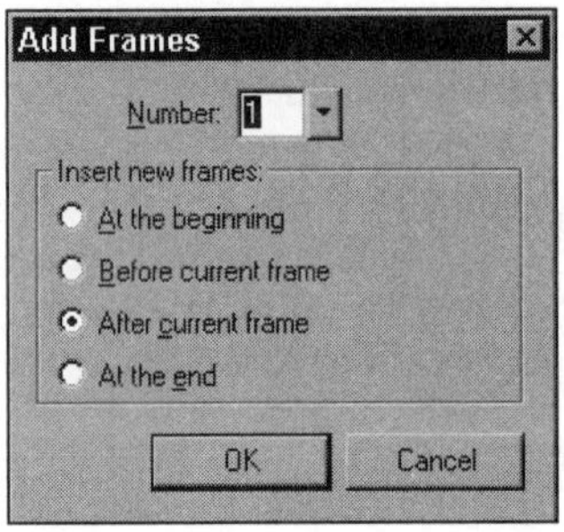

Figure 23-3: The Add Frames dialog box gives you careful control over how many frames you add and where you add them.

2. Enter the number of frames to add in the Number box, or use the slider to add up to ten frames.

3. Choose where to insert the new frames. The options are At the beginning, Before current frame, After current frame, and At the end. Click OK when you're done.

The new frames are created and added to the Frame list at the point you specified.

Deleting a frame

The most important thing to remember when you delete a frame is that you also delete all the objects that it contains, except for those that are on a shared layer. Take care to identify and delete the correct frame.

Tip   If you delete a frame accidentally and want to restore it to the Frame list, choose either Edit ➪ Undo or the keyboard shortcut Ctrl + Z (Command + Z).

To delete a frame, select it on the Frame list and do one of the following:

✦ Click the Delete Frames button (a Trash icon) at the bottom of the Frames panel.

✦ Drag the frame to the Delete Frames button at the bottom of the Frames panel.

✦ Choose Delete Frame from the Frames panel options pop-up.

Reordering frames

As you continue to work on your animation, you might want to change the order of your frames by moving them earlier or later in the animation.

To reorder a frame, click and drag it up or down the Frame list in the Frames panel.

Note From working with layers in the Layers panel, you may be accustomed to seeing the layer retain its name as you change its stacking order by dragging it up or down the layers list. When you reorder a frame, though, all frames are renumbered to reflect their new positions. The first frame in your animation will always be Frame 1.

Duplicating frames

One way to save a significant amount of time and effort is to copy a sequence of frames that you've already created and then modify the copies further. If you have created an animation sequence of a sunrise, you can copy those frames and then reverse their order to get an automatic sunset. This not only saves you the time and effort of creating the sunset animation from scratch, but also has the added advantage that the sun will set in the same place from which it rose.

To duplicate a single frame, drag it from the Frame list onto the Add Frames button at the bottom of the Frames panel. Fireworks inserts the copy into the Frame list right after the original.

To duplicate one or more frames and place the copies in a specific place in the Frame list, follow these steps:

1. Choose Duplicate Frame from the Frames panel options pop-up.

   Fireworks displays the Duplicate Frames dialog box.

Note The Duplicate Frames dialog box is very similar to the Add Frames dialog box, shown previously in Figure 23-3.

2. Enter the number of frames to duplicate in the Number box, or use the slider to duplicate up to ten frames.

3. Choose where to insert the copies. The options are At the beginning, Before current frame, After current frame, and At the end. Click OK when you're done.

The frames are duplicated and the copies are added to the Frame list at the point you specified.

Animating objects

A significant part of creating animation is managing how objects in your document change over time. If you are creating a simple, animated sunrise, the sun starts out at a low point on the canvas and, over time (through later frames), moves to a higher point on the canvas. At the same time, a cloud might move from left to right, while the ground and sky stay the same.

You certainly don't want to draw each of these objects numerous times. Aside from being a lot of extra effort, you would probably end up with objects that are not exactly the same dimensions or properties from frame to frame. If the sun were to change size slightly in each frame, it would detract from the illusion that the animation contains just one moving sun.

Instead, when you create an animation, draw objects once and then copy or distribute them from frame to frame, where the copies can be moved or modified slightly to give the appearance of the same object moving or changing over time.

Keeping similar objects on their own layers makes working with just those objects easier as you copy objects to frames. In the animated sunrise example, you might keep the sun on its own layer, the clouds on another layer, and the unchanging background objects on another.

Copying objects to frames

Most of the time, you'll be adding objects to other frames by copying them. To copy an object or objects to another frame, follow these steps:

1. Select the object(s).

2. Choose Copy to Frames from the Frames panel options pop-up.

   Fireworks displays the Copy to Frames dialog box (see Figure 23-4).

3. Choose where the selection will be copied. The available options are All frames, Previous frame, Next frame, or Range, which is used to specify a specific range of frames. Click OK when you're done.

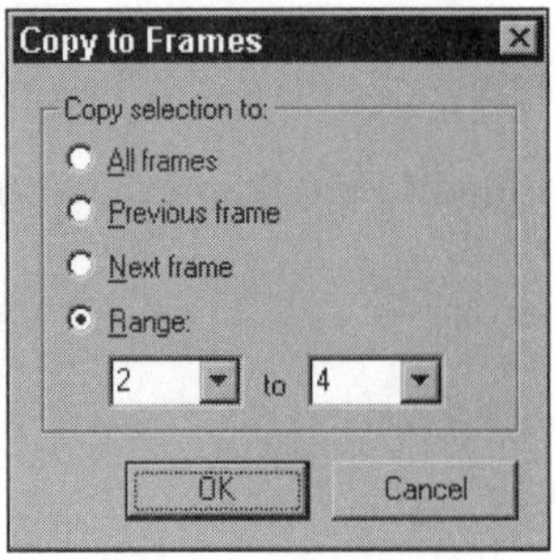

Figure 23-4: Use the Copy to Frames dialog box to copy objects to all of your frames or just a specific range of frames.

Distributing objects to frames

When you choose to distribute a group of objects to frames, the objects are distributed after the current frame, according to their stacking order. The bottom object in the group stays on the current frame, the next one up goes to the next frame, the next one above that goes to the frame after that, and so forth. If you start with a blank canvas and create three objects, such as a square, circle, and star, the star will be on top, because it was created last. If you select those objects and distribute them to frames, the star — which was created last — will now be in the last frame of your animation. New frames are added to contain all the objects, if necessary. For example, if you distribute ten objects to five frames, five more frames will be added to contain all the objects.

You can quickly turn a static document into an animation in this way. Objects that were created first on the canvas end up first in the animation.

To distribute a selection of objects across multiple frames, select the objects and then do one of the following:

✦ Click the Distribute to Frames button (a filmstrip icon) at the bottom of the Frames panel.

✦ Choose Distribute to Frames from the Frames panel options pop-up.

✦ Drag the blue selection knob on the object's bounding box to the Distribute to Frames button.

Managing static objects

Fireworks simplifies management of the objects in your animation that aren't animated, because any layer can be shared across every frame of your animation. For example, if you create a background in Frame 1, you can share the layer that contains the background, and that background will appear in every frame. After the layer is shared, you can modify the objects it contains in any frame, and the modifications will show up everywhere. Any static element in your animation needs to be created or edited only once.

To share a layer across all the frames of your animation, follow these steps:

1. In the Layer panel, double-click the layer that you want to share.

   Fireworks displays the Layer Options dialog box.

2. Check Share Across Frames and then click OK.

   Fireworks warns you that any objects on this layer in other frames will be deleted. Click OK to delete those objects and share the layer.

To stop sharing a layer across all frames of your animation, follow these steps:

1. In the Layer panel, double-click the layer that you want to stop sharing.

   Fireworks displays the Layer Options dialog box.

2. Uncheck Share Across Frames and then click OK.

   Fireworks asks whether you want to leave the contents of the layer in all frames or just in the current frame. Choose Current to leave the contents of the layer just in the current frame. Choose All to leave the contents of the layer in all frames.

Note   Another way to modify whether or not a layer is shared is to select the layer in the Layers panel and check or uncheck Share Layer on the Layers panel options pop-up.

Using the VCR controls

While building your animations in Fireworks, you'll no doubt want to play them to get a feel for the motion between frames. Fireworks offers VCR-style controls available in the status bar on Windows, and along the bottom of each document window on Macintoshes, so that you can preview your animations (see Figure 23-5).

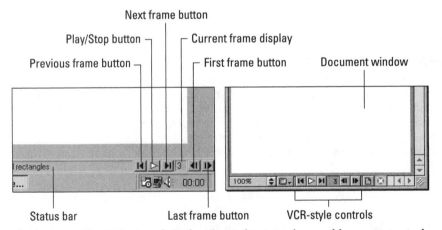

Figure 23-5: The VCR controls in the Fireworks status bar enable you to control your multi-frame Fireworks document like a movie.

When you click the Play button, Fireworks plays your animation, using the timing that is specified in the Frames panel or on the Animation tab of the Export Preview dialog box. If you don't set the timing yourself, your animation plays at the default of $\frac{20}{100}$ of a second between frames. We'll look at frame delay in the next section.

While the animation is playing, the Play button turns into a Stop button. Fireworks also displays the current frame, and has buttons available to jump quickly to the previous or next frame, or to the first or last frame of your animation.

Tip You can also stop a running animation by clicking your mouse inside the document window.

When you play your animation in the document window, it always loops, whether you have looping enabled in the Frames panel or not. The setting in the Frames panel controls looping only in the animated GIF file your animation eventually becomes.

Frame delay timing

The first thing to remember about controlling animation speed is that the settings you specify are ultimately approximate. While Fireworks is perfectly happy to follow your directions, once your animation becomes an animated GIF, timing is in the virtual hands of the playback software, usually a browser. Internet Explorer tends to play animations faster than Navigator, and both browsers play animated GIFs faster on faster computers.

Tip As if approximated GIF timing isn't enough, an animation that is currently being downloaded staggers along with no attention to timing, because each frame is displayed as it arrives. A couple of tricks for getting around the staggering playback of a downloading animated GIF are detailed later in this chapter, under "Web Design with Animated GIF Images."

The default frame delay setting for new frames is 20, specified in hundredths of a second. For example, a setting of 25 is a quarter second, 50 is a half second, and 200 is two seconds.

To change a frame's delay setting, follow these steps:

1. If the Frames panel is not already open, choose Window ➪ Frames or use the key shortcut Ctrl + Alt + K (Command + Option + K) to open it.

2. Double-click the frame you'd like to modify in the frame list. Fireworks displays a pop-up edit window with the frame's delay settings (Figure 23-6).

3. Type a new setting in the Frame Delay field.

4. Uncheck Include when Exporting if you want this frame delay setting to affect the way the animation is viewed in Fireworks without being included in the animated GIF you export.

Figure 23-6: Double-click a frame in the Frame panel to view a pop-up edit window with the frame's delay settings.

5. Click anywhere outside the pop-up edit window or press Enter (Return) to dismiss it.

Alternatively, if you're using the Export Preview dialog box to export your animated GIF, you can alter frame delay by choosing the frame from the list on the Animation tab and changing the value in the Frame Delay field.

Using Onion Skinning

Most of the time, your document window displays the contents of a single frame. By flipping back and forth from frame to frame, you can get a feel for how the animation is flowing, but this is just a rough guide. To get a more precise view of the changes from one frame to the next, turn on Onion Skinning to view, and even edit, multiple frames simultaneously.

Note   *Onion skinning* is the traditional animation technique of drawing on translucent tracing paper — like an onion skin — to view a series of drawings simultaneously.

The Onion Skinning button in the lower-left corner of the Frames panel enables you to access the Onion Skinning menu (see Figure 23-7) and select which frames you want to view. You can choose to view any range of frames within your animation, or all of them.

Onion skinning range selector

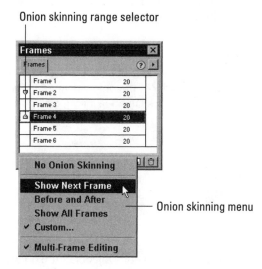

Onion skinning menu

Figure 23-7: The Onion Skinning menu on the Frames panel provides various ways to select which frames you want to view, and even edit, simultaneously.

When Onion Skinning is turned on, objects on the current frame are displayed normally, while objects on other frames are shown slightly dimmed. When playing an animation by using the Frame controls at the bottom of the document window, Onion Skinning is switched off temporarily.

Setting the range of frames to onion skin

You can turn on Onion Skinning and choose a range of frames to display in any one of three ways:

✦ Specify a range of frames by using the Onion Skinning range selector, located in the Frame list's left margin in the Frames panel (refer to Figure 23-2). This is the quickest way to specify a range of frames, especially for shorter animations. To expand the range to include earlier frames, click inside an empty box above the selector. To expand the range to include later frames, click inside an empty box below the selector. To contract the range, click inside the selector itself. To turn off Onion Skinning, click the bottom end of the selector.

✦ Choose predefined ranges from the Onion Skinning menu on the Frames panel. To show the current frame and the next frame, choose Show Next Frame. To show the previous frame, the current frame, and the next frame, choose Before and After. To show all frames, choose Show All.

✦ Choose Custom from the Onion Skinning menu to display the Onion Skinning dialog box (see Figure 23-8), which gives you precise control over the frames that you view, all the way down to the opacity of other frames. Fill in the number of frames Before Current Frame and After Current Frame that you want to view, and specify an Opacity setting for those frames. A setting of 0 makes frame contents invisible, whereas a setting of 100 makes objects on other frames appear as though they're on the current frame.

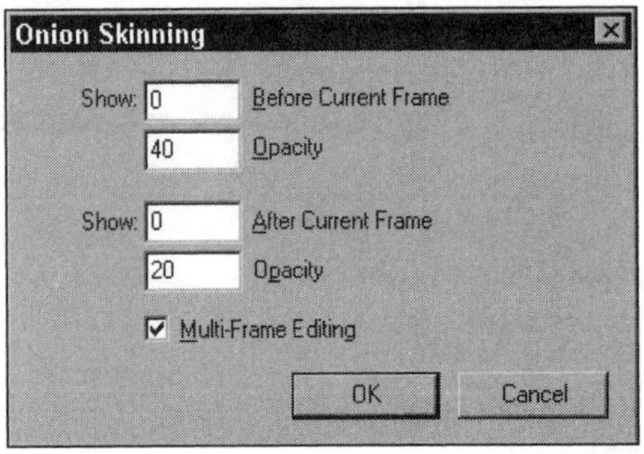

Figure 23-8: Select a specific range of frames to onion skin, and control the opacity of the onion-skinned frames with the Onion Skinning dialog box.

Multi-Frame Editing

When Multi-Frame Editing is enabled, you can select and edit objects in the document window that are on different frames. Whether an object is on the current frame and displayed regularly or on another frame and dimmed makes no difference. You can easily select all versions of a particular object across multiple frames and move or scale them as one.

To enable multi-frame editing, check Multi-Frame Editing on the Onion Skinning dialog box or the Onion Skinning menu. To switch off multi-frame editing, uncheck Multi-Frame Editing. on the Onion Skinning dialog box.

Export settings and options

The animated GIF format contains support for frame delay timing, looping, and various frame disposal methods. These options are built right into the Frame panel itself, or the Animation tab of the Export Preview dialog box.

New Feature   Export settings for animated GIFs—frame delay, disposal method and looping—can now be changed right in the Frame panel, consistent with Fireworks 3's new in-place export settings and previews.

The first export setting that you must specify is the animated GIF format itself. Choose Window ➪ Optimize to view the Optimize panel if it isn't already visible, and choose Animated GIF from the format options pop-up, as shown in Figure 23-9.

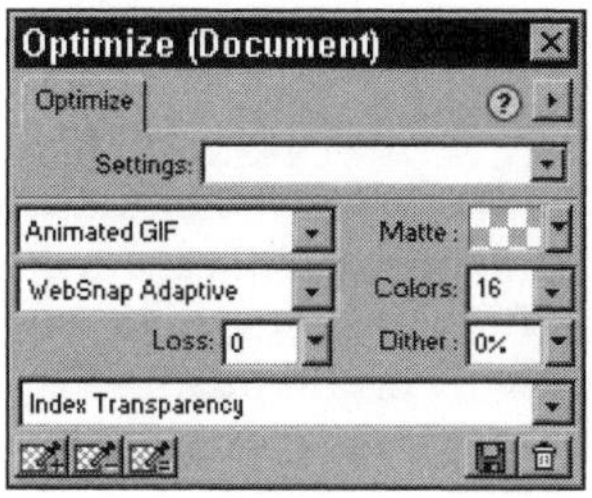

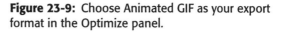

Figure 23-9: Choose Animated GIF as your export format in the Optimize panel.

As usual, the last step before publishing Web media is to put that media on a "diet." All the same rules for exporting a regular, static GIF also apply to animated GIFs. Limiting the number of colors reduces file size, and specifying a transparent background makes for easier compositing with the browser's background when your animated GIF becomes part of a Web page.

Cross-Reference   For more on specifying GIF export options, like number of colors and transparency, see Chapter 15.

Frame disposal

In addition to regular GIF options, the animated GIF format has a special trick up its sleeve for reducing file size: frame disposal. For the most part, you can use Fireworks' default frame disposal settings to produce very lightweight animated GIF images. Learning to tweak the Export settings might save you some valuable kilobytes here and there, though, depending on the type of animation you've created.

The frame disposal options are only available from the Frame Disposal menu on the Animation tab of the Export Preview dialog box. Access the Export Preview dialog box by choosing File ➪ Export Preview. Choose from one of these options:

✦ **Unspecified:** Fireworks automatically selects the disposal method for each frame. This is the default and generally creates the lightest animated GIF images.

✦ **None:** Overlays each frame on top of the previous frame. The first frame is shown, and then the next frame is added on top of it, and the following frame is added on top of that, and so forth. This is suitable for adding a small object to a larger background, if the object doesn't move throughout the animation. For example, this technique works well with an animation that features parts of a logo that steadily appear until the animation is complete.

✦ **Restore to Background:** Shows the contents of each new frame over the background color. For example, to move an object in a transparent animated GIF.

✦ **Restore to Previous:** Shows the contents of each new frame over the contents of the previous frame. For example, to move an object across a background image.

In addition to the Frame Disposal menu, two related options greatly affect the export file size:

✦ **Auto Crop:** Causes Fireworks to compare each frame of the animation with the previous frame and then crop to the area that changes. This reduces file sizes by saving information in each animated GIF only once, and avoids a situation in which, for example, a patch of blue in a certain position is saved repeatedly in each frame.

Tip If you are exporting your animated GIF for editing in another application, turning off Auto Crop is recommended. Some applications don't handle this type of optimization very well, and you may end up with artifacts. Macromedia's Director 7 is one such application.

✦ **Auto Difference:** Converts unchanged pixels within the Auto Crop area to transparent, which sometimes reduces file size further.

Auto Crop and Auto Difference can be checked or unchecked on the Frames panel options pop-up, or from the Animation tab of the Export Preview dialog box.

Looping

Looping is fairly straightforward. An animated GIF can loop any number of times, or it can be set to loop "forever," which means it never stops. If the last frame of your animation is a final resting point that looks good all on its own, setting your animation to loop a finite number of times is a good option.

If you're creating an animated rollover button, set looping to Forever for best results. Roll over to an animated GIF that plays once, and you may find that it doesn't play at all, or you may catch it in mid-play. Different browsers treat preloaded animated GIF images in different ways.

To change the looping setting for your animated GIF, do one of the following:

✦ Choose No Looping, a specific number, or Forever from the Looping menu in the Frames panel (shown in Figure 23-10).

New Feature The Frames panel now contains a Looping menu. Previously, looping options could only be set in the Export Preview dialog box.

✦ Select the Play Once button or the Loop button from the Animation tab of the Export Preview dialog box while exporting your animation. If you choose the Loop button, choose Forever or a number from the Number of Loops options list, or type your own number directly into the box.

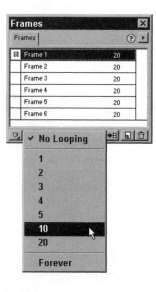

Figure 23-10: Choose your looping option from the Frames panel's Looping menu.

Exporting with the Export Preview dialog box

Although you can specify most of the options for your exported animated GIF within the Optimize and Frames panel, the Export Preview dialog box centralizes animation options and also provides a more realistic preview than Fireworks provides in the document window.

To export your animation with the Export Preview dialog box, follow these steps:

1. Choose File ⇨ Export.

   Fireworks displays the Export Preview dialog box, as shown in Figure 23-11.

2. On the Options tab, choose Animated GIF from the format options list.

3. On the Options and File tabs, specify settings such as Bit Depth and Transparency, just as you would for a regular, static GIF image.

4. On the Animation tab, choose each frame from the list, in turn, and enter a number (in hundredths of a second) in the Frame Delay field. Set the Frame Delay to 0 to make frames display as quickly as possible. Preview the results of your timing settings by using the VCR controls, located below the Preview window in the bottom-right area of the Export Preview dialog box.

Cross-Reference

For more about optimizing GIF Export settings, see Chapter 15.

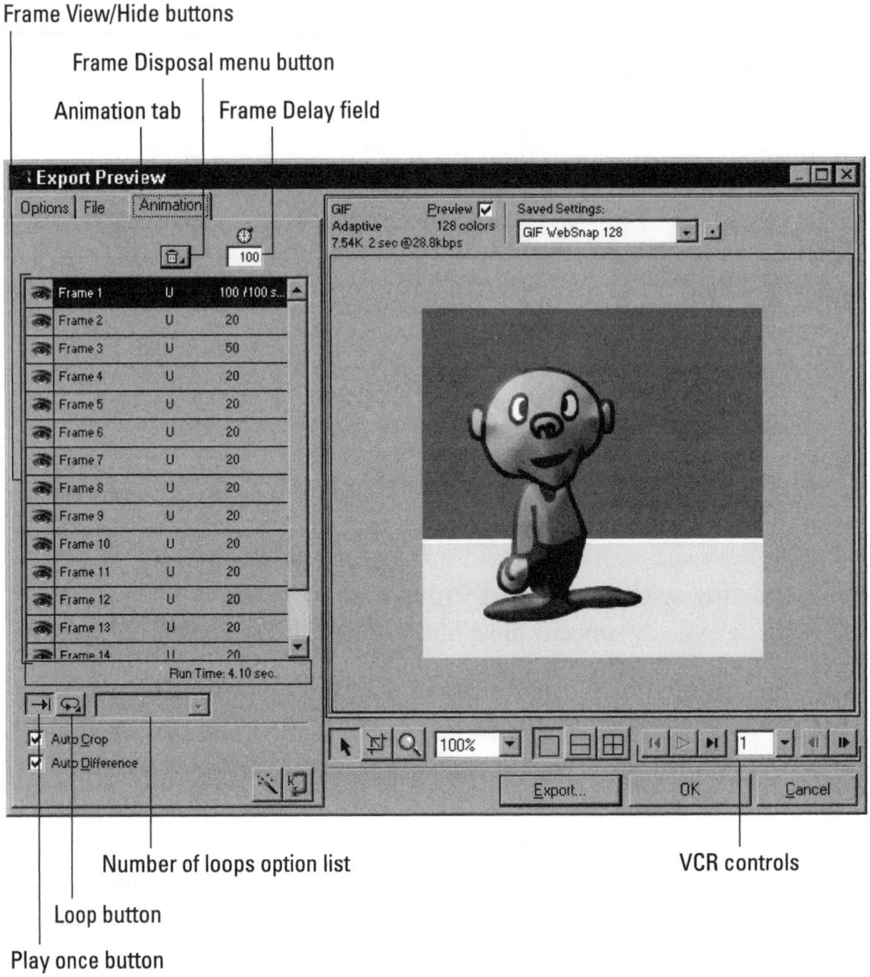

Frame View/Hide buttons

Frame Disposal menu button

Animation tab   Frame Delay field

Figure 23-11: The Export Preview dialog box's Animation tab centralizes animation export settings.

Number of loops option list

VCR controls

Loop button

Play once button

5. If necessary, click the Frame View/Hide buttons (the eye icons) at the left of each frame on the list to show or hide a frame. If a frame is hidden, it isn't exported, and thus isn't shown when the animation is played in Fireworks.

Note   The Frame Delay settings are saved with your file after you export. Fireworks will continue to use these settings when you play your animation in the document window using the VCR controls.

6. Specify a method for frame disposal by clicking the Frame Disposal menu button (the Trash icon next to the Frame Delay field) and choosing an option.

7. Choose whether or not your animation will loop, by clicking either the Play Once or the Loop button. If you click the Loop button, specify the number of times to loop in the Number of Loops options list. You can either choose a number from the list, type another number, or choose Forever to loop continuously. Click the Next button when you're done.

   Fireworks displays the Export dialog box.

8. Choose the target folder and filename for your animated GIF and then click Save.

Your animation is exported as an animated GIF image.

Web Design with Animated GIF Images

One of the nicest things about animated GIF images is that you can place them in a Web page just as easily as you can place regular GIF images. This section describes some ways you can incorporate animated GIF images into your Web pages to create a complete presentation.

Animating background images

Version 4 and up browsers can display an animated GIF as a background image. A small animated GIF will be tiled across the whole page, creating a very dynamic presentation with a very low weight.

Reusing animations

A viewer has to download your animated GIF only once. If you use it again on the same page or on another page, it will play from their browser's cache. This is especially useful for an animated logo or for animated buttons.

Scaling an animation

Use the `height` and `width` attributes of the `img` tag to present an animation at a larger size without increasing its weight. The slight reduction in quality that comes from scaling an image to double its size — in effect, you're halving its resolution — is a very small price to pay for the impact of a large animation. For example, if you create an animation that is 200 × 200 pixels, you can put it in a page at 400 × 400 pixels with the following `img` tag:

```
<img src="example.gif" width="400" height="400">
```

You can also use a percentage width or height to make an animation fit a page. This works better for some animations than others, but again, it can create quite an impact. Set the width and height to 100% and fill the entire browser window. The img tag would look like this:

```
<img src="example.gif" width="100%" height="100%">
```

Using the browser's background image

One of the limitations of animated GIF images is the small number of colors that the GIF format can contain—and the high price you pay in weight for each extra color. However, you can give your animation a colorful background by making it transparent and then placing it in a Web page with a JPEG background. The weight of the whole presentation remains low, because you combine the strengths of the GIF format—animation and transparency—with the strengths of the JPEG format—lots of colors with a low weight.

Preloading an animation

Two ways exist to preload an animated GIF, to avoid the staggering playback that you see when an animation plays while it's downloading:

✦ **Use the** lowsrc **attribute of the** img **tag.** The browser will show the lowsrc image until the regular image finishes downloading. The following line of code tells the browser "Show shim.gif until animated.gif has downloaded, and then replace shim.gif with animated.gif":

```
<img src="animated.gif" lowsrc="shim.gif" width="200"
height="200">
```

The file shim.gif is the transparent 1-x-1-inch image that Fireworks uses to space tables. You've seen it and have a few copies of it on your hard drive if you've ever exported a sliced image from Fireworks. If you haven't, you can make your own by creating a 1-x-1-inch image with a transparent canvas and exporting it. Because it's lightweight, it doesn't affect the weight of your page too much. Because it's transparent, the background color shows through until the animation starts.

Note   Internet Explorer does not support the img tag's lowsrc attribute.

✦ **Use a Fireworks Swap Image behavior to swap a static image or** shim.gif **with your animated image.** Modify the Event that triggers the Swap Image behavior to onLoad. When the entire page's content has loaded, the onLoad event fires and the static image is replaced with your fully-downloaded animated GIF.

For more about using Fireworks behaviors, see Chapter 21.

Animated rollovers

Replacing the Over state of a rollover button with an animation of the same size can create an exciting effect. When the viewer's mouse hovers over your button, the animation begins. When it stops hovering over your button, the animation stops.

Some browsers have problems with complex animated GIF images in rollovers. A small, simple animation that loops forever will likely work best.

To create a simple animated rollover, follow these steps:

1. Create a rollover button with at least three states (Up, Over, and Down) and export it as a GIF in the usual way. (A rollover with two states appears to flash rather than move.) Note the filename that Fireworks gives the Over state of your button; it will be something like button_r2_c2_f2, where f2 stands for frame 2, where you created the Over state.

For detailed instructions about creating rollover buttons, see Chapter 21.

After you export your file once as a rollover, you need to export it again as an animated GIF. The individual frames that served as each state of the rollover button will now serve as the frames of an animation.

2. To export your file again as an animated GIF, choose File ➪ Export Preview.

Fireworks displays the Export Preview dialog box.

3. On the Options tab, choose Animated GIF from the format options list.

4. On the Animation tab, click the Loop button, choose Forever, and then click Next.

Fireworks displays the Export dialog box.

5. Under Slicing, select No Slicing.

6. Under HTML Style, select None.

7. Choose the filename of the Over state of your rollover button and click Save to save your animated GIF with that name.

Fireworks asks whether you want to replace the original file. Click Yes.

When you open the HTML file that Fireworks created, you'll find that hovering your mouse over the button makes the button start cycling through its Up, Over, and Down states.

Tip You can also make an animated rollover button that stops animating when the user places their mouse over it. Instead of replacing the f2 image with an animation, as before, replace the f1 image. The animation plays as the page loads, but stops with a hover of the mouse over the button.

Slice up animations

Don't be afraid to unleash Fireworks' formidable slicing tools on your animations.

Caution In the Object panel, set static slices to GIF, JPEG, PNG, or whatever format you desire. Set animated slices to export as Export Defaults and then choose Animated GIF as the format when you export the whole document.

Some ideas for things you might do with slicing and animation:

✦ **Add extra colors:** Slice colorful, static areas and set the slice to export as a JPEG or PNG, and your animation will appear to have sections of 24-bit color.

✦ **Add interactivity:** Replace a blank slice of your animated GIF with an HTML form element, such as an options list or a set of radio buttons.

Cross-Reference For more information about slicing images in Fireworks, see Chapter 20.

Tweening with Fireworks

You can really unleash your animations in Fireworks by incorporating Symbols and Instances. Symbols are reusable objects that have been placed in a Fireworks Library. Copies of Symbols placed onto the canvas are called Instances. Instances maintain a link to their Symbols so that changing certain properties of a Symbol also updates all of its Instances.

Cross-Reference A basic knowledge of Symbols and Instances will serve you well for the rest of this Chapter. Read more about Symbols and Instances in Chapter 17.

Two or more Instances of the same Symbol can be "tweened" automatically by Fireworks. Tweening is a traditional animation term that refers to generating intermediate frames be*tween* two images to create the effect of the first image changing smoothly into the second image. In Fireworks, you provide the starting point for an animation with one Instance, and the ending point of the animation with another, and Fireworks creates the intermediate steps between them. Each new Instance is slightly changed from the one before it, so that the first Instance seems to evolve into the last. You can also tween more than two Instances (Figure 23-12), in which case it might be helpful to think of each Instance as a resting point, or a keyframe.

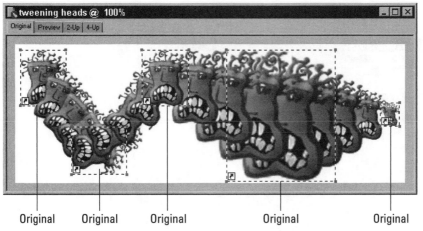

Original   Original   Original   Original   Original

Figure 23-12: Each Instance is a resting point, or a keyframe. Fireworks automatically creates the rest of the objects with tweening.

You can obviously use tweening to simulate motion, but by tweening object properties, you can also make an object appear to change over time. If you scale an Instance to a larger size and then tween it with another that's not scaled, the tweened Instances will be sized to create a smooth transition, as was the case in Figure 23-12. Any property of an Instance that can be independently modified can be tweened. These include:

✦ Transformations such as width, height, and skew made with the Transform tool or with the Modify ➪ Transform submenu.

Note

Fireworks always tweens two or more Instances of the same Symbol, and as such, can't tween shapes (morphing) because the shapes of the Instances are always the same. If you want to tween shapes, you can do a blend in Macromedia FreeHand and then import the file into Fireworks, and distribute the shapes to frames. You can also do a shape tween in Macromedia Flash, save the result as an Adobe Illustrator document, and then import that document into Fireworks in order to retain the vector information.

✦ Opacity and/or Blending modes adjusted in the Object panel.

✦ Live Effects. As long as all of the Instances have the same Live Effect applied, you can tween the properties of that Live Effect. If you want to make an object appear to go from not having an effect to having one, set the effect's settings to 0 on one of the Instances and a higher value on another.

Fireworks always tweens from the canvas up; the lowest object in the stacking order is first, and the highest object last, as shown in Figure 23-13. If you're tweening more than two objects, adjust their stacking order to make sure that they tween in the order that you want them to.

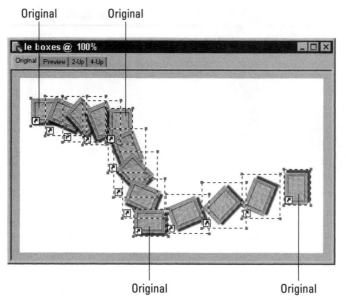

Original   Original

Original   Original

Figure 23-13: Four Instances become an entire animation after tweening. Note that Fireworks tweened according to the stacking order. The start of the tween is the object closest to the canvas, and the highest object in the stacking order is the end.

Tip   Don't be confused into thinking that objects tween from left to right across the canvas. The stacking order is always the guideline for tweening order.

After you set the stacking order to determine the order that objects get tweened, you also have to decide how many steps Fireworks should fill in between each object. Refer again to Figure 23-12. The number of steps in that tween was three, so Fireworks filled in three objects between each of the original Instances.

So far, we've tweened objects and created an interesting display across the canvas. Usually, though, you'll want to distribute your tweened objects to frames to create a real animation. You have the option to do this at the same time as the tweening, or you can select your tweened objects and click the Distribute to Frames button on the Frames panel at any time. Fireworks distributes objects to frames from bottom to top, the same way that it tweens, so that your objects stay in the correct order.

To tween Instances, follow these steps:

1. Create an object or a group of objects and convert it to a Symbol. Select the object and choose Insert ➪ Convert to Symbol. Name your Symbol in the Symbol Properties dialog and click OK when you're done. Your object is converted into a Symbol and stored in the Library. An Instance is left in its place on the canvas.

2. Choose Edit ➪ Duplicate or use the key shortcut Ctrl+Alt+D (Command + Option + D) to create a copy of the Instance. A copy of an Instance is also an Instance. Keep in mind that the duplicate will be one higher in the stacking order.

3. Position the duplicate Instance to a spot on the canvas where you want the tween to stop.

4. Select both Instances either by dragging a selection box around them with your mouse or by holding down the Shift key and clicking each one in turn.

5. Choose Modify ➪ Symbol ➪ Tween Instances.

Fireworks displays the Tween Instances dialog box (see Figure 23-14).

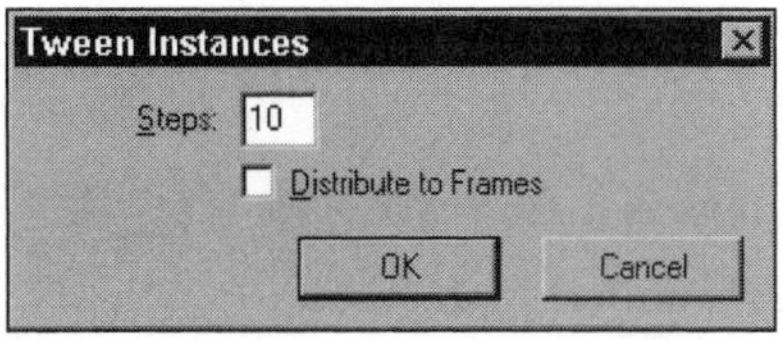

Figure 23-14: Set the number of steps to tween, and choose whether or not you want to distribute the objects to frames in the Tween Instances dialog box.

6. Enter the number of steps to tween. A setting of 3 makes Fireworks create three new objects between each of your original Instances.

Caution

If you are tweening between two Instances of a text object Symbol and you apply a skew to one Instance, apply a small skew to the other Instance as well. Otherwise, a bug in Fireworks 3 causes it to create a slight rotation in the middle Instances.

7. Check Distribute to Frames to distribute the tweened objects to frames and make them into an animation. Click OK when you're done.

Fireworks creates the new objects, and you have an instant animation.

Fireworks technique: tweening Xtras

Unlike Live Effects, you can't really tween Xtras, because they're applied directly to image objects only. Applying them to linked objects also breaks the link and leaves you with regular image objects. You can use tweening, though, to create an animation quickly, in which the only changes are the settings of the Xtra as it's applied to each frame.

Cross-Reference

This example uses an Xtra called Fire, which is part of a third-party package called Eye Candy, from Alien Skin. If you don't have Eye Candy, use one of the Eye Candy LE filters that are included with Fireworks, or another third-party Xtra — many are available free on the Web. For more information about Xtras and about Eye Candy, see Chapter 12.

To animate Xtras in Fireworks, follow these steps:

1. Create the basic object or group to which you're going to apply the Xtra, and then make the group or object into a Symbol using Insert ➪ Convert to Symbol. Name your Symbol in the Symbol Properties dialog and click OK when you're done. The Symbol is placed in the Library and an Instance is left in its place.

2. Select your Instance and create another Instance directly on top of it by choosing either Edit ➪ Clone, or by using the key shortcut, Ctrl + Shift + C (Command+Shift+C).

3. Select both Instances by dragging a selection box around them. Alternatively, if they are the only objects in your document, you can select them both by choosing either Edit ➪ Select All or Ctrl + A (Command+A).

4. Create tweened Instances between your two Instances by choosing Modify ➪ Symbol ➪ Tween Instances.

   Fireworks displays the Tween Instances dialog box.

5. Set the number of steps to a small number, such as 5.

6. Uncheck the Distribute to Frames checkbox and then click OK.

   Now we have a stack of identical objects, to which we're going to apply an Xtra, changing the settings slightly each time so that each object looks slightly different.

7. Select all the Instances by dragging a selection around them with the mouse.

8. Choose Xtras ➪ Eye Candy 3.1 ➪ Fire.

   Fireworks displays the Fire dialog box for the first Instance.

9. Specify the settings that you want, and then click OK.

   Fireworks displays the Fire dialog box for the second Instance.

10. The controls are set the same way you left them after the first Instance. Modify the controls slightly to create a difference between this Instance and the previous one. Click OK when you're done.

    Fireworks displays the Fire dialog box for the third Instance.

11. Continue to change control settings slightly in each box as it appears, until you have modified all the Instances.

Tip   Clicking Cancel at any time in the Xtra's dialog box cancels the operation for all the Instances.

12. With your Instances still selected, click the Distribute to Frames button (the filmstrip icon) on the Frames panel.

All Instances are distributed over frames to create an animation such as the one in Figure 23-15. Preview your animation with the VCR controls in the status bar on Windows or at the bottom of the document window on a Macintosh. Alternatively, you can choose File ➪ Export Preview and preview your animation in the Export Preview dialog box, or choose a browser from the File ➪ Preview in Browser submenu to see your work in a browser.

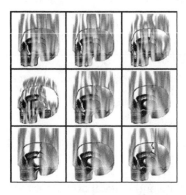

Figure 23-15: This animation depends entirely on the slight changes in the Fire effect applied to each Instance to make our subject's skull appear to be vigorously aflame.

Fireworks technique: tweening depth

A quick and useful effect that you can create with tweened Instances is 3D depth, wherein your object appears to fly out from the canvas.

To create a depth effect with tweened Instances, follow these steps:

1. Create the basic object or group that you're going to work with, and then convert it into a Symbol using Insert ➪ Convert to Symbol. Name your Symbol in the Symbol Properties dialog box and click OK when you're done. The Symbol is placed in the Library and an Instance is left in its place.

2. Move the Instance near the top of the canvas.

3. Choose Edit ➪ Clone or use the key shortcut, Ctrl + Shift + C (Command + Shift + C), to create another Instance directly on top of the first.

4. Hold down Shift key and, at the same time, use the arrow down key to move the new Instance down the canvas without moving it left or right. A few hundred pixels is usually all you can get away with while still keeping the depth effect looking like depth.

5. With the Instance still selected, choose Modify ➪ Transform ➪ Numeric Transform.

   Fireworks displays the Numeric Transform dialog box.

6. Scale the Instance to 30 percent of its size by selecting Scale from the options list, checking Scale Attributes, checking Constrain Proportions, and entering 30 in one of the fields. Click OK when you're done.

7. Set the Instance's opacity to 10 percent by double-clicking it and entering 10 in the Opacity field of the Object panel.

8. With the Instance still selected, choose Modify ➭ Arrange ➭ Send to Back or press Ctrl + B (Command + B).

9. Hold down Shift and click each Instance to select all of them. If they are the only objects in your document, you can choose Edit ➭ Select All or press Ctrl + A (Command + A).

10. Choose Modify ➭ Symbol ➭ Tween Instances.

   Fireworks displays the Tween Instances dialog box.

11. Set the number of steps you want in between the two Instances, uncheck Distribute to Frames, and then click OK.

   Fireworks tweens the Instances.

> **Tip** You can choose Edit ➭ Undo and then do Steps 12 and 13 again if you find that you want to change the number of steps.

12. If you like, you can select the original Instance and make it stand out by adding a Live Effect such as glow or inner bevel to it.

Your object now appears to fly out from the canvas (see Figure 23-16).

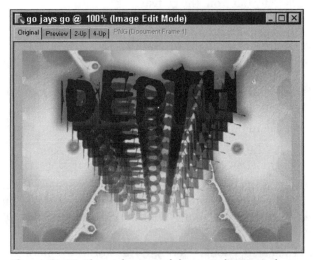

Figure 23-16: Fireworks created the steps between the front and back Instances with tweening. A little of the Glow Live Effect was then added to the front object to make it stand out.

> **Tip** To change this depth effect into an animation, select all of the Instances by drawing a selection around them with the mouse (or, if they are the only objects in your document, choose Edit ➭ Select All), and then click the Distribute to Frames button on the Frames panel. Your object animates its way toward you.

Fireworks technique: fading in and out

Fading an object in and out is a common effect that's easy to create in Fireworks. Tweening two Instances that are positioned in the same place on the canvas, one with an Opacity setting of 0 percent and one with an opacity of 100 percent, produces a fade. Which Instance is higher in the stacking order determines whether it's a fade-in or a fade-out. In this section, we create an animation in which the object fades in, then fades back out, and then loops, so that it seems to fade in and out continuously.

To fade an object in and out, follow these steps:

1. Create the basic object or group to which you're going to apply the fade, and then convert the object or group into a Symbol. Select it and choose Insert ⇨ Convert to Symbol. Name your Symbol in the Symbol Properties dialog box and click OK when you're done. Your new Symbol is stored in the Library and an Instance is left in its place.

2. Select the Instance and choose Edit ⇨ Clone or press Ctrl+Shift+C (Command+Shift+C) to create another Instance directly on top of it.

3. Open the Object panel and set the Opacity of the new Instance to 0 percent.

Note The Opacity setting might not seem to have any effect, because you will be able to see the original Instance through the newer Instance, which is now transparent.

4. Choose Modify ⇨ Arrange ⇨ Send to Back to send the transparent Instance directly behind the original Instance.

5. Select both Instances by dragging a selection box around them. If they are the only objects in your document, you can select them by choosing either Edit ⇨ Select All or by using the key shortcut Ctrl+A (Command+A).

6. Choose Modify ⇨ Symbol ⇨ Tween Instances.

   Fireworks displays the Tween Instances dialog box.

7. Set the number of steps to 5.

Note You can choose a different number of steps, if you prefer, but during this example, I'll count steps and frames as if you've chosen 5.

8. Check the Distribute to Frames checkbox and then click OK.

   Play your animation. Your object should appear to fade in. You should have seven frames. In the first frame, the Instance is completely transparent (opacity of 0); in the second frame, the Instance is slightly more opaque, making it appear to fade in; and so on until the seventh frame, in which the Instance is fully opaque.

Note At this point, you can choose to either leave your animation as is or continue on and make your animation appear to fade out as well.

9. Open the Frames panel and select the final frame in your animation, to display it in the document window. This frame contains your fully opaque Instance.

10. Select the Instance and choose either Edit ➪ Clone or use the key shortcut Ctrl + Shift + C (Command+Shift+C) to create another Instance directly on top of the first.

11. Open the Object panel and set the Opacity of the Instance to 0 percent..

12. Select both Instances by dragging a selection box around them. If they are the only objects in this frame, you can select them by choosing either Edit ➪ Select All or by using the key shortcut Ctrl + A (Command + A).

13. Choose Modify ➪ Symbol ➪ Tween Instances.

   Fireworks displays the Tween Instances dialog box.

14. Set the number of steps to the same number you used when fading the object in (in this case, 5).

15. Check the Distribute to Frames checkbox and then click OK.

16. Select the final frame of your animation in the Frames panel and remove it by clicking the Delete Frame button (the Trash icon). This final frame is redundant, because the first frame is also a fully transparent object. Your animation will loop more smoothly without it.

Click Play to preview your animation. The object appears to fade in and then fade out (see Figure 23-17). If you like, you can double-click the fully opaque frame in the middle of your animation (Frame 7 in the example) and specify a longer frame delay so that the pause between the fade-in and fade-out is longer. Choose File ➪ Export Preview to preview your animation in the Export Preview dialog box, where it will often run more smoothly than in the document window.

Figure 23-17: Fading an object in and out is easy with tweening.

Summary

Fireworks enables you to create and edit animation by using a variety of techniques, most of which revolve around the Frames panel. When working with animation in Fireworks, keep these points in mind:

✦ The overall weight of your animated GIF is always a consideration. Every creative decision must be examined for its effect on file size.

✦ The Frames panel is the heart of Fireworks' animation tools, but the Layers panel is also important.

✦ Each frame in your Fireworks document is like a frame of a film strip. Copy objects to other frames by using the Frames panel, and then change the objects' locations on the canvas or their properties to create animation.

✦ Layers can be shared across multiple frames, to manage static objects better in an animation.

✦ Onion Skinning enables you to view and edit multiple frames simultaneously.

✦ The Web design opportunities for animated GIF images are numerous, such as animated rollover buttons, sliced animations, and animated browser backgrounds.

✦ Tweening is a great time- and work-saver, because Fireworks fills in the middle elements of an animation automatically. Any selection of two or more Instances of the same Symbol can be tweened.

✦ Fireworks tweens objects starting at the bottom of the stacking order, nearest the canvas, and moving up.

✦ Distribute a tweened sequence to frames to create an instant animation.

✦ You can use tweening to create advanced effects, such as objects fading in and out or flying out from the canvas.

In the next chapter, you'll look at how you can apply animation techniques to create that most common species of animated GIF: the banner ad.

Animating Banner Ads

✦   ✦   ✦   ✦

In This Chapter

Banner ad standards

Putting banners ads
in a Web page

Advertising lingo

Creating banner ads
in Fireworks

Using blur to save
frames

✦   ✦   ✦   ✦

Banner ads are nearly ubiquitous on today's Web, and
have been a valuable contributor to the rapid growth of
the World Wide Web. Once you have a sponsored banner ad
on a page, the page begins to pay for itself, and you crave
hits — requests for files made to your server — rather than
worrying about the bandwidth costs of a page that grows
too popular.

Banner Ad Basics

Banner ads are where animated GIF images really shine. You
want a Web advertisement to be eye-catching and universally
viewable, and animated GIF images are really the only choice.
When does an animated GIF stop being an animated GIF and
start being a banner ad? Four elements are involved:

  ✦ It is a certain size in width and height.

  ✦ It is below a certain weight in kilobytes.

  ✦ It is placed on a Web page.

  ✦ It advertises something.

We take a closer look at each of these points in the following
sections.

Size — IAB/CASIE standards

When banner ads started to proliferate on the Web, it became
apparent that some sort of standard sizing scheme would benefit both the advertisers and the sites displaying the advertising. If you have a Web site on which you leave a 450 × 50-pixel
space in your design for a banner ad, and I then send you one
that's 460 × 60, we have a problem. If ten other people send
you ten other ads, all slightly different in size, then the problem becomes a big problem.

To solve this, the Standards and Practices committee of the Internet Advertising Bureau (IAB) and the Coalition for Advertising Supported Information and Entertainment (CASIE) got together, looked at the sizes everybody was using, and came up with a list of standard sizes. They offered this list as a recommendation to the ad buyers and sellers, who overwhelmingly accepted the list. Almost all ads on the Web now follow the IAB/CASIE standards.

Note   For more about the IAB/CASIE standards, visit the IAB at `www.iab.net` or CASIE at `www.casie.com`.

Table 24-1 details the standard banner ad sizes and their names. Full Banner is by far the most common type of ad, with Micro Button probably in second place, but other sizes are gaining popularity as Web sites display advertising into newer and smaller spaces, such as margins and even inline with content. If you don't know which size to choose, choose Full Banner, 468 × 60.

On the CD-ROM   You'll find on the companion CD-ROM a set of Fireworks PNG format files, one for each banner ad size, that you can use as templates when creating banner ads in Fireworks.

Table 24-1
IAB/CASIE Advertising Banner Sizes

Pixel Dimensions	Name
468 × 60	Full Banner
392 × 72	Full Banner with Vertical Navigation Bar
234 × 60	Half Banner
125 × 125	Square Button
88 × 31	Micro Button
120 × 90	Button 1
120 × 60	Button 2
120 × 240	Vertical Banner

Weight

In addition to making sure your banner ads are the correct dimensions, you need to consider their weight (file size). No "one true standard" exists for banner ad file sizes. Many Webmasters set an upper limit on weight, beyond which they won't accept your ad. If you're designing an ad for a specific site, check with its Webmaster first to see what the limit is, or at least check the weight of some of the ads that are already on that site. If you're not designing for a specific site, a general rule is to aim for less than 10K, and certainly keep it under 12K. If you can produce an exciting ad in 8K, so much the better. Your ad downloads quickly and more viewers see your entire message.

Putting it in the page

Obviously, a banner ad is as much an image as any other GIF, and the most basic way to place a banner ad in a page is with an ordinary <img> tag. When you export HTML from Fireworks, this is exactly the way you find your banner ad displayed.

Typically, though, most Web sites that depend on advertising have some sort of dynamic scheme for rotating through a series of banner ads, so that ads are added to pages on-the-fly by the server, and visitors who return to a page get an entirely new ad instead of seeing the same one again. The server also keeps track of how many times it displays each ad, because the sponsor pays for the ad to be displayed a certain number of times.

Implementing a banner ad rotation system is not nearly as hard as it might sound. The Web has many low-cost and even free CGI (Common Gateway Interface) scripts. A few hours of work and even the smallest site can start serving ads like the big guys.

Tip   A good place to start looking for the appropriate CGI script for your needs is the CGI Resource Index at <http://www.cgi-resources.com>.

Advertise it

While a complete course in Madison Avenue methods is well beyond the scope of this book, it doesn't hurt to at least know the lingo:

✦ A *page view* or *page impression* is one Web page served with your ad on it.

✦ A *hit* is one request by a browser for one file — an HTML document, or an image or multimedia file — from your server. Many people use "hits" and "page views" interchangeably, but one Web page might be made up of 20 individual files while another page is only 10 files. As a result, it's best to define your terms and seek common ground when discussing "hits."

✦ *CPM* is the cost per one thousand (Roman numeral M) page views. This is the standard way that ad space is bought and sold on the Web. A site with excellent demographics could demand a higher cost-per-one-thousand ads served.

✦ A *click-through* is one specific time when a viewer is interested enough in a banner ad to click it and go to the advertiser's site. The Web average for click-throughs might be less than 1 percent.

✦ The *click rate* is the percentage of people who click-through a particular ad.

✦ *Mindshare* is basically brand recognition. Even though Web users don't click-through banner ads the way advertisers once hoped they would, studies have shown that people do look at banner ads and take the brand away with them.

Fireworks Technique: Creating a Banner Ad

Although banner ads are often created by a chain gang of ad people, copywriters, producers, Web artists, and others, a good way to work on the techniques involved is to just dive in and start creating ad campaigns for fictional companies of your own creation. This is exactly what we do as we go step-by-step through the process of creating a banner ad in Fireworks.

On the CD-ROM   You'll find the "Mundane Magazine" example banner ad created for this section in both the original Fireworks PNG format and the exported animated GIF.

Step one: Set the stage

The very first step in creating a banner ad is to make sure you know what size it should be. Although you may sometimes come up with a creative idea that would dictate using a certain size, most of the time when you sit down to make a banner ad, the space has already been alotted. I follow the IAB/CASIE standards with my banner ad, and make a 468 × 60 Full Banner which can be displayed on almost any Web site that accepts advertising.

Step two: Write the script

Now that you have a suitable "blank page" of the right size and shape, you are ready to sit and stare at it while you come up with an idea. All the same things that apply to regular animations apply to banner ads with regard to making a concise statement, planning ahead, and watching file size.

Let's face it: a 10K or 12K banner ad is not going to get into serious character development or include a lot of scene changes or scenery. If you can't express your idea in a few lines, it probably won't fit into the banner. Think "bumper sticker," and you'll probably be more successful.

My ad is for a fictional magazine called Mundane Magazine. It's a hip, youth-oriented magazine about the Web. I want to make something that attracts the attention of the target audience of young, hip Web surfers. Here's the pitch for my ad: "A UFO crash lands on a barren alien landscape. The pilot thinks, '&*/$.'" Not much of a plot line, but again, what do you want from 12K?

Step three: Create the cast of characters

Our little movie has a stage and a script. Now it needs a cast.

Banner ads are deliberately sized as small as can be, and I find the dimensions a bit of a constraint when I'm drawing. Objects in banner ads are often cropped, scaled down, or halfway off the canvas anyway, so I like to draw and build objects in a second, larger document window (see Figure 24-1); sort of a scratchpad—or, to keep the showbiz analogy going, a backstage area where objects wait to be placed in their scenes. Because Fireworks objects always remain editable and can be easily dragged and dropped between documents, this backstage area is a convenient way to work.

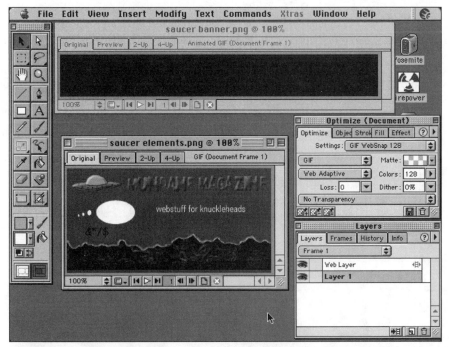

Figure 24-1: Use a second document as a scratchpad or backstage area when building objects for use in a banner ad, to avoid working entirely within the puny confines of the ad itself.

Complex effects such as drop shadows and glows increase the weight of the final animated GIF quite a bit because flat colors compress better in the GIF format. Concentrate on drawing good-looking objects, and leave the effects for later. If your final animation is underweight (yeah, right), then you can easily go back and add some effects to objects.

These elements make up the "cast" in my ad:

✦ Some rugged, otherworldly mountains to serve as a setting

✦ Some text of the magazine's name and catchphrase

✦ A flying saucer to do the crash-landing

A thought bubble with the word "&/$." in it

Each of these elements can be thought of as a cast member, an independent entity that we need to tell what to do as we make our ad.

Reusing Design Elements

The tiny face that banner ads present to the world can be very limiting creatively, but there is one major advantage: design elements and even bitmap images that were originally created for a Web site or print media are easily scaled down and reused without losing quality. Creating a banner ad for a Web site often means you have no end of big logos and artwork readily available for repurposing in a banner ad, as shown in the following figure.

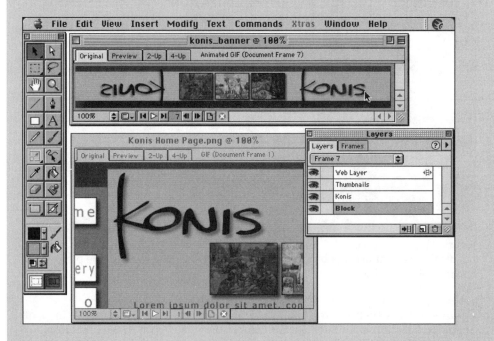

While this strategy is efficient from a production standpoint, it's also valid from a design perspective to maintain a consistent look between a Web site and a banner ad that advertises it.

Step four: Direct the action

Now you're ready to start putting the objects where they go. Create a layer for each of your cast members. I have four cast members, and I have a pretty good idea of the order in which they should be stacked: the background should be on the bottom and the text should be on the top, so I made four layers:

✦ text

✦ bubble

✦ saucer

✦ background

Figure 24-2 shows these layers and shows that the mountains are placed into the layer called background, which is then shared so that it appears in every frame. I can lock the background layer now and forget about it.

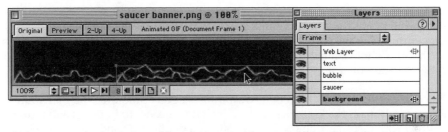

Figure 24-2: The background is going to stay the same throughout the animation, so the background layer is shared. This layer is now the same in every frame.

Tip   To share a layer, double-click its name in the Layers panel to view the Layer Options dialog box and check the Shared Across Frames box.

Splitting up objects onto their own layers enables you to share a layer at any time, if you decide that a cast member should be static. I'm not sure yet whether the text with the name of the magazine and the catch phrase is going to be static. It probably will be, but I might get to change that after I see my animated GIF's weight. For now, I place the text in the banner and share its layer too.

At this point, the first frame is basically done. The mountains and logo are in place, and the UFO hasn't appeared yet. I like to build the last frame next, which is where the animation rests before looping. I want to make sure that the UFO and the thought bubble are the right size, so that they hang together nicely in that frame, before I animate them through a bunch of middle frames (see Figure 24-3). Creating the first and last frames before the others often makes filling in the middle frames a lot easier.

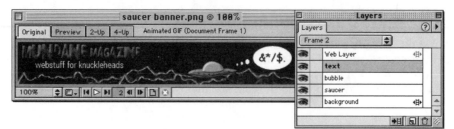

Figure 24-3: After you finish the first frame, create a new frame in which to build the last frame. Your two-frame animation now has a start and finish, which makes building the middle much easier.

Finally, we're ready to start some serious animating. In the first frame, the UFO hasn't appeared yet; in the last frame, it has landed. I'm going to copy the UFO from the last frame, paste it into the first frame, and then move it to the top of the canvas, so that it's just peeking in.

So, in Frame 1, the saucer is just appearing. I want the next frame to be almost identical, except that the saucer should move a little bit closer to its landing site. The saucer doesn't have far to travel, and I'd like it to do so in seven or eight frames, so that the whole animation is nine or ten frames long. Keeping the animation in a small area and on a small number of frames limits its file size.

You can distribute objects to their own frames at any time with the Distribute to Frames button on the Frames panel, so it's often easiest to build an animation entirely within Frame 1. In my case, I just keep duplicating and arranging copies of the saucer in the correct positions on the canvas. Eventually, Frame 1 contains a bunch of saucers in the correct positions on the canvas, but in the wrong frames, as shown in Figure 24-4.

Tip   The quickest way to duplicate objects is to drag them while holding down the Alt (Option) key.

Figure 24-4: Duplicating the saucer and moving the copies into the correct positions on the canvas gets them ready to be distributed to their own frames.

Cross-Reference   If your animation features an object that moves in a straight line, use tweening to generate the intermediate steps. Tweening is covered in Chapter 23.

Because the last frame is already done, I want to manually create frames before clicking the Distribute to Frames button so that Fireworks doesn't have to create any frames and overlap my final frame. I have seven saucers in Frame 1, so I need six new frames after Frame 1.

After distributing the saucers to frames, I can preview my animation by using the VCR controls, and tweak the saucer's descent by moving it a bit to the left or right in certain frames if necessary until I get the effect that I want, which is a bit of a rough landing.

Once you get to the point where your animation is actually playing, the inevitable rewrites begin. In my case, I decided that I didn't want the thought bubble to be the last frame. Instead, the last three frames should go: saucer lands, thought bubble appears, and then thought bubble disappears. I also realized that the "landed" saucer needs a little chewing up to emphasize that it has "crashed."

Chewing up the saucer is pretty easy, but it appears in Frame 7 and Frame 8. After modifying it in Frame 7, I selected it on the canvas and Alt-dragged (Option-dragged) its selection icon in the Frames panel (Figure 24-5) from Frame 7 to Frame 8. This copies the selection from Frame 7 to Frame 8.

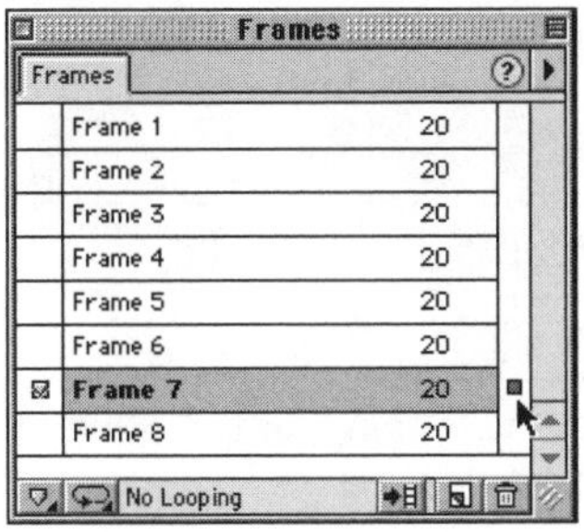

Figure 24-5: Dragging the selection icon in the Frames panel from frame to frame moves a selection. Alt-dragging (Option-dragging) copies the selection.

The quickest way to get that extra frame I want on the end is simply to duplicate the last frame and then delete the thought bubble out of it. I lose very little in bandwidth this way, because the last two frames are almost identical, and the only addition to the final frame is more flat color where the thought bubble was. Duplicating the last frame is as simple as dragging it in the Frame panel to the New Frame button.

The only thing that's left now is to set the frame timing so that the last three frames are a little slower. The frame timing, looping, and such are set either in the Frames panel or on the Animation tab of the Export Preview dialog box. Working in the Export Preview dialog box, shown in Figure 24-6, provides smoother animation play-back than the document window, and a centralized access point for animation controls. You can see that the last three frames are set to one second, two seconds, and one second, specified in hundredths of a second. I tested a few combinations of speeds by using the VCR controls in the Export Preview dialog box. Looping is set to 10 times, which is long enough that it loops for about a minute, because my banner takes a little over five seconds to play. At that point, it becomes a static banner that still invites the viewer to visit Mundane Magazine, without annoying them by continuing to flash away.

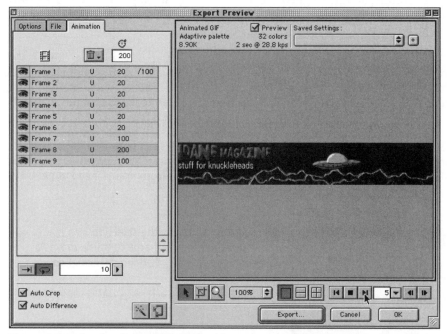

Figure 24-6: Set the timing of individual frames and set the looping for the whole animation. Note that the animation is playing in the Export Preview.

Tip   If you don't set looping to forever, make sure the last frame of your animation has all the pertinent details, so that it provides enough information to get your message across on its own.

Step five: Leave the excess on the cutting-room floor

Don't be afraid to be brutal when exporting your animation and creating the animated GIF image itself. Remember that your focus is to get a message across quickly — not to win awards for the most colors or the most profound use of animation. My banner came in just under 12K, but if it were any bigger, I would definitely have to consider one of the following options:

✦ Cut some frames, which might make the animation less smooth.

✦ Move the saucers closer together from frame to frame, so that the area that's animated is smaller.

✦ Flatten some areas, such as the bumpy, textured mountains. Areas of solid, flat color compress better.

✦ Take out some colors by cutting the palette further.

✦ Remove effects, such as the inner bevel on the text and the saucer, again to gain more areas of flat color.

✦ Make some objects smaller, such as the text, so that more of the flat, blue background is showing, resulting in better compression.

Sometimes, swallowing your creative pride can lead to a better overall presentation and a fast-loading, attention-attracting banner ad that's ready to take a message to the Web.

The final Mundane Magazine banner is exploded in Figure 24-7.

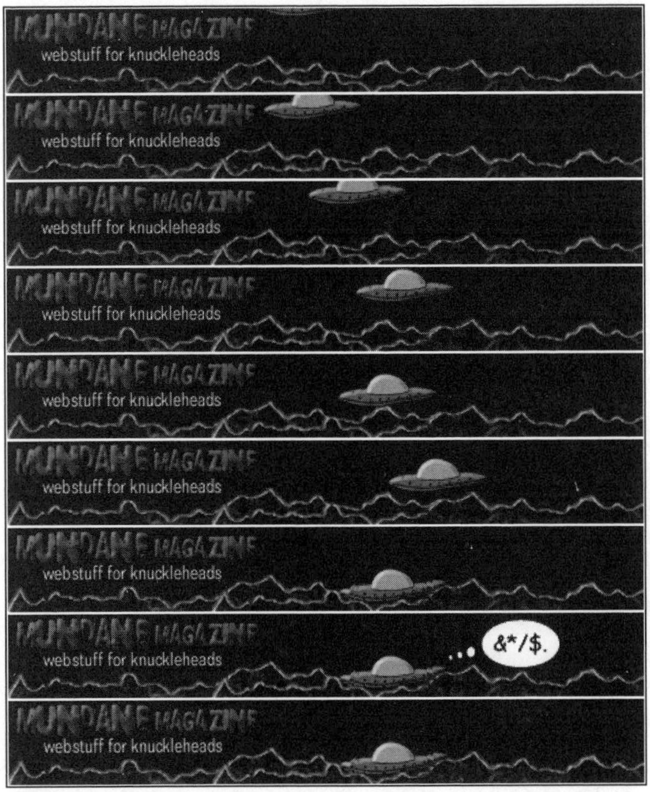

Figure 24-7: The finished banner ad keeps the animation in a small area and in a small number of frames. The flat color background compresses well. The banner weighs under 12K.

Cross-Reference   Turn to the color insert for another look at the example banner ads from this chapter.

Fireworks Technique: Using Blur to Save Frames

Generally, you want your ads to be dynamic and fast-moving, but as with everything on the Web, bandwidth is always an issue. Every frame that you add to your banner increases the file size.

A common technique for creating a feeling of action and speed in a banner ad without increasing the frame count and file size drastically is to use a motion blur filter — such as the Eye Candy Motion Trail filter included with Fireworks 3 — to get an object from point A to point B, as shown in Figure 24-8. Instead of moving across the banner in five or six frames, the saucer takes three steps from when it first appears to when it stops moving, but still seems to fill the intervening space. Without the Motion Trail filter, spacing the saucer so far apart would give it the appearance of disappearing and reappearing instead of moving.

Figure 24-8: The saucer seems to quickly fly across the banner, at the meager expense of just three frames.

Tip   This second Mundane Magazine banner reuses elements from the banner created earlier in this chapter. Creating banner ad "sequels" is a pretty common practice, building on the recognition of an earlier ad.

You can also make objects seem to be moving more quickly by altering their opacity settings. The motion-blurred saucers in Figure 24-7 have an opacity setting of 70 percent. Experimenting with the opacity setting and the controls in the Eye Candy Motion Trail filter can lead to impressive results.

On the CD-ROM Find the animated GIF banner ad detailed in this section, as well as the Fireworks PNG file.

Summary

Banner ads are a practical and popular application of the animated GIF. When creating banner ads in Fireworks, keep these things in mind:

✦ Standard sizes exist for banner ads. Before you create a banner ad, make sure that you've selected the correct size so that your banner ad can be used on the widest variety of Web sites.

✦ Many Web sites have upper limits on the file sizes accepted. Generally, banner ads should be under 12K.

✦ Use motion blur to cut out frames without slowing down the action.

In the next chapter, we look at customizing Fireworks.

✦   ✦   ✦

Programming with Fireworks

In This Part

Chapter 25
Customizing
Fireworks

Chapter 26
Fireworks API

Customizing Fireworks

In This Chapter

The HTML and
JavaScript engine

The Settings folder

Adding new
extensibility files

Fireworks 3
Preferences file

Web development has become an incredibly diverse field. It spans the range from the person building a personal home page all the way to incredibly complex Web applications that generate pages on the fly and provide functionality that has traditionally only been found in stand-alone applications. With the variety of technologies in use on the Web today, it's hard to imagine a Web development tool that could be all things to all people without demonstrating an amazing degree of flexibility.

Macromedia has certainly demonstrated with Fireworks 3 that it believes an extensible Web tool is a good Web tool. Almost every feature can be accessed through the extensive JavaScript API, while many features are executed in easy-to-modify HTML and JavaScript. Preferences are easily exposed in a simple text file. Extensions are added by dropping them in the appropriate Settings subfolder.

In this chapter, we'll look at some of the ways that you can customize Fireworks and create your own ultimate Web graphics editor.

The HTML and JavaScript Engine

Part of the explosive growth of the Web is due to the relative accessibility of the underlying code. HTML is — as programming languages go — extremely easy to learn and abundantly available. Whereas JavaScript is more difficult, it is far more open than any compiled programming language, such as C or C++. The Fireworks engineers applied this accessibility to a novel approach: portions of Fireworks itself are written in HTML and JavaScript, stored as simple text files in the Fireworks Settings folder.

New Feature Fireworks 3 offers you access to almost every feature of the program through a greatly-expanded JavaScript API, and also offers a Commands menu for running Scriptlets from within Fireworks.

Fireworks uses JavaScript and HTML Templates to output JavaScript and HTML code; scripts that automate tasks in Fireworks are written in JavaScript. This open approach makes it easy for a Web designer to customize many aspects of their Fireworks workflow completely.

Scriptlets are stand-alone JavaScript files that run on Fireworks itself. They can be placed in Fireworks' Commands folder and run from the Commands menu, run with the File ➪ Run Script command, or opened like any Fireworks document — with a double-click. Scriptlets have their own icon, as shown in Figure 25-1. Double-clicking a Scriptlet, or dropping it onto the Fireworks icon, launches Fireworks and executes the Scriptlet.

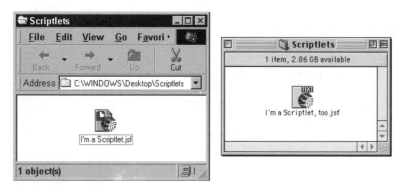

Figure 25-1: Fireworks Scriptlets — JSF files — are stand-alone JavaScripts that run on Fireworks.

On Windows machines, Scriptlets are their own file type, with the .jsf filename extension. Create or edit a Scriptlet as a regular text file, and then change the filename extension from .txt to .jsf when you're ready to run it.

On the Mac, a Scriptlet is a text file with a Fireworks Creator code, just as a Fireworks document is a PNG image with a Fireworks Creator code. Create or edit a Scriptlet as a regular text file. Compile the following AppleScript as an application in Script Editor, and drop files on it to convert them to Fireworks' Creator code. Dropping a text file converts it to a Scriptlet. Alternatively, use a utility such as File Buddy or FinderPop to change Mac Creator and/or File Type codes.

```
on open
   tell application "Finder"
      set creator type of every file of selection to "MKBY"
   end tell
end open
```

You can use Scriptlets to do an amazing range of tasks. Anything that the Fireworks API can access is fair game, and with Fireworks 3, that's a fair number of things. Scriptlets can change preference settings, automate tasks, batch process files, and more.

Scriptlets are also Commands. Placing Scriptlets in the Commands folder and choosing their name from the Commands menu runs them from within Fireworks. Alternatively, you can run a Scriptlet from within Fireworks by choosing File ➪ Run Script and navigating to a Scriptlet within the Open dialog box that follows.

Cross-Reference
To make your own Scriptlets, study the JavaScript API in Chapter 26.

The Settings Folder

The geographic heart of Fireworks extensibility and customization is the Settings folder, shown in Figure 25-2. Subfolders of the Settings folder contain files that relate in a certain way to extending a particular feature of Fireworks. Placing additional files in these folders can add new textures to your texture list, more Commands to your Commands menu, or more Xtras to your Xtras menu. Many of these files are text files containing HTML and JavaScript that you can easily customize.

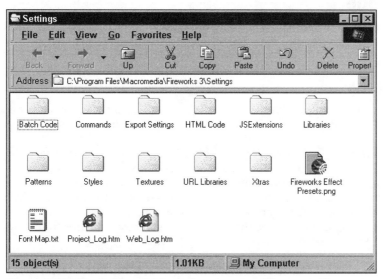

Figure 25-2: The Settings folder is the place to add custom files.

You can usually find the Settings folder in these locations:

✦ On Windows, look in `C:/Program Files/Macromedia/Fireworks 3/Settings`.

✦ On the Mac, look in `Macintosh HD/Applications/Fireworks 3/Settings`.

Dreamweaver users have long been making and trading Dreamweaver Objects, Behaviors, and Commands on the Web. Some of the same sources for Dreamweaver extensions are good for Fireworks Commands, Templates, and other files. There are some Fireworks-only spots as well. Some good sources:

✦ Macromedia's Fireworks Support Center at `www.macromedia.com/support/fireworks/` (click on Extensibility)

✦ Joseph Lowery's Fireworks, etc. at `www.idest.com/fireworks/`

✦ Simon White's Fireworks page at `www.simonwhite.com/geek/fireworks/`

✦ Massimo Foti's excellent site at `www.massimocorner.com`

As well as using extensions created by others, you can, of course, create your own. Modifying existing code is the easiest way to get quick results and better understand Fireworks capabilities. Always work on a copy of the file you are customizing so that the original is still available, though.

Batch Code

Batch code templates are placed in the Batch Code folder. By default, the Batch Code folder contains just two files: BatchGen.jst and BatchTemplate.jst.

Commands

The Commands folder contains Scriptlets. Each Scriptlet in the Commands folder appears as a menu command in Fireworks' Commands menu.

Open up a Command Scriptlet and you'll see that it contains simple JavaScript code. Almost every feature of Fireworks is accessible through the Fireworks JavaScript API. Custom Functions such as `dom.applyEffects()` and `dom.setDocumentCanvasSize()` give Commands the capability to automate otherwise repetitive tasks, extending the native Fireworks feature set. Even with all that, my favorite thing about Commands is that you don't even have to write code to make them, thanks to the History panel.

By default, Fireworks includes 16 Commands organized into five folders, with two individual Commands staying in the Commands folder itself. To add a new Command, drop the file into the Commands folder. Any JSF files within the Commands folder itself, or within subfolders one level down, are displayed in the Commands menu in Fireworks, so that you can run them by choosing a menu item. New additions are immediately available without restarting Fireworks.

Cross-Reference

Learn more about Commands in Chapter 19, and study the Fireworks API in Chapter 26.

Export Settings

The Export Settings folder is empty by default. When you save export settings as a preset in the Optimize panel — using the Save Settings command on the pop-up menu — Fireworks creates a similarly-named text file in the Export Settings folder. The file contains a description of the saved setting, and can be copied to another machine in order to standardize export settings across a workgroup, for example.

HTML Code

Fireworks HTML output Templates are stored in the HTML Code folder. HTML output Templates are actually folders that contain HyperText Templates and MapText Templates.

Fireworks includes six Templates by default, but an increasing number of Web designers, savvy in both design and code, are building HTML templates of their own to fit a variety of circumstances. Fireworks' open HTML Template architecture enables multiple HTML styles to coexist, so you can switch from one to another whenever necessary.

Tip

Adding .html to the names of the default Template folders — or to copies of them — causes them to output HTML files with the standard .html filename extension.

Typically, an HTML template consists of three files, as shown in Figure 25-3:

Figure 25-3: A Fireworks HTML output Template is actually a folder.

✦ **metafile.htt:** This HyperText Template creates the code necessary for making client-side image maps and for implementing the Set Text of Status Bar Behavior, if no slices are used.

✦ **slices.htt:** Any exported image that uses slices accesses this HyperText Template to create the necessary code.

✦ **ServerMap.mtt:** Server-side image maps use this MapText Template to generate the required code.

All three files are not necessary for every template (the ServerMap.mtt file could be omitted if no server-side image map output was planned), but a typical template includes them all.

Changing from one style of HTML to another when exporting is as easy as making a selection from an option list. Adding new templates is just as straightforward.

To add a new Template, follow these steps:

1. Using Windows Explorer or the Macintosh Finder, create a new folder within the HTML Code folder. The new folder should have a unique name to identify the template easily, and an optional filename extension to specify a filename extension other than .htm for exported HTML files. The folder's name is what appears in the HTML Style option list found on the Export dialog box.

2. Copy the new template files — metafile.htt, slices.htt, and ServerMap.mtt — to your new folder.

It's not necessary to restart Fireworks to use the newly installed Template. Perform your export procedure as normal and choose your new Template from the HTML Styles option list in the Export dialog box.

JSExtensions

Most computer programs are written in the C or C++ languages, and compiled into impenetrable object form before release. Fireworks leaves many functions accessible by JavaScript. More JavaScript functionality can be added through the use of C Libraries, added to Fireworks by dropping them into the JSExtensions folder.

Libraries

The Libraries folder contains Fireworks PNG images that typically contain Symbol Libraries. It contains just three files, initially, containing example Button and Graphic Symbols. Symbol Libraries are regular Fireworks documents that contain Symbols, created by exporting Symbols from the Library panel. Commonly used buttons, graphics, and clip art can be converted into Symbols and stored in Symbol Libraries. Symbol Libraries that are placed in the Libraries folder are easily accessed within Fireworks from the Insert ➪ Libraries subfolder. Each file is displayed as a menu item.

Cross-Reference

Explore Libraries in Chapter 17.

Patterns

Patterns are full-color images saved in standard Fireworks PNG format. Initially, the Patterns folder contains 14 Patterns, featuring things like bricks, jeans, and wood. You can create any image in Fireworks and save it in the Patterns folder. After a Fireworks restart, it's available for use as a Pattern from the Patterns option list in the Fill panel.

Cross-Reference

Patterns are detailed in Chapter 11.

Styles

Fireworks Style files are given the filename extension .stl and, on the Mac, have the Creator code MKBY and File Type STYf.

Although the Styles panel contains numerous default Styles, many Styles can easily be stored in one Fireworks Style file. Although Style files are typically stored in the Styles folder, that doesn't make them immediately accessible within Fireworks. To use the Styles from a particular Style file, import the file using the Styles panel in Fireworks.

When you first install Fireworks, the Styles folder contains one file called Style Defaults.stl. As the name implies, this file contains the default Styles that can be reloaded into the Styles panel by choosing Reset Styles from the Styles panel pop-up menu. Copy the Style Defaults.stl file to another name and replace it with your own favorite to make those favorites quickly accessible with the Reset Styles command.

Cross-Reference

Styles are covered in Chapter 16.

Textures

The Textures folder contains Fireworks PNG images that are used as textures in Fireworks. Files in the Textures folder show up as textures on the Textures option list in the Fill and Stroke panels.

Textures are images that are overlaid on objects in Fireworks using the Fill panel to give the appearance of a textured surface. Although the images themselves can be full color, a Texture is always converted to grayscale when it's applied in Fireworks. PNG images you add to the Textures folder are available for use after a Fireworks restart. Fireworks includes 26 Textures by default, including things like sand, grass, and smoke.

Cross-Reference

Learn to create your own Textures in Chapter 11.

URL Libraries

When you first install Fireworks, the URL Libraries folder contains the single, completely empty file called URLs.htm.

An important part of any Web development is obviously the creation and management of hyperlinks. Rather than laboriously typing URL after URL into Fireworks whenever they're needed, you can list them in an HTML document and drop the document into the URL Libraries folder. Access the file from the URL Panel and easily apply URLs to Web objects by pointing and clicking.

Find out more about URL Libraries in Chapter 18.

Xtras

The Xtras folder contains Fireworks Xtras and Photoshop-compatible effects plug-ins. Adding Photoshop plug-ins to Fireworks is as simple as dropping them — or shortcuts (aliases) to them somewhere else on your computer — into the Xtras folder. Typically, they live in their own subfolders. Where they sit on the Xtras menu is determined by settings contained within the plug-ins themselves. Restart Fireworks after adding plug-ins and access them from the Xtras menu or the Effects Category option list on the Effect panel.

Initially, the Xtras folder contains six Xtras that allow Fireworks to import certain file types, as well as the two Photoshop plug-ins that make up Eye Candy LE.

Xtras are covered in Chapter 12.

The Fireworks 3 Preferences File

Fireworks offers you a graphical look into its preference settings with the Preferences dialog box, accessed within Fireworks by choosing File ➪ Preferences. While the choices it offers are extensive, they are just a subset of the complete preference settings contained in the Fireworks 3 Preferences file.

The Preferences dialog box is detailed in Chapter 3.

The Fireworks 3 Preferences file is found at the following locations:

- ✦ On Macintosh, the Fireworks 3 Preferences file can be found with your other preference files, at Macintosh HD/System Folder/Preferences/Fireworks 3 Preferences.

- ✦ On Windows, find the Fireworks 3 Preferences file in the Fireworks program folder, typically at C:/Program Files/Macromedia/Fireworks 3/Fireworks 3 Preferences.txt.

There are two ways to edit the contents of the Fireworks 3 Preferences file. The first is to open the file in a text editor such as Windows Notepad or SimpleText on the Mac (Figure 25-4). By default, the Fireworks 3 Preferences file opens in those applications when double-clicked.

```
🖉 Fireworks 3 Preferences.txt - Notepad          _ □ ×
 File   Edit   Search   Help
(TextEditorPos) (50 100)
(TextEditorSize) (420 345)
(ExportPreviewPos) (0 0)
(ExportPreviewSize) (0 0)
(DefaultDocSize) (500 500)
(DefaultDocRes) (72)
(DefaultDocResUnitName) (inch)
(DefaultDocColorState) (1)
(ExtraPhotoshopPluginsDir) ()
(ExtraTexturesDir) ()
(ExtraPatternsDir) ()
(PrimaryScratchDisk) (c:)
(SecondaryScratchDisk) (c:)
(PasteImportOrder) ((FreeHand 8.0) (FreeHand
(PasteExportOrder) ((PNG) (#8))
(CheckAssociationOnStartup_png) (false)
(CheckAssociationOnStartup_jsf) (false)
(Text_Font) (Arial)
(Text_Editor_DefaultFont) (Arial)
(LastExportDirectory) ()
(InternalWinSetting06) (10)
(ExportSlicesImageFolder) (images)
(InternalWinSetting07) (48)
```

Figure 25-4: Edit the Fireworks 3 Preferences file in a text editor.

The preferences file is formatted like this:

```
(PreferenceKeyword) (value)
```

A small section of it looks like this:

```
(FindReplaceOptions_LogChanges) (1)
(FindReplaceOptions_ReplaceThenFind) (1)
(StylesOptions_LargePreview) (0)
(InfoPanelColorModel) (1)
(InfoPanelRulerUnits) (0)
(ColorMixerColorModel) (1)
(CurrentFavoritesFile) (URLs.htm)
```

To change a particular preference setting, find its keyword and alter the value next to it in the second set of brackets. Save the file when you're done and restart Fireworks.

Caution As you can imagine, changing preference values haphazardly can prove very disruptive to the program. Many of the preferences are not intended to be altered by the user, such as the DragTab positions. If you ever mistakenly damage your preferences, you can restore the defaults by deleting (trashing) the Fireworks 3 Preferences file and restarting Fireworks.

The other approach to altering the Fireworks 3 Preferences file is to attack it with the Fireworks API. The getPref() and setPref() methods of the Fireworks App object enable you to read or alter any preference setting. For example, the following code pops up a dialog box with the path to the Primary Browser:

```
alert(App.getPref('PrimaryBrowser'));
```

Note that the specific preference setting is passed as a string. Just as you can get a preference with App.getPref(), you can set a preference with App.setPref(). The following code uses setPref() to tell Fireworks not to ever ask the user to register:

```
App.setPref('NeverBugForRegistration', 'true');
```

The preceding techniques could be used to create a Scriptlet that offers the user a list of browsers and asks them to choose a primary and secondary, or to create a Command that simply changes the primary and secondary browsers from two version 4 browsers to two version 3 browsers, depending on the browser generation you're targeting. Of course, another similar Command could change them back.

The primary preference settings are detailed in Table 25-1; all of the settings can be found in the Fireworks 3 Preferences file.

Table 25-1
Key Preferences and Their Settings

Preference	Value Type
AllowFilePreviewInOpenDialog	True | False
AllowPictRgba	True | False
AllowTweeningOf3rdPartyEffects	True | False
AlwaysAppendFileExtensions	True | False
AnimGifDangerousOpt	True | False
AntiAliasFillAmount	Number
ApplyNPreviewVisible	True | False
ArtyFileExportType	Number
ArtyWriterFH8Compatible	True | False
AskWhenDuplicatingSymbols	True | False
AutoGenBehaviors	True | False
AutoGrowImages	True | False
AutoImageEdit	True | False

Preference	Value Type
BatchDoBackup	Number
BatchDoExport	Number
BatchDoReplace	Number
BatchExpFileFitHeight	Number
BatchExpFileFitWidth	Number
BatchExpFileHeight	Number
BatchExpFileMod	Text
BatchExpFileModType	Number
BatchExpFilePct	Number
BatchExpFileScaleType	Number
BatchExpFileSettings	Export Setting
BatchExpFileWidth	Number
BatchGenName	Filename
BatchIncrementalBackup	True | False
BatchTemplateName	Filename
BatchWhichFiles	Number
BezFitCornerAngle	Number
BezFitExtraTightTolerance	Number
BezFitExtraTightToleranceStep	Number
BezFitMaxPctLenDiff	Number
BezFitTolerance2	Number
BezHandlePickDist	Number
BezInterpMaxErr	Number
BlackAndWhiteForDirector	True | False
BrushCurrentColor	Red-Green-Blue-Alpha numbers
BrushDefaultColor	Red-Green-Blue-Alpha numbers
BucketFillsSelection	True | False
BucketMouseOverPreview	True | False
ButtonEditor_Pos	X, Y coordinates
ButtonEditor_Size	X, Y coordinates
CheckForMissingStuffDuringScripts	True | False

Continued

Table 25-1 *(continued)*

Preference	Value Type
ColorMixerAutoApply	True | False
ColorMixerColorModel	Number
ContractSelectionAmount	Number
CopyAsPathsFH8Compatible	True | False
CropDocCropsImages	True | False
CropTool_Constraint	Number
CropTool_Horiz	Number
CropTool_Vert	Number
CropToolStickiness	Number
CurrentFavoritesFile	URLs.htm
CustomCanvasColor	Red-Green-Blue-Alpha Numbers
DefaultDocColorState	Number
DefaultDocRes	Number
DefaultDocResUnitName	"inch" or "cm"
DefaultDocSize	X, Y coordinates
DefaultJsMaskCompression	Number
DontShowWebHelpDialog	True | False
DragOutThreshInPixels	Number
EditGradDialogPos	X, Y coordinates
EditTransformMode	Number
EditURLChangesAll	True | False
EraserToolDiameter	Number
EraserToolEraseMode	Number
EraserToolIsCircle	True | False
EraserToolSoftEdge	Number
EraserToolStampSpacing	Number
ExpandAnimatedGifFrames	True | False
ExpandCapType	Number
ExpandJoinType	Number
ExpandMiterLimit	Number
ExpandSelectionAmount	Number

Preference	Value Type
ExpandWidth	Number
ExportPngWithAdam7Interlacing	True | False
ExportPreviewPos	X, Y coordinates
ExportPreviewSize	X, Y coordinates
ExportSilently	True | False
ExportSlicesImageFolder	Path
ExportTransformMode	Number
ExtraPatternsDir	Path and filename
ExtraPhotoshopPluginsDir	Path and filename
ExtraTexturesDir	Path and filename
EyeDropperExtraSamples	Number
FeedbackColor	Red-Green-Blue-Alpha Numbers
FFReplaceFont	Font name
FFSearchFont	Font name
FillCurrentColor	Red-Green-Blue-Alpha numbers
FillDefaultColor	Red-Green-Blue-Alpha numbers
FindReplaceOptions_BackupOpts	Number
FindReplaceOptions_LogChanges	Number
FindReplaceOptions_ReplaceThenFind	Number
FindReplaceOptions_SaveNClose	Number
FreeFormGravDiameter	Number
FreeFormGravDiameter_Sens	True | False
FreeFormGravity_Preview	True | False
FreeFormGravPower	Number
FreeFormGravPower_Sens	True | False
FreeFormPushNPull_Preview	True | False
FreeFormPushNPullLen	Number
FreeFormPushNPullLen_Sens	True | False
GridGuideSnapDist	Number
GuidePickDist	Number
HideEdgesAutoResets	True | False

Continued

Table 25-1 *(continued)*	
Preference	**Value Type**
HtmlCharSet	Label
IgnorePNGGammaOnRead	True | False
ImageMapInspOpen	True | False
ImageMapInspPos	X, Y coordinates
ImageMapInspSize	X, Y coordinates
ImageResampleMode	Number
ImageSizeTransformMode	Number
InfoPanelColorModel	Number
InfoPanelOpen	True | False
InfoPanelPos	X, Y coordinates
InfoPanelRulerUnits	Number
InitialSettings_Alt	Text
InitialSettings_DoDemo	True | False
InitialSettings_ExportUndefined	True | False
InitialSettings_ImageMap	Number
InitialSettings_NameMode	Number
InitialSettings_ShimMode	Number
InitialSettings_URL	URL
InsetAmount	Number
InsetDirection	Number
InsetJoinType	Number
InsetMiterLimit	Number
InspectorsAutoApply	True | False
JsHeapLimit	Number
JsInterpIdleThreshInMilliseconds	Number
JsStackSize	Number
LassoToolAntiAliased	True | False
LassoToolFeatherAmount	Number
LastExportLocation	Path
LastImportLocation	Path
LastOpenLocation	Path

Preference	Value Type
LastSaveLocation	Path
LegLookForPNG	Number
LocalGamma	Number
LockGuides	True | False
LoptLookForPNG	Number
LZWSmoothingAmount	Number
MakeDocsDirtyOnOpen	True | False
MarqueeToolAntiAliased	True | False
MarqueeToolFeatherAmount	Number
MarqueeToolMode	Number
MarqueeToolModeRatioX	Number
MarqueeToolModeRatioY	Number
MarqueeToolModeWidthX	Number
MarqueeToolModeWidthY	Number
MaxFolderDropDepth	Number
MaxUndos	Number
MoveBitsWithPtrToolUsesFillColor	True | False
MultiFileBatchTypes	Format list
MultiFileSearchTypes	Format list
MultiFrameEditing	True | False
NeverBugForRegistration	True | False
NewDocHTMLTemplate	Filename
NewDocSlicing	True | False
NewWindowsShowRulers	True | False
NumericXformXformsBFE	True | False
NumFloatingInspectors	Number
ObjectMgrOpen	True | False
ObjectMgrPos	X, Y coordinates
OnionSkin_AfterOpacity	Number
OnionSkin_BeforeOpacity	Number
OnionSkinInButtonEditor	True | False

Continued

Table 25-1 *(continued)*

Preference	Value Type
OpenAsAnimation	True | False
OpenAsUntitled	True | False
OriginalFilesFolderName	Original Files
OtherGamma	Number
PasteExportOrder	Format list
PasteImportOrder	Format list
PencilAntiAlias	True | False
PencilAutoErase	True | False
PixelTrimThreshold	Number
PolygonToolIsAuto	Number
PolygonToolIsStar	True | False
PolygonToolSides	Number
PolygonToolSpikiness	Number
PreserveAlpha	True | False
PreviewDrag	True | False
PreviewDragThreshInMilliseconds	Number
PreviewInBrowserOpensNewWindow	True | False
PrimaryBrowser	Path and filename
PSLayersAsFrames	True | False
PSSharedLayers	True | False
PSTextEditable	True | False
RectToolCornerRadius	Number
ReplaceLogFileName	Filename
ResizeConstrain	True | False
ResizeResample	True | False
SaveAsMinimalFileWithBogusPngData	True | False
SaveMkb1CompatFiles	True | False
SavePngWithAdam7Interlacing	True | False
ScriptFilesSaveAsText	True | False
ScrubPressure	True | False
ScrubRate	Number

Preference	Value Type
ScrubVelocity	True | False
SecondaryBrowser	Path and filename
SecondaryFeedbackColor	Red-Green-Blue-Alpha Numbers
SelectionAdjustTolerance	Number
SelectionMouseOverPreview	True | False
ShowAllFontsInMenu	True | False
ShowAllPreview_Up	True | False
ShowGrid	True | False
ShowGuides	True | False
ShowSliceGuides	True | False
SimplifyAmount	Number
SingleLayerEditing	True | False
SliceGuideColor	Red-Green-Blue-Alpha Numbers
SmoothSelectionAmount	Number
SnapToGrids	True | False
SnapToGuides	True | False
StampToolEdge	Number
StampToolMode	Number
StampToolSize	Number
StampToolSource	Number
StampToolStampSpacing	Number
StopImageEditModeInPixels	Number
StylesOptions_LargePreview	Number
SwapFileChunkSize	Number
SwapFileReclaimThreshFraction	Number
SwapFileReclaimThreshInMegabytes	Number
SwfExportAllFrames	True | False
SwfExportFromFrame	Number
SwfExportToFrame	Number
SwfFrameRate	Number
SwfJpegQuality	Number

Continued

Table 25-1 *(continued)*	
Preference	**Value Type**
SwfMaintainObjEditable	True | False
SwfMaintainTextEditable	True | False
SymbolEditor_Pos	X, Y coordinates
SymbolEditor_Size	X, Y coordinates
Text_AntiAliasedFill	True | False
Text_AntiAliasLevel	Number
Text_AutoKern	True | False
Text_BaselineShift	Number
Text_Bold	True | False
Text_Editor_DefaultFont	Font name
Text_Font	Font name
Text_HorizScale	Number
Text_Italic	True | False
Text_Justification	Number
Text_Leading	Number
Text_LeadingMode	Number
Text_Orientation	Number
Text_RangeKerning	Number
Text_Size	Number
Text_Underline	True | False
TextEditor_AutoApply	True | False
TextEditor_AutoApplyTime	Number
TextEditor_RememberALLSettings	True | False
TextEditor_ShowFont	True | False
TextEditor_ShowSizeAndColor	True | False
TextEditorPos	X, Y coordinates
TextEditorSize	X, Y coordinates
TextToolRevertsToPointer	True | False
ToolboxOpen	True | False
ToolboxPos	X, Y coordinates
TransformConstrain	True | False

Preference	Value Type
TransformToolsAutoTrim	True | False
Transmogrify	Number
TryInterleaveSwapFiles	True | False
TryToRetainLayers	True | False
TwainSource	Path
UseExtraPatternsDir	True | False
UseExtraPhotoshopPluginsDir	True | False
UseExtraTexturesDir	True | False
UseLastExportDirectory	True | False
UsePrecisionCursors	True | False
UseSliceGuides	True | False
UseSmallVectorImportPages	True | False
WandToolAntiAliased	True | False
WandToolFeatherAmount	Number
WandToolTolerance	Number
WarnOnFlattenPathForFilter	True | False
WebsnapRange	Number
WriteThumbnailPreview	True | False
XformToolXformsBFE	True | False
XPDPaletteFeedback	True | False

Summary

For me, the true power of any tool is demonstrated when it adapts to my own way of working. Fireworks 3 can be greatly extended with custom Commands, Scriptlets, and more. When customizing Fireworks, keep these points in mind:

✦ Fireworks can be extensively customized just by including files in subfolders of the Settings folder — adding Commands, Xtras, and more.

✦ Scriptlets are stand-alone JavaScript files that run on Fireworks. On Windows, all Scriptlets must have the filename extension .jsf. On Macintosh, Scriptlets should have the Fireworks Creator code of MKBY and the File Type code of TEXT.

✦ You can run custom templates without relaunching Fireworks. Once the files have been copied to a folder within the Settings/HTML Code directory, the new files appear in the Export dialog box.

✦ Fireworks stores your preferences in a simple text file that you can modify in a text editor or through the use of Scriptlets or Commands.

In the next chapter, we'll look closely at the Fireworks JavaScript API.

✦   ✦   ✦

Fireworks API

◆ ◆ ◆ ◆

In This Chapter

Fireworks extensions

Nonstandard data types

Fireworks API

Developing Commands

◆ ◆ ◆ ◆

How is a graphics engine like Fireworks able to process JavaScript code? Fireworks has a JavaScript 1.4 interpreter built in. JavaScript is the Web scripting lingua franca, and as such, is an excellent choice for a scripting language for controlling Web development tools. The Fireworks JavaScript API (application programming interface) includes an amazing array of special objects with properties and methods for accessing, controlling, and modifying a Fireworks document.

New Feature

Fireworks 3 includes far more objects and methods than did Fireworks 2. The possibilities for the JavaScript author are extended beyond export templates and Scriptlets into complex scripts that can control virtually every aspect of Fireworks.

The Fireworks API employs both *static* method and properties, as well as *instance* methods and properties. A static method or property (also called a *class* method or property) is associated with the object itself, rather than an instance or copy of the object. As the name implies, an instance method or property is associated with an instance of the object. Instance methods and properties can therefore use the this keyword.

Keep these points in mind as you work through this chapter:

✦ This chapter deals with advanced HTML and JavaScript concepts. If you're just getting started with JavaScript, you might want to keep a good resource nearby as you look over this chapter. I like and use *JavaScript Bible, 3rd Edition*, by Danny Goodman, published by IDG Books Worldwide, Inc.

✦ Throughout this chapter, I followed certain conventions in the descriptions of each Fireworks API item. Arguments for methods are italicized; optional arguments are in square brackets.

✦ Because of the great number of objects and methods that the Fireworks API now includes, you are occasionally referred to Macromedia's Extending Fireworks documentation, which is available in PDF on your Fireworks installation CD-ROM, or on the Fireworks Web site at `http://www.macromedia.com/software/fireworks`; a hard-copy version of Extending Fireworks is also available for ordering.

Nonstandard Data Types

Because Fireworks deals with graphics-related objects, for example, masks, and specific Fireworks settings, such as resolution, that aren't commonly accessed with JavaScript, some common ways to format this data are required. Macromedia provides guidelines for formatting colors, file URLs, masks, matrices, points, rectangles, and resolution.

Colors

Colors are specified in the Hexadecimal RGB (red-green-blue) color model, which is one of the models accessible from the Color Mixer panel in Fireworks. This is the standard method for defining colors in HTML, and is formatted "#RRGGBB", where each color channel is written with a hexadecimal number. For example, pure red is "#FF0000". Additionally, an alpha channel can be specified by adding an extra hexadecimal number in the format "#RRGGBBAA".

Note   If the alpha channel value is not specified, Fireworks automatically assumes that the alpha channel is fully opaque. For example, a solid red fill color with a hexadecimal value of #FF0000 is interpreted by Fireworks to have a value of #FF0000FF.

File URLs

Fireworks specifies file and pathnames in scripts as file URLs. For example, the Windows path to the Fireworks Commands folder

```
C:\Program Files\Fireworks 3\Settings\Commands
```

looks like this when written as a file URL:

```
file:///C|Program%20Files/Fireworks%203/Settings/Commands
```

Note that all slashes are forward slashes, and that the pipe character (|) replaces the colon after the drive letter, and the %20 escape code is substituted for the space.

On a Mac, the path to the Commands folder would be written like this (if the hard drive was named Grover):

```
Grover:Applications:Fireworks 3:Settings:Commands
```

As a file URL, it's written like this:

```
file:///Grover/Applications/Fireworks%203/Settings/Commands
```

Again, %20 is substituted for a space, and forward slashes are used, but there are no drive letters on the Mac, so the C| is unnecessary.

Tip   When you're writing scripts to be cross-platform, use the platform property of the App object to determine whether your script is running on Windows or Macintosh and write file URLs appropriately.

Masks

Alpha masks are defined using the following properties:

✦ maskBounds specifies a rectangle which is the area of the mask.

✦ Choose from five types of masks with maskKind: rectangle, oval, zlib compressed, rle compressed, or uncompressed.

✦ maskEdgeMode is either "hard" or "antialiased".

✦ The value for featherAmount is a number between 0 and 1000, representing the feather value in pixels. A value of 0 means no feathering.

✦ For rectangle and oval masks, the maskData value is ignored. For other masks, maskData should contain 8-bit mask data in hexadecimal format.

Masks are specified in the format {maskBounds: **rectangle**, maskKind: **string**, maskEdgeMode: **string**, featherAmount: **int**, maskData: **hex-string**}.

Matrices

In programming, computer graphics are described using a three-by-three array of numbers called a *matrix*. In Fireworks, the format for a matrix is {matrix: [*float, float, float, float, float, float, float, float, float*]}. Discussion of matrices is beyond the scope of this book.

Points

Specify a point in the format {x: *number*, y: *number*}. For example, when the Pen tool is used, the placement of the initial point is coded like this:

```
fw.getDocumentDOM().addNewSinglePointPath({x:124, y:37},
{x:124, y:37}, {x:124, y:37}, true);
```

In this example, all three point coordinates are the same and correspond to the preceding Bezier control point, the point itself and the following Bezier control point.

Note   In the previous example, and throughout the book, the code `fw.getDocument DOM()` is used to refer to the current active document in Fireworks.

Rectangles

Define a rectangle {left: *number*, top: *number*, right: *number*, bottom: *number*}. If, for example, I drew a rectangle 100 × 50 pixels, starting at the upper-left corner (0, 0 coordinates), the code looks like this:

```
fw.getDocumentDOM().addNewRectangle({left:0, top:0, right:100,
bottom:50}, 0);
```

Resolution

The format for specifying resolution with the Fireworks API is {pixelsPerUnit: *number*, units: ["inch" or "cm"]. Setting the resolution of the current document to 72 dpi is accomplished with this code:

```
fw.getDocumentDOM().setDocumentResolution({pixelsPerUnit:72,
units:"inch"})
```

Global Methods

Global methods are always available for use in Fireworks scripts. The user interaction functions are helpful in debugging code and in helping to guide the user. The two file output functions — WRITE_HTML() and write() — are only available during an exporting operation.

alert(*message*)

The alert() method displays a simple dialog box (Figure 26-1) to the user with a Fireworks title, a *message* and an OK button. The message can be a text string or the contents of a variable or the result of a JavaScript statement. The `alert()` dialog box must be dismissed before the user can continue; this type of dialog box is referred to as *modal*.

Figure 26-1: The alert() method is a simple way to tell the user something.

For example, the following code informs the user that the batch process job is completed:

```
alert("All done!");
```

confirm(*message*)

The `confirm()` method displays a string in a modal dialog box and waits for the user to select either the OK or Cancel button, as shown in Figure 26-2. The function returns true if OK is selected and false if the user clicks Cancel.

Figure 26-2: Use the confirm() method to get a confirmation from a user during an export or batch processing procedure.

The following code asks if the user is ready to proceed with a particular operation; if not, the operation is not carried through:

```
function doConfirm(curBeh) {
 var message = "Ready to proceed with integrating " + curBeh;
 if (confirm(message)) {
 doFile(curBeh)
 }
}
```

prompt(*caption, text*)

The prompt() method enables the user to enter information in a modal dialog box (Figure 26-3) that can be incorporated in the JavaScript code or HTML output. The prompt() dialog box includes a text field (with a default value) and OK and Cancel buttons. If OK is selected, the contents of the text field are returned; otherwise null is returned.

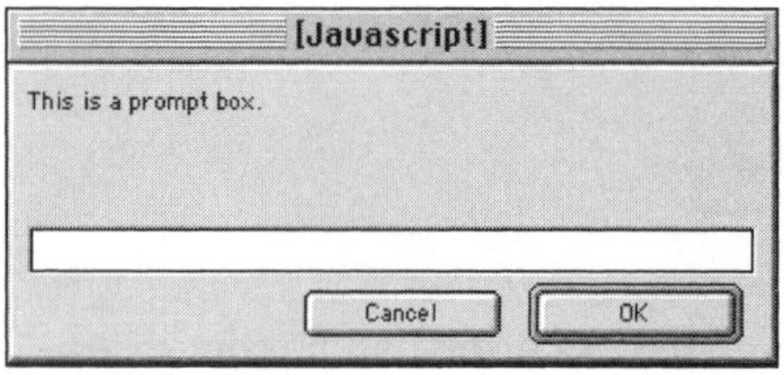

| [Javascript] |
| This is a prompt box. |
| |
| Cancel   OK |

Figure 26-3: The user can type text into the dialog box that's provided with the prompt() method.

In this example, the code lets the user select the exported slice's basename during the script's runtime:

```
function getName() {
 var baseName = ""
 prompt("Enter the basename for the slice now being ù
exported.", baseName)
 }
```

Note   Currently, the prompt() method is the only native mechanism available to Fireworks extension authors for gathering parameters from a user. Some extension creators use multiple prompts or a single prompt with comma separated values in order to get user input. One other possible route for advanced extensions is to open a parameter form in Dreamweaver and use it's values to run a Fireworks command. For an example of this, see the BulletBuilder command available on this book's CD-ROM (requires Dreamweaver 3).

WRITE_HTML(*arg1[, arg2, ..., argN]*)

The WRITE_HTML() method converts each argument to a string and outputs the string to the currently open HTML file during export. This method is available only when exporting. The arguments are written one after the other, which enables you to easily concatenate text and variables. To create an end-of-line character, use \n, which is automatically converted to Carriage Return Line Feed (CR LF) for Windows and Carriage Return for Macintosh systems. Quotations within the string should be escaped by prefacing them with the backslash character; therefore, they will be interpreted as part of the string, rather than as quotations.

For example, the following code writes out the ⟨title⟩ tag for an HTML page using a supplied filename and the first ⟨meta⟩ tag:

```
WRITE_HTML("<title>", exportDoc.filename, "</title>\n");
WRITE_HTML("<meta name=\"description\" content=\"Fireworks¬
  Splice HTML\">\n");
```

If the filename was MuseumPiece, this code would be output:

```
<title>MuseumPiece</title>
<meta name="description" content="Fireworks Splice HTML">
```

write(*arg1[, arg2, ..., argN]*)

The write() method is exactly the same as the WRITE_HTML() method. Macromedia recommends that WRITE_HTML() be used instead of write() to avoid confusion with the document.write() method of JavaScript.

Global Objects

Fireworks' global objects enable you to manage files, initiate a find-and-replace operation, report errors in a localized language, and uncover almost any detail about documents or the current application settings. These objects and their associated methods and properties are extremely valuable and used throughout Commands, Templates, and Scriptlets alike.

App

The App object accesses information about the Fireworks application as it is installed on the user's system. Through the App object, the programmer can determine the operating system being used, where specific folders, such as Commands or Templates, are located, and what files are currently open among many other items.

Two of the most powerful methods of the App object are the getPref() and setPref() pair. With these two methods, you can control virtually every aspect of Fireworks' interface, setting, and restoring options.

Properties

Most of the properties of the App object are read-only — you can get them, but you can't set them — except for batchStatusString, dismissDialogWhenDone, progressCountCurrent, and progressCountTotal.

appBatchCodeDir

This property returns the pathname to the Batch Code folder.

appDir

This property returns the pathname to the folder containing Fireworks.

appExportSettingsDir

This property returns the pathname to the Export Settings folder.

appFavoritesDir

This property returns the pathname to the URL Libraries folder.

appHelpDir

This property returns the pathname to Fireworks' Help folder.

appHtmlCodeDir

This property returns the pathname to the HTML Code folder.

appJsCommandsDir

This property returns the pathname to the Commands folder.

appJsExtensionsDir

This property returns the pathname to the JSExtensions folder.

appMacCreator

A Macintosh identifies which application a particular file belongs to by its Creator code. On a Mac, the `appMacCreator` property returns Fireworks' Creator code of `MKBY`.

appMacJsfFileType

A Mac identifies the file type of a particular document by its embedded File Type code. On Macintosh systems, `TEXT` is the File Type code for text files. Because Fireworks Commands and Scriptlets are text files, the `appMacJsfFileType` property returns the string `TEXT`.

appPatternsDir

This property returns the pathname to the Patterns folder.

appPresetsDir

This property returns the pathname to the Presets folder.

appSettingsDir
This property returns the pathname to the Settings folder.

appStylesDir
This property returns the pathname to the Styles folder.

appSymbolLibrariesDir
This property returns the pathname to the Libraries folder.

appTexturesDir
This property returns the pathname to the Textures folder.

appXtrasDir
This property returns the pathname to the Xtras folder.

batchStatusString
The `batchStatusString` property—which is not read-only—is used to display the current string in the Batch Progress dialog box. You can establish a new message in the dialog box by setting this property to the desired string. For example, the following code from the `BatchTemplate.jst` file displays the filename of each file as it is being processed:

```
App.batchStatusString = Files.getFilename(sourceDocumentPath);
```

dismissBatchDialogWhenDone
If you display the Batch Progress dialog box, you can cause it to be dismissed automatically by setting the `dismissBatchDialogWhenDone` property—which is obviously not read-only—to true at some point in the code, as in the following code:

```
App.dismissBatchDialogWhenDone = true;
```

documentList
The `documentList` property returns an array object with a Document object for every document currently open in Fireworks.

The following code makes the first Fireworks document active and brings it to the front for editing:

```
var editFirst = App.documentList[0].makeActive();
```

platform
The platform property returns win if Fireworks is running on a Windows system and mac if Fireworks is running on a Macintosh.

progressCountCurrent

When a batch process is running, the dialog box keeps track of how many files have been completed, displaying something like "1 of 6 files processed." The `progressCountCurrent` property—which is not read-only—represents the first number in this message and is used in a loop that increments the number each time a file is completed.

progressCountTotal

The `progressCountTotal` property is not read-only and represents the second number in the Batch Progress dialog box—the total number of files to be processed. This value can be set from the number of documents selected in the dialog box, which is presented at the beginning of the operation; the `chooseScriptTargetDialog()` method returns such a list. Therefore, to determine the total number of files to be processed, use code similar to this:

```
var theDocList = App.chooseScriptTargetDialog(PNG);
App.progressCountTotal = theDocList.length;
```

Methods

The functions associated with the App object are all extremely useful. With them, you can do everything from opening a specific file to altering any Fireworks preferences, or even closing Fireworks itself.

Note   All of the App methods are static.

chooseScriptTargetDialog(*formatlist*)

Similar to `locateDocDialog()`, the `chooseScriptTargetDialog()` method displays the same dialog box so that the user can select the files to be targeted for an operation. Unlike `locateDocDialog()`, here the formatlist is a required argument and no maximum number of documents can be specified. In this example, file formats are limited to BMP files:

```
var theFiles = App.chooseScriptTargetDialog¬
("kMoaCfFormat_TIFF")
```

Tip   To restrict the resulting dialog box from the `chooseScriptTargetDialog()` method to multiple file types, use the same array structure as `locateDocDialog()`.

findOpenDocument(*pathname*)

The `findOpenDocument()` method checks to see if Fireworks already has the given pathname open in a document window. If so, that Document object is returned. If not, it returns null. Usually `findOpenDocument()` takes the pathname argument from an array of filenames, as in the following code:

```
theDocList = App.chooseScriptTargetDialog(App.getPref("PNG"));
for (var i = 0; i < theDocList.length; i++) {
```

```
theDoc = App.findOpenDocument(theDocList[i]);
if theDoc == null {
alert("No file found");
}
}
```

getPref(*prefname*) and setPref(*prefname, prefval*)

The getPref() and setPref() methods enable you to read — and alter — the current program settings for almost every aspect of Fireworks. From the default fill color to the *x* and *y* coordinates for the Edit Gradient dialog box, these two methods provide a powerful peek into the program.

The prefname and prefval arguments are set keywords contained in the Fireworks 3 Preferences file.

Cross-Reference See Chapter 25 for more about the Fireworks 3 Preferences file and specific preference settings.

locateDocDialog(*maxnumdocs [, formatlist]*)

The locateDocDialog() method presents the user with a dialog box (Figure 26-4) that enables them to choose one or more files. The maxnumdocs argument tells Fireworks whether to use the standard Open dialog box to open a single file or to use the Open Multiple Files dialog box for loading more than one file. Use 1, 0, or –1 to open the standard Open dialog box and any number higher than 1 to specify the Open Multiple Files dialog box. The number used as an argument does not limit the number of files that can be opened in any other way.

Figure 26-4: Pop up a dialog box to enable users to select which files will be targeted for a custom operation with the locateDocDialog() method.

The formatlist argument is an optional list of acceptable file types to open. If formatlist is omitted, then all files will be listed. The formatlist argument is in the form of an array. For example, to specify just the PNG and TIFF file formats for a single file dialog box, use the following code:

```
var formats = [ "PNG", "kMoaCfFormat_TIFF" ];
var theFiles = App.locateDocDialog(1, formats);
for (f in theFiles) {
alert(theFiles[f]);
}
```

Note   The resulting dialog box also permits the user to select All Readable Files and All Files.

The `locateDocDialog()` method returns an array of filenames, or, if the dialog box is canceled, it returns null.

Tip   You can also access whatever file types the user's system has available by determining the `MultiFileBatchTypes` setting with code like this:

```
var thePrefs = App.getPrefs(MultiFileBatchTypes);
var theFile = App.locateDocDialog(1,thePrefs);
```

Table 26-1 details the `formatlist` arguments.

Table 26-1
Fireworks formatlist Arguments

Argument	Document	Filename Extension	Mac File Type Code
ADOBE AI3	Adobe Illustrator	.ai	uMsk
Fireworks JavaScript	Fireworks JSF	.jsf	TEXT
kMoaCfFormat_BMP	Microsoft Bitmap	.bmp	BMP
kMoaCfFormat_ FreeHand7and8	Macromedia FreeHand 7.0 or 8.0	.fh7 or .fh8	AGD3
kMoaCfFormat_GIF	GIF image	.gif	GIFf
kMoaCfFormat_JPEG	JPEG image	.jpg or .jpeg	JPEG
kMoaCfFormat_PICT	Macintosh Picture	.pict, .pic or .p	PICT
kMoaCfFormat_RTF	Rich Text Format	.rtf	RTF
kMoaCfFormat_Text	Plain text file	.txt	TEXT
kMoaCfFormat_TIFF	TIFF image	.tif or .tiff	TIFF
PNG	PNG image	.png	PNGf
PS30	Photoshop Document (3.0 or higher)	.psd	8BIM

Note   Fireworks 3 no longer supports the xRes LRG format, so the kMoaCfFormat_LRG argument from Fireworks 2 is not available.

openDocument(*pathname[, openAsUntitled]*)

The `openDocument()` method opens the specified file in the pathname argument. Because `openDocument()` opens another instance of an already opened file, the `openDocument()` method is often used in conjunction with `findOpenDocument()`. If the file cannot be opened, `openDocument()` returns null. If the optional `openAsUntitled` argument is set as true, the document is opened in a new Untitled window.

quit()

The `quit()` method, when invoked, closes Fireworks. No further confirmation is offered unless an open document has been modified, but not saved. You can use the `confirm()` global method to create a confirmation routine in this way:

```
if (confirm("Ready to Quit?")) {
 App.quit();
}
```

Document

The Document object in Fireworks is similar to the Document object in JavaScript. Both deal with a document on a precise, exacting level. The Fireworks Document object is used to define the export parameters, as well as the basis for a find-and-replace operation.

Because most of this object is concerned with a specific document, it has no static properties and only two static methods, `findExportFormatOptionsByName()` and `makeGoodNativeFilePath()`.

Properties

The Document object has numerous properties that enable you to determine whether a file is open, whether it's been modified, gather the current filename, and much more.

Because all of the Document object properties work with a specific document, they must be associated with a specific instance of the Document object and not the Document object itself. To get an instance of the Document object, use the `getDocumentDOM()` function, as in this code:

```
var theDoc = fw.getDocumentDOM();
```

Now the properties of the current document are accessible. To see the current background color, for example, your script would include this code:

```
var theDoc = fw.getDocumentDOM();
alert(theDoc.backgroundColor);
```

backgroundColor
The background color of the document.

backgroundUrl
The relative or absolute URL for the Background link.

brushes
The brushes property is read-only and contains an array of Brush objects available for use in the document. The Brush object has properties such as `antiAliased`, `diameter`, and `flowRate` that enable you to control aspects of the strokes used in a document. For a complete list of Brush object properties and values, see Macromedia's Extending Fireworks documentation.

currentFrameNum
The current frame selected in the Frames panel.

currentLayerNum
The current layer selected in the Layers panel.

defaultAltText
If a single or sliced image doesn't have alt text specified, it is given this default.

exportFormatOptions
Identical to `exportOptions` (detailed next). Included for backward compatibility with Fireworks 2 scripts.

exportOptions
Although all of the properties of any object are important, certainly the most complex — and arguably the most useful — property of the Fireworks Document object is `exportOptions`. The `exportOptions` property returns an object that contains the current export settings. Most of the export settings are expressed as a number, rather than as a string. For example, the following code

```
var theFormat = theDoc.exportOptions.exportFormat
```

returns a 0 if the format is GIF and a 1 if it is JPEG. Several settings — `paletteInfo`, `paletteEntries`, and `frameInfo` — are expressed as arrays.

Table 26-2 details the `exportOptions` settings.

Table 26-2
exportOptions Settings

Setting	Possible Values
exportFormat	0 (GIF), 1 (JPEG), 2 (PNG), 3 (Custom, including TIFF and BMP), or 4 (GIF-Animation)
macCreator	"XXXX" (a Macintosh Creator code, Fireworks is "MKBY")
macFileType	"XXXX" (a Macintosh File Type code, used to choose format if exportFormat = Custom)
colorMode	0 (Indexed), 1 (24-bit color), or 2 (32-bit color)
paletteMode	0 (Custom), 1 (Adaptive), 2 (Grid), 3 (Monochrome), 4 (Macintosh System), 5 (Windows System), 6 (Exact), or 7 (Web 216)

paletteInfo (array)
  colorModified
  colorLocked
  colorTransparent
  colorDeleted
  colorSelected
	
	True | False
	True | False
	True | False
	True | False
	True | False

paletteEntries (array) colorstring1 colorstring2 etc.	Red-Green-Blue-Alpha numbers where each number is in the range 0-255. Example: "255 0 0 255". If Alpha is 0, the color is transparent.
numCustomEntries	0-256
numEntriesRequested	0-256
numGridEntries	0-256
ditherMode	0 (None), 1 (2 × 2), or 2 (Diffusion)
ditherPercent	0-100
paletteTransparency	0 (None), 1 (Index), 2 (IndexAlpha), or 3 (RGBA)
transparencyIndex	0-255, or -1 if none
webSnapTolerance	Always set to 14
jpegQuality	1-100
jpegSmoothness	1-8
jpegSubsampling	1-100
percentScale	1-100000

Continued

Table 26-2 *(continued)*	
Setting	**Possible Values**
xSize	-100000 to 100000
ySize	-100000 to 100000
cropTop	0-Image Height minus 1
cropLeft	0-Image Width minus 1
cropBottom	0-Image Height minus 1
cropRight	0-Image Width minus 1
applyScale	True | False
useScale	True | False
crop	True | False
optimized	True | False
progressiveJPEG	True | False
interlacedGIF	True | False
animAutoCrop	True | False
animAutoDifference	True | False
localAdaptive	True | False
webSnapAdaptive	True | False
name	Text-Name of Setting
frameInfo (array) gifDisposalMethod delayTime	0 (Unspecified), 1 (None), 2(Background), or 3 (Previous) 0-100000
savedAnimationRepeat	0-1000000

The useScale and applyScale settings of the Document object are dependent on each other to determine the type of scaling that is actually used. The following rules determine the scaling type:

✦ If useScale is false, and applyScale is false, no scaling is done on export.

✦ If useScale is true, then percentScale is used, regardless of the setting of applyScale.

✦ If useScale is false and applyScale is true, then xSize and ySize are used to determine the scaling in the following manner:

- If the value is positive, the value is used as specified for the *x* or *y* axis.

- If the value is zero, the *x* or *y* axis varies without limit.

- If the value is negative, the *x* or *y* axis varies, but it may be no larger than the absolute value of the specified number.

Note that if one value is positive and one is negative, the positive value is always used.

ExportSettings

The ExportSettings object has properties such as htmlDestination ("same", "one up", "custom", "clipboard") and shimGeneration ("none", "transparent", "internal", "nested tables"). See the Extending Fireworks documentation for a complete list of the properties and associated values of the ExportSettings object.

filePathForRevert

The filePathForRevert property returns the pathname from which the Revert operation reads — in other words, the file opened to create the current document. Use filePathForRevert to determine an original pathname for non-Fireworks native files or documents opened as "Untitled." This property returns null if the document was newly created and not read from a file.

filePathForSave

The filePathForSave property is used to find and set the filename of the current document. This property is essential for creating backup files. If the file has never been saved, the result is null. The following code relies on the filePathForSave property to store a filename for later use during a backup operation.

```
function saveName(theDoc) {
 var sourcePath
 if (theDoc.filePathForSave != null) {
 sourcePath = theDoc.filePathForSave
 }
}
```

fills

The fills property is read-only and contains an array of Fill objects available for use in the document. The Fill object has properties like gradient and pattern. See the Extending Fireworks documentation for a complete list of Fill object properties and values.

frameCount

The number of frames in the document.

frameLoopingCount

Possible values for the `frameLoopingCount` property are:

+ 0: Loop forever
+ 1: Don't loop (just play once)
+ 2 or more: Loop this number of times

frames

The `frames` property is read-only and is an array containing the Frame objects in the document. The Frame object has properties such as `layers` and `delay`. Refer to Extending Fireworks for a complete list of Frame object properties and acceptable values.

gammaPreview

The `gammaPreview` property can be either true or false. On a Windows machine, true indicates that View ➪ Macintosh Gamma is enabled. On a Mac, true indicates that View ➪ Windows Gamma is enabled.

gradients

The `gradients` property is read-only and is an array that contains the Gradient objects that are available to the document. See Extending Fireworks for a list of Gradient object properties and values.

gridColor

The color in which the grid is displayed, which can also be set in the Grid dialog box.

gridOrigin

The point that corresponds to the grid origin. The origin of the grid can also be set by dragging it from the intersection of the horizontal and vertical rulers.

gridSize

The horizontal and vertical grid size for the document. The horizontal grid size is `gridSize.x` and the vertical grid size is `gridSize.y`.

guides

The guides property is read-only, and it corresponds to the Guides object. The Guides object has properties such as `color` and `locked`. See Extending Fireworks for a complete list of Guides properties and values.

height

The height of the document in pixels.

isDirty

It's often necessary to determine whether a file has been modified before deciding how to act on it. The isDirty property returns true if the document has been modified since the last save or if it has never been saved; otherwise, the property returns false.

isSymbolDocument

A read-only property that returns true if the document is a Graphic Symbol or Button Symbol, and false if not. The Symbol-editing window is an open document like any other.

isValid

The isValid property returns true if the current document is still open and false if it has been closed.

lastExportDirectory

The target folder for the last export operation, expressed as a file URL.

lastExportFile

The target file for the last export operation, expressed as a file URL.

layers

A read-only property that is an array containing the Layer objects in the document. Properties of the Layer object include sharing and layerType. Refer to Extending Fireworks for a complete list of properties and values.

left

The left property is a value in pixels that specifies how far from the left border of the canvas the farthest-left object is located.

mapType

The type of image map that the document creates. Possible values are client, server, or both.

matteColor

The Matte color value for the document, also specified in the Optimize panel.

onionSkinAfter

The number of frames after the current frame to be displayed using onion skinning. This value is also specified in the Onion Skinning dialog box, accessed from the Frames panel.

onionSkinBefore

The number of frames before the current frame to be displayed using onion skinning.

pathAttributes

This property corresponds to the PathAttrs object, which has properties such as brush and fill. See Extending Fireworks for a complete list of properties and values.

pngText

The pngText property is the text contained in a Fireworks document.

resolution

The document's print resolution setting. Possible values are between 1 and 5,000.

resolutionUnits

The measurement unit for the document's print resolution setting (resolution property). This can be either "inch" or "cm", for inches or centimeters, respectively.

textures

The textures property is read-only and is an array of Texture objects available to the document. The Texture object has one read-only property, name, which contains the name of an associated texture.

top

The top property is how far in pixels the topmost object is from the top of the document.

useMatteColor

Can be either true or false. When true, the Matte color specified in the Optimize panel or defined in the matteColor property is used when exporting.

width

The width of the document in pixels.

Methods

The Document object methods provide a great deal of functionality. These functions activate, save, and close files — and more. The findExportFormatOptions() and makeGoodNativeFilePath() methods are static, and the rest are instance methods.

exportTo(pathname [, exportOptions])

The actual export operation is handled by the exportTo() method. The full path-name argument is mandatory, and if the optional exportOptions argument is omitted, the current export settings are used. Should exportOptions be specified, they are used without affecting the document's exportOptions property. The exportTo() method returns true if it is successful.

findExportFormatOptionsByName(name)

This static method is used to access any preset Export Settings. If an Export Setting is preset with the given name, a Document object is returned with the same settings as the exportOptions property. If there is no preset by the given name, null is returned.

makeActive()

Use the makeActive() method to make the referenced document the active one in Fireworks. The active document is then brought to the front of all other documents.

makeGoodNativeFilePath(pathname)

To make sure that a given pathname ends in a proper Fireworks .png extension, the makeGoodNativeFilePath static method is applied. When used, it converts any filename extension to a .png. For example, the following code snippets all return "file:///images/logo.png" as the filename:

```
var theFile =¬
  Document.makeGoodNativeFilePath("file:///images/logo.ping")
var theFile =¬
  Document.makeGoodNativeFilePath("file:///images/logo.bmp")
var theFile =¬
  Document.makeGoodNativeFilePath("file:///images/logo")
```

save([okToDoSaveAs])

The save() method is used to store the document in its default location. If the optional okToDoSaveAs argument is true, then the user will be prompted for a file location if the document has never been saved. If okToDoSaveAs is false and the file has never been saved, the operation will fail and return false. Upon a successful save, the document's dirty flag is cleared. The save() method returns true if the save operation completes successfully, and false otherwise.

Tip To force a Save As dialog box to appear, set the App.filePathForSave property to null before calling Document.save().

saveCopyAs(pathname)

To store a duplicate of the current document, use the saveCopyAs() method. The full pathname, for example, "file:///images/logo.png", must be used. With this method, neither the filePathForSave nor isDirty property are affected.

Errors

To help keep the user informed when something goes wrong, the Fireworks API includes an Errors object. The Errors object includes 62 static properties. Each property of the Errors object returns a string, localized for the language of the program. For example, the code

```
var theError = Errors.EFileIsReadOnly;
```

returns "File is locked." in English. Table 26-3 lists all the Errors properties and their messages in English.

Table 26-3 Errors Properties	
Property	*English Message*
EAppAlreadyRunning	An internal error occurred. Fireworks is optimizing an image.
EAppNotSerialized	An internal error occurred.
EArrayIndexOutOfBounds	An internal error occurred.
EBadFileContents	Unsupported file format.
EBadJIsVersion	This script does not work in this version of Fireworks.
EBadNesting	An internal error occurred.
EBadParam	A parameter was incorrect.
EBadParamType	A parameter was not the correct type.
EBadSelection	The selection was incorrect for this operation.
EBufferTooSmall	An internal error occurred.
ECharConversionFailed	An internal error occurred.
EDatabaseError	An internal error occurred.
EDeletingLastMasterChild	A symbol must contain at least one object.
EDiskFull	The disk is full.
EDuplicateFileNname	File name is already in use.
EFileIsReadOnly	File is locked.
EFileNotFound	The file was not found.

Property	English Message
EGenericErrorOccurred	An error occurred.
EGroupDepth	An internal error occurred.
EIllegalThreadAccess	An internal error occurred.
EInternalError	An internal error occurred.
ELowOnMem	Memory is nearly full.
ENoActiveDocument	This command requires an active document.
ENoFilesSelected	At least one file must be selected for scripts to operate.
ENoNestedMastersOrAliases	Although symbols may contain other symbols, a symbol can not contain a copy of itself. Symbols may not contain Instances or other Symbols.
ENoNestedPasting	The JavaScript contains a paste step, which would create an endless loop.
ENoSliceableElems	No paths were found. Objects were cut.
ENoSuchElement	An internal error occurred.
ENotImplemented	An internal error occurred.
ENotMyType	An internal error occurred.
EOutOfMem	Fireworks is low on memory.
EResourceNotFound	An internal error occurred.
ESharingViolation	An internal error occurred.
EUnknownReaderFormat	Unknown file type.
EUserCanceled	An internal error occurred.*
EUserInterrupted	An internal error occurred.
EWrongType	An internal error occurred.

Generating Errors on Purpose

If you're programming in Fireworks, it's helpful to gain a full understanding of the errors a user might encounter. When a user reports a problem, most often they'll mention the error code generated, if any. Fireworks does a terrific job of avoiding numeric error codes that are only meaningful to someone who has a decoding manual.

Continued

Continued

The Errors collection, as documented in Extending Fireworks, is presented only as an alpha-betized list of the properties:

```
EAppAlreadyRunning, EAppNotSerialized, EArrayIndexOutOfBounds,
EBadFileContents, EBadJsVersion, EBadNesting, EBadParam,
EBadParamType, EBadSelection, EBufferTooSmall,
ECharConversionFailed, EDatabaseError, EDeletingLastMasterChild,
EDiskFull, EDuplicateFileName, EFileIsReadOnly, EFileNotFound,
EGenericErrorOccurred, EGroupDepth, EIllegalThreadAccess,
EInternalError, ELowOnMem, ENoActiveDocument, ENoFilesSelected,
ENoNestedMastersOrAliases, ENoNestedPasting, ENoSliceableElems,
ENoSuchElement, ENotImplemented, ENotMyType, EOutOfMem,
EResourceNotFound, ESharingViolation, EUnknownReaderFormat,
EUserCanceled, EUserInterrupted, EWrongType
```

The Error messages presented in Table 26-3 are the errors coded for the English release of the program. So how does a programmer uncover what the messages are in their own language? I used Fireworks itself—and a little macro magic—to help decipher the Error properties.

I often use Microsoft Word whenever I need to massage text from one format to another. In this situation, I needed to take the comma delimited list from Extending Fireworks and ultimately put it into a code that would generate a visible error message. The syntax for my error generator was

```
var theError = Errors.errorCode
alert(theError)
```

where *errorCode* was one of the 37 properties. To accomplish this, first I used Microsoft Word's Find and Replace feature to convert every comma-and-space combination (which separated the properties) into a paragraph return. This gave me a one-property-per-line list. Next, I used Word's Macro Recorder feature to add the necessary text before—`var theError = Errors.`—and after—`alert(theError)`—each property. So what was

```
EAppAlreadyRunning
EAppNotSerialized
EArrayIndexOutOfBounds
```

became

```
var theError = Errors.EAppAlreadyRunning
alert(theError)
var theError = Errors.EAppNotSerialized
alert(theError)
var theError = Errors.EArrayIndexOutOfBounds
alert(theError)
```

and so on until all properties were converted. This file was then saved as a standard text file with a .jsf extension, thus, creating a Fireworks command. Upon running the command, each error was reported in sequence and could be copied and included in Table 26-3.

Find

Within the Fireworks API, a separate Find object exists for running a find-and-replace operation. To link the Find object to a particular document, use the `MakeFind()` method to make the Find object and specify the criteria. Just as the Fireworks find-and-replace facility is capable of searching four different types of elements — text, font, color, and URLs — the `findParms` argument can take four different array forms.

For example, a text find-and-replace operation that searches for "FW" using the Whole Word option, and replaces it with "Fireworks" is defined with code like this:

```
var findParms = {
whatToFind: "text",
find: "FW",
replace: "Fireworks",
wholeWord: true,
matchCase: false,
regExp: false
};
var theFinder = Document.makeFind(findParms);
```

Note the use of quotation marks and parentheses to delineate the parameters.

Different properties are available depending on the type of Find and Replace operation, specified with the `whatToFind()` method. Table 26-4 details the four types of Find parameters: text, font, color, and url.

Table 26-4
Find Object Properties and Methods

Type of Find	Property or Method	Possible Values
text	whatToFind	"text"
	find	"Any text string"
	replace	"Any text string"
	wholeWord	(True | False)
	matchCase	(True | False)
	regExp	(True | False)

Continued

Table 26-4 *(continued)*		
Type of Find	**Property or Method**	**Possible Values**
font	whatToFind	"font"
	find	"fontname-to-find"
	replace	"fontname-to-replace"
	findStyle	(-1 to 7) where -1 (StyleAnyStyle), 0 (StylePlain), 1 (StyleBold), 2 (StyleItalic), 3 (StyleBoldItalic), 4 (StyleUnderline), 5 (StyleBoldUnderline), 6 (StyleItalicUnderline), or 7 (StyleBoldItalicUnderline)
	replaceStyle	(-1 to 7) as described under findStyle
	findMinSize	(0-9999)
	findMaxSize	(0-9999)
	replaceSize	(0-9999, or -1 for "same size")
color	whatToFind	"color"
	find	RGB Alpha values from 0-255
	replace	RGB Alpha values from 0-255
	fills	(True | False)
	strokes	(True | False)
	effects	(True | False)
URL	whatToFind	"url"
	find	"url-to-find"
	replace	"url-to-replace"
	wholeWord	(True | False)
	matchCase	(True | False)
	regExp	(True | False)

Note

When defining color strings for use in the color find-and-replace operation, it's often easier to define a few key variables to reuse again and again, such as these:

```
var kSolidWhite = "255 255 255 255";
var kSolidBlack = "0 0 0 255";
var kTransparent = "255 255 255 0";
var kRed = "255 0 0 255";
var kGreen = "0 255 0 255";
var kBlue = "0 0 255 255";
```

Files

The Files object of the Fireworks API is robust and covers more than 20 functions that permit you to perform most any file operation. All of the Files methods are static and must be called from the Files object itself, except for close(), readline(), and write(). No properties are associated with the Files object.

close()

As you might suspect, this Instance method closes the associated file. Although close() is not necessary because all files opened or created as a File object are closed when the script terminates, the close() method enables you to control access to a file within a script.

copy(*sourcePathname, destinationPathname*)

To quickly copy a file to a new location — including on another drive — use the copy() method. This function fails if the file named in the destinationPathname argument already exists. In other words, copy() won't overwrite a file. You can't copy folders with this function.

createDirectory(*pathname*)

It's not uncommon to need new folders (directories) when running batch procedures; the createDirectory() method handles this procedure for you. If the folder creation was successful, the function returns true; if not, it returns false.

createFile(*pathname[, mactype [, maccreator]]*)

To create a new file of any type, use the createFile() method. This method fails if the file already exists. The mactype (file type) and maccreator (associated application) arguments are necessary for properly making a new permanent file on a Macintosh system.

Cross-Reference See Chapter 14 for Fireworks-related Macintosh File Type codes.

deleteFile(*pathname*)

To remove a file or directory, use the deleteFile() method. If the deletion is successful, true is returned. False is returned if the pathname supplied in the argument does not exist or if the file or directory could not be deleted.

deleteFileIfExisting(*pathname*)

Rather than run a separate function to see if a file exists before removing it, you could use the deleteFileIfExisting() method. With this method, in addition to returning true if the file is successfully removed, true is also returned if the supplied pathname does not exist. The only circumstance in which false is returned is if the found file could not be removed.

enumFiles(*pathname*)

The enumFiles() method returns an array of pathnames for every file specified in the argument. The pathname argument should not, however, point to a file; if it does, enumFiles() returns just the single pathname for the file.

exists(*pathname*)

You can check the existence of either a file or directory with the exists() method. True is returned unless the file or directory does not exist or the supplied pathname is invalid.

getDirectory(*pathname*)

To extract just the folder — or directory — portion of a pathname, use getDirectory(). This code returns file:///images/winter:

```
var theFolderName =¬
  Files.getDirectory("file:///images/winter/seasonal.png");
```

getExtension(*filename*)

To retrieve just the filename extension, use the getExtension() method. If the filename has no extension, an empty string is returned. This code returns ".png":

```
var theExt = Files.getExtension("logo.png");
```

getFilename(*pathname*)

To parallel function to getDirectory() is getFilename(), which extracts a filename from a fully qualified pathname. This code returns seasonal.png:

```
var theFileName =¬
  Files.getFilename("file:///images/winter/seasonal.png");
```

getLastErrorString()

If the last call to a method in the Files object resulted in an error, getLastErrorString() returns text describing the error. If the last call

succeeded, this method returns null. The following example code returns
an error if a copy operation was unsuccessful:

```
if (Files.copy(sourcePath, destPath) == false) {
 return Files.getLastErrorString();
}
```

The error returned is taken from the Fireworks API Errors object, described later in
this chapter. Note that getLastErrorString() is dedicated to errors committed
by methods of the Files object; the Errors object is used for displaying error messages resulting from other situations.

getTempFilePath([*dirname*])

The getTempFilePath() method returns a pathname in the system temporary
files directory. This function does not create a file; it simply returns a unique pathname that does not conflict with any existing file. If the dirname argument is given
(and is not null), the pathname will indicate a file in the given directory rather than
in the temporary files directory. The dirname argument is taken literally and no
other path information is appended.

On a Windows system, getTempFilePath() generally returns file:///C|/
windows/TEMP/00000001, depending on your system settings; on a Macintosh it
returns file:///Macintosh%20HD/Temporary Items/00000001, where
Macintosh HD is the name of your Startup Disk.

isDirectory(*pathname*)

To verify that a supplied pathname is a directory and not a file, use the
isDirectory() method. If the pathname is not a valid directory, true is returned.

makePathFromDirAndFile(*dirname, filename*)

Often, during a batch operation, Fireworks is called upon to take a directory from
one source and a filename from another and put them together to store a file. That
is exactly what makePathFromDirAndFile() does. The directory is specified in the
first argument, the filename in the second, as shown in this example:

```
var dirname = "file:///fireworks";
var filename = "borg.png";
theNewFile = Files.makePathFromDirAndFile(dirname, filename)
```

In this example, "file:///fireworks/borg.png" is returned.

open(*pathname, wantWriteAccess*)

A basic function of the Files object, the open() method opens a specified file for reading or writing. To write to a file, the wantWriteAccess argument must be true. If open() is successful, a Files object is returned, otherwise null is returned. The open() method is intended for use with text files.

readline()

Text files are often read in one line at a time; in Fireworks, this function is handled by the readline() Instance method. The lines are returned as strings without the end-of-line character. Null is returned when the end-of-file is reached (or if the line is longer than 2,048 characters).

rename(*pathname, filename*)

Use the rename() method to change a full pathname to a new one. For example, the following code

```
Files.rename("file:///images/logo.png", "newlogo.png");
```

renames the file "logo.png" to "newlogo.png" and returns file:///images/newlogo.png.

setFilename(*pathname, filename*)

The setFileName() method replaces a filename in a pathname with another specified filename. For instance, the code

```
Files.setFilename("file:///images/logo.png", "newlogo.png" );
```

returns file:///images/newlogo.png. Note that this function does not affect the file on disk in any way, but it is just a convenient way to manipulate pathnames. Whereas setFileName() appears to perform the same operation as rename(), only rename() actually alters the name of the file on the drive.

swap(*pathname, pathname*)

Fireworks provides numerous methods for moving files around during an export operation; the swap() method switches the contents of one pathname for the contents of another. This function is helpful when you need to exchange a source file for a backup file.

Caution

The swap() method has two limitations: First, you can only swap files, not folders. Second, both files to be swapped must be on the same drive.

write(*string*)

To insert text in a file, use this Instance method. No end-of-line characters are automatically appended after each string; it's necessary to attach a \n to generate a proper end-of-line character, as in the following code:

```
theString = "Log Report\n";
theFile.write(theString);
```

Hotspot Objects

Hotspots — alternatively known as image maps — are one of two types of Web objects in Fireworks. Along with slices, hotspots enable a wide range of user interactivity to occur. The Fireworks API hotspot objects are, for the most part, read-only properties that enable you to gather any needed bit of information about image maps embedded in the Fireworks document.

Note   Because hotspots and slices employ many of the same mechanisms, several Fireworks API objects — exportDoc, BehaviorInfo, and BehaviorsList — listed under Hotspot Objects are also valid for use with slices.

exportDoc

The `exportDoc` object is available for use in all the exporting Templates — slices.htt, metafile.htt, and Servermap.mtt. However, `exportDoc` cannot be outside of these files. All of its properties are read-only and relate to the current document and its Document Properties, detailed in Table 26-5.

<table>
<tr><td colspan="3" align="center">Table 26-5
exportDoc Properties</td></tr>
<tr><td>*Property*</td><td>*Possible Value*</td><td>*Description*</td></tr>
<tr><td>altText</td><td>Text</td><td>The text string set as the Alt Text for the document.</td></tr>
<tr><td>backgroundColor</td><td>Hexadecimal String</td><td>String that is the hex color for the document canvas.</td></tr>
<tr><td>backgroundIsTransparent</td><td>True | False</td><td>True if the canvas is set to transparent, or if the export settings area transparent GIF.</td></tr>
</table>

Continued

Table 26-5 *(continued)*

Property	Possible Value	Description
backgroundLink	URL	The relative or absolute URL for the Background Link.
clientMap	True | False	True if the Client Side Image Map option is selected for the document.
filename	Relative URL	Simple URL for the exported image, relative to the HTML output—for example, images/Button.gif. In slices.htt, this property is the image basename plus the base extension—for example, Button_r2_c2.gif.
generateHeader	True | False	True if an HTML file is exported, false if the HTML output is sent to the clipboard.
hasAltText	True | False	True if alternate text has been specified in the HTML Properties dialog box.
hasBackgroundLink	True | False	True if a Background Link has been set through the HTML Properties dialog box.
height	Number	Height of the exported image in pixels. In slices.htt, it is the total height of the output images.
htmlOutputPath	URL	The complete file URL to which the HTML is being written.
imagename	Text	The image basename, without a filename extension—for example, Button.
numFrames	Number	The number of frames in a file.
pathBase	Pathname without filename extension	The filename with the extension removed—for example, images/Button.
pathSuffix	Filename Extension	The filename extension. For example, ".gif".
serverMap	True | False	True if the Server Side Image Map option is selected for the document.

Property	Possible Value	Description
startColumn	Number	Indicates the column of the slice when generating HTML for a single slice. Used only in metafile.htt.
startRow	Number	Indicates the row of the slice when generating HTML for a single slice. Used only in metafile.htt.
width	Number	Width of the export image in pixels. In slices.htt, it is the total width of the output images.

Image maps

Two objects relate to image maps: ImageMap and ImageMapList. Not only can the shape and number of coordinates of a hotspot be uncovered by using these two objects, but you can also determine what, if any, Behaviors are linked to them.

ImageMap object

Like several of the Fireworks API extensions, most of the work with the ImageMap object is handled though an array. Each element in the ImageMap array represents one hotspot in the current document. Get a particular ImageMap object with code like this:

```
var theHotspot = imagemap[0];
```

Properties

The properties of the ImageMap object are all read-only instance properties and are detailed in Table 26-6.

Table 26-6
ImageMap Instance Properties

Property	Possible Value	Description
altText	Text	The specified alternative text.
behaviors	A BehaviorsList object (described later in this chapter)	Details regarding the Behavior attached to the hotspot.

Continued

	Table 26-6 *(continued)*	
Property	**Possible Value**	**Description**
hasAltText	True | False	Returns true if alternative text has been specified.
hasHref	True | False	Returns true if the hotspot has a URL assigned.
hasTargetText	True | False	Returns true if the hotspot has a target specified.
href	Relative or Absolute URL	The assigned URL.
numCoords	1 for circle, 2 for rectangle, and any number for polygon	The number of coordinates used to describe the hotspot in HTML.
radius	Number	The radius of the circle area hotspot.
shape	circle, rectangle, or polygon	The type of hotspot.
targetText	An HTML frame name	The specified target.

Note   The ImageMap object has one other property associated with it: Behaviors. Because the BehaviorInfo object can also work with slice objects, it is described in detail in the following section.

Methods

The only ImageMap methods are those concerned with gathering the *x* and *y* coordinates for the hotspot, xCoord( ) and yCoord( ).

Both xCoord( ) and yCoord( ) work identically. Each gets one coordinate, in pixels, for the index point. These methods are used together in conjunction with the numCoords property to list the coordinates for the entire image map, as shown in this code:

```
for (var j=0; j<curImagemap.numCoords; j++) {
 if (j>0) WRITE_HTML(",");
 WRITE_HTML(curImagemap.xCoord(j), ",", curImagemap.yCoord(j));
 }
```

ImageMapList object

The ImageMapList object is an array of ImageMap objects, describing the areas in an image map. The ImageMapList object has only one property, numberOfURLs, and it is a read-only, static property.

The `numberOfURLs` property is important because it contains the number of hotspots in a particular image map. As such, `numberOfURLs` is often used to loop through an ImageMap object array, as with this code:

```
var i = 0;
while (i < imagemap.numberOfURLs) {
 hasImagemap = true;
 }
 i++;
```

If there are no image maps in the document, the `numberOfURLs` returns zero.

Behaviors

Behaviors, in Fireworks, are effects that are exported as JavaScript code to be included in an HTML page. A Behavior is attached to a Web object (a hotspot or a slice) and triggered by a specific user event, such as a mouse click or rolling over an image. Two objects deal with Behaviors: BehaviorsList and BehaviorInfo.

BehaviorInfo

All of the properties of the BehaviorInfo object are read-only and no methods are associated with the BehaviorInfo object.

Although the Behaviors panel lists four main Behavior groups — Simple Rollover, Swap Image, Set Nav Bar, and Set Text of Status Bar — from the BehaviorInfo object perspective, there are six different Behaviors: Status Message, Swap Image, Button Down, Swap Image Restore, Button Highlight, and Button Restore. Only four possible events are recognized: `onMouseOver`, `onClick`, `onMouseOut`, and `onLoad`.

Table 26-7 lists the BehaviorInfo object properties and their possible values.

Table 26-7
Properties for the BehaviorInfo Object

Property	Possible Value	Description
action	1 (Status Message), 2 (Swap Image), 4 (Button Down), 5 (Swap Image Restore), 6 (Button Highlight), or 7 (Button Restore)	The type of Behavior.
downHighlight	True | False	For Button Highlight Behaviors, returns true if there is a highlight image.

Continued

Table 26-7 *(continued)*		
Property	**Possible Value**	**Description**
event	0 (onMouseOver), 1 (onClick), 2 (onMouseOut), or 3 (onLoad)	The event that triggers the Behavior.
hasHref	True | False	For Swap Image Behaviors, returns true if the swap image swaps in an external file as opposed to a Fireworks frame.
hasStatusText	True | False	For Status Message Behaviors, returns true if the status text is not empty.
hasTargetFrame	True | False	For Swap Image Behaviors, returns true if the swap image swaps in another frame in the Fireworks file, as opposed to an external file.
href	A file URL	For Swap Image Behaviors, the URL for the swap image file for an external file swap image.
preload	True | False	For Swap Image Behaviors, returns true if the image is going to be preloaded.
restoreOnMouseout	True | False	For Swap Image Behaviors, returns true if the original image is to be restored onMouseOut.
statusText	Text string	The text used in the Status Message Behavior.
targetColumnNum	Number	For Swap Image Behaviors, the column in the slices table that will be swapped.
targetFrameNum	Number (0 to number of frames minus 1)	For Swap Image Behaviors, if hasTargetFrame is true, this is the frame number that will be swapped. The first frame is 0.
targetRowNum	Number	For Swap Image Behaviors, the row in the slices table that will be swapped.

BehaviorsList object

The one property of the BehaviorsList object, `numberOfBehaviors`, is used in the same fashion as `numberOfURLs` is used with the ImageMap object, to determine how many Behaviors are included in the current document. In the following code, the `numberOfBehaviors` property is used to loop through the array of Behaviors:

```
for (var i=0; i<theCurBehaviors.numberOfBehaviors; i++) {
 var curBehavior = theCurBehaviors[i];
 if (curBehavior.action == kActionRadioGroup) {
  groupName = curBehavior.groupName;
 }
}
```

Slice Objects

Slices make it possible to divide one graphic into several different files, each of which can be saved separately with its own export settings or Behaviors. Two objects relate directly to slices: SliceInfo and Slices.

SliceInfo object

The SliceInfo object enables you to examine every aspect of the separate slices of an overall image.

Properties

All properties of the SliceInfo object are read-only, and are detailed in Table 26-8.

Table 26-8
Properties of the SliceInfo Object

Property	Possible Values	Description
altText	Text	The alternative text for this slice.
behaviors	A BehaviorsList object	The BehaviorsList object describing any Behaviors attached to the current slice.
cellHeight	Number in pixels	The height of the current HTML table row.
cellWidth	Number in pixels	The width of the current HTML table column.
downIndex	Number	The index for this slice, if it is a multiple file export down button.

Continued

Table 26-8

Property	Possible Values	Description
hasAltText	True | False	Returns true if the slice has an alternative text description.
hasHref	True | False	Returns true if the slice has a URL.
hasHtmlText	True | False	Returns true if the slice is a text-only slice.
hasImage	True | False	Returns true if the current slice includes an image; text-only slices return false.
hasImagemap	True | False	Returns true if hotspots are associated with the current slice.
hasTargetText	True | False	Returns true if a target is specified for the current slice.
height	Number in pixels	The height of the image in the slice, including row spans.
href	URL	The URL for the current slice.
htmlText	Text	The text string for a text-only slice.
imagemap	An ImageMapList object	The ImageMapList object describing any hotspots attached to the current slice.
imageSuffix	Filename extension	The filename extension for the image in the current slice, including the period.
isUndefined	True | False	Returns true if the current slice does not have a user-drawn slice associated with it. Fireworks automatically generates slices to cover these undefined cells.
left	Number in pixels	The left side of the cell in pixels, starting at 0.
nestedTableSlices	Slices object (detailed later in this chapter)	Slices object describing a nested table that occupies the current table cell. Returns null if the cell doesn't contain a nested table.
skipCell	True | False	Returns true if the table cell for the current slice is included in a previous row or column span.
targetText	HTML frame name	The specified target for the current frame.
top	Number in pixels	The top of the cell in pixels, starting at 0.
width	Number in pixels	The width of the image in the slice, including column spans.

Methods

The SliceInfo object has two methods associated with it: `getFrameFileName()` and `setFrameFileName()`. Both are instance methods.

getFrameFileName(*frame*)

The `getFrameFileName()` method reads the filename for the slice and frame. The returned name does not include any path information, such as folder or filename extension. For example, using the Fireworks defaults, the name of the first slice for a file named newLogo.gif would be newLogo_r1_c1. The first frame in an image file is 0; generally all slices in frame 0 are named. For frames 1 and higher, only slices that are rollovers or that are targeted by a swap image are named.

The following code shows how the `getFrameFileName()` method is used both with a constant and with a variable:

```
var curFile = SliceInfo.getFrameFileName(0);
for (var curFrame = 0; curFrame < exportDoc.numFrames;¬
 curFrame++) {
 var curFile = SliceInfo.getFrameFileName(curFrame);
// processing code for each slice goes here
}
```

setFrameFileName(*frame, filename*)

To change the filename of a slice, use the `setFrameFileName()` method. Specify the frame number and the new name of the slice in the two arguments, as in the following code:

```
SliceInfo.setFrameFileName(swapFrame, fileName);
```

> **Note**
>
> An interesting side effect of `setFrameFileName()` is that this method determines which images is written. By default, Fireworks sets it up so that all slices on frame 0 are named, and no other frames are named. If a Swap Image Behavior uses a slice at row 2, column 3 on frame 2, the export Templates set the frame filename so that that image gets written. You can also set slices on frame 0 to an empty string, and they won't get written. This is how the "Don't export undefined slices" option gets implemented.

Slices object

The Slices object is an array of SliceInfo objects. Because slices exist in a table, each slice can be identified by its location in the row and column structure. A two-dimensional array holds these row and column values and marks each instance of a slice object. For example, the slice in the first row, first column position is `slices[0][0]`. To process all of the individual slices, use code similar to the following:

```
var curRow;
var curCol;
for (curRow = 0; curRow < Slices.numRows; curRow++) {
```

```
for (curCol=0; curCol < Slices.numColumns; curCol++) {
var curSlice = Slices[curRow][curCol];
// do whatever processing with curSlice.
}
}
```

Notice how both the numRows and numColumns static properties must be used to properly loop through all of the slices. Once the individual slice has been identified by its two-dimensional array, the properties of the instance slice can be read.

Several of the static properties of the slices object—doShimEdges, doShimInternal, and doSkipUndefined—refer to options. These options are all set in the HTML Properties dialog box. To find out if the user has selected the No Shims option, use code like this:

```
if (Slices.doShimInternal || Slices.doShimEdges) {
//create shim code here
}
```

Table 26-9 details the static properties of the slices object.

Table 26-9
Properties of the Slices Object

Property	Possible Values	Description
demoindex		The index for each file generated for a multiple-file button export.
doDemoHTML	True | False	Returns true for a rollover, mulitple-file button export.
doShimEdges	True | False	Returns true if the Table Shims option is set to Transparent Image in Document Properties.
doShimInternal	True | False	Returns true if the Table Shims option is set to Shims from Image in Document Properties.
doSkipUndefined	True | False	Returns true if the Export Undefined Slices is not enabled in Document Properties.
imagesDirPath	Relative URL	Path to the folder used to store the images in the sliced table. If the images and the HTML file are in the same folder, returns an empty string.
numColumns	Number	The total number of columns, excluding the shim column, in the HTML table.
numRows	Number	The total number of rows, excluding the shim column, in the HTML table.
shimPath	Relative URL	Path to the GIF file used for shims, for example, images/shim.gif.

Accessing the Fireworks API

The new History panel feature in Fireworks 3 had a major effect on the Fireworks API. In order to display each user action as a separate repeatable step, each action had to be accessible as a separate function. There are currently 264 documented JavaScript functions, which can be categorized in three groups: Document functions, History Panel functions, and general Fireworks functions. With these functions, you can programmatically repeat virtually every Fireworks command.

The Fireworks JavaScript API — as well as the all the other Fireworks methods and properties — is documented in the Extending Fireworks manual from Macromedia. Rather than repeat the information found in that resoure, the balance of this chapter will focus on how to best apply that information.

Document functions

As noted previously, the Fireworks extensability model relies heavily on the Document Object Model (DOM). In the Fireworks API, every Document function requires the DOM of a specific document in order to work correctly. The `getDocumentDOM()` function is used to retrieve the DOM in one of two ways. First, the function can be written out for every action, like this:

```
fw.getDocumentDOM.align(top);
```

This method is used in the History panel, as you can see by selecting any action, choosing the Copy Selected Steps to Clipboard button, and then pasting your clipboard in any text editor. While it's perfectly suited for single-line functionality, spelling out the entire function call each time is considered too wordy for general programming, and this syntax is often used:

```
var theDOM = fw.getDocumentDOM();
```

Once this variable is declared and set to the DOM, all future references to the DOM use the variable instead. For example, a series of statements could read:

```
var theDOM = fw.getDocumentDOM();
theDoc.addNewOval({left:20, top:20, right:100, bottom:50});
theDOM.applyStyle(stylename, 0);
theDOM.setDocumentCanvasSizeToDocumentExtents(true);
fw.exportDocumentAs(theDOM, exportPath, exportOptionsGif);
fw.closeDocument(theDOM, false);
```

The variable used here, theDOM, is completely arbitrary, and you can feel free to choose your own.

The Fireworks API Document functions are, by far, the largest, most comprehensive group of functions. The quickest way that I've found to code a specific action is through the Copy Selected Steps to Clipboard button found on the History panel.

Follow these steps to avoid searching through the Extending Fireworks manual for a likely function:

1. Perform the desired action—such as drawing an oval or adding new frames.

2. If necessary, open the the History panel by choosing Window ⇨ History.

3. Selected the steps in the History panel that represent your action(s).

4. Choose the Copy Selected Steps to Clipboard button.

5. In your favorite text editor, paste the steps.

The steps copied from Fireworks will include all the code necessary to replicate your action, exactly. Usually, the next step in creating a command is to generalize the parameters so that the command can be applied in many circumstances. For example, when an oval is created in a Fireworks document, the Fireworks generated code looks like this:

```
fw.getDocumentDOM.addNewOval({left:20, top:20, right:100,
bottom:50});
```

When I've finished incorporating the function into a command, the same code looks like this:

```
theDOM.addNewOval({left:theLeft, top:theTop, right:theRight,
bottom:theBottom});
```

In addition to substituting a variable for the getDocumentDOM() function, I've done the same for Fireworks' absolute numbers for the left, top, right, and bottom values. These new variables can then be altered by a user prompt or another programming function.

Fireworks functions

One group of API functions is generically referred to as the Fireworks functions. These functions are concerned with general document manipulation—creating, exporting, saving, closing, and reverting—as well as executing find-and-replace operations and controlling floater accessibility. You'll also find the often used getDocumentDOM() function in this category.

Note The general Fireworks functions must be prefaced with either fireworks or fw— the initial fireworks and fw are interchangeable.

The `getDocumentDOM()` function isn't the only way to access the Document Object Model of a document. Both `createDocument()` and `createFireworksDocument()` return the DOM when they used in this manner:

```
var theDOM = fw.createDocument();
var theDOM =
fw.createFireworksDocument({x:400,y:500},{pixelsPerUnit:72,unit
s,"inch"},"#ffffff");
```

These two functions serve exactly the same purpose — to make a new document — but differ in that `fw.createDocument()` uses the current defaults, while with `createFireworksDocument()`, the size, resolution, and canvas color must be expressly stated.

Several functions in this category are used for connecting to files outside of Fireworks. With the `browseDocument()` function, you can view any HTML or other compatible file in the user's primary browser. One possible use for the `browseDocument()` function is to display a help file or programmatically preview an exported file in the browser. Two other functions aid in saving Fireworks files: `browseForFileURL()` and `browseForFolderURL()`. The `browseForFileURL()` function displays an Open or Save dialog box and returns a file URL like this:

```
file:///C|images/clientlogo.gif
```

Note   On a Macintosh, the drive letter (here, C) would be replaced by the drive name.

The `browseForFolder()` function, on the other hand, returns a path to a folder. This function is useful when you want to store a group of generated graphics in a common folder and will be naming them programatically. The `browseForFolderURL()` function returns a string like this:

```
file:///C|images
```

Note that the final forward slash is not provided; it's up to the programmer to add that character when saving files.

History Panel functions

As you might suspect from the name, the History Panel functions are concerned solely with the operations of that particular Fireworks' floating palette. These functions enable you to programmatically execute every function capable with the History panel, including the following functions:

✦ Clear all History steps.

✦ Find the number of current steps.

✦ Replay selected steps.

Although these functions might appear arcane at first glance, the History panel functions greatly extend the automation possibilities of Fireworks. As an example, I built a Repeat History command, which enables the user to repeat any series of selected steps — or just the last action taken — any number of times. The Repeat History command uses the History panel functions almost exclusively.

Here's the code for the entire command:

```
var theSteps = fw.historyPalette.getSelection();
  if (theSteps.length == 0) {
    alert("No steps selected.\nPlease selected at least one
step and repeat command.");
  } else {
  var theNum = prompt("Repeat History\nEnter the Number of
Repetitions Desired");
    for (i=0;i < parseInt(theNum);++i) {
      fw.historyPalette.replaySteps(theSteps);
    }
  }
```

The first line uses the History panel function to get the array of steps currently selected in the History panel:

```
var theSteps = fw.historyPalette.getSelection();
```

Next, a check is made to see if any steps are selected. If no actions are selected in the History panel, the user is asked to select one or more steps and then to reissue the following command:

```
if (theSteps.length == 0) {
    alert("No steps selected.\nPlease selected at least one
step and repeat command.");
  }
```

Because at least one step has been chosen, the user is then asked with the following function for the number of times the selected steps should be repeated :

```
var theNum = prompt("Repeat History\nEnter the Number of
Repetitions Desired");
```

The number of desired repetitions is stored in the variable, theNum, as a string. The next — and final — bit of code alters that string to a number and then replays the selected steps for the requested number of times.

```
for (i=0;i < parseInt(theNum);++i) {
    fw.historyPalette.replaySteps(theSteps);
  }
```

The Repeat History command is useful when combined with Fireworks Clone or Duplicate command. If, for example, I wanted to make ten stars, each rotated 5 degrees from one another, I would create the initial star, clone it, and then with the Modify ➪ Transform ➪ Numeric Transform command, rotate the clone 5 degrees. Next, I would select the Clone and Rotate steps from the History panel and issue the Repeat History command, specifying ten repetitions. A starburst effect is created.

You'll find the Repeat History command on the CD-ROM that accompanies this book, under Additional Extensions ➪ Joseph Lowery.

Building on the built-in Commands

One example of an application where a little code can go a long way is customizing Fireworks' built-in Commands. As useful as the Commands on the Animation sub-menu are, they're both locked at 12 frames; no matter what kind of animation you want to create, it will be 12 frames long.

When you run an animation Command, it displays a confirmation dialog box that explains the function of the Command. The confirmation dialog box is generated by the `confirm()` function, as you can see in the complete code for the Rotate Command:

```
// Tell the user what is going to happen
var message = confirm("This command creates a multi-frame¬
 animation by rotating the objects in the document.");

if (message == true)
{
   // Add frames for the animation
   var kNumFrames = 12;
   fw.getDocumentDOM().addFrames(kNumFrames, "after¬
current");
   fw.getDocumentDOM().selectAll();
   fw.getDocumentDOM().duplicateSelectionToFrames("all");
   var angle = 30;
   for (frameNum = 1; frameNum <= kNumFrames; frameNum++) {
      fw.getDocumentDOM().currentFrameNum = frameNum;
      fw.getDocumentDOM().selectAll();
      fw.getDocumentDOM().rotateSelection(angle,¬
"autoTrimImages transformAttributes");
      angle += 30;
   }
   // Set the export options
   fw.getDocumentDOM().setExportOptions({ exportFormat:"GIF¬
animation" });
}
```

The original code sets the variable "message" to the value returned by the confirm() function. If the user clicks OK, the confirm() function returns "true". If the user clicks Cancel, the confirm() function returns null (nothing). Either way, the value of the confirm() function is stored in the variable "message". The next step is "if the variable message is equal to true then run the code that's contained in the following braces." If the message variable is true, the first task within the braces is to set the number of frames—the kNumFrames variable—to 12.

Replacing the confirm() function in line 2 of the Command with a prompt() function will provide an excellent opportunity for users to specify how many frames they'd like their animation to cover. The two dialog boxes are contrasted in Figure 26-5.

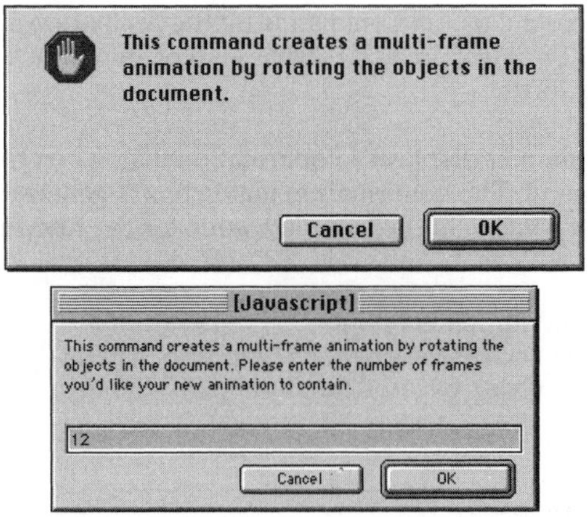

Figure 26-5: The original Animation Commands use a confirm() function to display a simple confirmation dialog box (top). If you substitute a prompt() function in the modified Command, it displays a dialog box (bottom) that enables you to input a number, which you will use as the number of frames for the resulting animation.

The primary task of the new code that you create is to set the kNumFrames variable—and, thus, the number of frames the Command creates—to a value that's input by the user when the Command runs. With the prompt() function, we can also prefill the text entry area with a default value.

It's also a good idea to try to anticipate unusual actions that the user may take. If the user enters anything other than a number, Fireworks ignores it, and the Command does nothing. It's easy, though, for the user to input 50, 100, or 500 frames and then regret it as Fireworks adds frame after frame after frame to their document, which could take quite a while on a slower computer system. Because the animation will eventually be an animated GIF, anything over 30 frames is probably unnecessary. A GIF of that size will create a slow animation with a huge file size. If users input a number more than 30, a confirmation dialog box appears that warns them and gives them the opportunity to cancel the Command before it begins.

You also need to set the angle variable so that regardless of how many frames are input, the animation always goes through one complete rotation. In the original Command, the number of frames is "hardwired" at 12, and the angle is hardwired at

30. It's no coincidence that 12 multiplied by 30 is 360, the number of degrees in one full rotation. In order to keep an animation limited to 360 degrees, you need to create the proper angle for each step in the rotation. Create the proper angle by dividing 360 degrees by the number of steps.

Tip

Before writing any code, it's a good idea to completely plan out the steps that you will create. I often start by writing what will eventually be the comments in the final script. A plain English explanation of the code is helpful when you read the code later, but it can also be helpful when writing the code.

The final code for the updated "RotatePlus" Command looks like this:

```
// This script was based heavily on the Rotate Command
// that shipped with Fireworks 3
// Tell the user what is going to happen and prompt them
// for the number of frames to create
var kNumFrames = prompt("This command creates a multi-frame¬
 animation by rotating the objects in the document. Please¬
 enter the number of frames you'd like your new animation¬
 to contain.", "12");
// if the number of frames is more than 36, ask the user
// for confirmation
if (kNumFrames > 36) {
   message = confirm("The number of frames you have asked for¬
 may take a while to generate. Continue?");
}
else { // if less than 37 frames, just go ahead
   message = true;
}
// Find the right rotation angle by dividing 360 degrees by
// the number of frames, so that our animation always makes
// one complete, 360 degree rotation
// this variable replaces "30" in the original script, which
// was appropriate only for 12 frames
var oneStepAngle = (360 / kNumFrames);
// if more than zero frames, and user said OK if over 36
// then get down to business
if (kNumFrames > 0 & message == true)
{
   fw.getDocumentDOM().addFrames(kNumFrames, "after current");
   fw.getDocumentDOM().selectAll();
   fw.getDocumentDOM().duplicateSelectionToFrames("all");
   // originally, this line set the angle to 30, which
   // is only appropriate for 12 steps
   // now, we set it to the oneStepAngle variable, which is
   // 360 degrees divided by the number of frames the user
   // asked for
   var angle = oneStepAngle;
   for (frameNum = 1; frameNum <= kNumFrames; frameNum++) {
      fw.getDocumentDOM().currentFrameNum = frameNum;
      fw.getDocumentDOM().selectAll();
      fw.getDocumentDOM().rotateSelection(angle,¬
```

```
"autoTrimImages transformAttributes");
    // originally, this line added 30 to the angle
    // now, we add the oneStepAngle variable in order to add
    // one more step
    angle += oneStepAngle;
}

// Set the export options
fw.getDocumentDOM().setExportOptions({ exportFormat:"GIF¬
animation" });
}
```

The nice thing about the resulting Command is (if that's all the user wants) that it works just like the original Command: click OK, and the user gets a 12-step, 360-degree, animated rotation of all of the objects in the document. But, if users want a different number of frames, they can have that, too.

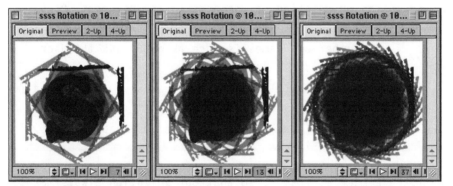

Figure 26-6: A modified Rotate Command becomes RotatePlus, enabling you to create animations with any number of steps. Starting from the left, these are 6-, 12-, and 36-step rotations of a stylized "S," shown with onion skinning.

Tip   When modifying another Command, a good first step is to copy and rename the original file. Always working on a copy prevents you from destroying the original, and it also ensures that you have an original copy to refer to if you run into trouble with your new Command. Before I modified the Rotate Command, I copied it to a file called RotatePlus and left it in the Commands/Animation folder while I worked on it. To test my Command as I went, all I had to do was save it and run it from the Commands menu in Fireworks.

Here are some points to keep in mind when you're developing Commands, or any kind of Scriptlet:

✦ Remember, Fireworks has a built-in JavaScript 1.4 interpreter built in. Therefore, many more Commands are available than just those offered by the Fireworks API, as robust as that is. JavaScript 1.4 offers regular expressions, search-and-replace functions, and much more.

✦ Be sure to end your scripts with a return on the final line of code. If you don't, Fireworks does not execute that line and errors could result.

✦ You can start building a script by performing the actions in Fireworks, selecting the corresponding steps in the History panel, and then copying the code to the clipboard with the Copy Steps to Clipboard button on the History panel. Paste the steps into a text editor and modify the code as desired.

Cross-Reference For more about the History panel, see Chapter 19.

Summary

Fireworks includes a comprehensive — to say the least — JavaScript API that allows scripted access to almost all of the application's features. Keep the following points in mind when you use Fireworks:

✦ Fireworks provides scripting access to almost every feature of the program.

✦ Nonstandard data types, such as colors, masks, and points, must be formatted correctly within your scripts.

✦ Five global methods are always available: `alert()`, `confirm()`, `prompt()`, `WRITE_HTML()`, and `write()`. Use these methods to display dialog boxes and receive user input, and to write text or HTML into exported documents.

✦ Fireworks provides five global objects that are always available:

✦ The App object provides access to many features of Fireworks itself, such as preferences and the platform that Fireworks is running on.

✦ The Document object provides access to individual documents, enabling you to change layers, set export options, or find out if a document has been changed since it was opened.

✦ The Errors object enables your scripts to provide meaningful error messages, regardless of which localized version of Fireworks they run on.

✦ The Files object can be used to copy files, create folders, and perform many other file-related tasks.

✦ The Find object provides access to Fireworks search-and-replace functionality.

✦ Objects, such as `BehaviorInfo`, `BehaviorsList`, `exportDoc`, `ImageMap`, and `ImageMapList`, provide control of exporting options within HTML export templates.

✦ Modifying Fireworks' built-in Commands is a good way to begin building your own scripts.

A Web Primer

◆ ◆ ◆ ◆

If you grew up in graphics using Photoshop, you're savvy with alpha channels and gradients, but the subtleties of Internet protocols and HTML code may have escaped you. With Fireworks you can make HTML and JavaScript as easily as GIFs and JPEGs, so you may find yourself creating whole Web sites — or at least prototypes — directly in Fireworks. A good grounding in the ways of the Web will help you to take full advantage of these powerful Fireworks features.

Note A significant portion of becoming truly Web-savvy is just knowing what the acronyms mean. While your eyes may glaze over at the mere mention of Protocol Suites, the ideas behind these lofty-sounding technical terms are actually fairly simple. Don't let unfamiliar technobabble deter you.

Formatting the Web

HyperText Markup Language, or HTML, is the page description language of the World Wide Web. Viewed in a browser, an HTML document such as the one shown in Figure A-1 is a formatted and readable page similar to a page in a printed magazine, complete with an assortment of typefaces and styles, images, and even multimedia such as streaming audio or movies.

But opening an HTML document in a text editor reveals the HTML code itself: formatting specifications called tags that tell the browser how to display text and how to link to media such as images and movies.

To view a Web page as HTML code, open it in your Web browser and

　　◆ If you are using Netscape Navigator or Communicator, choose View ➪ Page Source.

　　◆ If you are using Microsoft Internet Explorer, choose View ➪ Source.

✦ If you are using another browser, look for commands similar to the above, or consult the browser's documentation.

Typically, the HTML code for the current page will appear in your text editor or a special HTML code window, and will look something like the code in Figure A-2.

If what you see looks like Greek to you, don't worry. The seeming complexity of HTML hides a very simple structure.

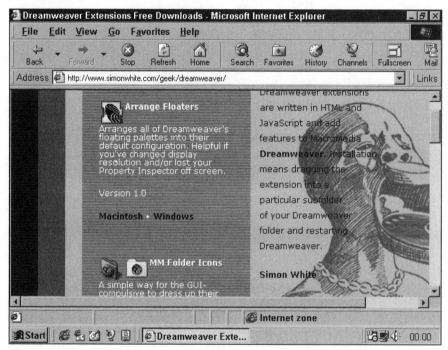

Figure A-1: Viewed in a browser, an HTML document is displayed with formatting such as typefaces and styles.

Tags and attributes

You can identify tags in HTML code by the angle brackets (<>) that surround them. Everything in an HTML document is either a tag, or is contained inside a tag. Tags specify whether a passage of text is a heading, a paragraph, or how that passage should be formatted. For example, to display *We Got the Funk* in bold text, you would surround it with the Bold tag, which is a letter *b*, like so:

```
<b>We Got the Funk</b>
```

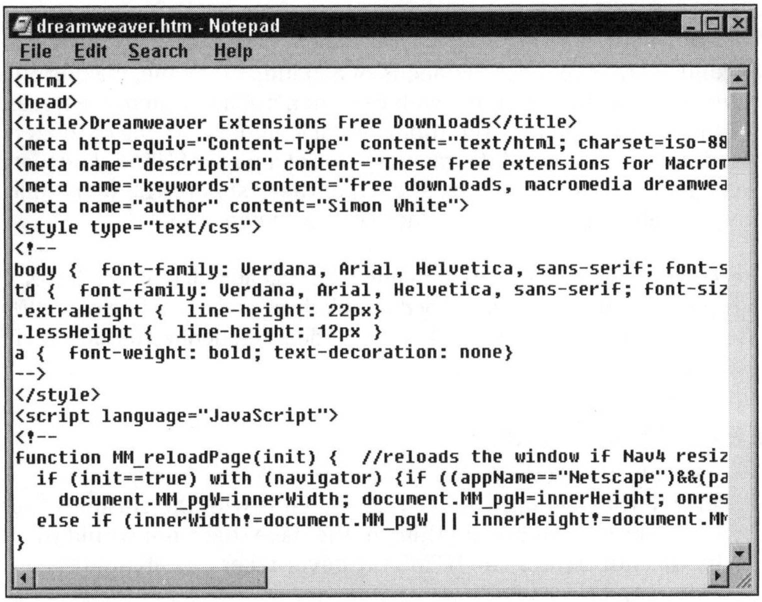


```
<html>
<head>
<title>Dreamweaver Extensions Free Downloads</title>
<meta http-equiv="Content-Type" content="text/html; charset=iso-88
<meta name="description" content="These free extensions for Macrom
<meta name="keywords" content="free downloads, macromedia dreamwea
<meta name="author" content="Simon White">
<style type="text/css">
<!--
body {  font-family: Verdana, Arial, Helvetica, sans-serif; font-s
td {  font-family: Verdana, Arial, Helvetica, sans-serif; font-siz
.extraHeight {  line-height: 22px}
.lessHeight {  line-height: 12px }
a {  font-weight: bold; text-decoration: none}
-->
</style>
<script language="JavaScript">
<!--
function MM_reloadPage(init) {  //reloads the window if Nav4 resiz
  if (init==true) with (navigator) {if ((appName=="Netscape")&&(pa
    document.MM_pgW=innerWidth; document.MM_pgH=innerHeight; onres
  else if (innerWidth!=document.MM_pgW || innerHeight!=document.MM
}
```

Figure A-2: Viewed in a text editor, the HTML document from Figure A-1 takes on an entirely different appearance.

Note the forward slash (/) in the previous code that marks the second tag as a closing tag. This convention is repeated again and again in HTML, although some tags don't require a closing tag.

An opening and closing tag pair says "anything within me is *this.*" For example, the `<title></title>` pair says "anything within me is the title." The `<b></b>` pair shown previously says "anything within me is bold."

Many tags can also have attributes that modify the formatting of the tag further; a tag that says "insert a table here" (the `<table>` tag) can have attributes that specify the width of the table, how thick the border should be, and more. Attributes are just placed within a tag. So a plain, bare-minimum opening `<table>` tag looks like this:

```
<table>
```

A `<table>` tag that specifies that the table should be 400 pixels wide and have a 3-pixel border looks like this:

```
<table width="400" border="3">
```

Although there are almost one hundred different HTML tags, the overwhelming majority of Web pages are created using only a handful of them.

Top ten tags

HTML has all kinds of tags to meet the needs of all kinds of people, making all kinds of pages. Fortunately for the beginning Web designer, not all of them are necessary to build almost everything on the Web today. A basic understanding of the ten most commonly used tags takes a lot of the mystery out of a page of HTML code, and Web pages in general. As we take a look at each of these super-tags, we'll build a simple example Web page in order to place the tags in context.

Note Don't necessarily worry about remembering every tag and all of its attributes. This section is primarily meant to demystify the underlying code structure of the World Wide Web. Even the most advanced HTML coders frequently consult an HTML reference guide to refine their work.

The HTML tag: <html></html>

The `<html>` tag simply says "everything within me is HTML." Every HTML document starts with the opening `<html>` tag, and ends with the closing `</html>` tag. Web browsers generally ignore anything in the page that's not within the `<html>` tag. Why? It's not HTML. The HTML tag never takes any attributes.

Tip XML (Extensible Markup Language) documents also contain an `<xml></xml>` tag pair that encloses all of the XML. Similarly, SMIL (Synchronized Multimedia Integration Language) documents have a `<smil></smil>` pair that holds all the SMIL code. These languages also use the / in their tags to specify closing tags.

Starting to build a Web page by adding the <html> tag looks like this:

```
<html>
</html>
```

The head tag: <head></head>

You can think of the `<head>` tag as a Web page's way of introducing itself to the browser. It's behind-the-scenes info that isn't displayed in the browser window itself. The `<head>` tag contains the title of the page and indexing information for search engines. Adding the `<head>` tag into our example Web page gives us this (new code is shown in bold text):

```
<html>
<head>
</head>
</html>
```

Note Other things you might find in a `<head>` tag are script functions that will be referenced by scripts in the body of the page (within a `<script>` tag) and CSS (Cascading StyleSheets) formatting information (contained in a `<style>` tag).

The title tag: <title></title>

The <title> tag simply contains the plain-language title of the page. This is a very important tag, because search engines often give the title a lot of weight when they index a page. In other words, if a user searches for *Pokemon,* the list of sites they receive from a search engine is more likely to contain sites with Pokemon in the title than sites that mention Pokemon in the body text but not in the title. The <title> tag always goes inside the <head> tag and should always be the first one right after the opening <head> tag; otherwise, some search engines won't find it. Adding a title to our Web page looks like this:

```
<html>
<head>
<title>An Example Page</title>
</head>
</html>
```

The meta tag: <meta></meta>

The <meta> tag allows you to store information about the page within the page itself. Think of <meta> tags as fields in a database. You can add as many <meta> tags to a page as you like, giving each one a unique name (the type of data) and content (the data). The most commonly used meta names are *description,* which contains a description of the page that some search engines show after the title in their results; and *keywords,* which contains keywords — separated by commas — that search engines use to index your page in their databases. Accurate and descriptive keywords in a keywords meta tag will lead to more interested users finding your page. Use as many as you like, but the first 16 are often given special weight, and repeating keywords (spamming the index) may cause a search engine not to index your page. There are also other <meta> tags in use, such as ones that contain the page's author. Now our example page looks like this:

```
<html>
<head>
<title>An Example Page</title>
<meta name="description" content="A Web page built as an¬
  example of the most common tags and where they go.">
<meta name="keywords" content="HTML, code, examples, learning,¬
  tags, markup languages, hypertexts, Web designs, Web¬
  authoring">
<meta name="author" content="Simon White">
</head>
</head>
</html>
```

Tip   Make your keywords plural. If you include the keyword mp3s, then Web surfers looking for mp3 or mp3s will find your page. Include common misspellings, too.

The body tag: <body></body>

The <body> tag is where the stuff you actually see in the browser window lives. Text, images, plug-ins, Java applets — it's all contained in the <body> tag. The <body> tag comes right after the <head> tag. The <body> tag almost always has some attributes that specify the background color and the text color of the page; otherwise, the page will be displayed in the user's default colors (which vary from user to user). Colors in HTML are usually specified in RGB color, written in hexadecimal notation. In this case, we'll use a white (#FFFFFF) background and black (#000000) text, so the code for our example page now looks like this:

```
<html>
<head>
<title>An Example Page</title>
<meta name="description" content="A Web page built as an¬
 example of the most common tags and where they go.">
<meta name="keywords" content="HTML, code, examples, learning,¬
 tags, markup languages, hypertexts, Web designs, Web¬
 authoring">
<meta name="author" content="Simon White">
</head>
<body bgcolor="#FFFFFF" text="#000000">
</body>
</html>
```

Now that it has a <body>, our example page could be displayed in a Web browser, but the only thing that would be shown would be the white background color.

The paragraph tag: <p></p>

Each opening and closing set of <p> tags contains a paragraph. Paragraphs can contain text, images, and just about anything that can appear on a Web page. Browsers leave a line space between paragraphs. You can add an align attribute to a paragraph tag to specify that it be aligned left, center, or right, as in the example code. If you leave the align attribute out, the paragraph is aligned left.

```
<html>
<head>
<title>An Example Page</title>
<meta name="description" content="A Web page built as an¬
 example of the most common tags and where they go.">
<meta name="keywords" content="HTML, code, examples, learning,¬
 tags, markup languages, hypertexts, Web designs, Web¬
 authoring">
<meta name="author" content="Simon White">
</head>
<body bgcolor="#FFFFFF" text="#000000">
<p>Here is a paragraph full of text.</p>
<p align="right">Here is a right-aligned paragraph full
 of text.</p>
</body>
</html>
```

Tip A closing </p> tag is not required by Web browsers, but it's good practice to use one anyway. XML, SMIL, and other HTML-like languages always require a closing tag, and the HTML 4 specification demands closing tags for complete compliance.

Viewed in a browser, as shown in Figure A-3, our Web page finally has some content.

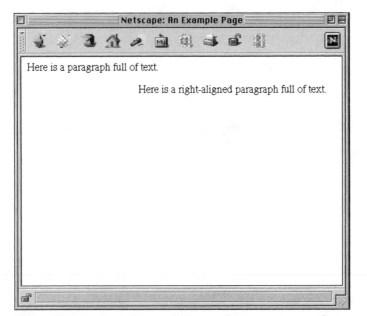

Figure A-3: Browsers leave a line space between paragraphs and align them according to the <p> tag's align attribute.

The anchor tag: <a></a>

The <a> (anchor) tag is the heart of the World Wide Web, because it's used to make hyperlinks. What kind of HyperText would we have without hyperlinks? It's easy to make a link: Simply surround text or images that you'd like to make into a link with an opening and closing <a> tag and give the tag an href attribute, like so:

```
<a href="http://www.google.com">Search at Google!</a>
```

The href attribute tells the browser what page to go to when the user clicks on *Search at Google!* Links are usually underlined and displayed in dark blue. Adding a link to the word *text* in our example page gives us this:

```
<html>
<head>
<title>An Example Page</title>
<meta name="description" content="A Web page built as an¬
 example of the most common tags and where they go.">
<meta name="keywords" content="HTML, code, examples, learning,¬
```

```
tags, markup languages, hypertexts, Web designs, Web¬
authoring">
<meta name="author" content="Simon White">
</head>
<body bgcolor="#FFFFFF" text="#000000">
<p>Here is a paragraph full of¬
 <a href="http://www.dictionary.com">text</a>.</p>
<p align="right">Here is a right-aligned paragraph full¬
 of text.</p>
</body>
</html>
```

The previous code looks like Figure A-4 when shown in a browser.

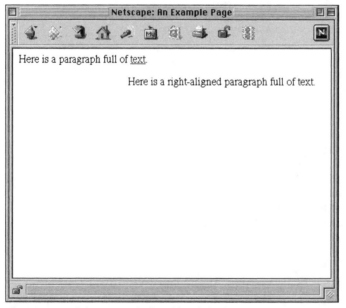

Figure A-4: Links are underlined by default.

The image tag: <img>

The <img> tag is the way you tell a browser, "display this particular image
file at this point in the page." Note that there is no closing tag for an <img> tag,
because it doesn't wrap around other tags or content. It's an image, plain and
simple. Although you don't have to put the width and height of the image as width
and height attributes, doing so will enable pages to load faster. An alt attribute is
also a good idea; it provides alternate text for text-only browsers, users who have
turned images off in their browsers, and visually impaired Web surfers. An <img>
tag can be placed within other tags, typically within paragraphs or tables, and
can even have an <a> tag wrapped around it to make the image into a link.

Images are placed in Web pages as illustrations, obviously, but they are also the only reliable way to put certain types of formatting into a page, and thus are often used for titles, logos, and such. In our example page, we will use one image as an illustration, and one as a page title.

Typically, image files are stored near the HTML file they belong to, either in the same folder, or in their own nearby folder, often called *images* or something similar. The ones for our example page are in the same folder, so the src attributes just contain their names, like so:

```
<html>
<head>
<title>An Example Page</title>
<meta name="description" content="A Web page built as an¬
 example of the most common tags and where they go.">
<meta name="keywords" content="HTML, code, examples, learning,¬
 tags, markup languages, hypertexts, Web designs, Web¬
 authoring">
<meta name="author" content="Simon White">
</head>
<body bgcolor="#FFFFFF" text="#000000">
<p><img src="example_title.gif" width="400" height="50"¬
 alt="An Example Page"></p>
<p>Here is a paragraph full of¬
 <a href="http://www.dictionary.com">text</a>.</p>
<p align="right">Here is a right-aligned paragraph full¬
 of text.</p>
<p><img src="mona.gif" width="125" height="160" alt="A¬
 generic placeholder image of the Mona Lisa."></p>
</body>
</html>
```

And the result will look something like Figure A-5.

You can also use an image from another folder or anywhere on the Web by supplying a valid URL to that image in the href attribute.

The font tag: <font></font>

Plain text can get pretty boring. Placing a <font> tag around text allows us to alter its formatting and specify a typeface with the face attribute, and a color with the color attribute. Colors are specified with RGB color names in hexadecimal notation, but which fonts you can use bears special attention. Fonts are typically specified with a list, such as "Arial, Helvetica, sans-serif," because the user must actually have the font you specify on their system. If not, then the browser goes to the second choice on the list, then the third, and so on. The options *serif* or *sans-serif* should always be the last choices in your font lists. These generic terms tell the browser to use a default serif (such as Times Roman) or sans-serif font (such as Helvetica).

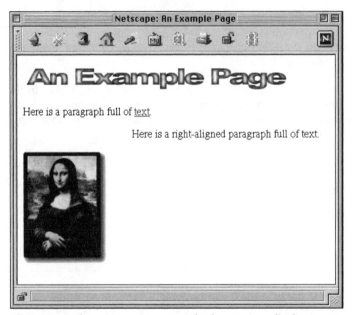

Figure A-5: The `<img>` tag causes the browser to display an image file, such as this Mona Lisa, within a Web page.

Tip   You can also use Bitstream's Dynamic Fonts to download any font with your page. They're viewable natively in Netscape 4+ and with the addition of a small ActiveX Control in IE 4+.

I'm going to bend the rules and go a bit beyond ten tags by also introducing you to two related tags: To make text bold, wrap it in `<b>` tags; to make it italicized, wrap it in `<i>` tags.

With the addition of `<font>`, `<b>`, and `<i>` tags, our example page now looks like this:

```
<html>
<head>
<title>An Example Page</title>
<meta name="description" content="A Web page built as an¬
 example of the most common tags and where they go.">
<meta name="keywords" content="HTML, code, examples, learning,¬
 tags, markup languages, hypertexts, Web designs, Web¬
 authoring">
<meta name="author" content="Simon White">
</head>
<body bgcolor="#FFFFFF" text="#000000">
<p><img src="example_title.gif" width="400" height="50"¬
 alt="An Example Page"></p>
```

```
<p><font face="Verdana, Helvetica, sans-serif"¬
color="FF0000"><i>Here</i> is a <b>paragraph</b> full of¬
<a href="http://www.dictionary.com">text</a>.</font></p>
<p align="right">Here is a right-aligned paragraph full¬
of text.</p>
<p><img src="mona.gif" width="125" height="160" alt="A¬
generic placeholder image of the Mona Lisa."></p>
</body>
</html>
```

Figure A-6 shows what our example page now looks like in a browser.

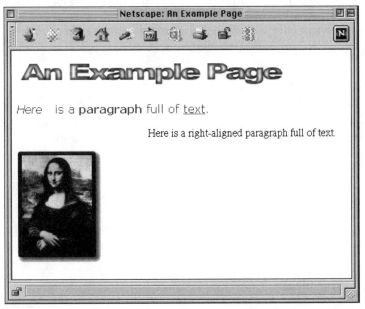

Figure A-6: The `<font>`, `<b>`, and `<i>` tags make the first paragraph of text look quite different from the second.

The table tag: <table></table>

The `<table>` tag was originally developed so that tables of data—similar to what you'd find in a spreadsheet—could be more easily displayed in Web pages. These days, it's more commonly used as a way of providing a formatting skeleton for an entire Web page, where elements such as text and images are placed within table cells so that they can appear at an approximate point on a page. The `<table>` tag is probably the hardest of the top 10 tags to grasp just by looking at it, which is why table tags are often created in visual editors, rather than by hand-coding.

Stretching the ten-tag limitation again, the `<table>` tag always contains two helpers: the `<tr>` (table row) tag and the `<td>` (table data) tag. The `<tr>` tag simply says, "everything within me is a table row." The `<td>` tag, which always goes within a `<tr>` tag, is a table cell. Columns aren't specified; they're implied by the number of cells in a row. An empty table with two rows and three columns would look like this:

```
<table>
<tr> <td></td> <td></td> <td></td> </tr>
<tr> <td></td> <td></td> <td></td> </tr>
</table>
```

Note that the string of three `<td></td>` pairs in each row implies the columns. If all tables were completely empty, formatting tables by hand would be much simpler, but once you start to fill them with things, they're a little harder to grasp at first glance. Wrapping the content in a table with three rows and two columns gives us this:

```
<html>
<head>
<title>An Example Page</title>
<meta name="description" content="A Web page built as an¬
 example of the most common tags and where they go.">
<meta name="keywords" content="HTML, code, examples, learning,¬
 tags, markup languages, hypertexts, Web designs, Web¬
 authoring">
<meta name="author" content="Simon White">
</head>
<body bgcolor="#FFFFFF" text="#000000">
<table width="500" border="0">
  <tr>
    <td colspan="2"><img src="example_title.gif" width="400"¬
height="50" alt="An Example Page"></td>
  </tr>
  <tr>
    <td> </td>
    <td> </td>
  </tr>
  <tr>
    <td><p><img src="mona.gif" width="125" height="160"¬
alt="A generic placeholder image of the Mona Lisa."></p></td>
    <td><p><font face="Verdana, Helvetica, sans-serif"¬
color="FF0000"><i>Here</i> is a <b>paragraph</b> full of¬
<a href="http://www.dictionary.com">text</a>.</font></p>
        <p align="right">Here is a right-aligned paragraph¬
full of text.</p>
    </td>
  </tr>
</table>
</body>
</html>
```

The finished example page, shown in Figure A-7, includes a title, indexing information, formatted text, a hyperlink, an image, and a table; all created with the most commonly used tags.

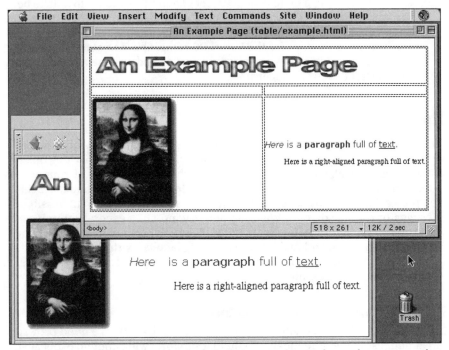

Figure A-7: Looking at the example page in Dreamweaver shows the structure that the <table> tag provides. Behind Dreamweaver is the same page in Navigator.

Tip If you hunger for even more tags, the next ones to learn might be <style>, <form>, <script>, and the comment tag. Consult an HTML reference such as Rob Schluter's HTML Tag List at http://utopia.knoware.nl/users/schluter/doc/tags/index.html.

Web Browser Variety Show

On an ideal Web, there would be a minimum set of things you could ask any Web browser to do and be guaranteed that they'd all do those things in a similar fashion, and do them well. If you stick to authoring for the feature set of Netscape Navigator 3.0, you can pretty much expect most browsers to provide most of the goods, but that still leaves you bumping up against different bugs in individual browsers or browser versions. If you author for a current Web standard such as CSS 1 (Cascading Style Sheets 1.0), then you will find browser support to often be sporadic and buggy. Either way, testing your work in as many browsers as possible is highly recommended, early in the design phase and often.

Tip   A Macintosh with Virtual PC installed is the ideal testing computer for any Web design shop, because you can run multiple versions of every Netscape, Microsoft, and AOL browser for Windows, Macintosh, and Linux, and also the WebTV viewer, all on the same machine (without multiple hard drive partitions or rebooting). The key to this is getting around IE and AOL for Windows' insistence that there be only one version of the same browser on each computer. Virtual PC circumvents this problem by allowing you to maintain multiple configurations, each corresponding to a different boot drive for the Virtual-PC-compatible computer, and each containing a different Windows or Linux configuration and a different browser (and/or set of installed browser plug-ins).

The browsers

Different projects may require you to target different audiences with different types of browsers. For example, if you're authoring a site that provides tips for using Windows 2000, you can expect the overwhelming majority of your audience to be using Internet Explorer 5 running on Windows 2000. An online magazine for Web professionals might have an audience that's using very current versions of IE or Navigator running on both Windows and Macintosh. A general shopping site will probably target pretty much anybody, including users of multiple versions of Macintosh, Windows, and AOL browsers. Being familiar with the capabilities and quirks of the browsers you're targeting and — as always — testing, testing, testing will avoid ugly surprises later.

Netscape Navigator (Communicator)

Navigator 1 and 2 are virtually nonexistent now. Navigator 3 is a good browser to target and test in if you're looking to build a site for a wide audience, because it was a very popular browser whose feature set was mimicked by browsers that came later. For the most part, if your page works well in Navigator 3, it may not need much more than a little tweaking to look very much the same in Navigator 4 and IE 4 and 5.

Navigator 4.x supports some CSS features, including layers, but not to World Wide Web Consortium (W3C) standards. It contains a widely-known bug that causes it not to reload a page without CSS formatting if the user resizes the browser window. Navigator 4.x is available for Windows, Macintosh, OS/2, Linux, and many, many other UNIX platforms. Keep in mind that browser plug-ins are platform dependent, and most exist only in Windows and Macintosh versions. When combined with a complete Internet suite, it's called Netscape Communicator, but the browser component is still the same.

Tip   Visit the World Wide Web Consortium at www.w3.org.

Navigator 5 will be a completely new product based on the open source work of the Mozilla.org team, which promises to provide complete support for HTML 4 and CSS

1 standards without exception, but as of this writing it is not yet available. Current builds look promising, though, and its open source status means that the HTML rendering engine — called *Gecko* — will likely be built into a range of software and hardware products such as other Web browsers or set-top boxes. Web professionals should definitely keep an eye on these developments.

Microsoft Internet Explorer

IE 1 and 2 were very limited in their feature sets and not widely used, and can be ignored completely. IE 3 includes some basic CSS features, but implemented poorly and in a completely different way than IE 4, so targeting CSS at IE 3 is not recommended. The Windows version doesn't support image swaps, but they fail without error. Keep this in mind if you create complex image swaps that don't make sense if they don't happen.

Tip   IE 3 is pretty rarely used now — at least some versions were not Y2K compatible or may require a patch — but the feature set survives in many AOL browsers based on it.

IE 4 for Windows generally renders HTML pages very well, and supports — albeit incompletely — a number of advanced Web technologies. It's reputation is marred by its forced integration with Windows and its refusal to play nice with a Netscape browser installed on the same machine.

Unfortunately, IE 4 for Windows and IE 4 for Macintosh are entirely different animals as far as the technologies they support and the way they render HTML. IE for Windows uses Windows-only technologies like ActiveX and VBScript (although it has shoddy support for Netscape Plug-ins and excellent JavaScript support as well). The Mac version uses Netscape Plug-ins and JavaScript exclusively, although its support for both in the 3 and 4 versions is the worst of any major browser. IE 4 for Macintosh and IE 5 for Macintosh are quite different as well, the latter based on Microsoft's new *Tazman* rendering engine, the most standards-based they've developed so far.

Note   There is also a UNIX version of IE 4, but it is not widely used or promoted.

America Online

AOL 3, 4, and 5 browsers are modified versions of Microsoft's Internet Explorer, but, unfortunately, the version numbers do not correspond. In other words, an AOL 4 browser may be based on IE 3 or IE 4. The major modification to keep in mind is that AOL browsers are single-window — they do not allow a second window to be opened.

Tip   For more about authoring for AOL see AOL's Webmaster page at `http://webmaster.aol.com`.

WebTV

WebTV has not exactly taken the world by storm, and its users remain a very small minority of the Web. Accessing the Web with a TV and a set-top box may be much more popular in the future, though, and future devices will no doubt learn some lessons from WebTV.

WebTV renders Web pages in a fairly unique way in order to account for the very low resolution of TV screens. The major point to note is that its "browser window" is fixed at 544 pixels wide and 378 tall. If your page is wider, it is squeezed to fit. If your page is longer, the user scrolls (a lot) to see the rest. WebTV only allows one browser window, and supports frames in a unique way: your frameset is converted to a table and then squeezed to fit into 544 pixels. WebTV will let you use any font you want to as long as it's 14-pixel bold sans-serif. Flash is Flash 2.0, and RealAudio is 3.0. One thing that WebTV does very well is play back MIDI files — in a software synthesizer based on technology from Beatnik, Inc.

There's no substitute for actually viewing your work as a WebTV user would see it. Thankfully, the WebTV people offer a free WebTV Viewer for Windows or Macintosh that goes a long way towards helping you make your pages WebTV-savvy. You can find it at `http://developer.webtv.net` and view it in Figure A-8.

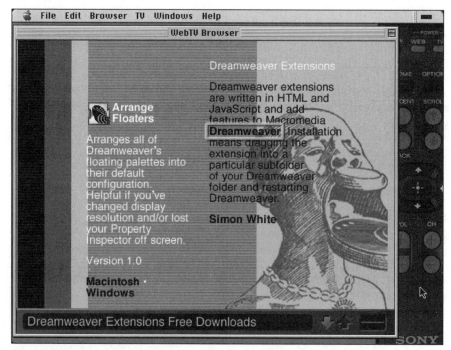

Figure A-8: The Web page from Figure A-1 is revisited in the WebTV Viewer 2.0 for Macintosh.

Cross-platform concerns

The Web can be surprisingly cross-platform, when you consider that Netscape browsers act similarly on Windows, Macintosh and Linux, but there are a few major caveats to keep in mind if you'd like your Web pages to look similar on different platforms.

Fonts

Before the Web existed, computer-based publishing was primarily print publishing. Choosing a font in a computer program has therefore traditionally meant choosing a point (pt) size. Displaying a 12pt font on a pixel-based computer display requires that the computer convert points, which are 1/72 of an inch, into pixels (px); the smallest dots a computer monitor can display.

Figure A-9 shows a Web page displayed on a Macintosh, where the specified 10pt font is displayed as a 10px font, because the Mac assumes 72dpi.

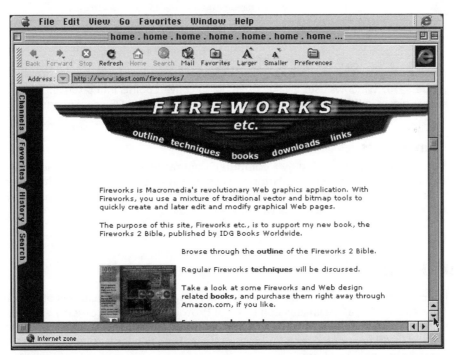

Figure A-9: Mac OS uses a value of 72 dpi to convert points into pixels, so fonts appear smaller in Mac OS browsers than they do in their Windows counterparts.

Figure A-10 shows the same Web page on a Windows computer, where the specified 10pt font is displayed as an 12-pixel font, because Windows assumes 96dpi.

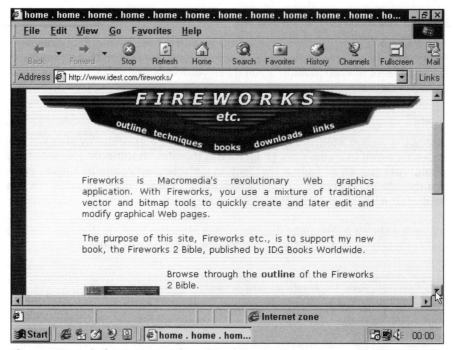

Figure A-10: Windows uses a value of 96 dpi to convert points into pixels, so fonts appear bigger in Windows browsers than they do in their Mac OS counterparts.

Form widgets

Form widgets are provided by a computer's operating system, not by the browser, and so are different on each platform, as shown in Figure A-11. Web authors need to be aware of this and allow for it in their designs, leaving extra space as necessary and testing on other platforms whenever possible.

Protocols

Information travels across the Internet according to the specifications of a protocol suite called TCP/IP (Transmission Control Protocol/Internet Protocol). A protocol suite is, quite simply, a collection of protocols, or agreements on how to do something. TCP/IP contains over a hundred of them, but we'll look at just the most commonly used ones here.

HTTP and HTTPS

HTTP, or HyperText Transfer Protocol, carries requests for HTML pages from Web browsers to servers, and carries HTML pages back from servers to browsers. As you may well imagine, this is a pretty common function on the World Wide Web. When a browser and server want to talk privately—during an e-commerce transaction, for example—they use the HTTPS protocol instead: HyperText Transfer Protocol Secure. When a browser is using HTTPS, a closed lock or similar icon is displayed for the user and information is encrypted before it's sent. All Web browsers support HTTP; most support HTTPS. An HTTP URL is written `http://opensrs.com`. An HTTPS URL is similar, except it uses an `https://` prefix.

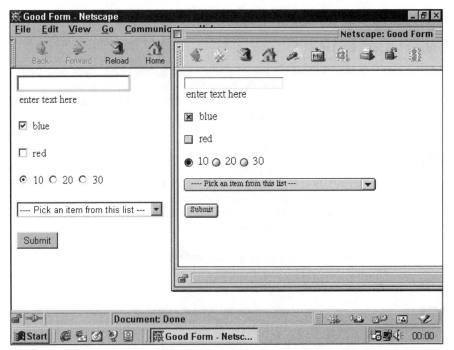

Figure A-11: Form widgets look different and are even slightly different sizes on each operating system.

FTP

FTP (File Transfer Protocol) allows for copying files between computers — even different kinds of computers — and for basic file manipulation functions, such as listing a folder of files on a remote computer. Browsers support rudimentary FTP, but a dedicated FTP Client such as WS FTP for Windows or Anarchie for Macintosh is needed to take full advantage of the control that FTP allows. Many FTP servers allow anonymous guest logins, where your e-mail address is your password and you have limited privileges. FTP URLs look like this: `ftp://ftp.panic.com`.

Tip   It may seem like *ftp* is specified twice in the URL `ftp://ftp.panic.com`, but that is not the case. The first ftp is the protocol, and the second ftp is the name of panic.com's FTP server. In the same way, HTTP servers are often named `www`, as in `http://www.panic.com`.

SMTP and POP

SMTP, or **S**imple **M**ail **T**ransfer **P**rotocol, allows different computers on a network to route e-mail to each other. POP, or **P**ost **O**ffice **P**rotocol, is a newer method for receiving mail. E-mail clients such as Netscape Messenger or Microsoft Outlook Express use SMTP and POP to send and receive e-mail.

NNTP

NNTP (Network News Transfer Protocol) is used by Internet news readers to query news servers, and by news servers to deliver news messages. NNTP is responsible for the Usenet news we all know and love. An NNTP URL looks like this: `news://forums.macromedia.com/macromedia.fireworks`.

Note   Other protocols use prefixes that are the same as their names — `ftp://` for FTP, for example — but NNTP URLs use the `news://` prefix.

RTSP

RTSP, or **R**eal-**T**ime **S**treaming **P**rotocol is perhaps the sexiest Internet protocol, allowing for the efficient transfer of streaming multimedia files such as audio or video over the Internet. The real-time refers to the fact that audio and video files need to get to the client in a timely fashion so as not to interrupt the presentation. Server software such as QuickTime Streaming Server or RealServer use RTSP to send information to the QuickTime Player or RealPlayer respectively (see Figure A-12). An RTSP URL starts with an `rtsp://` prefix.

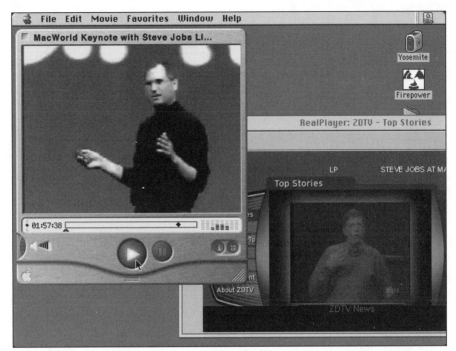

Figure A-12: QuickTime Player (left) and RealPlayer both use RTSP to receive streaming multimedia (in this case video) over the Internet.

✦   ✦   ✦

Keyboard Shortcuts

Fireworks includes a full complement of keyboard shortcuts to cut down on the time and trouble it takes to
access commonly used commands. We'll go menu by menu in
the first of the tables that follow. In Table B-11, you'll find key
shortcuts for the Fireworks Toolbox that will aid in quickly
selecting commonly-used tools. In Table B-12, you'll find my
Top Ten Fireworks Key Shortcuts.

Note Commands in **bold** text are new or have changed menu
locations in Fireworks 3.

The File Menu

The File menu contains commands for file handling and
import and export functions. Table B-1 details its keyboard
shortcuts.

Table B-1
File Menu Keyboard Shortcuts

Command	Windows	Macintosh
New	Ctrl+N	Command+N
Open	Ctrl+O	Command+O
Open Multiple	Ctrl+Shift+O	Command+Shift+O
Scan ➪ Twain Acquire	n/a	n/a
Scan ➪ Twain Source	n/a	n/a
Scan ➪ Your Photoshop Acquire Plug-Ins (Macintosh only)	n/a	n/a
Close	Ctrl+F4	Command+W
Save	Ctrl+S	Command+S
Save As	Ctrl+Shift+S	Command+Shift+S
Save a Copy	n/a	n/a
Update HTML	n/a	n/a
Revert	n/a	n/a
Import	Ctrl+R	Command+R
Export	Ctrl+Shift+R	Command+Shift+R
Export Special ➪ Selected Slice	n/a	n/a
Export Special ➪ Layers/Frames to Files	n/a	n/a
Export Special ➪ CSS Layers	n/a	n/a
Export Special ➪ Lotus Domino Image Well	n/a	n/a
Export Special ➪ Flash SWF	n/a	n/a
Export Special ➪ Illustrator 7	n/a	n/a
Export Preview	Ctrl+Shift+X	Command+Shift+X
Export Wizard	n/a	n/a
Batch Process	n/a	n/a
Run Script	n/a	n/a
Preview in Browser ➪ Preview in Primary Browser	F12	F12
Preview in Browser ➪ Preview in Secondary Browser	Shift+F12	Shift+F12
Preview in Browser ➪ Set Primary Browser	n/a	n/a
Preview in Browser ➪ Set Secondary Browser	n/a	n/a
Page Setup	n/a	n/a

Command	Windows	Macintosh
Print	Ctrl+P	Command+P
HTML Properties	n/a	n/a
Preferences	n/a	n/a
Recent Files (Windows Only)	n/a	n/a
Exit (Quit)	Alt+F4	Command+Q

The Edit Menu

The Edit menu allows you to select, duplicate, or remove objects. Cut, Copy, and Paste are standard on all programs; others, such as Paste Attributes, are unique to Fireworks. Table B-2 details the Edit menu's key shortcuts.

Table B-2 Edit Menu Keyboard Shortcuts		
Command	**Windows**	**Macintosh**
Undo	Ctrl+Z	Command+Z
Redo	Ctrl+Shift+Z	Command+Shift+Z
Cut	Ctrl+X	Command+X
Copy	Ctrl+C	Command+C
Copy as Paths	n/a	n/a
Copy HTML Code	n/a	n/a
Paste	Ctrl+V	Command+V
Clear	Backspace (or Delete)	Delete
Paste Inside	Ctrl+Shift+V	Command+Shift+V
Paste Attributes	Ctrl+Alt+Shift+V	Command+Option+Shift+V
Select All	Ctrl+A	Command+A
Deselect	Ctrl+D	Command+D
Superselect	Ctrl+Up Arrow	Command+Up Arrow
Subselect	Ctrl+Down Arrow	Command+Down Arrow
Select Inverse	Ctrl+Shift+I	Command+Shift+I

Continued

Table B-2 (continued)

Command	Windows	Macintosh
Feather	n/a	n/a
Select Similar	n/a	n/a
Modify Marquee ⇨ Expand	n/a	n/a
Modify Marquee ⇨ Contract	n/a	n/a
Modify Marquee ⇨ Border	n/a	n/a
Modify Marquee ⇨ Smooth	n/a	n/a
Duplicate	Ctrl+Alt+D	Command+Option+D
Clone	Ctrl+Shift+C	Command+Shift+C
Find and Replace	n/a	n/a
Crop Selected Image	Ctrl+Alt+C	Command+Option+C
Crop Document	n/a	n/a

The View Menu

With the commands on the View menu, you can zoom in or out on your work or view a grid or guides to assist with layout. Table B-3 details its key shortcuts.

Table B-3
View Menu Keyboard Shortcuts

Command	Windows	Macintosh
Zoom In	Ctrl+Plus	Command+Plus
Zoom Out	Ctrl+Minus	Command+Minus
Magnification ⇨ 6%	n/a	n/a
Magnification ⇨ 12%	n/a	n/a
Magnification ⇨ 25%	n/a	n/a
Magnification ⇨ 50%	Ctrl+5	Command+5
Magnification ⇨ 100%	Ctrl+1	Command+1
Magnification ⇨ 200%	Ctrl+2	Command+2
Magnification ⇨ 400%	Ctrl+4	Command+4

Command	Windows	Macintosh
Magnification ⇨ 800%	Ctrl+8	Command+8
Magnification ⇨ 1600%	n/a	n/a
Magnification ⇨ 3200%	Ctrl+3	Command+3
Magnification ⇨ 6400%	Ctrl+6	Command+6
Fit Selection	Ctrl+Zero	Command+Zero
Fit All	Ctrl+Alt+Zero	Command+Option+Zero
Full Display	Ctrl+K	Command+K
Macintosh Gamma (Windows only)	n/a	n/a
Windows Gamma (Macintosh only)	n/a	n/a
Hide Selection	Ctrl+M	Command+M
Show All	Ctrl+Shift+M	Command+Shift+M
Hide Edges	Ctrl+H	Command+H
Hide Panels	Ctrl+Shift+H	Command+Shift+H
Rulers	Ctrl+Alt+R	Command+Option+R
Grid	Ctrl+Apostrophe	Command+Apostrophe
Grid Options ⇨ Snap To Grid	Ctrl+Shift+Apostrophe	Command+Shift+Apostrophe
Grid Options ⇨ Edit Grid	Ctrl+Alt+G	Command+Option+G
Guides	Ctrl+Semicolon	Command+Semicolon
Slice Guides	Ctrl+Alt+Shift+Semicolon	Command+Option+Shift+Semicolon
Guide Options ⇨ Lock Guides	Ctrl+Alt+Semicolon	Command+Option+Semicolon
Guide Options ⇨ Snap to Guides	Ctrl+Shift+Semicolon	Command+Shift+Semicolon
Guide Options ⇨ Edit Guides	Ctrl+Alt+Shift+G	Command+Option+Shift+G
Status Bar (Windows only)	n/a	n/a

The Insert Menu

The Insert menu contains objects you can insert into your documents. Table B-4 details the items available on the Insert menu and their key shortcuts.

Table B-4 Insert Menu Keyboard Shortcuts		
Command	Windows	Macintosh
New Button	n/a	n/a
New Symbol	Ctrl+F8	Command+F8
Convert to Symbol	F8	F8
Libraries ⇨ Your Libraries	n/a	n/a
Libraries ⇨ Other	n/a	n/a
Hotspot	Ctrl+Shift+U	Command+Shift+U
Slice	n/a	n/a
Behaviors	n/a	n/a
Image	Ctrl+R	Command+R
Empty Image	Ctrl+Alt+Y	Command+Option+Y
Layer	n/a	n/a
Frame	n/a	n/a

The Modify Menu

The Modify menu lists commands for altering existing selections. Its key shortcuts are detailed in Table B-5.

Table B-5 Modify Menu Keyboard Shortcuts		
Command	Windows	Macintosh
Image Size	n/a	n/a
Canvas Size	n/a	n/a
Canvas Color	n/a	n/a

Command	Windows	Macintosh
Trim Canvas	n/a	n/a
Rotate Canvas ⇨ Rotate 180°	n/a	n/a
Rotate Canvas ⇨ Rotate 90° CW	n/a	n/a
Rotate Canvas ⇨ Rotate 90° CCW	n/a	n/a
Symbol ⇨ Edit Symbol	n/a	n/a
Symbol ⇨ Tween Instances	Ctrl+Alt+Shift+T	Command+Option+Shift+T
Symbol ⇨ Break Link	n/a	n/a
Image Object	Ctrl+E	Command+E
Exit Image Edit	Ctrl+Shift+D	Command+Shift+D
Path Edge ⇨ Hard	n/a	n/a
Path Edge ⇨ Anti-Alias	n/a	n/a
Path Edge ⇨ Feather	n/a	n/a
Transform ⇨ Free Transform	Ctrl+T	Command+T
Transform ⇨ Scale	n/a	n/a
Transform ⇨ Skew	n/a	n/a
Transform ⇨ Distort	n/a	n/a
Transform ⇨ Numeric Transform	Ctrl+Shift+T	Command+Shift+T
Transform ⇨ Rotate 180°	n/a	n/a
Transform ⇨ Rotate 90° CW	Ctrl+9	Command+9
Transform ⇨ Rotate 90° CCW	Ctrl+7	Command+7
Transform ⇨ Flip Horizontal	n/a	n/a
Transform ⇨ Flip Vertical	n/a	n/a
Transform ⇨ Remove Transformations	n/a	n/a
Arrange ⇨ Bring to Front	Ctrl+F	Command+F
Arrange ⇨ Bring Forward	Ctrl+Shift+F	Command+Shift+F
Arrange ⇨ Send Backward	Ctrl+Shift+B	Command+Shift+B
Arrange ⇨ ⇨ Send to Back	Ctrl+B	Command+B
Align ⇨ Left	Ctrl+Alt+1	Command+Option+1
Align ⇨ Center Vertical	Ctrl+Alt+2	Command+Option+2

Continued

	Table B-5 (continued)	
Command	**Windows**	**Macintosh**
Align ➪ Right	Ctrl+Alt+3	Command+Option+3
Align ➪ Top	Ctrl+Alt+4	Command+Option+4
Align ➪ Center Horizontal	Ctrl+Alt+5	Command+Option+5
Align ➪ Bottom	Ctrl+Alt+6	Command+Option+6
Align ➪ Distribute Widths	Ctrl+Alt+7	Command+Option+7
Align ➪ Distribute Heights	Ctrl+Alt+9	Command+Option+9
Join	Ctrl+J	Command+J
Split	Ctrl+Shift+J	Command+Shift+J
Combine ➪ Union	n/a	n/a
Combine ➪ Intersect	n/a	n/a
Combine ➪ Punch	n/a	n/a
Combine ➪ Crop	n/a	n/a
Alter Path ➪ Simplify	n/a	n/a
Alter Path ➪ Expand Stroke	n/a	n/a
Alter Path ➪ Inset Path	n/a	n/a
Merge Images	Ctrl+Shift+Alt+Z	Command+Shift+Option+Z
Merge Layers	n/a	n/a
Group	Ctrl+G	Command+G
Mask Group ➪ Mask to Image	Ctrl+Shift+G	Command+Shift+G
Mask Group ➪ Mask to Path	n/a	n/a
Ungroup	Ctrl+U	Command+U

The Text Menu

The Text menu allows you to change the formatting options for text objects, or convert them to paths. Table B-6 details Text menu key shortcuts.

Table B-6
Text Menu Keyboard Shortcuts

Command	Windows	Macintosh
Font ⇨ Your Font List	n/a	n/a
Size ⇨ Other	n/a	n/a
Size ⇨ 8 to 120	n/a	n/a
Style ⇨ Plain	Ctrl+Alt+Shift+P	Command+Option+Shift+P
Style ⇨ Bold	Ctrl+Alt+Shift+B	Command+Option+Shift+B
Style ⇨ Italic	Ctrl+Alt+Shift+I	Command+Option+Shift+I
Style ⇨ Underline	Ctrl+Alt+Shift+U	Command+Option+Shift+U
Align ⇨ Left	Ctrl+Alt+Shift+L	Command+Option+Shift+L
Align ⇨ Center	Ctrl+Alt+Shift+C	Command+Option+Shift+C
Align ⇨ Right	Ctrl+Alt+Shift+R	Command+Option+Shift+R
Align ⇨ Justified	Ctrl+Alt+Shift+J	Command+Option+Shift+J
Align ⇨ Stretched	Ctrl+Alt+Shift+S	Command+Option+Shift+S
Align ⇨ Top	n/a	n/a
Align ⇨ Center	n/a	n/a
Align ⇨ Bottom	n/a	n/a
Align ⇨ Justified	n/a	n/a
Align ⇨ Stretched	n/a	n/a
Editor	Ctrl+Shift+E	Command+Shift+E
Attach to Path	Ctrl+Shift+Y	Command+Shift+Y
Detach from Path	n/a	n/a
Orientation ⇨ Rotate Around Path	n/a	n/a
Orientation ⇨ Vertical	n/a	n/a
Orientation ⇨ Skew Vertical	n/a	n/a
Orientation ⇨ Skew Horizontal	n/a	n/a
Reverse Direction	n/a	n/a
Convert to Paths	Ctrl+Shift+P	Command+Shift+P

The Commands Menu

The Commands menu is completely new in Fireworks 3. Fireworks Commands are written in JavaScript and can be added to Fireworks by the user in order to customize the feature set to taste. Although the Commands menu does not include any key shortcuts, it is detailed in Table B-7 for the sake of completeness and for those using this section as a command reference.

For more about the new Commands menu, see Chapter 19.

Table B-7 Commands Menu Keyboard Shortcuts		
Command	**Windows**	**Macintosh**
Edit Command List	n/a	n/a
Animation ⇨ Rotate	n/a	n/a
Animation ⇨ Rotate and Scale	n/a	n/a
Batch a Command	n/a	n/a
Creative ⇨ Convert to Grayscale	n/a	n/a
Creative ⇨ Convert to Sepia Tone	n/a	n/a
Creative ⇨ Create Picture Frame	n/a	n/a
Document ⇨ Center in Document	n/a	n/a
Document ⇨ Hide Other Layers	n/a	n/a
Document ⇨ Lock Other Layers	n/a	n/a
Document ⇨ Reverse All Frames	n/a	n/a
Document ⇨ Reverse Frame Range	n/a	n/a
Panel Layout Sets ⇨ Your Panel Layout Sets	n/a	n/a
Panel Layout Sets ⇨ 1024x768 / 800x600	n/a	n/a
Panel Layout	n/a	n/a
Web ⇨ Create Shared Palette	n/a	n/a
Web ⇨ Set Alt Tags	n/a	n/a

The Xtras Menu

Xtras are add-on image filters (usually Photoshop-compatible) that expand the capabilities of Fireworks. Table B-8 details the standard Xtras that are included with Fireworks. Your Xtras menu will have additional options if you have installed third-party Xtras.

Table B-8
Xtras Menu Keyboard Shortcuts

Command	Windows	Macintosh
Repeat Xtra	Ctrl+Alt+Shift+X	Command+Option+Shift+X
Adjust Color ⇨ Auto Levels	n/a	n/a
Adjust Color ⇨ Brightness/Contrast	n/a	n/a
Adjust Color ⇨ Curves	n/a	n/a
Adjust Color ⇨ Hue/Saturation	n/a	n/a
Adjust Color ⇨ Invert	n/a	n/a
Adjust Color ⇨ Levels	n/a	n/a
Blur ⇨ Blur	n/a	n/a
Blur ⇨ Blur More	n/a	n/a
Blur ⇨ Gaussian Blur	n/a	n/a
Other ⇨ Convert to Alpha	n/a	n/a
Other ⇨ Find Edges	n/a	n/a
Sharpen ⇨ Sharpen	n/a	n/a
Sharpen ⇨ Sharpen More	n/a	n/a
Sharpen ⇨ Unsharp Mask	n/a	n/a
Eye Candy 3.1 LE ⇨ Cutout	n/a	n/a
Eye Candy 3.1 LE ⇨ Motion Trail	n/a	n/a

The Window Menu

The Window menu manages document windows and also Fireworks panels and inspectors. Through this menu you can open, close, arrange, bring to the front, or hide all of Fireworks' windows. The Window menu key shortcuts are detailed in Table B-9.

> **Tip**
>
> All the commands for the various panels and inspectors are toggles. Select once to view a floating window; select again to hide it.

Table B-9
Window Menu Keyboard Shortcuts

Command	Windows	Macintosh
New Window	Ctrl+Alt+N	Command+Option+N
Toolbars ⇨ Main (Windows only)	n/a	n/a
Toolbars ⇨ Modify (Windows only)	n/a	n/a
Toolbars ⇨ View Controls (Windows only)	n/a	n/a
Toolbox	Ctrl+Alt+T	Command+Option+T
Optimize	n/a	n/a
Object	Ctrl+I	Command+I
Stroke	Ctrl+Alt+B	Command+Option+B
Fill	Ctrl+Alt+F	Command+Option+F
Effect	Ctrl+Alt+E	Command+Option+E
Color Table	n/a	n/a
Swatches	Ctrl+Alt+S	Command+Option+S
Color Mixer	Ctrl+Alt+M	Command+Option+M
Tool Options	Ctrl+Alt+O	Command+Option+O
Layers	Ctrl+Alt+L	Command+Option+L
Frames	Ctrl+Alt+K	Command+Option+K
History	n/a	n/a
Info	Ctrl+Alt+I	Command+Option+I
Behaviors	Ctrl+Alt+H	Command+Option+H
URL	Ctrl+Alt+U	Command+Option+U
Styles	Ctrl+Alt+J	Command+Option+J
Library	n/a	n/a
Find and Replace	n/a	n/a
Project Log	n/a	n/a
Cascade	n/a	n/a
Tile Horizontal	n/a	n/a
Tile Vertical	n/a	n/a
Your Open Documents List	n/a	n/a

The Help Menu

The final menu, the Help menu, offers access to Fireworks' online manual, tutorial, and even the Fireworks Web site. Table B-10 details its key shortcuts.

Table B-10 Help Menu Keyboard Shortcuts		
Command	**Windows**	**Macintosh**
About Balloon Help (Macintosh only)	n/a	n/a
Show Balloons (Macintosh only)	n/a	n/a
Using Fireworks	F1	n/a
Index	n/a	n/a
Tutorial	n/a	n/a
What's New in Version 3 (What's New)	n/a	n/a
Fireworks Support Center	n/a	n/a
Fireworks Product Web Site	n/a	n/a
Register Fireworks	n/a	n/a
About Fireworks (Windows only)	n/a	n/a

Tip Mac OS 8/9 users can display the About Fireworks dialog box by choosing Apple Menu ⇨ About Fireworks.

The Toolbox

As well as providing key shortcuts for menu commands, Fireworks also enables you to use the keyboard to change the active tool quickly and easily. Table B-11 describes each tool's key shortcut.

Note Some of the key shortcuts act as a toggle between tools that are similar. For example, V (or Zero) toggles between the Pointer and the Select Behind tools, and M toggles between the square and ellipse marquee tools. The R key is even more special: it cycles through a list of seven tools.

Table B-11
Toolbox Keyboard Shortcuts

Button	Name	Shortcut
	Pointer	V or Zero
	Select Behind	V or Zero
	Export Area	J
	Subselection	A
	Marquee	M
	Ellipse Marquee	M
	Crop	C
	Lasso	L
	Polygon Lasso	L
	Magic Wand	W
	Hand	H or press and hold the spacebar
	Magnify	Z
	Line	N
	Pen	P
	Rectangle	R
	Ellipse	R
	Polygon	G
	Text	T

Button	Name	Shortcut
	Pencil	Y
	Brush	B
	Redraw Path	B
	Scale	Q
	Skew	Q
	Distort	Q
	Freeform	Period
	Reshape Area	Period
	Path Scrubber (+)	U
	Path Scrubber (–)	U
	Eyedropper	I
	Paint Bucket	K
	Eraser / Knife	E
	Rubber Stamp	K
	Hotspot	R
	Ellipse Hotspot	R
	Polygon Hotspot	R
	Slice	R
	Polygon Slice	R

Top Ten Fireworks Key Shortcuts

Of course, you'll want to learn universal key shortcuts such as Open, Save, and Close (see Table B-1), and Select All, Cut, Copy, and Paste (see Table B-2). But once you've got those down, Table B-12 contains my recommendations for the most useful Fireworks-specific key shortcuts, presented with the Toolbox first, and then going across the menus from left to right.

Table B-12 Top Ten Fireworks Key Shortcuts		
Command	Windows	Macintosh
Pointer / Select Behind Tool	V or Zero	V or Zero
Text Tool	T	T
View ⇨ Magnification ⇨ 50%, 100%, 200%, 400%	Ctrl+5, 1, 2, 4	Command+5, 1, 2, 4
Deselect	Ctrl+D	Command+D
Edit ⇨ Duplicate	Ctrl+Alt+D	Command+Option+D
Modify ⇨ Image Object	Ctrl+E	Command+E
Modify ⇨ Transform ⇨ Free Transform	Ctrl+T	Command+T
Modify ⇨ Transform ⇨ Numeric Transform	Ctrl+Shift+T	Command+Shift+T
Modify ⇨ Align ⇨ Center Vertical	Ctrl+Alt+2	Command+Option+2
Modify ⇨ Align ⇨ Center Horizontal	Ctrl+Alt+5	Command+Option+5

✦   ✦   ✦

What's on the CD-ROM

The CD-ROM accompanying the *Fireworks 3 Bible* contains the following:

+ Fully functioning trial versions of Macromedia's Fireworks 3, Dreamweaver 3, Flash 4, and FreeHand 9

+ Fireworks-compatible filters from leading manufacturers, such as Alien Skin and Xaos Tools

+ A time-limited demo of Pantone's ColorWeb Pro

+ Sample online courses in both Fireworks and Dreamweaver from eHandsOn

Also included are a wide range of commands, strokes, gradents, textures, and custom HTML templates designed to make your work more productive from some of the finest designers working with Fireworks today. Finally, you'll also find several sample graphics from the book, for you to inspect, modify, and experiment with at your leisure.

Using the CD-ROM

The CD-ROM is a "hybrid" CD-ROM, which means that it contains one section for Windows and one section for Macintosh. Your Operating System will automatically choose the correct section.

Several files, primarily the Macromedia trial programs and the additional commercial programs, are compressed. Double-click these files to begin the installation procedure. Most other files on the CD-ROM are not compressed and can be simply copied from the CD-ROM to your system by using your file manager. A few of the Fireworks extensions that include files that must be placed in different folders are also compressed.

Where possible, the file structure of the CD-ROM replicates the structure that Fireworks 3 sets up when it is installed. For example, textures are found in the Fireworks 3/Settings/Textures folder on both the CD-ROM and the folder that the Fireworks 3 installer creates on your computer.

Files and Programs on the CD-ROM

The *Fireworks 3 Bible* companion CD-ROM contains a host of programs and auxiliary files to assist your exploration of Fireworks, as well as your Web page design work in general. A description of the files and programs on the CD-ROM follows.

Fireworks 3, Dreamweaver 3, Flash 4, and FreeHand 9 trials

If you haven't had a chance to work with Fireworks (or Dreamweaver, Flash, or Free Hand), the CD-ROM offers fully functioning trial versions of four key Macromedia programs for both Macintosh and Windows systems. Each of these trials can be used for 30 days; they cannot be reinstalled for additional use time.

To install a trial, simply double-click its installer icon in the main folder of the CD-ROM and follow the installation instructions on your screen.

Caution The trial versions of the Macromedia programs are very sensitive to system date changes. If you alter your computer's date, the programs will "time out" and will no longer be functional.

The full Fireworks version comes with a wonderful assortment of styles. To sample this work, visit the Fireworks Web site at www.macromedia.com/software/fireworks.

Additional programs

Fireworks 3 is definitely one program that "plays well with others." Virtually any Photoshop-compatible plug-in can be used as a Fireworks Effect — good news if you're a Photoshop user or have Photoshop-compatible filters from another application. Several of the leading filter developers have kindly loaned their programs for inclusion on this CD-ROM. In addition to the filters described in this section, the world-renowned color specialist, Pantone, has contributed a program, ColorWeb Pro, to help ease the transition for designers from the world of print to the Web.

Xenofex from Alien Skin

Alien Skin Software has contributed a trial version of a filter collection: Xenofex. Xenofex is a collection of inspirational special effects that will energize any graphics project. Realistic natural phenomena and sophisticated distortions have never been easier to create.

Xaos Tools's Total Xaos Filters

Total Xaos is a bundle of three Fireworks-compatible plug-ins: Paint Alchemy, Terrazo, and TypeCaster. Paint Alchemy is great for painterly special effects, Terrazo makes superb seamless tiles, and TypeCaster turns any text into a 3D wonder—without any 3D experience required.

ColorWeb Pro from Pantone

Many new Web designers are not new to design at all and bring a rich history— as well as a client list—from their print backgrounds. One constant in print color reproduction is the Pantone Color System. Many clients require that all of their graphics, whether intended for print or for the Internet, conform to a specific selection of Pan-tone colors. The ColorWeb Pro application translates Pantone colors into their RGB equivalents.

You'll find a special technique for using ColorWeb Pro with Fireworks in Chapter 7.

Online learning

What better place to learn an Internet technology than online? eHandsOn is an online learning company that brings students together with the Web's leading experts. It specializes in media-rich content delivered by industry experts. Lisa Lopuck, a professional Web graphics designer and instructor, founded eHandsOn. Included on the CD-ROM are two sample courses—one on Fireworks 3, taught by Lisa, and another on Dreamweaver 3, taught by myself. You can find out more about eHandsOn by visiting their Web site at www.ehandson.com.

Fireworks Extensions

Fireworks is blessed with a robust community that not only creates great artwork and utilities, but also shares it. Included on the CD-ROM are numerous extensions— commands, styles, and textures—from the Fireworks community. Not only can these tools ease your workflow, but they can also vary and enhance your designs.

On the CD-ROM, you'll find contributions from the following Fireworks designers, in addition to myself:

- ✦ Kleanthis Economou
- ✦ Massimo Foti
- ✦ Linda Rathgeber
- ✦ Eddie Traversa
- ✦ Simon White

Fireworks Commands

With the availability of the Fireworks graphics engine through its JavaScript API and Document Object Model, Fireworks commands are really taking off.Commands are undeniably powerful, whether they are used to automate tedious production or produce fun effects. You can access a Fireworks commandfrom anywhere bychoosing File ⇨ Run Script. If you prefer to centralize your commands, copy any desired ones from the CD-ROM to the Fireworks/Settings/Commands folder. The next time you run Fireworks, you'll find your new tools under the Commands menu.

Note   There are two commands, created by me, which require both Dreamweaver and Fireworks to work: StyleBuilder and BulletBuilder. These commands are installed in Dreamweaver by using Macromedia's Extension Manager, available from the Macromedia Web site (or on this CD-ROM). To run them, open Dreamweaver and select the desired one from under the Commands menu.

Fireworks styles and textures

Part of the power of Fireworks is the ability to extend both its image-creating capabilities and its HTML output. Making a set of textures available is as simple as copying a folder from one location to another. For the textures included with this CD-ROM, you simply need to copy the images in any of the Textures folders found under the various contributors' names to the equivalent Fireworks folder and then relaunch Fireworks. The CD-ROM includes over 50 new textures.

Tip   You can also use an individual texture without having to copy it to your Textures folder by selecting Other from the Textures list in Fireworks and then choosing the texture from another folder on your computer.

Gradients, strokes, and image libraries

Fireworks also gives you the ability to add many other components of an image, such as the stroke or gradient fill. For your graphic-creation pleasure, the CD-ROM includes a useful compendium of various gradient fills, strokes, and image libraries, each in their own self-named folder. Although these are fairly simple to create in Fireworks, why reinvent the wheel when you have so much other work to do? Included in this collection is a wide variety of dotted and dashed strokes as well as an arrowhead library.

Fireworks 3 Bible examples

Example images used in the Fireworks 3 Bible can be found in the Examples folder of the CD-ROM, organized by the chapter in which they appear in the book. You'll find examples of everything from alpha transparency to a pseudo banner ad that conforms to industry-wide specifications.

Web resource directory

The Web is a vital resource for any Web designer, whether you're a seasoned professional or a beginner. The CD-ROM contains an HTML page with a series of links to resources on the Web; the series contains general as well as Fireworks-specific references.

✦   ✦   ✦

Index

SYMBOLS AND NUMERICS

$, 568, 569–570
(p), 570
*, 568
+, 568
body section, 514, 616
head section, 652
head section, 616
img tags, 616, 644, 652, 725
map section, 616
meta tags, 653
table tag, 633
title tags, 653
?, 568
[abc], 569
B, 568
b, 568
D, 567
d, 567
S, 567, 568
s, 567
W, 567
w, 567
–, 568
, 568
, 568
|, 761
16-bit computers, color depth, 195
2-bit computers, color depth, 194
2-Up tab
    described, 29–30
    Workspace preview, 477–478
24-bit computers, color depth, 195
32-bit computers, color depth, 195
3D
    Alien Skin Eye Candy, 390
    corners, 281
    effect, 361–364
    Emboss effects. See Emboss effects
    Glow unnatural stroke, 234–235
    gradient fills, 321

light sources, simulated, 425–426
Live Effects, 353
perspective shadow (Alien Skin Eye Candy), 389–390
pixel selection, 380
rollover images, 646
ShapeShifter (Kai's Power Tools 5), 394–395
tweening, 717–718
tweening depth, 718
unnatural stroke, 234–235
4-bit computers, color depth, 195
4-Up tab
    described, 29
    Workspace preview, 478–480
8-bit computers
    color depth, 195
    Color Table panel, 54–55
    flat color, 481
    GIF format, 484

A

About Balloon Help command, 96
About Fireworks command, 97
accessing
    application information, 765–771
    Color Mixer models, 201–204
    History list, 557–558
    often-used libraries, 549–550
    swatches in system color picker, 206–208
    temporary files, 787
Acquire plug-in scanning process, 442–443
Acrobat 4 (Adobe), 114
ACT. See Active Color Table (ACT) palettes
actions, 640, 793
Active Area tab, 658
Active Color Table (ACT) palettes, 211
acute angles, 151
adaptive color palette, 483
Add Color command, 486

adding
    behaviors, 640–643
    color, 54
    colors, 209
    Commands, 601–602
    control handle to Bézier curve corner point, 161–162
    CSS layers to Dreamweaver, 676–678
    depth to images, 366–367
    files to Project Log, 68, 576
    frames, 60, 695–696
    history to URL library, 559
    layers, 59, 399–400
    palettes, 56
    paths, 265–267
    Pattern fill, 330–331
    Photoshop plug-ins, 106
    points, 265–267
    Project Log files, 69
    texture fills, 341
    URLs to URL Library, 65, 558–560, 559
additional materials, Folder preferences, 106
addresses, Web. See URLs
Adjust Color commands, 91–92
Adobe Acrobat 4, 114
Adobe GoLive
    customizing workflow with, 102–105
    exporting rollover images, 649
    HTML style, 614
    image maps, exporting, 620–621
    slices, inserting, 636
    Web page, inserting rollover code, 652–653
Adobe Illustrator
    application filter, 383
    clip art, 461
    exporting files, 72, 509
    formatlist arguments, 770
    importing Flash animation, 469
    tweening animation, 713
    vectors, exporting, 515–517
    vectors, inserting, 450

Adobe Illustrator 7
    command, 72
    document format, 122
    exporting, 72
    importing files into, 517
    vector graphics files, 459–460
Adobe Palettes, 212
Adobe Photoshop
    adding plug-ins, 106
    blurring, 734
    color model, 203–204, 211
    compatibility, 8
    creating new documents, 116
    Drop Shadow effect, 368
    File menu commands, 70
    Fireworks versus, 5
    folder, 746
    image filters, 348
    importing files, 20, 107–108,
        451, 454, 455–458
    layers, 58, 398, 512
    locating Plugins, 375
    opening existing images, 169
    opening files, 125
    saving customized effects, 376
    scanner plug-ins, 438–440
    shared palettes, 591
    Styles, 522
    third-party filters, 382–395
    tweening Xtras, 715–717
    Xtras menu, 352–353
Adobe Photoshop Acquire plug-
        ins, 71, 438, 446
Adobe Photoshop document
    described, 122
    formatlist arguments, 770
Adobe Photoshop-compatible
        image filters
    bitmap compatibility, 8
    blurring, 734
    browser animation support,
        692
    Convert to Alpha, 367
    Effect panel, 52–53
    File menu commands, 70
    folder, 746
    installing, 382
    listed, 382–395
    Live Effects, 10
    locating, 375
    photograph edges, 419
    Photoshop, 348

Photoshop, adding, 106
PNG, 502
scanner, 438–440
shortcuts (aliases), 384
Styles, 522
third-party, Photoshop-
        compatible, 382–395
tweening, 715–717
using with multiple
        applications, 383–384
Web color, 193–194
Xtras menu, 352–353
Adobe Plug-In Source, 382
Adobe Swatches, 212
Adobe Type Manager, 463
advertising
    banner ads, 725–726
    repetition, importance of, 519
Agfa ScanWise, 442
Air Brush
    described, 49
    flow rate, 241
    illustrated, 141
    stroke, 227
alert() method, 762–763
aliases, filters, 384
Alien Skin Eye Candy
    blurring, 734
    compatibility, 8
    described, 384–386
    filters, listed, 387
    Fire filter, 379
    Jiggle, 388–389
    perspective shadows, 373,
        389–390
    tweening animation, 715–717
Align Bottom button, 40
Align Left button, 40
Align Right button, 40
Align Top button, 40
aligning
    commands, 84–85, 87–88, 403
    font, 297
    objects, 402–405, 594
    text, 294–296, 307, 566
Aligning button, 39
alpha mask, 92
Alpha slider, 393
alpha transparency, 492–493, 502
Alpha, filter, 367
alpha, Live Effects, 353

alphanumeric characters,
        wildcards, 567
Alt tags
    hotspots, assigning links, 612
    setting, 591
Alter Path commands, 85–86
Alternate Image Description text
        box, 607–608
AltText
    default, 772
    hotspots, 789
Ambrosia Software Snapz Pro, 466
American Standard Code for
        Information
        Interchange. See ASCII
anchor, 557
Anchor grid, 130
angles
    Bevel effect, 362
    control handle, 163
    Emboss effect, 365
    frames, 804
    polygons, 150–151
    stroke stamp, 245, 246
animation
    background images, 709
    bandwidth, importance of, 690
    banner ads, 723–735
    browser background image,
        710
    commands, 89, 582–583, 803
    completing, 587
    controls, 33
    CSS layers, 676
    described, 11–12
    document controls, 33
    embedded, 622
    Export Preview dialog box, 504
    exporting, 704–709
    formats, 691–693
    frame delay timing, 701–702
    frames, managing, 59–60,
        693–697
    image maps, 622
    importing multiple files,
        467–468
    indexed color export format,
        482
    Instances, 534
    objects, 698–700
    onion skinning, 702–704
    opening, 169–170, 466–469

preloading, 710
reasons, 690–691
reusing, 709
rollovers, 711–712
scaling, 709–710
slices, 636–637
slicing, 712
status bar, 41
tweening, 712–720
VCR controls, 700–701
Web, described, 689
Another Behavior, 678
anti-aliasing
    basic stroke, 226–227
    fill, 316
    Lasso edge, 179
    paths, 82, 140
    selecting pixels, 180
    text, 296
Antimatter filter, 387
API (application programming
        interface)
    commands, building on built-
        in, 803–807
    data types, handling
        nonstandard, 760–762
    described, 759–760
    document functions, 799–800
    Errors object, 780–782
    file URLs, 760–761
    History Panel functions,
        801–803
    hotspot objects, 789–795
    JavaScript, 740
API (application programming
        interface) methods,
        listed
    alert() method, 762–763
    behaviors, 793–795
    colors, 760
    confirm() method, 763
    masks, 761
    matrices, 761
    points, 762
    prompt() method, 764
    rectangles, 762
    resolution, 762
    write() method, 765
    WRITE_HTML() method,
        764–765
API (application programming
        interface) objects, listed

App objects, 765
    Document object, 771–779
    exportDoc object, 789–791
    Files object, 785–789
    Find object, 783–784
    image map objects, 791–793
    SliceInfo object, 795–797
    Slices object, 797–799
apostrophe key, 410
App object
    described, 765
    methods, 768–771
    properties, 765–768
Apple Display Software, 208, 214
AppleScript, 591
application programming
        interface. See API
        (application
        programming interface)
applications
    accessing information,
        765–771
    Dreamweaver, bringing in
        front, 685
    editing preferences, 105
    filters, using with multiple,
        383–384
    Fireworks, bringing in front,
        685
    image-edit, 508
    inserting objects, 450–453
    moving images between, 121
    screen capture, 466
applying
    color, 36, 120
    Styles, 521–522
arcs, 277
areas, image map object, 792–793
arguments, converting to string,
        764–765
Arrange commands, 83–84
Arranging button, 39
array, returning files, 786
arrow button, stroke color, 50
arrows, expander, 47
ASCII
    importing, 298, 462
    inserting objects, 450
    text format, 123
aspect ratio, stroke stamp, 245
asterisk (*), 568
Attach to Path command, 88

Auto Levels
    Live Effect, 354
    photographs, adjusting,
        356–358
Auto-crop Images option, 257
automating
    batch processing graphics
        files, 577–579
    tools, production, 16–17
    workflow, 581–602

B

background
    banner ads, 729
    browser image, 710
    color, 772
    layer, hiding, 135
    link, hotspots, 790
    restoring frames, 705
    selecting, 187
    tile, 601
backslash character (), 568
backups
    Find and Replace operations,
        565
    layers, 399
balloons, word, 691
bamboo calligraphy, 228
banding, 202
bandwidth
    animation, importance of,
        690
    banner ad animation, 734
    limitations, 471
banner ads
    advertising, 725–726
    creating, 726–734
    frames, saving with blur,
        734–735
    GIFS, animated, 689
    placement, 725
    size (IAB/CASIE standards),
        723–724
    weight, 724
Barnett, Don, 319
barrel roll, RadWarp (Kai's Power
        Tools 5), 392–394
Bars gradient fill, 51, 322, 323
baseline shift, text spacing,
        292–293
basename, hotspots, 790
Basic stroke, 49, 221, 226–227

Batch a Command
    Commands menu, 583–584
    described, 90
Batch Code
    returning pathname, 766
    Settings folder, 742
Batch Process
    completion, dialog box, 763
    confirming, 763
    described, 73
    display string in dialog box,
        767
    tools, production, 17
    tracking files, 768
    Web graphics, 577–579
BehaviorInfo object, 793–794
Behaviors
    adding and removing, 640–643
    API (application programming
        interface), 793–795
    Button Symbols, 533
    command, 81, 95
    described, 639–640
    Dreamweaver integration, 667,
        678–680
    image map, 790
    images with, 13–15
    inserting, 81
    Nav Bar, 654–659
    Object Inspector, 49
    preloading animation, 710
    rollovers, 643–654, 659–663
Behaviors Inspector
    described, 63–64
    Dreamweaver, 679
    opening, 49
Behaviors Panel
    adding, 641–642
    deleting behaviors, 643
    described, 640–641
    modifying, 642–643
BehaviorsList object, 795
Beta slider, 393
bevel
    corners, 281
    effect, 361–364
    Live Effects, 353
    pixel selection, 380
    rollover images, 646
    tweening depth, 718
Bézier control handles
    API, 761

viewing, 265
Bézier curves
    adjusting, 160–162
    described, 156–157
    drawing with Pen, 157–158
    keyboard modifiers, 162–163
    mixing lines and, 159–160
    perspective shadows, 374
    smooth, 158–159
bicubic interpolation, 102, 171
bilinear interpolation, 102, 171
bit depth
    channels, 414
    exporting photographic
        images, 498
    Web, color considerations,
        194–195
bitmap images
    banner ads, 728
    Image Edit mode, 166–169,
        173–185
    importing, 453–458
    inserting empty, 172–173
    inserting into document, 172
    opening, 169–170
    scaling, 170–171
bitmaps
    creating, 172–173
    edges, mask groups, 418–420
    exporting, 497–503
    feathering selections, 427–428
    JPEG, 498–501
    PNG 32 and 34, 502–503
    selecting pixels, 180
    tonal range, adjusting, 355–361
    Web photo album, 681–683
    Web-safe colors, 197
black & white, Adaptive color
        palette, 284
black, bit depth, 194
blending
    Bevel effect and, 363
    Color mode, 424
    comparison, 423–424
    Darken mode, 424
    described, 420–421
    Difference mode, 424
    edges, 177
    Erase mode, 425
    fill, 51, 316
    groups, 413
    Hue mode, 424

images, 188
Instances, 542
Invert mode, 425
Lasso edge, 179
light source, simulating,
        425–427
Lighten mode, 424
Luminosity mode, 424
modes, 421–423
Multiply mode, 424
objects before compositing,
        420
path edges, 83
pattern fills, 334
photograph edges, 419
photographs, 427–428
Saturation mode, 424
Screen mode, 424
selecting pixels, 180
stroke edges, 222
strokes, 220
Tint mode, 425
tweening animation, 713
blur
    animation, described, 365–366
    banner ads, saving frames,
        734–735
    color, 92
    described, 92
    Live Effects, 353
    perspective shadow, 389
    seamless patterns, 336–337
Blur Live Effect, 354
Blur More Effect, 354
Blur filter, 392
BMP
    digital camera images, 450
    exporting, 497
    files, 454
bold
    Styles, 524
    text, 87, 290, 462
Bookmark files, 560
borders
    Expand to Fill document
        option, 104
    Glow effect, 371
    HTML tables, 629
    image, 168–169
    Image Edit mode, 167
    left side, 777
    marquee selection, 189

pattern fills, 334
photograph, 418–420
sizing image objects, 173
bounding box
    aligning text objects, 294–295
    circles and ellipses, 147–148
brands
    color, 213
    recognizing, 726
    repetition, importance of, 519
bricks pattern, 745
brightness and contrast
    adjusting, 91
    JPEG, 499
    Live Effect, 354
    photographs, adjusting,
        355–356
    scanned images, 445
Bring Forward button, 40
Bring Front button, 40
bristle oil stroke, 231
broad splatter oil stroke, 231
broken links, images, 605
browseDocument() function, 801
browsers
    animation, 691
    background image, 710
    client-side image maps, 607
    color, 194, 196–197
    color palette, 210
    Dynamic-HTML, 509
    faster display, 623
    file format limitations, 471
    Frame delay timing, 701
    Help, 96
    hit, 725
    hotspots, 112, 612
    photo album, 683
    photographs, 197
    PNG alpha channel, 414
    preferences, 748
    preloading animation, 710
    previewing in, 73, 553–556
    printing Project Log, 576
    rollover GIF images, 711
    rollover images, 660
    rollover states, 645
    screen capture, 465
    status bar, 662
    transparency, 482
    Web formats, comparing, 692
Brush Strokes filter, 419

Brush tool
    color default, 101
    described, 35, 152
    documents, 772
    freeform lines, drawing,
        154–156
    Image Edit mode, 190
    Save as Command limitations,
        595
    Stroke panel, 49–50
    stroke stamps, viewing,
        239–240
bubble
    banner ads, 729
    described, 392
    jiggle, 387–389
    size slider, 388
build-up, strokes, 241
BulletBuilder command, 683, 764
Butt Cap, 281–282
Button Area, Link Wizard, 548
button banner ad, 724
Button Editor, 543–544
Button presets
    Bevel effect, 362
    Bevel effects, 363–364
Button Symbols, 533
buttons
    animating, 690
    banner ad sizes, 724
    clip art, 460
    Cookie-Cutter Text, 304–305
    creating, 14
    displaying frames, 67
    Find and Replace, 563
    hotspots, 790
    image export, 508
    inserting, 80
    inside strokes, 252
    Instances, 546–547
    Library, adding to, 559
    Link Wizard, 547–548
    Main toolbar, 38
    Modify toolbar, 39–41
    Nav Bar, 654–659
    Object Inspector, 48
    preset Bevel effects, 363–364
    reversing frames, 586
    rollover, 645, 706
    styles, 520–521
    symbols, making and
        modifying, 543–546

C

C, 739
C++, 640, 739
Calligraphy stroke, 49, 228
camcorders, 449–450
canceling, Instances operations,
    716
canvas
    aligning objects to, 404–405
    border, 777
    centering objects, 586
    color, 119–120, 135, 428
    commands, 586–587
    creating new documents, 115,
        116, 117–120
    erasing, 184–185
    exporting image against
        different, 487–489
    increasing/decreasing size, 34
    modifying, 128–135
    resolution, 118–119
    rotating, 135
    size, altering, 129–134
    trimming, 81, 134
    tweening animation, 713
    width and height, 118
Canvas Color command, 81
Canvas Size command, 81
capturing
    images, 437–450
    screen images, 464–466
carat (–), 568
Carriage Return Line Feed, 568,
    764
cartoons. See animation
Carve filter, 387
Cascade command, 95
Cascading Style Sheet. See CSS
    layers
Casey, Donna, 528
CASIE standards. See IAB/CASIE
    standards
catalogs, 681
categories, stroke, 221–222
CD-ROM, back of the book
    animated banner ad, 735
    banner ad example, 726
    BulletBuilder command, 764
    Commands, 602
    Dreamweaver 3 trial version,
        665
                        Continued

CD-ROM (continued)
    Fireworks folder icon, 27
    HTML templates, 614, 649
    Repeat History command, 803
    Styles, 11
    textures, 223, 342
    Textures folder, 495
cell spacing, HTML tables, 629
center
    drawing from, 610
    drawing rectangle from, 145
    drawing slice from, 624
Center Horizontal Axis button, 40
Center Vertical Axis button, 40
centering
    alignment, 404
    commands, 601
    gradient fills, 323
    objects, 84
    objects on canvas, 586
    paths, 142–143
    pattern fill, 332
    text, 87
    warping effect, 393–394
centimeters, measurement display, 62
CERN, 112
CGI (Common Gateway Interface) scripts, 725
Chameleon unnatural stroke, 234–235
changes, tracking, 68, 69, 575–576
changing, colors throughout site, 572–573
channels, bit depth, 414
characters
    banner ads, 727–728
    positions, regular expression searches, 568
    ranges, regular expression searches, 569
    wildcard, regular expression searches, 567–568
Charcoal stroke
    described, 49, 228–229
    velocity, 154
check boxes, 47
chemical formulas, 292–293
choosing, color, 200–201

Chrome filter, 387
circle
    bounding box, imaginary, 147–148
    commands, automating, 594
    drawing, 148, 174
    Eraser tool, 184
    hotspot, 608, 610
    hotspots, 606
    image map, 791
    text on, 308
    tool, 190
Clear All button, 409
Clear command, 75
clearing
    guides, 409
    Project Log selection, 576
    stroke selections, 221
click rule, 726
click-and-drag method, 298
click-through, 725
Client Side Image Map
    described, 607
    hotspots, 790
clip art, 460–462
clipboard
    copying HTML code, 651, 652
    copying steps to, 596–598
    cut, copy and paste, 38, 74, 75
    Document Object Model (DOM), 799–800
    exporting rollover images, 649, 651
    HTML style, 615
Clone command
    described, 76
    rollover images, 645
Close command, 71
close() method, 785
closing
    files, 128, 785
    Library palette, 675
    paths, 142
    paths, structuring, 267–268
CMY
    choosing, 203
    color slider, 201
    described, 57, 62
CMYK
    defined, 194
    Macintosh color picker, 207

Coalition for Advertising Supported Information and Entertainment (CASIE), 724
code. See also HTML; JavaScript
    commands without, 593–596
    Dreamweaver 3, 15
    Dreamweaver, exporting, 672–678
    image map, exporting, 613–622
    rollover, 650–654
collage, 172
color
    API (application programming interface), 760
    applying, 36
    bandwidth considerations, 690
    banner ad animation, 732–733
    batch processing, 578
    Bevel effect, 362
    blending, 421
    canvas, 81, 117, 119–121, 135, 428
    documents, 772
    effects, listed, 355
    Ellipse Marquee tool, 177
    erasing, 184–185
    export options, 773
    fill, 51, 142
    Find and Replace, 17, 68, 563, 564, 572–573, 784
    font attributes, 290
    GIFs, 710
    gradient fills, 321–329
    grid, 410–411, 776
    guides, 408–409
    hexadecimal, 789
    hotspots, 608, 612
    JPEG, 498
    limiting, 705
    Live Effects, 353
    locking, 480
    matte, 777, 778
    mixing. See Color Mixer
    Pantone, converting to Web-safe, 213–216
    Pencil tool, 155
    perspective shadow, 389
    preferences, setting, 101–102
    previews, 43
    removing unused, 47

selecting similar pixels,
   179–180
slice guides, 626–627
slicing animations, 712
stroke, 50
Styles panel, 65–66, 524
swatches, selecting, 205–213
text objects, 301
texture fills, 341
Web considerations, 193–199,
   199, 691–692
Web-safe, 318–321, 573–574
color depth
  grayscale images, 445
  images, 445
  line art, 444, 445
  scanning, 444–445
Color Mixer
  button, 38
  choosing color, 200–201
  command, 94
  described, 56–57, 199–200
  models, accessing, 201–204
  RGB, 358, 760
  slides, 200–201
  stroke color, 219
Color mode
  blending, 424
  opacity and blending, 423
color picker
  color wheels, 360
  Find and Replace colors, 573
  guides, 409
color ramp, gradient fills, 321,
   323, 325
Color Table
  accessing, 212–213
  command, 94
  creating shared palettes,
   590
  described, 54–55
  file type, 591
  optimizing, 474
  optimizing files, 472
  panel layout, 589
color wells
  described, 47
  gradient fill, 325
  illustrated, 316
  swatches, choosing from,
   205–206
color wheels, 360

color, indexed
  dither, 489
  exporting, 481–496
  GIF-friendly images, creating,
   494–496
  Interlaced option, 493–494
  lossy GIF compression,
   487–489
  matte, 487
  number of, 484–487
  palette, 483–484
  Remove Unused Colors option,
   493
  saved settings, 494
  transparency, 489–493
colored pencil, 225, 226
ColorSync, 199, 214
ColorWeb Pro
  functions, 213
  Macintosh, 215–216
  Windows, 214–215
column
  hotspots, 790
  HTML table, 798
Combine commands, 85
comics, 691
Command Menu, layers, 401
commands
  Behaviors panel, 63–64
  building on built-in, 803–807
  Color Table panel, 54–55
  Color Table pop-up, 486
  creating without coding,
   593–596
  Dreamweaver 3, 15
  Dreamweaver hybrid, 683–685
  Dreamweaver integration, 667
  Effect panel, 53
  File menu, 70–73
  File Type code, 766
  Fill panel, 52
  Find and Replace panel, 68
  History panel, 61
  Info panel, 62
  Layers panel, 59
  Library panel, 67
  Object Inspector, 49
  Project Log, 69
  scriptlets, 741
  Settings folder, 742–743
  Styles panel, 66
  Swatches panel, 56

Commands folder
  path, 761
  returning pathname, 766
Commands menu
  adding steps, 16–17
  animation, 582–583
  Batch a Command, 583–584
  Create Web Photo Album
   command, 681
  Creative submenu, 584–586
  described, 89–91, 581–582
  Document submenu, 586–587
  Optimize Image in Fireworks,
   668
  Panel Layout command, 589
  Panel Layout Sets, 587–588
  Web submenu, 589–591
commands, listed
  Commands menu, 89–91
  Edit menu, 74–76
  File menu, 70–73
  Help menu, 96–97
  Insert menu, 80–81
  Modify menu, 81–86
  Text menu, 87–89
  View menu, 77–79
  Window menu, 93–95
  Xtras menu, 91–93
Comments, transferring, 618
commercial Web sites, 519
Communicator 4.x, 555
complimentary color, 244
compositing, 397
compression
  bandwidth, 690
  exporting image files, 509
  JPEG, 499
  lossy GIF, exporting indexed
   color, 487–489
  masks, 761
  smoothing, 500
  Web optimizing, 14
  Web photo album, 682
computer system
  querying, 767
concentric shapes, 283
Cone gradient fill, 51, 322, 323
Confetti stroke, 233–234
confirm() function, 803–804
confirm() method, 763
Connectix Virtual PC, 556
consistency. *See* Styles

contracting, marquee selection, 189
contrast. *See also* Brightness/Contrast
adjusting, 91
Bevel effect, 362
Emboss effect, 365
photographs, adjusting, 355–356
control handle
Bézier curves, 160–162
keyboard modifiers, 163
controls, VCR, animation, 700–701
Convert to Alpha Effect, 354
Convert to Grayscale command, 339
Convert to Paths command, 89
Convert to Symbol command, 80
converting
arguments to string, 764–765
Button Symbols to Graphic Symbols, 546
color to grayscale texture, 341
object palettes, 584–586
objects to Button Symbols, 545
objects to hotspots, 49, 613
objects to images, 190–191
objects to symbols, 536–537
Pantone to Web-safe color, 213–216
symbols, 536
text to images, 303
text to paths, 303
cookie-cutter text, 304–305
cookies, 654
copy and paste, objects from other applications, 450–451
Copy as Paths command, 74
Copy button, 38
Copy command, 74
Copy HTML Code command, 74
copy() method, 785
copying. *See also* Symbols
banner ad objects, 730
command, 37
comments, 618
CSS layers, 678
documents, 779
files, 785
foreground images, 427
frames, 60, 646, 697

gradient fills, 327
History panel steps, 61
image portions, 182–183
image to slice, 627
Instances, 541
layers, 59
objects, 76
objects to create simulated light sources, 426
objects to frames, 698
rollover images, 645
saving, 592
steps to clipboard, 596–598
Symbol, 67
Symbols. *See* Instances
symbols, 538–539
tweening depth, 717
copyright footer, 594
Corel Photo-Paint, 383, 458
CorelDRAW, 8, 383, 461
CorelDRAW 8
document files, 123
vector graphics files, 459–460
corner point
Bézier curve control handles, 161–162
extending control handle, 163
corners
expand stroke, 281
rectangle, 601, 602
rounded rectangles, 146–147
cost per one thousand. *See* CPM
counting, frames, 481
CPM, 725
Crayon stroke
described, 49, 223, 229–230
Macintosh color picker, 207
creamy charcoal stroke, 228–229
Create Shared Palette command, 590–591
Create Web Photo Album command, 681
creating
banner ads, 726–734
bitmaps, 172–173
button symbols, 543–546
document, 38
files, 785
GIFs, animated, 125
guides, 406
Instances, 541
Nav Bar, 655–656

square, 145
strokes, 235–247
Styles, 522–525
styles, 66
Symbol, 67
Symbols, 536–539
Creative commands, 90
Creative submenu, Commands menu, 584–586
Creator code, 766
crescent, smooth bitmap, 177
crop
correcting, 417
deleting objects while, 104
Export Preview dialog box, 504–506
frames, 60
mask groups, 417–418
objects, 85
optimizing, 669
path operations, 279
restoring frames, 706
Crop Document command, 76
Crop Selected image command, 76
Crop tool
altering canvas size, 130–131
described, 34
crosshair pointer
described, 103–104
toggling, 180
CSS layers
adding to Dreamweaver, 676–678
Export special command, 72
exporting, 72, 512–514
exporting image files, 509
Current frame display, 700
cursor
changing path, 36
endpoints, 152
Freeform Path tool, 271
precise, 103–104
rollover states, 645
Rotator, 260
curves
color, 92
control handle, 163
selecting areas, 178–179
uneven, drawing, 160
Curves filter, adjusting photographs, 359–360
Curves Live Effect, 354

curves, Bézier, 156–163
custom color palette, 284
Custom Color radio button, 120
customizing
    batch processing, 577
    gradient fills, 323–327
    HTML and JavaScript engine,
        739–741
    HTML properties, 108–112
    preferences, 99–108
    Preferences file, 746–757
    print options, 113–114
    Settings folder, 741–746
    storing Live Effect, 376–377
Cut button, 38
Cut command, 37, 74
Cutout filter, 387
cutting
    correcting, 417
    deleting objects while, 104
    Export Preview dialog box,
        504–506
    frames, 60
    mask groups, 417–418
    objects, 85
    optimizing, 669
    path operations, 279
    restoring frames, 706
    sliced images, 634

D
Darken mode
    blending, 424
    opacity and blending, 423
data entry, 764
data types, nonstandard,
    760–762
date, Time and Date Stamp
        command, 601
debugging, 762
defragmenting, hard drives, 107
Delete Color command, 486
deleting
    behaviors, 63, 643
    color, 54
    commands, 599
    curve endpoints, 359
    custom colors from palette,
        209
    export settings, 47
    files, 785–786
    frames, 60, 696

gradient fill, 52, 326
History panel steps, 61
Instances, 543
layers, 59
links, 558
Live Effects, 375
new strokes, 236
objects while cropping, 104
palette colors, 210
pixels, 36
points, 265–267
points on a path, 267
Project Log files, 69
stroke settings, 50
Styles, 525
styles, 66
Symbols, 67, 535, 540–541
URL libraries, 562
URLs, 65
depth
    color, 444–445
    CSS layers, 676
    Glow effects, listed, 370–371
    images, adding, 366–367
    shadow effects, 367–370
    sharpening images, 371–372
    tweening, 717–718
descreen setting, 445
Description, 41
Deselect command, 75
Design Notes
    images, 669
    recognizing in Dreamweaver,
        671–672
design, reusing elements in
        banner ads, 728. See
        also Styles
designers, work methods, 4
Detach from Path command, 88
DHTML
    browser support, 692
    Web formats, comparing, 691
dial-up connection, 471, 476, 690
dialog boxes
    Batch Process, displaying
        string, 767
    completion, 763
    confirming, 763, 803–804
    users to enter information, 764
Difference mode
    blending, 424
    opacity and blending, 423

digital camera. See also
        photographs
    camcorders, 449–450
    capturing images into
        Fireworks, 447–448
    described, 447
    image capture, 437–438
    selecting, 438–439
dimensions
    animation objects, 698
    Bevel effects, 361–364
    canvas, 117
    Emboss effect, 364–365
    shapes, precise adjustment,
        152
    source and exported files,
        671
    swapped images, 644
direction, paths, 143
Director (Macromedia)
    Behaviors, 640
    described, 383
    PNG format, 414, 502
directories
    checking, 787
    creating, 785
    deleting, 785
    extracting, 786
    file storage, 787
    patching with, 787
    temporary files, 787
    verifying, 787
dirty edges, cleaning, 392
disjointed rollovers, 659–660
Disk Defragmenter, 107
disk space, recording steps, 593
dismissing, Batch Process dialog
        box, 767
display
    behaviors, 64
    browser speed, 623
    button frames, 67
    Color Table panel, 474
    document controls, 31–32
    Export Preview dialog box, 29
    Find and Replace options, 68
    layers, 401
    Library panel, 534
    Panel Layout Sets, 588
    panels, 38
    panels on dual monitors, 42
                        Continued

display *(continued)*
　rulers, 405
　saved effects, 377
　Symbol properties, 67
　Tool Options panel, 57
　tooltips, 41
Distance slider, 369
distort
　barrel roll, 392
　Instances, 542
　objects, 83
　photograph edges, 419
　tool, described, 36
Distort tool
　dragging corners, 264
　Image Edit mode, 190
　objects, 259–261
　text objects, 302, 303
Distribute Heights button, 40
Distribute to Frames checkbox,
　716
Distribute Widths button, 40
distributing
　objects, 402–404
　objects to frames, 699
dither
　color models, viewing, 202
　exporting indexed color, 489
　fill, 318
　illustrated, 490
　Web color, 197, 315
DitherBox filter, 353
docking
　Layers panel, 695
　URL panel, 558
　View Controls toolbar, 28
document
　background color, 772
　commands, 90, 583–584
　commands menu, 89, 90
　copying, 779
　creating, 38, 117–121
　Edit menu commands, 74–75
　exporting, 34, 772–774
　File menu commands, 70–71, 73
　filename, 775
　Frames panel, 772
　gradient fills, sharing, 326–327
　height, 777
　importing, 38, 454–455
　interface, document window,
　　25–27

Layers panel, 772
modifying canvases, 128–135
objects from top of, 778
opening, 38, 121–127
organizing open, 26
panning view, 35
printing, 38
resolution, 778
saving, 38, 779
sharing new strokes among,
　237
storing, 127–128
text changes, 566
texture fills, 342
trimming canvas, 134
undo, 591–593
view menu commands, 77–79
width, 778
document controls
　animation, 33
　display options, 31–32
　Exit Image Edit Mode button,
　　33
　illustrated, 24
　magnification settings, 30–31
　Original tab, 29
　Page Preview, 32
　Preview tab, 29–30
document functions, API
　　(application
　　programming interface),
　　799–800
Document Object Model (DOM)
　Commands, building, 803–807
　document functions, 799–800
　extending Fireworks, 684
　Fireworks functions, 800–801
　History panel functions,
　　801–803
Document objects
　API (application programming
　　interface), 771–779
　array object, 767
　properties, 771–780
Document Properties. *See* HTML
　　Properties command
Document submenu, Commands
　　menu, 586–587
document window
　described, 25–27
　illustrated, 24
　multi-frame editing, 704

dollar sign ($), searching with,
　569–570
DOM. *See* Document Object Model
　　(DOM)
domain name, 557
Domino (Lotus), 509
Domino Designer (Lotus), 514–515
Domino Image Well (Lotus), 72
dots per inch. *See* dpi
Dots stroke, 233–234
dotted lines
　creating, 241
　strokes, 247–250
Down rollover state, 645
Down state, 544, 680
download speed
　colors, 195
　Polygon slices, 625
　previewing, 476
downloads
　animation, 701
　Dreamweaver commands, 683
　JPEG, 498
　Polygon slices, 625
　slices, 622
dpi, 440
Draft Display, 31–32
drag-and-draw method, polygons,
　149
drag-and-drop method
　creating Instances, 541
　objects from other
　　applications, 451–453
　opening files, 124
dragging, slice guides, 627
Draw Fill over Stroke option, 250
drawing
　circles and ellipses, 148
　freeform pencil and brush,
　　154–156
　graphics tablet, 144
　hotspots, 608–611
　limiting area, 185–186
　lines, straight, 153
　polygons, 149–150
　shapes, 35
　slice objects, 36
　strokes, 219–253
　tools, crosshair cursor,
　　103–104
Dreamweaver (Macromedia)
　Behaviors, 640

behaviors, Fireworks, 678–680
code, exporting, 672–678
commands, hybrid, 683–685
creating new documents, 115
customizing workflow with,
    102–105
exporting image files, 509
History panel, 591
image-edit, 508
integration, overview, 15–16,
    665–667
Web photo album, creating,
    681–683
Dreamweaver (Macromedia)
    images
    editing in Fireworks, 670–672
    optimizing in Fireworks,
        667–669
Dreamweaver 2 (Macromedia)
    exporting rollover images, 649
    HTML style, 614
    image maps, exporting,
        617–618
    slices, inserting, 634
    Web page, inserting rollover
        code, 652–653
Dreamweaver 3 (Macromedia)
    exporting rollover images, 649
    image maps, exporting,
        617–618
    inserting rollover code,
        652–653
    slices, inserting, 634
    Web page, inserting rollover
        code, 652–653
Dreamweaver 3 Library
    (Macromedia)
    exporting rollover images, 649
    HTML style, 614
    image maps, exporting,
        618–620
    repeating elements, 654
    slices, inserting, 634–635
    working with, 673–676
drop shadow
    copying image to slice, 627
    described, 368–370
    fitting canvas size, 130–131
Drop Shadow Effect, 354
Drop Shadow filter, 387
Duplicate command, 76
duplicating

banner ad objects, 730
command, 37
comments, 618
CSS layers, 678
documents, 779
files, 785
foreground images, 427
frames, 60, 646, 697
gradient fills, 327
History panel steps, 61
image portions, 182–183
image to slice, 627
Instances, 541
layers, 59
objects, 76
objects to create simulated
    light sources, 426
objects to frames, 698
rollover images, 645
saving, 592
steps to clipboard, 596–598
symbols, 538–539
tweening depth, 717
dust removal, 445
Dynamic HTML
    browser support, 692
    described, 509
    Web formats, comparing, 691

E

e-mail protocol, 556
edge
    crayon, 229–230
    dirty, cleaning, 392
    Eraser tool, 184
    fill, 51, 344
    finding, 92
    hiding, 104
    Lasso tools, 179
    mask groups, 418–420
    paths, 82–83
    Rubber Stamp tool, 184
    selecting pixels, 180
    sharpening, 47
    size, 245
    Solid fill, 318
    stroke, 50
    strokes, 222, 241–243
    texture, 241–242
Edge object, fill, 316
Edit button, 670
Edit Color command, 486

Edit Command List command, 89
Edit menu
    commands, 74–76
    creating Instances, 541
    fading in and out, 719
    Preferences, 670
    rollover images, 645
    selecting objects, 186–189
    sliced images, 634
    Symbols, creating, 536
    tweening animation, 715
    tweening depth, 717
    undo, 591
editing
    applications, working with
        other, 105
    behaviors, 63
    Behaviors in Dreamweaver,
        678
    bitmaps, 166
    color, 54, 55
    colors, removing, 486
    Commands menu, 599
    cursors, precise, 103–104
    delete objects while cropping,
        104
    Dreamweaver Library items,
        675
    effects, applied, 351
    gradient fill, 52, 324–326, 326
    images in Fireworks, 670–672
    layers, 58, 59
    Mask Group text, 311
    mask groups, 413
    multi-frame, 704
    new strokes, 236
    objects in layers, 400–401
    optimized files, 669
    paths, structuring, 269–283
    Photoshop image filters, 348
    pixel-based image options, 104
    preferences, described,
        102–105
    strokes, 238–247
    Styles, 525–526
    styles, 66
    Symbols, 67, 538, 539
    text, 297
    text objects, 287
    URLs, 65
Editor command, 88
editor, graphics, 670–671

editor, HTML, 102–105
editor, text
    described, 285–287
    fonts, choosing basic
        characteristics, 288–290
    options, enabling, 296
    previewing on the fly, 287–288
    spacing, adjusting, 290–296
Effect command, 94
Effect panel
    described, 52–53, 348–349
    expander arrow, 47
    Xtras menu versus, 378
effect, stroke edges, 241–243
effects
    Cookie-Cutter Text, 304–305
    defined, 347
    Effect panel, 348–349
    imported files, 463
    perspective shadows, 372–375
    rollover images, 646
    rollovers, 514–515
    Styles, 524
    third-party plug-in filters,
        382–395
    Xtras menu, 352–353, 378–381
Effects panel, rollover images,
    646
effects, listed
    Bevel, 361–364
    blurring, 365–366
    color, adjusting, 355
    Emboss, 364–365
    Glow, 370–371
    Knock Out shadow, 370
    shadow, 367–370
    sharpen, 371–372
    table, 354
    tonal range, adjusting,
        355–361
effects, Live Effects
    built-in, 353–372
    described, 349–351
    managing, 375–378
Ellipse gradient fill, 51, 322, 323
Ellipse Hotspot tool, 36
Ellipse Marquee tool
    color, 177
    described, 34
Ellipse tool
    described, 35
    Image Edit mode, 190
    Stroke panel, 49–50

ellipses
    bounding box, imaginary,
        147–148
    drawing, 148
    hotspots, 610
embedded
    animation, 622
    rollovers, 622
Emboss
    effects, listed, 364–365
    Live Effects, 353
Empty Image command, 81
End Caps, 281–282
end-of-line, searching for, 568
endpoints, cursor, 152
Enter (Return) key, 62
enumFiles() method, 786
equilateral polygon. See polygon
Erase mode
    blending, 425
    opacity and blending, 423
Eraser tool
    described, 36, 184–185
    options, 58
    Tool Options panel, 277
errors
    Batch a Command, 584
    files, handling, 786–787
    opening folders with
        Macintosh, 126
    text describing, 786–787
Errors object
    API (application programming
        interface), 780–782
    properties, 780–782
events, 640, 679
existence, files, 786
exists() method, 786
Exit command, 73
Exit Image Edit command, 82
Exit Image Edit Mode button
    described, 33
    document controls, 33
Exit Image Mode button, 41
exiting, Image Edit Mode, 349
Expand to Fill document option,
    104
Expand, objects, 86
expander arrow, 47
expanding
    marquee selection, 189
    stroke path operations,
        280–282

Export Area tool
    cropping, 504–506
    described, 34
Export button, 38
Export command, 71
Export Preview
    command, described, 72
    frame disposal, 705–706
    working in, 503–507
Export Preview dialog box
    API (application programming
        interface), 707–709
    cropping, 504–506
    described, 503–504
    displaying, 29
    scaling exported images,
        506–507
Export Settings
    returning pathname, 766
    Settings folder, 743
Export Special dialog box
    CSS layers, exporting as,
        512–514
    described, 510
    Flash SWF files, 515–517
Export Wizard
    command, 73
    described, 507–509
    Optimize Panel, 47
exportDoc object, API
    (application
    programming interface),
    789–791
exporting
    Alt tags, 591
    animation, 691, 704–709
    banner ad animation, 732–733
    batch processing, 578
    buttons, 547
    color, indexed, 481–496
    confirmation, 763
    CSS layers, 512–514
    documents, portions of, 34
    Dreamweaver code, 672–678
    Export Wizards, 507–509
    files, 511–512, 671, 788
    Frame Delay settings, 708
    image against different canvas
        colors, 487–489
    image map code, 613–622
    Image Wells, 514–515
    libraries, 550–551
    method, 779

Optimize panel, 46–47
options, 509–510, 772–774
parameters, defining, 771–780
photographs, 497–503
Project Log, 69, 576
reduced color palette,
212–213
rollovers, 648–654, 711
shared palettes, 590–591
slices, 111–112, 510–511, 629,
631–636
Styles, 66, 378, 526
Symbols, 67
URL libraries, 562
URLs, 65
vectors, 515–517
Web commands, 589–591
Web dither fill, 321
working in Export Preview,
503–507
exportTo() method, 779
expressions, regular
searching with, 566–570
updating URLs, 575
Extending Fireworks, 684
extensions, filename
API (application programming
interface), 790
bitmap image files, 453–454
HTML files, 650
Styles, 745
supported file formats,
122–123
Extensis, 462
External Editors, 670
external rollovers, 660–661
Eye Candy (Alien Skin)
blurring, 734
compatibility, 8
described, 384–386
filters, listed, 387
Fire filter, 379
Jiggle, 388–389
perspective shadows, 373,
389–390
tweening animation, 715–717
Eye symbol, frame visibility, 512
EyeCandy 3.1 LE commands, 8–9,
93, 746
Eyedropper tool
activating, 160
color application, 120
color ramp, 199–200

color wells, 205
described, 36
Find and Replace colors, 573
levels, 357
matte, 487
specialty, 359
stroke color, 50
Swatches, adding color to, 209
swatches, color, 206
temporary switch to, 37

F
fading in and out, tweening,
719–720
Fantastic Corporation, 223
faux-wood picture frame, 585
Feather command
described, 75
Solid fill, 318
feathering
Bevel effect and, 363
edges, 177
fill, 51, 316
images, 188
Lasso edge, 179
objects before compositing,
420
path edges, 83
photograph edges, 419
photographs, 427–428
selecting pixels, 180
stroke edges, 222
Felt Tip stroke, 49, 230–231
Fiber fill, 495
FiberOptix filter, 392
File Buddy, 527, 591
File Exchange Control Panel, 527
file format
extensions, seeking, 786
mixed, 622
opening existing images,
122–125
Optimize panel, 46–47
unsupported, 780
File menu
animation preview, 717
animation, exporting, 691, 707
batch processing graphics
files, 577–579
browsers, defining, 555
commands, 70–73
CSS layers, 677
HTML style, exporting, 614

New command, 115, 120
Preferences, 669, 746–757
Preferences dialog box, 99–108
printing, 113–114
Reverse All Frames command,
587
rollover images, exporting, 650
running scriptlets, 579
slices, exporting, 631, 632
updating images, 671
file optimization, 14–15
file size
banner ads, 723, 724–725,
732–733
colors, 195
editing/optimizing, 105
exporting image files, 509
image quality, balancing, 472
JPEG, 499
file type
returning array, 770
unknown, 782
File type, code, 766
file, Export Preview dialog box,
504
filename
buttons, 547
current document, 775
extension, seeking, 786
hotspots, 790
reading slices, 797
replacing, 788
slice, 797
filename extension
hotspots, 790
HTML code, 650, 743
Macintosh color, 211
retrieving, 786
slice, 796
Styles, 745
filenames
returning array, 770
slice, 797
thumbnail images, 683
files
array, returning, 786
Batch a Command, 583–584
browser format limitations,
471
checking, 787
choosing one or more, 769
closing, 128, 785
Continued

files *(continued)*
  combining with different
      directory, 787
  copying, 785
  creating new, 785
  deleting, 785–786
  directories. *See* directories
  displaying recent, 73
  error-handling, 786–787
  exporting, 69, 511–512
  extensions, seeking, 786
  file URLs, 760
  Find and Replace, 564
  Flash animation, 468–469
  importing, 38, 453–464,
      467–468
  locked, 780
  opening, 788
  Project Log, adding to, 68, 576
  reading lines, 788
  renaming, 788
  replacing, 788
  reverting to saved, 128
  server-side image maps, 607
  storing, 127–128
  swapping, 788
  target of last operation, 777
  temporary, 787
  text, inserting, 789
  tracking in Batch Process, 768
  transmitting via FTP, 556
  URLs, 760–761
Files to Process option list, 584
Fill button, 38
Fill command, 94
Fill panel
  described, 51–52
  expander arrow, 47
  gradient fills, 326
  layout, 589
  Pantone color, 215, 216
  picture frame, 586
  rollover images, 646
  Style 37, 529
  text objects, 301
  Textures, 745
  Web-safe colors, 197
fills
  accepting, 152
  built-in, 315–321
  color, 56, 101, 199–200, 206
  described, 142

gradient, 36, 321–329
  hotspots, 611
  imported files, 463
  No color option, 208–209
  Paint Bucket tool, 342–344
  Patterns, 329–338
  property, 775
  Styles. *See* Styles
  text, transforming, 301
  texture, 339–342
  turning off, 316–317
film, 449–450
filters
  bitmap compatibility, 8
  blurring, 734
  browser animation support,
      692
  Convert to Alpha, 367
  Effect panel, 52–53
  File menu commands, 70
  folder, 746
  installing, 382
  listed, 382–395
  Live Effects, 10
  locating, 375
  photograph edges, 419
  Photoshop, 348
  Photoshop, adding, 106
  PNG, 502
  scanner, 438–440
  shortcuts (aliases), 384
  Styles, 522
  third-party, Photoshop-
      compatible, 382–395
  tweening, 715–717
  using with multiple
      applications, 383–384
  Web color, 193–194
  Xtras menu, 352–353
filters, listed
  Alien Skin Eye Candy, 384–390
  Alien Skin Eye Candy 3.1, 387
  Kai's Power Tools 5 (KPT 5),
      390–395
Find and Replace
  API (application programming
      interface), 783–784
  batch processing, 577
  changes, tracking, 575–576
  described, 76, 95
  panel, 68
  timesaver feature, 17

Web graphics, updating,
      562–575
  Web-safe colors, 197
Find Edges Effect, 354
Finder, 744
FinderPop, 527
finding
  edges, 92
  pathname, 768–769
findParms argument, 783
Fire filter, 379, 387, 715–717
FireWire. *See* IEEE 1394 interface
Fireworks
  banner ads, animating,
      723–735
  color, managing, 193–217
  customizing, 99–114, 739–758
  documents, setting up,
      117–136
  Dreamweaver, integrating
      with, 665–686
  exporting and optimizing,
      471–518
  image maps and slices,
      605–638
  introduction, 3–21
  paths, structuring, 255–284
  styles, 519–530
  symbols and libraries, 531–551
  text, composing, 285–312
  workflow, automating, 581–602
Fireworks 1.0, 122
Fireworks 2
  Crop tool, 131
  JavaScript, 579
  previews, 14
  toolbox changes from, 34
Fireworks 2.0, file format, 122
Fireworks animation
  background images, 709
  bandwidth, importance of, 690
  banner ads, 723–735
  browser background image,
      710
  commands, 89, 582–583, 803
  completing, 587
  controls, 33
  CSS layers, 676
  described, 11–12
  document controls, 33
  embedded, 622
  Export Preview dialog box, 504

exporting, 704–709
formats, 691–693
frame delay timing, 701–702
frames, managing, 59–60,
    693–697
image maps, 622
importing multiple files,
    467–468
indexed color export format,
    482
Instances, 534
objects, 698–700
onion skinning, 702–704
opening, 169–170, 466–469
preloading, 710
reasons, 690–691
reusing, 709
rollovers, 711–712
scaling, 709–710
slices, 636–637
slicing, 712
status bar, 41
tweening, 712–720
VCR controls, 700–701
Web, described, 689
Fireworks API (application
    programming interface)
    commands, building on built-
        in, 803–807
    data types, handling
        nonstandard, 760–762
    described, 759–760
    document functions, 799–800
    Errors object, 780–782
    file URLs, 760–761
    History Panel functions,
        801–803
    hotspot objects, 789–795
    JavaScript, 740
Fireworks API (application
    programming interface)
    methods, listed
    alert() method, 762–763
    behaviors, 793–795
    colors, 760
    confirm() method, 763
    masks, 761
    matrices, 761
    points, 762
    prompt() method, 764
    rectangles, 762
    resolution, 762

write() method, 765
WRITE_HTML() method,
    764–765
Fireworks API (application
    programming interface)
    objects, listed
    App objects, 765
    Document object, 771–779
    exportDoc object, 789–791
    Files object, 785–789
    Find object, 783–784
    image map objects, 791–793
    SliceInfo object, 795–797
    Slices object, 797–799
Fireworks Behaviors
    adding and removing, 640–643
    API (application programming
        interface), 793–795
    Button Symbols, 533
    command, 81, 95
    described, 639–640
    Dreamweaver integration, 667,
        678–680
    image map, 790
    images with, 13–15
    inserting, 81
    Nav Bar, 654–659
    Object Inspector, 49
    preloading animation, 710
    rollovers, 643–654, 659–663
Fireworks Behaviors Inspector
    described, 63–64
    Dreamweaver, 679
    opening, 49
Fireworks Behaviors Panel
    adding, 641–642
    deleting behaviors, 643
    described, 640–641
    modifying, 642–643
Fireworks Creator code, 591
Fireworks fills
    accepting, 152
    built-in, 315–321
    color, 56, 101, 199–200, 206
    described, 142
    gradient, 36, 321–329
    hotspots, 611
    imported files, 463
    No color option, 208–209
    Paint Bucket tool, 342–344
    Patterns, 329–338
    property, 775

Styles (See Styles)
text, transforming, 301
texture, 339–342
turning off, 316–317
Fireworks functions, API
    (application
    programming interface),
    800–801
Fireworks graphics
    Behaviors (See Behaviors)
    creation, 18
    creation, Fireworks 3 new
        features, 18
    editor, Dreamweaver,
        670–671
    matrices, 761
    Object Inspector, 48
    text rendered as, 298
Fireworks images
    capturing and importing,
        437–470
    working with, 165–191
Fireworks interface
    application programming. (See
        API (application
        programming interface)
    described, 23
    document controls, 27–33
    document window, 25–27
    Fireworks environment, 18,
        24–25
    floating panels, 41–69
    menus, 70–97
    toolbars (Windows), 37–41
    tools, 33–37
Fireworks JSF, 770
Fireworks Live Effects
    applying, 349–352
    Bevel, 361–364
    blurring, 365–366
    buttons, 546–547
    color, adjusting, 355
    Cookie-Cutter Text, 304–305
    described, 9–10
    Effect panel, 53
    Emboss, 364–365
    Glow, 370–371
    groups, 411–413
    Instances, 532, 542
    Knock Out shadow, 370
    managing, 375–378
                        Continued

Fireworks Live Effects *(continued)*
missing, 377
rollover images, 646
shadow, 367–370
sharpen, 371–372
storing custom, 376–377
Styles. *See* Styles
table, 354
tonal range, adjusting, 355–361
tweening, 713, 718
vectors, exporting, 516
Fireworks objects
arranging and compositing, 397–433
creating and transforming, 139–163
Fireworks Products Web Site command, described, 97
Fireworks strokes
Air Brush, 227
applying, 140–141
Basic, 226–227
built-in, 224–235
Calligraphy, 228
Charcoal, 228–229
color, 56
color selection, 206
color wells, 199–200
Crayon, 229–230
creating, 235–247
described, 152
dotted lines, 247–250
drawing, 35
editing, 238–247
erasing canvas, 184–185
Felt Tip, 230–231
imported files, 463
managing, 236–238
No color option, 208–209
Oil, 231–232
orienting, 250–252
Pencil tool, 225–226
Random, 233–234
Styles. *See* Styles
text, transforming, 299–300
texture fills, 340
thickness, 268
Unnatural, 234–235
Watercolor, 232–233
Fireworks Support Center command, 96

Fireworks textures
adding, 341
assigning additional folders, 341–342
banner ad animation, 733
color, 316
command, 601
converting color to grayscale, 341
described, 51, 339–340, 339–342
documents, adding to, 342
images, 340
light sources, simulated, 426
new strokes, 239
random strokes, 234
Settings folder, 745
strokes, 50, 220, 222–223, 241–242, 340
Style 37, 528–529, 529
Styles, isolating from, 528–529
Unnatural strokes, 234
Fireworks Xtras
color, 193
commands, 91–93
described, 352–353
Effect panel, 52–53
Effect panel versus, 378
false pixel selections, 380–381
fixing, 371
image objects, 379
Instances, 542
multiple objects, 381
Path objects, 379
pixel selections in image object, 379–380
returning folder pathname, 767
selection tool, 185
Settings folder, 746
Styles, 522
tweening, 715–717
fish-eye effect. *See* barrel roll
Fit All commands, 78
Fit Selection commands, 78
fitting, animation on page, 710
fixes
crops, 417
stray pixels, 496
Flash (Macromedia)
browser support, 692
buttons, 658
importing files, 451, 468–469

PNG browser support, 414
PNG format, 502
tweening animation, 713
Web formats, comparing, 692
Flash SWF (Macromedia)
command, 72
exporting files, 509
exporting format, 72
vectors, exporting, 515–517
FlashPlayer (Macromedia), 517
flat color, 481
flat fill. *See* Solid fill
Flip Horizontal button, described, 41
Flip Vertical button, 41
flip, objects, 83
floating panels
configurations, saving, 587–588
described, 41–69
illustrated, 24
Window menu, 93–95
flow rate, strokes, 241
Fluid Spatter unnatural stroke, 234–235
folder
Batch code, 742, 766
browsing for Web photo album, 682
Commands, 583, 599–600, 742
creating, 785
creating shared palettes, 590
Dreamweaver 3 library, 634–635
Export Settings, 743
file URLs, 760–761
FrontPage documents, 620
HTML code, 743–744
HTML output templates, 650
HTML style, 615
JavaScript functionality, 744
libraries, 550, 744
opening, 126
patterns, 331–332
plug-ins, shortcuts to, 384
preferences, 105–107
Settings/Styles, 520
Styles, 745
target of last operation, 777
texture fills, 341–342
Textures, 745
URL libraries, 562, 746

Xtras, 352, 382, 746
Folds gradient fill, 51, 322, 323
Font command, 87
fonts
    batch processing, 578
    Find and Replace, 17, 563, 784
    listing, 297
    missing, imported files,
        462–463
    outline, 299–300
    preserving, 305–306
    spacing, imported files, 463
    Styles, 524
    Web graphics, altering
        characteristics, 570–572
footer, formatting, 594
foreground images, copying, 427
form feed character, wildcard, 567
format, file
    animation, 691–693
    browsers, 471
    color, indexed, 482
    digital cameras, 447
    errors, 782
    exploring slices as different
        image types, 631
    Flash SWF, 72
    mixed, 622
    moving images between
        applications, 121
    opening existing images,
        122–125, 169–170
    photographs, exporting, 497
    unsupported, 780
    Web animation, 691–602
formatlist arguments, 770
formatting
    footer, 594
    RTF, 298
    view Styles before applying,
        526
Foti, Massimo, 223, 742
Frame command, 81
Frame Counter control, 481
frame delay timing, animated
        GIFs, 704
frame disposal, animated GIFs,
        704
Frame panel
    animation controls, 33
    export settings and options,
        704–705

frames
    adding, 695–696
    animation, 583, 693–697, 694,
        701–702
    bandwidth considerations, 690
    banner ads, 730, 734–735
    button, displaying, 67
    commands, 94, 586–587
    controls, optimizing, 481
    copying objects to, 698
    counting, 776
    creating, 81
    deleting, 696
    disposal, export setting,
        705–706
    distributing objects to, 699
    download time, 476
    duplicating, 697
    editing multiple, 704
    exporting, 509, 511–512
    Find and Replace, 564
    Frames panel, 59–60
    hotspot rollovers, 662
    hotspots, 612, 790
    image map, 791
    Onion Skin property, 777–778
    opening existing images,
        169–170
    reordering, 697
    setting range to onion skin,
        703–704
    target, 796
    VCR controls, 700–701
Frames panel
    animation, 467, 693, 695, 699
    current, 772
    duplicating frames, 646
    layout, 589
Frax4D filter, 392
FraxFlame filter, 392
FraxPlorer filter, 391, 392
Freeform and Reshape Area,
        paths, 270–275
freeform selection, 178–179
Freeform tool
    described, 36
    Image Edit mode, 190
FreeHand (Macromedia)
    clip art, 461
    compatibility, 8
    described, 116, 383
    document files, 459

document format, 122
formatlist arguments, 770
importing files into, 517
importing images, 437
inserting vector art, 450
opening existing images, 169
frequency, grid, 410–411
FrontPage (Microsoft)
    exporting rollover images, 649
    HTML style, 614
    image maps, exporting, 620
    slices, inserting, 635
FTP (File Transfer Protocol), 556
Full Display, 31–32
function keys, 536, 619, 654
functions
    custom, 742
    document, API (application
        programming interface),
        799–800
    Dreamweaver, 684
    execution, 685
    Fireworks API (application
        programming interface),
        800–801
    History Panel, API (application
        programming interface),
        801–803
Fur filter, 387
Fur stroke, 233–234
FVPicker, 208
fw.createDocument() function,
        801
FWLaunch JSExtension, 684–685

G
gamma
    commands, 78
    correction, scanned images,
        445
    cross-platform, 475
    PNG correction, 502
    preview, 776
    setting, 197–198
Gaussian blur
    color, 92
    depth, adding to images, 366
    described, 354
    Live Effects, 353
General preferences
    color defaults, 101–102
                                    Continued

General preferences *(continued)*
  interpolation defaults, 102
  undo levels, 100–101
Generic HTML code
  exporting rollover images, 649
  image maps, exporting,
    616–617
  slices, inserting, 633
  Web page, inserting, 652–653
getDirectory() method, 786
getDocumentDOM() function,
  800–801
getExtension() method, 786
getFilename() method, 786
getFrameFileName() method,
  797
getLastErrorString() method,
  786–787
getTempFilePath() method, 787
GIF
  animating slices, 637
  browser format limitations,
    471
  Color Table panel, 54–55, 474
  compression, 487–489
  creating images, 494–496
  download time, 476
  editing, 127
  export options, 773
  exporting image files, 509
  file path, 798
  format, 123
  formatlist arguments, 770
  Frame delay timing, 701
  halos, 487
  hotspots, 789
  hyperlinks, 644
  importing, 454
  indexed color export format,
    482
  moving images between
    applications, 121
  opening, 466–469
  opening existing images, 169
  optimizing, 472, 668
  rollover images, 660–661
  saved settings, 494
  shims. *See* shims
  slicing animations, 712
  transparency, 413–414,
    489–493
  Web photo album, 682

GIFs, animated
  banner ads, 689, 723
  browser support, 692
  creating, 11, 125
  export options, 773
  image export, 508
  indexed color export format,
    482
  looping, 706–707
  other formats versus, 691–693
  Web formats, comparing, 691
Glass filter, 387
glow
  fitting canvas size, 130–131
  Live Effects, 353
  tweening depth, 718
Glow Effect, 354, 370–371, 627
Glow filter, 387
Glow panel, Kai's PowerTools,
  395
Go to First Frame control, 481
Go to Last Frame control, 481
GoLive (Adobe)
  customizing workflow with,
    102–105
  exporting rollover images, 649
  HTML style, 614
  image maps, exporting,
    620–621
  slices, inserting, 636
  Web page, inserting rollover
    code, 652–653
Goodies folder, 461
gradients
  altering, 323–326
  applying, 36, 321–323
  available, 776
  color, 316
  described, 51, 142, 321–323
  perspective shadows, 374
  saving, 326
  Styles, 327
  transparent, 328–329
  using in another document,
    326–327
Graphic Symbols
  converting from Button
    Symbols, 546
  described, 533
graphics
  Behaviors. *See* Behaviors
  creation, 18

  creation, Fireworks 3 new
    features, 18
  editor, Dreamweaver, 670–671
  matrices, 761
  Object Inspector, 48
  text rendered as, 298
Graphics Interchange Format. *See*
  GIF
graphics tablet
  Freeform tool, pressure, 273
  freehand drawing, 154
  reasons to use, 144
  simulating lighter touch
    without, 275
  stroke stamp speed, 247
  strokes, 224
graphics, Web
  batch processing, 577–579
  browser, preview in, 553–556
  Project Log, working with,
    575–576
  updating with Find and
    Replace, 562–575
  URL Panel, maintaining links
    with, 556–562
Graphire (Wacom), 224
graphite pencil, 225, 226
grayscale, 90
  Adaptive color palette, 284
  color ramp display, 201
  convert to command, 584
  texture fills, 341
Grayscale color model, 56, 57,
  204, 210
  channels and bit depth, 414
grid
  color, 776
  color and frequency, 410–411
  Curves filter, 359
  seamless patterns, 335
  snap to, 410
Grid command, 79
Grid Options commands, 79
Group button, 40
Group command, 86
group, selecting objects, 34
grouping
  behaviors, 64
  described, 411–412
  mask groups, 413–418
  objects, 40, 411–420
  panels, 42

regular expression searches,
    569–570
subselecting and
        superselecting objects,
        413
Grouping button, 39
Guide Options commands, 79
guides
    clearing, 409
    colors, 408–409
    creating, 406
    exporting rollover images,
        650
    locking or hiding, 406–407
    property, 776
    slice, 623, 625–627, 632
    snapping to, 408
Guides command, 79

H

halo effect
    described, 370
    GIF transparencies, 487
Hand tool
    described, 35
    panning images, 478–480
handles
    Skew object, 258
    text, 287
handwriting. *See* calligraphy
hard disk
    defragmenting, 107
    Find and Replace operations,
        565
    full, 780, 782
hard edge, fill, 316
hard line basic stroke, 226–227
Harsh wet edge effect, 243
Heavin, Bruce, 319
height
    canvas, 117, 118, 121
    document, 32, 777
    hotspots, 790
    HTML table row, 795
    Instances, 542
    scaling animation, 709–710
Help button, 45
Help folder, returning pathname,
    766
Help menu
    commands, 96–97
    described, 95–96

hexadecimal color model
    choosing, 202–203
    color ramp display, 201
    described, 57, 62
    Web color considerations,
        195–196, 197
hexadecimal strings, hotspots,
    789
HiColor, 195
Hide Edges command, 79
Hide Panels command, 79
Hide Selection command, 78
hiding
    animation frames, 708
    background layer, 135
    CSS layers, 676, 678
    guides, 406–407
    layers, 59, 401, 586
    panels, 38, 44
    tool pointers, 180
    Web layer, 662
highlight
    area, 344
    button behaviors, 793
    color, 101, 220
    modifying, 358
Highlight button, 364
Highlight eyedropper, 357, 359
highlighter felt tip stroke, 230–231
History command, 94
History list, accessing URL,
    557–558
History Palette. *See* History panel
History panel
    automation, 16
    commands without coding,
        593–596
    converting objects to images,
        191
    described, 60–62, 581–582
    Document Object Model
        (DOM), 799–800
    Find and Replace, 564
    functions, API (application
        programming interface),
        801–803
    steps, copying to clipboard,
        596–598
    undo and redo, super, 591–593
    undo levels, multiple, 100
hit, 725
Hit area, 658

HLS color model, 204, 207
horizontal scale, text spacing, 292
HotJava, 554
hotspots
    API (application programming
        interface), 789–795
    Behaviors, 641
    commands, 49, 80
    converting object to, 613
    described, 12–13, 606–608
    image map objects. *See* image
        map objects
    inserting, 80
    layer, 398, 401–402
    links, assigning, 611–613
    Object Inspector, 48
    rollovers, 661–662
    slice, 631, 796
    tools, 36, 608–613
    updating URLs, 574–575
    URL history list, 557
    Web Layer, 58
hotspots, listed
    circle, 610
    polygon, 611
    rectangular, 608–610
HSB color model
    choosing, 203–204
    color slider, 201
    described, 57, 62
    Noise filter, 387
HSL color model, Hue/Saturation
        filter, 360
HSV, Macintosh color picker, 207
HTML code
    anchor, named, 557
    API, 740–741
    code templates, 743–744
    copy wizard, 74
    CSS layers, 677
    described, 12
    Design Notes, 671–672
    Dreamweaver integration, 15
    editing/optimizing, 105
    File menu commands, 71
    Fireworks 3 changes, 19
    folder pathname, 766
    hotspots, 12–13, 606, 662, 790
    image map, 112–113, 607, 791
    image optimization technique,
        507

                    Continued

HTML code *(continued)*
 images with behaviors, 13–14
 images, slicing, 108–112
 links, 556
 Macintosh color picker, 207
 optimizing, 14–15
 output with images. *See*
  behaviors
 outputting Dreamweaver,
  672–678
 properties command, 73
 rollovers, 643–644, 711
 setting tags, 591
 Settings folder, 743–744
 slices, 622–623
 Style option, 512
 styles, 614
 table, 109–111, 795, 798
 text, 285
 URL Library, 559
 URL panel, 13
HTML code, exporting
 CSS layers, 512–514
 Image Map code, 613–622
 image maps, 613–622
 slices, 631–636
HTML code, importing
 links, 560
 text, 297–298
HTML editor, 102–105
HTML engine, 739–741
HTTP (HyperText Transfer
  Protocol), 556
hue
 blending, 424
 JPEG, 499
 opacity and blending, 423
 stroke stamp, 246
 stroke tips, 244
Hue/Saturation filter, adjusting
  photographs, 360–361
Hue/Saturation Live Effect, 354
Hybrid-Safe Colors, 319
hyperlinks
 creating and maintaining, 746
 mimicking, 290
HyperText Template, 743

I

i.Link. *See* IEEE 1394 interface
IAB/CASIE standards, banner ads,
  723–724
IBM PC-compatible emulator, 556

icons
 clip art, 460
 No Color, 101
 shared palettes, 591
 Styles, 65–66, 520, 526, 527
 Symbols, 534–535
IEEE 1394 interface, 449
illustrations, JPEG, 496
Illustrator 7 (Adobe)
 command, 72
 document format, 122
 exporting, 72
 importing files into, 517
 vector graphics files, 459–460
Ilustrator (Adobe)
 application filter, 383
 clip art, 461
 exporting files, 72, 509
 formatlist arguments, 770
 importing Flash animation,
  469
 tweening animation, 713
 vectors, exporting, 515–517
 vectors, inserting, 450
image cropping, mask groups,
  417–418
Image Edit mode
 bitmap images, 104
 described, 165, 166
 Eraser tool, 184–185
 exiting, 349
 Lasso and Polygon Lasso tool,
  178–179
 leaving, 167–169
 Magic Wand tool, 179–182
 Marquee tool, 174–177
 opacity and blending, 422
 pixels, changing with Pencil
  tool, 156
 Pointer tool, 173–174
 Rubber Stamp tool, 182–184
 Select All command, 187
 selecting pixels, 75–76
 starting, 167
 tools, 190
 Turn Off "Hide Edges"
  preference, 169
image filters
 adding, 106
 bitmap compatibility, 8
 blurring, 734
 browser animation support,
  692

Convert to Alpha, 367
Effect panel, 52–53
File menu commands, 70
folder, 746
installing, 382
listed, 382–395
Live Effects, 10
locating, 375
photograph edges, 419
Photoshop, 348
Photoshop, adding, 106
PNG, 502
scanner, 438–440
shortcuts (aliases), 384
Styles, 522
third-party, Photoshop-
  compatible, 382–395
tweening, 715–717
using with multiple
  applications, 383–384
Web color, 193–194
Xtras menu, 352–353
image map object
 3D effects, 394–395
 API (application programming
  interface), 791–793
 areas, describing, 792–793
 client side, 790
 described, 605, 606–608
 drawbacks, 622
 exporting code, 613–622
 Find and Replace, 563
 hotspot tools, 608–613
 HTML properties, 112–113
 methods, 792
 pixel selections , Xtras menu,
  379–380
 properties, 791–792
 server-side, 744, 790
 type, 777
 Xtras menu, 379
Image Object command,
  described, 82
image objects, perspective
  shadows, 374
image quality, file size, balancing,
  472
Image Size command, 81, 113
image slices, shims, 110
Image Well, 509, 514–515
Image, command, 81
image-edit applications, 4, 508
ImageMapList, slice, 796

images
    bandwidth considerations, 690
    batch processing, 17
    behaviors, 640
    behaviors with, 13–15
    bitmap, 453–458
understanding, 166–185
    browser's background, 710
    canvas size for single, 131–134
    clipboard, dimensions of, 121
    copying to slice, 627
    depth, 366–371
    drawing area, limiting, 185–186
    Dreamweaver, 680
    editing in Fireworks, 670–672
    exporting, 506–507, 508, 631
    feathering selections, 427–428
    importing, 81
    internal error, 780
    listing changes, 69
    masking with text, 310–311
    Nav Bar, 641
    non-path based, described,
        165
    Object Inspector, 48
    Object Tools, applying,
        189–190
    objects, converting to, 190–191
    opening, 121–127
    opening multiple, 125–127
    optimizing, 19, 667–669
    output code with. See
        behaviors
    patterns, 745
    pixel-based, examining, 104
    resampling, 132
    rollover, 640
    selecting, 186–189
    selecting areas, 35
    selecting elliptical portion, 34
    sharpening, 371–372
    slice, 796
    slicing, 108–111
    swapped, dimensions of, 644
    text, converting to, 303
    texture fills, 340
    tonal range, adjusting, 355–361
    tools, 173
    writing, 797
img tag, 660, 709–710
Import button, 38
Import command, 71
Import preferences, 457

Import URL feature, 613
importing
    animations, 466–469
    bitmap image files, 453–458
    external files, 453–464
    gradient fills, 326–327
    images, 450–453
    libraries, 548–550
    palettes, 56
    preferences, 107–108
    Styles, 66, 526
    Symbols, 67
    text, 297–298, 462
    URLs, 65, 559, 560
    vector art files, 458–462
inches, measurement display, 62
incremental backups, Find and
        Replace operations, 565
incremental download, slices,
        622
index
    command, 96
    slice objects, 795, 798
Info command, 94
Info panel
    described, 62
    drawing rectangles, 145
    layout, 589
    object dimensions, 152
ink amount, strokes, 239, 246
Inner Bevel filter, 387
Inner Bevel Live Effect, 354
Inner Glow Effect, 354
Inner Shadow Effect, 354
inner shadows, 368–370
Insert Image command, 172
Insert menu
    accessing often-used libraries,
        550–551
    buttons, building, 543–544,
        656
    commands, 80–81
    converting object to Symbol,
        536–537
    creating new Symbols, 537–538
    CSS layers, 677
    hotspots, 610, 613
    Symbols, creating, 536
inserting
    bitmap images into document,
        172
    empty bitmap images, 172–173

image map code into Web
        page, 616–622
    rollover code in Web pages,
        652–654
    slices into Web pages,
        633–636
inset button, 364
Inset Emboss Live Effect, 354
Inset Path operation, 282–283
installing
    filters, 382
    Styles, 745
Instances
    animation, 693
    buttons, 546–548
    creating, 541
    deleting, 540–541
    described, 531–534
    fading in and out, 720
    Library panel, 66–67
    modifying, 542–543
    tweening, 82, 712, 714–716
integration, Dreamweaver,
        665–667
interactivity
    slicing animations, 712
    Web formats, comparing,
        691–692
interface
    application programming. See
        API (application
        programming interface)
    described, 23
    document controls, 27–33
    document window, 25–27
    Fireworks environment, 18,
        24–25
    floating panels, 41–69
    menus, 70–97
    toolbars (Windows), 37–41
    tools, 33–37
interlaced option
    described, 47
    exporting indexed color,
        493–494
Internet Advertising Bureau, 724
Internet Explorer (Microsoft)
    animation, 691
    client-side image maps, 607
    color palette, 210
    Frame delay timing, 701
    JPEG, 498
                        Continued

Internet Explorer *(continued)*
  PNG, 502
  preloading animation, 710
  previewing, 555
  Progressive JPEG, 501
  versions, 556
  Web animation, 692
Internet Explorer 4.x (Microsoft)
  location, 554
  status bar, 662
Internet Explorer 5.x (Microsoft),
  554
interpolation
  default preferences, setting,
    102
  resolution, 441
  scaling images, 170–171
intersect
  objects, 85
  path operations, 278
inverse images, selecting, 187
Invert Live Effect, 354
Invert mode
  blending, 425
  opacity and blending, 423
inverted button, 364
Invisible elements, 617
IP (Internet Protocol) address,
  557
isDirectory() method, 787
isDirty property, 777
ISExtensions, Dreamweaver
    integration, 667
isValid property, 777
italic text, 87, 290
  Rich Text Format, 462
  Styles, 524
iView Multimedia (Script
    Software), 462

J
JavaScript. *See also* Commands
    menu; History panel
  alert box, 763
  animation commands, 582–583
  API, 740–741
  automation tool, 16–17
  Batch a Command, 583–584
  Behaviors, 640, 793–795
  browser support, 692
  Creative submenu, 584–586
  described, 12, 759–760
  Document commands, 586–587

Dreamweaver integration, 15,
  665
  engine, customizing, 739–741
  errors, 781
  execution, 685
  exporting rollover images,
    648–654
  functionality, 744
  hotspots and slices, 12–13
  image export, 508
  images with behaviors, 13–14
  inserting rollover code,
    652–653
  links, 556
  Nav Bars, 654–659
  optimizing, 14–15
  output with images. *See*
    behaviors
  Panel Layout command, 589
  Panel Layout sets, 43, 587–588
  repeating elements, 654
  rollovers, 643–648
  running scriptlets, 579
  URL panel, 13
  Web formats, comparing, 691
  Web submenu, 589–591
jeans pattern, 745
Jiggle filter, 387, 388–389
Join button, 40
Join commands, 85
JPEG (Joint Photographic Experts
    Group)
  4-up view, 478
  animation, exporting, 691
  background images, 710
  browser format limitations,
    471
  color ranges, 180
  described, 498
  digital cameras, 447
  edges, sharpening, 500
  editing, 127
  export options, 773
  format, 123
  format, exporting, 497
  formatlist arguments, 770
  hyperlinks, 644
  image files, exporting, 509
  image maps, 622
  importing files, 454
  moving images between
    applications, 121
  opening existing images, 169

  optimizing, 47, 472, 668
  progressive, 501
  quality, 498–500
  rollover images, 660–661
  sharpening edges, 500
  slicing animations, 712
  smoothing, 500–501
  stray pixels, 496
  transparency, 489
  Web photo album, 682
JSExtensions
  returning folder pathname, 766
  Settings folder, 744
justify, 88, 295, 296, 307

K
Kai's Power Tools
  described, 8, 390–391
  filters, listed, 392
  RadWarp, 392–394
  ShapeShifter, 394–395
kerning
  auto kern, 290–291
  described, 290
  imported files, 463
keyboard modifiers
  adding/removing pixels, 180
  Bézier curves, 162–163
  control handle, extending, 162
  hotspots, drawing, 608
  rectangles, 145
keyboard pressure, simulating,
    224
keyboard shortcuts
  bitmaps, creating, 172
  browser preview, 555
  clearing selections, 221
  closing files, 128
  Convert to Paths option, 304
  converting objects to images,
    190
  converting symbols, 536
  copying selections, 366
  drawing ellipses and circles,
    147, 148
  drawing rectangles, 145, 146
  Exiting Image Edit mode, 167
  false pixel selections, 380
  fills, 315
  function keys, 654
  grids, modifying, 410
  grouping objects, 412
  guide colors, 408

guides, 407, 408
Insert Image command, 172
magnification, 31
mask, 416
Mask Group, 311, 328, 419
menu commands, creating, 595–596
Open Multiple command, 467
opening files, 123
opening multiple images, 125
Replay button, 593
return to object mode, 381
saving History panel steps, 594
selecting objects, 186, 187, 188, 189, 419
starting Image Edit mode, 167
Styles, creating, 378
toggling between Full and Draft Display, 32
URL Library, 558
Web dither fill, 319
keyboard shortcuts, filters
brightness/contrast, 355
Curves, 359
Hue/Saturation, 360
Levels, 357
keyboard shortcuts, panels
Behaviors, 641
Control, 619
Effect, 350
Fill, 325
Frames, 701
hiding and revealing, 44
Stroke, 219
Styles, 521
keyboard shortcuts, tools
Eraser, 184
Freeform tool, 272
Knife, 277
Lasso, 178
Magic Wand, 179
Numeric Transform, 261
overview, 34–37
Paint Bucket, 323
Pen, 157, 266
Rubber Stamp, 183
rulers, 405
Skew, 263
Text, 286
keywords, Preferences file, 769
Knife tool
described, 36

Eraser tool versus, 184
Path Scrubber, 276–277
Knock Out shadow effects, 370
Kodak color management, 199
KPT 5. See Kai's Power Tools 5 (KPT 5)
Krause, Kai, 390

L
labeling, stroke settings, 50
Lasso and Polygon Lasso tool, 35, 178–179
Launcher, Behavior button, 679
launching, Fireworks, 685
Layer command, 81
Layer panel, animation objects, 699
layers
adding, 399–400
animation, 694
banner ads, 729
changing stacking order, 400
commands, 94, 586–587
creating, 81
described, 397–398
distributing selection, 601
drawing hotspots, 609
editing by, 400–401
exporting, 72, 509, 511–512
hotspots, 608, 662
merge, 86
moving objects between, 400
Photoshop, maintaining, 107
property, 777
Web, 401–402
Layers button, 38
Layers panel
animation, 693, 695
CSS layers to Dreamweaver, 677
described, 58–59
document, 772
sharing animation layers, 700
layers, CSS
adding to Dreamweaver, 676–678
exporting, 512–514
Layers/Frames to Files, Export Special command, 72
layout tools
grid, 410–411
guides, 406–409
rulers, 405–406

leading
imported files, 463
text spacing, 292
left property, 777
left side, slice, 796
legal footer, 594
lenses, 392
letters, spacing
auto kern, 290–291
described, 290
imported files, 463
levels
color, 92
photographs, adjusting, 356–358
Levels Live Effect, 354
libraries
adding URLs, 65
command, 95
commands, 80
exporting and sharing, 550–551
importing, 548–550
libraries, URL
adding URLs, 558–560
described, 746
managing, 560–562
Library panel
deleting Symbols, 540–541
described, 66–67
display, 534–536
duplicating Symbols, 538–539
modifying buttons, 545
modifying Symbol properties, 540
light source, simulating, 425–427
Lighten mode
blending, 424
opacity and blending, 423
lighting angle, buttons, 364
lightness, stroke stamp, 246
line art, color depth, 444
line feed character, wildcard, 567
Line tool
described, 35, 152
Image Edit mode, 190
using, 153
Linear gradient fill, 51, 322, 323
lines. See also paths
Bézier curves, 156–163
freeform, 154–156
paths, 140–143

Continued

lines *(continued)*
  searching for beginning, 568
  straight, 153
  stroke, 338
  strokes (*See* strokes)
  text, 788
  texture, 495
Link Wizard
  buttons, 547–548
  Nav Bar buttons, 658
  new buttons, 544
links. *See also* URLs
  adding, 560
  breaking, 82, 542
  buttons, 547
  creating and maintaining, 746
  deleting, 558
  document, 772
  hotspots, assigning, 611–613
  Instances, breaking, 542
  maintaining, 556–562
  setting URLs in slices, 627–631
  updating, 560–561
  updating imported libraries,
    550
  without image maps, 622
  Xtras as Instances, 542
Linux, 556
list
  events, available, 679
  font, 297
  images, altered, 69
  open documents, 767
  option, 45
  Symbol, 534
  URLs, 64–65
Live Effects
  applying, 349–352
  buttons, 546–547
  Cookie-Cutter Text, 304–305
  described, 9–10
  Effect panel, 53
  groups, 411–413
  Instances, 532, 542
  managing, 375–378
  missing, 377
  rollover images, 646
  storing custom, 376–377
  Styles. *See* Styles
  tweening, 713, 718
  vectors, exporting, 516
Live Effects, listed
  Bevel, 361–364

  blurring, 365–366
  color, adjusting, 355
  Emboss, 364–365
  Glow, 370–371
  Knock Out shadow, 370
  shadow, 367–370
  sharpen, 371–372
  table, 354
  tonal range, adjusting, 355–361
Load Palette command, 486
location
  browser, 554–555
  Commands folder, 600
  Fireworks, 670
locking
  color, 54, 485
  files, 780
  guides, 406–407
  layers, 58, 59, 401, 586
logos
  animating, 690
  applied compositing, 428–430
  banner ads, 728
  color, 213, 572
  JPEG, 496
  Web dither fill, 320
looping
  animation export setting,
    706–707
  banner ad animation, 732
  frames, 776
  GIFs, animated, 704
lossless file formats, digital
    cameras, 447
lossy GIF compression, exporting
    indexed color, 487–489
Lotus Domino, 509
Lotus Domino Designer, 514–515
Lotus Domino Image Well, 72
lowercase text, 601
Lowery, Joseph, 683, 742, 803
luminance values, 55, 486
luminosity. *See* HLS
Luminosity mode
  blending, 424
  opacity and blending, 423

M

Macintosh
  Bézier curves, 163
  browser locations, 554–555
  Commands folder location, 600
  Commands menu, 89–91

  converting symbols, 536
  display resolution, 442
  document controls, 28
  dual monitors, 43
  Edit menu, 74–76
  exit/enter Image Edit Mode, 33,
    349, 350
  File menu commands, 70–73
  Fireworks interface, 24
  Fireworks location, 670
  function keys, 654
  gamma, 197–198, 475
  guides, 409
  hard drive, 106–107
  Help menu, 96–97
  HTML authoring, 513
  IBM PC-compatible emulator,
    556
  Insert menu, 80–81
  layers, 398
  libraries folder, 550
  magnification, 31
  Modify menu, 81–86
  navigating preferences box, 99
  OLE, 451
  opening document view, 27
  Page Preview button, 32
  panels, 44
  path to Commands folder, 761
  photographic images,
    exporting, 497
  Photoshop Acquire plug-ins,
    438
  platform property, 767
  PNG, 502
  resolution, 119
  screenshot tools, 465–466
  scriptlets, 740
  Settings folder, 742
  slice guides, 627
  steps, recording, 593
  templates, adding, 744
  Text menu, 87–89
  toggling between Full and
    Draft Display, 32
  Undo, 61, 101
  URL libraries, exporting, 562
  VCR controls, 33
  View menu, 77–79
  Web pages, building by hand,
    616–617
  Window menu, 93–95
  Xtras, 91–93, 382

Macintosh color
    Adaptive color palette, 284
    ColorWeb Pro, 215–216
    creating shared palettes, 591
    Eyedropper tool, 206
    filename extensions, 211
    indexed export format, 482
    management, 199
    palette, 56
    system color picker, 206–208
    WebSnap Adaptive color
        palette, 483
Macintosh Creator, 766, 773
Macintosh files
    bitmap image, 453–454
    Bookmark, 560
    creating, 785
    File Type code, 766, 773
    formats, 122–123
    importing to Windows
        platform, 464
    open multiple Fireworks
        documents, 125
    opening folders, 126
    Styles from Windows
        (Microsoft), 527
    temporary, 787
    vector graphics, 459–460
Macintosh Picture, 770
Macintosh System color palette,
    210
macro recorder. See also History
    panel
Macromedia
    Fireworks design scheme, 4
    registering product, 97
Macromedia Director
    Behaviors, 640
    described, 383
    PNG browser support, 414
    PNG format, 414, 502
Macromedia Dreamweaver
    Behaviors, 640
    behaviors, Fireworks, 678–680
    code, exporting, 672–678
    commands, hybrid, 683–685
    creating new documents,
        115
    customizing workflow with,
        102–105
    exporting image files, 509
    History panel, 591
    image-edit, 508

integration, overview, 15–16,
    665–667
Web photo album, creating,
    681–683
Macromedia Dreamweaver 2
    exporting rollover images, 649
    HTML style, 614
    image maps, exporting,
        617–618
    slices, inserting, 634
    Web page, inserting rollover
        code, 652–653
Macromedia Dreamweaver 3
    exporting rollover images, 649
    image maps, exporting,
        617–618
    inserting rollover code,
        652–653
    slices, inserting, 634
    Web page, inserting rollover
        code, 652–653
Macromedia Dreamweaver 3
        Library
    exporting rollover images, 649
    HTML style, 614
    image maps, exporting,
        618–620
    repeating elements, 654
    slices, inserting, 634–635
    working with, 673–676
Macromedia Dreamweaver images
    editing in Fireworks, 670–672
    optimizing in Fireworks,
        667–669
Macromedia Fireworks. See
        Fireworks
Macromedia Flash
    browser support, 692
    buttons, 658
    importing files, 451, 468–469
    PNG browser support, 414
    PNG format, 502
    tweening animation, 713
    Web formats, comparing, 692
Macromedia Flash SWF
    command, 72
    exporting files, 509
    exporting format, 72
    vectors, exporting, 515–517
Macromedia FlashPlayer, 517
Macromedia FreeHand
    clip art, 461
    compatibility, 8

described, 116, 383
document files, 459
document format, 122
formatlist arguments, 770
importing files into, 517
importing images, 437
inserting vector art, 450
opening existing images, 169
Macromedia Shockwave
    browser support, 692
    PNG format, 502
    Web formats, comparing, 692
macros, History panel, 16
magazine images, scanning, 445
Magic Wand tool
    background selection, 187
    described, 35, 179–182
    entering Image Edit mode,
        165
    pixel selection, 380
    Select Similar command, 188
magnification
    buttons, 35
    document settings, 30–31
    Magnify tool, 35
    view, 480
Mailto, 556
Main toolbar, described, 37–38
maintaining, Web links, 556–562
makeActive() method, 779
MakeFind() method, 783
makePathFromDirAndFile()
        method, 787
managing
    frames, 695
    Live effects, 375–378
    static objects, 699–700
    strokes, 236–238
    Styles, 525–527
map, image
    API (application programming
        interface), 791–793
    areas, describing, 792–793
    described, 605, 606–608
    exporting code, 613–622
    hotspot tools, 608–613
    HTML properties, 112–113
    methods, 792
    properties, 791–792
markers, felt tip. See Felt Tip
        stroke
marking, document locations. See
        guides

marquee
    Edit menu commands, 76
    modify submenu, 189
    tool, 174–177
Marquee tool
    accessing Crop tool, 131
    blurring, adding depth with,
        366–367
    described, 34
    seamless patterns, 337
mask
    API (application programming
        interface), 761
    images with text, 310–311
Mask Group
    applied compositing, 429, 430
    commands, 86
    described, 413–416
    image cropping, 417–418
    Object Inspector, 48
    paths, 417
    transparency, 328
masks, ShapeShifter effect, 395
matching, character positions in
        searches, 568
matrices, API (application
        programming interface),
        761
Matte color
    exporting, 487
    use, 777, 778
Max box, slider, 571
Maximize button, 26
memory
    bit depth, 195
    errors, 781, 782
    Find and Replace operations,
        565
    full, 781
    pixels, 166
    recording steps, 593
    scratch disks, 106
    undo operations, 101
menus
    Behaviors panel, 63–64
    Color Table panel, 54–55, 474
    Commands, 89–91
    Edit, 74–76
    Effect panel, 53
    File, 70–73
    Fill panel, 52
    Find and Replace panel, 68

Help, 95–97
History panel, 61
illustrated, 24
Info panel, 62
Insert, 80–81
Layer panel, 399
Layers panel, 59
Library panel, 67, 534
Modify, 81–86
Optimize Panel, 47
pop-up, 45
Project Log, 69
Styles panel, 66
Swatches panel, 56
Text, 87–89
View, 77–79
Window, 93–95
Xtras, 91–93
Merge Images command, 86
Merge Layers command, 86
messages
    confirm dialog box, 803–804
    mode-shifting, 166
    status, 794
    status bar, 662–663
    writing user alerts, 762–763
methods
    App object, 768–771
    global, API (application
        programming interface),
        762–765
    image map object, 792
    URL, 556
Micro Button banner ad, 724
Microsoft Bitmap
    files, 454
    formatlist arguments, 770
Microsoft FrontPage
    exporting rollover images, 649
    HTML style, 614
    image maps, exporting, 620
    slices, inserting, 635
Microsoft Internet Explorer
    animation, 691
    client-side image maps, 607
    color palette, 210
    Frame delay timing, 701
    JPEG, 498
    PNG, 502
    preloading animation, 710
    previewing, 555
Progressive JPEG, 501

versions, 556
    Web animation, 692
Microsoft Internet Explorer 4.x
    location, 554
    status bar, 662
Microsoft Internet Explorer 5.x,
        554
Microsoft Windows
    Adobe Illustrator, 450
    Bézier curves, 163
    bitmap format, 123
    building Web pages by hand,
        616–617
    ColorWeb Pro, 214–215
    Commands folder location, 600
    Commands menu, 89–91
    converting symbols, 536
    document controls, 28–29
    Edit menu, 74–76
    exit/enter Image Edit Mode, 33,
        349, 350
    export options, 773
    Fireworks interface, 24–25
    Fireworks location, 670
    font attributes, 289
    gamma, 197–198, 475
    hard drive, 106–107
    Help menu, 96–97
    HTML authoring, 513
    image format, 123
    Insert menu, 80–81
    layers, 398
    libraries folder, 550
    magnification, 31
    Modify menu, 81–86
    monitors, dual, 43
    navigating preferences box, 99
    OLE, 451
    opening document view, 27
    options lists, 46
    Page Preview button, 32
    panels, 44
    panels, floating, 44
    platform property, 767
    PNG, 502
    recording steps, 593
    screenshot tools, 465
    scriptlets, 740
    Settings folder, 742
    slice guides, 627
    status bar messages, 662
    templates, adding, 744

Text menu, 87–89
toggling between Full and
    Draft Display, 32
toolbars, 37–41
Toolbox, 34
Undo, 61, 101
VCR controls, 33
View menu, 77–79
Window menu, 93–95
Xtras, 91–93, 382
Microsoft Windows color
    Adaptive color palette, 284
    Adobe Color Tables, 212
    color picker, 208
    ColorWeb Pro, 214–215
    Eyedropper tool, 206
    No color option, 209
    palette, 56
Microsoft Windows Explorer, 744
Microsoft Windows files
    Bookmark files, 560
    browser locations, 554–555
    File menu commands, 70–73
    importing Macintosh, 464
    temporary, 787
    viewing only specific, 124
Microsoft Windows Meta File,
    458
Microsoft Word
    importing files, 451
    text format, 123
midtone eyedropper, 357, 359
millions of colors, 195
Min box, slider, 571
mindshare, 726
Minimize button, 26
mitered corners, 281
mixing
    color, 199–205
    gradient fills, 321–329
MKBY, 591
modal dialog box, 763
models, color, 201–204
modems, 471, 476, 690
modification tools, 103–104
modifiers, keyboard
    adding/removing pixels, 180
    Bézier curves, 162–163
    control handle, extending, 162
    hotspots, drawing, 608
    rectangles, 145
Modify Marquee commands, 76

Modify menu
    animating slices, 636
    Canvas color command, 119
    commands, 81–86
    editing Symbols, 539
    external rollovers, 660
    hotspot rollovers, 662
    Image size command, 113
    Instances, 542
    opacity, 719
    tweening animation, 713, 715
    tweening depth, 718
Modify toolbar
    described, 39–41
    illustrated, 25
modifying
    behaviors, 642–643
    button symbols, 543–546
    Instances, 542–543
    rollover images, 646
    Styles, 525
    Symbols, 538, 539–541
moiré removal, 445
monitor
    bit depth, 194–195
    color management, 199
    color models, viewing, 202
    dual, 42, 43
    gamma settings, 197–198
    Panel Layout Sets, 588
    resolution, 5, 441, 442
Motion Blur effect, 259, 392
Motion Trail filter, 387, 734
motion, tweening animation, 713
mouse
    behaviors, modifying, 642
    freehand drawing, 154
    highlighting, 344
    hovering buttons, 659
    rollover GIF images, 712
    rollover states, 645
    rulers, 406
    stopping running animation,
        701
mouse cursor, Dreamweaver, 680
mouse movement. See buttons;
    rollovers
mouseover. See rollover
movement
    CSS layers, 676
    lines illustrating, 691
movie cameras, 449–450

movies. See animation
moving
    files during export, 788
    image objects, 172, 174
    images among applications,
        450–451
    images between applications,
        121
    objects, 34, 40, 257
    objects between layers, 400
    panels, floating, 42
    points with Subselection tool,
        264–265
multiple paths, structuring,
    268–269
multiple previews, Workspace
    preview, 474–476
Multiply mode
    blending, 424
    opacity and blending, 423

N
names
    changes, Find and Replace,
        566
    domain, 557
    layers, 401
    path to Batch Code folder, 766
naming/renaming
    buttons, 547
    commands, 599
    CSS layers, 677
    effects, 53
    files, 788
    gradient fill, 52, 326
    HTML code, 743
    Live Effects, 375
    new strokes, 236
    Panel Layouts, 589
    pathnames, 788
    slices, 108–109, 629–630, 797
    stroke settings, 50
    Styles, 745
    Symbols, 536–537, 539
National Center for
    Supercomputing
    Applications. See NCSA
    protocol
Nav Bar
    Behavior, 641
    buttons, building, 656–659
        Continued

Nav Bar *(continued)*
    creating, 655–656
    described, 654–655
    Dreamweaver, 667, 678, 680
navigating, Commands, 741
navigation bar, banner ads, 724
navigation page, Web photo
        album, 683
navigation system, hotspot
        rollovers, 661
Navigator
    animation, 691
    Frame delay timing, 701
    location, 555
    Web animation, 692
NCSA protocol, 112, 607
Nearest Neighbor interpolation,
        102, 171
neon edge effects, 243
Netscape Bookmark files, 560
Netscape Navigator
    client-side image maps, 607
    color palette, 210
    importing files, 451
    PNG, 502
Network Solutions, 557
New button, 38
New Button command, 80
New command, 70, 115, 120
New Document dialog box, 121
New Layer button, 426, 677
New Style button, 525
New Symbol command, 80
New Window command, 93
News protocol, 556
newsgroup servers, 556
newspaper images, scanning, 445
Next Frame button, 700
Next Frame control, 481
No Color button, 317
No Style.stl, 527
Noize filter, 392
Normal mode, opacity and
        blending, 423
Norton Utilities Speed Disk, 107
Notepad, 513, 616–617
notes, recognizing in
        Dreamweaver, 671–672
number of colors, exporting,
        484–487
numbering, animation frames,
        697

numeric characters, wildcards,
        567
numeric sliders, described, 47
Numeric Transform
    dialog box, 660
    objects, 83, 261–263

O
Object button, 38
Object Inspector
    described, 47–49
    mask group, 417
    opacity and blending, 421, 422
Object mode
    entering, 417
    opacity and blending, 422
Object palette, Dreamweaver, 674
Object panel
    Alternate Image Description,
        607–608
    animating slices, 636
    hotspots, assigning links,
        611–613
    opacity, 432, 719
    slicing animations, 712
    stroke orientation, 300
    URL Library, 558–559
    URLs in slices, 627–631
object tools, applying to images,
        189–190
objects
    aligning, 39, 402–405
    animation, 698–700
    arranging and compositing,
        397–433
    background, 139–140
    Behaviors, 642
    Bézier curves, 156–163
    Button Symbols, converting to,
        545
    centering on canvas, 586
    creating hotspots, 402
    cut, copy and paste, 38
    deleting while cropping, 104
    fills and textures. *See* fills;
        textures
    frames, copying to, 698
    freeform paths, 154–156
    global API (application
        programming interface),
        765–789
    grouping, 39, 40, 411–420

hotspot, converting to, 613
images, converting to, 190–191
inserting from other
        applications, 450–453
layout assistance, 405–411
lines, 152–153
merge, 86
orientation, 6
palettes, converting, 584–586
paths, 140–143
perspective shadows, 373–374
pixel selections, Xtras menu,
        379–380
position, 39, 62
selecting and moving, 34
shapes, 143–152
size, 35, 62
skew, 36
slices, 49, 632
Stroke panel, 49–50
Styles panel, 65–66
symbols, converting to,
        536–537
text, inserting, 35
tools, 173
transforming and combining.
        See paths, structuring
Xtras menu, 379
obtuse angles, 151
official papers, 364
Oil stroke, 49, 231–232
OLE, 451
on/off, Live Effects, 375
onClick event, 642
onion skinning
    animation, 702–704
    box, 657
    multi-frame editing, 704
    property, 777–778
online image
    resolution, 441
    scan resolution, 443
onLoad event, 642
onMouseOut event, 642
onMouseOver event, 642
opacity
    animation, 720
    buttons, 546–547
    controlling, 421
    described, 420–421
    groups, 413
    Instances, 532, 542

Mask Group, 328
new strokes, 239
perspective shadow, 389
stroke stamp, 246
tweening animation, 713
Open as Animation option, CSS
    layers, 678
Open button, 38
Open command, 70
open files, batch processing, 577
Open Multiple command
    animations, 467
    CSS layers, 678
    described, 70
Open Multiple Files dialog box,
    769
open() method, 788
opening
    animations, 466–469
    another instance of an open
        file, 771
    bitmap images, 169–170
    document, 38
    Edit Stroke dialog box, 50
    existing images, 121–127
    files, 788
    folders, 126
    multiple images, 125–127
    Open in Image Edit mode
        preference, 169
    paths, 142
Opera, 555
operating system. See also
        Macintosh; Microsoft
        Windows
    color pickers, 206–208
    sharing Styles, 527
operations, path
    crop, 279
    expand stroke, 280–282
    Inset Path, 282–283
    intersect, 278
    punch, 279
    simplify, 279–280
    union, 277–278
optical resolution, 441
Optimize Image, 620
Optimize panel
    animating slices, 637
    described, 472
    Export Settings, 743
    exporting slices, 631–632

GIFs, animated, 704
layout, 589
optimizing, 473–474
reduced color palette,
    212–213
optimizing
    Color Table panel, 474
    defined, 472
    described, 471–473
    Fireworks, 685
    frame controls, 481
    images in Fireworks, 667–669
    Optimize command, 94
    workspace preview, 474–480
opting for no color, swatches,
    208–209
Option lists, 45
Options panel
    Path Scrubber tools, 276
    transform tools, 257
Options tab, strokes, 239–244
options, Text Editor, 296
Orb-It filter, 392
orientation
    commands, 89
    print, 113
    scanned images, 445
    stroke, 250–252, 300
origin, grid, 776
Original tab, document controls,
    29
OS/2, browsers, 556
Other commands, described, 92
Other menu, DitherBox filter, 353
Outer Bevel filter, 387
Outer Bevel Live Effect, 354
outline
    font, 299–300
    stroke, applying, 140–141
Outline unnatural stroke,
    234–235
oval
    drawing, 174
    masks, 761
Over Down rollover state, 645
Over rollover state, 645
Over state, rollover images, 646
Over While Down state, new
    buttons, 544
overlapping
    area, 278
    path lines, 272

overview, document, 32
overwriting, Find and Replace
    operations, 565

P
padding, HTML tables, 629
Page Preview
    button, 32
    document controls, 32
Page Setup
    command, 73
    dialog box, 113
pages
    animation to fit, 710
    impression, 725
    name of Web, 557
    saving, 668
    scanning, 440–442
    size, 113
    view, 725
Paint Bucket tool
    described, 36
    fills, 342–344
    gradient pattern, 323
    light sources, simulated, 426
    Swatches panel, 210
Paint Splatter unnatural stroke,
    234–235
Paintbrush tool, 344
Painter, 458
painting, simulated. See Oil
        stroke; Watercolor
        stroke
palette
    Color Table, 54–55, 486
    Fireworks additions, 675
    History. See History panel
    indexed color, exporting,
        483–484
    Library, 654
    objects, converting, 584–586
    shared, creating, 590–591
    Styles, 520
    Web, shared, 91
Palette button, 205
Palette icon, Find and Replace
    colors, 573
Palettes (Adobe), 212
Panel Layout command
    Commands menu, 589
    described, 91
Panel Layout Sets, 90, 587–588

panels, floating
  Behaviors inspector, 63–64
  Color Mixer, 56–57
  Color Table, 54–55
  common features, 44–46
  described, 41–42
  Effect, 52–53
  Fill, 51–52
  Find and Replace, 68
  Frames, 59–60
  grouping and moving, 42
  hiding and revealing, 44
  History, 60–62
  Info, 62
  Layers, 58–59
  Library, 66–67
  Object inspector, 47–49
  Optimize, 46–47
  Project Log, 69
  saving arrangements, 43–44
  Stroke, 49–50
  Styles, 65–66
  Swatches, 55–56
  Tool Options, 57–58
  URL, 64–65
  Windowshading, 44
panning
  view, 35
  workspace preview, 478–480
Pantone, converting to Web-safe
    color, 213–216
paper punch. See Punch tool
paper source, 113
parameters, errors, 780, 781
parentheses, Find and Replace
    operations, 783
Paste Attributes command, 75
Paste button, 38
Paste command, 37, 74
Paste Inside command, 75
pastel charcoal stroke, 228–229
pasting
  CSS layers, 678
  sliced images, 634
path
  completing, 163
  Object Inspector, 48
  returning name to Batch Code
    folder, 766
  selecting points, 34
  server, 557
  Stroke panel, 49–50

Styles. See Styles
text, 88–89
text on, Object Inspector, 48
Path Edge commands, 82–83
path objects
  perspective shadows, 373
  Xtras menu, 379
Path Scrubber tool, 36, 190, 268,
    275–277
PathAttrs object, 778
pathname
  checking, 787
  file URLs, 760
  files, 786
  finding, 768–769
  naming/renaming, 788
paths
  adding points, 35
  altering with cursor, 36
  center point, 142–143
  custom strokes, 238
  described, 140
  direction, 143
  dividing, 276–277
  errors, 782
  joining, 40
  mask groups, 417
  open and closed, 142
  Paint Bucket tool, 343
  redrawing, 35
  selecting, 173
  strokes, applying, 140–141
  text on, 306–309
  text, converting to, 303
paths, structuring
  adding and removing points,
    265–267
  closing, 267–268
  described, 255
  editing, 269–283
  moving points with
    Subselection tool,
    264–265
  multiple, 268–269
  numerically transforming
    objects, 261–262
  perspective, creating, 262–264
  visually transforming objects,
    255–261
Pattern fill
  adding new, 330–331
  altering, 332–333

color, 316
described, 51, 329–330
document, adding to, 332
fill, 142
gradient, 321
gradient, customizing, 323–324
light sources, simulated, 426
seamless, 334–336
Settings folder, 745
Style 37, 529
Styles, isolating from, 528–529
pattern-matching. See regular
    expressions
patterns
  applied compositing, 428, 430
  applying, 36
  command, 601
  PNG, 142
Patterns folder
  adding, 106
  returning pathname, 766
PCT file format, 123
PDF files, 114
Pen tool
  adding points on path, 266
  Bézier curves, drawing with,
    157–158
  closing open paths, 267–268
  described, 35, 152
  Image Edit mode, 190
  path scrubber setting, 36
  perspective shadows, 374
  points, specifying, 762
  Stroke panel, 49–50
Pencil stroke
  flow rate, 240
  spacing option, 240
Pencil tool, 49, 140
  clean up stray pixels, 496
  cursor shape, 103
  described, 35, 152
  drawing freeform lines,
    154–156
  illustrated, 141
  Image Edit mode, 190
  strokes, 225–226
Perspective Shadow filter, 387
perspective shadows
  Alien Skin Eye Candy, 389–390
  described, 372–375
  paths, structuring, 262–264
perspective, skew, 36

Photo-Paint (Corel), 383, 458
photographs
    edges, mask groups, 418–420
    exporting, 497–503
    feathering selections, 427–428
    JPEG, 498–501
    PNG 32 and 34, 502–503
    selecting pixels, 180
    tonal range, adjusting, 355–361
    Web photo album, 681–683
    Web-safe colors, 197
Photoshop (Adobe)
    adding plug-ins, 106
    blurring, 734
    color model, 203–204, 211
    compatibility, 8
    creating new documents, 116
    Drop Shadow effect, 368
    File menu commands, 70
    Fireworks versus, 5
    folder, 746
    image filters, 348
    importing files, 20, 107–108,
        451, 454, 455–458
    layers, 58, 398, 512
    locating Plugins, 375
    opening existing images, 169
    opening files, 125
    saving customized effects, 376
    scanner plug-ins, 438–440
    shared palettes, 591
    Styles, 522
    third-party filters, 382–395
    tweening Xtras, 715–717
    Xtras menu, 352–353
Photoshop (Adobe) document
    described, 122
    formatlist arguments, 770
Photoshop Acquire (Adobe) plug-
        ins, 71, 438, 446
Photoshop-compatible image
        filters
    bitmap compatibility, 8
    blurring, 734
    browser animation support,
        692
    Convert to Alpha, 367
    Effect panel, 52–53
    File menu commands, 70
    folder, 746
    installing, 382
    listed, 382–395

Live Effects, 10
    locating, 375
    photograph edges, 419
    Photoshop, 348
    Photoshop, adding, 106
    PNG, 502
    scanner, 438–440
    shortcuts (aliases), 384
    Styles, 522
    third-party, Photoshop-
        compatible, 382–395
    tweening, 715–717
    using with multiple
        applications, 383–384
    Web color, 193–194
    Xtras menu, 352–353
PICT
    compatibility, 454, 464
    digital camera images, 450
    exporting, 497
    indexed color export format,
        482
picture element. See pixel
picture frame
    convert to command, 585
    creating, 90
pictures. See images; objects;
        photographs
pipe character (|), 761
pixel
    Alien Skin Eye Candy, 386
    banner ad sizes, 724
    changing with Pencil tool, 156
    defined, 166
    eliminating in JPEG, 498
    filters, 353
    magnification, 30
    measurement display, 62
    object dimensions, 152
    objects, 140
    scaling images, 170–171
    selecting, 173
    selecting adjacent of similar
        color, 179–180
    selecting in Image Edit mode,
        75–76
    stray, JPEG original, 496
    Web color, 194
Pixel Radius slider, 372
pixel-based image options, 104
pixels
    Dimensions settings, 133, 134

placement, banner ads, 725
platforms, computer
    gamma, 475
    querying, 767
    scripts, 761
    sharing files across, 464
    sharing Styles, 527
    Web color, 197–199
Play button, 657, 720
Play Once button, 706
Play/Stop button, 481, 700
plug-in image filters
    adding, 106
    bitmap compatibility, 8
    blurring, 734
    browser animation support,
        692
    Convert to Alpha, 367
    Effect panel, 52–53
    File menu commands, 70
    folder, 746
    installing, 382
    listed, 382–395
    Live Effects, 10
    locating, 375
    photograph edges, 419
    Photoshop, 348
    Photoshop, adding, 106
    PNG, 502
    scanner, 438–440
    shortcuts (aliases), 384
    Styles, 522
    third-party, Photoshop-
        compatible, 382–395
    tweening, 715–717
    using with multiple
        applications, 383–384
    Web color, 193–194
    Xtras menu, 352–353
Plug-In Source (Adobe), 382
Plugin Com HQ, 382
plus sign (+), 568
PNG, 453, 454
    API (application programming
        interface), 779
    browser format limitations,
        471
    browser support, 414
    Color Table panel, 474
    described, 122
    export options, 482, 691, 773
                        Continued

PNG (continued)
    formatlist arguments, 770
    gamma settings, 198
    hyperlinks, 644
    importing Flash animation, 468
    importing libraries, 548–550
    Kai's PowerTools, 395
    limitations, 471–472
    moving images between applications, 121
    optimizing images, 668
    patterns, 142, 330, 332
    rollover images, 660–661
    saving files, 127
    sharing libraries, 550–551
    slicing animations, 712
    textures, 339, 342
    using, 105
    Web photo album, 682
PNG 24, 497, 498
PNG 32, 497, 498, 502–503
PNG 34, 502–503
PNG files, 454
pngText property, 778
point, center, 142–143
Pointer tool
    adjusting image objects, 172
    color selection, 485
    described, 34, 173–174
    Export Preview dialog box, 504
    panning images, 480
    starting Image Edit mode, 167
    stroke color, 221
    switching to, 221
    temporary switch to, 37
pointers
    Lasso tools, 180
    Magic Wand tool, 180
    Rubber Stamp tool, 182
points
    adding to paths, 35
    API (application programming interface), 762
    selecting, 34
    star shapes, 149
polygon hotspot, 36, 608, 611
Polygon Lasso tool
    pixel selection, 380
    tool, 35, 178–179
Polygon Slice tool, 36, 623, 625–626

Polygon tool
    described, 35
    Image Edit mode, 190
    image map, 791
polygons
    automatic angles, 150–151
    creating, 148–149
    drawing, 149–150
    hotspots, 606
pop-up menus, 45
popularity, sorting colors by, 486
Portable Network Graphics. See PNG
position
    CSS layers, 676
    Info panel, 62
    objects, 39, 40
    shapes, precise adjustment, 152
PostScript fonts. See Type 1 fonts
Precise Cursors, 180
Preferences
    command, 73
    customizing, 99
    Editing, 102–105
    editing, 747–747
    Folder, 105–107
    General, 100–102
    Image Editing mode, 169
    Import, 107–108, 457
    Invisible elements, 618
    location, 746
    Open in Image Edit mode, 169
    optimizing source, 669
    settings for key preferences, 748–757
    Turn Off "Hide Edges," 169
prefname, 769
prefval, 769
preloading, animation, 710
Presets folder, returning pathname, 766
pressure
    Path Scrubber tool, 276
    strokes, 247, 268
preview
    Alien Skin Eye Candy, 386
    animation, 716–717
    browser, 73
    color palette, 212
    different resolutions, 43
    document controls, 29–30

    export, 503–507, 508
    Export Preview dialog box, 72, 707–709
    files before opening, 124
    Fireworks 2, 14
    Fireworks 3 improvement, 23
    gamma, 776
    gradient fill, 325
    levels/auto levels, 357
    Nav Bar, 656
    pages in other gamma settings, 198
    rollover images, 647, 648
    saved effects, 377
    scanned images, 445
    Shape tab, strokes panel, 244–245
    Styles before applying, 526
    Symbol, 534
    text, 287, 290, 296
    workspace, 474–480
Preview in Browser commands, 73
previous frame
    button, 700
    control, 481
    restoring frames, 705
printed image, scan resolution, 443, 444
printers, color management, 199
printing
    colors, 203
    options, selecting, 113–114
    Print button, 38
    Print command, 73
    print publishing, 440–442
    Project Log, 576
    resolution, 778
    Size settings, 133, 134
PrintScreen key, 465
production tools
    automation, 16–17
    batch processing, 17
program settings, 769
programming. See API (application programming interface)
Project Log
    Batch a Command, 583–584
    batch processing, 577
    command, 95
    described, 69

Find and Replace, 564
Web graphics, 575–576
Project Log panel, 68
prompt() method, API
(application
programming interface),
764
properties
App object, 765–768
Document object, 771–780
Errors object, 780–782
image map object, 791–792
Property Inspector
editing Dreamweaver Library
items, 675–676
editing images, 670
proportions, sizing image objects,
173
protocol, server, 556
PSD files, 454, 682
publishing
image-edit, 508
scanning for print, 440–442
punch
objects, 85
path operations, 279

Q

Quality slider, JPEG format, 472
question mark (?), 568
QuickTime
browser support, 692
Web formats, comparing, 692
quill calligraphy, 228
quit() method, 771
quotation marks, Find and
Replace operations,
783
quote (double) key, 410

R

Radial Gradient fill, 51, 322, 323,
426
radio buttons, 656
RadWarp filter, 392–394
raindrops, 392
raised buttons, 364
Raised Emboss Live Effect, 354
rake crayon stroke, 230
ramp, color, 56, 199–200
random color, stroke tips, 244
Random stroke, 49, 233–234

range
characters, regular expression
searches, 569
frames to onion skin, 703–704
raster graphics. See bitmaps
ratio, fixed, 176
reading
file lines, 788
files, 788
slice filenames, 797
readline() Instance method, 788
RealPlayer, 691, 692
Rebuild Color Table command,
486
Recent Files command, 73
recording, steps, 593
Rectangle gradient fill, 51, 322,
323
Rectangle Slice tool, 624–625
Rectangle tool, 140–141
described, 35
Image Edit mode, 190
Stroke panel, 49–50
rectangles
API (application programming
interface), 762
broken links, 605
commands, 601, 602
creating, 144–145
hotspot, 608–610
hotspots, 606
image map, 791
keyboard modifiers, 145
masks, 761
rounded corners, 146–147
slices, 623
theoretical, aligning objects
by, 402–404
red X, Save as Command
limitations, 595
redo. See undo/redo
Redo button, 38
Redo command, 74
Redraw Path tool, 35
redrawing, paths, 35, 269–270
Register Fireworks command,
97
register, adding color, 493
regular expressions
searching with, 566–570
updating URLs, 575
relative URL, 557

Remove Action button, 643
Remove Edit command, 486
Remove Unused Colors, 47, 493
removing, points, 265–267
rename() method, 788
reordering
animation frames, 697
frames, 697
Repeat Xtra command, 91
repeating, pixel images, 36
Replace functions
API (application programming
interface), 783–784
batch processing, 577
changes, tracking, 575–576
described, 76, 95
panel, 68
timesaver feature, 17
Web graphics, updating,
562–575
Web-safe colors, 197
Replace Options dialog box, 565
Replace Palette Entry command,
486
Replay button, 593
resampling, 132
Reshape Area tool
described, 36
Image Edit mode, 190
perspective shadows, 375
Reshape Path tool, 375
resolution
API (application programming
interface), 762
canvas, 117, 118–119, 121
Commands folder, 601
defined, 440
digital cameras, 447
document, 32, 778
dual monitors, 43
monitors, 5
Panel Layout Sets, 588
scanning, 443–444
returning folder pathname, 767
reusing. See also Styles
animation, 709
design elements in banner ads,
728
Reverse All Frames command,
587
Reverse Direction command, 89
reversing, frames, 586

Revert command
API (application programming interface), 775
described, 71
saved files, 128
RGB color model
Adaptive color palette, 284
API, 760
bit depth, 194–195
choosing, 202
color ramp display, 201
color slider, 201
defined, 194
described, 57, 62
hex number system, 196
levels, modifying, 358
Macintosh color picker, 207
selecting pixels, 180
ribbon calligraphy, 228
Rich Text Format (RTF)
formatlist arguments, 770
importing, 298, 462
opening, 123
Ripples gradient fill, 51, 322, 323
Roelofs, Greg, 502
rollover button
animation, 711–712
Behaviors panel, 640
Bevel effect, 362
Cookie-Cutter Text, 304–305
creating, 363–364
disjointed, 659–660
Dreamweaver, 678, 680
embedded, 622
exporting to Web, 648–654
external, 660–661
Frames panel, 59–60
hotspot, 661–662
image export, 508
image maps, 622
image wells, 514–515
images, creating, 645–647
looping, 706
mechanics, 643–644
reversing frames, 586
Shims from Image option, 111
simple behavior, applying, 647–648
slice objects, 798
slices, 629
states, 644–645
status bar message, 662–663

Rotate 90° CCW button, 40
Rotate 90° CW button, 41
Rotate Canvas commands, 82
rotating
canvas, 82, 135
center point, 142–143
Instances, 542
multiframe animation, 582
objects, 35, 40–41, 83, 89, 257, 259–261
pattern fill, 332, 333
text, 88, 308
Rotating button, 39
Round Cap, 281–282
round corners, 281
rounded, basic stroke, 226–227
row
hotspots, 790
slice, 796
RTF
formatlist arguments, 770
importing, 298, 462
opening, 123
Rubber Stamp tool
described, 36, 182–184, 187
seamless patterns, 336
rubber stamps. See Symbols
rulers, 405–406
Rulers command, 79
Run Script command, 73

S
Satin gradient fill, 51, 322, 323
saturation. See also HLS
color, 92
photographs, adjusting. See Hue/Saturation filter
stroke stamp, 247
Saturation mode
blending, 424
opacity and blending, 423
saucer, banner ads, 729
Save a Copy command, 71
Save As command, 71
Save As dialog box, 779
Save button, 38
Save command, 71
Save Palette command, 486
save() method, 779
saved files, reverting to, 128
saving
CSS layers, 677

digital camera images, 450
documents, 779
effects, 53
export settings, 47
exporting indexed color setting, 494
filePathForSave property, 775
floating panels, configurations, 587–588
Frame Delay settings, 708
gradient fills, 326
gradients, 52
History panel steps, 61
Live Effects, 375, 377–378
new strokes, 236–237
Optimize panel settings, 474
pages before optimizing, 668
palettes, 55, 56
panels, floating, 43–44
steps, 592
stroke settings, 50
scale
animation, 709–710
batch processing, 578
bitmap images, 170–171
export options, 506–507, 774–775
horizontal, text spacing, 292
Instances, 532
measurement display, 62
multiframe animation, 582
objects, 83, 256–258
optimizing, 669
thumbnail images, 683
Scale tool
described, 35
objects, 259–261
text objects, 303
scallop shapes, 162
scanning/scanners. See also photographs
color depth, 444–445
color management, 199
directly into Fireworks, 446
fixing bad, 371
image capture, 437–438
other options, 445–446
page scanning, 440–442
pages, 440–442
process, described, 442–443
resolution, 443–444
selecting, 438–439

ScanWise (Agfa), 442
scatter, stroke stamp, 246
scratch disks, Folder preferences, 106–107
scratch removal, 445
screen capture
    applications, specialized, 466
    described, 464–465
    tools, built-in, 465–466
Screen mode
    blending, 424
    opacity and blending, 423
script
    banner ads, 726
    Command, 598
Script Software iView Multimedia, 462
scriptlet
    adding to Commands folder, 601
    Commands folder, 742
    deleting commands, 599
    Dreamweaver, 684
    execution, 685
    File Type code, 766
    Fireworks, 740
    important points, 806–807
    preferences, 748
    Web processing, 579
scripts. *See also* API (application programming interface)
    CGI (Common Gateway Interface), 725
    errors, 780, 781
    File menu commands, 73
    file URLs, 760
Search and Replace
    API (application programming interface), 783–784
    batch processing, 577
    changes, tracking, 575–576
    described, 76, 95
    panel, 68
    timesaver feature, 17
    Web graphics, updating, 562–575
    Web-safe colors, 197
search engines, attracting, 653
searching, regular expressions, 566–570
Select All command, 75

Select Behind tool
    3D effects, 426
    described, 34
Select Inverse command, 75
Select Similar command, 76
Selected Slice, Export Special command, 72
selecting
    circles, 175
    errors, 780
    Find and Replace, 564
    freely drawn areas, 35
    images, 186–189
    indicator, 41
    irregularly shaped areas, 178–179
    objects, 34
    ovals, 175
    points, 34
    portion of images, 34
    rectangles, 175
    scanners, 438–439
    squares, 175
selection tools
    crosshair cursor, 103–104
    Exiting Image Edit mode, 167
    filling, 343
Send Backward button, 40
Send to Back button, 40
Sensitivity tab, strokes, 245–247
separator, Save as Command limitations, 595
sepia tone, 90
    convert to command, 585
sequels, banner ad, 734
server
    banner ads, 725
    formats, 112
    path, 557
    protocol, 556
server-side image maps, 607, 744, 790
set brackets, 569
setFileName() method, 788
setFrameFileName() method, 797
settings
    Optimize panel, 474
    preferences, key, 748–757
Settings folder
    Batch Code, 742
    Commands, 742–743
    customizing, 741–746

    described, 741–742
    Export Settings, 743
    HTML Code, 743–744
    JSExtensions, 744
    Libraries, 744
    Patterns, 745
    returning pathname, 767
    Styles, 527, 745
    Textures, 745
    URL Libraries, 746
    Xtras, 746
Settings/Style folder, 527
shadow
    copying image to slice, 627
    effects, listed, 367–370
    Live Effects, 353
    modifying, 358
    perspective, 372–375, 389–390
    pixel selection, 380
    stroke tips, 244
shadow eyedropper, 357, 359
shape
    described, 143–144
    dimensions, adjusting, 152
    drawing, 35
    ellipses and circles, 147–148
    hotspot rollovers, 661–662
    hotspots, 610
assigning links, 613
    masks, 761
    polygons and stars, 148–152
    position, adjusting, 152
    rectangles and squares, 144–147
    slices, 623
    transformations, Instances, 542
Shape tab, strokes, 244–245
ShapeShifter filter, 392, 394–395
sharing
    animation layers, 700
    files across platforms, 464
    layers, 59
    libraries, 550–551
    Styles across platforms, 527
sharpen
    edges, 47
    effects, listed, 371–372
    Live Effects, 353
Sharpen commands, 93
Sharpen Effect, 354
Sharpen More Effect, 354

shims
    images, slicing, 109–111
    slices, 630–631
Shockwave (Macromedia)
    browser support, 692
    PNG format, 502
    Web formats, comparing, 692
Shockwave Flash files, 458–459
shortcuts, keyboard
    bitmaps, creating, 172
    browser preview, 555
    clearing selections, 221
    closing files, 128
    Convert to Paths option, 304
    converting objects to images,
        190
    converting symbols, 536
    copying selections, 366
    drawing ellipses and circles,
        147, 148
    drawing rectangles, 145, 146
    Exiting Image Edit mode, 167
    false pixel selections, 380
    fills, 315
    function keys, 654
    grids, modifying, 410
    grouping objects, 412
    guide colors, 408
    guides, 407, 408
    Insert Image command, 172
    magnification, 31
    mask, 416
    Mask Group, 311, 328, 419
    menu commands, creating,
        595–596
    Open Multiple command, 467
    opening files, 123
    opening multiple images, 125
    Replay button, 593
    return to object mode, 381
    saving History panel steps, 594
    selecting objects, 186, 187,
        188, 189, 419
    starting Image Edit mode, 167
    Styles, creating, 378
    toggling between Full and
        Draft Display, 32
    URL Library, 558
    Web dither fill, 319
shortcuts, keyboard, filters
    brightness/contrast, 355
    Curves, 359

Hue/Saturation, 360
    Levels, 357
shortcuts, keyboard, panels
    Behaviors, 641
    Control, 619
    Effect, 350
    Fill, 325
    Frames, 701
    hiding and revealing, 44
    Stroke, 219
    Styles, 521
shortcuts, keyboard, tools
    Eraser, 184
    Freeform tool, 272
    Knife, 277
    Lasso, 178
    Magic Wand, 179
    Numeric Transform, 261
    overview, 34–37
    Paint Bucket, 323
    Pen, 157, 266
    Rubber Stamp, 183
    rulers, 405
    Skew, 263
    Text, 286
Show All command, 78
Show Balloons command, 96
SimpleText, 513, 616–617
simplify, objects, 85
Site menu, enabling Design Notes,
        672
size. See also optimizing
    altering canvas, 129–134
    altering font characteristics,
        570, 571
    banner ad, 726
    banner ads (IAB/CASIE
        standards), 723–724
    canvas, 81, 117
increasing and decreasing, 34
    commands, 87
    document windows, 478
    export settings, 47
    exporting image files, 509
    file, image quality, balancing,
        472
    fixed, style, 176
    font, 297
    font attributes, 289
    hotspots, 610
    image, 81
    image objects, 173

Info panel, 62
limiting file, 705
objects, 35
objects, changing, 256–259
optimizing, 669
pattern fill, 333
reducing file, 484–487
Rubber Stamp tool, 184
scan results at different
        resolutions, 443
stroke, 50, 222
stroke stamp, 245, 246
text, Styles, 524
Web formats, comparing, 692
sizing handles, transforming
        objects visually, 256
Sketch filter, photograph edges,
        419
skew
    gradient fills, 323
    Instances, 532, 542
    objects, 83
    pattern fill, 333
    text, 89
    text on a path, 308
Skew tool
    creating perspective, 263
    described, 36
    dragging corners, 264
    Image Edit mode, 190
    objects, changing, 258–261
    text objects, 302, 303
slanting, objects, 36
slashes, forward (/), 760–761
Slice command, 80
Slice Guides command, 79
Slice tool, 36
SliceInfo object, 795–797
slices
    animation, 636–637, 712
    API (application programming
        interface), 795–799
    Behaviors, 641
    creating, 49
    described, 12–13, 605, 622–623
    example, 623–631
    exporting, 72, 631–636
    exporting files, 511–512
    exporting image files, 509
    guides, working with, 626–627
    hotspots, 790
    HTML style, 614

inserting, 80
layer, 398, 401–402
Object Inspector, 48
single, exporting, 510–511
updating URLs, 574–575
URL history list, 557
Web Layer, 58
slide-show, 690
slider
Bubble Size, 388
color, 57, 199–200
Hue/Saturation, 361
Min and Max boxes, 571
numeric, 47
Quality, 472
stroke, 50
Undo Marker, 592
slides, Color Mixer, 200–201
SMIL, exporting animation, 691
Smoke filter, 387
Smooth neon edge effect, 243
smooth, marquee selection, 189
Smoothie filter, 392
Snap to Web Safe command, 486
snapping to guides, 408
Snapz Pro (Ambrosia Software),
466
soft charcoal stroke, 229
soft interpolation, 102, 171
soft line basic stroke, 226–227
softness
Bevel effect, 362
Emboss effect, 365
solid color, 315
Solid fill
described, 51, 317–318
light sources, simulated, 426
Sort by Luminance command, 486
sorting, Symbols, 535
sound, comparing Web formats,
691–692
space character, wildcard, 567
space, searching for, 568
spacing
fonts, imported files, 463
letter, imported files, 463
strokes, 239–241, 243–244
spacing, text
aligning, 294–296
auto kern, 290–291
baseline shift, 292–293
horizontal scale, 292

kerning, 290
leading, 292
speed
banner ad animation, 735
download, 195, 476
downloading Polygon slices,
625
Path Scrubber tool, 276
stroke stamp, 247
strokes, 268
Speed Disk, 107
spelling, links, 613
spheres, 392
spider programs, 653
spins, 392
spirals, 392
splatter oil stroke, 231
Split button, 40
Split command, 85
square button banner ad, 724
Square Cap, 281–282
Square tool, Image Edit mode, 190
squares
creating, 144–145, 145
drawing, 174
Eraser tool, 184
hotspots, 609
keyboard modifiers, 145
rounded corners, 146–147
stroke, 233–234
stroke stamp, 245
Squint filter, 387
squinting, 277–278
src attribute, 644, 660
stacking
animation objects, 699
commands, 601
CSS layers, 676
layers, changing, 400
open documents, 26
tweening animation, 714
stamp
stroke, 239–240
time and date, 601
standards, banner ad size
(IAB/CASIE), 723–724
Star filter, 387
Star tool, Image Edit mode, 190
Starburst gradient fill, 51, 322, 323
stars
creating, 151
hotspots, 613

starting, Image Edit mode, 167
static objects, managing, 699–700
status bar
command, 79
Exiting Image Edit mode, 167
illustrated, 25
rollover messages, 662–663
setting text, 641
text, 678, 743
VCR controls, 33
Status Message Behaviors, 794
Status toolbar, 41
stencils, 156
steps
recording as Command, 16–17
recording number, 593
saving, 592
Stop. See Play/Stop
Stop button. See Play/Stop button
storing
custom Live effects, 376–377
files, 127–128
gradient fills, modified, 326,
327
Symbols, 11
strands oil stroke, 231
streaming, comparing Web
formats, 691–692
stretch
alignment, 295, 296
text, 88
text on a path, 307
string
converting argument, 764–765
Find methods, 784
hotspots, 789
Stroke button, 38
Stroke command, 94
Stroke panel
buttons, 35
categories and types, 221–222
described, 49–50, 219–221
edge and size, 222
expander arrow, 47
layout, 589
rollover images, 646
texture, 222–223
strokes
applying, 140–141
Basic, 226–227
built-in, 224–235
Continued

strokes *(continued)*
   color, 56
   color selection, 206
   color wells, 199–200
   creating, 235–247
   described, 152
   drawing, 35
   editing, 238–247
   erasing canvas, 184–185
   imported files, 463
   managing, 236–238
   No color option, 208–209
   orienting, 250–252
   Styles. *See* Styles
   text, transforming, 299–300
   texture fills, 340
   thickness, 268
strokes, listed
   Air Brush, 227
   Calligraphy, 228
   Charcoal, 228–229
   Crayon, 229–230
   dotted lines, 247–250
   Felt Tip, 230–231
   Oil, 231–232
   Pencil tool, 225–226
   Random, 233–234
   Unnatural, 234–235
   Watercolor, 232–233
Style 37, 528–529
Style 51. *See* Style 37
StyleBuilder command, 683
Styles
   altering font characteristics,
      570, 571
   applying, 521–522
   commands, 87, 95
   creating new, 237–238, 522–525
   described, 10–11
   Find and Replace, 563
   folder, returning pathname,
      767
   font, 290, 297
   gradient fills, 327
   HTML, 614
   Live Effects, 377–378
   managing, 525–527
   panel, 65–66
   patterns and textures,
         isolating from, 528–529
   reasons for, 519
   Settings folder, 745

strokes, 65–66, 524
   understanding, 520–521
Stylize filter, photograph edges,
      419
Subselect command, 75
Subselection tool
   closing open paths, 267–268
   described, 34
   grouping objects, 413
   paths, structuring, 264–265
   starting Image Edit mode, 167
Superselect command, 75
superselecting, grouping objects,
      413
Swap Image behavior, 640, 794
   dialog box, 660
   Dreamweaver, 678
   preloading animation, 710
swap() method, 788
swapping, files, 788
swatches
   color wells, choosing from,
      205–206
   Eyedropper, 206
   opting for no color, 208–209
   panel, using, 209–212
   Swatches panel, 55–56
   system color picker, accessing,
      206–208
Swatches (Adobe), 212
Swatches command, 94
Swirl filter, 387
Symbol commands, 82
Symbol Editor, modifying
      Symbols, 539
Symbol list, 534
Symbol preview, 534
Symbols
   animation, 693
   buttons, making and
      modifying, 543–546
   copying (*See* Instances)
   creating, 536–539
   described, 531–534
   errors, 780, 781, 782
   inserting, 80
   libraries, 744
   Library panel, 66–67
   Link Wizard, 548
   modifying, 539–541
   Object Inspector, 48
   tweening animation, 712, 713

updating imported libraries,
      550
Symbols-Plus. *See* Button Symbols
system color picker, accessing,
      206–208

T

tab character, wildcard, 567
Tab key, 44, 62
Table Shims, 629, 798
tables, slice, 623, 796
tablet, graphics
   freehand drawing, 154
   path scrubber setting, 36
   reasons to use, 144
   strokes, 224
Tabs, described, 44
Tag Selector, 634
tags
   banner ads, 725
   image maps, exporting,
      613–622
   setting, 91
   setting Alt (HTML), 591
Targa files, 123, 454
target
   buttons, 547
   hotspots, assigning links, 612
   slice, 796
television
   gamma setting, 198
   Internet, 198
   Web TV Viewer, 555
template
   adding, 744
   Dreamweaver 3 library,
      634–635
   HTML, 614, 649, 650, 743–744
temporary files, 787
testing, animation, 467
text
   adding, 789
   banner ads, 729
   batch processing, 578
   button, 546–547
   commands, 601
   cookie-cutter, 304–305
   files, inserting, 789
   Find and Replace, 17, 68, 563,
      783
   fonts, 305–306
   hotspots, 789, 790

image map, 790, 791
importing, 297–298
inserting objects, 35
interpolation, 171
links, behaviors, 640
masking images with, 310–311
Object Inspector, 48
objects, perspective shadows, 373
on a path command, 306–309
on a path, Object Inspector, 48
Photoshop files, 457
property, 778
re-editing, 297
reading one line at a time, 788
regular expressions, searching with, 567
searching and replacing, 566
slices, 628–629, 795, 796
status bar, 641, 678
Styles, 65–66, 524
transforming, 299–303
text boxes, 47
Text Editor
building Web pages by hand, 616–617
described, 285–287
display dialog box, 88
fonts, choosing basic characteristics, 288–290
importing files, 298
options, enabling, 296
previewing on the fly, 287–288
spacing, adjusting, 290–296
Web page, inserting rollover code, 653
text file
File Type code, 766
formatlist arguments, 770
importing, 462
Text menu, commands, 87–89
text styles, 520–521
Text tool
described, 35
Image Edit mode, 190
Stroke panel, 49–50
Texture
banner ad animation, 733
color, 316
command, 601
new strokes, 239
random strokes, 234

Settings folder, 745
strokes, 50, 220, 222–223, 241–242
Style 37, 528–529, 529
Styles, isolating from, 528–529
Unnatural strokes, 234
Texture fill
adding, 341
assigning additional folders, 341–342
converting color to grayscale, 341
described, 51, 339–340, 339–342
documents, adding to, 342
images, 340
light sources, simulated, 426
strokes, 340
textured air brush stroke, 223, 227
textured bristles oil stroke, 231
textured charcoal stroke, 229
textures
applying, 36
charcoal strokes, 228–229
creating perspective, 263
folder, 106, 495, 767
pixel selection, 380
property, 778
thickness, stroke, 222, 268
think felt tip market stroke, 230–231
third-party, Photoshop-compatible image filters, 382–395
thousands of colors, 195
Threshold slider, 372
thumbnail images, 448, 681, 682
TIF, Web photo album, 682
TIFF
digital camera images, 450
export options, 773
exporting, 497
format, 123
formatlist arguments, 770
indexed color export format, 482
Kai's PowerTools, 395
moving images between applications, 121
opening existing images, 169
tile background, 601
Tile Horizontal command, 95

Tile Vertical command, 95
tiling, documents, 26
Time and Date Stamp command, 601
time, previewing download, 476
time-saving tips. See Libraries; shortcuts; Styles; Symbols
timing
animation, 467, 691
bandwidth considerations, 690
frame delay, 701–702
frames, 481
Tint mode
blending, 425
opacity and blending, 423
tips, strokes, 243–244
toggling
Full and Draft Display, 32
layers, 586
tolerance slider, 344
tonal range, adjusting effects, 355–361
Tool Options command, 94
Tool Options panel
corner percentage, 147
described, 57–58
Lasso edge, 179
toolbars
commands, 93–94
Window menu, 93–95
Windows interface, 25
Toolbars (Windows)
Main, 37–38
Modify, 39–41
Status, 41
Toolbox
Circle Hotspot tool, 610
command, 94
described, 33–37
illustrated, 24
Polygon Hotspot tool, 611
Polygon Slice tool, 625–626
Rectangle Slice, 624–625
Rectangular hotspot tool, 608–610
Slice tools, 623–631
stroke color, 219
tools
animation, 693–709
automation, 16–17

Continued

tools *(continued)*
   batch processing, 17
   Button Editor (*See* Button
      Editor)
   color wells, 205
   described, 33–37
   Image Edit mode, 190
   Polygon Slice, 623
   precise cursors, 103–104
   screen capture, 465–466
   Transform, Instances, 532
tools, listed
   Distort, 259
   Eraser, 184–185
   Hand tool, 478–480
   hotspots, 608–613
   Image Edit Mode, 190
   knife, 276–277
   Lasso and Polygon Lasso,
      178–179
   Magic Wand, 179–182
   Marquee, 174–177
   Paint Bucket, 342–344
   Path Scrubber, 275–277
   Pencil, 225–226
   Pointer, 173–174
   Rubber Stamp, 182–184
   slices, 624–631
   text transform, 301–303
tooltips, 41, 168
Toothpaste unnatural stroke,
   234–235
top
   property, 778
   slice, 796
touching up. *See* Redraw Path
   tool
Toxic Waste unnatural stroke,
   234–235
tracking, changes, 68, 69
trademarks, color, 213
Transform as Path option, 302
Transform commands, 83
Transform tools
   Image Edit mode, 190
   image objects, 256
   Instances, 532
   slices, 624
   text, 301–303
transformations
   text, 299–303
   tweening animation, 713

transparencies
   alpha, 502
   browsers, 482
   buttons, 546–547
   canvas color, 119, 184–185
   color, 54
   controlling, 421
   exporting indexed color,
      489–493
   fill, 344
   fill texture, 51
   GIFs, 413–414, 487, 710
   GIFS, animated, 705
   gradient fills, 328–329
   hotspots, 789
   Instances, 532, 542
   JPEG, 498
   new strokes, 239
   perspective shadow, 389
   restoring frames, 706
   seamless patterns, 338
   shims, 110
   slice objects, 798
   slices, 623
   strokes, 222, 246
   tweening animation, 713
   Watercolor strokes, 232–233
   Web dither fill, 321
   Web formats, comparing,
      691–692
triggering, behaviors, 642–643
Trim Canvas command, 82
Trim Images option, 512, 678
trimming, canvas, 134
True Color
   channels and bit depth, 414
   compatibility, 195
   optimizing, 472
TrueType fonts, 289
Turn Off "Hide Edges" preference,
   169
turning off, fills, 316–317
Tutorial command, 96
TWAIN
   defined, 437–438
   File menu commands, 70
   scanned images, 446
tweening
   animation, 712–720
   defined, 712
   depth, 717–718
   described, 11

fading in and out, 719–720
   Instances, 82, 534
   uses, 713–715
   Xtras, 715–717
twist, jiggle, 389
Type 1 fonts, 289, 463
Type Manager (Adobe), 463

U
underline text, 87, 290
underlines, Styles, 524
Undo button, 38
Undo command
   converting objects to images,
      191
   described, 74
Undo Marker, 592
Undo/Redo. *See also* History
      panel
   animation frames, 696
   Batch a Command, 584
   described, 37
   editing Symbols, 539
   Find and Replace, 564
   History panel, 16, 60–61
   setting preferences, 100–101
   super, 591–593
   tweening depth, 718
Ungroup button, 40
Ungroup command, 86
uniform color
   palette, 284
   stroke tips, 244
Uniform Resource Locator. *See*
      URLs
union
   objects, 85
   path operations, 277–278
Unix image format, 123
Unlock All Colors command, 486
unlocking, gradient pattern, 323
Unnatural fluid spatter, 221
Unnatural stroke
   described, 49, 234–235
   illustrated, 141
Unsharp Mask Effect, 354
Up rollover state, 645
Update button, optimizing
      images, 667
Update HTML command, 71
updating
   Color Table panel, 54

Dreamweaver Library items, 675
images, 622, 671
imported libraries, 550
links, 746
Symbols, 67
URLs, 574–575
Web graphics, 562–575
uppercase text, 601
URL
    background link, 772
    batch processing, 578
    Button Symbols, 533
    buttons, 547
    command, 95
    file, API (application programming interface), 760
    Find and Replace, 17, 68, 563, 564
    Find methods, 784
    History list, accessing, 557–558
    hotspot rollovers, 662
    hotspots, 112, 790, 792
    image map, 791
    regular expressions, searching with, 567
    rollover images, 648
    setting in slices, 627–631
    slices, 796, 798
    Swap Image Behaviors, 794
    target of last operation, 777
    updating, 574–575
    Web TV Viewer, 555
URL History list, 557–558
URL library
    adding URLs, 558–560
    managing, 560–562
    returning pathname, 766
    Settings folder, 746
URL panel
    described, 13, 64–65
    setting URLs in slices, 627–631
    Web graphics, maintaining links with, 556–562
USB port, digital cameras, 447
user interface
    buttons (See buttons)
    described, 23
    document controls, 27–33
    document window, 25–27

Fireworks 3 new features, 18
Fireworks environment, 18, 24–25
floating panels, 41–69
menus, 70–97
Nav Bar, 654–659
rollovers. See rollovers
toolbars (Windows), 37–41
tools, 33–37
users
    application information, 765–771
    data entry, 764
    entering information, 764
    shim creation, control, 631
    writing alerts, 762–763
    writing confirmation boxes, 763
Using Fireworks command, 96
utilities, URL management, 64–65

V
vanishing point, 389
VCR-like controls
    animation, 693, 700–701
    banner ad objects, 731, 732
    described, 33
    Export Preview dialog box, 504
    frames, 481
    preview animation, 716–717
    testing animation, 467
vector art
    drawing programs, 4
    exporting, 509
    importing, 458–462
    importing Flash animation, 468
    inserting, 450
    tweening animation, 713
vectors. See also paths
    exporting, 515–517
    indexed color export format, 482
versions
    Fireworks, 685
    Internet Explorer, 556
vertical text on a path, 308
video memory, bit depth, 195
VideoShop, 449
view
    Button Editor tabs, 657
    frames, 512

layers, 402
panning, 35
rulers, 405
View Controls toolbar
    illustrated, 25
    toggling, 94
    toggling between Full and Draft Display, 32
View menu
    commands, 77–79
    Invisible elements, 617
viewing
    animation frames, 708
    Color Table panel, 474
    CSS layers, 676, 678
    grid, 410
    JPEG, 498
    slice guides, 626–627
    Web graphics, 480
Virtual PC (Connectix), 556
Viscous Alien Paint unnatural stroke, 234–235

W
W3C. See World Wide Web Consortium (W3C)
Wacom Graphire, 224
warnings, mode-shifting, 166
Warp amount, jiggle, 388
warping. See Distort tool
Water Drops filter, 387
Watercolor stroke
    described, 49, 232–233
    velocity, 154
wave shapes, 162
Waves gradient fill, 322, 323
Wavy gravy edge effect, 243
Weave filter, 387
Web
    Export Wizard choice, 508
    image files, exporting, 509
    rollovers, exporting, 648–654
Web 216 palette, 56, 210
Web addresses. See URLs
Web commands, described, 91
Web connectivity, Fireworks 3 new features, 19
Web Dither fill, 51, 315, 318–321
Web graphics
    batch processing, 577–579
    browser, preview in, 553–556
                        Continued

Web graphics *(continued)*
   Project Log, working with, 575–576
   updating with Find and Replace, 562–575
   URL Panel, maintaining links with, 556–562
Web Layer
   described, 58, 398, 401–402
   hotspot rollovers, 662
Web links
   described, 12
   Dreamweaver integration, 15–16
   file optimization, 14–15
   hotspots and slices, 12–13
   images with behaviors, 13–15
   maintaining, 556–562
   URL panel, 13
Web objects. *See* image maps; slices
   Behaviors, 793–795
Web page
   banner ads, 723
   client-side image maps, 607
   CSS layers, 678
   exporting and optimizing files, 471–518
   inserting image map code, 616–622
   inserting rollover code, 652–654
   inserting slices into, 633–636
   photo album, 681–683
Web site, importing home page, 560
Web sites, addresses listed
   Adobe Plug-In Source, 382
   Alien Skin, 384
   banner ads, standards for, 724
   Casey, Donna, 528
   CGI (Common Gateway Interface) scripts, 725
   clip art, 462
   color picker, third-party, 208
   Dreamweaver commands, 683
   Extensis, 462
   Fireworks Support Center, 601, 684, 742
   IAB/CASIE standards, 724
   Joseph Lowery's Fireworks, etc., 742

Massimo Foti, 742
Plugin Com HQ, 382
PNG home page, 502
Simon White's Fireworks page, 742
Styles, 11, 520
TWAIN Working Group, 438
Web TV Viewer, 555
Web submenu, Commands menu, 589–591
Web TV Viewer, 555
Web-safe color
   Adaptive color palette, 284
   batch processing, 578
   bit depth, 194–195
   browsers, 196–197
   Color Table command, 486
   Color Table panel, 54
   described, 193–194
   dithering, 318
   Eyedropper tool, 206
   Find and Replace, 17, 564
   hexadecimal colors, 195–196
   managing, 199
   platform differences, 197–199
   snapping to, 573–574
   Web Dither fill, 318–321
webbot. *See* Front Page
WebSnap Adaptive color palette, 483, 494
weight, banner ads, 723, 724
Weinman, Lynda, 319
wells, color, 199–200
wet calligraphy, 228
What's New in Version 3 command, 96
White neon edge effect, 243
White neon no center edge effect, 243
white, bit depth, 194
White, Simon, 742
white-space characters, wildcards, 567
width
   Bevel effect, 362
   canvas, 117, 118, 121
   document, 32, 778
   Emboss effect, 365
   expand stroke, 281
   gradient fills, 323
   hotspots, 790
   HTML table row, 795

Instances, 542
   minimize panel, 535
   scaling animation, 709–710
   slice, 796
wildcard characters, regular expression searches, 567–568
Window menu commands, 93–95
windows
   dockable floating, 99
   document, 25–27
Windows (Microsoft)
   Adobe Illustrator, 450
   Bézier curves, 163
   building Web pages by hand, 616–617
   Commands folder location, 600
   Commands menu, 89–91
   converting symbols, 536
   document controls, 28–29
   Edit menu, 74–76
   exit/enter Image Edit Mode, 33, 349, 350
   export options, 773
   Fireworks interface, 24–25
   Fireworks location, 670
   font attributes, 289
   gamma, 197–198, 475
   hard drive, 106–107
   Help menu, 96–97
   HTML authoring, 513
   image format, 123
   Insert menu, 80–81
   layers, 398
   libraries folder, 550
   magnification, 31
   Modify menu, 81–86
   monitors, dual, 43
   navigating preferences box, 99
   OLE, 451
   opening document view, 27
   options lists, 46
   Page Preview button, 32
   panels, 44
   platform property, 767
   PNG, 502
   recording steps, 593
   screenshot tools, 465
   scriptlets, 740
   Settings folder, 742
   slice guides, 627
   status bar messages, 662

templates, adding, 744
Text menu, 87–89
toggling between Full and
    Draft Display, 32
toolbars, 37–41
Toolbox, 34
Undo, 61, 101
VCR controls, 33
View menu, 77–79
Window menu, 93–95
Xtras, 91–93, 382
WIndows (Microsoft) color
    Adaptive color palette, 284
    Adobe Color Tables, 212
    color picker, 208
    ColorWeb Pro, 214–215
    Eyedropper tool, 206
    No color option, 209
    palette, 56
WIndows (Microsoft) files
    Bookmark files, 560
    browser locations, 554–555
    File menu commands, 70–73
    importing Macintosh, 464
    temporary, 787
    viewing only specific, 124
Windows Explorer, 744
Windows System color palette,
    210
Windowshading, floating panels,
    44
wizards
    Copy HTML Code wizard, 74
    Export, 507–509
    Link, 547–548
wood pattern, 585, 745
Wood-Light Pattern fill, 263

Word (Microsoft)
    importing files, 451
    text format, 123
word balloons, 691
word boundary, searching for, 568
word processors, Styles, 521
words. *See* text
workflow, automating, 20, 581–602
Workspace preview
    2-Up tab, 477–478
    4-Up tab, 478–480
    multiple previews, 474–476
    optimizing, 474–480
    Preview tab, 477
World Wide Web Consortium
    (W3C), 502
write() method, 765, 789
WRITE_HTML() method, API
    (application
    programming interface),
    764–765
writing
    files, 788
    images, 797
    text to a file, 789

X

x coordinates, hotspots, 791
X-ACTO knife. *See* Knife tool
xRes files
    API (application programming
    interface), 770
    format, 123
    importing, 454
Xtras
    color, 193
    commands, 91–93

described, 352–353
Effect panel, 52–53
Effect panel versus, 378
false pixel selections, 380–381
fixing, 371
image objects, 379
Instances, 542
multiple objects, 381
Path objects, 379
pixel selections in image
    object, 379–380
returning folder pathname, 767
selection tool, 185
Settings folder, 746
Styles, 522
tweening, 715–717

Y

y coordinates, hotspots, 791
Yarn stroke, 233–234
Your Open Documents List, 95

Z

zero-point, 406
zlib compressed masks, 761
Zoom In command, 77
Zoom Out command, 77
Zoom tool
    Export Preview dialog box, 504
    selecting area for
        transparency, 492
    temporary switch to, 37
zooming
    described, 30–31, 392
    objects toward viewer, 582
    workspace preview, 480

IDG Books Worldwide, Inc.
End-User License Agreement

READ THIS. You should carefully read these terms and conditions before opening the software packet(s) included with this book ("Book"). This is a license agreement ("Agreement") between you and IDG Books Worldwide, Inc. ("IDGB"). By opening the accompanying software packet(s), you acknowledge that you have read and accept the following terms and conditions. If you do not agree and do not want to be bound by such terms and conditions, promptly return the Book and the unopened software packet(s) to the place you obtained them for a full refund.

1. **License Grant.** IDGB grants to you (either an individual or entity) a nonexclusive license to use one copy of the enclosed software program(s) (collectively, the "Software") solely for your own personal or business purposes on a single computer (whether a standard computer or a workstation component of a multiuser network). The Software is in use on a computer when it is loaded into temporary memory (RAM) or installed into permanent memory (hard disk, CD-ROM, or other storage device). IDGB reserves all rights not expressly granted herein.

2. **Ownership.** IDGB is the owner of all right, title, and interest, including copyright, in and to the compilation of the Software recorded on the disk(s) or CD-ROM ("Software Media"). Copyright to the individual programs recorded on the Software Media is owned by the author or other authorized copyright owner of each program. Ownership of the Software and all proprietary rights relating thereto remain with IDGB and its licensers.

3. **Restrictions On Use and Transfer.**

   (a) You may only (i) make one copy of the Software for backup or archival purposes, or (ii) transfer the Software to a single hard disk, provided that you keep the original for backup or archival purposes. You may not (i) rent or lease the Software, (ii) copy or reproduce the Software through a LAN or other network system or through any computer subscriber system or bulletin-board system, or (iii) modify, adapt, or create derivative works based on the Software.

   (b) You may not reverse engineer, decompile, or disassemble the Software. You may transfer the Software and user documentation on a permanent basis, provided that the transferee agrees to accept the terms and conditions of this Agreement and you retain no copies. If the Software is an update or has been updated, any transfer must include the most recent update and all prior versions.

4. **Restrictions On Use of Individual Programs.** You must follow the individual requirements and restrictions detailed for each individual program in the "What's on the CD-ROM" appendix of this Book. These limitations are also contained in the individual license agreements recorded on the Software Media. These limitations may include a requirement that after using the program for a specified period of time, the user must pay a registration fee or discontinue use. By opening the Software packet(s), you will be agreeing to abide by the licenses and restrictions for these individual programs that are detailed in the "What's on the CD-ROM" appendix and on the Software Media. None of the material on this Software Media or listed in this Book may ever be redistributed, in original or modified form, for commercial purposes.

5. **Limited Warranty.**

   (a) IDGB warrants that the Software and Software Media are free from defects in materials and workmanship under normal use for a period of sixty (60) days from the date of purchase of this Book. If IDGB receives notification within the warranty period of defects in materials or workmanship, IDGB will replace the defective Software Media.

   (b) **IDGB AND THE AUTHORS OF THE BOOK DISCLAIM ALL OTHER WARRANTIES, EXPRESS OR IMPLIED, INCLUDING WITHOUT LIMITATION IMPLIED WARRANTIES OF MERCHANTABILITY AND FITNESS FOR A PARTICULAR PURPOSE, WITH RESPECT TO THE SOFTWARE, THE PROGRAMS, THE SOURCE CODE CONTAINED THEREIN, AND/OR THE TECHNIQUES DESCRIBED IN THIS BOOK. IDGB DOES NOT WARRANT THAT THE FUNCTIONS CONTAINED IN THE SOFTWARE WILL MEET YOUR REQUIREMENTS OR THAT THE OPERATION OF THE SOFTWARE WILL BE ERROR FREE.**

   (c) This limited warranty gives you specific legal rights, and you may have other rights that vary from jurisdiction to jurisdiction.

6. **Remedies.**

   (a) IDGB's entire liability and your exclusive remedy for defects in materials and workmanship shall be limited to replacement of the Software Media, which may be returned to IDGB with a copy of your receipt at the following address: Software Media Fulfillment Department, Attn.: *Fireworks 3 Bible*, IDG Books Worldwide, Inc., 7260 Shadeland Station, Ste. 100, Indianapolis, IN 46256, or call 1-800-762-2974. Please allow three to four weeks for delivery. This Limited Warranty is void if failure of the Software Media has resulted from accident, abuse, or misapplication. Any replacement Software Media will be warranted for the remainder of the original warranty period or thirty (30) days, whichever is longer.

   (b) In no event shall IDGB or the authors be liable for any damages whatsoever (including without limitation damages for loss of business profits, business interruption, loss of business information, or any other pecuniary loss) arising from the use of or inability to use the Book or the Software, even if IDGB has been advised of the possibility of such damages.

(c) Because some jurisdictions do not allow the exclusion or limitation of liability for consequential or incidental damages, the above limitation or exclusion may not apply to you.

7. **U.S. Government Restricted Rights.** Use, duplication, or disclosure of the Software by the U.S. Government is subject to restrictions stated in paragraph (c)(1)(ii) of the Rights in Technical Data and Computer Software clause of DFARS 252.227-7013, and in subparagraphs (a) through (d) of the Commercial Computer — Restricted Rights clause at FAR 52.227-19, and in similar clauses in the NASA FAR supplement, when applicable.

8. **General.** This Agreement constitutes the entire understanding of the parties and revokes and supersedes all prior agreements, oral or written, between them and may not be modified or amended except in a writing signed by both parties hereto that specifically refers to this Agreement. This Agreement shall take precedence over any other documents that may be in conflict herewith. If any one or more provisions contained in this Agreement are held by any court or tribunal to be invalid, illegal, or otherwise unenforceable, each and every other provision shall remain in full force and effect.

Put a serious
dent
in your
workload with
Dreamweaver®
and Fireworks.®

Introducing Dreamweaver 3 and Fireworks 3

The newest versions of Dreamweaver and Fireworks
work together to give you the power to create
Web sites faster. Design buttons, animations
and page comps in minutes with Fireworks 3.
Mold your graphics and code into completed
Web sites in record time with Dreamweaver 3.
Streamline development with support for the
content creation and Web application software
you use. Together, Dreamweaver and
Fireworks are one awesome team
for rapid Web development.
www.macromedia.com

macromedia®

my2cents.idgbooks.com

Register This Book — And Win!

Visit **http://my2cents.idgbooks.com** to register this book and we'll automatically enter you in our fantastic monthly prize giveaway. It's also your opportunity to give us feedback: let us know what you thought of this book and how you would like to see other topics covered.

Discover IDG Books Online!

The IDG Books Online Web site is your online resource for tackling technology — at home and at the office. Frequently updated, the IDG Books Online Web site features exclusive software, insider information, online books, and live events!

10 Productive & Career-Enhancing Things You Can Do at www.idgbooks.com

- Nab source code for your own programming projects.

- Download software.

- Read Web exclusives: special articles and book excerpts by IDG Books Worldwide authors.

- Take advantage of resources to help you advance your career as a Novell or Microsoft professional.

- Buy IDG Books Worldwide titles or find a convenient bookstore that carries them.

- Register your book and win a prize.

- Chat live online with authors.

- Sign up for regular e-mail updates about our latest books.

- Suggest a book you'd like to read or write.

- Give us your 2¢ about our books and about our Web site.

You say you're not on the Web yet? It's easy to get started with IDG Books' *Discover the Internet*, available at local retailers everywhere.

CD-ROM Installation Instructions

The *Fireworks 3 Bible* CD-ROM contains a trial version of Fireworks, as well as a full complement of auxiliary files and additional programs.

Accessing the programs on the CD-ROM

Only the trial programs are compressed. Double-click these files to begin the installation procedure (Fireworks installation instructions are listed below). All other files on the CD-ROM are uncompressed and can simply be copied from the CD-ROM to your system by using your file manager.

For a detailed synopsis of the CD-ROM contents, see Appendix C.

Installing Fireworks

To install Fireworks on your Windows system, follow these steps:

1. Insert the Fireworks 3 Bible CD-ROM into your CD-ROM drive.

2. Double-click the Fireworks.exe file to unpack it and begin the installation process.

3. Follow the onscreen instructions. Accept the default options for program location.

Changing the Windows read-only attribute

You may not be able to access files on the CD-ROM after you copy the files to your computer. After you copy or move the entire contents of the CD-ROM to your hard disk or another storage medium (such as a Zip disk), you may get the following error message when you attempt to open a file with its associated application:

```
[Application] is unable to open the [file]. Please make sure
the drive and file are writable.
```

Windows sees all files on a CD-ROM drive as *read-only*. This normally makes sense because a CD-ROM is a read-only medium — that is, you can't write data back to the CD-ROM.

However, when you copy a file from a CD-ROM to your hard disk or to a Zip disk, Windows doesn't automatically change the file attribute from read-only to writable.

Installation software normally takes care of this chore for you, but in this case, since the files are intended to be manually copied to your disk, you have to change the file attribute yourself. Luckily, it's easy—just follow these steps:

1. Click the Start menu button.

2. Select Programs.

3. Choose Windows Explorer.

4. Highlight the filename(s) on the hard disk or Zip disk.

5. Right-click the highlighted filename(s) in order to display a pop-up menu.

6. Select Properties to display the Properties dialog box.

7. Click the Read-only option so that it is no longer checked.

8. Click the OK button.

You should now be able to use the file(s) with the specific application without getting the annoying error message.